THE PICADOR BOOK OF

Contemporary Scottish Fiction

PETER KRAVITZ lives in the Scottish Borders with his wife and three children. He was an editor at Polygon in Edinburgh between 1980 and 1990. He also edited the *Edinburgh Review* between 1984 and 1990.

THE PICADOR BOOK OF

Contemporary Scottish Fiction

Edited by Peter Kravitz

PICADOR

First published 1997 by Picador

This edition published 1998 by Picador
an imprint of Macmillan Publishers Ltd
25 Eccleston Place, London SW1W 9NF
and Basingstoke

Associated companies throughout the world

ISBN 0 330 33551 0

Introduction and this selection copyright © Peter Kravitz 1997

The acknowledgements on pages 557–60 constitute an extension of
this copyright page.

The right of Peter Kravitz to be identified as the
editor of this work has been asserted by him in accordance
with the Copyright, Designs and Patents Act 1988.

1 3 5 7 9 8 6 4 2

A CIP catalogue record for this book is available from
the British Library.

Typeset by CentraCet, Cambridge
Printed and bound in Great Britain by
Mackays of Chatham plc, Chatham, Kent

IN MEMORY OF EDWARD BOYD

(1916–1989)

Contents

Introduction xi

PART ONE

Agnes Owens – *When Shankland Comes* 3

Iain Crichton Smith – from *In the Middle of the Wood* 19

Duncan Williamson – *Mary and the Seal* 47

Joan Lingard – from *After Colette* 57

Bill Douglas – *My Childhood* 76

Alasdair Gray – from *Lanark* 97

Jeff Torrington – *The Fade* 110

William McIlvanney – *At the Bar* 119

Allan Massie – *In the Bare Lands* 122

Stanley Robertson – *A Monk's Tail* 128

John Herdman – *Original Sin* 134

Carl MacDougall – from *The Lights Below* 139

Douglas Dunn – *The Political Piano* 148

Thomas Healy – from *It Might Have Been Jerusalem* 160

Tom Leonard – *Honest* 174

Sian Hayton – from *Cells of Knowledge* 178

James Kelman – from *The Busconductor Hines* 190

PART TWO

Liz Lochhead – *Phyllis Marlowe: Only Diamonds Are Forever* 215

Alison Fell – *There's Tradition For You* 219

Margaret Elphinstone – from *A Sparrow's Flight* 223

Liz Heron – *Undue Haste* 236

Alan Spence – *Brilliant* 242

Andrew Greig – from *Electric Brae* 255

Frank Kuppner – from *A Very Quiet Street* 270

Brian McCabe – *Not About the Kids* 281

Ronald Frame – *La Plume de Ma Tante* 289

Dilys Rose – *All the Little Loved Ones* 294

Martin Millar – from *Dreams of Sex and Stage Diving* 299

Candia McWilliam – *Seven Magpies* 311

Janice Galloway – from *The Trick is To Keep Breathing* 321

Iain Banks – from *The Bridge* 336

Joseph Mills – *Watch Out, the World's Behind You* 342

PART THREE

Irvine Welsh – from *Trainspotting* 367

Robert Alan Jamieson – *The Last Black Hoose* 385

Ian Rankin – *A Deep Hole* 393

Andrew Crumey – from *Pfitz* 406

Jackie Kay – from *Trumpet* 413

Gordon Legge – *Life on a Scottish Council Estate Vol. I* 430

James Meek – *Get Lost* 439

Contents

Ali Smith – *The Unthinkable Happens to People Every Day* 442

Frank Shon – *The Farmer's Wife* 449

Duncan McLean – *Hours of Darkness* 460

Bridget Penney – *Incidents on the Road* 491

Alan Warner – *The Man Who Walks* 504

A. L. Kennedy – from *Looking for the Possible Dance* 508

Mark Fleming – *St Andrew's Day* 526

Andrew O'Hagan – *Glass Cheques* 542

Biographical Notes 549

Acknowledgements 557

Introduction

So you end up a typical Scotsman. Prejudiced, Christian (when
it suits you), well-educated, nostalgic, nationalistic, willing to
travel, pro-Irish (well they're in the same boat), aggressive,
proud, single-minded, occasionally pissed, occasionally singing,
not mean (as a nation we are rather generous, you'll find),
willing to accept second place too often, expecting to lose, easily
embarrassed, passionate and football daft, standing there,
thousands of us, in Wembley Stadium at the game. England 5
Scotland 1. A nation mourns – member at.

> Bill Bryden (1977)

We'll never do anything richt will we?
> (Scots supporter to William McIlvanney at the end of
> Scotland v. Iran in the 1978 World Cup)

In March 1979 the people of Scotland were asked whether they wanted
their own parliament separate from England. The majority said yes.
However, a last minute clause added to the bill stated that 40 per cent of
the total electorate had to be in favour. This took non-voters to be saying
no. Governments get elected on less.

In 1980 I started reading manuscripts for the Edinburgh publisher
Polygon. The backlist consisted mostly of books about Scottish failures.
There was one on the failure of the breakaway Scottish Labour Party,
another on the *Scottish Daily News* – a failed attempt at newspaper
publishing. And there were books about failures that failed to appear.
Someone was commissioned to write a fan's diary of the Scottish team's
failure in the Argentina World Cup of 1978.

Polygon was also due to publish Neal Ascherson's *Devolution Diaries*,
written during the referendum debacle, in which he referred to the post-
referendum years as 'the hangover of '79'. In some circles it was known
as the 'deferendum' due to the lack of nerve exhibited by the electorate.
In the end Ascherson decided they were too frank and instead deposited
them in the Public Record Office in Edinburgh under a 'Closed' mark.

Around the time I started at Polygon, publishers released a flood of histories, companions, dictionaries and encyclopedias of Scottish literature. In most cultures these reference works might have had quite a long shelf-life, but the publication of work by Alasdair Gray, James Kelman and others in the early 1980s rendered the volumes that had excluded them obsolete almost as soon as they were published. In retrospect they were marking the end of a former era in Scottish literature and the beginning of a new one.

Anyone looking for the country's authors in a Scottish bookshop at that time would have been pointed towards reprints of Neil Gunn and Eric Linklater. Publishers were more interested in resurrecting dead writers as opposed to looking for new ones and grants from the Scottish Arts Council encouraged this. When on behalf of Polygon I sent them Kelman's second novel *A Chancer*, they deemed it unworthy of a grant towards publication costs. They had received a complaint from a Conservative Member of Parliament, Alick Buchanan-Smith; one of his constituents had picked up Kelman's previous novel, *The Busconductor Hines*, in an Edinburgh bookshop, and was shocked that taxpayers' money was subsidizing such language. Those who claimed to represent culture had lost their collective nerve.

There was the publication of the long-delayed *New Testament in Scots* in 1982 and the *Concise Scots Dictionary* in 1985. These became surprise (to the bookshops) bestsellers and were products of decades of work. W. L. Lorimer's *New Testament in Scots*, like Gray's *Lanark* and Kelman's *Not Not While The Giro and other stories*, were completed long before publication in book form. Lorimer first had the idea of translating it in 1945, began in earnest in 1957 and completed it in 1966. It took until 1983 to raise sufficient interest and funds to secure publication. He uses different forms of Scots to show different authors in the New Testament and when the Old Testament is quoted he uses Old Scots. The book's raciness and hybridity made the attempts by various writers and academics in the decade before to sort out an agreed form of Scots laughable.

Later on in the 1980s books and pamphlets came out glossing Glasgow speech, such as Stanley Baxter's *Parliamo Glasgow* and Michael Munro's *The Patter*, which topped the Scottish bestseller charts for months and went into several editions. Words that were being taken out of speech and print in the past couple of centuries were now being put back in, in the case of anglicized Scots, or left in, in the case of others.

Derek in Kelman's story 'Events in yer life' says, on turning on the TV one morning, that 'it was only the Scottish accents made it interesting'.

Eck in John McKay's play *Dead Dad Dog* has the answer: 'It's not ma accent it's your ears.' In a nice reversal, Alasdair Gray used a transcription of upper class Oxbridge English for 'The Distant Cousin of the Queen' section in *Something Leather*. Here your is 'yaw', poor is 'paw', literature is 'litritcha', here is 'hia', nearly is 'nialy' and Shakespeare is 'Shakespia'.

The sudden appearance in print of many of these writers has been called a boom by many commentators. In reality, however, it was more the result of a process: Alasdair Gray, Jeff Torrington, Bill Douglas and James Kelman wrote for more than a decade before being published in book form in Scotland or England. Perhaps it took the failure of the Devolution Bill in 1979 to bring them to a wider public. There is, after all, a school of thought that says that when the politics of a country run aground, the people look for self-expression in culture.

The public acceptance or censorship of vernacular Scots has always been a symptom of political feeling in the country. In reaction to the Act of Union with England in 1707, there was a renewal of interest in the vernacular, followed by a reaction in Edinburgh around the middle of the eighteenth century when a guide book on how to excise Scotticisms from speech became popular amongst the literati. Its stated aim was 'to put young writers and speakers on their guard against Scotch idioms' and its influence is still obvious many generations later in the properly anunciated speech of Miss Jean Brodie. One exception was Robert Burns, whose writing was applauded in the 1780s by the same people who had set about removing Scottish words from their vocabulary.

In Glasgow during 1971 some writers had begun to meet every two weeks in a group coordinated by Philip Hobsbaum, a lecturer in the English Department at the university. This was the fourth time he had organized such a group. Besides an earlier one in Glasgow there had been groups in London and in Belfast (to which Seamus Heaney brought his poems) in the late 1950s and early 1960s. Here Gray and Kelman met each other and Tom Leonard and Liz Lochhead for the first time. Other writers at the group included the poets Donald Saunders, Aonghas MacNeacail and Robin Hamilton, and the science-fiction writer Chris Boyce. Each would submit a piece of writing in advance which would then be copied, circulated and read out during the meeting. The value of such encouragement and criticism at an early stage of a writer's career cannot be overemphasized.

Leonard's 'The Good Thief' had already appeared in the first issue of *Scottish International* back in January 1968. When he had tried to publish poems in *Glasgow University Magazine* the printer declined because of the language. A few years later a typesetter wanted 'foreign language rates' for some of his other Glasgow poems. Leonard was probably the most established writer attending the Hobsbaum group. *Six Glasgow Poems* and *A Priest Came on at Merkland Street* were published to some acclaim in 1969 and 1970.

J. B. Caird (one of Her Majesty's Inspector of Schools in Scotland) ended a talk to the Association for Scottish Literary Studies in 1972 with the question 'Is there a possibility in fiction – as has been done in verse by Tom Leonard and others – for the phonetic rendering of Glasgow speech in the way Raymond Queneau has used Parisian speech in *Zazie dans le Metro*?' Like most people, he was not to know that over in Glasgow James Kelman was doing just this.

When Kelman and Gray first met at Hobsbaum's group they did not particularly like each other's writing, but warmed to each other personally. Gray later acknowledged him for helping the first chapter of *Lanark* read smoother. He included a drawing of Kelman on the frontispiece of Book One of *Lanark* while printing his story 'Acid' in one of the footnotes to plagiarisms in the novel. Gray had been working on *Lanark* since the 1950s. When he completed one of the four books it comprises he sent it to the literary agent Spencer Curtis Brown, who rejected it in 1963.

An editor at Quartet bought an option on *Lanark* for £75 after reading a half-complete version in 1972. When Gray finished his work four years later it was turned down because it was 'too long'. Two other London publishers offered to publish it if he split it into two books. During this time Gray made a meagre living selling plays to television and radio. In between he would go back to painting. He did murals in restaurants and churches, and for more than a decade made portraits of Glasgow citizens for the People's Palace Museum. Finally, he offered *Lanark* to the Edinburgh publisher Canongate in February 1977, who accepted it a year later. They went on to publish it in 1981. *Lanark* had been twenty-four years in the making.

The index to the *Glasgow Herald* for 1984 has the following entry:

> GRAY, Alasdair
> Artist who painted for his supper on brink of
> literary fame and fortune, Jan 9, 9a, P;
> Jan 13, 8c, C; [Three editions of his work
> published], Mar 6, 4g; £500 [Frederick Niven]
> award for author, May 10, 5e; Author gives miners
> £500, May 14, 1b, P.

In 1987 Gray used the advances of two books to organize a touring exhibition of the painters John Connolly, Alan Fletcher, Carole Gibbons and Alasdair Taylor, whose work he felt had been unjustly neglected.

Kelman had been writing since about 1967 and by 1971 had enough stories for a book. Through Hobsbaum he met the American writer Mary Gray Hughes. She got a publisher in Maine interested in the manuscript of *An old pub near the Angel*, his first book of stories. It was published in 1973 by Puckerbrush Press and was little noticed in Scotland or England. His work was starting to appear in magazines and occasionally in the *Scottish Short Stories* annual volume. By the mid-1970s Kelman had another collection of stories ready, was completing one novel and was well underway with another.

A good deal of cooperation amongst these writers in the West of Scotland began at this time; writing circulated in manuscript and addresses of hard-to-come-by literary magazines were exchanged. The best of these was *Scottish International* which lasted from 1968 to 1974. At the beginning of the 1970s it ran extracts from *Lanark* and published Alan Spence's stories. Two poets – Edwin Morgan and Robert Garioch – were on the board of the magazine. Morgan sponsored Alasdair Gray's application to the Scottish Arts Council for money to finish *Lanark* (he received £300 in 1973).

Many of the new writers from the West of Scotland found Morgan's poetry an inspiration as it took in urban life (especially Glasgow) and embraced the new. These were themes not often found in combination at that time. *Scottish International* was strange for a Scottish cultural magazine in several respects. Guided by its editor Bob Tait, it treated Hugh MacDiarmid as a poet amongst equals instead of installing him high on a throne. It also tried to cover Glasgow comprehensively for the first time.

In 1970 the *Glasgow Herald* did two features on Thomas Healy entitled 'From the Pick to the Pen' and 'Labourer Who Writes Stories'. They reported that Healy 'whose most recent story "The Traveller" reflects his experiences as a navvy on a hydro-electric site in the Highlands, has won at the age of 28, a Scottish Arts Council bursary of £500.' This allowed him to work on a novel of Glasgow in the 1950s. Some stories appeared in an anthology of new writers put out by Faber, who took an option on the novel but never published it. Nothing more appeared in book form. Until in 1988, maybe aware of the work we were publishing, he sent Polygon his novel *It Might Have Been Jerusalem*. He had been writing for more than twenty years without having had a book accepted. In his second book, *Rolling*, his hero has a love affair with a schoolboy in Glasgow, gets dysentery in Madrid and ends up, via Germany and Australia, in a marriage of sorts. After publication, Healy was berated for creating a character who made everything secondary to drink. Many Scottish reviewers appear to seek redemption from books by Scottish writers. They approach them with different critical apparatus to that which they might bring to, say, an American writer. Like the councillors of Glasgow they prefer happy endings to hard-won self-determination.

In 1974, Bill Douglas wrote the novel *My Childhood* to raise money to allow him to complete his trilogy of films *My Childhood/My Ain Folk/My Way Home*, but it never found a publisher. The manuscript resurfaced nearly twenty years later. Apart from this, I have taken 'contemporary' to mean work published after *Lanark*. In addition I have made my selection from writers born after 1926. When I made a list of writers born between 1915 and 1930, there was a gap for five years after 1921 where none were born at all (although I can't quite believe it) so 1926 seemed like a good beginning. But any start date is arbitrary and all definitions are temporary and contingent. This means I have had to exclude writers as diverse as Alexander Trocchi and Elspeth Davie, Freddy Anderson and Robin Jenkins, or Naomi Mitchison and Alan Sharp.

In 1975 William McIlvanney, after winning the Whitbread Prize for *Docherty*, said he wanted 'to write a book that would create a kind of literary genealogy for the people I came from.' Meanwhile, Kelman was doing exactly this and getting rejection slips from London publishers who slammed the door on Scottish writers of fiction just as quickly as they had opened it. Not being published in book form, whether in Edinburgh or London, meant they had to build their own links with readers and other writers to avoid complete neglect.

If publishers in Edinburgh and London had their blinkers on when it came to manuscripts from new Scottish writers, the work was not sitting in drawers. Magazines and small presses evolved to plug the gap and they had an influence disproportionate to their size. For a couple of years from 1978 Kelman, Gray, Leonard, Lochhead, Spence and others distributed booklets of their work as the Glasgow Print Studio Cooperative with the help of its director Calum Mackenzie.

In 1979 Kelman began the first of two periods as Writer-in-Residence for Renfrewshire District Libraries. In an interview with the *Glasgow Herald* at the time Kelman said: 'I wanted to help ordinary people to become aware that books and writers are not sacred and unapproachable … Most people have something in them worth writing about if only they realized it, and I intend to have workshops in every local community to encourage people to both read and write.' In May of that year, five days after Margaret Thatcher's first election victory, Kelman put on – in his words to a reporter at the time – 'the first poetry reading to take place at Paisley Town Hall since W. B. Yeats in 1924'. Among those on the bill were Sorley MacLean, Iain Crichton Smith and Aonghas MacNeacail.

In the absence of interest from publishers or agents, authors in the west of Scotland continued to link up. More and more readings were organized. Here Kelman met Jeff Torrington, who had been a shop steward at the former Talbot/Chrysler car plant at Linwood. Torrington was in the middle of writing *Swing Hammer Swing*, part of which Kelman passed to me in 1983. It led to several Torrington stories appearing in *Edinburgh Review*. Torrington told me that when he first attended one of Kelman's writing groups in Paisley Kelman suggested that he knock all the stained glass windows out of his prose, referring to the adjectives and adverbs. But Torrington's favourite writers include Vladimir Nabokov and Ray Bradbury and as he enjoyed using these words they remained.

When Liz Lochhead ran a writing group in Alexandria, north of Glasgow, she met Agnes Owens who gave her the story 'Arabella'. Lochhead showed it to Gray and Kelman who loved it and soon became friends with the author. Several years on, in 1982, Gray passed me the typescript of the novel *Gentleman of the West* by Agnes Owens, which was published at Polygon.

I also heard about Janice Galloway from James Kelman. He had been judging a short story competition and photocopied some of her entry for me. I went on to publish several stories in *Edinburgh Review* and her novel *The Trick is To Keep Breathing* at Polygon. Later, Kelman was to bring Torrington and McLean to the attention of his publisher at Secker & Warburg. Galloway published the first work by Irvine Welsh as one of the editors of *New Writing Scotland*. He went on to be published by The Clocktower Press and then in Kevin Williamson's Rebel Inc. McLean suggested Welsh and later Alan Warner to the same editor at Secker & Warburg. There is a common strand here of writers using their own reputations to bring to people's attention the work of other writers. Just look at the cover puffs and you'll see how one writer praises another who in turn introduces another new writer's work. In his 'diplags' and 'implags' in the margins of *Lanark*, Gray uses a satire on academic footnotes to admit he has plagiarized sentences or parts of sentences from the work

of Kelman, Lochhead, Leonard, Spence and McCabe. This was an unsel-
fish support network proving the validity of Ezra Pound's comment that
no single work of art excludes another work of art. Tom Leonard made a
huge magic marker banner of this phrase and put it along one wall of the
room where his writing groups met in Paisley.

> Scotland will be free when the last Church of Scotland minister
> is strangled by the last copy of the *Sunday Post.*
>
>   Tom Nairn (1970)

> When I see one of these Free Church ministers on the street in
> Lewis, I feel like walking across the road and hitting him in the
> face.
>
>   Iain Crichton Smith (1985)

Most of the themes here – the art of keeping a fragile hold on sanity,
struggles against moral intolerance and the causes and effects of drinking
too much – would have made sense to another Glasgow writer, R. D.
Laing. His work has been an influence on some of the people published
here. What many of the writers have in common with him is rage,
intelligence, humour and a curiosity and frustration about the central
role of guilt in the Scottish psyche. His first book, *The Divided Self,*
published in London in 1959 after he left Glasgow, is a psychological look
at the everyday occurrence of split personality.

He felt that guilt develops when anger is not expressed but sent
inward and two selves are created. Scotland can lay some claim to being
one of the best purveyors in world literature of the *doppelgänger* or
double. Since James Hogg's *Confessions of A Justified Sinner* and Robert
Louis Stevenson's *Dr Jekyll and Mr Hyde* many Scottish writers have
explored this theme. Yet, what is remarkable about so much Scottish
writing of the past fifteen years is how the double has disappeared. There
is very little splitting. Some of the characters may be struggling to recover
from damage but they are *whole.* They may be alienated from the values
of society, but they are not alienated from themselves. They may be
angry, but this comes out as rage and is not left buried to form cycles of
bitterness and depression. They fight madness and avoid suicide: Patrick
Doyle in Kelman's *A Disaffection*; Roy Strang in Welsh's *Marabou Stork
Nightmares*; Jock McLeish in Gray's *1982 Janine*; Joy Stone in Galloway's

The Trick is To Keep Breathing; Helen Brindle in A. L. Kennedy's *Original Bliss* and Ralph in Iain Crichton Smith's *In The Middle of The Wood*. For these characters sanity is not given, but won. Then they are whole, not split people.

For his *Radical Renfrew* anthology Tom Leonard compiled a thematic list of contents which could be a thumbnail history of Scotland. The first five of the sixteen sections are religion, alcohol, emigration, employment and unemployment. Institutionalized religion still has a powerful hold on Scotland. Monty Python's *Life of Brian* is still banned from every cinema in Glasgow and in the early 1980s Glasgow University Union denied students permission to form a Gay Society.

In Alan Sharp's *A Green Tree in Gedde*, Moseby began to understand what being West Coast Scottish meant, with its preoccupations with guilt and sex and sin. Twenty-five years later, in *The Trick Is To Keep Breathing*, Janice Galloway sums up the prevailing ethos of Scottish schooling: 'apportion blame that ye have not blame aportioned unto you.' In *Looking For The Possible Dance*, A. L. Kennedy lists ten points that her protagonist Margaret, 'like many others, will take the rest of her life to recover from'. It is called 'The Scottish Method (FOR THE PERFECTION OF CHILDREN)' and includes the credo that 'guilt is good ... joy is fleeting, sinful and the forerunner of despair.'

There are more antecedents of these themes in the work of Glasgow writer Ivor Cutler (born before 1926 so outside the scope of this book). In *Life In A Scotch Sitting Room Vol. 2* his mother smells burning:

> 'Who's been playing with the matches?' asked Mother, looking into the
> box and shaking its contents.
>   I looked through the hole in my plate. You could have boiled a
> kettle on my cheek. ALL the children were busy looking guilty. It was
> our custom.

Not that long ago children in Scottish schools were still being punished by the tawse. The *Concise Scots Dictionary* defines it as 'a whip with tails; the lash for a whipping top; a leather punishment strap with thongs (since 1983 rarely and only in certain regions); also a child's word for penis.' Schools can oppress their teachers as much as their pupils. Teachers appear in contemporary Scottish fiction as people for whom sanity is no longer a given. Ralph in Iain Crichton Smith's *In The Middle of The Wood*, Joy Stone in *The Trick is to Keep Breathing*, Patrick Doyle in *A Disaffection* ('He just wanted something different. To not be a teacher perhaps!') are all burdened with the pressures put on the country's educational system.

Whether because of Calvinism or Catholicism, Scotland has had hangups in abundance – especially around sex and drink. Then there is anger. Then there is guilt about this anger. Then the depression that follows when anger is internalized. Nowhere is this clearer than in the rage of Scottish men. A good deal of contemporary Scottish fiction shows the pressure put on Scots men to be real hard men. In *Marabou Stork Nightmares*, in my opinion Irvine Welsh's best book so far, Roy Strang is abused by his racist uncle. A few years later he helps commit a gang rape. Strang has been 'running away from sensitivity ... a fucking schemie, a nobody, shouldnae have these feelings because there's fucking naewhair for them tae go.'

In the 1970s two plays dealt with this theme overtly. Tom McGrath wrote *The Hard Man* about convicted murderer Jimmy Boyle and Bill Bryden's play *Benny Lynch* tells the story of the Glasgow boxer who lost it all to drink. William McIlvanney's novel *The Big Man* traces the life of a man who loses his job in contemporary Ayrshire and turns to bare-knuckle fighting to earn a living. Even the title of his collection of short stories – *Walking Wounded* – tells us that we are entering the arena where damaged men do damage to each other and have damage done to them. It is as if only a decade, not centuries, has elapsed since the wars with England. The word 'manliness' occurs very regularly in Thomas Healy's fiction and it is not surprising that his most recent book, *A Hurting Business*, is a memoir of being a lifelong boxing fan in Glasgow.

The story 'At the Bar' by William McIlvanney in this anthology has parallels in the novel *Gentleman of the West* by Agnes Owens:

> Proctor's answer was to hurl a glass through the mirror behind the
> bar ... My mother gave a moan of fear. This excited Paddy's chivalrous
> instincts. He hurried up to Proctor and smashed a lemonade bottle on
> the counter over his head.

The main character of the book, Mac, describes the scars on his face, saying 'they were status for me'. Owens presents violence as a straight-forward fact of everyday life, with little comment or judgement. Violence and anger (and fondness, which can sometimes make the switch hilar-ious) come out in language too. Most violence between people never results in a fight but remains in language. Kelman has given the example of writing about a few men in a pub. You can either write using the dialogue that they might actually use or you can write using language they wouldn't use. If you do the latter then you end up censoring their whole existence. A writer has to make other decisions, such as, Does the narrator use the same language as the characters? In the prose of some writers in this anthology there is no such split.

In 1988 a magazine for English teachers in Scottish schools printed a review of *Gentleman of the West* which concluded that the book's 'usefulness as a school text is unfortunately limited by the realistic inclusion in the dialogue' of language associated with 'bouts of drinking and occasional houghmagandie'. The reviewer finished by warning teachers that 'the parents of your average "S" grade candidate would certainly be moved to protest.'

Censorship can take many different forms. I came across a peculiarly misguided example when I was editing *Towards The End*, a novel by the Glasgow writer Joseph Mills published in 1989 by Polygon. The job of an editor is to understand the author's intention and play devil's advocate to both the writer and to his or her own instinctive response. Although I didn't like some of Mills's florid metaphors, what made the book compelling was its attention to detail, its focus on the particular lived moments of the protagonist's life. Yet, whenever the character moved about the city, the Glasgow place and street names had been tipp-exed out on the manuscript.

'I'd like you to think about reinstating these names.'

'Are you sure?'

'Yes.'

'It's just that the publisher in London that almost took the book said if I took them out it would have more universal appeal.'

Needless to say he was delighted to reinstate them.

In December 1990, the *Scots Magazine* – a favourite read among Scots abroad – published an article by Maurice Fleming entitled 'Scotland the Depraved'. In it he called for a return to the values of the comic classics of Compton Mackenzie and more publicity for writers who could celebrate Scotland as opposed to those he labels 'the terrible twosome': Kelman and Welsh, joined by Duncan McLean. He describes his targets as 'desperate to plumb even deeper depths of depravity'. These writers, he said, 'appear to view Scotland with undisguised and malicious disgust ... [portraying the place as] a nation of drunks, drug addicts and dropouts.'

In 1992 the *Daily Record* printed the headline SEX SHOCKERS ON SCHOOL'S READING LIST and continued with reference to 'dirty books' and 'classroom porn shockers'. In response to the action of a retired chemistry teacher on the Johnstone High School board five books were removed from the library's shelves for sixteen- to eighteen-year-olds. The books were *A Chancer* and *A Greyhound for Breakfast* by James Kelman; *The Color Purple* by Alice Walker; *The Cider House Rules* by John Irving and *Perfume* by Patrick Süskind. The reason given was that they contained obscene language and/or depictions of rape and/or child abuse and/or violence. As a follow-up the paper had sent copies of pages from these books to the Strathclyde Region's Director of Education who commented 'I am shocked and appalled... I'm taking urgent steps to ensure that they are not available to children anywhere in the region.'

The next day, under the headline, CLEAN UP AT PORN SCHOOL, the director of education commented: 'It was utterly unacceptable that such filth should ever have become available in the first place.' Subsequently, Robert Gould, the Leader of Strathclyde Region, told the school to take all post-1970 grown-up fiction off the shelves to be vetted. He was later quoted in a paper as saying 'I'm not much of a reader... No one talks like that, f-ing and blinding all over the place... You can't use language like that in public; if I spoke like that I'd be f***ing hounded out of office.'

This is not that different from those who only want a rosy image of their city written or painted or filmed. A standard criticism from this direction in Scotland was trotted out during 1996 for the film of *Trainspotting* and goes something like this: 'Yes I'm sure the book/film accurately represents life as it is lived for a proportion of the population, but to put this out as art or entertainment makes me feel uneasy. The book/film seems to condone all that is bad about our society. He needn't have written it because we see it every day in our streets and estates'.

Many newspapers still put in asterisks or dashes or blanks when they take exception to what is simply language. The *Glasgow Herald* would print stories in censored versions – removing the words from view and leaving nothing in their place – even after guarantees to the author. These writers were too important for the paper to be seen to be ignoring them but that didn't stop them doctoring the language. Several anthologies published with the school market in mind have obviously gone out of their way to pick a Kelman story or a Leonard poem with no language they don't like in it. The radio stations in Scotland still omit words without bleeping them: 'Well,' they seem to be saying, 'would you prefer not to have your story broadcast at all?'

The *Scots Magazine* got one thing right and that is the connection between the so-called culprits. Duncan McLean has said, only half-jokingly, that he sees himself as the missing link between Lewis Grassic Gibbon and Kelman. McLean may come from rural Aberdeenshire but he has written about life in and around Edinburgh in a way that would simply not have happened unless he had come across Kelman's 'Not Not While The Giro' and *The Busconductor Hines*.

Some Scots do not believe a book is worth reading unless it has been praised in London. It often has to be published there as well. Bill Forsyth said his film *Gregory's Girl* was not given a proper cinema release in Scotland until it had the seal of approval from London. Many journalists, broadcasters and academics north of the border poured scorn on Kelman's experimentation and use of language until *A Disaffection* was shortlisted for the Booker Prize.

Whereas Kelman looked to America and Europe for a literary tradition, McLean, together with Gordon Legge, Alan Warner and Irvine Welsh – and to a lesser extent Janice Galloway and A. L. Kennedy – have been influenced by Kelman and Gray, in part for their tenacity and in part for formal and technical breakthroughs in their use of language. McLean says, 'When *The Busconductor Hines* came out in 1984 it just blew my mind. It was the voice. For the first time I was reading a book about the world I lived in. I didn't know literature could do that.'

Welsh also credits Kelman with 'setting the whole thing out so that people like myself can have more fun.' A. L. Kennedy has said that people like John Byrne, Tom Leonard and James Kelman 'made my generation of writers possible ... gave us permission to speak ... made us more ourselves – gave us the reality, life and dignity that art can at a time when anything other than standard English and standard address was frowned upon.'

The Busconductor Hines, Kelman's first published novel, did not reach the Booker Prize shortlist. However, Richard Cobb (the chairman of the judges), did express his shock that 'one of the novels seemed to be written entirely in Glaswegian' as if that was enough to pass judgement on it. Anne Smith, editor of the (then Edinburgh-based) *Literary Review*, said of it, 'Who wants to read 300 pages about the life of a busconductor where nothing much happens anyway?' When Kelman won the Booker Prize for *How Late It Was, How Late*, Simon Jenkins of *The Times* said the Booker Prize judges were glorifying a noble savage, a glib and conde-scending way of sidelining work that disturbs.

The *Edinburgh Magazine* once described Burns as 'a striking example of native genius bursting through the obscurity of poverty and the obstructions of laborious life.' The same sentiments in more modern language greeted many of the writers in this anthology on their first publication. More than a few of them have been described in profiles as coming from non-literary backgrounds, using Leith or Grangemouth or Gorbals or whatever argot, dialect, patois or demotic. Most critics go to extraordinary lengths to avoid using the word 'language'. The result is that writers are marginalized outside a constructed literary canon, built by those who think middle-class people in the English home counties have no accent whatsoever. Similarly, when Alasdair Gray gets described as 'eccentric', critic and reader can collude in not taking his political or historical arguments seriously.

In 1985, Douglas Dunn concluded his *Glasgow Herald* review of Kelman's *A Chancer* with a plea for a good middle-class novel set in the west of Scotland. Things have come a long way from the day when Neil Gunn, writing in the same newspaper nearly fifty years before, wrote that 'Glasgow needs a working class novel written from the inside'. Elsewhere, in his *Oxford Book of Scottish Short Stories*, Dunn talks of the 'bruising candour' of Kelman and McLean. His argument is that just as in the nineteenth century many Scottish writers escaped into writing kailyard (cabbage patch) stories of rural idylls, so now 'unfortunately, the emphasis on urban working-class stories can appear to be as exaggerated as the agrarian stresses of the past.' He goes on to refer to Alasdair Gray's 'eccentric, astonishing intelligence ... the politicized demotic challenge of James Kelman and ... feminist purposes of Janice Galloway.'

This is an anthology from a country where more people leave or die than stay or arrive. Scotland's biggest export in the nineteenth and twentieth centuries has been people. The net emigration that has been happening for most of this century stopped abruptly at the end of the 1980s. Now less Scots are leaving and more are coming back. The Public Record Office in Edinburgh has so many archives and exhibitions on the theme of emigration that it should consider changing its name to The Museum of Those That Went Away. Jim Sillars, the main force behind the breakaway nationalist Scottish Labour Party in the late 1970s, has made the point that 'going to Canada or Australia or Rhodesia or into the armed forces was an accepted fact of life. If you wanted to get on then you had to get out.'

The Scots, like the Jews and the Irish, are a small nation dispersed all over the world. They form a higher-than-average proportion of interpreters, mediators, football managers, athletics coaches and translators. Great writing was found at the margins amongst Scottish translators like Willa and Edwin Muir (Kafka), C. K. Scott-Moncrieff (Proust), Alastair Reid (Borges), Hamish Henderson (Holderlin and Gramsci), Stuart Hood (Pasolini, Buzzati and Busi) and Edwin Morgan (just about everyone).

Emigration is a theme that appears in the fiction of many writers in this anthology. In Thomas Healy's *It Might have been Jerusalem*, Rab is looking for somewhere to live and a job and the conversation turns inevitably to where to go to achieve his aim. 'Tae London,' he tells his friend. Renton in *Trainspotting* says: 'Ah huv tae get oot ay Leith, oot ay Scotland. For good. Right away, no jist doon tae London fir six months.'

The impossibility of staying and the difficulty of leaving is a constant refrain in Kelman's fiction. In *A Chancer* John asks Tammas:

Ever thought about emigrating?
Emigrating? Course.
Whereabouts?
Any fucking place!

and in *How Late It Was, How Late*, Sammy Samuels tells his son Peter:

I'm thinking of heading.
Aw da.
Back to England.
Da.
Trying to get a job and that ye know?

In 1983 a book was published in France entitled *L'Ecosse: une nation sans état*. A year later, *Invisible Country* by James Campbell was published in London. He visits his native Scotland to discover why he had left the place a couple of years before. He gave it that title – which infuriated reviewers in Edinburgh and Glasgow at the time – because he felt that at the heart of the place was a political void. These were the years immediately after the 'failure' of the referendum on devolution. Campbell wrote that 'in this queer stagnation, prospects for a thriving modern literature are pretty dismal'. Allan Massie's novel, *One Night in Winter*, came out in the same year as Campbell's travel book. In it, Ebenezer exclaims that Scotland is a 'withered culture'. He says, 'Let Scotland be as independent as they wish, it will not alter the fact that there's little ... to keep talent here. Of course a political framework would retain a few – but how many?'

Both echo the 1936 essay 'Scott and Scotland', where Edwin Muir argued that the writer who wants to stay in Scotland and add to the culture 'Will find there, no matter how long he may search, neither an organic community to round off his conceptions nor a literary tradition to support him.' Any writer working in Scotland in 1997 certainly has the community and tradition to draw on for support.

Alasdair Gray has said that during the 1950s and most of the 1960s the only writers living in Glasgow he knew were Joan Ure and Archie Hind. In the years that have passed a lot has changed. An outsider reading some of the new writing coming out of Scotland could be forgiven for thinking that independence had already come. Cultural self-determination is assumed like never before in the nation's history.

Maybe it's because of size that Scotland works well as a literary centre. People can meet face to face relatively easily. Through the Hobsbaum group, the Print Studio Press, readings at the Third Eye Centre and the small magazines, writers met one another frequently for mutual support and disagreement. This happened more in Glasgow than in Edinburgh. Some hostility between the two cities remains even though they are only 45 minutes apart by train. Glasgow is a large city, but at any one time there tended to be half a dozen pubs where people connected with literature could meet for a chat. This helped to create a context outside the institutions of higher education and away from the distractions of London, where writing could be talked about in full seriousness.

> There is very little written, acted, composed, surmised and
> demanded in Scotland which does not in some strand descend
> from the new beginning he made.
>   Leader, the *Scotsman*, 9th September 1978,
>   after the death of Hugh MacDiarmid

In the century before this anthology, Scottish writers often employed an alias. Hugh MacDiarmid was born Christopher Murray Grieve, George Douglas published as George Douglas Brown, James Leslie Mitchell used the pen-name Lewis Grassic Gibbon, Robert Sutherland called himself Robert Garioch, Thomas Douglas Macdonald wrote as Fionn MacColla and Morris Blythman as Thurso Berwick. If such a distancing mechanism was necessary for them to write in a free way, others sought *geographical* space. There was Alexander Trocchi (who had written *Young Adam* and some hack pornography under the pseudonym Frances Lengel) in Paris and New York, W. S. Graham in Cornwall, Muriel Spark in New York and Rome, Alastair Reid in New York and the Dominican Republic and Alan Sharp in Los Angeles and then New Zealand.

MacDiarmid had a memorable face off with Alexander Trocchi during the International Writer's Conference at the 1962 Edinburgh Festival. This was organized by the publisher John Calder who invited seventy writers from twenty countries. Trocchi had lived outside Scotland for many years and was familiar to the authors attending from France and America but was little known in the country of his birth. The debate came to an operatic climax when he said that anything that had any merit in the Scottish Literature of the preceding twenty years had been written by him. MacDiarmid countered by calling him 'cosmopolitan scum'. Trocchi replied, 'I am only interested in lesbianism and sodomy'. Americans, including William Burroughs and Henry Miller, lined up in support of Trocchi and East European Communist Party writers backed MacDiarmid. On the surface this could be read as Trocchi the internationalist versus MacDiarmid the nationalist, or modernist versus traditionalist. Yet MacDiarmid had experimented with language in his poetry and drawn on sources from all over the world. Maybe their differences were more cultural and generational: beatnik and bard, heroin and malt whisky, black polo-neck and tweed tie. Thirty-five years on, the division seems to endure with Irvine Welsh calling Trocchi 'a Scottish George Best of literature' and MacDiarmid 'a symbol of all that's perfectly hideous about Scotland.' The problem may lie not so much with Mac-Diarmid as with those that cling only to his aura.

For most of the twentieth century, there was such a lack of debate in Scottish letters that MacDiarmid would start arguments with himself, changing his mind from month to month as if only to open up areas to debate. In making all this noise he was being more deliberate than most thought. He once wrote that what Scottish literature needed most was bulk. MacDiarmid spoke at times as if he was the country personified, the embodiment of the spirit of Scotland. At the age of seventy-two he told his friend George Bruce that he felt his job had always been 'to erupt like a volcano emitting not only a flame but a lot of rubbish.' He certainly kept his foot in the door when those outside were trying to slam it shut.

A by-product of this massive effort to hold Scottish literary culture up and protect it from all comers was firstly to prioritize poetry at the cost of fiction, and secondly, to prioritize MacDiarmid in front of everybody else. After his death it was not always easy to get close to his *work*. Mac-Diarmid's own words about Burns in 'A Drunk Man Looks At the Thistle' could well be applied to himself: 'Mair nonesense has been uttered in his name/ Than in ony's barrin liberty and Christ.' Young male disciples and sycophants created an aura around his life and work which meant you inevitably came to it with massive preconceptions either in favour or against. A cultural magazine – *Cencrastus* – was named after one of his poems and a book of tributes was published called, not surprisingly, *The Age of MacDiarmid*. For writers interviewed in the early 1980s an early question would be, 'What do you think of MacDiarmid's poem about or essay on...?' Especially after the 'failure' of the devolution referendum his legacy was a lifeboat for young men. Now, in the late 1990s, his halo has receded and it is possible to appreciate his writing free from encumbrances.

It is hard to exaggerate the influence of his personality on those around him. At his funeral Norman MacCaig said that MacDiarmid would walk into his mind 'as if it were a town and he a torchlight procession of one.' Seven years later when signing a copy of his own collected poems he at first wrote 'Hugh MacDiarmid', crossing it out just before he reached the end of the surname. He was a standing stone that cast a large shadow. For several decades Scottish literature appeared to the world as a group of male poets sitting round a table covered in malt whiskies in The Abbotsford Bar in Edinburgh. A writer only got admitted if one of them died. And if you weren't a poet you might as well wait at the door.

For three decades or more Scottish Literature *was* Scottish Poetry, and Scottish poetry was claimed by Edinburgh. The poets met in Edinburgh in one of three literary bars after a reading. The atmosphere is best captured in a classic, often reproduced, photograph of Hugh MacDiarmid, Sydney Goodsir Smith, Norman MacCaig and Douglas Young, cigarette in one hand, malt in the other. The scene has become something of an archetype – also appearing in a novel, a painting and being echoed by more recent photographs of writers. In Alasdair Gray's *1982 Janine* Jock McLeish goes into a basement bar in Hanover Street for a pie and a pint: 'The bar was crowded except where three men stood in a small open space created by the attention of the other customers. One had a sombre pouchy face and upstanding hair which seemed too like thistledown to be natural, one looked like a tall sarcastic lizard, one like a small sly shy bear. "Our three best since Burns," a bystander informed me, "barring

Sorley of course." I nodded as if I knew what he meant then went out and bought a picturecard view of the castle.'

In his painting *Poet's Pub* (also the title of an Eric Linklater novel) Alexander Moffat merged three drinking places – Milne's Bar, The Abbotsford and the Cafe Royal – into one. It formed the centrepiece of the 1981 exhibition 'Seven Poets' and he put MacDiarmid in the middle of a single canvas with Iain Crichton Smith, George Mackay Brown, Edwin Morgan, Sorley MacLean, Norman MacCaig and Robert Garioch. In hindsight this mythic combination marked the end of an era where poetry eclipsed prose, Edinburgh lorded it over Glasgow and women were left outside the pub of Scottish literature. The idea that you could fit Scotland's best writers round one table is inconceivable now. Yet a sincere attempt was made in 1995 when the *New Yorker* sent Richard Avedon to Glasgow to capture Scotland's best in a single posed team shot at the Clutha Vaults, a pub in the East End of Glasgow. In the sixteen years between Moffat's painting and Avedon's photograph the public landscape of Scottish writing has changed beyond recognition.

A few months later the *New York Times* magazine had a reporter set up a similar scene in Robbie's Bar in Leith. The piece appeared with the headline 'The Beats of Edinburgh' and the sub-headline 'from the margins of Scottish society comes a new, beer-soaked, drug-filled, profanity-laced, violently funny literature.'

> Scotland doesnae mean much tae Glesca folk.
>
> > Robert McLeish, *The Gorbals Story* (1948)

> There was no feeling of being Scots. I was from Greenock and that was different even from being from 'the Port' or Gourock or Glasgow.
>
> > Bill Bryden (1977)

James Kelman's autobiographical note to the *Three Glasgow Writers* anthology (published by Molendinar Press in 1976) reads:

> I was born and bred in Glasgow
> I have lived most of my life in Glasgow
> It is the place I know best
> My language is English
> I write

> In my writings the accent is in Glasgow
> I am always from Glasgow and I speak English always
> Always with this Glasgow accent
>
> This is right enough

In 1982 his story 'Not Not While the Giro' was published in Penguin's first *Firebird* anthology. Contributors provided sixty- or seventy-word author biographies. He wrote:

> James Kelman is a citizen of Glasgow.

In the pages that follow about a third of the writers are from Glasgow. When my first issue as editor of *Edinburgh Review* came out at the end of 1984, the reviewer in the *Times Literary Supplement* said that there were so many writers from the west of Scotland it should be renamed the *Glasgow Review*. If there was a scepticism of centralized power in London, there was barely less suspicion of the power that Edinburgh presumed itself to have. To much of the outside world Glasgow was still a city of murderers and drunks.

This image had started to change through new representations of the place by writers and artists. The city fathers sought to accelerate the process by paying public relations experts vast amounts of money to dream up rapturous tautologies like 'Glasgow's Glasgow' and 'Glasgow: European City of Culture' and 'What's Glasgowing On' and 'Glasgow's Miles Better'. The latter was trying to point out that Glasgow was smiling again (the decline of heavy industry made for cleaner air but massive unemployment) and that it was miles better than Edinburgh. When the slogan was booked by an ad agency for the side of Edinburgh's maroon buses, the capital's politicians refused permission at the last minute.

While many Glasgow writers see themselves as natives of that city first and of Scotland second, the city's burghers have been far from happy to take them on board. A member of the festivals office during Glasgow's year as European City of Culture was asked by a journalist why so few writers were involved. He told him that 'the writers were too difficult to work with'. A piece in the *New York Review of Books* by expatriate historian Gordon Craig took the side of the writers. This was followed swiftly by a long letter from Glasgow City Council leader Pat Lally rubbishing his argument. When the city fathers have included them it has been in a belittling fashion. In 1995 Glasgow's Department of Performing Arts distributed a lavish colour brochure consisting of folding out posters in four languages. I picked up my copy on the Gourock ferry.

The section entitled 'Glasgow People' is so awful it is worth reproducing in its entirety:

> Glaswegians prefer life lived on the verge of the surreal.
> Theirs is a gallows humour – exuberant, extravagant,
> grotesque but sparkling like the sun on frosty glass.
> As Ken Dodd put it, 'the trouble with Sigmund Freud was
> that he never had to play the Glasgow Empire on a Saturday
> night.' It could have changed history.
>
> Look at some of the people GLASGOW has produced.
>
> James Watt
> Lord Lister   Lord Kelvin
> Tobias Smollett   James Bridie   James Kelman
>   Jimmy Maxton   Billy Connolly
> Liz Lochhead   Charles Rennie Mackintosh
>   Peter Howson
>
> SOME TEAM! as Glaswegians might say
> But Glaswegians are prone to talk about themselves in a
> language that could bamboozle visitors.

During this promotional hubbub Edwin Morgan commented that 'it's much harder to write about central Glasgow today, which has had its face lifted – this doesn't give rise to feelings from which poems come.' A lifetime of being ignored, spoken for, used and abused and patronized would be hard enough for one person to bear. The city of Glasgow was done in by England and Scotland ... and by the burghers of Glasgow.

On the frontispiece of Book One of *Lanark*, Alasdair Gray rewrote the Glasgow city motto. Instead of 'Let Glasgow flourish by preaching the word', it reads 'Let Glasgow flourish by telling the truth.' The truth about Glasgow is that it has the highest density of lung cancer, heart problems, suicides and alcohol use in western Europe. In Jeff Torrington's story 'The Sink' Brogan tells Jordan that his neighbour has been sent home from hospital as incurable: 'Liver's like a chunk of cardboard. An alky. Telling you, if they cremate 'm, he'll burn for a fortnight!' In Torrington's novel *Swing Hammer Swing*, Burnett suggests to Clay that a Gorbals House of History should be erected. Clay muses to himself that 'at Sales Points patrons would be able to purchase wee model slums that tinkled "I Belong Tae Glesca" when their roofs were raised.'

Fuckin failures in a country of failures. It's nae good blamin
it oan the English for colonising us. Ah don't hate the English.
They're just wankers. We are colonised by wankers. We can't
even pick a decent, vibrant, healthy culture to be colonised by.
No. We're ruled by effete arseholes. What does that make us?
The lowest of the fuckin low, the scum of the earth. The most
wretched, servile, miserable, pathetic trash that was ever shat
intae creation. Ah don't hate the English. They just git oan wi
the shite thuv goat. Ah hate the Scots.

from Irvine Welsh's *Trainspotting* (1993)

The Scottish National Party used this monologue by Renton for a
recruitment form in September 1996. The Commission for Racial Equality
received a complaint about it from a Labour Member of Parliament and
it was referred to a lawyer who said that they might be in contravention
of the Malicious Publications Act. The editor of *Chapman*, one of Scotland's literary periodicals that comes out most in favour of devolution
and independence, has said, 'I'm not a patriot, Scotland's a rotten country.'
This berating of Scotland from within shows a new self-confidence.
Scottish writers are more comfortable criticizing their own country than
ever before. This can only come from a degree of cultural security,
moving beyond the see-saw of self-love (in the form of blind patriotism)
and self-loathing. This was not the case twenty years ago.

During 1995, Mainstream Publishing had a runaway success with the
guidebook *Scotland the Best*. A year later Canongate, another Edinburgh
publisher, released its sequel *Scotland the Worst*, a clear sign of cultural
health. Frank Kuppner, represented in this anthology by an extract from
one of his hybrid novels 'of sorts', sent a cycle of poems called 'Albanian
Folk Songs' to the *London Review of Books*. The Scots-born editor asked
why he was writing about a distant south-eastern European country and
he had to point out that Alba was the Gaelic for Scotland. An interviewer
once asked him, 'Kuppner – that's not exactly a Scottish name is it?' To
which he replied, 'Well, it is now.'

Muriel Gray in her speech on being elected Rector of Edinburgh
University said: 'I am no staunch defender of the couthy heedrum
hodrum brand of marketable mock Scottishness.' She called her production company Gallus Besom. There used to be another called Big Star in a
Wee Picture. When Duncan McLean was part of the Merry Mac Fun Co
theatre company in the mid 1980s they wrote plays with titles like
Macattack and *Psychoshanter*.

In the Highlands on the road to Fort Augustus there is a grey concrete litter bin on which someone has written in huge black letters the words 'TARTAN TOURS BOX OFFICE'. Football fans, rugby fans and pipers busking on Princes Street in Edinburgh or Sauchiehall Street in Glasgow now paint the Braveheart-trademark St Andrew's Cross on their faces as a humourous and powerful rather than nationally obedient gesture. 'Roam the globe, not the glens' screamed a recent advert for the newspaper *Scotland on Sunday.*

In 1981 Barbara and Murray Grigor organized an exhibition called *Scotch Myths.* They gathered ephemera – from shortbread tins to whisky bottles – which showed the whole range of representations of Scottishness. A recent promotional postcard from the British wine-merchants Oddbins would have fitted nicely into their polemic. It highlights a range of rare malt whiskies 'bottled from precious and dwindling collections, each has been nurtured to perfection and carefully selected. Most are unlikely to be seen again.' This combines the two recurrent myths of visitors to rural Scotland. On the one hand it has some of the last stretches of wilderness left in Europe and somehow by peat bog through highland spring water we can sample this purity through a malt. On the other hand with more tourism and development you are less likely to be alone, or in the words of the Oddbins promo 'So small is each bottling that this may represent your first and last chance to see, let alone taste, them.' The reverse of the postcard has a Ralph Steadman drawing of three men with red hooked noses and beards leaning over a malt potstill, with the faces of two more like them wafting ghostlike into the air above the boiling pot.

For an insight into the competing myths that part of Scotland claims as its own, buy copies of *The Field* and *Country Life* in the month of August (the month the shooting season begins). Then look at the *Scots Magazine* with its ads for Burns paperweights, cassettes of music with titles like 'Blood in the Heart' and, understandably for a country that so many people leave, articles on tracing your Scottish ancestry by CD-ROM. They make odd bedfellows. What they have in common is a desire to keep Scotland as it was. Or as it never was.

As a nation we have what the Germans call *eine unbewaltigte Vergangenheit* – a past with which we haven't completely come to terms. (In this we are quite unlike the English, who have come to terms with their history so well that they have largely forgotten it.)

Hamish Henderson in the *Scotsman* (1966)

We have to become independent so that we become more Scottish and less anti-English.

Dick Gaughan (1995)

England player: You Scotch are just a shower of bloody animals.
Scotland player: Aye, and don't you bloody well forget it.
    (conversation reported between players at a Rugby international)

Scotland continues its fight for statehood in an era where nations are breaking up into ethnicities, satellite broadcasting and internet communication mock national boundaries, and individuals are united more by their enthusiasms than by the colour of their passports. Yet its intellectuals are broadening their parameters to cope with this. The historian Angus Calder says that you can be counted as Scots if you support one of the country's sporting teams. What nationality does that make a Chicago Bulls fan in Aberdeen (or Moscow for that matter)?

In 1994 a new cultural journal was launched called *Scotlands*. Its editorial foreword described the magazine as an atlas to the plural identities that form contemporary Scotland. When Alan Warner was interviewed in the style magazine *I–D* in a feature on young talent to watch for in 1995 he said, 'There are many Scotlands within Scotland. I wanted to capture the strangeness of the one I know.' This embracing of the plurality that is Scotland is a characteristic of the new writing coming from the country which goes way beyond a table in The Abbotsford Bar.

The relationship between Scotland and England is still commemorated from Jedburgh to Orkney in the annual 'Ba Game'. In a cross between the running with the bulls in Pamplona and the Eton wall game, a leather ball is moved through the streets. The 'ba' is said to represent an Englishman's head. Football matches between Scotland and England at Wembley were war by another name. Major pitch invasions followed the Scottish victories of 1967 and 1977. The Scottish National Party wanted to use footage of these in a political broadcast but were refused permission.

Scottish business embraced the Union because it offered access to riches to be mined, picked and exploited in the foreign lands throughout the British empire. The Scots were the empire's most loyal administrators, engineers, teachers, doctors and key missionaries, like David Livingstone. The image and reality of the Scot as the trusted subaltern lives on in characters like Scottie, the loyal servant in *Star Trek.* As the empire began to decline, the English aristocracy, accelerating a process that began with Queen Victoria building Balmoral, turned ever larger parts of rural Scotland into the huge sporting estates which still constitute a third of the country's landmass. People were evicted from their homes for the sake of sheep and sport. What would the population of Scotland be now if the Highland Clearances had never happened?

While travelling around Scotland in 1995, the journalist George Rosie had a chance meeting with a senior English civil servant from Whitehall. As they sat in a hotel overlooking Ben Loyal and the hills of Sutherland, Rosie asked him why English governments have been so unwilling to hand Scotland back to the Scots. The official ticked the reasons off on his fingers: 'One, oil. Two, gas. Three, fish. Four, water. Five, land. The oil and gas are self-explanatory, even now. Fish might not mean much to the British but it is a superb bargaining counter in Europe. Water will be important one day, I suspect. And as for all this [gesturing to the hills] well, this is our, how shall I say it, breathing space. That bit of elbow room that every country should have.'

There were clearances of another sort in the 1960s when planners and developers bulldozed tenements and sent the people up into modern but damp flats or to the new towns like Cumbernauld, Glenrothes or East Kilbride. In *Swing Hammer Swing,* Jeff Torrington writes that: 'Whole tribes of Tenementers had gone off to the Reservations of Castlemilk and Toryglen or, like the bulk of those who remained, had ascended into Basil Spence's "Big Stone Wigwam in the Sky"'. This was a time when – in the words of Burns Singer – Glasgow felt it was too big for its own boots and set about shaving down its foot to fit.

Scotland missed out on the great nation-building of the nineteenth century because the middle classes had such a good economic deal out of being England's junior partners in the empire. As the empire fell apart and former colonies won their independence, the Scots lost the foundation of their British identity. This led to the first real electoral impact of Scottish Nationalism in the late 1960s. Scotland would have been given back to the Scots by now had it not been for the discovery of North Sea oil. As the oil depletes, so does Scotland's chance of self-government increase. There is a strange dynamic at work here, though. The Scots have Scottish nationalism, the Welsh have Welsh nationalism, but English nationalism is about being British.

Scotland entered the Union with England in 1707 as some people enter an arranged marriage – without enthusiasm. David Black has said that 'she recognized in her partner qualities she needed to develop in herself, qualities of stability and tolerance.' Now it may be too late for marriage guidance. As this relationship nears its end, the two countries require a course of separation counselling. The place can no longer be described, in the words of one Scot who edited an anthology in the early 1980s, as 'a nation which has lost much of its original culture and invented or romanticized more.' For the first time in centuries of insecurity and strife, Scotland has begun to stop defining itself by what it is not – England – and is with good humour facing up to what it is, both bad and good. Future generations will applaud the contribution which the writers in this anthology played in this process.

Part One

Agnes Owens

When Shankland Comes

It was a raw March morning when Ivy came into the village hotel where she was employed as a cleaner. Sometimes she served in the public bar too, but at present she wasn't needed so often, for trade was always poor after the New Year. In summer, though, the hotel did well. It stood on the main road and was a good stopping point for tourists on their way to the mountains and lochs beyond. The village itself could be described as sleepy. Some folks said it was merely dull. On the side of the road near the hotel was a long stretch of mansions near the hotel, and on the other a grocery store, adjacent to a small scheme of neat one-storey council houses. Behind the scheme stood a church dated 1894, and refaced with pink modern brick. There was no school in the village. The kids, big and small, had to travel by bus to the one in the small town of Blairmaddie, five miles away.

There were only two customers in the public bar: Geordie Forsyth the builder, and Sam Ferguson, who was elderly and toothless. Geordie Forsyth watched Ivy wipe the bar counter. She was a tall, angular-faced woman with an abundance of dark curling hair and a slim figure which was hidden under a green nylon overall. Though not young, being almost forty, older men – including Geordie Forsyth – still found her attractive. 'Ye look fair scunnered,' Geordie said.

'That's no crime,' said Ivy, tossing her head. Her mind was on Dennett, her seventeen-year-old son. He had refused to get out of bed when she called him up for work, and he'd only just started the job on the farm two days ago. Admittedly it was on the side and the wage was poor, but between that and his social security money you'd have thought he would be doing fine. When she called him a lazy bastard he'd said, well it wasn't his fault if he was a bastard, was it? The remark had rankled then, and it still did now.

'Gie us a smile,' said Geordie, when she lifted his glass to wipe under it. 'Ye're braw when ye smile.'

'I'm no' in the mood for smilin',' said Ivy; nevertheless, her mouth softened. She liked Geordie well enough. He wasn't bad looking in a coarse way and he had a steady job, which said a lot in his favour, but she didn't trust him. He was a hard drinker. Everybody knew that was why his wife had left him. Anyway she'd never had any time for men since Dennett was born.

'Whit she needs is a man,' said old Sam, wheezing with laughter.

'That I don't need,' said Ivy, rubbing away furiously. 'Besides there's no men in this place, at least no' what I'd call one.'

'Come roon the back and I'll soon show ye,' said Geordie.

Sam laughed again. Ivy tutted and said to Geordie, 'You should be at your buildin' instead of standin' here drinking. I don't know how you get away wi' it.'

'Because I'm ma ain boss,' said Geordie complacently, just as Jim Carr, the barman, came in.

'Hurry up wi' that counter so as I can get servin',' he told Ivy. Geordie put down his empty tumbler on the counter and walked out. Old Sam faded into the background, holding a glass which still contained an inch of beer.

'Who is there to serve?' snapped Ivy, and headed for the kitchen. It was almost ten o'clock and time for her cup of tea. Going down the hallway she met Walter Sproul, the manager. Although he barely glanced at her, she noted the bags under his eyes. Likely been on the bottle last night, she thought, and fighting with his wife. They could be heard first thing in the morning, either bawling at each other or thumping on their bed in a frenzy of love-making. Ivy despised Sproul and also that wife of his, who did absolutely nothing in the hotel except come down the stairs in the afternoon, her hair all frizzed up and her make-up thick, and drive off somewhere in her blue Mercedes. Of course when Shankland came it was a different story. Then you'd see her hovering behind Sproul as he spoke to Shankland with a smarmy smile on his face. Albert Shankland had been manager when Ivy first started work, twenty years ago. She had been taken on part-time as a waitress, then full-time, when they'd asked her to clean. The hotel had done well in those days, and it had always been a pleasure to work for Shankland. Eventually he bought up the hotel and then another one further south. When, soon afterwards, he'd moved south himself, appointing a new manager in his place, it had been a bitter blow. But that was a long time ago now, and many managers had come and gone before Sproul took over. Sproul, though, was the worst of the lot. She wished Shankland would come and pay the hotel one of his flying visits to study the books and give a pep talk to the staff. He always took her aside when he came, and spoke to her in a warm and friendly way. Once he even enquired about Dennett's health. 'He's fine,' she'd answered, not knowing what else to say.

In the big kitchen, Babs, the cook, was pouring out two cups of tea. Ivy began to spread butter thickly on a roll. 'That Sproul gets on ma goat,' Babs said.

'What's he done this time?' said Ivy.

'He says we'll have tae put less meat in the sandwiches.' Staring hard at Ivy's roll, she added, 'He'll go mad if he sees that.'

'I'm no' takin' any meat,' Ivy pointed out.

'I've got tae account for the butter as well,' said Babs, her voice aggrieved.

Ivy shrugged, then sat up on a high stool with her back facing the table and her legs crossed. Babs frowned at the sight of Ivy's slim legs. Her own were short and fat. In fact she was fat all over, with a stomach that bulged out under her white overall. Her broad face was red from the heat of the kitchen. 'By the way,' she said, 'are ye goin' tae the dance in the church hall on Saturday?'

Ivy wrinkled her nose slightly. 'I don't know. They're gettin' awful stale nowadays.'

'Ye always get a laugh at somethin', and the punch is free.'

'I'm no' that desperate for a drink,' said Ivy.

'There's nothin' much else happenin' in this dump,' said Babs bitterly.

'If I go it means that Dennett's in the house by himsel' until dead late.'

'Surely Dennett's auld enough to stay in by hissel'.'

'I'll have to think about it,' said Ivy, picturing Dennett bringing his pals in and drinking cans of lager.

Ivy was washing her cup when Jim burst into the kitchen and asked her to take the bar while he had some tea, since Betty, the lounge bar waitress, hadn't come in yet.

'I don't know how she's kept on,' said Ivy. 'She's always late.'

'And she's that bloody cheeky wi' it tae,' said Babs.

'Yous two are just jealous because she's sexy lookin',' Jim said.

Ivy and Babs laughed simultaneously. 'She's as sexy lookin' as a coo lookin' ower a dyke,' said Ivy.

There was nobody in the bar except old Sam, still holding his tumbler with its inch of beer.

'Finish that pint and get anither one,' said Ivy. 'This is no' a bus shelter you're staunin' in.'

'I canny afford anither one,' said Sam. 'I've only got ma pension tae keep me.'

'Aye, I know,' said Ivy sighing. She was about to give him a free half pint when Betty came in, her blonde hair spiked at the top and long and flat at the back.

'I slept in,' she explained, as old Sam gave her a startled look. He finished his beer and walked stiffly away.

'I'm sure that hair-do must have taken a good hour to fix,' said Ivy.

'No really,' said Betty, 'it's quite easy when ye know how.'

Sensing that Betty was about to launch into a long explanation about why she'd slept in, Ivy said quickly, 'Now that you're in I'm away to clean the toilets.'

The day passed slowly for Ivy. Business was still poor in the afternoon apart from a few young lads from the Community Programme who came in to order coffee. She looked at them enviously as they came through the hotel door wearing their donkey jackets. She wished Dennett could have been one of them. Of course he was too young for the Community Programme, which mainly consisted of doing old folk's gardens. In the bad weather they didn't do much more than hang around the hotel entrance laughing loud and inanely, but at least they were obliged to get up in the morning. Dennett, on the other hand, had still been in bed when she went home at lunchtime.

Sproul's wife had left as usual in her Mercedes and Sproul was prowling about the hotel like a pregnant cat, his face sullen and brooding, as if he wanted to find someone to lash out at. Ivy affected to look busy by polishing the hallway twice before she went through to the kitchen to scrub the big table. Babs had gone off duty at four o'clock, and the room was empty. Ivy stared up through the kitchen window at the tormented-looking sky, thinking that it wouldn't be all that long until summer, when the place would be packed out. In the meantime she had only another hour to go.

On her way home she stopped at the grocery, which sold everything from a packet of pins to a jar of boiled mussels. The freezer near the door was filled with all sorts of frozen packets and half the counter was taken up with rolls, pies and doughnuts, all in separate cardboard boxes. Scarcely four people could stand inside the shop comfortably.

'My, it's a right cauld day,' said Mrs Braithwaite, the owner, from behind the counter. She was a small stout elderly woman who always wore a hairnet over her blue perm.

'I'm fair roastin',' said Ivy, and went on to ask for two pies and a tin of beans.

'It'll be a' that hard work ye dae in the hotel,' said Mrs Braithwaite. She put two pies in a poke, then, without turning round, lifted a tin of beans from the shelf behind her. The shop was so cramped that she scarcely needed to move an inch to put her hand on any item, except for the freezer, from which folk helped themselves. 'I've heard the manager's no' very easy tae work for,' she added.

'He's no' bad,' said Ivy, reluctant to say anything that could get to Sproul's ears.

'They tell me the wages are no' very good,' said Mrs Braithwaite, when Ivy handed over a pound note for the purchases.

'They're a lot better than what ye get off the social,' said Ivy promptly.

'That's true,' said Mrs Braithwaite, opening the till. 'Though I've heard there's plenty on the social and workin' forbye.' She looked directly at Ivy. 'I don't think that's fair, dae you?'

'I don't suppose it is,' said Ivy, wondering if the storekeeper knew that Dennett had worked two days on the farm. She asked for ten kingsize Regal before Mrs Braithwaite could pursue the subject any further, and headed for the door.

Outside, the wind blew cold in her face, but invigorating. Old autumn leaves stirred at the side of the pavement and in the distance she could see the peaks of the mountains covered in snow. She walked up the neat path of her council house noting the snowdrops under her window and reflecting that the village would be a nice enough place to stay in, if it wasn't for some of the folk.

When she came into the living room Dennett was sitting in the armchair facing the television with the gas fire turned up full.

'So, you've managed to get up then,' she said, turning the fire low. He stretched his legs and kept his sharp profile fixed ahead. She noticed with distaste that his hair was uncombed. It lay on his shoulders light brown and straggly. 'You might have washed yersel' at least,' she muttered, as she went through to the kitchenette to put on the kettle. A minute later she was startled to see him towering above her looking anxious. 'Did ye get my fags?' he asked.

'They're in my bag,' she said, exasperated. 'Do ye no' think it's terrible I should have to buy you fags and you'll no' even make an attempt to earn money to buy them yersel'?'

'I wisny feelin' well this mornin',' he said, ripping the cellophane from the packet. 'I'll go tae work the morra.'

'Well, ye'd better,' she said, a bit mollified by this statement. 'But mind,' she added, 'don't go near the store on your way to the farm. If auld Braithwaite thinks you're workin' she could report ye. She's that type.'

'Aye,' he said, then: 'Are ye makin' chips?'

'No,' she shouted, thinking that Dennett never seemed to give a damn about anything that really mattered.

'Did ye hear that Shankland's comin'?' Babs said to Ivy when she came into the hotel kitchen next morning.

'When?' said Ivy, trying not to look excited.

'Either Friday or Saturday,' said Babs. She added morosely, 'I hate it when he comes.'

'He's OK – a lot better than Sproul,' said Ivy. 'If Shankland has anythin' to say he tells ye fair and square, no' like Sproul wi' his snidy remarks for no good reason. Shankland doesny bother me.'

'It's a' right for you,' said Babs. 'You're mair familiar wi' him than me.'

'Whit dae ye mean "familiar"?' said Ivy, her voice sharp.

'I only mean that you've known him longer than any of us, that's a',' said Babs, her eyes wide and innocent. She poured out the tea while Ivy buttered her roll heavily. 'Anyway,' she went on, 'business is that bad I wouldny be surprised if he's up tae close the hotel. It's happenin' a' ower the place. I heard the hotel outside Blairmaddie's tae close and it only opened three years ago.'

Ivy made no comment on this, inwardly seething at the use of the word 'familiar'. It looked as though Babs was jealous of her long acquaintanceship with Shankland. She'd have to be careful of what she said to her in future. When she was washing her cup at the sink Babs said, 'Are ye still no' goin' tae the dance?'

'Definitely no',' snapped Ivy, marching off to dust and hoover the lounge, although she didn't think it would need much cleaning since it hadn't been opened since Monday.

Thursday was cold, but bright. The hotel was surprisingly busy with families tempted out for the day by the early spring sun, and some of the wealthy retired locals from the big houses. The lounge was opened and there were six men standing in the public bar, including Geordie Forsyth who came in every day anyway. Ivy was asked to serve in the bar while Betty did the lounge. All this and the fact that Dennett had got out of his bed and gone to his job at the farm put Ivy in a good mood. Jim hummed tunes under his breath as he pulled the pints, and Sproul walked between the lounge and the bar with his face less haunted looking than usual. Only Babs in the kitchen was grumbling when Ivy dashed in for a quick cup of tea; she hadn't time for a roll. 'If it's goin' tae be as busy as this,' she said, 'I'll need extra help.'

'I thought you said the hotel might be closin' down,' Ivy laughed.

'If it's no' one way it's another,' Babs shouted as Ivy dashed off. 'Don't forget one swallow doesny make a summer.'

Ivy didn't go home for lunch, since she had a lot of catching up to do with the cleaning. She took a snack in the kitchen, and then carried on with all her other jobs: the washing, the hoovering and dusting, the polishing. It was hard going, she thought, but it was worth it to see the place so busy. Maybe from now on business would pick up and every-one would be in a better mood. When she got home at half past five after stopping at the store to buy milk, bread and cheese, her face fell. Dennett sat in the chair facing the television with the gas fire turned up full.

'I thought ye didny stop until six,' she said, blinking nervously.

'I've been sacked,' he said.

'Sacked?' she said, throwing her message bag on the couch and sinking down beside it.

'Aye, sacked,' he said defiantly. 'It wis because I never came in yesterday. I've been in here since nine in the mornin'.'

'I knew this would happen,' she said bitterly.

Dennett's voice was equally bitter. 'I'm glad I wis sacked. You don't know whit it's like tae muck out dung all day, and then havin' tae eat your piece wi' yer haunds all smelly, and no' even a drap o' tea to wash it down. Anyway it wisny a real job, I'd only have got paid in washers.'

'Did you get yer two days' money then?'

'Naw, he said I wis tae come back on Saturday.'

'And I bet like hell you bloody well won't,' said Ivy, her temper rising. 'And here's me workin' my pan in to keep you in meals and fags and put a good face on everythin' and tryin' to keep decent and there you are tellin' me you're above muckin' out byres … Well I don't particularly like bein' a cleaner and gettin' paid in washers either, but I have to do it to keep a roof above our heids.'

Dennett sneered, 'That's up tae you.'

Enraged, Ivy jumped up from the couch and slapped him on the cheek. Dennett confronted her with eyes blazing. For a second she thought he was going to slap her back, but he only stared at her madly for a moment before he rushed out of the room. She heard his bedroom door slam hard, then silence. She sat down on the couch again, drained, vowing to herself that she would tell Dennett to get out. He was old enough to take care of himself, after all; why should she put up with his laziness and cheek? He could get himself a room or a bed and breakfast somewhere in Blairmaddie, and come to think of it Blairmaddie would suit him better, being full of licensed grocers and pubs.

Knowing him he'd likely just drift around spending his social money on booze or even dope: she'd heard there were junkies galore there. At least, she thought angrily, if he's out of the way he can't give me a showing up in the village. She sat for a while thinking of what could happen to Dennett in Blairmaddie or some other bigger place beyond. But she could never do it, of course. He was too feckless. It was quite beyond her to put him out at seventeen. Besides, he wouldn't go easily, and after all he might get a job with the Community Programme next September when he was eighteen. Sighing, she stood up and went through to the kitchenette to make some tea and toasted cheese. It was all she felt fit to cook. Ten minutes later she shouted from the living room, 'Dennett, come and get your supper.' When he came through he peered at the plate on the work top, saying in a perplexed manner, 'Toasted cheese? How did ye no' make chips for a change?'

On Friday it snowed and again there was hardly anybody in the bar except Geordie Forsyth who was at one of the tables in the small room, deep in discussion with two of the brickies he employed. He hardly glanced at Ivy when she came in to clean, which annoyed her in a way, especially when she had taken extra pains with her hair, brushing it hard so that it fell smoothly round her face, as well as putting on a touch of eye-shadow and lipstick. Although all this was for Shankland's benefit, she'd expected a compliment or two from Geordie. Betty came in right on time for once, and Ivy didn't doubt that it was because she too expected Shankland at any minute. Jim stood behind Betty polishing the glasses intently.

The morning passed and Shankland did not show up, nor was there any sign of Sproul in the hotel. This seemed strange to Ivy but she didn't remark on it, not even to Babs. In fact, they had scarcely a word to say to each other during the tea break. It was as if they had mutually decided to fall out.

Ivy came back home at lunch feeling thoroughly disgruntled. She was taken aback to see Dennett up and fully clothed, eating toast and scrambled egg. Then she remembered that this was his giro day.

'There's some egg left in the pot,' he said obligingly.

'Thanks,' she said curtly, thinking he'd have done better to make a slice of toast to go with it. Before she left she reminded him to leave his money on the sideboard after he had cashed the giro at Braithwaite's store.

'I always dae,' he answered with a touch of indignation.

In the afternoon when she took the hoover into the lounge she was surprised to see Sproul's wife standing behind the small lounge bar. 'Don't bother hoovering,' she told Ivy. 'The carpet's clean enough. Just separate the tables. They're far too close together.'

'I always hoover the carpet whether it's clean or no',' Ivy said hotly. 'That's how it's in such good condition.'

'Nonsense,' said Sproul's wife. 'Just do as I say.'

'Wait a minute,' said Ivy, her eyes blazing. 'Since when have you taken charge?'

Sproul's wife said tartly, 'As from today, I'm in charge of the lounge.' As Ivy stared at her in disbelief, Sproul's wife, her lips cyclamen pink and smiling, added, 'if you don't believe me, ask my husband when he comes in.'

'I'll no' bother seein' your husband,' Ivy retorted, 'I'll wait tae Shankland comes in. It seems to me he's the main one to see.'

'Do you think so?' said Sproul's wife, assuming an astonished expression. 'I'd hardly credit that, when my husband is paid to manage the hotel. However, if you want to see Mr Shankland you'll have to wait until tomorrow. He's down at Blairmaddie at the moment discussing business with my husband in the Riverbank Hotel. He thought it better to stay there for the night on account of the roads being so bad up here with the snow.'

Ivy gave Sproul's wife one black look, then turned on her heel, trailing the hoover behind her.

'What about separating the tables,' Sproul's wife called, but Ivy was off into the toilet to try and calm herself down.

On a Friday at tea-time the store was always busy, mainly with women rushing in at the last minute after collecting their husband's wages. Although there was less rushing in nowadays than there used to be, it was still busy enough to make Ivy fume with impatience as she waited at the end of the queue. She wanted to get home quickly to make sure that her share of Dennett's giro was lying on the sideboard, but over and above that, she had been completely thrown into confusion by her encounter with Sproul's wife. It seemed to her as she waited that Mrs Braithwaite was chatting longer than ever with the customers. When finally her turn came, she asked for bread, potatoes and half a pound of sausages in a clipped voice. But this didn't prevent the storekeeper informing her that Dennett had just been in to cash his giro. As Ivy nodded and opened her purse, Mrs Braithwaite added, 'It's a pity he canny get work, a big strong fella like that.'

Ivy was stung into saying, 'There's no work to be had, is there?'

'I don't know,' said Mrs Braithwaite deliberately. 'There's some that widny take a job if it was under their very nose.'

Ivy grabbed her change from Mrs Braithwaite's fat fingers and marched out past the queue that had formed behind her.

When she went in through the front door she heard Dennett running the tap in the bathroom. He usually celebrated his giro day with a bath and a hair wash before going out with his pals for a night in Blairmaddie. She put the kettle on then checked to see if her money was on the sideboard. It was – the whole twenty-five pounds of it. His dinner was on the plate when he came into the kitchen, rubbing his hair with a towel, his face pink and shiny.

'Good,' he said. 'Chips.'

'I'm glad somethin' pleases you,' she said drily, following him into the living room. Dennett stuffed chips into his mouth, gazing dreamily at the television. Ivy picked at her meal half-heartedly. Before she lifted the dishes to wash them she told Dennett to mind and go up to the farm on Saturday and get the money owed to him.

'Aye – so I wull,' he said reluctantly, frowning, as if he had no intention of going at all. Then he stood up and went into his bedroom. Within seconds the insistent beat of some pop group pounded on her ear drums. She debated whether to go through and tell him to turn the record down. Instead she took a pair of ear plugs from a drawer in the kitchen cabinet and sat down on the couch, staring blankly at a television she couldn't hear. An hour later he peeped into the living room to tell her that he was away. She took the ear plugs out and told him not to be late.

'Aye, so I wull,' he said. She knew she was wasting her breath.

On Saturday, rain turned the snow on the pavements to slush. Ivy came into the public bar wearing a blue woollen dress minus her nylon apron. She had decided to look good for Shankland, but when Jim turned to her and said, 'For a second I thought you wir Sproul's wife,' she began to wonder if the dress was a mistake.

'I should hope no',' she muttered, dying to ask him if Shankland had come in last night, but her pride kept her silent. She only asked if Sproul was around.

'No' yit,' he answered, pulling a face as if something was happening that only he knew about. When she began to wipe the shelves he said in a low voice, 'Sproul's wife is takin' over the lounge.'

'So I heard,' said Ivy. 'Well, maybe it's time she did something for her keep.'

'Looks as if there's gaun to be a lot mair changes,' said Jim darkly.

Curtly Ivy replied, 'It's all one tae me, I'm only the cleaner, thank God.' Jim turned away to serve one of the men who had come forward from a youngish crowd who sat at a table. Every Saturday morning they came in, deafening the place with their loud aggressive talk. Ivy was glad to get out of the bar whenever they arrived.

'Would ye like to gie us a hand?' Jim asked her when another two of the men came forward to the counter.

'I've got a lot to do,' said Ivy hurrying away: Betty would be in any minute and she'd be overjoyed to serve that boisterous lot.

'That's a nice dress ye've on,' Babs said to her in the kitchen, evidently prepared to be friendly.

'Actually it's quite an old one,' said Ivy.

'It doesny look it,' said Babs. 'How have ye no' got yer apron on? It'll get a' dirty.'

'I forgot to bring it. Anyway it doesny matter if it gets dirty,' said Ivy impatiently.

'Here, d'ye know that Sproul's wife's in the lounge?' said Babs, handing Ivy a cup of tea and a roll which she explained was already buttered.

'Thanks,' said Ivy, suspecting the roll would be buttered thin. 'She telt me herself yesterday.'

'Did she?' said Babs, her eyes wide. 'You must be well in. Naebody tells me anythin' except when it's history.'

'I wouldn't worry about it,' said Ivy. 'There's always bound to be changes at some time.'

'Aye, but changes are never for the best nowadays,' said Babs.

'Let's look on the bright side for once,' said Ivy, feeling anything but bright. She suddenly had a premonition: either Shankland wasn't going to come in at all, or maybe he had been in last night and gone away again. So if Sproul's wife was going to take over the lounge, where did that leave her? If Betty had only the public bar to do it meant that they wouldn't need her to serve at all and there definitely wasn't enough cleaning to justify her hours from nine to five. And if they cut her hours, she might as well be on the dole. She'd have to talk to Sproul about it immediately.

Suddenly Babs said, 'Are you still no' goin' tae the dance?'

'I've already told you I'm no',' said Ivy sharply.

'Then I don't think I'll go either,' said Babs. 'I hate goin' in the door masel'.'

'Don't then,' said Ivy. She felt like screaming.

Later, when she was coming out of the toilet, Betty told her in a casual way that she'd heard Shankland was coming in the afternoon. Ivy brightened up at that. She decided that there was no need to see Sproul. Shankland would allay her fears. So what if Sproul's wife was managing the lounge? She could come to terms with that as long as they didn't cut her hours.

When she got home at lunchtime she looked in at Dennett's room to see if he was all right. Heaven knows what time he'd come home last night, and in what condition. When she'd left this morning she had been so preoccupied by the affairs of the hotel that she'd forgotten all about him. She found him lying on his back, snoring his head off, his long legs sticking out from under the blankets. 'Dennett,' she called, but he continued to snore. When she called again, 'Do ye want something to eat?' he grunted 'Naw,' and turned on his side. She studied him for a while, almost envying his complete disregard for anyone but himself. He had no talent, no ambition and no pride, yet he looked so happy lying there with that slight smile on his lips.

The afternoon wore on and still there was no sign of Shankland. Sproul passed her once or twice as she was polishing the woodwork in the corridor, and ducked his head in an embarrassed way which made her wonder. But when Jim handed over her pay envelope at half past four she found out why. Inside was two weeks' money and a letter saying that due to increased overheads and poor trade, the management regretted that they no longer required her services. However, as soon as trade picked up they would send for her again.

Ivy scanned the letter twice to make sure she had read correctly. Then chalkfaced, she went off in search of Sproul. She found him behind the lounge bar standing close to his wife. They were studying a ledger and they looked conspiratorial. Ivy thrust the letter under Sproul's nose and said, 'You canny do this to me.'

Sproul and his wife looked up at her with pained expressions. Sproul said, 'I'm very sorry about this, but ...'

'Never mind bein' sorry,' Ivy interrupted. 'I'm goin' to see Shankland. When will he be in?'

Sproul's wife shoved her face forward. 'He won't be in,' she said spitefully. 'He's already spoken to us about everything. Isn't that right, Walter?'

'Yes,' Sproul said heavily.

Ivy's head swam. She said faintly, 'He canny know about this. Shankland would never sack me.'

'It was his instructions,' said Sproul.

'You're lyin',' said Ivy. 'Give me his address and I'll get in touch wi' him myself.'

Sproul and his wife exchanged weary glances. 'Look Ivy,' said Sproul, 'if you want to see him, try the church hall round about ten o'clock. He and his wife have been invited to the dance as special guests, but I can assure you that letter was written on his instructions.'

'I still don't believe you,' said Ivy, turning away to hide the tears in her eyes. A minute later she put on her coat and walked out of the hotel without saying a word to anyone.

Prompt on ten Ivy was inside the church hall, still wearing her blue woollen dress and fortified by two glasses of port from the bottle which had been in her sideboard since the New Year. She was dismayed to see that hardly anyone had turned up, apart from the minister and some church elders waiting by the door; the minister's wife and her cronies stood at the far end of the hall beside a table spread with food. The band sat on a platform in a corner near the entrance, wearing maroon shirts and dark suits. It was the same band that played every year, its members middle-aged and bespectacled. Hesitantly Ivy went over to the table and, for want of anything better to do, helped herself to a sandwich and a glass of punch from the big fruit bowl in the centre.

'How nice to see you, Ivy,' said the minister's wife, smiling horsily.

'Likewise, I'm sure,' said Ivy. She took a gulp of the punch and shuddered.

'Strong, isn't it?' said the minister's wife. 'There's a bottle of brandy in it. I made it myself.'

'It's very good,' said Ivy, forcing a smile. She added brightly, 'There's no' many turned up though.'

'They'll be fortifyin' themselves in the hotel,' said Mrs Braithwaite, who wore pink gingham and for once had no hairnet on.

'Do you mind if I sit down?' said Ivy. She was beginning to feel dizzy from drinking the strong punch on top of the port. She went over to the bench against the wall and sat there sipping from her glass until she calmed down a bit. A crowd of men and women thrust through the door like cattle from a stockade, and the band began to play a slow foxtrot.

The minister and his wife were the first on the floor, dancing awkwardly, their faces strained. Ivy decided to have just one more glass of punch. It would while away the time until Shankland arrived. Although by now her head was so foggy that quite honestly she didn't really care whether he came or not. When she turned round from the table she saw Babs sailing towards her like a gigantic balloon in her wide orange dress.

'I thought you wereny comin',' said Babs indignantly, helping herself to a sausage roll. With crumbs falling from her mouth, she added: 'Is it true ye've got the sack?'

'Is that what you heard?' said Ivy, taking a gulp of punch.

'Well, is it true?' Babs persisted.

'Nothing that's ever said in this place is true.' Ivy pointed to the bowl of punch. 'Try some of that. It's strong stuff. There's a whole bottle of brandy in it.' She heard herself laugh foolishly.

'It seems tae be,' said Babs, staring hard at Ivy. Then she walked off to talk to the minister's wife, leaving Ivy on her own.

Geordie Forsyth came up from behind then, and asked her for a dance. She was vaguely surprised to see him so smart in a grey pin-striped suit. 'Right,' she said, grateful for the rescue. As they waltzed round the hall she tripped over his feet, feeling quite giddy.

'Steady on,' said Geordie. He pulled her close, his hand pressing her waist. If it hadn't been for the half bottle in Geordie's pocket jamming hard into her hip, she would happily have floated round the hall for the rest of the night. When the dance ended, Geordie asked her if she'd like to come outside for a wee nip of whisky.

'I don't know...' she began. And then she saw Shankland standing in the doorway. With him was a small, plump, matronly woman in a black lace dress. Shankland was shaking hands with the minister, his heavy-jowled face lit by a smile. He was a big man with a thick waist. He had never been handsome, exactly, but you could tell he attracted attention wherever he went.

Without thinking, Ivy rushed forward. 'Mr Shankland,' she said, tugging at his sleeve, 'can I have a word with you? It's very important.'

Shankland turned round, frowning. 'Later, Ivy. Can't you see my wife and I are talking to the minister?'

His wife, who as far as Ivy could see hadn't been talking at all, looked her up and down with suspicion.

'I'm sorry,' said Ivy, 'but Sproul's sacked me from the hotel and I've been waitin' for you to come in.' The words came out slurred. She broke off, sick at heart at Shankland's expression.

'Yes, I'm sorry it had to happen,' he said guardedly. 'But you see, it was either that or closing down the hotel altogether. However, if the place does better in the summer we'll send for you again, don't worry on that score.' And with that he turned back to the minister, who had been listening anxiously.

Suddenly Ivy's rage erupted. 'You mean to say,' she said, her voice rising, 'that you were the one who sacked me, after all these years? All these years I've been loyal and kept my mouth shut?'

Shankland scarcely looked at her. 'Go away, Ivy,' he said wearily. 'You're drunk.'

'Yes, do go and sit down, Ivy,' the minister pleaded. 'You're not your usual self. Perhaps it's the punch. I told my wife not to put in so much brandy.'

'What do you mean – "kept your mouth shut"?' asked Shankland's wife, her face puckering.

'Don't listen to her,' Shankland said. 'She's just upset and a bit drunk. That's all there is to it.' He led his wife towards the table, bending over her slightly, while the minister followed close behind.

Ivy stood for a moment, dazed, her mind fuddled by the slow monotonous rhythm of the band. She noticed Geordie Forsyth dancing with Babs and looking genteel. A taste of bile was in her mouth and her head was in a turmoil. She saw Shankland turn his back on her and offer his wife a sandwich from a plate. Then all at once her mind was made up. She rushed across to the table.

'That's no' all there is to it!' she said in a voice loud and clear. 'What about Dennett, my son and yours, whom I've kept for seventeen years without a penny off ye? I took the blame on myself, aye, they say it's always the woman to blame, don't they. But since you think so little of me I might as well admit in front of everybody here that you're Dennett's father. I think ye owe me something for that.'

'You're crazy!' said Shankland, with a furtive look at his wife. Her face had turned white as a sheet. All around the table a hush had fallen, and people were staring. He grabbed his wife's elbow. 'Let's get out of here,' he whispered.

The small woman stood her ground, trembling. 'Leave me alone,' she said.

Shankland tugged at her urgently. 'Come on.'

And then his wife's arm jerked up and her eyes went blank and she threw the glass of punch straight into Shankland's face.

'Oh dear,' said the minister, his hands fluttering in the air, and

someone laughed. There were a few more titters. Then Shankland turned
and marched towards the door, his wife following a yard or two behind.

Ivy clutched at the table for support.

'Go over and sit down,' Mrs Braithwaite said in a surprisingly kind
voice. 'I'll see if I can get a cup of tea from somewhere.' She glared at the
minister's wife. 'That punch bowl's been a bloody curse!'

'I'm okay,' said Ivy, smiling wanly.

'I'm awful sorry',' said the minister's wife with an apologetic look at
Ivy. 'I shouldn't have put so much brandy in.'

'Don't worry yourself, I quite enjoyed it.' Ivy walked over to the bench
by the wall and sat down. Geordie Forsyth and Babs came off the dance
floor, red-faced and dripping with sweat.

'Have you been sittin' here a' night?' Babs sounded concerned.

'No' really,' said Ivy.

'I thought I saw Shankland come in.'

'So he did,' said Ivy. 'He's away now.'

'Did he say anythin'? I mean, about you gettin' the sack?'

'No' as much as I said to him.'

Geordie took the half bottle from his pocket. 'Do any of youse ladies
want a wee nip?'

'No' straight frae the bottle,' said Babs, aghast.

'I'll take one,' said Ivy, putting the bottle to her mouth.

'Will ye look at her!' Babs said. 'To think she's aye sae proud and
ladylike.'

'No' any more,' said Ivy. The rough whisky trickled down her throat.
She was about to tilt the bottle again when a sudden thought stopped
her. Dennett. It wasn't as if she only had herself to consider, after all.
Likely he'd be in on his own, watching the television, since he never had
any money left on a Saturday to go anywhere. Aye, Dennett. Somebody
had to set him an example, didn't they, and she'd been doing it for years
so she wasn't about to stop now. She handed the bottle back to Geordie
and struggled to her feet. 'I think I'll go home now.'

'Away, it's still early,' said Geordie, looking at his watch.

'I must get home,' Ivy said firmly. 'I've left Dennett in himsel' and he's
no' to be trusted.'

'There goes an awfy determined woman,' said Geordie, as he and Babs
watched her leave.

'The trouble wi' Ivy,' said Babs, 'is that she's aye been too big for her
boots, and now she's been sacked she canny take it.' She sniffed loudly.
'If you ask me, it serves her right.'

Iain Crichton Smith

from *In the Middle of the Wood*

In the ambulance the following day there was only himself and the psychologist. He rocked from side to side, and, as he did so, he looked out of the window at the beautiful autumn colours of the day. There were ordinary people walking along the streets with shopping bags in their hands, a boy cycling invulnerably along, a youth and a girl strolling hand in hand. The world that he would never enter again, that he must leave forever behind him. How dear it was, how little he had taken account of its freedom in the past. They left the town and raced along beside a moorland with lochs in it, the untroubled blue of water. How splendid and fine it all was, that heartbreaking picture of serenity. The psychologist smiled at him but didn't speak. Ralph drew his dressing-gown more closely about him as if he were cold. Now and again the ambulance driver waved to a passing van or bus, negligently, cordially.

They had been an hour on the road when they arrived at a large building, along whose side they drove. Eventually they were taken along to a room and told to wait there. Ralph looked up idly and saw that the lamp above the bed had been decorated with a Mexican hat: it was the only odd decoration in the room. This didn't surprise him, it was only another incident in the war of nerves that was being waged against him. Suddenly he saw Linda walking along a corridor and then coming in.

'I raced after you in the car,' she said. He was astonished to find her there at all. This appearance didn't seem part of the script he had worked out. According to the scenario he had modelled she should now be sitting with her fat lover drinking wine, being comfortable.

'What did you come here for?' he asked angrily.

'What do you mean what did I come here for? I had to see that you were all right.'

'Yes. Now that you have put me here.' He wanted to hurt her as badly as he could. He wanted to reduce his dependence on her but he couldn't. He was glad that she had come but he couldn't understand why. This of course was the reason for her visit: she wished to confirm that he had arrived in the Mental Home.

He looked up and saw a grey-haired woman patrolling the corridor.

She was going round and round the quadrangle which formed the central core of the hospital. The woman was gaunt, silent, studious: he immediately christened her Lady Macbeth.

'Have you got everything you need?' said Linda anxiously.

'I don't know. I don't care.'

'I brought you some money. There might be a shop here.' She handed him over some money and he placed it in a locker.

'Do you see that? That hat?' he said aggressively.

She considered it and said, 'It's odd right enough. The arm of the lamp looks broken.' She switched the lamp on and it emitted a pale light hardly to be seen in the daylight.

'At least it's working,' she said.

'Why must it always be something of mine that has something wrong with it?' he asked.

'I don't know. I don't understand. Perhaps it was a nurse's prank.'

'Huh.'

He was sure it wasn't a nurse's prank. There were too many wrong things, too many coincidences. But what was the inner meaning of leaving a Mexican hat? He was sure it must have some deep inner significance. An allegory, symbolism. But he couldn't work it out.

'You had better go,' he said firmly.

'Is that what you want me to do?'

'Yes. That's what I want you to do. You should never have come in the first place.'

She regarded him sadly. 'I won't be able to come so often now. This place is further away.'

'Naturally,' he said.

'But I'll do my best.'

'I'm sure you will,' he said ironically. 'How do you get sleep?'

'I don't know,' she whispered. Her voice was very low as if there was something wrong with her throat. He was sure that the reason for this was that she was wearing a bug and she wanted only his comments to be picked up.

'I don't want the nurses to hear us quarrelling,' she said.

'I don't care,' he said. 'I know what you're at.'

'What do you think I'm at?'

'You have a bug,' he whispered. Linda rose to her feet angrily. She was almost weeping but he thought this was her good acting.

'You obviously don't want me here,' she said.

'You're right.'

But when she did go it was as if his whole life was draining away from him.

Shortly after she had gone a thin tall unsmiling man entered the ward and began to pace from his bed to the opposite wall and then back again. He did this with an obsessive pertinacity, remorselessly, as if he were an automaton. Ralph smiled defensively at him but he didn't smile back. Again he felt fear as if this dour robot might attack him. First there was the grey-haired Lady Macbeth and now this tense unsmiling man from whom emanated an air of suppressed violence.

After a while a man came in with a stethoscope hung over his neck like a snake.

'I'm Doctor Malone,' he said in an Irish accent. 'If you will wait here for a moment I'll be back for you.' Of course he was another spy pretending to be a psychologist. He was handsome, debonair, careless. Suddenly it occurred to Ralph that this was Linda's lover, and not the taxi driver: the whole plot smelt of a psychologist's expertise. And this too was why Linda had come. The plan had been evolved from this very place: he had made a mistake: he hadn't fully realized the complexity of it.

He waited and waited while the thin tense man paced up and down, counting his steps, and when the doctor didn't come he decided that he would go to bed, even though he hadn't been told to. He sat up in bed and watched the relentless repetitive journey of his room mate who completely ignored him. The doctor had left his stethoscope on a neighbouring bed: there was silence everywhere, an oppressive silence. In the middle of it he could hear through the open window the humming of bees. Could he escape from here? Some people had. He couldn't sign himself out, that was certain. He wanted to write something but he couldn't for firstly he couldn't find pen and paper and secondly his concentration had gone.

After a while the doctor came back and said cheerfully, 'Come along now if you please.'

They sat in chairs opposite each other. The psychologist told him a story as the doctor in the hospital had done and he answered the questions correctly. He was told to remember a certain address which this time was 56 Osborne Street. He analysed it in his mind but couldn't find any connections hanging to it. The psychologist asked him about his novels but he didn't want to talk about them: he knew that Malone hadn't read any of them anyway. The whole place was very quiet: he could hear no violent noises, no mad ravings. The sun shone pleasantly through the windows.

'When will I be out of here?' he asked abruptly.

'Not long,' said the psychologist smiling. 'Not too long at all.' What a Celtic liar you are, thought Ralph. You are like all the Celts, a gentle hypocrite.

'Two weeks?' he probed.

'I wouldn't know about that, not at all,' said the psychologist, still smiling. Ralph stared unsmilingly back. In fact he couldn't smile at all nowadays. If he tried to, he felt that his face would crack. He felt like an agent under interrogation: he didn't want to give anything away. Dr Malone took him back to his own room and Ralph pointed to the stethoscope lying on the bed.

'I would forget my own head,' said the psychologist.

The thin man was still pacing obsessively up and down. Ralph wanted to ask him about the Mexican hat but decided not to. Suddenly with a brutally quick movement the thin man left the room and Ralph was alone in the overwhelming silence. He waited as if he expected that at any moment a violent madman would burst in, and kill him. The buzzing of the bee was loud in his head which felt as if it would break into pieces. He saw Lady Macbeth on her endless peregrinations. Who would have thought that she had so much blood in her? He stared down at his pyjamas whose stripes matched the stripes of the bee, yellow and black. A breeze stirred the curtains. It occurred to him that they had left him alone like this so that he would attempt to escape but he wasn't going to give them that pleasure.

He stared through the window. Two men with shaven heads and faces as blank and square as loaves were bending down, putting leaves in a wheelbarrow. They gave him a feeling of terrifying desolation. He knew at once that they were patients from the bad wards: they looked inhuman, their movements jerky as in an ancient silent film.

He turned away from the window. The psychologist, whom he had travelled with in the ambulance, was just coming in. He smiled at him and walked over and sat on his bed in the corner. It was all beginning again.

Having a desire to pee he walked along the corridor in search of a bathroom. He found one and went in. There was a man standing there washing his face. Ralph stared into the mirror: his face had become small like a monkey's and his eyes fixed and dull. He thought, So this is what a madman looks like. In the waste of the glass he looked frightened and brutal and vulnerable, all at the same time. He walked slowly back to his room.

The psychologist was sitting on his bed.

'Do you see that ray?' he said.

'No,' said Ralph. 'I don't see any ray. Where did you see it?'

'It's coming in through the window.'

'I don't see anything,' said Ralph.

'I have been here before,' said the psychologist. 'I took aspirins.'

'Oh?'

'I was working too hard. I work on a farm.'

'Aspirins,' said Ralph. 'I took sleeping tablets. They found me lying in the middle of a wood. I nearly died,' he concluded proudly.

'Aspirins I took,' said the psychologist. 'I work on a farm,' he repeated. 'Like hell you do,' said Ralph to himself. 'Do you think I'm simple?'

'I was here for three weeks,' said the psychologist. 'They're telling me they're sending me to Glasgow to have a look at my head.'

'What treatment is that?' said Ralph.

'I don't know.'

'I'd refuse that,' said Ralph. 'I don't want them to tamper with my brain. If they do that to you, you become like an idiot.'

The psychologist didn't answer. It was as if he had used up all his words for the moment.

Ralph felt that he was crossing swords with this psychologist who was pretending to be a farm worker. Why, look at his brow, it was too high for a farm worker's. The psychologist placed all his possessions tidily in his locker. Everything he had was neat and new. His shaving gear was in a black leather case.

Ralph felt like a small boy going to school for the first time. Even now the memory was sharp in his mind. He was wearing short trousers and his knees were bony and pale. There were prefects in uniform all about him. There was a smell of carbolic from the floors and light pouring through the windows as here. The season too was autumn.

The psychologist stared at his ray and then he too went to the bathroom.

That night Ralph sat in the television room along with four or five others, some of whom were sitting silent staring straight ahead of them, some of whom were talking. In the middle of a programme about nurses he suddenly saw three Japanese entering, and speaking in their own language: their faces looked alien and threatening. He knew that this wasn't part of the programme and was about to leave, feeling uneasy and disoriented, when a nurse sat beside him and said, 'I'm afraid you'll have to change your room tonight if that's all right. I should like to tell you about it. I'll be back later.' He turned his face away from the television set and waited for a long time but she didn't come. Later he walked along the corridor to his room. Finding no one there he sat down on his bed. He thought he might phone Linda but decided against it: he was no longer going to be a beggar asking for love. But he felt lonely and dispirited. The fact that the nurse hadn't come to the television room as she had promised bothered him. And he didn't like the idea of changing his room, which was much more comfortable and modern than he had expected. It was true that the patients didn't speak much but they did not look menacing and almost brutal, as the men collecting the autumn leaves had done.

A tall man strode along the corridor carrying a shaving case. He stopped and looked in.

'Hullo,' he said. 'My name's Heydrich.'

'Heydrich?'

'They say that Heydrich is dead but I am Heydrich,' the man repeated proudly. 'I'll tell you something,' he said confidentially. 'Hitler was far too lenient with the Jews. If it had been me I would have put them up against a wall and shot the lot of them. That's what they deserved. I told him that but he wouldn't listen.' All the time he was talking he looked smiling and pleasant and normal, and Ralph felt the ward spinning about him.

'I keep a Webley at home. I was home for a weekend last weekend. Have you just come? I haven't seen you before.'

'That's right,' said Ralph. 'I came today but they tell me I have to change rooms.'

'If I had control here that wouldn't happen,' said the tall man. 'There are too many Jews about. They're everywhere. Have you met Mr Manson yet? He's a scientist. He's very clever.'

'No, I haven't.'

'He talks at our meetings, you know. I never say very much. They don't believe I'm Heydrich. They want me to go home but I want to stay here. I've been here before. I was here five years ago, and there was a bulb missing from the bathroom. It's still missing. I don't want to go home. There aren't so many Jews here as you get outside. You'll like Bobby.'

'Bobby?'

'He's the male nurse. He's the one who keeps our razors.'

Ralph stared at him.

'Didn't you know? They take your razor from you and they keep it in the office. When you want a shave in the morning you have to collect it.'

'Should I hand it in just now then?'

'You can leave it for a while. I'm going to have a shower. I like to keep clean. That was one of the troubles with the Jews. They never washed, they smelt. In the Reich cleanliness was very important. I can't stand dirt.'

Suddenly Ralph said. 'Do you know anything about a Mexican hat?'

'Mexican hat?'

'Yes, if you look up there you'll see a Mexican hat. And there's something wrong with the arm of the lamp. It's been twisted.'

'I don't know about that. There might have been a fancy dress party. I don't like that myself. I prefer efficiency. Take yesterday now. The food in the canteen was rotten. I told the supervisor that she should put the staff up against the wall and shoot them. She reported me. It's very important to be efficient. That's how the Reich became so great. Sometimes in the office they can't find your razor right away or they put the wrong name on it. I gave them a row about that. But they are quite nice usually and I didn't notice any Jews among them. I like it here. I don't want to go home. I've been here five months. The other time it was four months.'

'Can you get newspapers here?'

'I don't get one. I used to get the *Record* but I stopped it. I'm not sure if they bring newspapers now. Some of us are allowed down town you know. You could ask someone to bring you one back from the shop.'

'When will we be allowed down town?'

'It might be a week or two. Or more. I go to the canteen but I don't often go down town.'

'Canteen?'

'There's a canteen. You can buy cigarettes and sweets there. I'll show you where it is if you like.'

At that moment Ralph saw a procession of men walking along the corridor, each carrying a cup of coffee or tea. He didn't want to mention it to the tall man in case he was imagining it. The men were holding the cups steady, staring ahead as if they were part of a moving frieze.

Heydrich? How could anyone be Heydrich? On the other hand the man might have been sent to further disorientate him. He was sure that Linda was now the Irish psychologist's lover and that they were staving together in a flat in this very town. If he phoned her she would not be at home.

'Can you phone from here?' he asked the tall man.

'There's a phone in the corridor. It's outside the television room.'

'I think I'll walk along then.'

'See you,' said the tall man waving his white towel. He must have decided that I'm not a Jew, thought Ralph.

When Ralph phoned it was a long time before anyone answered. Finally he recognized the voice of his mother-in-law.

'Where's Linda?' he asked.

'She's in bed.' His mother-in-law sounded hostile.

'I don't believe it. I don't believe she's there at all.'

'She's tired. She's in bed.' He slammed the phone down and walked back along the corridor. Of course she wasn't in bed. She had organized this with the Irish psychologist from the very beginning. He remembered her saying once, 'I've always wanted to be a nurse.' Maybe she had meant that she wanted to work in a hospital like this. 'They do a useful job. Their work is more important than yours.'

'I give pleasure to people,' he had said defensively.

'Well, maybe, but you're an élitist. You prefer books to people deep down.'

'That's right,' he had said. 'Their conversation is more interesting.'

He had never understood 'ordinary' people. For instance they were very conscious of precedence: no one was more reactionary than an 'ordinary' person. Once on a train travelling to Edinburgh he had met a drunk who had said to him, 'I don't like you. You think I'm not good enough for you. But I'll tell you something, I'm better than you.' The drunk had thrust his face at him like a damp torch and he had finally retreated to another compartment. Ordinary people were like another race: they read the *Sun* and the *Star*.

But he was sure that Linda had turned against him, against his egotism, his élitism. The Irish psychologist hadn't looked at all élitist but rather cheerful and relaxed. He couldn't bear the thought that Linda should be with him. Nor could he bear the thought that he would never be able to read again.

Through the window he could see birds flying about in the twilight. On the lawn there was an exotic tree with pink blossoms, but he couldn't identify it. It had a thick trunk and the blossoms flamed like candles. He didn't know much about trees or birds: all he knew about was words. Of course Linda was not in bed and that business about tiredness was an excuse. The light faded from the sky: he thought he could hear the distant sound of the television set.

A handicapped girl who walked to one side like a ship in a storm ran pale-faced to him and said, 'Are you Mr Simmons?'

'Yes.'

'There's a phone call for you.'

He knew it was from Linda but he didn't want to answer it. His mother-in-law would have phoned the Irish psychologist's flat and Linda would now be phoning from there. He was determined that he wouldn't phone her but in spite of his decision he found himself walking quickly along the corridor with the reproductions of Picasso and Klee on the walls. He picked up the phone. Her voice sounded far away and gentle.

'I just got up,' she said. She sounded punch drunk. But then she was a good actress.

'Where are you phoning from?' he asked.

'Where do you think I'm phoning from?'

'All right. Put the phone down and I'll dial your number,' he said.

'If you want.' And he did what he had said. The phone rang and she answered it. But he was sure that engineers had been hired to construct this piece of trickery: he wasn't speaking to the house at all. Linda's voice sounded far too remote and wavering. She began to weep at the other end of the phone. Satisfied, he put the phone down slowly.

That night he was shifted into another room where there was a full complement of patients, that is, four including himself. Nurses came in with a trolley and doled out tablets: and in the morning they were wakened at half-past six. He had to go along to the office to collect his razor, and he shaved with the others silently in the bathroom. When he returned to his room two young nurses were trying to waken the young boy in the adjacent bed.

'Come on now, Ronny,' they pleaded with him. But he crouched under the bedclothes and wouldn't obey them.

'Now, Ronny,' said one of the sisters who came in at this point as if she was doing it quite often, 'you must get out of your bed like the rest. Otherwise you know what will happen.' But he turned away from her, burying his head in the pillow. After a while the sister went out.

In the opposite bed to Ralph was a squat man of about sixty or so who had a white moustache like a ghostly officer from the First World War: he made up his bed very meticulously, a towel still draped about his neck. Ralph made up his own bed though he wasn't very satisfied with it; however he left it as it was.

'Look, I'll show you how you do it,' said the man who introduced himself as Hugh, Hugh Green. 'You didn't tuck it in at the bottom, you see.' He padded about in his bedroom slippers.

The youth turned and tossed restlessly in his bed. The psychologist, who had been shifted into this room as well, replaced the shaving articles in his leather case. Ralph was reminded again of his days in boarding school.

'Did you sleep well?' said Hugh Green.

'Yes.'

'I sleep till four o'clock in the morning. After that I don't sleep at all.' Hugh went and pulled the bedclothes away from the youth.

'This is Ronny,' he said. 'He never gets up in the morning. And he's very noisy when he is up, aren't you, Ronny? He won't take his tablets,' said Hugh. Ralph glanced across to Ronny's locker. On it there was a bottle of orangeade and a record called "Breakdown". The title of the record worried him as if it had been placed there like a theatrical prop to remind him of his illness. Hugh took out a cigarette and began to smoke. Restlessly he went out into the corridor and came back again. He slid his feet along as if he were on wheels.

'Have you been here before?' said Ralph to him.

'Yes, I took aspirins. I was here for three weeks about five years ago.'

It occurred to Ralph that all the people he had met had tried to commit suicide by means of an overdose: he wondered if the youth had done the same. Surely this wasn't a coincidence. On the contrary everything was a reminder of his own attempted suicide. He sat on his bed staring dully at the floor. Hugh padded out into the corridor again smoking furiously. The psychologist took a bag of sweets from his locker and offered them but Ralph didn't take any. Suddenly the sister came in again in a rush of white and blue.

'Now, listen,' she said to Ronny. 'You have to get up.' And she pulled the bedclothes to the floor leaving him cowering against his sheets in his striped pyjamas. Ronny rubbed his eyes and stared around him.

'You shouldn't be watching the tv till all hours,' she said. Ronny got up and made his way to the bathroom.

'That boy,' she said, shaking her head and going out again.

All this appeared to Ralph like a scene from a play. Around him were four actors. What organization it all required, what attention to detail.

'Listen,' he said to Hugh. 'I can't read. Are you like that?'

'Yes. I tried to read but I can't. My wife brought me a lot of history books. I should be making notes on them but I can't do it.' He put out his cigarette and lit another, offering Ralph one from his packet. Ralph took it.

'As a matter of fact,' said Hugh, 'you weren't supposed to take that cigarette. You're not supposed to lend or borrow money either. Did you not read the rules?'

'No,' said Ralph. He picked up the sheet with the rules: there were a number of misspellings and errors in punctuation. This too bothered him quite a lot. He was sure that they were fake, hastily put together for his benefit. He wondered whether Hugh had deliberately made him break the rules. He stubbed his cigarette in a blue scarred ashtray.

Ronny came back from the bathroom, tall and strutting. Ralph saw that his face was pale and spotty. It was really astonishing how an actor as young as this could be hired.

'I hope you washed yourself,' said Hugh. 'You needed a wash.' He walked over to Ronny on his slippered feet.

'Listen to him,' said Ronny in a high almost hysterical voice. 'He never washes himself. Do you, old man? You never wash do you, old man?' Hugh turned away, the cigarette between his lips, smiling.

'He just washes his moustache,' said Ronny in the same high voice, and went off into a paroxysm of laughter. 'He takes it off at night and leaves it beside his bed, don't you, old man?' He seemed very noisy and aggressive. Hugh smiled patiently and then went out of the room and along the corridor. He seemed constitutionally unable to sit still.

'Old man,' Ronny shouted after him. He made up his bed quickly and noisily drank some orangeade. Hugh came back and went over to him and punched him lightly in the chest.

'You know what's going to happen to you,' he said. 'You'll end up in another ward, one of the really bad ones, if you don't take your pills and if you don't get up in time in the morning. And if you don't wash.'

'Listen to him. He snores,' said Ronny and went off into another paroxysm of laughter. 'Did you hear him snoring? He snores like a horse. You're a horse, old man, a horse, a horse.'

'That's right, I'm a horse,' said Hugh calmly. He put out his cigarette and lit another one. 'You've taken my ashtray,' he said to Ronny. 'You don't smoke and you take my ashtray all the time. You're a thief, aren't you? Aren't you?'

'I'm a thief, I'm a thief, I'm a thief,' Ronny chanted.

What actors they are, thought Ralph. They have rehearsed this very carefully. What looks spontaneous is really planned and scripted. They're really very good.

Hugh walked over to Ronny again and said, 'I'm serious. If you don't watch out you'll end up in another ward.'

'I don't care,' said Ronny. 'I've been in one before. I don't mind. There's more action there. There's no action here, is there, old man?'

'Action?'

'And I'll tell you another thing. These pills you're taking make you impotent. That's why your wife doesn't visit you. His wife never comes to see him,' he said to Ralph. "Cos he's impotent and he smells. Don't you, old man?' Hugh smiled tolerantly. 'It's true though she never comes to see you. And you smoke too much. You'll die of smoking, old man.'

'Ronny watched the television till midnight,' said Hugh. 'What was it last night, Ronny? Was it *Frankenstein*? Ronny here never got his O levels, did you, Ronny? He wasn't in school long enough. You were jinking, weren't you, Ronny? You wait till that sister comes. She's got it in for you.'

'I did,' chanted Ronny. 'I did get my O levels. You don't even know what O levels are. They weren't invented when you were in school, old man.' And he doubled up with laughter.

'Run away and polish your head,' said Hugh calmly.

'Polish your head, polish your head,' Ronny chanted, laughing again with a high nervous noisy sound. Everything he did was tense and nervous and jerky as if he were a twanging wire, while all the time the psychologist smiled in the corner, now and again getting up to tidy his bed compulsively.

'Breakfast,' said Hugh, glancing at his watch.

'What kind of watch is that?' said Ronny. 'That's a Russian watch. The old man is a Communist. What Communist gave you that watch, old man?'

'I'm going for my breakfast,' said Hugh and padded out of the room. After a while, Ralph and the psychologist followed him.

'I don't want any breakfast,' shouted Ronny. Ralph and the psychologist walked along side by side past the office. Ralph wanted to speak to his companion: his silence bothered him. He hated being judged by that silence; and yet when he was writing there was nothing he liked better. He hadn't talked much to Linda thinking that in comparison with his own, her concerns were trivial. He would have liked to have been self-sufficient as a stone. Yet here he wished to speak.

'I wonder what they'll have for breakfast,' he said.

'I don't know,' said the psychologist, but didn't add to his statement. What a clever fellow he is, thought Ralph, he is doing this deliberately. And he was ashamed of himself for having spoken first as if it had been a culpable weakness.

They queued for their food and then sat at the same table. By now Ralph could recognize one or two people, including Lady Macbeth and the tall thin man whom he had seen pacing up and down in the ward the day before, and who had clearly been shifted. People stared morosely down at their plates. Opposite him sat an old man whose mouth moved continually, as if he were in the process of having a stroke. Now and again he would find someone staring at him and then he would remind himself that after all this was a drama group which had been hired to drive him mad.

'You must take your food,' said a nurse to a young girl who was standing at the door.

'I don't want to.'

'You must take it. The doctor said you had to take it.' The young girl sat sulkily at a table near the door but made no attempt to eat.

When they had finished their food the handicapped girl, who had told him about the phone call, cleaned all the tables and cleared the plates away. She looked white-faced and angry, as if the diners offended her by their slovenly manners. After breakfast was over, Ralph followed the others into the lounge.

When he had had his pills in the lounge carefully dispensed from a trolley, he walked back to his room. Ronny was sitting on his bed staring down at the floor.

'Should you not be taking some pills?' said Ralph.

'I'm not taking them.'

After a while he added, 'I'll get the bastard yet.'

'What bastard?'

'My stepfather.'

'Your stepfather?'

'That's right. He's a naval officer.'

Stepfather, thought Ralph. So they're at it again. And a picture of his own stepfather returned to him, silent and bookish, always disapproving. Perhaps that was why he himself had become a novelist, creating new worlds for himself to escape that terrible silence. If only his stepfather had once shouted at him but, no, whenever he did anything wrong or was too noisy, then that awful silence had descended: he had felt himself less important than one of his stepfather's books. What was the secret of those books, their calming cold secret mystery? He must try and find out. And so he had tried to read them, to placate his stepfather, as if by reading he might enter that world and, little by little, he had done so. Had he done the same with Linda, repeated the silences which he himself had endured? Had he cast his disapproval on her too? But, no, that did not excuse her, unless she had grown to hate him as much as he himself had hated his stepfather. And now he in turn had entered the kingdom of silence. It was his weapon as it had been his stepfather's. The sins of the stepfathers are visited on the children.

'He beat me up, the bastard,' said Ronny. 'But he won't do it again. I'm bigger than him now.'

'What did he beat you for?' said Ralph.

'For nothing. He took it into his head. Because of school sports. Report cards. Anything.'

'And what about your mother?'

Ronny snorted but didn't answer. Ralph thought of the mother as suave, svelte, ambitious, dressed in fine clothes, standing beside her husband at parties. He said, 'You should take your pills, you know, or they'll put you in a worse ward.'

'I don't care. I've been in one already. I like the nut cases.'

'As if you are not one yourself,' thought Ralph. But the cunning of the scheme almost overwhelmed him. Imagine putting him in with a stepson, just as he had been himself. Was there nothing that they hadn't thought of? The labyrinthine plot attracted him, repelled him. It was so huge, so luminous in its ramifications. It was almost beyond the scope of the human mind. How much he had underestimated Linda. It was she who was the novelist, not him.

'So one day I left the house and I swallowed a lot of aspirins,' Ronny was saying. 'I couldn't stand the bastard any longer.'

'I tried everything,' Ralph thought, 'I abased myself. I read his books even though I didn't understand them. I wanted to know his secret, to enter his world, to make him notice me. But he didn't notice me. There was nothing I could do that would make him notice me. There was only that terrible silence as cold as crystal. It was as if he hated me for existing, for being an interruption to his books.'

His head spun: he couldn't understand what was happening to him. It was as if, even while he was growing up, this plot was being woven about him: everything that had happened to him, everything that he was, contributed to this story which was torturing him.

And a kind of tenderness for Ronny overwhelmed him. 'Please,' he said. 'Please. Take your pills.'

Ronny raised his head as if the tone of Ralph's voice had attracted him: he hearkened like a dog that is listening to a sound that no human ear can hear.

'I might,' he said. 'I might at that.'

And suddenly Ralph began to tell him his own story. He told him of the hotel, of the black doctor, of the tapes, the taxi driver, he told him of his journey into the wood, and Ronny listened seriously.

But he did not really appear interested till Ralph told him about his own stepfather, of his silences, of his disapproval. Nevertheless while he was talking to him Ralph was thinking, This boy is an actor, he has been planted here. There can be no other explanation, there have been too many coincidences. Why should I be confiding in an actor, whose profession is being used to destroy me? Yet some impulse had made him break his silence, speak endlessly as if he were talking to himself.

'I'll tell you something, he makes me feel like shit,' said Ronny. 'I'll strangle the bastard.' And his face became ugly and angry so that Ralph felt frightened that the boy might attack him. And then it occurred to him, That is what they are gambling on, that this boy might confuse me with his stepfather, that in the middle of the night he might attack me with a banned razor. And he was frightened again and wanted to leave the ward, but he stayed. Sometimes now he didn't care whether he was killed or not. It might not last very long anyway, the fact of death, it might last only a moment, the stab in the stomach, the strangling, the throttling. And in any case what did he have to look forward to? This boy would be doing him a favour.

Should he not simply say to him, 'I am your stepfather,' and let events take their course? Should he not tender himself as a sacrifice to that desperate rage?

He remembered the night he had shouted at his stepfather, 'I'll burn the house down. Send for the police. I don't care.' And his father standing by the phone saying, 'I will. Don't think I won't.'

And himself, 'Do it then.' And at that moment if he had had a match he would have burnt the house down. His stepfather trembled and shook, his face was twisted with hatred and helplessness, and his mother had come between them and said, 'If you send for the police you'll ruin his life, don't you understand?' And he hated his mother then and always. How had she married this iceberg? Could she not see what he was like?

That he had no love in his bones? And sometimes in the night he had heard them whispering together and thought that they were talking about him.

Ronny was looking at him with a hostile gaze now. He was saying, 'I've changed my mind. I won't take the pills. They can do what they like.' And he stalked out of the ward with the careless stride of youth that does not think of consequences. And Ralph was left alone again.

He walked to the window. The leaves were stirring in a breeze and the two men were gathering them in their wheelbarrow. It was to a ward such as they inhabited that Ronny might be sent if he continued with his disobedience. Ralph glanced up at the hat which hung above the lamp but realized that this was not the ward it was in.

He took a pad from his locker and tried to write but he could write nothing. Then very seriously in the silence of the room he began to note down reasons why he believed there was a plot against him. He headed his notes THE PLOT and numbered his reasons as if he were a bureaucrat.

1. Why did the lawyer say, 'This is like a scene from a play'?
2. Why did the trolleys in the previous hospital have only two wheels instead of four?
3. Why was there a Mexican hat on the light?
4. Why have I been put in here with a boy who has a stepfather?
5. Why did the surgeon drop the match on my pillow?
6. Why is the psychologist always watching me?
7. Why did that nurse say, 'I could make a scene if I liked'?
8. Why did Linda pretend that she was tired? Why didn't she answer the phone?
9. Why is it that everyone I meet has taken an overdose?
10. How could a black doctor be called Emmanuel?

He studied what he had written and tried to think of other items to record but he seemed for the moment to have exhausted his questions. He would present his list to that lady psychologist when he had his first meeting with her. He would show her that he was not to be trifled with, that he had a clear cool brain, that he had read psychology and knew what he was talking about.

Finally he thought of another question, Why was there a procession of men carrying coffee cups in the corridor?

*

'Oh, that,' said Hugh. 'There's a coffee machine along there. Do you want to come along for a coffee?'

Ralph and Hugh and the psychologist walked along the corridor together, Hugh scuttling along very fast as was usual with him. They passed Lady Macbeth who was pacing up and down in her endless circles. A woman in a nightgown came out of a room and said, 'Why is my room full of tourists? They came on a bus and they are lying in the beds. Where did they come from? You tell me that.'

'Tourists?' said Hugh.

'Tourists. I can't understand their language. They came off the bus and into my room. Why did they choose my room? They didn't come for Bed and Breakfast, I can tell you.' She thrust her haunted face towards them. 'I've had Americans and I should know. There was a woman came to my house one day and she examined the sheets, and she said, "I think they will do." "Well," I said to her, and I grabbed her skirt and looked at her underskirt and I said to her, "Do you think that is clean enough for my sheets?" She didn't like it.'

'You'll be all right,' said Hugh. 'They're not tourists. What nationality do you think they are?'

'I think they're Germans.'

'They're not Germans anyway,' said Hugh. 'I was in the war.'

'Well then they might be Dutch. They're not so bad. I had a Dutch boy in my house and he took pictures all the time. Even when I was at the sink he was taking pictures. But then he began to steal my things. He stole my ornaments and then he stole my dog.'

'They're all right if they're Dutch,' said Hugh.

And the three of them walked along to the coffee machine.

'There was no one there,' said Hugh. 'No one at all.'

When they got back to their room Hugh lit another cigarette. 'I don't know if my wife will come today. I gave my sons my business, you know, after I came out of the hospital last time.'

The other two waited for him to continue.

'I have two sons and I divided the business between them. I wanted to get on with my writing.'

'Writing?' said Ralph.

'I'm writing a history of the world from a Communist point of view. I make notes all the time. I have a typewriter but I know a professional typist who will put a finish on the book for me.'

'How long will it take?' said Ralph.

'I don't know yet. It'll take a long time. It hasn't been done before. Wells wrote a history of the world but it wasn't from a Communist point of view. I'm a Communist. My sons aren't Communist though. I have a paper business.'

'Where is it?'

'In Bowling.' He paused and then said, 'Who built the pyramids? I ask you that. It was the ordinary people. It's always the rich who are written about, the kings and so on. But it's the poor who did the work. I've got hundreds of cards on which I've written notes. My wife threw some of them out; she said she couldn't move in her own house. She might come today, I don't know. My sons are too busy to come.'

'Why did you start on a book like that?' said Ralph.

'I don't know. Yet I had plenty of other hobbies. I used to bowl but I stopped that. And I used to be a curler. But that wasn't enough. I wanted to find out what history was all about. I left school at the age of fifteen but I always had an inquiring mind.' He stubbed out his cigarette and lit another one, padding restlessly about the room, oldish, restless with a grey moustache.

'I write books,' Ralph volunteered suddenly.

'You mean you publish them?'

'That's right.'

'You could maybe tell me what you have to do, then, to get a book published. I'll try and publish it when I'm finished.'

'You must have it neatly typed,' said Ralph, 'and then you send it away to a publisher. Some publishers specialize in certain subjects. I don't know who would publish your book. It's a big thing, isn't it?'

'It is. I don't know when I'll finish it. I wanted my wife to bring me some books last time but she forgot. I wanted to take notes but I can't seem to concentrate. I used to be able to concentrate. I used to work till four in the morning. But I can't concentrate here. I think it must be the drugs.'

The psychologist was listening carefully but not speaking. 'What's it like when you leave the hospital?' he asked eventually.

'What do you mean?'

'When you come out. What's it like? What do people think?'

'Nothing. They don't think anything of it nowadays,' said Hugh expansively. 'In the old days they did but not now. They think of it now as an illness. It didn't bother me. People used to come up and speak to me just the same. I started on my book again when I left the hospital. I worked very hard at it. And then I got another depression and tried to kill myself again. The house is full of these cards. My wife is always complaining. I'm working on the history of the Trade Unions just now. There's a lot in that.'

'I'm sure,' said Ralph. 'But the main thing is to have it typed neatly.' He couldn't imagine the appalling labour this man was involved in: it made him tired just to think about it. Why he couldn't even read a column of the *Daily Express* himself.

'What paper do you read?' he asked.

'I read the *Sun* and the *Star*. At one time I used to read the *Telegraph* but it gives you a wrong slant on things: it's very Tory. I used to read the *Financial Times* as well.'

So here was another actor who pretended to have delusions about authorship. First of all there was a stepson and then a potential author. What an extraordinary thing: the coincidences were bizarre and therefore not coincidences at all. And all the time the psychologist was silent: he had an infinite capacity for vigilance.

Hugh stopped talking and sat on his bed smoking. Then he walked out into the corridor again. Time passed so slowly, there was no end to it. He must ask that Irish psychologist again how long he was likely to be in. He might be here forever. And Hugh's wife would never come to see him, that was certain. She too had betrayed her husband, she would have mixed up all his cards while he was in hospital and when he arrived home there would be such a chaos that he would go mad again. And again, why had he been so silly as to hand over his business to his sons? Would men never learn the infinite greed of the human heart?

When the lady psychologist sent for him he took his list of complaints with him. She was sitting at a desk, a charge nurse beside her. Did she need a witness in case he attacked her?

'How are you feeling today?' she asked brightly. 'Do you still think you're being spied on?' Wordlessly he handed her the list and she glanced rapidly over it.

'What is this?' she said.

'Proof,' he answered tersely.

'Proof of what?'

'That I'm being spied on. That it's all a charade.' The charge nurse didn't smile or make any sign at all. He simply listened.

'What is this about a Mexican hat?' she asked the charge nurse.

'I don't know. I'll look into it.'

'On the light,' she said to Ralph. 'It must be a mistake. Nothing important. Someone playing a prank.'

'To you nothing is important,' said Ralph. 'That's where you're wrong. Everything is important. Everything is linked. You think I'm ignorant. I'm not. I've read Freud and Jung. I know more than you think.'

'And what is this about a surgeon dropping a match on a pillow? I don't understand any of this.'

'It was in the other hospital,' said Ralph. 'He obviously wanted to get me into trouble.'

'And what's this about a stepson. Do you know anything about this?' she asked the charge nurse.

'There's a patient called Ronny in the same room. He's a stepson.'

'Oh, I see,' and she smiled for the first time. 'And because you're a stepson you think that we.... Jolly funny.'

'Not at all funny,' said Ralph indignantly. 'More tragic than funny if you ask me.' He wanted to shout at this woman who didn't seem to be listening to anything he was saying.

'Tell me about your wife,' said the psychologist briskly.

'What about her?'

'Have you been making any bad phone calls to her?' Bad, as if he was a child.

'No.'

'But you must believe that she loves you. She is coming to see you tomorrow. She phoned to tell me.'

'I don't want her to come. I want her to stay away. When will I be out of here?'

'Oh, it won't be too long if you behave yourself. But you do believe that she loves you, that she worries about you.'

'Love,' he said, 'what does that mean? The world is so meagre. I saw that in Yugoslavia.'

'Meagre?' she said. He felt that he had already mentioned this to her but he couldn't remember. The desk in front of her was bare, meagre. That was how the world was. Flat, without depth. The bareness, the lack of ornament, the invincible presence of things, their demand to be heard.

The charge nurse was looking at him intently, and fiddling with a pencil.

'I don't understand what you mean by love,' said Ralph. 'How do we know?'

'How do we know what?'

'What people are thinking. They may be talking to you about one thing and thinking of something else. How can we see inside their heads? We have our own theatres inside our heads.'

'I see.' She glanced at the charge nurse. 'But you haven't been making threatening phone calls.'

'No.'

'I'm sorry about that stepson, that Ronny. I didn't realize.... You didn't like your stepfather, did you?'

'No.'

'He lived in a world of his own, didn't he? He was always reading.'

'Where did you get that from? Has Linda been talking to you?'

'No. You told me yourself.' The woman's glasses glinted in the sparse autumnal sunshine which shone through the window behind her.

'Did I?' said Ralph. 'I can't remember. But it's true. He did live in a world of his own. I tried to get into it but I couldn't.'

'And it wasn't a meagre world, was it?'

'No. Eventually I got into it. But when I was a child it was hard.'

'You mean as a child you never got into that world.'

'No, I didn't. I wondered about it. How he could be so self-sufficient. How he didn't need me. How he didn't seem to know my name. Sometimes when I spoke to him it was as if he was coming out of a trance. He had a large bald head.'

'What?'

'A large bald head. I used to watch. It was like a big marble with veins in it. And his eyes were always cold. As if he was saying to me that I had no right to exist. I used to wonder if he ever thought about me at all.'

'Did you think he was plotting against you?'

'I used to hear my mother and him whispering in their bed at night. I used to listen at the keyhole but I could never make out the words.'

'As in Yugoslavia?'

'What do you mean?'

'People talked around you there and you didn't know what they were saying. Isn't that right?'

For the first time he regarded her with a wary respect.

'That's true,' he said slowly. 'I didn't think of that.'

'You have a high opinion of yourself, don't you? You believe that no one can understand things except yourself. You under-estimate other people just as your stepfather did. You never listen to them. When did you listen to anyone last?'

'I listen to the characters in my books.'

'That's different. When did you listen to any living people? You despise me: you are surprised that I should have any interesting thoughts. You think you know more than I do about my own subject. And yet what I have said is quite obvious. In Yugoslavia you couldn't make out what people were saying any more than you could make out what your father and mother were saying in bed at night. What happened to you in Yugoslavia?'

'Nothing much. We visited a cave.'

'A cave?' The word hung hollowly between them.

'Yes,' he said, 'an icy cave. It was so cold.'

'An icy cave?' She echoed him.

'Yes,' he said. 'It was so cold. In the bowels of the earth.' After he had said the word 'bowels' he wondered why he had used it. It sounded like a cliché.

'And all around,' he said, 'there were faces and bodies, all of ice.'

'Did any of them remind you of your father?'

'He used to play chess. He never played against people. He played out problems from the *Observer* and the *Sunday Times*. There was a chess player among the figures.'

'In the cave?'

'Yes.'

'Anything else? Did you visit anywhere else?'

'We visited a sort of colosseum. There was no roof on it.' He stopped again, thinking.

'A building without a roof?'

'Yes.'

'Why wasn't it finished?'

'Because the fairies who had been building it flew away at dawn.'

'Jolly good.' The woman pushed papers about on her desk and said, 'Now don't you be rude or violent to your wife when she visits you. She is suffering a great deal and she loves you, whether you believe it or not. Otherwise she wouldn't come at all. She phones me up to find out how you are.'

'She would, wouldn't she?'

'What do you mean?'

'She wants to know how her play is progressing. In any case this place is a theatre not a real hospital.'

'Did your father take notes?' she asked him obliquely glancing down at the list he had brought her.

'When?'

'For instance, when he was reading a book?'

'Yes, he did. He left hundreds of notes in jotters when he died.'

'What did you do with them?'

'I kept them. I sometimes use them in my novels.'

'What were they about?'

'Oh, about lots of things. Comments on life. Notes on books he had read.'

There was another silence and then she said, 'Well, I think you're making progress. I'll see you again shortly. Meanwhile you can go along to your room.'

'There is one other thing,' he said. 'About King Lear.'

'What about King Lear?'

'A man in my ward says that he gave his business away to his children. They never come to see him.'

'Who is this gentleman?' said the psychologist to the charge nurse.

'I think he must be talking about Hugh. He comes from Bowling. He says that he gave away his business to his sons.'

'I know you're an actor as well,' said Ralph to the charge nurse, and for a moment there was a flicker of what might have been malice in the latter's eyes.

'Cut along now,' said the psychologist. 'I'll see you soon. But you are feeling better?'

'Yes. A little.'

'Jolly good.'

There was a flash of hockey sticks in his mind, girls in green uniforms, a green field with an umpire in it. And then he was out of the room.

'Excuse me,' he said to Lady Macbeth who was passing in her ashen helmet. It was as if she was sleepwalking, having surrendered a precious kingdom as well.

He got it into his head that he didn't have the courage of Ronny. Why, if he was a real writer at all, he should enter the other wards, the mad ones, the lower circles, he should listen to the mad songs, the elegies, but he was afraid. But surely before he left here he must enter these wards, he must find out what it was like to be at the extreme limits of existence. In the place without music, without harmony. He must talk to these two flat-faced crew-cut lunatics who walked about slowly, perpetually shovelling the autumn leaves into their barrows, gathering wounded nature from the world of wind and rain. He had not faced life: and this was what had happened to him. He had not looked into the darkest corners with his torch. He admired Ronny, large, noisy, careless.

'I don't care,' said Ronny. 'I'll go there but I won't take my pills.' It seemed to him that Ronny symbolized all those men of free spirit by which the human race had been impelled up the shaky ladder of evolution from the rank green nameless grass.

'The old men are funny,' said Ronny. 'I like them.'

When Linda came to visit him he told her about this. She looked at him with large dry eyes as if she were stunned.

'What are you talking about?'

'I know what I'm talking about. I haven't suffered enough yet. You started me on the road but I must go further along it.'

'I started you on it?'

'Yes. With your drama. I wish you would come out into the open.'

She was wearing her red velvet suit and looked neat and desirable. He regarded her with hopeless longing. She had brought sweets and oranges. He showed her the first verse of a poem he had written.

> And as we wave goodbye
> I know we shall not meet again
> either here or earnestly
> in another place beyond this pain.

He saw the tears springing to her eyes. Oh, how clever she was, what duplicity she had.

'You must know an engineer as well,' he said. 'He has done something to the phone.'

Through the window he could see Heydrich and the handicapped girl strolling among the autumn leaves hand in hand. Heydrich tall and blond talking to her in an animated manner.

'What kind of tree is that?' he asked Linda, pointing out to the lawn. The tree leaned like a cherry tree towards the ground with its umbrella of pink petals.

'I don't know. I haven't seen one like that before.' Heydrich and the girl passed under the splendid heart-breaking tree.

'The man there thinks he is Heydrich,' he said.

'Oh?'

'Apart from that he's okay. Of course he's an actor. He's trained for the part. I must say he's very good.'

For a moment there, there was a gap and he saw through it, and the gap closed again.

'The psychologist says you may not be long in here. Maybe another two weeks.'

'I know I'll be here a long time,' said Ralph. 'I know I'll be here forever.'

'Why do you say that?'

'The logic of the plot demands it.'

'What plot?'

'The plot has an invincible rightness. I've been caught in my own plot. My stepfather saw to that. And there's a boy here exactly like me. And a man who gave away his property just like King Lear. He's trying to be a writer too. And his wife mixes up his notes. There are too many things....' He rubbed his head. 'The comprehensive power of the plot. Sometimes I feel as if I'm inside a machine.'

'You know I love you,' said Linda tearfully. 'You know there is no one else but you. You know that, don't you?' Her voice echoed mockingly as if from the inside of a cave.

'So you say.'

'But it's true. I've always loved you.'

'Why should you love me? I can't see why you should. There's no reason for it.'

'Of course there's no reason for it. That's what you don't understand. That is what love is.'

'Love!'

'It's caring for someone. Surely you can see that. I care for you. I don't want to see you like this.' And she cried again, trembling and shaking. But he regarded her with a cold eye. Who could believe anything that anyone said. In the last analysis everyone was out for himself. All the ethical systems that had ever been woven like a spurious tapestry were a lot of crap: tiny men with tiny teeth had nibbled and nibbled till they had climbed the ladder from which they could see whole landscapes. The world was an eternal spy story with double agents, triple agents, secret scripts. A man must always look over his shoulder to check if he was being followed. Even the most innocent spectator, that one lounging by the lamp-post, was part of the plot.

'If you could only come straight out with it,' he said. 'Admit it.'

'Admit what?'

'That you've found someone else. It would be much simpler. That psychologist. You've said you always wanted to be a nurse. That you never liked being a secretary. That you didn't think it was useful.'

'But ... what psychologist? Who are you talking about?'

'The Irish one. The one who came to see me first. I suppose you could call him handsome. Perhaps even charming. He's certainly handsomer than the taxi driver. And something as complicated as this would require a psychologist. Then again your mother was a nurse. Perhaps there's a secret union which looks after its own. Look, how do we know what happens in hospitals? They've got the power of life and death over their patients. They can kill them, sign certificates. Hospitals are secret closed societies. The word goes out. This fellow is making a nuisance of himself. Let's get rid of him.'

She stared at him in astonishment as if the fertility of his imagination had stunned her. In her infernal reds, in which fires were burning, he saw the glow of the tree behind her. Petals lay on the ground below it. Everything was burning away, but was it being resurrected?

He saw a police car swing up the drive and draw up at the door of the bad wards.

A nurse swirling a red and navy-blue cloak passed like a foreign exotic bird along the pathway.

'Maybe you can't help what you're doing,' he said. 'Maybe none of us can.'

'I shan't be able to come tomorrow,' Linda said tiredly. 'I'll come the day after that. It's a long drive and mother isn't well.'

'I'm sure she isn't.'

'She isn't. She doesn't know what is happening. She doesn't understand.'

'But I do,' said Ralph proudly. 'I understand.'

'My mother likes you.'

'No, she doesn't. She doesn't understand what I do. She wishes you had married someone else. She has the old-fashioned idea that writing isn't work, not like nursing. It's not respectable.'

'Well, you've got to make allowances for that.'

'Why should I be making allowances all the time?'

'I don't know. I make allowances too,' said Linda. 'We all have to make allowances. That among other things is what marriage is.'

Like Dante I must enter the final circle, he thought. I must burn there and find out about the fire and the mad shadows. That is what the Inferno is, the seethe of lost egos burning in their pain.

'Do you remember Mrs Hunter?' said Linda briskly. 'She phoned Annie Macleod and asked her who had hired Judas to betray Christ. Would you believe that?'

'And who did?'

'What?'

'Who did hire him? She has a point there. She's no fool.'

Linda ignored this comment and proceeded. 'And Mary Mason has a black baby. Her husband is a black doctor in Liverpool, I think it is.'

Ralph thought of the house surrounded by its gravel. It seemed to him that the ferns and grasses were rising up to swallow him. Once he had been hacking at ferns when his glasses, which he kept in his top jacket pocket, fell into the greenery. Blindly he had searched for them but couldn't find them. Such a failed scholar among famished nature he was. There was some deep meaning in the incident. Nature which he had seen by means of his glasses now became a blur as he thrust his arms into the luxuriant greenery, which had closed over them. Sometimes he had felt the vegetation was devouring even his manuscripts, turning them first green and then brown. And on rainy days he watched the water pour into the brimming barrel which stood under the rone. Another day he had seen two rabbits playing in the garden. No, he said to them, this is not an Irish missal, the real weasel is waiting for you. Even now he is feeling his way towards you, he is preparing his dance of luminous rings.

'Is there anything you want me to bring you?' said Linda.

'No, nothing. There is a man in here who's writing a history of the world. An amateur. A fool. He walks about all the time, he can't sit still. And he wears bedroom slippers. He's expecting his wife to bring him books and notes but of course she won't.'

'Why not?'

'Why do you think he's here? She didn't care about his book. God knows what will happen to his notes while he's away from home.'

'Ralph,' said Linda tenderly.

'What?'

'Come back to me.'

He turned his face away from her towards the two lunatics with their wheelbarrow.

There was a silence and then Linda said, 'I'll have to go.'

'Yes.'

'Do you want to come to the car?'

'I don't know if I'm allowed out.'

'Give me a wave then.'

He didn't speak. She kissed him lightly on the lips and then left. She waved to him but he gazed back at her stonily. She seemed to be smaller than usual as she entered the car. So the strain was getting through to her. This huge plot took a lot of thinking out, no wonder she was tired.

There must even be a place for the feeding rabbits and the tenuous redbreast on the branch. The car turned away in a shower of pebbles and then she was gone. The car was red as an expiring ember. Oh God, when would there be an end to this? To cut cleanly away from the world, that was what he should do. Only he didn't have the courage.

Duncan Williamson

Mary and the Seal

Many years ago in a little isle off the West Coast of Scotland – it could be Mull, Tiree, or any island – there lived an old fisherman and his wife. And the old fisherman spent his entire life fishing in the sea and selling whatever fish he couldn't use himself to keep him and his wife and his little daughter alive. They lived in this little cottage by the sea and not far from where they stayed was the village, a very small village – a post office, a hall and some cottages. But everyone knew everyone else. And his cousin also had a house in the village.

This old man and woman had a daughter called Mary and they loved her dearly, she was such a nice child. She helped her father with the fishing and when she was finished helping her father, she always came and helped her mother to do housework and everything else. The father used to set his nets every day in the sea and he used to rise early every morning. Mary used to get up and help her father lift his nets and collect the fish. After that was done she used to help her mother, then went off to school. Everybody was happy for Mary. And her father and mother were so proud of her because she was such a good worker. But she was such a quiet and tender little girl and didn't pay attention to anyone … she did her schoolwork in school. But the years passed by and Mary grew till she became a young teenager.

This is where the story really begins, when Mary was about sixteen or seventeen. She always used to borrow her father's boat, every evening in the summertime, and go for a sail to a little island that lay about half a mile from where they stayed, a small island out in the middle of the sea-loch. And Mary used to go out and spend all her spare time on the island. Every time she'd finished her day's work with her father and helped her mother and had her supper, she would say, 'Father, can I borrow your boat?' Even in the wintertime sometimes, when the sea wasn't too rough, she would go out there and spend her time. Her father and mother never paid any attention because Mary's spare time was her own time; when her work was finished she could do what she liked. Till one day.

Her mother used to walk down to the small village to the post office where they bought their small quantity of messages and did their shopping, it was the only place they could buy any supplies.

She heard two old women nattering to each other. Mary's mother's back was turned at the time but she overheard the two old women. They were busy talking about Mary.

'Och,' one woman said, 'she's such a nice girl, but she's so quiet. She doesn't come to any of the dances and she doesn't even have a boyfriend. She doesn't do anything – we have our ceilidhs and we have our things and we never see her come, she never even pays us a visit. Such a nice quiet girl, all she wants to do, she tells me, is to take her boat and she rows over to the island and spends all her time there on the island. Never even comes and has a wee timey – when our children have their shows and activities in school she never puts in an appearance! And her mother and father are such decent people ... even her Uncle Lachy gets upset!'

This was the first time her mother had heard these whispers so she paid little attention. She came home, and she was a wee bit upset. And the next time she went back to the village she heard the same whispers again – this began to get into her mind, she began to think. But otherwise Mary was just a natural girl: she helped her daddy and she asked her mummy if there was anything she could do, helped her to do everything in the house, and she was natural in every way. But she kept herself to herself.

One evening it was suppertime once more, and after supper Mary said, 'Daddy, can I borrow your boat?'

'Oh yes, Mary, my dear,' he said, 'you can borrow the boat. I'm sure I'm finished – we've finished our day's work. You can have the boat.' It wasn't far across to row the little boat, maybe several hundred yards to the wee island in the loch. And the old woman and the old man sat by the fire.

Once Mary had walked out the door and said good-bye to her father and mother, the old woman turned round and said to her husband, 'There she goes again. That's her gone again.'

Mary's father turned round and he said, 'What do you mean? Margaret, what do you mean – you know Mary always goes off, an-and-and enjoys herself in the boat.'

She said, 'Angus, you don't know what I mean: it's not you that has got to go down to the village and listen to the whispers of the people, and the talk and the wagging tongues.'

He says, 'Woman, what are you talking about?'

She says, 'I'm talking about your daughter.'

Angus didn't know what to say ... he said, 'What's wrong with my daughter? I'm sure she works hard and she deserves a little time by herself – what's the trouble, was there something that you needed done that she didn't do?'

'Not at all,' she said, 'that's not what I'm talking about.'

'Well,' he says, 'tell me what you're trying to say!'

She said, 'Angus, it's Mary – the people in the village are beginning to talk.'

'And what are they saying,' he said, 'about my daughter!' And he started to get angry.

'They're talking about Mary going off herself in her boat to the island and spending all her time there, she's done that now for close on five years. And they say she doesn't go to any dances, she doesn't go to any parties and she doesn't accept any invitations to go anywhere and she has no boyfriend! And the wagging tongues in the village are talking about this. It's getting through to me and I just don't like it.'

'Well,' he said, 'Mother, I'm sure there's nothing in the world that should upset you about that; I'm sure Mary's minding her own business! And if she's out there, she's no skylarking with some young man – would you rather have her skylarking around the village with some young man or something? And destroying herself and bringing back a baby or something to you – would you enjoy that better?'

'It's not that, Angus,' she said, 'it's just that Mary is so unsociable.'

But anyway, they argued and bargued for about an hour and they couldn't get any further. By the time they were finished Mary came in again. She was so radiant and happy.

She came over, kissed her mother and kissed her daddy, said, 'Daddy, I pulled the boat up on the beach, and everything's all right.'

He says, 'All right, Daughter, that's nice.'

'And,' she says, 'Daddy, the tide is coming in and some of the corks of the net are nearly sunk, so I think we'll have a good fishing in the morning. I'll be up bright and early to give you a hand.'

He said, 'Thank you, Mary, very much.'

And she kissed her mother and said, 'I'll just have a small something to eat and I'll go to bed.'

But anyway, the old woman was unsettled. 'There she goes again,' she says, 'that's all we get.'

'Well,' he says, 'what more do you expect? She's doing her best, Mother. She's enjoying herself.'

'What is she doing on that island? That's what I want to know.'

Said the old man to Margaret, 'Well, she's no doing any harm out there.'

So the next morning they were up bright and early, had their breakfast. And Mary went out with her father, collected the nets, collected the fish, and they graded the fish and kept some for themselves. Then they went into the village and sold the rest, came back home, had their supper. It was a beautiful day.

And Mary said, 'Is there anything you want me to do, Mother?'

'Well no, Mary,' she says, 'everything is properly done: the washing's finished and the cleaning's finished, and I was just making some jam; and I'm sure your father's going to sit down and have a rest because he's had a hard day.'

Mary turned round and she said, 'Father, could I borrow your boat?' once again.

'I'm sure, my dear,' he says, 'you can have the boat. Take the boat. Now be careful because there might be a rise of a storm.'

'I'll be all right, Father,' she said, 'I don't think it's going to – the sky looks so quiet and peaceful. I doubt if we'll have a storm the night.' And away she goes.

But as soon as she takes off in the boat, oh, her mother gets up. 'That's it, there she goes again,' she said. 'To put my mind at rest, would you do something for me?'

Angus says, 'What is it you want now, woman?'

'Look,' she said, 'would you relieve my mind for me: would you go down and borrow Lachy's boat, your cousin Lachy's boat, and row out to the island and see what Mary does when she goes there? It'll put my mind at rest.'

'That's no reason for me to go out,' he said. 'Let the lassie enjoy herself if she wants to enjoy herself! There's no reason for me to go out – I'm sure there's no one within miles. Maybe she's wading on the beach and she sits there, an-and-and maybe she has some books with her, and she – she likes to be by herself.'

But no. She says, 'Look, do something for me, husband! Would you go out, Angus, and see what she does?'

So Angus said, 'Och, dash it, woman! To keep you happy, I'll go out and see what she's doing. It's only a waste of time anyway.'

So he walks down; it was only about two hundred yards down to Lachy's cottage. Lachy had the same kind of boat. He was sitting at the fire; he had never married; their fathers had been brothers. Lachy stayed in this cottage, he was an old retired seaman and he always liked to keep a boat.

'Well, it's yourself, Angus!' he said. 'Come away in. And come you, sit down and we'll have a wee dram.'

'No,' he said, 'Angus, I'm not here for a dram.'

'Well,' he said, 'what sent you down? It's not often you come for a visit.'

'I was wondering,' he said, 'if you would let me borrow your boat for a few minutes?'

And Lachy said, 'Well, what's the trouble?'

'Ach, it's no trouble, really,' he said, 'I was just wanting to borrow your boat for maybe half an hour or so.'

'Well, what is wrong with your own boat?'

'Och,' he said, 'Mary's using it.'

And Lachy said, 'Och, that's Mary off on her gallivant to the island again. And you want to follow the lassie and see what she's doing. If I was you I would leave her alone. Come on, sit down and have a dram with me and forget about it.'

But old Angus was so persistent, 'I want to borrow your boat.'

'Well,' he said, 'take the dashit thing and away you go!'

He takes the boat and he rows across to the island and he lands on the small beach. There was Mary's boat beached. And he pulls his cousin Lachy's boat up beside Mary's, and beaches it. And he walks up a path – it was well worn because Mary had walked up this path many many times – he follows the path up, goes over a little knowe. There are some rocks and a few trees, and down at the back of the island is a small kind of valley-shaped place that leads out to the sea. Then there's a beach, on the beach is a large rock. And beside the rock is a wee green patch.

Old Angus came walking up, taking his time – looked all around and looked all around. There were a few seagulls flying around and a few birds wading along the beach because the tide was on the ebb. And he heard the laughing coming on. Giggling and laughing – this was Mary, carrying on. And he came up over the knowe, he looked down – here was Mary – with a large seal, a grey seal. And they were having the greatest fun you've ever seen: they were wrestling in the sand, carrying on and laughing, the seal was grunting and Mary was flinging her arms around the seal!

So Angus stopped, he sat down and watched for a wee while. He said, 'Ach, I'm sure she's doing no harm, it's only a seal. And her mother was so worried about it. She's enjoying herself; probably she's reared it up from a pup and she comes over to feed it, and I'm sure it won't do her any harm. She's better playing with a seal than carrying on with a young bachle as far as I'm concerned!'

So, he takes his boat and he rows home, gives his cousin Lachy back the boat, lights his pipe and walks up to his own home. He comes in through the door and his old wife, old Margaret, is waiting on him.

She said, 'You're home, Angus.'

'Aye, I'm home,' he said, 'Margaret, I'm home. And thanks be praised to God I am home!'

She said, 'Did you see Mary?'

'Of course,' he said, 'I saw Mary. She's out on the island.'

'And what is she doing? Is she sitting – what is she doing?'

He said, 'She's enjoying herself.'

Old Margaret said, 'What way is she enjoying herself – is she wading on the beach or something?'

'No,' he said, 'she's not wading on the beach.'

'Is she reading?'

'No, she's not reading.' He said, 'She's playing herself with a seal.'

She said, 'What did you say?'

He said, 'She's playing herself – she has the best company in the world and she's enjoying herself – she's playing with a seal! A large grey seal. They're having great fun and I didn't interfere.'

She said, 'Angus, Mary's enchanted. It's one of the sea-people that's taken over. Your daughter is finished – ruined for evermore. I've heard stories from my grandmother how the sea-people take over a person and take them away for evermore, they're never seen again – she's enchanted. What kind of a seal was it?'

He said, 'It was a grey seal and they were having good fun so I didn't interfere.'

She said, 'If you want to protect your daughter and you want to have your daughter for any length of time, you'd better get rid of the seal.'

He says, 'Margaret, I couldn't interfere with them. It's Mary's pet.'

'I don't care if it's Mary's pet or no,' she said, 'tomorrow morning you will take your gun and go out, instead of going to the fish you'll go out and you'll shoot that seal and destroy it for evermore!'

'But,' he said, 'it's Mary's pet – she probably reared it up unknown to us, she probably reared it up from a young pup, and it's not for me to destroy the seal, the thing she has to play with.'

'I'm sure she can find plenty of company in the village instead of going out there to the island!'

But the argument went on, and they argued and argued and finally old Margaret won. He lighted his pipe to have a smoke before going to bed.'

'Well,' he said, 'in the morning I'll go out and see.'

Then Mary came home and she was so radiant and so bright, so happy. She came in and kissed her daddy and kissed her mummy. She had a cup of tea and asked Mummy and Daddy if they needed anything or wanted anything done.

And they said, 'No, Mary.'

The old woman was a wee bit kind of dubious. She wasn't just a wee bit too pleased. And Mary saw this.

She said, 'Is there something wrong, Mother?'

'No, Mary,' she said, 'there's nothing wrong.'

'Well, I'm going off to my bed.' Mary went to her bed. In these cottages in times long ago in the little crofts, the elderly people stayed down on the floor and there was a small ladder that led up to the garret in the roof. If you had any children they had their beds in the garret. Mary lived upstairs.

So the next morning Angus got up early. And before he even had any breakfast, he went ben the back of the house and took his gun. He loaded his gun and took his boat and he rowed out to the island, before Mary was up. And he walked up the path, the way Mary usually went, over the little hillock, down the little path to the little green part beside the bare rock – sure enough, sitting there sunning himself in the morning sun was the seal.

Angus crept up as close as he could – he fired the shot at the seal, hit the seal. And the seal just reared up – fell, and then crawled, made its way into the sea, hobbled its way into the water and disappeared. 'That's got you,' he said.

And then he felt queer. A funny sensation came over him. And he sat down, he felt so funny – as if he had shot his wife or his daughter. A sadness came over him. And he sat for a long while, then he left the gun down beside him and he looked at the gun ... he felt that he had done something terrible. He felt so queer.

So he picked up the gun, walked back to his boat and he could barely walk, he felt so sick. He put the gun in the boat. He sat for a while before he could even take off in the boat and he had the queer sensation, a feeling of loss was within him, a terrible feeling of loss – that something he had done could never be undone … he could hardly row the boat. But he finally made his way back to the mainland, tied up his boat, picked up the gun, and put it back in the cupboard. He walked in and old Margaret was sitting there.

She said, 'You're back, Angus.'

He said, 'Yes I'm back.'

She said, 'Did you do what I told you to do?'

'Yes, Mother,' he said, 'I did what you – what you told me to do.'

She said, 'Did you see the seal?'

'Yes,' he said, 'I saw the seal. And I shot the seal.'

She sat down. 'Are you wanting…'

'No, I don't want any breakfast,' he said.

She says, 'Are you feeling…'

'No, I'm not feeling very well. I'm not feeling very well at all.'

She says, 'What's wrong with you?'

'Well,' he says, 'I feel terrible, I feel queer and I feel so kind of sad … I've done something wrong and you forced me to it, I hope in the future that you'll be sorry for it.'

'Och,' she said, 'it's only a seal!'

But they said no more. By this time Mary had come down.

She said, 'Good morning, Father; good morning, Mother,' and she sat down at the table as radiant as a flower and had some breakfast. 'Are you not eating, Daddy?'

'No,' he said, 'Daughter, I don't…'

She said, 'Are you not feeling very well?' And she came over and stroked her father's head. 'Are you not feeling very well, Father?'

'Oh,' he said, 'I'm feeling fine, Mary. I'm just not, just – what I should be.'

And the mother tried to hide her face in case Mary could see something in her face that would – a give away in her face, you know.

'Well,' she says, 'Father, are you ready to go out to lift the net?'

'Well, Mary, to tell you the truth,' he said, 'I don't think the tide'll be on the – the out-going tide won't be for a while yet. No, I think I'll sit here and have a smoke.'

'Mother,' she says, 'are you needing anything done?'

'No, Mary,' she said, 'we don't need anything done.'

Now they wanted to try and be as canny with her as possible. They didn't want to upset her in any way.

And the mother said, 'No, Mary, I think everything's done. There's only a little cleaning to be done and I think I'll manage.'

Mary says, 'Well, after I milk the cow, Father, would it be all right if I take the boat?'

'Och, yes, daughter, go ahead and help yourself to the boat,' he said, 'I'm sure you can have the boat any time. You don't need to ask me for the boat, just take it whenever you feel like it.'

So Mary milked the cow, brought in the milk and set the basins for the cream, and did everything that was needing to be done. She said, 'Goodbye, Mother, I'll see you in a while. I'm just going off for a while to be by myself – I'll be back before very long.'

Mother said, 'There she goes again! If you tell me it's true, she'll be home sadder and wiser.'

But old Angus never said a word. He just sat and smoked his pipe. And he still had this – as if a lump were in his heart. And he was under deep depression, just didn't want to get up, just wanted to sit. He had this great terrible feeling of loss.

So Mary rowed the boat over to the island. And he sat by the fire and he smoked and he smoked and he smoked. Maggie called him for dinner and the day passed by, but Mary never returned. Evening meal came, Mary never returned. Her mother began to get worried.

She came down and she said, 'Angus, has Mary come home? It'll soon be time for milking the cow again.'

'No,' he said, 'Mary has never come.'

'Perhaps,' she said, 'she – would you go down and see if the boat's in? Has she tied up the boat? Maybe she walked down to the village.'

Angus went out and there was no sign of the boat. 'No,' he said, 'the boat – '

'Well, she's not home. If the boat's not home, she's not home,' she said. 'I doubt* something's happened to her … I doubt something's happened to her – Angus, you'll have to go and see what, you'll have to go out to the island. Go down and get Lachy's boat and go out to the island and see.'

So Angus goes down, just walks down and takes Lachy's boat, never asks permission, just pulls the rope, unties the rope and jumps in the boat. He doesn't – he had the feeling that he doesn't even worry what happens, he's so upset. And he rows out to the island and there's Mary's boat. And he pulls the boat in because the beach was quite shallow. And he lays the boat beside Mary's boat, his own boat. And he walks up the path, over the little hillock, down by the big rock to the little bay and the

* I doubt – I fear

green patch beside the big rock, and walks right down where he saw the seal. He looks. The side of the rock was splattered with the blood where he had shot the seal. And he walks round the whole island, which wasn't very big, walks the whole island round – all he saw was a few spots of blood. Nowhere did he find Mary. Mary had completely disappeared, there wasn't a sign of her, not even a footprint. And he walked round once, he walked round twice and he went round a third time; every tree, every bush, every rock he searched, but Mary was gone.

And he felt so sad, 'What could happen to Mary, my poor wee Mary, what happened to her?'

Then at the very last he came back once again to the rock where he had shot the seal – and he looked out to sea, the tide was on the ebb. And he stood, looked for a long long while. And he looked at the rock, saw the blood was drying in the sun. And he looked again, then – all in a moment up come two seals, two grey seals, and they come right out of the water, barely more than twenty-five yards from where he stood! And they look at him. They look directly at him – then disappear back down in the water. And he had this queer feeling that he was never going to see Mary any more.

So he took his boat and he rowed home, tied up his boat. Just the one boat, took his own boat, left Lachy's boat on the island. He sat down beside the fire. His wife Margaret came to him.

She said, 'Did you see Mary?'

'No,' he said, 'I never saw Mary. I never saw Mary, I searched the entire island for Mary and Mary is gone. And look, between you and me, she's gone for ever. We'll never see Mary again.'

And they waited and they waited, and they waited for the entire days of their lives, but Mary never returned.

And that is the end of my tale.

That was a Gaelic tale from the Western Isles. That story was told to me when I was only about fifteen years of age, doing the stone-dyking in Argyll at Auchindrain with a mason, Mr. Neil McCallum. He was from crofting stock; he was a crofter, his brother was a crofter. And, just to sit there listening . . . I can still hear his voice in my ears; you know, his voice is still there after, maybe, nearly forty years. And every little detail is imprinted in my memory. And when I tell you the story, I try to get as close as possible to the way that he spoke to me. Do you understand what I mean?

Joan Lingard

from *After Colette*

'I belong to a country that I have left.'
Jours gris

From the beginning, Eugénie was determined that her daughter should be fully aware of her French inheritance. The stories of Saint-Sauveur started early. Amy's first words were in French. At the age of five she went to Stockbridge School and there spoke Anglicized Scots in the classroom (broad dialect was strongly discouraged) and playground Scots outside in the company of other children. She played Scottish street games, called a top a peerie, and skipped to the chant of 'One, two, three, a leerie...' Eugénie did not mind the street games, but she did object to the street language. It sounded so coarse. After hearing Amy rowing with another girl in the street below from her third-floor window, Eugénie reproved her.

'But she ca'ed me a Frog! I only tellt her she was a ba'-faced tatty-heid!' Amy had said a few other things as well, but those she would not repeat to her mother. 'And so she is. She's got a face like a ba'.'

'Ball,' said Eugénie, who had never imagined she would be trying to teach a daughter of hers to speak *English*. And they didn't even live in England! Her own command of the language still had its holes: she always forgot that it should be people, for instance, not peoples, her 'th's were difficult, and her accent caused smiles. Tolerant, even indulgent, smiles. Men had told her that her voice was 'attractive'. Not George, of course.

Eugénie hated her daughter arguing and fighting in the street. George was no support to her in that; he said he was glad the lassie wasn't feart and could stand up for herself, the way he'd had to do.

'I want you to speak nicely, Amy,' said her mother. 'Say head, not heid!' That was one of the few Scots words Eugénie could understand. The rest sounded like double Dutch to her. Now she knew how he felt, said George, when she rattled on in French!

'Granny Balfour says heid,' said Amy. 'And ba'.'

Eugénie did not respond.

'I like French better than anything, though,' said Amy, knowing how to make her mother smile.

Amy longed to go to France. 'One of these days!' said her mother. But when Eugénie returned to Saint-Sauveur for a visit after an interval of nine years, she did not take Amy with her.

Amy begged to be allowed to go to Burgundy with her mother, but her father was adamant. She couldn't take time off her schooling, she had to 'stick in at her lessons' or she'd 'never get on in life'.

'It's only two weeks. I won't be able to *bear* it if you don't let me go! I'll die!'

'Don't talk rubbish!'

'Have you never wanted anything so badly you could've died for it?'

'I've said no, haven't I? And where do you think we'd get the money from?'

'All right, I know it doesn't grow on trees.'

'Don't be cheeky, madam!' Her father raised his hand, and Amy backed away. Not that he had ever struck her. When he hit her mother, Amy ran out of the house along the street to her Aunt Janet's, where no one ever raised their voice.

Amy and her mother had two places of refuge: the home of my parents, James and Janet Balfour, and that of her mother's friend Liane. Her father did not know about Liane. Amy and Louise, Liane's eldest child, had been born on the same day. Liane was French, too, and married to a Scot, and she taught piano. She gave Amy a weekly lesson, and in return Eugénie would do some of her ironing. Liane had four children, and would have more; she was a Roman Catholic.

'You mustn't fret while I'm gone, now, Aimée,' said Eugénie. This would be their first separation; they had never been apart for a single night. 'The time will pass quickly.'

'For you, maybe. But not for me.'

'Don't pout, love. It spoils your pretty face.' Eugénie put her arms around her daughter and held her close. 'You know I love you, don't you?'

'If you did, you wouldn't leave me!'

'Now, don't be silly! You know I have to go and see *my* mother. You know I'll come back.'

George Balfour saw his wife off at the station. Amy did not go with them; from an early age, she hated standing on cold draughty station platforms waving goodbye. She went instead down to the Water of Leith, where she sat on the bank and fired stones at a rusted oil-drum bobbing about in the scummy water. It was quiet down there in the valley, away from the traffic, with the high green trees screening her; there was only the sound of the smack of the stones as they hit their target and the swoosh of the water as the drum swirled. As she fired she imagined that the drum was her father. 'Take that!' she muttered. 'And *that*!'

She heard feet slithering down the bank behind her and turned to see Danny McGrath, who lived in the flat below hers. His curly hair stood out around his head like a bush.

'You're no a bad shot fer a lassie.'

'What do you mean, fer a lassie? Are you wanting yer heid in yer haunds to play wi'?'

'Hey, hang on! No need to lose your rag.'

'I could beat you any day!'

'You're on!'

Amy jumped up. Swiftly they gathered stones and piled them into small cairns at their feet. They stood higher up the bank to fire, to get better aim. Amy went first. Her eyes narrowed, her lips protruded in a characteristic pout of concentration, then her arm came up and over in a wide arc and her stone went crash! right into the side of the drum, sending it into a frightful tizzy.

'The de'il seems to be in you the day!' said Danny, squaring up to take his turn.

Amy won the contest. And she was a whole year younger than Danny McGrath!

'You pitch like a laddie,' he said, and went sloping off, with his hands in his pockets.

For a few minutes Amy enjoyed her triumph, then she thought again of the train steaming south, snaking round long bends, sounding its mournful hooter, leaving a long plume of smoke trailing behind it. She trudged back along the path to the bridge at Stockbridge.

Granny Balfour was coming past, pushing the old pram she kept for transporting her washing to and from the steamie. She stopped when she saw Amy and put on the foot-brake.

'Where have you been?'

'Down by.'

'You shouldne go down by the river on yer ain. A bad man might get ye. Ye're no greetin', are ye?'

Amy had not realized that her face was wet. She wiped it with the back of her arm. She knew her grandmother thought she was 'tied to her mother's apron strings'; she had overheard her saying so to Aunt Nan. Aunt Nan had said, 'She's only a bit lassie yet.' Some said that Aunt Nan was still tied to *her* mother's apron strings. And she was forty!

Granny Balfour had on her thick hairnet and underneath her coat, which gaped open, her big wrap-around apron sprigged with blue and black flowers on a grey ground. She was seldom to be seen without the apron or the net: only on special occasions – christenings, funerals, visits to the panto at the King's Theatre and the like. For these celebrations she had her hair set at the hairdresser's in Raeburn Place, where Bunty MacFarlane's sister Jessie worked. Then Amy would find the sight of her grandmother's hair odd: like steel wool set in marcel waves. Amy preferred hers netted and aproned.

'C'mon, hen, ye can chum me to the steamie. It'll dae ye guid to learn to work the mangle and fold sheets the richt way. Ah ken you've got some fancy notions in that wee heid of yours – put there by your mammy, no doot! – but ye micht still need to dae washin' when you grow up. Whit woman doesne?'

'I thought you were at the steamie yesterday.'

'This is your Aunt Janet's washing. She's no feeling so well the day.' She was pregnant, Amy knew; her mother had told her. Her grandmother thought that matters of that nature should not be spoken of in front of children; when Jinty Smith along the street, who was unmarried, had had a baby, Granny Balfour had given Amy some guff about her finding it under a gooseberry bush. As if there were any gooseberry bushes in Stockbridge!

Granny Balfour fished in her apron pocket and brought out a poke of sweets, black-and-white-striped balls, half of them stuck to the paper. 'Put one of them in yer gob and that'll cheer you up!' Amy did as she was told; she felt in need of some sweetness. The hard round ball, spiced with peppermint, bulged agreeably in her cheek.

'Bonjour, Aimée!'

Amy whipped round to see Louise, Liane's daughter. She was swinging her pink dancing pumps by their tapes. She went to ballet lessons on a

Saturday morning. Amy's mother had asked her father if Amy might learn to dance – she yearned to dance – but he'd given a predictable answer.

'Bonjour, Louise,' muttered Amy, well aware that Granny Balfour's eyes and ears were on alert.

'Et ta mère? Elle est allée en France, n'est-ce pas?'

'Oui.'

'Veux-tu jouer avec moi cet après-midi?'

'Pas aujourd 'hui.'

'Au 'voir, Aimée!'

'Au 'voir.'

Louise sped off.

'Who in the name was yon?'

'A girl.'

'I could see that! A Frog? What was she on about?'

'Nothing.'

'Do ye ken her?'

Amy shrugged. 'I just sort of see her about.'

Amy understood, without her mother having to tell her, why they kept quiet about their friendship with Liane and her family: it saved rows, being cross-questioned, as Amy had just been. So she learnt early on the art of concealment, of withholding pieces of information that she did not wish others to possess, thereby avoiding having to descend into the outright telling of falsehoods.

Granny pressed no further. She put out her foot and released the pram brake. Amy rested one hand on the handle. They waited for a tram to swing past, then they crossed the road into Hamilton Place.

As they drew near St Cuthbert's bakery, they saw that Aunt Nan was standing on the step talking to Jessie MacFarlane. Jessie's coat made a splash of red against the grey stone. Her sister Bunty had married and gone to live in Fife, and so they saw less of her now. Jessie too had been married, to a fisherman at Newhaven, and widowed. The fisherman had fallen into the dock when drunk; at least, that was how the story went in the street. Jessie was still only twenty-four. 'The Merry Widow', Granny called her.

'Look at the two o' them! Bletherin' their heids aff! I've tellt Nan her tongue'll fall aff yin o' these days.'

Jessie was smoking a cigarette; she held it perkily, at shoulder level. Amy saw that Aunt Nan was smoking too, but she was holding her cigarette behind her back; little feathers of smoke were curling round the edges of her white overall. Granny Balfour thought that women who smoked in the street were common.

'Hello there, Mrs Balfour!' Jessie was quick with a greeting. She spun around on her high heels, her earrings birling. 'How're you doin' the day?'

'I'm takin' Amy tae the steamie. She's missin' her mammy.'

'What a shame! Thick as thieves, the pair of you, aren't you, you and your mammy?'

'I'll take you to the pictures, hen,' said Aunt Nan. She loved going to the cinema. They had a picture house – the Grand – in their own street and then there was the Savoy just down past the bridge and the Ritz over in Rodney Street, not far away. Aunt Nan spent nearly all her pocket money in these palaces of pleasure. She sat through most programmes twice. 'There might be a Roy Rogers on.' She particularly liked Roy Rogers; she'd sit right in the front row if he was in the film and talk to him. 'Ride 'em, cowboy!' she'd say. 'Give Trigger a pat for me, Roy.' 'Would you fancy going to the pictures tonight?' she asked Amy.

Amy nodded. She liked going to the pictures, but she didn't like it when Aunt Nan talked to the screen. People would snigger and glare at them and hiss 'Shush!', and worse.

'I'll come along for you after, then.'

'I don't know aboot the two of youse,' said Granny Balfour, shunting the pram forward, 'but Amy and I have got work tae dae.'

The steamie was full of steam. It didn't get its name for nothing, Granny would say. The steam snatched them into its damp embrace as soon as they opened the door and stepped inside, laying droplets of moisture on their faces and hair. No wonder Granny wore a net. The women's faces were brick-red and their hair clung in wet snakes to their heads. They were calling to each other across the deep-sided tubs. 'The boxes', Granny called them. They were wood on the outside, stone on the inside. Amy found it all strangely comforting, even though she'd hated the place when she'd come in before with her mother. But today she liked the way the women joked with one another and she liked the slap of the sheets and the whirr of the mangles as their big rollers turned. She felt half-hypnotized by the sounds and the steamy heat.

Granny Balfour was putting her waterproof apron on top of the other one and rolling her sleeves up her stout forearms. Then she ran hot water into a box and threw in a fistful of gritty soap powder.

'Git the sheets in then, hen, and dinne staund there lookin' glaikit! If ye keep yersel' busy yer mammy'll be hame in nae time, ye'll see.'

Amy was thinking about love when her mother came home; she had been to the pictures with Aunt Nan the evening before. They'd gone to the pictures five times in the two weeks that her mother was away. And nearly all the films that they'd seen had been about people – men and women – falling in love. She'd asked Aunt Nan if she'd ever been in love and her aunt had gone all coy and hinted that she might have been. 'What happened?' asked Amy. 'Why didn't you marry him? Would Granny not let you?' 'I love Roy,' said Aunt Nan. 'But that's not *real*,' said Amy. Aunt Nan looked huffed.

Eugénie brought back for Amy two books by the French children's writer the Comtesse de Ségur, *Les Malheures de Sophie* and *Les Petites Filles modèles*. Eugénie had read them when she was a child. Amy wrote her full name on the flyleaves: Gabrielle-Amélie Bussac Balfour.

For herself, Eugénie had bought Colette's novel *La Chatte*.

'I could read that, too, Maman, if it's about a cat. I like cats.

'No, it's not suitable for you yet, love.'

'But why not?'

'It's a book for grown-ups. It's not so much about the cat as the man who owns it.'

'What does he do, this man?'

'He marries.'

'Is that all?'

'No, of course not. It's complicated.'

'Is he in love with his wife?'

'Their marriage is not what is called a love-match. It was arranged by their families – it is something that used to happen more.'

'But why is the book called *La Chatte*?'

'He is very attached to his cat, you see. And the cat does not like his new wife.'

'Does the cat win?'

'I suppose one would say that it does.'

'Maman, was yours a love-match, with Father?'

'Of course.' Eugénie's colour was high.

'Did you ever fall in love – before you married Father, I mean?' Her mother was looking away, towards the window where the light was failing. 'Did you, Maman?' asked Amy again.

'Well, yes ... I did, once.'

They heard the key in the front-door lock. Eugénie got up, smoothing back her hair, which she now wore in a chignon, and went to meet her husband.

Three years later, Amy was allowed to go to France with her mother. On their way to Saint-Sauveur they were to spend a few days in Montmartre with the Lebruns.

'Can we go and see your friend Colette when we're in Paris?' asked Amy.

'Oh, I don't know ...'

'Please, Maman!'

'It's a very long time since I've seen her. Must be eighteen years! She's probably forgotten all about me.'

'How could she forget? When she and Grand-mère were almost like twins. Write to her, Maman, *please*!'

Colette's answer came on blue paper. She was living now on the top floor of the Marignan building on the Champs-Elysées, with her third husband, Maurice Goudeket.

'Every time I see you, you're in a different place,' said Eugénie.

'I have moved thirteen times. Unlucky thirteen!' Colette did not sound troubled. 'How would you like to live on the eighth floor, Aimée?'

'I should love it. Especially if it looked over the Champs-Elysées.'

'Which floor do you live on in Edinburgh?'

'The third.'

'We do have a view,' said Eugénie. 'Of the Fife hills.'

'But it's nothing like this,' said Amy, irritated that her mother should even compare the two.

'Let me take you up on to my roof terrace and show you the view from there.'

Colette led the way up the ladder, which she said made her think of a ship's ladder. She liked it when it swayed in the wind. She had a cat on one shoulder and the other hand grasped a bulldog by the scruff of its neck. Amy, following behind, saw that Colette's feet moved surely and the calves of her legs looked muscled and strong, even though she was getting to be quite an old lady. She was sixty-four, the same age as Amy's French grandmother. Her mother had brought back a photograph of

Grand-mère Bussac from her last trip, and she had looked grey and elderly then. She'd had a hard life, her mother said. 'Hadn't Granny Balfour's life been hard?' Amy had asked. 'Yes, but perhaps not in the same way. She's always been in control.' That was the thing to aim for, said Amy's mother: to be in control of one's life. Not that that was easy, she had added, and closed the conversation before Amy could ask any more questions.

'Look at the clouds, Aimée!' Colette's ringed hand swept upward and silver bangles slid down her arm. 'See how the horizon shimmers! Look at Sacré-Coeur – wouldn't you think it was made of sugar candy? And there's the Opéra. I feel as if I have the whole of Paris at my feet when I come up here. I come in all seasons. Even on wild winter days. I like to watch the storm-clouds gathering and the rain advancing on the city like a curtain. Tell me, Aimée, how do you like Paris?'

Amy thought it wonderful, but felt too overwhelmed to say so. Looking at Colette, who was smiling broadly, her wiry hair lifted by the breeze, the cat sitting on her shoulder sniffing her neck, she realized that she did not need to. Colette understood the whirl of sensations going on inside her. Their eyes met; it was a moment of contact for Amy that was to stay with her for ever. She said she felt as if she had received an electric shock.

She went to the balcony rail and looked down into the avenue of the Champs-Elysées. 'The finest thoroughfare in the world', her mother called it. The street buzzed with traffic, the wide pavements swarmed with pedestrians. The pavement cafés too were busy; the customers lounged in their chairs their faces turned towards the street so that they might watch the passers-by. They looked as if they had nowhere to go, nothing to do other than sit and stare and drink café crème and eat tartelette de fraises and smoke long, pungent-smelling cigarettes. They looked as if they might well sit until the sun went down. It would be good to have cafés like that on Princes Street, Amy had suggested to her mother as they'd walked down the avenue, but her mother had said that the wind was too cold in Edinburgh. You'd be blown to bits in no time. Besides, it was not a Scottish sort of thing. The Scots preferred to hug themselves inside their own houses. They didn't like exposing themselves to the stares of passers-by.

Colette came to stand alongside Amy. She leant both arms on the rail and the cat arched and curled its claws deeply but gently into the shoulder of its mistress's jacket. 'There's always something to see. Processions, military parades, funerals, traffic jams! I have a lot to amuse me.'

'When I grow up I shall come and live here on the top floor and I'll spend all day up on the terraces looking down into the Champs-Elysées!'

'And why not, Aimée? One must have dreams. But come, let us go back downstairs and I shall make you some hot chocolate.'

'Mother said you would give us hot chocolate.'

Colette's laugh was whipped away by the breeze.

The telephone was ringing as they came back into the apartment. While Colette talked to someone called Marguerite (who appeared to be an actress, judging from the conversation), Amy let her eyes feast on the sitting room. Everything delighted her: the profusion of flowers, the bowls of fruit, the books, the crystal-glass paperweights, the lamps. She especially liked a mauve crystal lamp etched with lilac flowers. Some day she would have such a lamp. And she would fill her room with flowers like these flowers: curly-headed dahlias, velvet-petalled roses, glowing geraniums. She got up to look more closely at the paperweights; she did not think that Colette would mind or consider her nosy.

'Look, Maman, there's a paperweight almost like yours!'

The phone rang again, and the caller this time was called Nathalie. Colette must have millions of friends, thought Amy; they probably called from morning till night and had long, interesting, literary conversations.

'Ring me later, Nathalie,' said Colette. 'I have visitors.'

Amy smiled, pleased that Colette would put them before her friend Nathalie.

Pauline, the maid, brought in hot chocolate and Colette served it in blue-and-white cups. Amy sipped hers slowly, wanting to make it last for ever. She had never tasted anything so delicious. They had chocolate at home every morning, she and her mother, even though her father thought they would be better off drinking tea, like him, but it never tasted quite like this. Perhaps the milk was different. Or the cocoa powder.

'You speak French very well, Aimée,' said Colette.

'With a Scottish accent!' Eugénie smiled.

'There's Burgundy in it, too. Oh yes, I can hear it! You sound like a true Burgundian girl.'

Amy blushed. 'Maman and I always speak French when we're together. When Father isn't listening.'

'He doesn't like you to speak French?'

'It seems to make him angry, doesn't it, Maman?'

Eugénie shrugged. 'Men are sometimes like that.'

'That is true. But not all, thankfully. My Maurice is not, I am happy to say. I could never stay long with a man who did not like me to speak my mother tongue. With whom I could not *speak* in my mother tongue.'

Amy saw her mother look suddenly sad, bereft almost. They were closely attuned to one another's moods. She said quickly to Colette, 'Maman has all your books.'

'Not every single one, Aimée. Colette has published so many. I have just been reading *La Naissance du jour*.'

'Ah.'

'I liked the opening – you know, where you quote your mother's letter saying that she can't come and visit you because her rose cactus is about to bloom? And if she doesn't see it this time she may never see it again.'

'Shall I let you into a secret? I actually reversed what she said.'

Eugénie looked nonplussed.

'Oh yes, novelists are often guilty of turning their material around! That's how it becomes fiction. My mother wrote that not *even* the rare blooming of her cactus would keep her from visiting her daughter.'

'She must have loved you very much,' said Amy.

'Yes, I think she did. I still miss her.' For a moment Colette looked sombre, then she brightened and lifted the jug, asking if they would like more chocolate. She replenished their cups and produced a plate of chocolate éclairs. 'Do you like éclairs, Aimée?'

'Oh, yes!'

'I do, too.' Colette bit into one with relish, then licked a sliver of cream from her top lip. 'I have an excellent appetite. What about you, Aimée? You don't look as if you eat enough – you have those telltale little salt-cellars in your neck. Not that they are not attractive. Now mine have long since vanished, alas. I love food. I like meat and crabs and apples and chocolate éclairs – am I not disgusting? – and ripe bananas and freshly ground coffee and mangoes. You might even say I'm a bit of a glutton!' She patted her stomach. 'It shows, eh? Do you like sugared almonds, child? You *must* like sugared almonds!'

'I've never tried them.' They were Aunt Nan's favourite sweet. Aunt Nan bought herself a poke of sugared almonds every Saturday afternoon as a treat, on her way home from the bakery, and ate them in the Grand Picture House on Saturday nights. Amy had always thought of them as old maid's sweets, along with peppermint pan drops, which old men and women sucked in church to stop them coughing.

'Try one now.' Colette held out a dish. 'Look at their soft sweet-pea colours; that is why I like them so much.'

Amy looked up, startled. Aunt Nan called them her sweet-pea sweeties. Maybe Aunt Nan wasn't as daft as some people liked to make out.

'Feel how smoothly they lie on the tongue,' said Colette.

From then on Amy shared with her Aunt Nan a preference for sugared almonds over all other forms of confection.

'You have such a lot of new things to look forward to, Aimée,' said Colette. 'How old are you?'

'Twelve.'

'Ah. On the brink.'

On the brink, thought Amy, liking the idea, even though she was not sure exactly what it was that she was on the brink of. Real life, she supposed. She felt suddenly older, on the way to being grown up, sitting here in this room high above Paris, drinking hot chocolate, three women together, talking.

'You have a good thick braid there,' said Colette, putting out her hand. 'Turn around and let me see it! You must be able to sit on it! Can you release it and let me see your hair? Would you, for me?'

Amy, blushing a little, fumbled to undo the blue satin ribbon at the end of the plait, then her fingers scrabbled through the three intertwined strands, running rapidly up to the nape of her neck. With a flick of her head she shook out her hair.

'What a glorious colour! Like a beech tree in autumn, with the sun lighting it. You are blessed to have such beautiful hair.'

'She wants to have it cut,' said Eugénie. 'All her friends are having their hair cut.'

'Don't!' said Colette. 'Not yet.' She glanced from mother to daughter. 'You seem close, you two?'

Eugénie nodded. 'We're good friends.'

'Where is your daughter?' asked Amy.

'Wherever she wants to be – a not unreasonable thing at her age. She is twenty-four now, my Colette. She spends most of her time on the Jouvenel estate in the Corrèze. She comes to Paris only occasionally. She comes and sees me when she wants to. She'll arrive unexpectedly and we'll talk for hours and then she'll go away and I won't see her for months.'

'*Months!* I should hate not to see Maman for months. I couldn't bear it.'

'Bel-Gazou married, didn't she?' said Eugénie.

'That lasted only two months. She divorced him, for physical disgust. An unimpeachable reason, would you not agree?'

Eugénie did not have time to comment before the door opened and a man put his head round.

'Maurice, come and meet some old friends!' Colette smiled warmly at him. 'Eugénie and Aimée, this is my best friend!'

Amy could not help feeling a little disappointed at the appearance of Colette's husband. He was quite dapper in appearance, but otherwise she thought him fairly ordinary: he was neither tall nor particularly handsome, and he had a largish mouth and ears that stuck out. She had expected him to look more *romantic*, more like a Chéri. He was sixteen years younger than Colette. He did seem to be nice, however, and he had very good manners; he gave them each a little bow when he shook hands and said 'Enchanté!', and he took the hand his wife was holding out to him and spoke to her in a kindly, affectionate way, which Amy had seldom heard her own father do to her mother. Her father seemed forever to be complaining, hectoring. Something was not right. The kitchen was untidy; there was a stain on the tablecloth; they had banked the fire too high, or not high enough; the dinner was late. She had started to notice it more in the last year and when she had commented on it her mother had said that his complaining was a bit like a nervous tic: on coming home, on opening the door, he seemed to be overcome by a compulsion to criticize. She had seen him standing in the doorway, looking round, looking for areas in which to attack her. Why does he want to attack you? Amy had asked. Her mother had shrugged. Her father hated it when her mother shrugged. 'You French!' he would say. 'Why can't you just *answer*?'

Her mother was gathering up her bag and gloves from the floor beside her chair. She was anxious that they should not overstay their welcome.

'Let me give you my new book,' said Colette. Goudeket fetched a copy from a shelf and put it into his wife's hands, along with a pen. 'It's called *Bella-vista*.' Colette inscribed it on the flyleaf: 'A Eugénie et Aimée, amies de Bourgogne et d'Ecosse, affectueusement, Colette.'

She embraced them both, told them never to visit Paris without coming to see her.

Going down in the lift Amy asked her mother, 'What does Monsieur Goudeket do?'

'I am not sure. Odile said she thought he was a dealer in pearls at one time. He's half-French and half-Dutch. Half-Jewish, too. He used to write a little himself, it seems.'

'But he's not famous, like Colette?'

'Oh no.'

'I wonder if he minds.'

'He doesn't seem to.'

'Maman, what does physical disgust mean?'

Eugénie blushed. 'It's difficult to explain. It's when a woman doesn't like to have a man near her.'

'But if Colette's daughter didn't like her husband why did she marry him?'

'Sometimes a woman doesn't find out until afterwards.'

On the Métro, Amy opened *Bella-vista.* 'C'est folie de croire que les périodes vides d'amour sont les "blancs" d'une existence de femme,' she read. She contemplated the sentence. 'It is mad to think that the periods in a woman's life which are empty of love are blanks.' She was glad of that, otherwise her mother's life would be one long blank. Excepting, of course, that *she* loved her. But Amy knew that Colette meant *romantic* love. Men and women. As they sped through the tunnels underneath Paris, Amy thought about Colette's daughter, who lived by herself on a big estate in the Corrèze. Odile said the house was like a castle.

'Maman, Colette doesn't seem to mind if she doesn't see her daughter.'

'Her life is very crowded, of course, what with her writing and her friends. She travels, too. They go all over the place – to Belgium, Italy, Tunisia. They sailed in the *Normandie* on its maiden voyage to New York. Odile saw their picture in the newspaper. But she must miss her daughter sometimes. You'd think so, anyway. Her daughter was brought up differently – differently from you, that is. She had a nanny, and after that went to boarding school. It is what people in their milieu do. You've always been at home with me; I wouldn't have had it any other way. I'd never want to be separated from you.'

That was what made it so difficult for Amy to understand when her mother left her just over a year later.

They were on a train from Paris to Auxerre, Amy and Eugénie, on their way to Saint-Sauveur, having been seen off at the Gare de Lyon by Yvonne and Odile. They were alone together in the compartment. They had just finished a lunch of crusty bread and a ripe Camembert and peaches and were brushing the crumbs off their laps, when the door opened. Eugénie had been talking about Odile, saying what a pity it was that her husband had died so young, that she'd never had children, and had had to live so many years alone. It was as well she'd had Yvonne and Giles to turn to. Now there was a good marriage! They had always been so considerate – Eugénie stopped in mid-sentence. A man stood framed in the doorway. Amy felt conscious of him being framed; it was as if the moment was frozen. Yellow light seemed to encircle his head. He had dark, greying hair and dark, thickly lashed eyes. A handsome man, much more handsome than Maurice Goudeket. He might have been a Chéri when he was younger. He was wearing a pale jacket and a deep-blue shirt with a lighter-blue tie. He stood there staring at Amy's mother. She stared back at him.

'Claude,' she said, rising to her feet. 'Claude Laroche.'

Like a sleepwalker, she moved out into the corridor. The door closed behind her. Amy stayed in her seat, motionless, paralysed by a nameless fear, the last of the breadcrumbs sticking to her lap. When she got out at Auxerre, they trickled down her legs, into her white ankle socks. That night, taking off her socks in her grandmother's flat above the bakery, feeling the crumbs disintegrate between her fingers, the fear repossessed her.

They stood to one side of the compartment door, the man and her mother, so that she could not see them, though she could hear their voices murmuring, rising and falling, mingling with the rumble of the train wheels. The train swayed and rocked. She swayed and rocked like a stocking-doll.

After some time her mother came back. Amy could not say how long she had been in the corridor. Ten minutes. Or a lifetime? Eugénie said nothing. She sat down. She stared at the dusty velour back of the seat opposite. From time to time her top lip twitched and she seemed about to break into a smile, then, with a sideways glance, to think better of it.

Amy's mother did not speak the name of Claude Laroche again, not in her daughter's hearing. And Amy could not bring herself to ask, 'Who was that man? That man on the train?: The one you called Claude Laroche?'

Amy both loved and hated Saint-Sauveur. The village and its surrounding countryside had featured much in her daydreams: she had wanted desperately to come here, to see her grandmother and the Saracen tower and the ruined château and the garden behind the Colette house; to walk the streets; and take the paths through the woods. But something had shifted imperceptibly in her life, between stepping into the train at the Gare de Lyon and stepping out at the station in Auxerre. A remembrance came to her of a day at home when, riding her bicycle, the chain kept falling off. She had dismounted and, kneeling on the hard pavement, getting her hands covered with sticky black oil, carefully eased the chain back on to the ratchets until, finally, she had been able to spin the pedals freely between her hands. Then she had remounted and ridden off, but a few turns of the pedals later her foot lurched sickeningly down and there was the chain hanging loose again! She put it back three times, then in frustration flung the bicycle aside. Later her Uncle James had told her that it was the back wheel that needed adjusting.

She did not know what it was that needed adjusting now; she had only this sense of dislocation and an awareness that something which had once been taut was now slack. Walking in the woods one afternoon outside Saint-Sauveur, conscious that her mother's thoughts were not with her, Amy tried to take her hand and was reproved, gently and with a little laugh but firmly.

'You're too big a girl to take my hand now, Aimée!'

Later, looking back, Amy's most vivid memories of that holiday were of the times when her mother had gone off on her own to meet Florence or Sylvie, old school friends, or Anne-Marie, with whom she had nursed at the Front. Her mother would talk too much and too rapidly before going out. 'You remember me talking about Anne-Marie, don't you, Maman? We were at Cambrai together. She met George – your father, Aimée – she's from Sens, married now, to a man, an engineer, from Nantes, they have four children. They are living in La Rochelle, they have come to visit Anne-Marie's sister in Auxerre.' Berthe Bussac seemed not to notice the difference in her daughter. She said, 'Anne-Marie? I don't remember. You knew so many girls.' And on one occasion Eugénie simply disappeared. She went to the pharmacy, she had a headache ... She did not come back for hours. Amy paced the streets. Two women standing at the intersection of the rue de l'Hospice and the rue des Gros Bonnets thought the girl looked a little demented with all that red hair streaming out behind her. Surely not another Juliette Colette? But then Eugénie Bussac had mingled her blood with that of a foreigner, and who knew what strange concoction could result from that? Amy passed her Uncle Robert in the square with his son Alphonse and did not even see them.

Eugénie came back as dusk was shrouding the street. She said, 'I felt like some air. I went for a walk...'

After that visit to France Amy felt as if a shadow had appeared at the edge of her eye. Whichever way she turned her head, whatever she looked at, it was there.

On their return to Edinburgh, Eugénie paid regular visits to the General Post Office up in Waterloo Place, to the Poste Restante counter. She would then go into Princes Street Gardens to read her letter if the weather was fine, and Crawford's Tea Rooms on North Bridge if it was not. Amy knew because she followed her. She told no one.

Amy went to the hairdressing salon where Jessie worked.

'I want my hair cut,' she said. 'Short.'

'Does your mammy know?'

Amy held out her hand. 'I've got the money.'

'I wouldne like to touch it without your mammy – '

'I want it *cut*! It's *my* hair.'

Amy swept some black hairs off the red mock-leather chair and sat herself down, facing the mirror. 'I'm ready,' she said, and folded her arms over the upper part of her chest.

Jessie covered her with a voluminous grey cloak and tied the tapes at the back.

'Are you sure now?' She held the scissors suspended.

'Sure,' said Amy fiercely.

'All right, keep your – !' Jessie stopped, realizing that what she had been about to say would be inappropriate, given the circumstances.

Afterwards, Jessie was uneasy about what she'd done. There sat the girl, glowering at her shorn head in the mirror, with a sea of dark-red tresses washing around the legs of her chair. Jessie told my mother that she hadn't realized before just how strong-willed Amy was.

She asked her if she'd like to keep her hair. Amy said that she never ever wanted to see it again.

When she had gone out Jessie gathered it up in a bag, in case Eugénie should come asking for it. But Eugénie never even mentioned it to her.

Years later, Jessie brought out the hair; we looked at it, faded and lifeless then. Dead hair, Jessie called it. Next day, she threw it out in the bucket.

It was a full day before Amy's mother noticed the transformation that had taken place to her daughter's head, and it was her husband who drew her attention to it.

'I'm surprised you let the lassie cut her hair,' he said. 'Now that it's gone, she'll never get it back.'

The following year, 1938, Berthe became seriously ill. She had not been well for some months – a kidney complaint – but now her condition was deteriorating. Eugénie's brother Robert wrote to say that his sister should come, his wife could not cope, she had her own elderly father to look after. Eugénie prepared to go, leaving Amy with her father and Granny Balfour. It was early summer.

'Please let me come with you!'

'How could I?'

'*Please*, Maman! Don't leave me!' Amy clung to her mother.

'You can't take time off school. You know your father would never allow it.'

Berthe lingered, dying eventually in late August. Eugénie did not return to Scotland until the beginning of November. She wrote, saying that she had her mother's affairs to sort out. Granny Balfour snorted. What affairs could *her* mother have had? She hadn't even owned her house, had she?

When Eugénie did come back, there was a big row in the kitchen between her and George. Amy's mother emerged afterwards with the usual half-shut eye and next day her father said that he was sorry. Amy heard them behind the closed door of their room.

'You can say sorry once too often, George.'

'You'll forgive me, Jeanie, won't you?'

There was no reply.

Eugénie resumed her visits to the GPO. She hugged her secret to herself, did not confide in anyone. She stayed away from our house, fearing perhaps that my mother might plead for George. My mother often would speak up for him; she said he was his own worst enemy – not that that excused him. But she thought he loved Eugénie, in his own way. When he struck his wife, it was out of frustration; my mother did not condone it, but she understood.

Eugénie took to walking in the King's Park and on Arthur's Seat in stormy weather as well as fair. She was seen standing on the top of Salisbury Crags while the rain pelted down and others ran for cover. She began to look like a wild woman, with her muddied shoes and long hair tangled by the wind. On wet days she came in sodden. Placing her coat lengthwise over the rails of the pulley, she winched it up to the ceiling, where it hung like a spreadeagled scarecrow and dripped navy-blue water at irregular intervals on to their heads. She'd kick off her shoes and sit as close to the range as she could get, her hair hanging down over her shoulders like rats' tails. Her serge skirt steamed, giving off a wet-woollen, fusty smell. Her stockinged feet were stained.

The sight of her on those occasions inflamed George Balfour even more. She was a disgrace to him, to the name of his family. They were a laughing stock in the street. On coming home from work, he ranted about unwashed dishes, picked them up and threw them. Shards of broken china speared the carpet, tea spattered the ceiling, milk ran down the walls. His wife watched impassively. It was Amy who, trembling, jagging her fingers on the broken china, cleared up the mess.

In March, Claude Laroche arrived in town. Amy knew that he had without seeing him: her mother became transformed, looked years younger. She washed and brushed her hair. She smiled. She laughed. She stuck yellow daffodils in a blue-and-white jug. She pushed the kitchen window up high to let in the spring air.

George Balfour came upon his wife and Laroche behind the ruined chapel of St Margaret in the King's Park. Now he wore a bruise like a badge on his cheek. He had a broken knuckle too, on his right hand, which he had to take to the Infirmary to get set and plastered. For several weeks he carried a clenched white fist. The Frenchman left Edinburgh, taking Eugénie with him. She was not even allowed to come back to the house to collect her clothes.

From some points of view it might have been seen as romantic, this elopement, but not from Amy's. She saw her mother once more, at the school gate. It was lunchtime. The playground was milling with pupils, many of whom knew the story of Amy's mother and her fancy Frog. They formed a sniggering cluster a few yards from the gate. 'French kisses!' 'French knickers!' 'Hoor! Hoor! Hoor!'

Amy and her mother put their backs to them. Eugénie had come to say goodbye and to tell Amy that she would send for her. She did not say how the sending would be done, nor how Amy's father would be induced to let her go. 'As soon as we have an apartment. I promise! I'll write to you at the Poste Restante in Waterloo Place. We're going to live in Paris. Won't that be nice? You like Paris, don't you?' Eugénie looked distraught, and happy. She embraced Amy, holding her close. 'Courage, mon enfant! Je ne t'oublierai pas.' 'I won't forget you.'

It was 1939, and Hitler was gathering strength in Europe.

Bill Douglas

My Childhood

The Story takes place towards the end of the war.

Scotland. 1945. Sounds of an air raid siren whining. We descend through a shaft of black sky with the noise in our ears. Then gradually the darkness turns to light and the siren dies away. After a moment's silence come softer sounds of breeze and bird song. Suddenly, our downward journey comes to a halt. The first thing we notice is the landscape stretching to the horizon. Then fields. Closer, a deserted mining village.

Closer still, the school. The playground is empty except for the solitary figure of an old woman in black. Age has withered her. She is quite static. She is cold. She is wearing all the clothes she possesses with the exception of her coat which, in her absentmindedness, she has left at home where it also serves as a blanket. She is wearing slippers because she has no shoes. She clutches a black shawl to her head.

Her face has the abstracted look of a mind given to wandering. She has forgotten her reason for coming. She is lost for one brief ecstatic moment in the memory of her own girlhood. But then the children are singing.

The children are gathered together in the assembly hall, hymn books in hand.

> All things bright and beautiful
> All creatures great and small
> All things wise and wonderful
> The Lord God made them all.

The teacher is not singing. She is keeping a look out for drifting heads.

> Each little flower that opens
> Each little bird that sings
> He made their glowing colours
> He made their tiny wings.

At that moment the door opens and in comes the janitor. As quiet as a mouse he relieves himself of his bucket and mop and tip-toes inside. The quickness of his movement suggests urgency.

The janitor approaches the teacher, inclines close to her ear and whispers his message. The teacher nods while casting a glance at one of her pupils.

This is Tommy. He is twelve years old. He appears strangely out of place. His eyes have the seriousness of a person double his age. It is as if the carefree pleasures of childhood had passed him by. Like the others he is poorly dressed, only more so. But he has pride and keeps his head high.

The janitor takes his leave. The teacher progresses amongst her pupils causing some of them to turn with curiosity.

The teacher comes to whisper in Tommy's ear.

The boy goes out of the assembly hall.

> The mountain and the valley
> The river running by
> The sunset and the morning
> That brightens up the sky.

Tommy steps into the playground as weary as an old man. He stands before his grandmother saying nothing. No need to ask questions. He understands. He will take her home where she belongs.

And so these two silent figures make their way through the school gate towards the village.

Their private pain is dwarfed by God's gigantic earth.

> He gave us eyes to see with
> And lips that we might tell
> How great is God Almighty
> Who hath made all things well.

Tommy helps his grandmother up the open stairs. The old woman keeps an anchor hold on the railing. Home is at the top of the landing and that seems a very long way away.

At the top there is a wooden door that looks a thousand years old. Tommy shuts it keeping the world outside.

A fierce wind rages against the mountain of coal dust. It carries us upwards until we can see its crater-like surface.

There is a boy crouched there on his knees. He is grubbing for coal and nearby there is an old newspaper carrying some of his finds. This is Jamie.

On closer inspection we can see he is about nine years old and dirty and that he has worn the elbows of his jumper down so that his shirt peeps through. Jamie is quite lost in his search for coal. No sound of human voices here, no hints of animal life either, just the wind curving and the scrape-scraping of small hands. Then quite suddenly the pit horn moans out like a tired cow. The boy looks up from his chore with more than passing interest. He has every reason to.

Down at the pit shaft gate come the miners weary from their shift.

And from the entrance a rush of children shouting excitedly

> Pit pieces da'
> Pit pieces

This is the circus of their day. There must be something extra tasty about a piece of bread when it has made a long journey into the earth and back.

Jamie moves quickly, snatches up his newspaper package. The headlines hint at news of war.

The boy reaches the edge of the tip just in time to witness the happy moment.

In one joyous surge the children meet with their fathers. There are new imploring cries

> Lift me up da'
> Lift me!

Some get hunch-backs, some fireman's lifts. Others are content to be enclosed in arms. How happy they are.

But not so Jamie. No need for him to go down. He has seen it all before, been there. No lifts for Jamie. Oh well, there is no harm in watching.

So here we have this lonely boy watching the passing of this joyous parade. In a moment the laughter will die away and there will be silence.

Jamie, left there on his own, can only think of one thing. And this thought becomes uppermost in his mind, takes on vast proportions. So much so that he quite forgets his real reason for coming here. He makes off.

He helter skelters down the tip letting the package fall from his grasp. He is too busy thinking about Helmut.

The German POWs can be seen spread out across the field. All is silent except for the clicking sounds of their knives.

Helmut roots a turnip, casting the good vegetable to one side and its waste to the other. He is doing the job without thinking about it. He is thirty. He has an open friendly face. He glances across the field, catches sight of someone and smiles.

Young Jamie is there leaning on the gate.

Helmut goes to join him.

And there they stand with the gate between them. Not a word passes from man or boy but there is an immediate warmth that tells us they are great friends. Helmut winks.

He swings the boy merrily through the air and into the field beside him.

The guard is watching them intently. He looks like the kind of man who has the rule book implanted in his memory, knows how to enforce orders. And there is a suggestion in his eyes that tells us he does not like Germans. Still, he has been known to look the other way.

Helmut wipes Jamie's running nose with his sleeve in a fatherly gesture. Then he crouches low and taps his shoulder. It is his way of telling the boy he is going to give him a lift. Suddenly a voice rackets the silence. It is the guard. 'We're going now!' 'Eine minuten, bitte,' answers Helmut. 'Keine Zeit,' replies the guard. He is saying there is no time.

The workers move wearily towards the tractor wagon.

Jamie settles himself on Helmut's shoulders and 'woosh' in no time at all he is ten foot tall.

They go to join the others in the wagon. The most immediate sound we hear is the clatter of Jamie's tackety boots on the boarding. Finally, they sit down and there is no visible movement at all.

Helmut has his arm round Jamie's shoulders. The boy looks happily content.

Two farm women stroll away across the field giggling at something between themselves.

A group of prisoners have already fallen asleep inside the wagon.

One man stares bored into space.

The guard's rifle lies abandoned against a side flap.

The guard himself is in the field urinating. He seems in no hurry.

The group sleep on, oblivious to the sound of water.

Now the guard turns, whistles his signal and the tractor starts up.

The guard comes to take possession of his rifle. The vehicle pulls away bumping and grinding over lumps of hard earth. We are left with the empty field.

A group of villagers, an old man and two women are standing on the landing of one of the village's open stairs when the tractor makes its entry.

One of the vehicle's large wheels splashes a puddle.

The engine stops. The group on the stairs look on the Germans with a hateful stare.

Helmut swings a reluctant Jamie back to earth and takes back his hat.

Jamie looks numb.

Helmut smiles trying to cheer the boy up.

But the young face looks more miserable than ever.

The tractor pulls away leaving Jamie behind. Helmut waves. 'Auf Wiedersehn, Jamie.' Then he goes leaving a terrible silence.

Jamie feels like crying. He will not see his friend again until tomorrow and that seems a very long way away. Now he must go home. He moves away looking very sorry for himself.

On the village green a scraggy black cat, a stray, wondering where to go. Now and again he meows to himself for company. Jamie eyes the creature from a secret position behind a row of hanging sheets. He progresses silently until he is quite close to the animal. The cat seems unaware of the prowler. Suddenly, Jamie darts out, his arms outstretched, his voice screeching for all the world like a bomber plane. The frightened creature disappears in a flash.

We are now inside the house. We are close to this door that looks a thousand years old when the latch goes up. Jamie peers inside. He is revealing only one eye and it expresses guilt.

The living room, which is all there is, is so poor, so spare it echoes the smallest sound. Tommy is kneeling on the floorboards busily axeing an old drawer to pieces. He gathers up some of the wood and carries it towards an empty hearth.

The old woman is sitting in a rocking chair. She is perfectly still except for her shivering hands.

Jamie's face is now completely visible. He looks afraid. He feels like running away. But he comes inside.

The wallpaper is so old there are places where it no longer sticks to its surface. Tommy rips off a piece, crunches it up and puts it in the grate.

Jamie is hovering self-consciously beside the bare wooden table. He remembers having stored two pieces of coal in each of his trouser pockets. He fetches out his small offering and puts them on the table top.

The sound of the coals attracts Tommy. He turns to offer Jamie one brief accusatory glance and continues with his chore. Finally, in his own good time, he confronts Jamie.

There is an agonising silence at the table. Jamie, unable to bear the penetration of the accuser's eyes, considers his offering.

Tommy studies the four coals, then the giver. He looks grave.

Jamie decides the best thing to do is not to appear afraid, perhaps even to change the subject. 'I'm hungry.' 'You're selfish!' answers Tommy. And with that he throws himself at Jamie, pulling and pushing, kicking and punching. The boys tumble crazily to the floor.

Their grandmother tries in vain to separate them.

That night a friendly fire burns in the grate. Little flickers of light dart to and fro across the dark room. The family huddle together hypnotised by the flames. The old woman's lips are moving to silent words only she can hear. They are content for a moment. Tommy puts his arm around Jamie's shoulder; all their warring forgotten in the heat.

Much later that night the family lie in bed. They are lying inside what are called bedcupboards. Once they had wooden doors attached that enclosed them inside but Tommy burned them for fuel. Jamie is sharing with his grandmother while neighbouring them lies Tommy. They are wearing all their clothes because there is nothing else to wear.

Jamie draws himself up and leans on his elbow. He appears deep in thought. He looks at his grandmother. 'Granny, where's my ma' and da'?' asks Jamie. But there is no answer. The old woman is fast asleep.

Tommy has been lying awake listening. 'Ma's dead,' he answers.

Jamie is confused. 'What does dead mean?' 'You go up to heaven,' answers

Tommy. There is a long silence. 'What's heaven?' Tommy sighs. This is no time for questions. 'My teacher said it's a beautiful house in the sky.' Jamie thinks about that. He understands nothing. 'Go to sleep!' orders Tommy. And silence falls about the room.

Dawn. On the wall just above the old woman's bed there hangs a double portrait in a single frame. We see the faces of two young women, one smiling, the other a little sad. We can hear low sounds of a convoy drifting by. Silence. Then the voice of the old woman. 'Oh, my poor girls.' She is crying quietly to herself. She is lost in the memory of a very private pain. 'What have they done to you?'

A tear lies on the old woman's cheek.

Jamie is fast asleep.

Tommy is lying awake. He hears the old woman say 'God curse them'. He understands everything. He will never tell anyone least of all Jamie. But time will unfold the mystery.

A large billowing cloud covers the sun.

Young Jamie is staring up at the sky in absolute wonder.

The cold winter sun stretches itself across the fields eating up hard frost. The boy is still looking up when Helmut comes. He lifts Jamie, swirls him through the air in circles of delight and deposits him inside the truck.

The others are as still as corpses. Helmut and Jamie no sooner take their seats than up goes the rear flap.

The vehicle moves away leaving behind an empty field. The spluttering engine lingers for a while then fades.

Inside the truck Jamie is sharing his ABC book with Helmut. As this will be Helmut's first lesson in English the boy begins at the beginning. 'A is for apple,' says Jamie. 'A is for apple,' answers Helmut with not too much difficulty. 'B is for boy,' says Jamie. 'B is for....' Helmut appears stuck. 'Boy,' repeats Jamie with a lot of emphasis. 'Boy,' answers his friend in a very German way. 'C is for Cat.' 'C is for Cat,' repeats Helmut. He is doing well. Jamie is delighted.

The truck travels merrily up a sloping field.

The boy continues his lesson. 'Dooog' answers Helmut, a little unsure. 'Dog,' repeats Jamie. 'Dog,' answers Helmut again. 'Good,' says Jamie. And he smiles.

The vehicle thunders into the village and stops.

Helmut flits a miserable Jamie back to earth. Then he hands down the ABC book. The boy shakes his head. 'No, it's for you, Helmut.' The man seems to understand this simple gesture. He thanks Jamie and asks in German if he is going home to his mother. Jamie does not really understand but he nods just the same. 'Auf Wiedersehn,' says Helmut clutching the gift. The boy waves trying to keep up his spirits. In a moment the truck will go away and he will be a little figure left behind.

A young POW goes towards the farmhouse to collect his dinner.

The farmer's wife arrives promptly with the food.

She places in the hands of the young German an enamelled basin piled high with mashed potato.

He carries the meal away.

He goes to lean on the truck where a friend is waiting. The rest of the soldiers are spread out across the grass preoccupied with the business of eating. Helmut remains quite separate. He is sitting on an old oil drum perusing his book. Over at the truck the young German nudges his friend to look. Helmut is completely lost in his newly acquired ABC, and has forgotten his food. The two Germans chuckle to each other.

A blustering day in the village graveyard. Tommy is looking down at his mother's grave. The headstone is overgrown with weeds. There is complete disillusion on his young face. A crow squawks hauntingly in the silence. A fresh bunch of poppies adorns a grave nearby. Tommy steals them.

The boy strolls down the village street with the flowers in his hand. He is going to make a present of them to his grandmother to cheer her up. Some distance ahead of him comes a man with a dog, a whippet on a lead. The man has a round face and his name is Mr Knox. Mr Knox is completely absorbed in himself. The man and the boy pass one another without a word or a glance.

Barely a moment later Tommy turns to give his full attention to the man.

Mr Knox reaches the top of the street. Ahead of him there are two neighbouring houses. The house on the left has a window with eight panes of glass, the one on the right, two panes, both equal size just different in design. Outside the house with two panes stands a woman of advanced age. This is Mrs Knox. Mr Knox advances towards his mother.

The woman nudges her son to look. At closer inspection she has a face like a hawk. Mr Knox turns as directed and for some reason he looks a trifle uneasy.

There is an expression of hate on Tommy's face. He spits on the ground in order to make his feelings more felt. Then he departs.

The poppies are withered now. They hang limp from a tea cup.

The flowers are made insignificant by the table top and, in turn, the table by the room. The latch clacks up on the living room door. Jamie comes in carrying a kettle which he places on the table.

The boy has need of the tea cup and so he sploshes the dead poppies on to the floor. That done, he proceeds to fill the cup with boiling water. Up and up the water goes until it overflows on to the table. Now he empties the cup itself.

Jamie goes to kneel before his grandmother. He places the warm cup inside her hands.

He encloses her hands in his for extra warmth and pats them gently.

One day there is a strange bicycle at the foot of the stairs. There is a moment's silence, then the sound of the door closing.

Inside the old woman looks agitated. From somewhere in the room comes the voice of a man. 'How are you, old one?' asks the visitor, kindly. 'Getting along all right, are you?' The old woman does not answer.

Jamie and Tommy are standing behind their grandmother's chair. They feel safer there. They have never set eyes on the man before.

Mr Brown is nearing forty. He holds a birdcage in his hand. He looks more and more uncomfortable. He fetches the canary into sunlight on the table.

The boys are fascinated by the small yellow creature. But they remain where they are, hiding their feelings.

The canary flutters to and fro inside its cage whistling a happy tune.

'It's for your birthday, son. Like birds, do you?' asks Mr Brown.

Jamie glances up at Tommy. He is not sure to whom the visitor is referring.

'Come on then, son,' encourages Mr Brown. 'Not frightened of me, are you?'

Tommy, feeling the man must be talking to him, releases himself from his grandmother's grasp.

He goes towards the visitor. He plays for a moment with the canary.

Jamie is feeling very sorry for himself. He hides his face inside his grandmother's shoulder. The old woman comforts the jealous boy.

'Is it really my birthday?' asks Tommy, shyly. The man smiles warmly. 'Did you not know that? A big laddie like you?' He ruffles the boy's hair affectionately. At that moment Tommy feels instinctively the man before him must be his father. But he is too frightened to ask. Mr Brown's eyes have a long-lost look in them. They suggest a hint of private pain, regret, an infinite sadness. What are you going to be when you grow up, son?'

Suddenly, the old woman explodes with energy. It is as if she has been given a new lease of life. 'I hope he won't be anything like you. Now get out!' Mr Brown is nervous. 'I brought him a birthday present because I was thinking about him.' But the old woman is thoroughly at war. 'He is not needing anything from the likes of you. Go on, get out!'

'Right!' says Mr Brown, thus fetching the argument to a close. He turns to go. On his way out he glances briefly at the photograph of his wife.

The young woman appears not to be smiling now, but laughing at him.

Mr Brown pulls the door behind him. Young Tommy looks disconsolate. 'What did you do that for?'

'Because he's no earthly good to man or beast,' answers his grandmother. Jamie smiles with satisfaction.

Tommy bolts out of the house. There is no time to lose.

He reaches the landing, shouts, 'Da?'

Down in the street Mr Brown is already on his bicycle.

The boy scrambles down the stairs as fast as his legs will carry him.

He hurries breathlessly after the bicycle. 'Da, come back. Da, come back!' But his father does not respond.

Mr Brown journeys alone down a country lane. His anger causes the machine to shake. He turns a corner and disappears.

Tommy is beside himself with grief. He is crouched in a corner beside some railway sleepers. This is where he comes when he wants to be on his own.

That night the old woman is standing on the stair landing waiting for the boy to come back. A lonely dog howls in the silence.

The howl spreads across the dark landscape and dies.

In the very early hours of the morning Jamie hangs the birdcage up in the window. He is hoping to attract Tommy.

A little later the boy returns, though not immediately to the house. He goes to sit on an opposite step.

The canary comes to life behind the window, flits back and forth. It too must be wanting him to come back.

Tommy looks up at his pet. His eyes are tired and his face is very dirty. But for all that, he appears happy to see his canary. Then, quite suddenly, the boy's expression turns to horror. He is wondering if he is seeing things.

Behind the widow – there are no curtains, so there is a clear view – there is a hint of disturbance. The old woman has a broom in her hand and she is trying to dislodge the cage. She has no trouble and boom down it comes with a crash.

The boy springs up.

He races upstairs.

He bursts into the room. There is a terrible noise inside. The old woman is bashing the cage with her broom. Tommy wrenches the weapon free, rescues his birthday present and puts it on the table. Then he turns to his grandmother and says angrily, 'Just you leave my birdcage alone. I'll give it away if you want but just leave it alone.' He pauses a moment so that she might understand. 'Okay?' He picks up his gift and leaves the house. The old woman sobs like a little child.

The boy descends the stairs, panting. In the well of the staircase there is a coal cellar. He disappears inside and slams the door shut.

Tommy huddles in the darkness with the birdcage on his lap. The canary is perfectly still but unharmed. The boy prods the cage trying to encourage his pet to flutter happily again. 'Joey, what's wrong?' The bird remains silent. 'Never mind. I'll look after you,' says Tommy. Then they remain content with each other's company.

Jamie approaches the coal cellar door, tries to open it. 'Go away!' snarls Tommy, holding the door fast. 'Tommy, Granny's lost,' says Jamie. He means she has wandered away. And he is worried because being old she has been known not to remember her way back home. 'I'm not bothered,' shouts Tommy. Jamie turns away. He is busily wondering what to do when he hears a cat meowing.

It is the same scraggy black stray. The animal senses Jamie's presence and runs off. It reaches the edge of the pavement and ponders the best way to go.

Jamie is hypnotised by the creature. He decides to have the animal for a pet.

The stray charges off.

Jamie in hot pursuit.

The old woman is standing in grass that reaches to her waist. She is perfectly lost. Jamie hurries towards his grandmother with the protesting animal firmly locked under his arm. He takes the forlorn woman by the hand and gently leads her away.

A Spitfire haunts the sky.

Jamie is now sitting on the stair landing. His hand shields his eyes while he watches the plane.

The Spitfire drones deep into the sky and disappears. Out of the silence comes the sound of heavy footsteps.

Jamie turns his attention to the street below.

Mr Knox, the man who keeps the whippet, is there looking up. He beckons Jamie forward.

The boy descends with caution. He reaches the end of the railing then holds back shyly. There is no reason to, the man looks friendly enough. Jamie finally comes forward and as he does so Mr Knox stoops to his level.

The man smiles warmly.

Jamie looks puzzled. He has never seen the man before.

Mr Knox holds forth a shining sixpenny piece between two fingers.

The coin tantalises Jamie. He completely forgets the man, grabs the money and bolts upstairs.

Mr Knox looks a little disappointed by their short encounter. Perhaps he wanted to talk.

Jamie remains watching from the safety of the landing.

The man goes away through an alley. There is something very lonely about him.

Jamie and his friend, Helmut, are huddled together on a grassy slope. Now it is Helmut's turn to teach his young pupil a lesson in German. 'Das ist mein Buch, Jamie,' says Helmut holding the ABC book open. The boy listens intently. The man turns a page. 'Apfel.' 'Apfel,' echoes Jamie without the slightest difficulty. 'Katte,' continues the German. 'Katte,' repeats Jamie. He is surprised how similar the words sound in a foreign language. But Helmut, always ready for fun, has a surprise in store for his young friend. The next thing he says is very long and complicated. Jamie leaps up on to his knees, protesting. 'I want something easy.' Helmut laughs. He throws himself back on to the grass and pulls Jamie towards him. 'Auf Wiedersehn, Jamie,' says Helmut. And before the startled boy knows what is happening, he and his friend are toppling head over heels, merrily down to the bottom of the hill.

A makeshift cover hangs over Tommy's bedcupboard. The boy is hiding inside in the company of his canary. The bird chirps sweetly.

The old woman is fast asleep in her rocking chair. Jamie is sitting by the table with the scraggy black cat on his knee. Clearly the creature does not want to play and with an angry snarl it leaps on to the floor. Jamie folds his arms. He looks bored. He comes to his grandmother and touches her cheek but the old woman shows no reaction. Jamie moves quietly away.

He comes to sneak a peep at the canary. Tommy's head appears instantly through a hole in the cover. 'Get away,' he orders. This is too much for Jamie to bear. 'If you don't let me play I'll tell granny you've got the canary,' says the disappointed boy. 'You're just jealous because it was my da' who gave it to me.' Jamie looks very hurt. 'He's my da' too.' 'No he's not,' charges Tommy. He worries for a moment in case Jamie is going to cry. That would surely put an end to the canary. 'I know a secret,' offers Tommy. 'What?' asks Jamie. Tommy draws close to the other's ear.

Their grandmother remains asleep.

The whispering is over. 'Well?' asks Jamie. 'Okay,' answers Tommy. He slides off his bed.

He accompanies Jamie towards the door. He pauses briefly to whisper in Jamie's ear. 'He's got a whippet.' 'A whippet?' exclaims Jamie. 'Sssh.' The old woman wakes up. She looks angry. The boys leave the house.

Once in the street, Tommy points a finger. 'Jamie, your da' lives over there.' He is indicating the window with two panes. But they are a little distance away from the place in question and Jamie is unsure. 'Where?' he asks. 'There,' says Tommy. Only now he has had second thoughts. Perhaps he is afraid of his grandmother for his hand drifts to the neighbouring window with eight panes.

And so Jamie comes to this house in search of his father. He knocks on the door but there is no answer. He goes to tap on the window but still no answer.

Tommy is sitting at the bottom of the stairs feeling very sorry for himself. It appears he and his grandmother have had more than words.

Jamie is standing some distance away tugging aimlessly at a loose chain on a coal cellar door. He is looking equally sorry for himself.

Tommy glances up still nursing a sore ear. 'Get away,' he says angrily.

Jamie gives a wounded look at his aggressor.

'Get away. I got hit because of you,' adds Tommy.

Jamie goes away.

A group of old men are keeping themselves company in the village street. They are laughing and talking amongst themselves.

Jamie is watching them through a stair railing. But he can hear nothing. He is far too lost inside himself thinking about his father.

The old men drift across the square in silence.

Jamie continues watching them. They are like figures in a dream.

Finally, the group disappear round a corner leaving the place deserted.

The field is a happier place because Helmut is there. The man is sitting on a wall eating bread.

Jamie is crouched on the soft earth sharing the same food.

They are both perfectly quiet, perfectly content to be in each other's company. The boy finishes eating. He sneaks up behind Helmut who pretends not to notice. The boy throws his arms round the man's neck and hugs him tight. 'I love you, Helmut,' whispers Jamie. Helmut smiles. He understands perfectly.

That night there is an air raid in the area surrounding the village. We hear the drone of planes then sounds of bombs booming on the horizon. From inside the air raid shelter comes the voice of an old man singing.

> Oh! Rowan tree. Oh! Rowan tree.
> Thou'lt aye be dear to me
> Entwin'd thou art wi many ties
> O hame and infancy.

The two boys and their grandmother huddle together inside. Tommy is fast asleep.

The face of the old man radiates happiness. His song is about the home of his youth.

> Thy leaves were aye the first o' spring
> Thy flow'rs the summer's pride
> There wasna sic a bonny tree
> In a the countryside.
> Oh! Rowan tree.

Jamie turns away from his grandmother.

On a bunk nearby there is a little girl. She is fast asleep and next to her, close to her open hand, is a rosy apple.

Jamie sneaks a look at his grandmother to make sure she is not watching him.

The apple is tantalising.

Jamie, unable to bear it any longer, stretches out his hand. Nearer and nearer the fruit he goes. He is about to pick up the apple when suddenly his grandmother pulls him back. She shakes a finger angrily. A long wailing cry sounds the All Clear.

The sound explodes into the cold light of the morning. Drowsy figures emerge on to the green going their own separate ways.

The sound follows Tommy and his grandmother into the house. Then it dies. Jamie's tackety boots clatter up the stairs.

Jamie slams the door shut.

Tommy's face is contorted in silent agony.

The old woman stares dumbfounded.

The birdcage lies abandoned on the floor.

The scraggy black cat is eating the canary's innards. Tommy's hand jerks the creature up by the scruff of the neck. Jamie springs forward to rescue his pet. 'Give me back my cat!' screams Jamie. 'He was hungry.' The poor animal, finding itself pulled to and fro, snarls and spits.

The old woman is too tired to separate them.

Tommy thrusts Jamie away. 'I'm going to kill it!' He drags the cat across the room.

Jamie looks numb. We can hear the swing of Tommy's arm and a dull thump as the cat reaches a wall.

On the stair landing Tommy has the dead creature by the tail. He throws it over the railing.

The animal lands in the gutter.

Tommy slides down the stair railing, scampers off through an alley.

A steam train trailing coal wagons crashes forward.

Tommy hoists himself above the fence of sleepers.

The train gathers speed.

Tommy lowers himself into a pathway.

The engine chugs and sways. Steam billows from its funnel.

Tommy races behind the sleepers, legs and arms crazily flying.

Mountains of steam.

Faster legs, faster arms.

Tommy dives towards the bridge.

He bursts on to the bridge landing. And within seconds he is lost in steam. It is as if he had ascended to the clouds. He spreads out his arms like a bird in flight. His face is ecstatic. He remains there long after the steam has dispersed, too thrilled to break this magic spell.

Jamie sneaks a look round a corner in the village.

Ahead of him Mr Knox is walking his whippet. He is progressing towards the house which has the window with eight small panes. Jamie watches this man who once gave him sixpence whom he now thinks must be his father.

The boy decides to follow.

Mr Knox pauses for a moment to pat his dog. On his left is the window with eight panes and on his right the house which has the window with only two panes. When Mr Knox moves again he veers right. He snaps the door shut behind him. Jamie comes to hover around outside.

Mrs Knox is watching Jamie from behind her window curtain. The boy, sensing her gaze, looks uncomfortable. Mrs Knox utters the word 'sixpence' with a touch of irony and moves away.

Mr Knox looks uncomfortable. He had been aware of the boy following him. He was hoping the boy would give up, go away, because he did not want his mother to notice. Now he had had to admit the incident of the sixpence. Mrs Knox was not happy. She preferred to keep the past forgotten. She wanted her son to stay with her. Mrs Knox comes to her son where he is sitting by the fireside. She smoothes him as one would a child.

She remembers a time when he was a child just like Jamie. He had been an orphan and she had brought him up as her own son. She loved him, possessed him. 'You're mine,' says Mrs Knox. 'I took you in and cared for you when nobody in the world cared. God in heaven, the dreams I had for you.' She thinks about Jamie's mother. 'She was a whore, son.'

Jamie remains outside looking more and more unwanted. Mrs Knox continues, 'All women are whores.'

Mrs Knox smiles affectionately at her son. 'You're a King,' she says, embracing him. 'How can they know?' Mr Knox resigns himself.

Jamie waits for a long while, then he gives up.

Jamie is looking through a bus window. The engine throttles, gathering speed.

Helmut is in a field. He becomes a small figure drifting away.

Jamie watches after his friend with a numb face.

Then Helmut is gone and there is just emptiness.

Jamie is sitting beside his grandmother when the bus conductress approaches. 'Where to?' she asks. The old woman has no money. She pretends not to hear. The conductress sighs. The boy unpins a letter from inside his grandmother's coat and hands it to the young woman. She scans the letter with an even deeper sigh. She is too busy to care. 'That will be one and three.' She hands Jamie back the paper. Jamie searches for money inside his grandmother's pocket. The conductress stares through the window, gathering impatience. Jamie fetches out a rosy apple. He is mesmerised. The bus conductress runs off two tickets. Her manner is gruff but she understands. 'Never mind, we'll pay for it.' She goes.

Jamie looks at his grandmother. He is thinking it is the same apple from the air raid shelter. The old woman senses what is in the boy's mind. She says nothing, just smiles and winks.

The bus continues its journey.

The old woman is fast asleep, lulled by the bus's rhythmic sway. Jamie is reading the letter. He looks puzzled. 'Granny, who's Mary?' Getting no answer, he goes back to his letter. He turns to his grandmother once more. 'Granny, I don't want to go to a hospital.'

The hospital has an appearance more like an ancestral home. In front of its colonnades there is a spacious lawn trimmed with flower beds.

Inside, the first sound we hear is a nurse's clapping hands. Her voice is bright and breezy. 'Come on, Mary.' In a bed, in the raw summer light of sun on frosted glass, lies a figure completely hidden under covers. Then we see fists clutching the covers fast. The nurse tugs at the covers but they won't give.

Jamie and his grandmother are standing quite close to the bed. The nurse wrenches off the covers. 'Now, Mary, this is no way to behave when you've got visitors, is it?' She might be speaking to a child. 'No, it isn't.'

The nurse turns to smile at Jamie. We notice she has healthy apple-blossom cheeks.

Jamie, feeling a little shy, does not return the smile. His grandmother puts the apple in his hand and nudges him forward.

The fruit is placed on the bed.

Jamie returns to his grandmother's side. The nurse tucks in the bed-covers while taking notice of the apple. She proceeds to tend her patient, combs her hair. 'We've got to make you look pretty, haven't we?' She pats the pillow. 'Yes, we have.' She progresses towards the apple, patting and tucking the covers as she goes. 'There, there, that's better. Now

we're all nice and comfy.' In a flash the nurse pockets the apple. She
finishes her chores, then approaches Jamie. The boy is horrified. The
nurse smiles warmly as if nothing unusual had taken place. 'And what's
your name?'

'Jamie,' says the boy. 'You stole my apple.' But the nurse pretends not to
hear. 'Jamie, that's a very nice name. Would you like to say hello to your
mother, Jamie?'

The nurse ushers the boy towards the bed. Then she withdraws in a
hurry, tapping her pocket like a schoolgirl with a choice sweet.

Jamie's face is numb. He understands nothing.

His mother stares abstractedly into space. Her face is ghost-white from
lack of fresh air.

The old woman cries tears of anguish.

Jamie turns to look at his grandmother. He feels miserable. He returns to
his mother. But it is too late. She has hidden her face beneath the covers
again.

That night the old woman and Jamie come to the house of the boy's
father. She spits on the doorstep, releasing feelings of hate.

One bleak day the old woman is stranded in a field. She moves in circle
upon circle not knowing who she is or where she is going.

She wails like a wounded animal. She sways to and fro cradling a grubby
newspaper parcel.

Tommy and Jamie hurry down the field as fast as their legs can carry
them. Tommy comes to a halt. He looks worried.

The old woman shows no signs of recognition.

Tommy comes to his grandmother's side.

Jamie stands a short distance away.

Tommy takes the parcel from the old woman and studies its contents. He
looks horrified by what he sees. He throws the parcel to the ground.

A dead bird clings to the newspaper.

Jamie looks sadly at the old woman.

Tommy embraces his grandmother, holds her tight. Then he takes her
by the hand and leads her away.

Night. The war has ended. There is a huge bonfire on the village green. Crowds surround the flames, rejoicing.

In the morning smouldering ashes and silence.

There is a bus waiting at the edge of the field. The POWs are inside.

A blustering day. Helmut and Jamie are seen high on a hill preparing to fly a kite.

A colourful kite dancing in the sky.

Jamie and his friend descend into a ditch. Helmut is wearing civilian clothes. He passes the string to Jamie. 'Nice kite,' says Helmut. 'For you, Jamie.' Jamie expresses delight.

The kite flaps merrily in the air, then it takes a giant swoop. The guard's voice is heard shouting. 'We're going now!'

Helmut glances across the field. He must go now. 'Auf Wiedersehn, Jamie,' says Helmut. He hurries away. Jamie is distraught. He is so stunned by Helmut's departure he lets the kite go.

The kite falls from the sky.

Jamie tears across the field trying to keep up with the bus. 'Helmut!' he screams. 'Helmut!' The sound spreads across the landscape and dies and nobody hears but himself.

Jamie is beside himself with grief. He is crouched in a corner beside some railway sleepers. This is where he comes when he wants to be on his own.

Jamie lies in bed feeling sorry for himself. His hand covers his face. Tommy comes to sit beside him. 'What's wrong, Jamie, aren't you feeling well?' Jamie does not answer. 'Is it because of your da?' Silence. 'Never mind, granny and me will look after you.'

Jamie is inconsolable. He knows nothing in the world will bring Helmut back. He draws a cover over his face.

One cold winter's day, Jamie is sitting at the table. Tommy comes into the room carrying a bottle containing some milk. On the table there is a cooking pot, two bowls and a lump of bread.

Tommy divides the bread between the three. He soaks one of the bowls of bread with milk and passes it to Jamie. He lifts the second bowl for his grandmother.

Jamie eats in silence using his fingers. A little while later it occurs to him that there is not another sound in the room. He looks across at his grandmother. He moves away from the table.

He comes to stand beside Tommy, who is still holding the bowl of food in his hand.

Jamie picks up his grandmother's hand.

There is no response, so he lowers her hand back to her lap.

The old woman's head is tilted back in the chair. Her mouth hangs open, static. She is dead.

The two boys stare at their grandmother as if they could not believe this could happen. 'I'd better go and fetch your da,' says Tommy mournfully. He puts the food back on the table and leaves the house. Jamie continues to look at the lifeless figure, then, unable to bear it any longer, he runs away.

He runs towards the railway bridge.

He emerges on to the railway lines through a gap in the sleepers.

He presses his ear to the line listening for a train. Everywhere is silent.

The boy crouches by the sleepers and cries. From the distance comes the sound of a train. Jamie hears it, looks up.

Steam billowing from the engine's funnel.

Jamie hurries on to the bridge landing as the train bursts underneath.

The boy climbs over the bridge rail, steadies himself, and jumps through the steam.

Jamie is lying on his back in a coal wagon. He struggles himself up to a crouched position.

The village recedes.

Jamie spits at this place that has caused him so much pain.

The village disappears.

The wagons drift away all sound and sway towards the horizon.

Alasdair Gray

from *Lanark*

Kenneth McAlpin

Once a week they queued outside the lecture theatre for a talk on the history of art. Everyone seemed friendly; lightly chattering currents of emotion flowed easily between them and Thaw stood in the flow feeling as dense and conspicuous as a lump of rock. One day he arrived when the queue had gone in but before the lecturer came. Pausing outside the door he made his face expressionless, softened it with a thoughtful frown and entered. There was an explosion of laughter and someone shouted, 'This was the noblest Roman of them all!' The theatre confronted him with a collection of grinning, glaring and roaring heads. The mirth crashed like a wave into his shell of loneliness and gravity. He grinned and said, 'Is my nose green or something?' sitting down beside the fair-moustached student he had once instinctively hated.

'No, but you looked like Caesar pondering over the head of Pompey.'

After the lecture they walked to the refectory together. The moustached student was called Kenneth McAlpin. Thaw said, 'It's queer to be enjoying a coffee here.'

'I've noticed you hardly ever use the place.'

'I never know where to sit. The world sometimes seems a chessboard where the pieces move themselves. I'm never sure what square to go to. Yet it can't be a difficult game, most folk play it instinctively.'

'The rules are fairly simple,' said McAlpin. 'You stick near pieces like yourself and move along with them. The people at that table are in the school choir. The clan over there are highlanders. These four in the corner are serious Catholics. After the second year your group is usually decided by the subject you specialize in.'

'Have you a group?'

McAlpin pursed his lips then said, 'Yes. I suppose I'm a snob. My family used to be rather well off so I've grown up feeling a bit grander than the majority, and I'm slightly uncomfortable when I'm in a group who don't feel the same. I suppose the people I sit with are snobs too. They'll be here soon, so you can judge for yourself.'

Thaw smiled and said, 'I'll leave when they come. I don't want to embarrass you.'

'Actually I'd be glad if you stayed. I enjoy your conversation more than theirs. With the exception of Judy, of course.'

'Judy?'

'My girlfriend. Don't mistake me, they're nice people, you know some of them already. But it's snobbery which keeps us together, I sometimes think.'

Judy and Rushford arrived. Judy was a handsome, sturdy girl with a vaguely displeased expression. Rushford wore an embroidered waistcoat copied from one worn by Benjamin Disraeli.

'The Victorians were far from being the stuffy monsters we used to assume,' he said in a fluting, meticulous voice. Molly Tierney arrived followed by Macbeth and some others, and the group was complete. Macbeth looked lost and unhappy because Molly ignored him but Thaw felt perfectly comfortable. The conversation was about people he never met and parties he never visited but his occasional remarks were heard politely.

After this Thaw and McAlpin worked side by side in the studio, drank coffee together, brought to school books they enjoyed and read the best parts aloud to each other. Thaw preferred poetry and drama, McAlpin music and philosophy. They discussed these but avoided politics in case their opinions divided them. Once or twice they had tea in each other's homes. McAlpin lived in the small posh suburban town of Bearsden. The house had a garden round it and warm well-carpeted rooms. The furniture was large and beautifully kept with Indian cabinets and Chinese ornaments. Mrs. McAlpin was small, brisk and cheerful. 'This is the tiniest of the houses we owned when Kenneth's father died,' she said with a faint sigh, pouring tea into thin cups. 'Not that I wanted the others, even if I could have afforded to keep them. We really were rather prosperous once. Kenneth, for instance, had a nanny when he was small...'

'We keep it, stuffed, in a cupboard under the stairs,' murmured McAlpin.

'... we had a chauffeur too, Stroud, a delightful character, a real Cockney. I do miss the car. Still, if I had it I would probably use it all the time because I'm naturally terribly lazy. I suppose running up and down to the shops helps keep me young. Another thing we don't do much nowadays is entertain. Still, I want Kenneth's twenty-first birthday party to be one he'll really enjoy. You'll come to it, Duncan, I hope? Kenneth often talks of you.'

'I'd like to,' said Thaw. He sat on a sofa so deep that it supported the whole length of his legs, and he sipped tea and wondered why he felt so much at home. Perhaps when he was small his own house had seemed as spacious and secure.

At the refectory table he often heard parties and excursions planned. McAlpin took little share in the plans for in that group practical details were left to the girls, but Judy brought him in by asking, 'What do you think, Kenneth?' or 'Have you any ideas about that?' while Thaw sat hoping to be invited and wondering why Aitken Drummond was always invited. Aitken Drummond was not a member of the group. He was over six feet tall and usually wore green tram conductor's trousers, a red muffler and an army greatcoat. His dark skin, great arched nose, small glittering eyes, curling black hair and pointed beard were so like the popular notion of the Devil that on first sight everyone felt they had known him intimately for years. Drummond was always asked to parties and next day stories were told of him amid mocking, slightly horrified laughter. Thaw envied him, but the question 'Can I come to the party, Kenneth?' though often in his mind, was never asked. He was sure McAlpin would answer 'Yes, why not?' with hurtful coolness. Yet coolness was the quality in McAlpin he most admired. It showed in his polished solidity, his relaxed confidence which nothing, nobody, seemed to perturb. It showed in his calm robust body, his good manners and good clothes, in the finely rolled umbrella he carried with careless ease when the weather was cloudy. It showed most of all on the few occasions he spoke of his private life, as if that life were entertainment he watched, with ironical sympathy, from a distance. One day he said to Thaw, 'I behaved badly last night.'

'How?'

'I took Judy to a party. I got rather drunk and started kissing the host's daughter on the floor behind the sofa. She was drunk too. Then Judy found us and was furious. The trouble is I was enjoying myself so much I couldn't even pretend to be sorry.'

He frowned and said, 'That was bad, wasn't it?'

'If Judy loves you, yes, of course it was bad.'

McAlpin looked gravely at Thaw for a moment, then flung his head back and roared with laughter.

One morning Thaw and McAlpin went into the Cowcaddens, a poor district behind the ridge where the art school stood. They sketched in an asphalt playpark till small persistent boys ('Whit are ye writing, mister? Are ye writing a photo of that building, mister? Will ye write *my* photo, mister?') drove them up a cobbled street to the canal. They crossed the shallow arch of a wooden bridge and climbed past some warehouses to the top of a threadbare green hill. They stood under an electric pylon and looked across the city centre. The wind which stirred the skirts of their coats was shifting mounds of grey cloud eastward along the valley. Travelling patches of sunlight went from ridge to ridge, making a hump of tenements gleam against the dark towers of the city chambers, silhouetting the cupolas of the Royal infirmary against the tomb-glittering spine of the Necropolis. 'Glasgow is a magnificent city,' said McAlpin. 'Why do we hardly ever notice that?'
'Because nobody imagines living here,' said Thaw. McAlpin lit a cigarette and said, 'If you want to explain that I'll certainly listen.'
'Then think of Florence, Paris, London, New York. Nobody visiting them for the first time is a stranger because he's already visited them in paintings, novels, history books and films. But if a city hasn't been used by an artist not even the inhabitants live there imaginatively. What is Glasgow to most of us? A house, the place we work, a football park or golf course, some pubs and connecting streets. That's all. No, I'm wrong, there's also the cinema and library. And when our imagination needs exercise we use these to visit London, Paris, Rome under the Caesars, the American West at the turn of the century, anywhere but here and now. Imaginatively Glasgow exists as a music-hall song and a few bad novels. That's all we've given to the world outside. It's all we've given to ourselves.'
'I thought we had exported other things – ships and machinery, for instance.'
'Oh, yes, we were once the world's foremost makers of several useful things. When this century began we had the best organized labour force in the United States of Britain. And we had John McLean, the only Scottish schoolteacher to tell his students what was being done to them. He organized the housewives' rent strike, here, on Clydeside, which made the government stop the landlords getting extra money for the duration of World War One. That's more than most prime ministers have managed to do. Lenin thought the British revolution would start in Glasgow. It

didn't. During the general strike a red flag flew on the city chambers over there, a crowd derailed a tramcar, the army sent tanks into George Square; but nobody was hurt much. Nobody was killed, except by bad pay, bad housing, bad feeding. McLean was killed by bad housing and feeding, in Barlinnie Jail. So in the thirties, with a quarter of the male workforce unemployed here, the only violent men were Protestant and Catholic gangs who slashed each other with razors. Well, it is easier to fight your neighbours than fight a bad government. And it gave excitement to hopeless lives, before World War Two started. So Glasgow never got into the history books, except as a statistic, and if it vanished tomorrow our output of ships and carpets and lavatory pans would be replaced in months by grateful men working overtime in England, Germany and Japan. Of course our industries still keep nearly half of Scotland living round here. They let us exist. But who, nowadays, is glad just to exist?'

'I am. At the moment,' said McAlpin, watching the sunlight move among rooftops.

'So am I,' said Thaw, wondering what had happened to his argument. After a moment McAlpin said, 'So you paint to give Glasgow a more imaginative life.'

'No. That's my excuse. I paint because I feel cheap and purposeless when I don't.'

'I envy your purpose.'

'I envy your self-confidence.'

'Why?'

'It makes you welcome at parties. It lets you kiss the host's daughter behind the sofa when you're drunk.'

'That means nothing, Duncan.'

'Only if you can do it.'

'Ten weeks is a long, long holiday,' said Mr. Thaw that summer. 'What's your friend Kenneth doing?'

'Working on the trams. Almost everyone I know is taking some kind of job.'

'And what are you going to do?'

'Paint, if you let me. There's an exhibition when we go back with a competition for a picture of the Last Supper. The prize is thirty pounds. I think I can win it.'

He walked the streets looking at people. He used the underground railway where passengers faced each other in rows and could be examined without seeming to stare. Folk near the river were usually gaunter, half a head shorter and had cheaper clothes than folk in the suburbs. He had not seen the connection between physical work, poverty and bad feeding before because he came from Riddrie, an in-between district: where tradesmen and petty clerks like his father lived. He noticed too that the sleek office faces and roughened workshop ones had the same tight mouths. Nearly everyone looked anxious, smug or grimly determined. Such faces would suit the disciples, who had been chosen from labourers and clerks, but they wouldn't suit Jesus. He began looking for harmonious faces whose mouths closed serenely. Most children had these when they sat still, but the people who kept them after adolescence were usually women with a mild, mysterious, knowing look. For a while he thought this might be the incarnate God's expression, for Leonardo and the carvers of oriental Buddhas had thought so. One morning he found it on the face of a three-inch embryo in the university medical museum. The huge little head nodding over the bent-up knees, the great closed eyes and subtly smiling mouth seemed dreaming of a satisfying secret as big as the universe. And he saw such an expression could not belong to Christ, who had looked steadily at the people around him. He needed the face of a mature, sane, outward-looking man whose love abolished all advantage over whom he beheld, a face without triumph or blame in it because triumph is smug and condemnation is Devil's work. He raked for a Christian expression among old drawings. A sketch of Coulter showed a calm unafraid friendly face but was far too wistful, and one of McAlpin was calm and strong but had disdainful eyelids. He decided to steal a face from a masterpiece, but in Glasgow Art Gallery the only good Christs were infants, apart from Giorgione's 'Christ and the Adulteress', where the painter's modesty or restorer's cowardice had kept the holy face in shadow. He took a day trip to the National Gallery in Edinburgh and at last found the face in a trinity by Hugo Van der Goes. It came from the fifteenth century when the Flemish masters discovered oil paint and made brown the subtlest colour of all while keeping the crisp brightness of tempera. God sat on a clumsy gold and crystal throne floating among gaudy turbulent clouds. He wore a plain red robe with green lining and was preventing, by a hand under each armpit, a pained, thin, dead, nearly nude Christ from sliding off the seat beside him. A white pigeon hovered between their heads. God had the same ordinary thin brown face as his son and a look of pure sorrow without bitterness or blame. In spite of the golden seat neither he nor his son looked like well-paid men. They had the thin faces of providers, not owners or directors. And the suffering father, not the dead son, had Thaw's sympathy. This was the face of his Christ, and he knew he could never paint it. Nobody can paint an expression that is not potentially their own, and this face was beyond him.

In the end he decided to imagine the supper as Jesus would see it from the head of the table. On each side of the board the disciples, anxious, hopeful, doubting, delighted, hungry, replete, were craning and leaning for a glimpse of the viewer's face. The only visible part of Jesus was his hands on the tablecloth. They entered the picture from the bottom margin, and Thaw copied them from his father. He took so long preparing this picture that there was no time to paint it so he submitted the black and white cartoon.

The picture won no prize but was easy to photograph, and *The Bulletin* showed Molly Tierney and Aitken Drummond in front of it. A caption said, 'Art students discuss Douglas Shaw's interpretation of the Last Supper at the opening of Glasgow Art School's summer exhibition.' Thaw took a copy of the paper into a lavatory cubicle to gloat over it. Though sick of the picture the published photograph gave him a moment's pleasure of almost sexual potency. He went over to the refectory in a mood of unusual confidence and sat by Judy, who asked in a friendly way, 'Duncan, did you enjoy drawing those unpleasant people? Or does your picture shock you as much as us?'
Her interest delighted him. He said, 'No, I didn't try to paint unpleasant people. After all, Christ picked his disciples at random, like a jury, so they must have been an ordinary representative lot. I may have drawn them grotesque. Not many of us are as we should be, even in our own estimations, so how can we help being grotesque? But we aren't often unpleasant.'
Judy said, 'Draw a portrait of me Duncan, here, on the tabletop.' She kept her head still while Thaw scribbled on the Formica surface. He said, 'I've finished, but it's not a success.'
Judy said, 'You see, you've made me look evil. You've shown my bad qualities.'
Thaw looked at the drawing. He thought he had only shown the shape of her face, and not well. She said, 'I know I have more bad qualities than good. . . .' He started to protest but she said, 'Look at Kenneth!'
Thaw looked across at McAlpin who had put his head back to laugh at a joke. He had grown a beard over the holidays and the gold spire of it

wagged at the ceiling. Judy said, 'Kenneth has no bad qualities. If he hurt anyone it would be from stupidity, not deliberately.'
'He's a gentleman,' said Thaw. 'It's civilizing to know him.'

In the tramcar that evening he felt unusually conscious of his appearance: the paint-stained trousers like a labourer's below the waist, the collar and tie like an office worker above. Passing the park someone plucked at his sleeve. He turned and saw a plump pretty girl who said, 'Hullo there. How are you doing?'
'Fine thanks. And yourself?'
'Not too bad. D'ye live out here?'
'Aye. Opposite the Chapel.'
'I'm visiting my auntie. I'll be seeing you.'
She went downstairs and Thaw wondered who she could be. Suddenly he realized she was Big June Haig who had been to Whitehill School. He went downstairs and stood beside her on the platform. She said, 'Oh, there you are.'
'I usually get off farther up the hill,' said Thaw, as if explaining something.
'Your house faces the Chapel?'
The tram halted and they got off.
'No, it's in the street which runs into the road just opposite the Chapel.'
He stood still, describing this geography with his hands. She gripped his lapel and drew him onto the pavement out of the path of a lorry, saying, 'I don't want to be held as a witness to a road accident.'
'Where are you working just now?'
'Brown's. I'm a waitress in the dining room.'
'Oh I go there sometimes, but downstairs to the smokeroom.' Thaw described his eating habits in detail and she seemed to listen intently. He showed her the photograph in the paper and she was less impressed than he expected. There were gaps in the conversation in which he expected her to say cheerio, but she stayed quiet until he thought of something new to say. He said, 'I'll walk you to your auntie's house,' and they set off side by side. June moved with chin held up and vivid mouth set haughtily as if disdaining herds of admirers, and Thaw's heart thumped hard against his ribs. They turned some corners and stopped at a close. June explained that she visited her aunt twice a week; the aunt was an old lady who had recently had an operation. Thaw made an unsubtle reference to her unselfishness. There was another silence. He said desperately, 'Look, could I meet you sometime?'
'Oh sure.'

'Where do you live nowadays?'

'Langside, near the monument.'

'Hm ... Where will we meet?'

After a pause she suggested Paisley's corner near Jamaica Street Bridge.

'Good!' said Thaw firmly, then added, 'But we haven't fixed the night or the hour have we?'

June said, 'No. We haven't.'

After some silence she suggested Thursday night at seven o'clock.

'Good!' said Thaw firmly again. 'I'll see you then.'

'Yes.'

'Well ... cheerio.'

'Cheerio, Duncan.'

That night Thaw kept stopping work to walk up and down the living room, chuckling and singing. Mr. Thaw said, 'What's got into ye? Did a lassie look at ye sideways?'

'My painting aroused a certain interest.'

Next morning Thaw told McAlpin about June as they sat in the school library. McAlpin studied the page of a glossy magazine, then said, 'Does she smell of the bakery, the brewery, or the brothel?'

Thaw felt shocked and cheapened and cursed himself for speaking. McAlpin glanced at him and said, 'All women have an odour, you know. The deodorant adverts pretend it's a bad thing, which is all balls. If the girl is clean it's a very attractive thing. Judy has an odour.'

'Good.'

'What you need, Duncan, is a friendly, experienced older woman, not a silly wee girl.'

'But I don't like being condescended to.'

'I admit she'd have to handle you cleverly. I'm sure there are many women in continental brothels who could do it. Of course there are no brothels deserving the name in Scotland. This is such a bloody *poor* country.'

Thaw said, 'Your mind is full of brothels this morning.'

'Yes.... What do you think will happen to you when you leave art school?'

'I don't know. But I can't teach children and I won't go to London.'

McAlpin said, 'I don't want to teach but I probably will. I would like to travel and have freedom before I settled down, visit Paris, Vienna, Florence. There are a lot of quiet little cities in Italy with frescoes by minor masters in the churches and their own wine served under awnings in the squares outside. I'd like to wander around exploring these with a girl, not necessarily a girl I'd marry. Think! After sunset the air is as warm as a fine summer afternoon here ... but I can't leave my mother for long. At least when I do leave her it will be to marry Judy, which – as far as freedom is concerned – will be leaving the frying pan for the fire. Meanwhile I'm getting older.'

'Blethers.'

'Does time never worry you?'

'No. Only feelings worry me, and time isn't a feeling.'

'I feel it.'

After a moment McAlpin said on a baffled note, 'I suspect that if I started living in a slum, and consorting with a prostitute, and wore nothing but a leopard skin, Judy and my mother would visit me four days a week with baskets of food.'

'I envy you.'

'Don't.'

That afternoon in the lecture theatre Thaw's body came to an uneasy compromise with the wooden bench and he dozed. Later he heard the lecturer say '... something of a thug. In fact he broke Michelangelo's nose once, in a brawl, when they were young. It is consoling to remember that he died, most unhappily, a raving lunatic in a Spanish prison, ha-ha. However, that will do for today.'

The lights went on and people crowded to the exits. Thaw noticed McAlpin and Judy ahead of him; they ran hand in hand across the street to the annexe and he followed slowly. They were not in the refectory. He sat down at a table near Drummond and Macbeth. Drummond was saying, 'I can't understand why I've been asked. I hardly know Kenneth.'

'When is it?' said Macbeth.

'Tomorrow night. We go to his house for a meal and a booze-up, then to a fancy-dress party at a hotel.'

'How old is he?' said Macbeth.

'Twenty-one.'

A sad kind of shock flowed through Thaw like water. He sat still, not saying much, then went to the counter and brought food back to the table. Drummond left and Macbeth sat in a way which told Thaw he was depressed at not being asked to the party. Macbeth said, 'You're quiet tonight, Duncan.'

'I'm sorry. I was thinking.'

'I suppose you've been asked to Kenneth's party tomorrow?'

'No.'

Macbeth became cheerful. 'No? That's queer. You and Kenneth are always about together. I thought you were friends.'

'I thought that.'

He walked a lot around the streets that evening and let himself into the house after midnight.

'Is that you, Duncan?' said his father from the bed settee in the living room.

'I think so.'

'Is anything wrong?'

Thaw explained what had happened. He said, 'I can't get used to this. An acquaintance becomes a friend in a gradual, genial way. The reverse is . . . shocking.'

'What's that noise?'

'I'm fiddling with ornaments on the lobby table. In God's name how can I face him tomorrow? What can I say?'

'Don't say much, Duncan. Quietly and politely wish him many happy returns of the day.'

'That's a good idea, Dad. Goodnight.'

'And go straight to sleep. No writing.'

He went to bed, grew breathless, took two grains of ephedrine, slept for an hour and woke feeling excited. He opened his notebook and wrote, *The future demands our participation. To participate willingly is freedom, unwillingly is slavery.*

He scored this out and wrote:

The universe compels cooperation. To cooperate consciously is freedom, unconsciously is. . . .

Nature always has our assistance. To assist eagerly is freedom, resistingly is. . . .

God needs our help. Giving it joyfully is freedom, resentfully is. . . .

We have God's help. To know this is freedom, not to notice is. . . .

He snarled and threw the notebook at the ceiling where it rebounded onto the top of the wardrobe, dislodging an avalanche of books and papers. He lay feeling happy about the changes in life, then masturbated and fell asleep. His happiness had gone when he awoke.

McAlpin was not at school that day. At tea break Judy, Molly Tierney and Rushford discussed the costumes they would wear at the fancy-dress dance. Thaw was unsure how to behave. He drew on the tabletop and grinned with the left side of his mouth.

'You should see my costume!' said Molly gleefully. 'It's terrible. All pink and nineteen-twentyish, with a cigarette holder three feet long. Here, give me a pencil.'

She seized the pencil from Thaw's fingers and drew the costume on the tabletop. That evening he went into town to meet June and stood in an entry to a clothes shop looking at suave dummies in evening dress and sportswear. Grey dusk became black night. The entrance was a common place for appointments, and he often had the company of people waiting for boy or girlfriends. None waited longer than fifteen minutes. When it was not possible to pretend June would come he walked home feeling horribly insulted.

McAlpin entered the classroom briskly next day with a new book in one hand. He hooked his neatly rolled umbrella on a radiator, laid his coat and bag on a pedestal and came briskly to Thaw. He said, 'Listen to this!' and read out the first paragraph of *Oblomov*.

Thaw heard him with embarrassment then said, 'Very good' and went into a corner to sharpen a pencil. That morning he and McAlpin worked apart from each other. At lunchtime Thaw went to the main building and obtained an interview with the registrar. In a careful voice he said he thought the school's anatomy course inadequate, that he was going to ask permission to sketch in the dissection room of the university, that he would be grateful for a letter from the registrar saying that such permission would be useful to his art. The registrar swung reflectively from side to side in his swivel chair. He said, 'Well, I'm not sure, Thaw. Morbid anatomy certainly was in our curriculum till shortly after the fourteen-eighteen war. I was trained in it myself. I don't think I benefited from it, but of course I was not so dedicated an artist as you. But would such training do you good psychologically? I honestly think it would do harm.'

'I am not—' Thaw said, then cleared his throat and knelt before the electric fire near Mr. Peel's desk. He stared into the red-hot coal and plucked fibres out of the coconut matting.

'I am not a complete person. A good painter one day, mibby, but always an inadequate man. So my work is important to me. If that work is to develop I must see how people are made.'

'Your "Last Supper" showed a detailed grasp of anatomy, gained, I assume, by the usual methods?'

'Yah. That detail was bluff. I padded out the definite things I knew with imagination and pictures in books. But now my imagination needs more detailed knowledge to work on.'

'I am not convinced that morbid anatomy will be good for you, Thaw, but I suppose you must convince yourself of that. I'm remotely acquainted with the head of the university medical faculty. I'll get in touch with him.'

'Thank you, sir,' said Thaw, standing up. 'Some sketching in the vivisection room is really necessary at this stage.'

'Dissection room.'

'Pardon?'

'You said vivisection room.'

'Did I? I'm sorry,' said Thaw, confused.

He ran back to the classroom to work off his exhilaration. McAlpin stood at an easel near the door. Thaw stopped and muttered to him, 'Peel's getting me permission to sketch in the university dissection room.'

'Good! Good!'

'I've not felt so happy since I invented the bactro-chlorine bomb.'

McAlpin bent over and emitted muffled bellowing laughter. Thaw went to his seat thinking what a waste of time unfriendliness was. Later on their way to the refectory he said to McAlpin,

'Why didn't you ask me to your party?'

'We had only a few tickets for the fancy-dress ball and had to give them to people who had asked Judy and me to their parties. I wanted to invite you but – er, it just wasn't possible. I thought you wouldn't mind because you were taking out that girl you picked up. How did you get on with her?'

Jeff Torrington

The Fade

McQuirr, scarcely half-awake, trudged to the clocking-on point. Once there, a yawn froze in his mouth. The Tardis had vanished! The chunky oak and brass machine had been ousted by a newcomer, a computerised whippet with a nasty slit of a mouth and luminous red numerals dancing like madness on its brow.

'Stick it in there,' Fawcett, the seats section greyback, ordered.

McQuirr stared at him.

'Your card.' Fawcett was pointing to the machine's slot.

McQuirr searched the rackful of unfamiliar cards. The greyback frowned. 'Forgotten our number, have we?'

'Two thousand and one!'

'You were issued with a new one – remember?'

McQuirr shook his head.

'In your pay-packet, last week.'

Fawcett's forefinger riffled down the shiny tabs. An irate queue of ops had formed behind McQuirr.

'Does it dish out fivers?' one of them asked.

'Be "late-warnings" unless that dozy bastard gets a jildy on,' shouted another.

The greyback located McQuirr's card. He handed it to'm. 'Get on with it!'

McQuirr fumbled the operation and the machine began immediately to bristle with warning lights before finally playing its 'VOID!' card.

Fawcett groaned. 'You've got it arse-for-elb ... That's better!'

The new time-machine gave an electronic burp and the card popped up.

Tommy Farr, the section shoppy, stopped McQuirr as he trudged towards the seats-hoist. 'Don't forget, there'll be an IE in your section today, John,' Farr warned. 'So, no buckshee breaks, no getting ahead of the game. You know the score. Anyway, Glover'll keep you right.'

'These clock numbers,' McQuirr said.

'What about'm?'

'Look at it,' he grumbled, waving a scrap of paper. (Fawcett'd made

McQuirr take note of his new number.) 'Like a machine-part number. How'd the union let'm away with it? Shower of diddies. Organisers? They couldn't organise a piss-up'n a brothel.'

'Brewery, John.'

'What?'

'It's a piss-up'n – never mind. Just remember, soon as you drop that bit of plastic your name lights up'n five places. Don't be on the "late" print-out, that's all.'

The industrial engineer, Austin Seymour, had settled himself near a stack of seat-frames. Equipped with stopwatch, a selection of coloured pens, clipboard, and time-sheets, he beadily observed the operations taking place in the seats-build area. McQuirr glowered at'm. A locust, that's what he was, sitting there on a twig munching minutes.

'Wish I'd stuck in at borstal,' McQuirr said.

'So's you could be a wank wi' a watch, eh?'

'As long as my bloody arm.'

'Eh?'

'New clock number.'

Glover shook his head. 'You still bitching about that–?'

'Diabolical, so it is.'

'Slow down a bit,' Glover cautioned, 'that bugger's getting excited.'

McQuirr stacked polythene-wrapped seats alongside others on the floor. He hauled a Sultan rear seat from the unwrapped pile.

'Years, I had that number. Years. That's how I got my nickname.'

'Nickname?'

'Sputnik.'

'What-nik?'

McQuirr cut open a bag and tipped a slithering mass of polythene covers onto the bench. 'After yon Arthur C. Clarke movie: "2001" – remember?'

Glover checked off a sequence number on the telex print-out sheet. 'Never heard anybody call you "Sputnik" before.'

'It sort of faded away.' McQuirr took an armful of covers and folded them neatly over the stretched rope. 'It was when I worked on the wet-deck. The lads got to hear my clock number, and – bingo, I'd a nickname!'

'They called you Bingo, did they?'

'No, I told you – "Sputnik".'

'Bingo suits you better,' said the grinning Glover. 'Seeing's you haven't got a full house upstairs.'

'Bugger off!' McQuirr grunted.

During the break McQuirr waylaid 'Gentleman' Jim Corbett as he was passing the snack area. With his neatly-clipped moustache and his impeccably-groomed grey hair he looked like a debonair con man.

'Thought you'd be redundant,' McQuirr said.

Corbett removed his blue-tinted glasses. (For some reason he couldn't speak with them on.) 'Never been busier,' he said. 'Haven't a minute.'

A timekeeper without a minute!

Corbett began to edge around McQuirr. 'Well, must press on.'

'Listen, Jim, do's a favour.'

Alarm spread in Corbett's grey eyes. When a punter wanted a favour it usually involved time or money. The glasses, already halfway to his nose, paused. 'A favour?'

McQuirr nodded, then, dropping his gaze, mumbled something.

'What's that?' Corbett bent closer to catch the words.

McQuirr cleared his throat. 'I was, well, you know, kinda wondering who'd got two thousand and one . . .'

'Two thousand and one what?'

'It's my old clock number. I was just curious who had it.'

'Why?'

'Daft, I know, but—' McQuirr drew Corbett to one side as a forky laden with seat-springs honked past.

'Nobody has it,' Corbett told'm. 'It's gone to that Big Time-Office in the Sky.'

'You sure about that?'

Corbett nodded. 'New system: Plant's been zoned off so that each zone has a max of 300 ops.' He began to explain the ramifications of the introduced system but McQuirr had stopped listening. The timekeeper's glasses slipped over his eyes, then he was off. McQuirr watched him disappearing into the murk of Zombie-land, where a welding operation was lobbing lucid blue sparks into the air.

Like a probe, Seymour's penpoint sank into each squandered minute, extracted its essence, then wrote its epitaph in brisk fashion on the time-sheets. The industrial engineer seldom smiled, nor did he allow his scrutiny to wander far from its given task – to locate parasitic growths in the human energy fields: the wasted moment; the extra step; the blight of bad coordination; every input of misused muscle power; anything at all which checked or baulked the surging gallop of the Centaur Car Company.

McQuirr sheathed seats, stacked them, marked them off on the sequence sheet, barrowed them across to the hoist. The IE, he suspected, was paying particular attention to him; he could feel his gaze following his every movement as he juggled the three essential elements of his exercise – time, motion, and pause.

Seymour seemed to be relishing the complexity of the equation he was so precisely developing so that the consequences of McQuirr's removal could be gauged. McQuirr sped another surly glance towards the IE. There was no doubting what the twat in the tweed sports jacket was there for – quite simply it was to figure the means of his elimination. This wasn't the first time the Company'd tried to get shot of him. There'd been other 'hangman's rehearsals', as McQuirr called them – a description which brought to mind a movie he'd once seen in which the public hangman had peered through the Judas of the condemned man's cell to determine the prisoner's 'dropistics' – a term the urbane executioner had used, accompanied by a gallows grin. Although less covert about it, the IE was similarly assessing McQuirr.

A trapdoor, its bolts well oiled with use, dropped open in McQuirr's mind, plunging him once more into the void of 'that bitch of a morning' as he'd tagged it, the one when he'd returned home to find a letter awaiting him. It'd been sent to'm by the Company.

In a few terse lines it thanked him for his job application but regretted its inability at this time to grant him employment at Centaur ... For McQuirr, who'd been working at the plant for over a decade, this was mind-bending news. His wife had chosen to see the comical side of the screw-up. 'My, my,' she'd laughed, 'you must be really important down there – ten years, and they don't even know you're around!' McQuirr had found nothing laughworthy in the event. In fact, he'd taken it to be not only an insult but also a warning. Just like the movie's public executioner going through the grisly preliminaries of his profession, using a sandbag as a substitute for the real thing, so the Centaur (the farcical letter'd had been but one of its ploys) measured McQuirr for the drop.

He'd never forget the hour he'd endured trawling the wet streets in search of an unvandalised phonebox. Even yet he remembered the odd sensation he'd had of being adrift from his body, of having to break into a run to catch up with it, for the further he'd got separated from it, the more he'd seemed to vaporise, to become nothing but a trick of light. People – how enviably solid they'd looked! – had seemed to pass through the evaporating cloud-man he'd become. Panic, like pronged lightning, had speared him to the core as his body had given its harried phantom the slip at a pedestrian crossing. Luckily he'd seen his flesh'n bone twin go into a laundrette, where he'd managed to pounce on the wayward body and inveigle himself back into it. A bizarre experience it'd been, one he'd divulged to no one, not even his wife. It was the stuff madness was made from. There was a public phone in the laundrette. While he'd watched a grey shirt having soapy convulsions behind a machine's glass porthole, his identity had been restored. An administrative cock-up, that's all it'd been. He'd accepted the apology but, nevertheless, the obsession had continued to haunt him that the Centaur Car Company was still intent on striking him from its payroll.

Glover nudged McQuirr. 'C'mon for chrissake, John – you're miles away!'

Snapped from his reverie, McQuirr realised that he'd been staring into space, his hands idle. For how long he'd been in this trance he wasn't sure. But Seymour would know; that voracious locust feasted on every unproductive moment, sucked it dry.

McQuirr's hands writhed in the slippery polythene, sought to grapple with its slick nothingness. He drew envelope after transparent envelope over velour-trimmed seats, and the more he dealt with, piling them up to his left, the more seats streamed of the carousel. His movements were jerky, uncoordinated. Quite often the polythene wrapper split and he'd to rip it off, junk it. From the corner of his eye he caught Glover's puzzled-looking glances. He was probably trying to work out whether he was putting on an act for the IE or was genuinely uptight about something. Was he ever anything else but uptight these days? The other night, for instance, while watching TV, the image of a fissuring iceberg had sent him panicking from his armchair. His alarmed wife reckoned it was high time he visited a head-doctor.

But the Centaur Car Company didn't employ an industrial psychologist. When faced with the mental casualties that came off-track with their cars, the Company tended to rely upon the 'it-never-happened' strategy. So, should a disturbed operator sit down one day by the edge of the flowing track and give way to an unrestrainable fit of sobbing, or if a cackling greyback in the canteen took the notion to fill his shoes with custard, the remedy was to deny it'd ever occurred. With a blanket of secrecy thrown over him, the unfortunate 'breakdown' would be taken to the edge of some administrative ravine and hurled over. Now and again the wan phantom of a victim might be seen wandering in its old working area but inevitably it would fade away. McQuirr, Glover, and a chaser called Troy usually did the crossword during the lunchbreak. But not today, it seemed. Rising suddenly to his feet, as if reacting to the clue

Troy'd just read out – 'Has this Wellsian character been overdoing the vanishing cream? (3,9,3)' – McQuirr jettisoned the remaining tea from his mug, making a black star on the concrete floor.

'Where're you off to?' asked Glover.

'Breath of air.'

'It's pissing out there, man!'

McQuirr shrugged his shoulders. As he walked away, he overheard Glover say: 'If you ask me – the bugger's cracking up!'

As if the rain wasn't flooding the yard fast enough, the wind was cuffing water over the storage tank's rim. McQuirr stood near the half-shut doors of the loading bay. He watched the water's white leaping, saw it cascading down the sides of the tank. It was in that black funnel that Alf Sheridan had done away with himself. Yeah, he'd climbed the ladder and, dressed in chains, had taken the freedom plunge. He hadn't so much as scribbled a line to explain his bizarre exit. It was generally accepted though that the sudden death of his wife had triggered his actions. Grief was the planet's deadliest and most-to-be-feared poison: compared to its slow, agonising effects the mamba with its sudden black lightning was a mercy-killer.

McQuirr went into the body'n white section and paused between lines of raw, unpainted Sultan saloons, the metal blemishes of which had been blue-circled for the discers. A roof leak tapped out a tattoo on an empty paint drum. From the snack areas came the low rumble of men's voices and the occasional yelps of triumph from card winners. Some of these ops turned in their seats to rake McQuirr with suspicious stares. Conscious of their scrutiny, he felt a bit foolish as he pawed his way down a rackful of glossy new time-cards. It seemed that Corbett hadn't been having him on, after all: there was no card to be found with a higher numerical value than 300.

'You there! Where's your permit?'

The question was volleyed from behind a group of Sultan Estate shells. Stricken motionless by it, McQuirr suddenly relaxed. 'Jeez, Biggles, you scared me shitless there!'

Biggles Blane, the Sequencer, emerged from the shells. He approached McQuirr with fists raised and did a bit of mock-sparring. 'How goes it, Sputnik, me old son?' He dropped his hands. 'What're you arsing around here for?' He mimed a casting motion with an invisible fishing rod. 'You still drowning worms?'

'Had to get shot of my gear,' McQuirr told'm. 'Rheumatics.'

Biggles' grin widened. 'Don't come the fanny. You've already used that one to work your ticket from the wet-deck.' They walked on together. 'You should see the rod I'm packing now,' Biggles said. 'A right cracker. Telling you, take out a pike like it was a sardine.' This was the prelude to a fishy tale that kept Biggles' mouth busy until they'd reached the main door of the stores area. They looked out at the rain. Biggles nodded in the direction of the nearby Broadmoor.

'Fancy a squint at your redundancy?'

McQuirr frowned. 'Redundancy?'

'Yeah. Them Daleks. Bastards'll weld anything that moves. C'mon, let's have a shufty.'

Battered by the rain, they skirted around puddles and dripping pallet stacks and went into Broadmoor. A group of ops stood in the area where the unimates had been installed. In all there were twenty-two of these robot welders, eleven to each side of the track. McQuirr eyed one. It looked more like a praying mantis than a Dalek, standing there with beaky head poised, awaiting the power that would have it pecking out welds at a rate no human could hope to match. An engineer who'd apparently elected himself as tour-guide was rapping out impressive stats: 'They can handle over one hundred car-shells an hour.' He reached to finger the skeletal neck of the unimate nearest to'm. 'For that level of output you'd require over two hundred operatives...'

A grey-haired op who stood near McQuirr said, 'You should see'm when they get going: like hens in a byre midden!'

McQuirr and Biggles walked around the machines, squinting at them from different angles. 'Soon won't need us, eh?' said Biggles. He shrugged. 'I guess we're for the broth pot.'

Maybe it was this remark or perhaps the sight of those brutish muzzles poised, waiting, that'd sent the pellets of dread skittering down the slope of McQuirr's mind. There was no restraining them as they gathered velocity, prising loose old fears as well as an avalanche of new anxieties.

'Give you the creeps, eh?' Biggles went on, completely unaware that he was speaking to a phantom which despite desperate resistance was being slowly ejected from its body. 'A lick of oil'nd a tap'n the arse with a spanner, that's all they need. Never strike, never shit, and never get hangovers.'

Back'n the body'n white, they passed swiftly amongst the crates and pallets of metal stampings, and skirted puddles in which dull rainbows glimmered. McQuirr's runaway body was now well clear of its former occupant. It capered around, waving its arms and looking slyly about itself; clearly, it was plotting mischief. Biggles Blane, still oblivious of the bewildered spook at his elbow, dropped out when a punter from the plant's angling club stopped him for a bit crack.

Meanwhile, McQuirr's body had brought a painter's ladder crashing to the concrete floor before it began to hurl door hinges up at the complaining tradesman, who quickly ducked for cover amongst the roof girders. McQuirr's body now sent a forky driver tumbling from his seat and commandeered the vehicle itself. With its rightful driver shouting in pursuit it charged the rubber doors that led to the paintshop, where it was afforded not only the props to make mischief on an unprecedented scale but also to make it in glorious colour!

McQuirr, who'd given up all hope of reconnection with his body, wandered around the plant. He felt himself fading, becoming progressively drained of energy, so much so that soon he was looking for a corner in which to hide himself. But everywhere he turned he found a clone of Austin Seymour, complete with stopwatch, pens, clipboard, and time-sheets, waiting for him. Such obscenities plagued the place, breeding, hatching out. Those things in Broadmoor with their fiery beaks and their staunchless energies would multiply too. Able to outweld two hundred men, from them would come a flux of inhuman power that, like a bore tide, would surge up the metal rivers that ran throughout the plant, and all the hourly-paid minnows who swam in those streams would be swept away.

Officially, the incident in which McQuirr was involved that afternoon never happened. The personnel records might show, 'Dismissed due to industrial misconduct' or, more accurately, 'Discharged for medical reasons', but the details of what actually 'never happened' remain oral. Since Glover was McQuirr's working partner, his version of what really took place was judged to be nearest the mark:

'Well, as I said, he'd been jumpy all morning. It was obvious after chuck time that he'd been out'n the rain. I mean any daft bugger who'd go out in the piss when he didn't have to, well, he's got t'be one short of the full deck – right? So, he starts going on about them auto-welders they've stuck'n Broadmoor, only he calls 'em Daleks. They were going to take over, that's all he kept saying. Nothing the unions could do 'bout stopping 'em – that kinda shit. To listen to'm you would've thought they was out t'have his job in particular.

'Any roads, he clams up for a bit. Done that a lot, McQuirr. One minute it's gab-gab, the next it's the "broodies". Y'know, go into trances, stare into space. Gave me the creeps it did. Well, it happened this way: Seymour, who's doing the watch number on us, slopes off for a riddlemeree or something. Leaves his clipboard'n time-sheets on a crate, don't he? And that's when it happened. It was like something went twang inside McQuirr's noggin. Next I knows, don't he go rushing across to where Seymour's sheets are, lifts the whole batch and, before you could blink, he's made confetti of it! But he's not finished. He grabs a can from the glue table and scampers with it towards the new time-puncher. But the loopy bugger'd gone'nd lumbered himself with a duff can that should've been binned on account of its glue having hardened off. He could've stood there till kingdom come waiting for a pour.

'Clueless, as well as glueless now, he takes to bashing the time-puncher with the can. Brained the bloody thing. Put its lights out. By then, of course, the Bull comes charging from his office and sticks an arm-lock on McQuirr, What's that? Took a swing at the Bull? No way. That's crap! I'll tell you what the poor sap did – began to blub, that's what. Pathetic.

'They took'm into the office but couldn't get tuppence-worth of sense out of'm. All the time he keeps parroting his clock number, his old one, that is – 2001. Eh? Come back here? No chance! By the time he gets out of the booby-hatch he'll be on two wheels and zombie's zube-zubes. Come again? Miss'm? I suppose so. He could be a bit of diddy at times but he was quite good at crosswords...'

William McIlvanney

At the Bar

The pub was quiet. When the big man with the ill-fitting suit came in, the barman noticed him more than he normally would have done. The suit was slightly out of fashion yet looked quite new and it was too big for him. He could have come back to it after a long illness. Yet it wasn't that either. Whatever had happened to him had tightened him but not diminished him. The charcoal grey cloth sat on him loosely but that looked like the suit's problem. You wouldn't have fancied whoever the suit might fit to come against the man who wore it.

He came up to the bar and seemed uncertain about what to order. He looked along the gantry with a bemused innocence, like a small boy in a sweet-shop.

'Sir?' the barman said.

The big man sighed and shook his head and took his time. His face looked as if it had just come off a whetstone. The cheek-bones were sharp, the mouth was taut. The eyes were preoccupied with their own thoughts. His pallor suggested a plant kept out of the light. Prison, the barman thought.

'Uh-huh,' the big man said. 'Fine day. I'll have.' It seemed a momentous choice. 'A pint of heavy.'

He watched the barman pull it. Paying, he took a small wad of singles from his pocket and fingered them deliberately. He studied his change carefully. Then he retreated inside himself.

Making sure the patch of bar in front of him was clean, he spread his *Daily Record* on it and started to read, the sports pages first. His beer seemed to be for moistening his lips.

Before turning back to the television, the barman checked the pub in his quick but careful way. The afternoon was boringly in place. Old Dave and Sal were over to his left, beside the Space Invader. As usual, they were staring past each other. Dave was nursing half-an-inch of beer and Sal had only the lemon left from her gin and tonic, her thin lips working against each other endlessly, crocheting silence. That should be them till they went home for their tea. At the other end of the bar, Barney, the retired schoolteacher, was doing *The Times* crossword. Did he ever finish it? In the light from the window his half-pint looked as stale as cold tea.

The only other person in the pub was someone the barman didn't like. He had started to come in lately. Denim-dressed, he looked nasty-hard, a broad pitted face framed in long black hair. He was a fidgety drinker, one of those who keep looking over both shoulders as if they know somebody must be trying to take a liberty and they're determined to catch him at it. Just now, standing at the bar, he kept glancing along at the big man and seemed annoyed to get no reaction. His eyes were a demonstration looking for a place to happen. He took his pint like a penance.

The television was showing some kind of afternoon chat-show, two men talking who made the pub seem interesting. Each question sounded boring until you heard the answer and that made you want another question very quick. The barman was relieved to see Old Dave come towards the bar as if he was walking across America. It would be good if he made it before he died.

'Yes, Dave,' the barman said to encourage his progress. 'Another drink? What is this? Your anniversary?'

The barman noticed the big man had the paper open at page three. He knew what the man was seeing, having studied her this morning, a dark-haired girl called Minette with breasts like two separate states. But the big man wasn't looking at her so much as he was reading her, like a long novel. Then he flicked over to the front page, glanced, sipped his beer till it was an inch down the glass and went to the lavatory.

'Same again,' Dave said, having arrived. 'Tae hell wi' it. Ye're only young once.'

The barman laughed and turned his back on him. He had to cut more lemon. He had to find one of the lemons the pub had started getting in specially for Sal. After brief puzzlement, he did. He cut it carefully. He filled out gin, found ice, added the lemon. He turned back, put the drink on the counter, pulled a pint. As he laid the pint beside the gin and opened the tonic, pouring it, he noticed something in among the activity that bothered him. He suddenly realised what it was. The big man's pint-dish held nothing but traces of froth.

The barman was about to speak to the hard-faced man in denim when the big man walked back from the lavatory to the bar. His arrival froze the barman. The big man made to touch his paper, paused. He looked at his empty pint.

'Excuse me,' he said to the barman. 'Ah had a pint there.'

The moment crackled like an electrical storm. Even Old Dave got the message. His purse hung in his hand. He stared at the counter. The barman was wincing.

'That's right,' the man in denim said. 'Ye had a pint. But Ah drank it.'

The silence prolonged itself like an empty street with a man at either end of it. The barman knew that nobody else could interfere.

'Sorry?' the big man said.

'Ye had a pint, right enough. But Ah felt like it. So Ah drank it. That's the dinky-dory.'

So that was the story. The big man stared and lowered his eyes, looked up and smiled. It wasn't convincing. Nonchalant surrender never is. But he was doing his best to make it look as if it was.

'Oh, look,' he said. 'What does it matter? Ah can afford another one. Forget it.'

The barman was grateful but contemptuous. He didn't want trouble but he wouldn't have liked to go to sleep in the big man's head. And when the big man spoke again, he could hardly believe it.

'Look. If you need a drink, let me buy you another one. Come on. Give the man a pint of heavy.'

The barman felt as if he was pouring out the big man's blood but he did it. It was his job to keep the peace. The man in denim lifted the pint, winked at the barman.

'Cheers,' he said to the big man, smiling at him. 'Your good health. You obviously value it.'

He hadn't managed his first mouthful before the side of the big man's clenched right hand had hit the base of the glass like a demolition-ball. There was a splintered scream among the shards of exploding glass and the volleying beer.

Not unused to fast violence, the barman was stunned. The big man picked up his paper. He laid the price of a pint on the counter and nodded to the barman.

'If he's lookin' for me,' he said, 'the name's Rafferty. Cheerio. Nice shop you run.'

He went out. Lifting a dish-towel, the barman hurried round the counter and gave it to the man in denim. While he held his face together with it and the cloth saturated instantly with blood and he kept moaning, the barman found his first coherent reaction to the situation.

'You're barred,' he said.

Allan Massie

In the Bare Lands

'No, you most certainly can't see him.'

Giles was accustomed to flat refusals. They didn't faze him.

'I don't want to intrude,' he said. 'I did write, you know, and I've come a long way.'

It was cold on the steps of the seedy-looking house which had certainly seen better days.

The woman – you could imagine from her cheek-bones she had once been beautiful – didn't seem impressed.

'You didn't get a reply, did you?'

Giles nodded.

'I know he's very old,' he said. 'I would have telephoned but you're not in the book.'

'Are you surprised?' she said.

'I'm a perfectly respectable person. I'm not a journalist if that's what you're afraid of.'

'I don't care who you are. Can't you see that?'

'I'm afraid it's beginning to rain.'

The wind which had been blowing for the last two days was now swirling heavy gouts of rain with it. The house – why had it been built facing north – lay or, rather, crouched directly in its path. Further up the mountain it might be snowing.

'Couldn't you just let me in to explain myself. It reminds me of trying to sell encyclopaedias, standing here.'

He turned up the collar of his Donegal tweed coat.

'That couldn't do any harm, could it, Miss Urquhart? You are Miss Urquhart, aren't you, his daughter, I mean?'

When she didn't reply, he turned for a moment and looked back down the valley. There were meadows a couple of hundred feet below and a sort of byre or bothy standing alone. It was a limestone country.

'I've got very respectable credentials,' he said, 'even a letter of introduction. Mr Alkins said he would write too.'

'Henry Alkins?'

'Yes, of course.'

It was the first sign that she might relent and he followed it up, though he knew well that what would really count was his docile dejection – his air of a spaniel that isn't being taken for a promised walk.

'I know there's been a postal strike,' he said, 'perhaps both our letters got lost that way.'

'I don't know what you want,' she said. 'You can't have sold encyclopaedias.'

'Not very successfully, I'm afraid.'

There was no point in telling her that he'd never come near to needing to do anything like that; friends' accounts had only established it in his mind as the most pathetic of imaginable holiday jobs.

'Well,' she said, 'he's out just now.'

'In this weather?'

'It's the lambing season.'

She pointed to the byre below.

'You can come in and talk to me if you like. I'll give you some tea. It's English.'

They entered a narrow hall. There was a heavy oak chest and the walls were painted white. The paint had been done a long time ago.

Miss Urquhart said,

'We'll go in here. There are no comfortable rooms in this house. I sometimes think that's why my father chose it.'

'The bare lands the surgeon's scalpel,' said Giles.

'Oh,' she looked at him with surprise, 'you do know a little then. I promised you tea. Or would you rather have kirsch? It's local.'

'I'd love both. I'm afraid that's very greedy.'

Giles gave her his little boy smile – he had been brought up by a maiden aunt while his parents were on a tea-plantation in Assam.

'There is whisky,' she said, 'but that's his.'

She went out through a door at the back of the small room to make the tea. Giles stood by the fire and looked around. It was like a Victorian art photograph – 'Cottage in the Hebrides', perhaps. There should be an old woman with a shawl round her head sitting at her spinning-wheel by the fire. The only thing that spoiled the effect was the book-case which ran along the wall beside the door they had come in by. Giles examined it. There were two shelves of Urquhart's books – poetry, history (damned tendentious history he could imagine), political philosophy, social studies, six volumes of autobiography – Christ, he hadn't realised he'd written so much, and most of it crap. He pulled one out, not bothering to choose.

'The warder had knowledge of which my fellow-prisoners were ignorant. He knew he was a prisoner more closely confined than they.'

What bloody arrogant nonsense. He put the book back.

He had a feeling, rare to him, of being out of place. If Judkins thought
up any more of these bright assignments he could bloody well follow
them up himself.

He sat down – the chair had a straight back and the seat was too short
– and pulled out Simon Lumsden's letter. It was brief and badly typed, the
signature barely legible. He supposed it might do, though he, remembering Lumsden's animosity, could read reluctance between the lines.

'Simon Lumsden's the man to go to,' Judkins had said.

'Isn't he dead?' – his memory of Lumsden was very vague – his name
surely hadn't appeared in the papers for at least a decade.

'No, he lives in Gravesend, but he isn't dead.'

It was the nearest approach to a joke Judkins could assemble from his
card-index mind.

'And what if he won't see me?'

The whole project was unattractive – he would far rather stay in
Venice instead of having to drive into the mountains above Bolzano. It
was typical of Judkins to come up with something like this – 'we've got
the unit there, kill two birds with one stone,' he could just hear him say
it, even though Judkins was more the type of sentimental moron who
would put out a bird table in his suburban garden.

'Lumsden'll see you,' he had snickered. 'All you need do is go along
with a bottle of brandy in one hand and a bottle of Scotch in the other.'

'But I thought they quarrelled. Will Lumsden's letter do any good?'

'You can get off your arse and try.'

Miss Urquhart came back into the room and set a tray down. She
poured two cups of very dark tea.

'Milk and sugar?'

'Both, please.'

She handed him the cup and a small glass of kirsch and passed a plate
with caraway-seed cake on it.

'It's a little stale, I'm afraid. He's finished with politics. You know that?
That's why we live out here. He doesn't even like to talk about them. I
don't know when he last wrote to the newspapers.'

'Well, he's eighty-five, isn't he?'

'The last visitor we had, sometime back in the autumn, didn't realise
that. He was still looking for a lead from him. He was a boy from Glasgow
University. I'm Edinburgh myself.'

'I'd better explain why I've come.'

'There's no point in that. I only asked you in because it's pleasant to talk English now and then.'

She must have seen surprise on Giles's face.

'He'll only talk Gaelic to me. That shows what he feels.'

'I didn't realise...'

'He only learned it in prison, you know. In the second war, not the first.'

'I thought,' Giles had done his homework, 'he belonged to the Lallans school at one time.'

'That was before the working-man let him down.'

'You sound bitter.'

'Bitter? You're quite a wit, aren't you?'

Giles began to feel his resentment deepen.

'I've a letter from Simon Lumsden,' he said, handing it over.

'Poor Simon,' she replied. She only just glanced at the letter and laid it aside. 'How is he?'

It wasn't really a question to be answered.

'We haven't seen him for years. Simon had no ideas, you know. He just wanted a cause to attach himself to. Don't look at me like that, please. What do you imagine I think about when I'm sitting here? What have I to think about? The Workers' Republic of Scotland or the Union of Celtic Commonwealths?'

'I haven't said anything. I thought you said he was finished with politics' – if you call that sort of nonsense politics, he nearly added.

'Precisely.'

'Look,' said Giles, 'I didn't want to come here.'

'I used to think I was in love with Simon,' she said. 'I wanted to be. He did too. Oh well, do you know my fate? I chose the wrong man to save.'

She started to try to laugh and then to light a cigarette and then to cry – she stopped frozen between the attitudes.

Giles said,

'It's a television programme. My boss thought of calling it "A Leader in Search of a Party". It's his notion of Pirandello, half-baked, you know, but that's his style, it needn't be as awful as it sounds...' – he was speaking too fast, almost unaware of what he was saying and at any moment the ice would break and she would cry.

But instead the door opened and a very tall old man came in. He walked very erect, no suggestion of a stoop. He was wearing a plaid and looked ... Giles had once spent a wet afternoon in Aberdeen and between closing and opening time gone into the Municipal Art Gallery (it was a choice between that and 'Sex – Swedish-Style', and though he detested great Galleries and would run a mile rather than visit the Uffizi or the Prado, he had in certain moods a weakness for provincial ones) and there seen a Landseer of truly impressive ineptitude entitled 'Flood in the Highlands', depicting what he took to be a Laird surrounded by family and retainers with assorted livestock perched on cliffs or struggling in the flood-waters ... yes, Urquhart looked exactly like Landseer's conception of a Highland chief. He might even have modelled for the painting, or, more probably, based his conception of himself on it.

He didn't look at Giles but said something in what was presumably Gaelic to his daughter. She replied in the same language. Giles couldn't avoid the impression that hers sounded more fluent, even more natural.

Urquhart's hand disappeared somewhere under his plaid and emerged with a key. He unlocked a heavy deal cabinet, took out a bottle of whisky (Talisker, Giles enviously observed) and poured himself a half-tumbler which he swallowed at one gulp. He made another brief remark to his daughter, filled his glass, replaced the bottle, locked the cabinet and marched out of the room.

'Well?'

'I told you it was pointless.'

'What in fact did he say?'

'He told me to tell you to get the hell out of here. That's a paraphrase. It's more vivid in the Gaelic.'

'I see.'

They could hear footsteps overhead.

'Well, I never really thought anything would...' He tried to think of just what he'd like to do to Judkins. 'Do you think I could have another drop of kirsch before I go. It's really rather good.'

The footsteps marched up and down like a man pacing his cell.

'He'll live to be a hundred, I know he will,' she said, but she filled his glass. 'You can buy it in the village below.'

Giles drank it quickly and shrugged himself into his overcoat. Or something in a cage.

'Thanks, I will, I certainly will.'

He might as well get something out of the trip. Mind you, for the first time he conceded that Judkins had a point. Visually it would be damned good, but, still, if the old loony would only speak Gaelic – well, there were bloody few Gaelic speakers and most of them probably had no TV reception. He'd tell Judkins he'd sent him on a two hundred mile round trip to interview a monoglot Gael – that'd puzzle him.

'And give my love to Simon. For what it's worth.'

'He won't live to be a hundred, that's for sure. I'm not likely to see him again. He didn't like me much.'

'No,' she said.

It was sleet that was being blown on a diagonal by the wind now. He got into the hired Fiat, and turned, surprising himself, to say something, he didn't quite know what, something to bring life to her, even perhaps just thank you, but the door was already shut, and he drove down into the valley, the sleet changing to a thin rain as he descended.

Stanley Robertson

A Monk's Tail

There wis anither mannie hid a placie nae far frae whar I worked and he aye deen a big order for filleted monks tails. Noo he usually aye kept the same loons for cutting these fish but during a 'flu epidemic baith his loons were aff nae weel, so he asked me tae come roon and help him oot. I wisnae that braw a hand at daeing monks cos I very seldom worked amongst them but I said I wid come roon and gie him a hand.

Monks are ugly looking fish. They mind ye on yon tropical angler fish. A big head like Humpty Dumpty and a cavernous mooth with rows of aa the sharpest teeth ye could ever find. If ye stuck yer hand in the mooth by mistake then the razor sharp teeth jist tore living lumps oot of yer hands. Whit awfy things tae poison yer hands with. The teeth were slanted back intae the mooth and if ye caught yer fingers or hands intae them then ye couldnae get them oot. It wis like being bit by a rattler or some strange snake. So it wis a maitter of being very careful whin ye messed aboot with monks. Even experienced monk filleters hae gied themselves bonnie sair hands with these fish.

Noo, although I wisnae that great a monk cutter, I did ken how ye done them. The body of a monk is very wee in comparison with the swalt napper. Ye hid tae cut aff firstly the big heid and the wee body seemed tae hae layers of slimy membranes aa through it. The skin wis slimy and the hale fish hid a funny texture. Folks said it wis a delicacy but I didnae fancy eating them cos of their scunnering appearance. Sometimes they're selt as scampi. For that they are cut intae wee penny pieces.

Frunkie, frae the place across the road, came intae gie us a hand as weel and he wis nane better than mysel at daeing the monks, but at least we were helping the mannie oot.

The wee bodies of the monks, which ye caw the tails, are firstly filleted and then ye kind of split the fillet so it looked like a finnian, and then sometimes they were smoked or else sent awa as freshlets. The only trouble wis there wis an awfy lot of them tae be deen and it teen us a lang time tae get through them.

If the mannie's usual boys hid bin in then they were crack hands at their jobs but Frunkie and me plodded on. We baith started tae speak aboot the names of the different kinds of fish ye get. We wondered how they got sic strange names. There were coley, saith, megrims, laithe, cats, dogs, witches, dabs, flounders, skate, cod, ling, whitings, haddocks, herrings, mackerel, gowdies, bars, dovers, breem, trout, salmon and hundreds of ither species. Yet the fish we were cutting were cawed monks. Noo with us speaking aboot monks we started tae speak aboot religion. Frunkie and me hid baith very different ideas aboot religion but I wisnae gan tae get intae ony arguments aboot religion or ye wid never get oot of it. Wid ye believe it. Fa dae ye think came intae the door but auld Fanny. She wis coming doon tae dae some pickling of wee whiting cutlets which hid been sent roon by anither boss, cos his place wis chockablock as weel.

'My goodness Fanny, yer nae still working at nights?' I cried oot tae her.

'Faith, aye!' she cried. 'I'm nae ower auld tae gang oot tae pasture yet!'

Fine weel did I ken that she wis aboot eighty. She didnae look that age for she wis a hardy auld culloch, but whit a grafter. I often wished that I hid half of her energy. Never mind it wis fine tae see her again cos I hid worked many nights with that auld wifie.

Fanny joined in oor conversation aboot religion and things pertaining tae churches.

Jist as we were speaking a laddie popped his heid in looking for the boss but we telt him he wis awa and that he widnae be back until aboot ten at night. The fella, wha wis a right hardy-looking boy says, 'Tell him that Andy called by, and that I'll come back in the morning tae see aboot the job he wis offering mi.' Then he wint awa.

Frunkie says tae us, 'See that loon, weel he jist newly finished a three year sentence in prison. I dinnae ken whit it wis he daen, but it must be bad enough for tae get aa that time. I widnae feel safe working with an ex-convict cos ye wid never ken whin ye might end up with nine inches of steel in yer back!'

'Dinnae speak rubbish!' I replied. 'Why wid the fella bother onybody. He is nae that auld. Probably got himsel intae trouble as a loon and he's got the dunt.'

Auld Fanny blurted in, 'Ye shouldnae condemn a person cos they hae bin in the nick, cos sometimes circumstances gets folks put ower the water.'

Frunkie replied, 'If ye are nae with the craws then ye winnae get shot.'

'Rubbish,' cried Fanny. 'I kent a loon wha got the wrang end of the stick every time; and eence he got the name for being a bad een then his reputation preceded him everywhere he wint.'

She then wint on tae tell us the story of Stony.

The Jail Bird

Since the time he wis a wee laddie Stony wis forever in trouble. He couldnae help it and I suppose it wis mair or less the environment he wis brought up in that made him the wye he wis. Ye see, jist afore the second world war times were awfie difficult for folks and aabody wis still suffering frae the effects of the Great Depression. Very few folks hid lowdy intae their pooches and that made a lot of people turn tae crime as a means of getting by. If ye got awa with cheating then ye were aaright but if ye were silly enough tae get caught then ye wid hae tae pay the penalty.

In the case of Stony, his mither wis a drunkard and his faither wis a pure guffie and mony's the battering Stony wid get frae his faither. Noo his mither wis aye that peevie that she wisnae aware of the ills of her wee laddie. Stony started his life of crime frae an early age with stealing little things like frae sweeties oot of shoppies, and things aff the stallies intae the mairkets.

Whin he wis twelve Stony and three ither loons got pit tae a remand home for a year and that made him come oot a wee hardened bachle. He wisnae big in stature, but he wis a gallus wee gadgie and he wid fecht with his shadow. By the time he wis sixteen he wis living a life of crime and he wis never oot of the juvenile courts. His mither died with aa her peeving whin he wis seventeen, and there wisnae onybody wha wanted tae ken aboot him. Folks were really scared whin he walked aboot the toon of Dundee.

He wis a very smairt laddie cos he wid plan jobs and then cairry them oot and he never got caught. The sad thing for which he did get caught, and done for, wis giving his faither a right sair layin-on. His faither made a darriach at him een night and Stony jist gaed him laldy. He kicked him sae saft that he pit his faither intae the hospital for three weeks. The swine deserved whit he got, cos that wis naething compared with the tunkins he hid gaed tae Stony. In court Stony wis cawed a wretch and a danger tae guid society, and he wis pit intae prison for a year. Mind ye, his faither cliped tae the hornies, and Stony got deen for a lot of things. That wis his first real time ower the waater but it wisnae his last.

Aye, Stony wis tae experience a lot of prison life. Every time he came oot of een nick he wis back again a few weeks later on ither charges. The police kent him and whin onything wis wrang it wis sure tae be pinned ontae Stony. He wisnae a guid person but he wisnae aye tae blame every time. There were times whin he wis completely innocent. Many a hiding he got frae the hornies whin they wid lift him aff the street drunk. It wis jist like this – he hid a label ontae him and he became the scapegoat for everything.

By the time he wis twenty-four, Stony hid spent almost seven years intae the prison. In between that times he got hitched tae a very bold, brazen hizzie wha cairried on with gadgies whinever he wis awa onywye. She hid one bairnie but Stony hardly ever saw it. It wis a wee lassie. Stony loved his bairnie but its mither poisoned her mind against him.

Stony became very bitter and hardened against everybody. If folks showed him kindness he wis apprehensive aboot them and he thought folks aye hid an ulterior motive for daeing a guid turn. A lot of anger wis raging inside him. These feelings were bad and festering in his soul. There seemed tae be nae escape frae this life of imprisonment.

Then aboot ten weeks afore his twenty-fifth birthday Stony wint tae the prison library and he teen oot a book aboot a fella wha wis a gypsy – and it wis tae hae an everlasting effect on him. The story wis aboot a gypsy laddie wha hid a very difficult time as a wee loon, but as he grew aulder this young fella turned tae be a great preacher. Somehow this book touched Stony's heart and he could identify many traits of the young gypsy laddie's tae his ain young life. He admired whit the young gypsy hid accomplished and the book seemed tae hae a calming influence upon him. Firstly, he wanted tae ken whit made the young gypsy fella change frae haeing an empty life tae a life of fulfillment. It brought tears tae the yaks of Stony wha wis noo a very hardened person. Yet this book made him decide that he wanted oot of prison and dae something useful with his life.

Stony decided that he wid reform himsel for the sake of his wee lassie, but firstly he needed tae prove tae the prison that he could be a changed person. Whin at first he tried being quiet the screws were very careful, cos they thought that he wis planning something coorse, but aifter a while they could deek a change of heart within Stony. Een night aifter listening tae the chaplain gieing a talk, Stony decided tae read the Bible and tae fin oot for himsel whit it wis that the young gypsy and the chaplain hid found. He teen a Bible oot of the library. He hid never read the Bible afore and tae him it wis jist a load of rubbish. He started tae read the new Testament and while he read aboot the life of Jesus a warm sensation came ower his soul. This wis a new experience for him. A spiritual conversion wis taking place on Stony.

Then, aye night, he awoke aifter haeing a very beautiful dream whar he dreamt that he saw the Lord with his airms ootstretched and beckoning him towards him. He felt a great surge of love that wis new tae him. It wis like the love that he felt for his wee lassie. This experience wis a spiritual witness tae him and he couldnae hud back the tears. This new warmth of feeling made Stony tak a new course.

Whin he wis released frae the prison he decided tae mak new life for himsel. He wint back tae his wife but she wis shacking up with anither gadgie, and she widnae let him near the wee quinie. Stony wis heartbroken but somehow he accepted it withoot ony struggle or madness. Before, he wid hae killed the bloke and battered her tae pulp. She wis ready tae get the police but as he walked awa quietly frae the hoose he couldnae be charged again. Yet een of the policemen met him in the street and wis very cheeky tae him. He wis trying tae provoke Stony by gieing him a dreadful tear of lip. Stony wis aware noo that the least thing he did wid be fairly for this gadgie, so he remained silent. He kent that they wid hae hit him.

This hornie said tae Stony, 'We will soon get ye back inside again.'

That wis enough tae mak Stony move awa frae Dundee and start afresh intae anither toon whar he widnae be recognised.

Weel, the fella moved up tae Fraserburgh tae mak a start with the new happy life that he had found. It wis hard at first, but Stony never looked back tae his days of crime. As naebody kent him there in the Broch he wis able tae get a decent job and he worked hard and honestly tae earn his keep. The lady wha he bade with thought the world of him, and he wis guid tae her in return. This woman attended een of the kirks intae the toon; Stony aye wint with her, and wis happy living in Fraserburgh.

Things were gan fine until een day he wis walking hame frae his work and, wid ye believe it, that same mean policeman frae Dundee wis moved tae Fraserburgh.

'So here's whar ye hiv wint tae, Stony, weel I will soon catch up with ye and pit ye inside again and I will easily plant evidence against ye.'

Stony turned white. He kent he wid hae tae leave this place whar he wis sae happy. The lady whar he bade with wis very disappointed at him leaving. He telt her the truth aboot himsel but he telt her that Jesus hid changed his life and noo all he wanted wis tae live a peaceful life, tae work for his keep and pay money for his young daughter. The lady wis shocked, but she knew him tae be a nice fella.

'Dear laddie, ye winnae be able tae rin awa frae yer past life forever.'

Stony wis very sad but he telt the lady that he must go awa or this hornie wid dae him a deprivation. So he moved intae Aiberdeen.

Aifter settling doon tae a new life intae Aiberdeen, Stony wis happy again. He joined a church and he worked very hard intae it. He wis liked and respected. He kept his past a secret. He didnae want folks tae find oot aboot his seven years in prison. Aifter a time Stony wis chosen tae be an elder of the Kirk. Two great emotions ran through him. Een wis of deception and the ither wis for joy. Could he be honest and tell the church dignitaries aboot his past life and wid it mak a difference tae them? He felt that he wid hae tae be honest above all things. He decided tae come clean.

The Bishop interviewed him and he telt the truth aboot himsel and his past life and how the influence of the young gypsy hid turned his life tae Christ. He wanted tae be fully converted. The Bishop, wha wis a wise and sensible man, listened and he said, 'You have worked very hard in the service of this church and community. We are all very impressed with your honesty and sincerity. We prayed for weeks before asking you to be an elder. If you have truly repented of your past life then that is acceptable to us.'

'I have never in these last few years done anything that is contrary to the laws of the gospel, and I have tried very hard to live the commandments. I am striving tae make up for those stupid years.'

A new life did arise for Stony. He married a guid-living girl and they had a wonderful family, and whin his eldest girl became old enough to understand, she came to live with him and his wife, who showed her much love.

He became a successful graphic artist and he never looked back again.

John Herdman

Original Sin

I

Full-length on his stomach in the ditch-like depression, his chin resting among the coarse grass on its verge, fingers dug deep into moss, soft muddy dampness beneath his thighs, peering through the tufts of heather; almost panting as he strove to hear, panic at his heart. The group of figures moving to and fro among the pine trees two hundred yards ahead of him, the reservoir lying leaden beyond them under the dull sky, the voices mostly muffled but every now and again rising sharply for an instant only to fall again before he could distinguish the words. Then 'Here!' came a sudden shout from a poking, prodding shape in a donkey jacket, and again, sharp with rising excitement, 'here!' His breath was halted with horror in his throat and he gripped compulsively at the tufts of grass. From all directions the dark figures came hurrying to where the man who had shouted had been digging. The latter held something up for all to see, and while some jostled up to gaze at it others fell to scrabbling with frenzied energy around the spot where it had been found. Very soon a new, loud and concerted shout arose and at once a further find was held up to view. This time he could make it out clearly from where he lay watching, an elongated stick-like thing showing up pale in the mirkiness of the pine wood – a bone, a long thin pale bone, and, as he knew all too well, a human bone. He moaned. The helpless terror of discovery was upon him and his brain and his body were numbed. He struggled to rise from the pit in which he lay, to rise and flee into the enveloping dusk, but his limbs failed him, his arms had no strength in them and they could not raise him up...

He was awake. He opened his eyes in the dim light of dawn, and lay on in the irremediable sickness of his soul. He knew that he had dreamed, that the discovery had not taken place, but the full horror and foulness of his deed overwhelmed his spirit. How had he ever forgotten it? How was that possible? How could he have lived with this act for all those years, repressed it and erased it so successfully that his waking life had not known of it at all? How had he walked about on the face of the earth with this weight inside him, how had he moved among people, how had he laughed and worked and eaten and loved? When all along, deep within him, he had known?

He moaned aloud and tried to move. He was nearly off the edge of the bed, his right arm was dead. He became aware of his immediate situation. The woman he loved lay beside him, turned away from him, he could feel her back against his front, feel the silkiness of her buttocks against his belly, make out the contour of her body and the darkness of her head on the pillow. His dead right arm was pinioned under her neck. He tried to concentrate, and a thin flash of hope illuminated his consciousness. This deed, had he dreamt that too? No, no, he had not dreamt that: the illumination receded into dimness and despair flooded his mind. Think, think, it was necessary to think. Yes, but yes, that idea wanted to re-establish itself, to assert its plausibility. It wanted to lie to him, to perpetuate that old lie, to whisper to him that he had never killed. He tried to move the fingers of his dead hand but he could feel nothing, it was as if his arm had been cut off below the shoulder. Back and forth went these ideas in his mind: it's true, it isn't true, it's true, it isn't true. After about five minutes he was finally sure. No, it was not true. He had never killed anyone in his life.

He sighed with weakness and weariness. He endeavoured to raise himself but could not get a purchase: he had almost been pushed out of his own bed, the woman lay solidly in the middle and he was half hanging over the edge. He began to try to pull his arm out from under her; it was not easy. She stirred and made a noise in her throat. He cursed and pulled again. At once she moaned and half turned over on her back, covering more of his arm. As she did so she tossed her head from side to side on the pillow: 'No,' she said, 'no!' 'Sorry,' he replied, but she sighed and was still. He tried again and she whimpered. He peered into her face and saw that she was asleep, but that her brows were pulled together in a look of distress. He was moved and felt an access of love for her, and with it a thin tugging of desire. He held his breath and pulled his arm out sharply from under her; this time she did not stir.

Carefully he climbed out of bed and walked over to the window, moving his arm about to get the circulation going. He drew the curtain back further and looked out over the neighbouring gardens; it was quite light but the sun was not yet up and there was a dampness in the air. He felt chilled. He was greatly relieved now in the knowledge that what he had dreamt had no solid reality, yet somehow not so relieved as he ought to have been: a nasty taste remained in the mouth of his spirit. He had a powerful impression that he had experienced that crushing sense of guilt before. When ... when? The memory was not too far away, there was some connection with his standing here at the window, looking down into the garden ...

He had it. He was four years old. His parents had taken him on a visit to some friends. He remembered a large house surrounded by a beautiful garden, away out somewhere on the edge of town. Two boys, much older than himself, and a girl, only a little older. There was something funny about the girl: although she was older than him she did not seem to be able to talk properly. She kept pointing to him and saying 'Bibby'. He felt somehow insulted and wanted to protest in some way, but he did not know how to set about it. He looked at the boys as if for guidance, but they seemed to be very tolerant of the girl and unaware of his distress and embarrassment.

The next thing he remembered he was out in the garden with the girl at the back of the house. The boys had disappeared. They were supposed to be playing but he was feeling very useless and unhappy. He could not make the girl understand anything he said or do anything sensible at all, she just kept running aimlessly to and fro and shouting. She looked very odd and his already fastidious nature shrank from her in fear and disgust. Suddenly she stopped running about, stood still and pointed at him. 'Bibby!' she cried, 'Bibby!' Rage sprang up in him. A long clothes pole lay on the thick grass. He made for it and began to pick it up. He wanted to annihilate the girl. He was going to hit her on the head with the pole and if possible kill her. 'Bibby!' she shouted again. He struggled to raise the pole; it was very heavy, but he had it round the middle. Just at that moment he heard his mother's voice calling – he did not take in the words. Guilt flashed in his heart. He let go of the pole as if it had been red-hot and looked up: his mother and the mother of the girl were standing looking down at them from an upstairs window. They were both smiling and he could not understand why: he stood before them exposed and naked, caught in the act, his face on fire. The two mothers seemed to be pretending not to know what he intended, but he knew that it could only be an act to save embarrassment all round, for his guilt was everywhere about him; unhidden, he was certain, from those smiling eyes. Yes, this shame and terror of exposure was the very feeling of his dream: what he had purposed secretly and in safety, in the private places of his heart, was openly known.

II

The terror, the terror: nights of long darkness and encroaching cold, the short bitter days. We sit in front of the log fire, the two of us, crouching towards its crackling heat. Heaping on more fuel, inadvertently I move one of the logs so that it is not burning properly, and the other is angry. As I try to shove it back into place it seems to move of its own accord, what seems like an eye appears and then a rudimentary ear. 'My God,' I cry, 'that log's alive!' No surprise to him, though; he savagely pokes the fire while the log twists and moans. He has always known that logs can live, and this one he means to kill. I see now what it is, this log, it is the head and neck of a horse which writhes in agony! Somehow it tells its story – how it was cut down by human cruelty and taken from its home.

Things are different now: a plastic surgeon has been at work. This former log, this erstwhile horse, he has converted it into human form, the incisive one, recreated it in his own image; the image of a repulsively handsome and decadent young man, an actor who struts forth his arrogance upon the stage. He holds the log in subjection as his servant (oh yes, you can still tell, from certain lumps and scars about the forehead, that this was once a log). The log is murderously resentful: a fight to the death will break out between these twins.

III

The baby lies there, looking up and smiling, a plump and happy baby with nothing but love in its heart. In the shaded room the people pass in and out, looking at the baby and admiring it, making friendly noises, sometimes leaning down and chucking it under the chin. The baby responds delightedly, it coos and gurgles with joy.

It is the dark man's turn: his form overshadows the cot, he gazes down into the baby's eyes, smiling, his purpose complete within him. He smiles to let the others know his good intent, he smiles at the baby to establish as it were a conspiracy between them; the shame of his perfidy gnaws him like a worm. Yes, the baby knows all right, but will it betray him? Will it remember, and will it forgive him? He gently fondles the infinitely soft and delicate skin beneath the baby's chin, all the time smiling his gentle love ... But the baby's smile is less certain now, a cloud passes over, at any moment it may cry. At once, gritting his teeth, he digs the nails of his thumb and forefinger deep within that unresisting flesh.

IV

Crawl, crawl on, lump. On your belly, arms pinioned at the sides, snaking onwards, gasping and panting. Tighter and tighter. Through the tortuous passageways of this castle. Is there space in the distance? Is there breath? On, then, tighter and tighter til wriggling and squirming. This creeping thing, going on its belly. This slimy squirming thing, eating dust. This tiny piece of contemptible obscene matter, this living bird-dropping. I. Crush it beneath the heel.

Carl MacDougall

from *The Lights Below*

Sometimes he couldn't sleep.

For the first few weeks he slept twelve hours a night, sometimes dovering for twenty minutes or half an hour in the early evening, wakening in time for the evening concert.

Then for no reason the pattern changed. He slept for four hours or five, wakened for a few hours and slept again, relaying throughout the day and night. This was broken by fighting sleep, by sitting up till eleven o'clock, going to bed with a book and chocolate or camomile tea and rising with his alarm at eight. He could understand the temptation of staying awake at night and sleeping through the day, of finding no good reason for rising.

He was called to the dole office at eleven o'clock. The lad with the shell suit and trainers in the next seat kept yawning. 'I was supposed to've been here at ten,' he said. 'Slept in.' Claimants were called in the morning for that very reason.

'Are you still looking for work?' the girl asked. She had lipstick on her teeth and a ribbon in her hair. 'And are you prepared to travel to find work?'

It was best to provide the answers they needed; otherwise benefit was automatically stopped. Then a reclaim procedure would have to be instigated; the claimant would need to appeal and appeals could take four or five weeks.

'Are you prepared to take whatever work is offered?'

'Yes.'

'Thank you, Mr Paterson.'

The lad in the shell suit was smoking a roll-up. 'I'm waiting for wee Mickey,' he said. 'Fancy a score?'

'No, thanks.'

'Nae bother, big man. Thought you'd fancy it, know what I mean.'

'Another time. What happened up there?'

'Benefit stopped. Another fucken hassle. That's how I've got to sell the stuff, know what I mean. Win some, lose some.'

At first he thought it was the room temperature; if he was disturbed in the first few minutes of sleep he was awake for at least a couple of hours. He used to read till he ran out of books; he listened to the World Service till neighbours complained.

So he started walking, rising rather than staring at the ceiling with the bed too warm, remembering snatches of conversation, missed opportunities, the dancer's legs and a past that always ended in jail. At first he imagined he was crazy. The illusory disapproval made him do it. He walked round the block, got back to bed and slept. The third time a policeman stopped him.

'Where are you off to?'

'Nowhere.'

'What do you mean nowhere?'

'I'm out for a walk.'

'At this time in the morning; around here?'

'I live here.'

'Where?'

So it went on, ending when the policeman said, 'Right, then. On your way, but watch it. Okay. Just watch it.' His breath smelled of whisky and peppermint.

Andy loved the night and was slightly scared. He was like his Granny, loved what could never happen in daylight, loved the possibilities, which also scared him. Night was frantic and a little nervous, night was alone. The city changed. There was an easier, carefree attitude, another play in the same setting, different lights and shadows, different players. What was easily ignored by day was obvious at night, easily seen and hard to avoid.

He was walking by the river, once a source of commerce, manufacture and storage, now a relic, a river like any river, passing through any city, a place of no significance. The docks were ruined or turned to sites for brick-built tenements, three storeys high, a joint venture. The district council sold the land, a developer built the houses.

Sometimes, to wonder what went on, to visualise lives behind the curtains, because he tried to imagine what sleepers would think if they knew he was passing, he wandered through a residential area, usually in the west end. He did not expect houses by the river and wandered around the small estate.

An environmental health van was parked at the end of a small street. A man in overalls and a donkey jacket watched him walk down the road.

'Help you?'

'Just passing. Out for a walk.'

'You live here?'

'No.'

'Fucken lucky. See they hooses, riddled wi rats. This was the docks, right? And what've docks got plenty of? Rats. Big as dugs, so they are, fucken rats yon size.'

He had been rolling a cigarette. He lit it and shook his head. 'See if they folk sleeping nice and cosy knew what was going on, they'd shite themselves. They took away the docks and the sheds, so the rats had nae place tae stay. But rats don't go away and the company that bought this place, the fucken developers spent a fortune on a private firm that was supposed tae get rid of them. But the rats is still here. You'll never shift them. Rats'll survive a holocaust. Look at it. The rats think their coupon's up. They build centrally heated houses with a chute for flinging your rubbish down into a big midgie. Perfect conditions for breeding rats, food, warmth and shelter all in the one place. So what do the rats do; they're sitting down there with wee napkins roon their necks at the bottom of the chute, waiting for the mugs to send the grub down. They're the best-fed rats in the world. They don't need to go looking for grub. The punters send it doon to them, doon the chute. The rats are the only thing on the increase here, rats and beggars, there's fucken thousands of them. And guess what: we're here because a woman saw a rat in broad daylight. Jesus Johnny, it must've been one of their relations coming doon tae Glesca for a feed, or else it was a rat that was lost, cause I can assure you any rats around here know they're on a good thing. There's two main packs to every building. Unless the yuppies never sent the vol-au-vents doon the chute in time and this was a wee warning party coming out to check them.'

He laughed. 'Fancy a hoose here? Seventy-five thow for a three apartment facing the river and aa the rats you can catch.'

Was it then or later, around that time or nearly, he read about the new city, the emerging place. Consumerism's victory over manufacture promoted a tourism and conference centre, with no extra facilities to support the influx. Millions were coming to the city, using the same sewers, the same water, gas and electricity as served the population prior to the goldrush.

A couple of weeks later and further upstream, a man was trembling by Glasgow Green, a blanket and a carrier bag beside him. 'Polis've flung us aff the Green,' he said. 'Nae place tae sleep.'

In the jail they'd talked of a good skipper on the Paisley Road West or maybe out Duke Street. 'Come on. I'll get you a cup of tea, auld yin,' Andy said. They walked up the Saltmarket towards Glasgow Cross.

The man was talking. Andy could not make out what was being said. The man kept talking. His wife was dead. He was glad she didn't have to see him like this, with the family scattered.

'There's a bit to go for the tea, auld yin.'

The man said something Andy didn't understand. He went to move off and the man grabbed his arm. Andy almost vomited as he caught the smell, bending his ear towards the voice. 'I'm not an old man,' he said. 'I'm fifty-three.'

They were on Argyle Street. A young man, maybe in his twenties, with spiky hair, three earrings on the lobe of his left ear, a raincoat tied to his neck and a dog on a bit of string, was standing in a doorway. 'Where yous off to?' he asked.

His hands and fingers were covered with the do-it-yourself tattoos Andy recognised from jail, boredom or both, like schoolbag graffiti. 'There's a skipper doon here,' he said.

His name was Davie. He had a sign: HOMELESS. NO DOLE. HUNGRY. PLEASE GIVE SPARE CHANGE PLEASE. THANKYOU. Four hours a night at the Central Station and he splits the take with the lookout. Begging's illegal on railway property, though it's worth the risk; the station's a good pitch, especially if you have a dog. People feel sorry for the dog, he said. He gets about twelve quid and finishes by nine. No point after that.

'The businessmen and yuppies give you fuck all,' he said, going down Stockwell Street towards the river. 'And the casuals give you a kicking. I got a doing off them last week. The trouble's getting worse, on both sides. Sometimes when somebody stops you in the street to tap you, they're sizing you up for a mugging.'

They work the grid, Central Station, Argyle Street, Clyde Walkway, St Enoch Square. 'I'm fed up eating they Dunkin Donuts and McDonalds shite. Carry-oot food's all you can take. By the way, have you any grub on you, auld yin?'

The other man shook his head.

'Fine. Just checking. There's rats where we're going. They'll no touch you as long as you've nae grub on you. You get bitten bringing grub in. They run over your body looking for it. There's aye too many for the dug to get.'

The skipper was a hut beneath the bridge. 'Better than the Queens

Park, though that wee lane up there's no bad. This hut's moving soon. Every night I expect it'll be gone. The corporation workmen left it.'

'See you,' said Andy.

Davie said, 'Please yourself.' The older man went into the hut without speaking.

Next time he couldn't sleep, Andy went to Charing Cross and stood opposite the casino. He didn't see anyone he knew.

He had finished his tea and was reading a book about hillwalking. The man in the next-door room who worked funny shifts and sometimes sang to himself while shaving, little songs in Gaelic, knocked on the door and looked at the wall.

'There's a woman to see you,' he said.

Myra smiled self-consciously. She wanted him to think she'd come straight from work, or maybe she was passing, but he knew she had taken some trouble with her appearance. 'Can I come in?' she asked.

Ten minutes later she sipped a mug of tea. 'Hasn't changed much,' she said. 'You've still got the birds.'

'It's nice to see you.'

'Are you still listening to that music on the wireless?'

Nerves made her talk. She used her left hand as a saucer for the mug and looked at the tea every once in a while, thinking of something to say. She obviously wanted to appear as natural as possible, as though they had seen each other recently or were renewing a casual acquaintance.

She sat on the chair with her knees together and filled the room with her scent. Andy knew the chatter was preamble; he was content to wait, happy she was talking because he did not know what to say. Her fingernails were filed to an oval shape and painted with an opalescent varnish which caught the light like a piece of jewellery. She finished the tea and put the mug on the carpet beside the chair.

'So, what's been happening?'

'Nothing much.'

'Still not found a job?'

'Not yet.'

Maybe she wouldn't tell him. Maybe she would go away feeling foolish and never come back. He would have to say something. He would have to tell her.

'You never come into the café.'

'I didn't think you'd want to see me.'

'I thought you'd've come in.'

'I will then. I'll come in tomorrow.'

'Have you put your name down on the housing list?'

'I didn't think it was worth it. I don't know what to do. One minute I think I'll go, then I don't know where I'll go to or what I'll do when I get there.'

'You must have a lot to straighten out. I was thinking, it must be hard trying to get your life together after all that time.'

He looked away and hoped she didn't notice. He felt angry: there was a sudden flash, a tightening like fear in his stomach and a numbness around the mouth when he narrowed his lips. Later, he would not know why he had felt angry, nor why it had happened so suddenly.

'What's the matter?'

'Nothing.'

'You looked angry. Did I say something?'

'No. I'm okay.'

'Listen, I'd better go. Maybe, if you like, I could come with you when you're putting your name down, if you want to that is?'

'No, of course, that's great. And thanks for coming round. I'm really glad to see you.'

'Good. I'm glad I came now. So, you'll come into the café?'

He nodded.

She stood up and gentle as a pickpocket kissed him goodbye.

Possil had hardly changed. One or two shops had different owners, but it was still the same straight semi-treeless street. The Lido Café was there with the same sign, black lettering on a green background; Andy wondered if they made their own ice-cream, but was too cold to try.

The Blind Asylum had been demolished; it always looked a rickety structure, twentieth-century and temporary, unlike the red sandstone Rockvilla Church and the wee hall on the other side of the street. Sometimes, just before sleep, he would remember the frozen sermons, the wooden pews with long, padded crimson cushions and the other boys restless in their heavy uniforms.

After a while he never went back, long after Watson left. This was an unpredictable cause of misfortune, easily explained in the hours before sleep when it returned like a debt collector. He always excused himself, said he was adolescent, had lost his father, mother and sister, in the emotional confusion he clutched at comfort, warmth or maybe someone showing an interest. It was all over quickly. Billy Watson was in a hurry, the toilet was small and the caretaker might find them. He wondered how he got there, why he went; was he asked or did he go into the toilet and find Billy Watson waiting? There was the pain, the impossibility of it all, even while it was happening, there was fear. It was the terror he remembered most, the anxiety of his cheek rubbing against plaster, the smell of dampness and the sound of the cistern. Watson never spoke. He wiped himself and closed the door; Andy heard the snap of the lock and let out a yell. 'You've hurt your face,' the caretaker said when he found him. 'What happened? Did you fall?' Andy nodded.

Next week Watson was back for more. He walked Andy along to Saracen Cross and took him into a close, the close beside the Balmore Bar; again Andy's face was to the wall, again the pain and the stickiness, again the useless feeling. He never went back.

'Is that you done wi the Scouts?' said Granny.

Now there was a new church, a new hall and a new name, built of brick like most new buildings. The lime leaks after a rain and it does not catch the light. There are no shadows on brick buildings.

Orlando warmed his hands on the fire. Geordie Anderson was living in Andy's room and writing poetry. This was the first time Andy had seen him without make-up.

'You'll need to let me hear some of your poetry,' said Andy.

'There's some good stuff,' said Orlando. 'He took to verse when the parties stopped. Somebody wrote them down for him and now he goes to a wee writing group. He's written poems in praise of the Mosshouse and Keppochhill Road, one about Saracen Street and one about Life. There doesn't seem to be a shortage of subject matter. He wrote one I liked called Grace: *Thank you God and make us good / As we sit down to eat our food*, something like that at the beginning. Food is still an important subject for Geordie.'

Geordie carried in the tray with three mugs of tea. Andy had brought a wee Dundee Cake and a packet of digestive biscuits which Orlando liked to dip in his tea. They were bought in Saracen Street.

Two girls were standing near a bus-stop beside the shop, giggling and pushing each other. They were pale girls, maybe fourteen, no more than fifteen, in their panstick make-up and high-heeled shoes. Andy was looking down the road towards the Mosshouse, watching the light as it crossed the street and lit the lamp posts, flattered the tenements and sparked in the hair the girls had backcombed together, laughing at each other's reflection in the mirror. He realised he was staring. One of the girls was nodding towards him, a single downward jerk of her head, mouthing a word whose meaning he could not understand.

'Business.'

They looked at him. The girl on the left put a hand on her hip and opened her legs. The other's smile changed to a slightly menacing stare, brimming with confident bravado; she had obviously mistaken his confusion for innocence or fear. From a close, a young man, whose hair was matted and whose back was stooped, moved between them, his back to Andy, who went into the shop. When he came out with the cake and biscuits all three were gone.

He told Orlando. 'Ten pounds each,' he said, 'or the two for fifteen. Am I alone in thinking there was a time when drugs were not an issue, when whatever threat or problem they represented was easily containable because we live on an island. Look at it now, our only growth industry. How did this happen? How did they cease to become containable? What was the springboard to their undoubted success, apart from cutting the customs staff, and where does all the money go if it doesn't go into the economy?'

The house was the same, smelling of cats. Granny's wedding photograph was on the mantelpiece in its leather frame, Granny and Grandpa, stern-faced and shy. Andy expected her to come in with the shopping. He expected to hear her complain.

'The changes are all very well,' Orlando said. Geordie poured more tea. 'They are the same as any other of this city's so-called changes. Did you hear about the woman who gave birth to a heid? No arms, legs or body, just a heid. She visited the heid in hospital every week and on its twenty-first birthday said "I've brought a nice surprise for your birthday. Will I open it?" The heid said "Yes please" and watched the parcel being unravelled, first the ribbon, then the tape and finally the wrapping. "Oh, Mammy," it said, when the parcel was opened, "Oh Mammy. No another bunnet."'

Orlando went into the lavatory. He was older, stooped and walked with an old man's limp. Geordie handed him another piece of cake and a sheet of paper:

> In the field near St Theresa's chapel
> There's a balloon as big as a corporation building,
> A balloon with stars.
> I get in the balloon and float
> Above the city,

Rising into the warm darkness
With stars all around me.
I could be anywhere,
America, Perth or Russia,
On the other side of the world.
When I come back to reality
I do not know if I've seen it
Or dreamed it.
You would need to be there,
You'd need to see it for yourself
To know.

He waited three hours. By the time his number was called he had finished the novel he brought and exhausted conversational possibilities with the people on either side, he had become accustomed to the tension, noise and smells. The noise was the perpetual grind of voices, crying children and complaint.

'Paterson?'

'That's right. Andrew Paterson.'

'What is it?'

'I live in a bedsit with shared facilities and get housing benefit. I am thinking of changing my house, or rather, of applying for a house and – '

She leaned her left forearm on the counter and raised herself up by pushing her right hand down on the chair. She said nothing, opened the door and walked away. Five minutes later, she was back.

'Here.' She handed him three forms printed in different colours; plum, orange, puce. 'Fill these in and send them back in this envelope.'

Douglas Dunn

The Political Piano

The countryside of the Scottish Borders was wearing its winter tweeds. Here and there, on the pastures, patches of unmelted snow, decorated with frost, formed their crusty tiaras on clumps of rough grass. Snowdrops grew along the line of the rusted iron fence that escorted the long drive to the house of Alois Hanka, the Czechoslovak composer, who had settled there with his wife.

On the hills, snow was impressively pure against a blue sky. To meditate on that beautiful house, its pleasing proportions, and on the farms dotted over the lower slopes of the hills, was to think of an older but visually benign civilization at peace in a benevolent wilderness.

As they sat in their parked car, looking at the countryside, and at Hanka's house, Lucy Williams said, 'Is it Georgian? I've never been in Scotland before. Is there such a thing as "Scottish Georgian?"'

'Something like that,' Paul Salmon said. He heard what Lucy said without taking it in. His thoughts were turning over the practical opportunities which the delightful house and its pastoral setting offered him. 'It really makes its point.' He smiled with satisfaction 'No need to say very much on the soundtrack about a house like that. Thirty seconds of careful planning and all anybody'd think about is money, and more money. And how did Hanka get it? Nervous?' he asked Lucy Williams.

'Very,' she said, although Paul Salmon failed to notice that her single, spoken word expressed her distrust of him.

Paul Salmon made television profiles of celebrities in the arts. At one time he had been a senior producer on the staff of a television company. Now he was freelance, successful, and busy.

Former associates and acquaintances of Hanka's, a few in London, two or three in New York, some in Los Angeles, others in Paris, Geneva and Rome, had suggested to Salmon that the composer was hardly likely to co-operate in the making of Salmon's film. Confidence, which Salmon possessed the way other people have degrees and qualifications, had led him to start work on the film without Hanka's participation. A contract had been signed with a television company which was attracted by what was already known of Hanka's controversial past. Money had been spent on travel and research.

A bigger budget was almost guaranteed now that Hanka had surprised Salmon by agreeing to see him, expressing in his reply to Salmon's letter a willingness to help, mentioning old photographs and manuscripts. For the film-maker, it was a scoop. For years, the reclusive composer had refused to see journalists, interviewers and broadcasters, and now he was opening his front door.

'Even if he turns nasty, there's nothing he can do to stop me filming the outside of the house,' Salmon said to his girlfriend as they approached the front of Hanka's home. 'It says so much!'

'You could make a picture say anything,' Lucy Williams said derisively.

'So? I'm a film-maker!'

Alois Hanka was affable and welcoming. He was a small, round man in his mid-seventies. He looked to be in excellent health; his skin was unwrinkled, smooth, tight and plump. His eyes were a clear blue-grey and he did not wear spectacles. His hair, though, was thin and white. He wore a tweed suit, the colours of which imitated the countryside. A waistcoat drew attention to his corpulence. For a man of his years and size – he was five foot four and fat – he appeared unusually elegant, fastidiously dressed and well.

'I once met a cousin of yours,' Hanka said to Salmon, after he had shown the couple into a sitting room, introduced them to Mrs Hanka, and exchanged courtesies about the comfort of their long drive.

'A cousin of *mine*?' Salmon was seriously surprised.

'Mousse. Salmon Mousse!'

Hanka laughed loudly at his feeble joke. 'And do you know the Smoked-Salmons?' He laughed even more vigorously.

No one else laughed. Mrs Hanka shoved her husband, and he squealed as if it hurt.

'He thinks he has a sense of humour, but he is mistaken,' Mrs Hanka said in a mid-European accent, more marked in her voice than it was in the composer's. If anything, there was a slight intonation of American in Hanka's voice, and a queer suggestion of a Scottish accent, barely percep-tible – no more than a dash of the spoken colouring of his adopted country.

Mrs Hanka presented the disconcerting appearance of having been taller than she was now. Hers was a presence of withered beauty. She was slender and precise, but the straightness of her back looked like the willed demeanour of someone who had once been beautiful and elegant and whose temperament did not accommodate itself to the inconveniences of age. Her face was wrinkled vividly. But she was still graceful, her hair carefully ordered, her suit smart and its jacket waisted. The brooch that held a silk scarf to her neck was distinctive and antique.

'Hanka-chief,' the composer said, still smarting from his wife's chastising push, sniffing sadly, like a clown, and pointing to himself as the victim of his own jest. Then he waved his arms as if to dispel any taint of juvenile merriment from his chintzy sitting room, driving jokes out by the tall, ornately draped and swagged windows.

'Why is sweet wine so unfashionable?' he said to Lucy Williams, who had been invited by Mrs Hanka to say what she would like to drink, and had asked for a dry sherry. 'Why so severe and dry? Why not sweet? Sweet is joy! Here, in Scotland, they call whisky "nippy sweeties". These Scots people eat sweeties all the time. Eat cakes. They die like flies! But maybe they die happy!'

'Don't believe him,' Mrs Hanka said censoriously. 'Alois is in love with his "nippy sweeties". You must not believe a word he says,' she added, to Paul Salmon.

'He's come to hear me tell the truth, and you say, "Don't believe a word he says!"' Hanka appealed to Salmon with a shrug and a wide gesture of arms, which might have meant 'Women! Wives! They're impossible!' And then Hanka winked, which could have been a hint of the composer's conviction that Salmon might try as hard as he liked, but he would not lead Hanka to say any more about his life than he wanted to disclose.

After small-talk about the house, an inspection of views from the sitting room windows, the indication of landmarks, Hanka said privately to Salmon, 'Lunch might be another hour, so maybe we should go for a walk, and talk about your film.' In a louder voice, he said, 'Would you like to see my garden?'

'Put on your coat if you go out,' Mrs Hanka said severely, her expression suggesting to Lucy Williams that Hanka had a long history of underclad walks in his garden. 'And your scarf and gloves.' Confidingly, she said to Lucy, 'He is a little boy – to be looked after, all the time, looked after.'

When the two men were in the hall, Mrs Hanka said, 'Your Mr Salmon is very tall.'

'Six feet and an inch.'

'Over six feet! Five foot four and over six feet together!' Mrs Hanka clapped her hands and laughed.

'We're not ready yet,' Hanka said in the hall. 'Before I go anywhere, there's an inspection. Coat, hat, gloves, shoes ... Do you know the joke? Spectacles, testicles, watch and wallet? No? Where have you been? You English! I have my watch. No wallet – won't need it. Don't wear glasses, thank God, because I eat carrots. Will I need my testicles, Mr Salmon? No? Maybe I'll take them off and leave them in the cupboard, but then I'd forget where I put them. "Alois! What do you mean, you have lost them?"' he said, singing an imitation of his wife's imagined alarm.

Salmon was amused by Hanka's good-natured crudity. No one, though, had forewarned him of the composer's manic humours. He wondered how one of Hanka's jests would look and sound on his film.

'Ah, here's my sergeant-major,' Hanka said, as Mrs Hanka came from the sitting room to check that her husband was dressed for the weather.

Although Salmon was too far away to hear her whisper in any language, Mrs Hanka took the precaution of speaking in German. 'I don't trust him. Remember, Alois – he is not your friend. He is handsome, English and sensitive, but I think he is cunning. He will be deferential and nice, but he might try to trap you. Be careful what you say.'

Hanka nodded his agreement and kissed her on the cheek.

'It is not only when men grow old, when their work is over, that they turn to their gardens,' Hanka said as the two men walked together. 'It is when they know that they are mature that they realize the peace and pleasure to be found in making things grow, and the great delight of being responsible for beautiful flowers and fresh vegetables. Oh, I love to eat. Most of all, I love my own fresh vegetables...'

'I'm thinking of the film, in a way that'll present a complete portrait...'

'Yes, Mr Salmon, I know the questions you want to ask me,' Hanka said.

'There was an article about you last year, more or less saying that you've written "the music of capitalism", and he tied this up...' Salmon's voice became unsure; it wavered as he stumbled on the unexpected difficulty of what he wanted to say. 'Your work during the war, and then that long stint in Hollywood.'

'I'm not any kind of an *ist! Isms!* These damned *isms* get everywhere!' Hanka said angrily, swatting the air energetically as if attacked by a swarm of insect isms. Visible breath flowed from them in the cold January air. 'Maybe they got into some people's music, but they didn't get into mine!'

'Did you read Lambourn's article about you?'

'Was it a long article? Do you know what Joseph Conrad said about reviews and articles? "Dear boy, I only ze measures zem!"' Hanka said, overdoing his mimicry. 'Good music in Poland. Penderecki, Baird, Lutoslawski...'

'Wooto?'

'OK, Lootoslavski. I am European. I pronounce. I speak languages. I am not English.'

'I suppose it's preferable for an artist of any kind to be on the truthful side of history. But it's not always possible, is it? Would you agree? Is that how you see it?' Salmon said, unnerved by the intensifying grimace with which Hanka greeted each question.

'History doesn't have any sides! That's how I see it!'

Hanka opened the door to a planthouse that was built against the south-facing wall of the garden.

'I see what you mean,' Salmon said. 'You were understating when you said you were an enthusiastic gardener. Marvellous!' he said, impressed by the size of the planthouse. 'Interesting to look at, yes. I'd like to film you in here, if it's all right with you.' He looked around for a minute. 'Then you don't accept Lambourn's view that your career's disabled by a profoundly right-wing political stance?' Salmon asked.

'Right-wing, left-wing, no, I wouldn't. I'm a wishy-washy liberal, that's what I've been, always, even before there was the phrase. No, I'm a wishy-washy *survivor*! Like all liberals, I'm a coward, and I admit it. Thank God for liberals! Can you see me as a soldier? History!' Hanka shouted with a violent upward jerk of his arms, as if the word exploded. He looked at the ground and sneered; the word 'history' writhed in the thin dust of the path between the beds of the planthouse. 'I'll tell you what history is. It's the political piano, and the noise it makes is *lies*! I am like Greta Garbo. "I want to be alone,"' he said, with an absurd shake of his hips.

'Yes, I was coming to that. I'll have to ask you why you've chosen to live up here, in Scotland, and why you hardly ever see anyone...'

'Dear, young Mr Salmon, there are five million people or more in Scotland! It's old. It's not going to run away. There are no earthquakes in Scotland. Malaria's unheard of. So far as I know, there have been no nasty camps in Scotland. There were prisoner-of-war camps – and do you know? Would you believe it? The prisoners come back to visit their old friends in the villages. Even the wild animals aren't so wild! As for "nippy sweeties",' he said, his face broadening on a grin, 'they don't even need grapes to make it!'

Salmon was unruffled by Hanka's preliminary evasions of the questions suggested to him. He was too enthusiastic for Hanka the man of talk, the man of gestures, that movable, expressive face, to be perplexed by what sounded like a lack of candour. If he could coax Hanka to speak on the film in what seemed to be his natural idiom, the composer would be a knockout.

Hanka looked at him over a plantpot which had been inspected for first signs of growth breaking the surface of the compost. 'I wonder how D-minor can be political. Or E-flat. Oh, those poor notes!'

'The film would give you a terrific chance to put your own case,' Salmon said. 'You could clear up what's been said and written about you.'

'You haven't asked me yet. You haven't said, "Mr Hanka, why did you work for the Germans?"' Hanka put the plantpot back on its table, and picked up another. 'All these are lilies. Did you know that the water-lily has more DNA than man himself, more than you have? No? It's true. The lilium is the most beautiful and significant of all the flowers. And in these parts, I am *famous* for my lilies. And my asparagus!' He kissed his fingers in appreciation of the good taste of asparagus, and blew the kiss to Salmon. 'A retired general of the British Army comes here, and I tell him about lilies. *Royalty* has eaten my asparagus in a house not ten miles from here. Do *they* care if I conducted Mozart, at concerts, to an audience of German soldiers, most of whom didn't even want to be there?'

'I think I can imagine your predicament at the time, and maybe how you feel about it now, but it surely isn't as easy to dismiss as you make it seem. *You did it*,' Salmon said emphatically, but with less triumph and judgemental sternness than he had rehearsed. 'Your career and reputation are absolutely steeped in controversy. Hardly a single work of yours has been performed ever since it came to light that you conducted German orchestras during the war. If you aren't frank on film, it'll show,' he warned.

'I don't deny anything,' Hanka said.

'It's just as well,' Salmon said.

In the house, Mrs Hanka and Lucy Williams visited the kitchen, where the Hankas' housekeeper was preparing lunch. Mrs Hanka pointed out treasured possessions in various rooms – china, furniture, ornaments and paintings. In the room where Hanka worked, Lucy asked if she could play his piano. Mrs Hanka nodded with approval at her playing.

'Where did you study?'

'Just at school, and with a private teacher, but I've practically given it up. I don't even have a piano.'

'Alois says, "Why should I write music? No one performs it any more. I am writing symphonies of silence."'

They wandered through the house. 'He was very thrifty. After the war, we had nothing, nothing. During the war we had next to nothing, but who cared then, so long as you were alive. In bed you could pretend that everything was normal and no one anywhere was being hurt. Even that became impossible, and you didn't even have that any more. But in America, Alois worked, and worked, and if I wanted to buy something, it was always, "How much is it? Good God, no, that's too much." He was a squirrel with money! And how he worked! Italy, Switzerland, Paris, London – he was some success in those days. I know what your friend, Mr Salmon, wants to talk to him about,' Mrs Hanka said, her voice austere with suspicion. 'Maybe you think we don't deserve to live in such a nice house, and so peacefully,' she said bitterly.

Mrs Hanka fitted a hand with a glove before trying to lift a log for the sitting room fire. The task was too strenuous for her and Lucy interceded, taking large logs from the fireside basket and placing them on the fire. She helped the kneeling Mrs Hanka to her feet. It was a courtesy Mrs Hanka seemed pleased with.

'If all your husband did was conduct an orchestra, then I don't find that so very terrible,' Lucy said, 'although I'd probably feel differently if I were Czech, and my family had suffered. Paul thinks it's pretty damning, though. I don't think Paul's cruel, or means to be, but he could be in spite of himself – all he's after are a few episodes to spice up a film and give it an edge, make it look "important". And money, of course: Paul's very interested in money.'

'Are you saying that your Mr Salmon might not be fair to Alois?'

'I'm saying, Mrs Hanka, that Paul's superficial. I've known him just a couple of months, but for someone who's making a film about a composer, you'd think Paul would know a bit about music, or have a decent record collection. About all he's got is party music, and a few token classics. God knows why, but he's got two LPs of the band of the Coldstream Guards. He can *talk* about anyone you like, Bach, Berg and Bartók, and he gets carried away about modern jazz, but he hasn't any records and he can't read a note let alone play an instrument.'

'If there is one thing Hanka can do, it is talk,' Mrs Hanka said, sitting back in her chair, looking relieved at Lucy's picture of Paul Salmon as shallow. 'I can rely on my Alois to explain to Mr Salmon everything that he needs to know.'

'I wouldn't be too sure,' Lucy said. 'Paul has contacts in Germany, and they've unearthed an old German propaganda film from some archive or other.' A tremor of fright showed on Mrs Hanka's face, followed quickly by a deliberately impassive stare. 'It's obviously your husband on the film conducting a German Army orchestra. When he acknowledges the applause, takes a bow and accepts the flowers, he looks as if he's enjoying it. I've seen it and it doesn't look good.'

'And it didn't feel good at the time,' the old woman said fiercely.

Mrs Hanka fidgeted in her chair. She put down her sherry glass and pulled a handkerchief from her sleeve. Wiping the sticky wine from her fingers looked like the action of a woman who was used to keeping her self-control, or retrieving its temporary loss through an act of calculated fastidiousness.

'I didn't mean to upset you, but I felt that you ought to know.'

'Why apologize to me? You weren't even born!'

'If he was *forced* to work for the Germans, then why doesn't he say it?' Lucy asked as Mrs Hanka dabbed at the smallest of tears with her handkerchief.

Very few people knew the real reason why Alois Hanka accepted the invitation of the German authorities in Prague and conducted and directed what started out as a joint Czech-German orchestra. Gradually, the Czech musicians dwindled in numbers. After only a month, no German civilian players remained, and the entire ensemble consisted of musicians in uniform.

'Because I made you guess that he did not want to work for them, does not mean that he was forced, Miss Williams,' Mrs Hanka said with difficulty.

'I don't understand.'

'It was a cultural lie. It was to look good. It was to look friendly. But they didn't mean it, and neither did Alois. I shall tell what happened. Alois is not proud of his secret.'

'But people have known for years,' Lucy said.

'I mean why he worked for them, not just that he did. What he is saying to Mr Salmon, I don't know; but I am tired of all this silence. Alois would like people to believe that because only music was involved, then there was no harm. Maybe he used to believe it himself, but I think he is tired of it, too. I am not Czech, you see, although I had citizenship there, from not long after I married Alois. My father was Austrian, my mother came from East Prussia, which is where they lived, although I was born in Vienna. Our home was in East Prussia. I met Hanka in Vienna. He wasn't a Nazi, he was never a Nazi, nor was I ever a Nazi. After we were married, 12 November 1935, we went to Prague – Hanka's city, his home, and I loved it. I was happy there. We kept it quiet that I was really a German. I did not *claim* to be anything else, but when I got my Czechoslovakian papers, I was proud. My father, you see – *he* was a Nazi – more German than the Germans, because of my mother, and her family, and business. Alois? He despised all politics. When we met, he didn't like me too much at first, because I said I was thinking of becoming a Communist; but I never did, you see, because of Hanka. After Czechoslovakia is occupied, then the war, the German authorities discover who I am, my family, my father, my mother; and they ask Hanka to work for them. He had a name as a composer and a conductor. His early compositions were admired. Not the most famous, but everyone respected him … He was talked about. People liked him. He knows what they know about me and so he accepts. He knows because they told him, but they don't say anything about what might happen to me, or to Alois, if he refuses. Alois asks them, but all they do is smile. I said to him, "No, never!" He says, "Why not, it's harmless?" But he made an arrangement with them. They stop thinking of Hanka's wife as a traitor German, a woman who hates her mother and father. So, you see, the shame is mine. Hanka did it to save me, but he tells no one. Instead, he says: "I wave a little stick, I keep time, I tell when the cellos come in. What's wrong with that?" And I still nag him, and I indulge in little extravagances that he says we can't afford, even now, when we can. "I am a soldier in the army of St Cecilia!" he says, but he doesn't know how stupid he makes himself seem, Miss Williams. Because of me, he has this terrible thing on his conscience. And now you'll tell your Mr Salmon, although if I took a whole day to explain, if we talk for a week, you will not understand,' Mrs Hanka said with cold passion.

'I won't tell Paul if you don't want me to,' Lucy said.

In the garden, Paul Salmon turned up the collar of his coat against the weather, wishing that he was inside by the fire. Hanka said, 'You say you'll give me fair play? There's no such thing! In the twentieth century?' he said, shrill with theatrical disbelief.

'I can't turn my back on the evidence,' Salmon said petulantly. 'As well as the old archive footage, we've even found a list of officers invited to one of the concerts.'

'*I* didn't invite them!'

'Five of them were convicted as war criminals,' Salmon stated.

'So? The man who shot Abraham Lincoln in the theatre was guilty – but they didn't execute the cast, did they? Did they hang the leading lady? Did they shoot the author? Maybe you want to dig up Mozart's bones and burn them?'

'But you performed the concerts,' Salmon said, exasperated with Hanka's refusals to submit to how damaging the evidence would look on the screen.

'Fiddlers played in the cafés the German soldiers went to, but nobody branded them as traitors!'

'That isn't the same thing, and you know it,' Salmon said, risking the sound of anger. 'All over Europe, artists, of one kind or another, didn't wait to find out what the Germans might ask them to do. They got away. They went abroad. Those who stayed, many of them, most of them, refused to have anything to do with the Nazis. Some of them suffered for it.'

'I am so very sorry – I am guilty of being alive. Forgive me, Mr Salmon, for not being dead. My own music was forbidden by the German authorities, you know. I used to play it in my head. I knew other composers who did the same. No one has forbidden my music in this country, or anywhere else, but it isn't played! I have no children and I have no philosophies – that's me, Hanka. Does it matter to your film that I wash the dishes? That I have always been faithful to my wife? No? Ah, poor Webern!'

'Webern...?'

'Do you like Webern's music?'

'No, not a lot, some, but...' Salmon was caught off-balance by Hanka's sudden change of direction. His discomfort was worsened by Hanka's closeness to him, the challenging earnestness with which the composer stared at him.

'He was shot by an American soldier who thought he was a blackmarketeer making his escape! And he wasn't. He was Anton Webern! He was modern music with a bullet in his back. Poor Anton! And that poor soldier! Even if all the music he knew was his own whistle, what a responsibility!'

'So, what was said?' Mrs Hanka asked in the hall, where her husband sat on a stool and his wife helped him off with his heavy outdoor shoes.

'You've heard of British fair play, this thing the world has never seen? Mr Salmon is full of it – promises, you never heard such promises! But his worst fault it banality, and after that comes ignorance. He knows as much about music as a rabbit.'

'Mr Salmon is a divorced person, aged thirty-six, and Miss Lucy Williams sleeps with him,' Mrs Hanka said. 'She is so nice, Alois, but she is not a happy woman. She told me that her Mr Salmon knows nothing about music.'

'What else did you talk about, other than who is sleeping with who?'

'About you, Alois; and about me. I told her the truth, but I trust her, and she will not tell her Mr Salmon.'

'The goody-goodies, they'll be coming in the windows! Ah, no, what have you done, Eva?'

'Shh. Not so loud,' she said. 'I have lived with my shame for a long time, Alois. We're old now. What harm can it do to tell the truth? Don't let me die ashamed, Alois.'

'But they'll *make* you feel guilty,' Hanka said.

'I did not want to do it. Did I ask? Did I plead with you for my life?'

'You stupid, brave woman, you would have done anything to have stopped me working for them. You were ashamed of *me*, for working to save you, and you were ashamed of yourself for being German, for something you couldn't help. I took your shame away from you, Eva! I waved the historical wand, I played the political piano, but all the time I was saying, "No, no, no!" Maybe you're too German to understand that "No" can be in your heart but not in your mouth.' He stood up. 'She'll tell him. If she sleeps with him, she'll tell him,' Hanka said. 'Who'll understand? No one!'

'It doesn't matter,' his wife said, smartening the sleeve of his jacket. 'I could not have asked you to work for them to save me. I could not have asked it, and did not need to. Can you imagine how much I have cherished what you did for me, and yet how I have hated myself that it was because of me that you had to make that choice? That is why I feel so guilty. You made yourself look like the enemy of so many people, because of me, not because of music.'

Paul Salmon stood before the fire, warming himself and looking displeased. He had been annoyed by Lucy's refusal to tell him what she had been talking about with Mrs Hanka.

'Go on, you can tell him!' Hanka shouted to the young woman as he walked past her on his way to the dining room. 'Tell him now, because he can't wait, then come and eat!'

Mrs Hanka followed her husband. She turned and opened her arms to Lucy Williams, and shrugged, as if to say, 'That man, Hanka, what am I to do with him?'

Thomas Healy

from *It Might Have Been Jerusalem*

It was a sawdust floor and red cheap wine. The barman was a beefy guy with his sleeves rolled up and tattoos on his arms. Rab admired them. He had often thought of a tattoo himself. A touch of manliness. Tattooed men were most manly.

Winnie sat in the far corner of the pub; a twilighted place and the sawdust thick for the feel of sand.

'A dump,' she said.

'It's handy, is a'.'

'But the wine's not bad.'

Rab looked at her glass, wine red as blood, for they did not in this place sell gin and tonic. 'They call it Dragon's,' he said.

Winnie made a face but drank it down. Greedily. Rab raised his eyebrows but, at least (Winnie's drooth, it must be the dust beneath the bed) the stuff was cheap.

'How did ye find me?'

'I traced ye back tae the dairy – ye know, the place ye worked when ye were a boy.'

'That was clever.'

'I got yer second name and it was easy after that.'

Rab looked at Winnie's empty glass. 'My throat's full of stoor,' she said.

'Ye don't want a beer?'

'Another wine. They gie ye a lot of wine in here, I'll say that for this pub.'

Rab went up to the bar.

'Another wine and beer, Stick?'

'Only the wine.' Rab felt bagged by what beer he had already drank and he did not like the nickname. The beefy tattooed barman. He looked a bruiser but was free with the wine, a half pint glass and sloshing over. 'That'll put some hair on her tits,' he said.

Rab paid his money and took Winnie's wine; he spilled a little, feeling so skinny: his trousers flapped around his legs and he should be out?

Winnie asked, 'Ye feel okay?'

'A wee bit light.'

'Ye looked a wee bit shaky at the bar.'

'I'm okay,' Rab said. But he had small taste for the bagging beer and wished to have bought himself a wine. The stuff, one glass, had put new sparkle in her eyes, good to laugh, it worked a treat with Winnie.

'Still it's good that ye're out,' she said, a swallow of her wine. 'It shows that ye're getting better.'

'I suppose,' Rab said, but he hardly felt the better; not, with hobo drinkers, they looked at him and the tattooed barman called him Stick.

It was enough for Rab, a sip of Winnie's wine.

'Ye like it?' Winnie asked.

Rab thought a hint of metal. 'But I don't like that barman,' he said.

Winnie looked. 'He's just a big fattie,' she said and laughed; a shade too loudly, a lot too widely, so that the fit of her dentures showed. 'Don't worry about him.'

'I'm not worried,' Rab said. 'At least not about him.'

'That doctor, she said that ye worry too much.'

'I was worried about ye.'

Winnie's hand caressed Rab's thigh.

'I thought tae have lost ye.'

'But I'm back again,' Winnie said.

'If I could,' Rab said, 'if I was fit enough I'd ask ye we run away the night.'

'I'd go.'

'Ye would?'

'Just ask me.'

'*If* I was fit enough.'

'Ye'll soon be fit again.'

'I have ye back,' Rab said, 'I think I will.'

'And quicker than ye know,' Winnie enthused. Her face was flushed and her eyes were bright, as burning with a fierce love. 'We'll hit the high spots, ye and me.'

'Ye bet,' Rab said, 'we will.'

Winnie pecked him on the cheek.

'A right couple of lovebirds yous are,' a tall tramp said. He stood swaying and a jug of wine. Looking at Winnie. 'Ye might kill him, hen.'

'I'll kill ye.' A ragamuffin woman, his mate, a dung-like waft, appeared to pull the tramp away. 'He gets a bit of wine in him,' she avoided Rab, a look at Winnie who looked to scratch her eyes out. 'I'm awful sorry.'

'I'm sorry tae,' the man said. He produced a dirty horny hand. 'Shake on it.'

But the woman, not so drunk, seeing the protective Winnie, cuffed his head and hustled him away.

'Phew,' Rab said. He held his nose. 'She smells like a fucking stable.'

'I don't like,' Winnie said, 'people poking their faces in where it doesn't concern them.'

'It's that I'm so skinny,' Rab said.

'But they'll not take advantage,' Winnie said. 'Not if I'm with ye.'

Rab thought (the barman) that it better Winnie went, for a couple more wines.

'I'll treat,' Winnie said.

Rab rolled a smoke while Winnie was at the bar. This dive of bums, the drunkards of Wine Alley. But early yet and a kind of hush, just scattered bodies here and there and a rag-glad snore on the floor, in the sawdust.

Winnie returned with the wines. 'It's a good full measure,' she said. 'I've never known a place where ye get so much wine.'

'Did *he* say anything?'

'Who?'

'The barman.'

'Naw. Should he?'

'I just wondered.'

'He never said a word.'

Rab drank his wine, a good, a manly, swallow to almost drain his glass. The half pint tumbler. The stuff spun his head, he felt his hair: an instant sprout, so that he sat a half-inch taller.

'Ye want another?' Winnie asked, Rab's empty glass.

'Why not?' Rab shrugged his shoulders. They felt not so slender nor fragile now. 'But don't speak tae that barman.'

'Ye don't like him?'

'He called me Stick.'

'But ye *are* thin, Rab.'

'He could have called me Slim.'

'It's something the same.'

'It's nothing the same,' Rab said. He was about to explain, how a whoremaster in Glasgow slang, was referred to as a stickman, when Winnie said, 'I think I understand.'

'Just don't speak tae him.'

'I won't.'

While Winnie was away Rab sneaked a drink of her wine. It did not taste so metallic now, rather he thought quite juicy. And it had lifted him all right, and not his hair alone. Rab a whole new confidence; the miserable wretch, like a cowardly freak, had tip-toed into this place. Indeed he almost felt for music, wild dancing now; Winnie returned, with two wines, which was just as well as Rab had all but drained her glass.

'He said nothing?'

'Not a dicky bird.' Winnie looked at Rab. 'I think he knew better.'

The wine was sticky on Rab's fingers, tackety stuff; but it wormed a treat his head. Rab was beginning to enjoy himself. It was, sitting in the pub, with Winnie, like old times again. So long ago. Aeons past his nightmare. 'Ye're a real wee smasher,' he told her. 'Ye don't know how ye've cheered me up.'

Winnie flushed her pleasure. Her sham teeth gleamed. Some sweat on her brow. As a soft dew. Rab felt to lick it off but the time, the place, was wrong; a dump like this, it was hard to be anything, anyway romantic. This drunken night. It was fast becoming. How Rab sat, his weakened state; his first night out, and he thought to be seeing things.

The pub had filled considerably; the swiftest time, a squeeze at the bar, a fight for wine, when, casually, almost dead centre in the sawdust floor, the rag-glad snore had risen up and lowered down his trousers. Rab held Winnie's hand. The drinkers, drunk as they were, full of glasses of wine, fell back from the man, who, with the rags he wore, had surprisingly clean white underpants – what *struck* Rab – raised his coat and squatted down as the most natural thing in the world.

There was a silence in the pub. The man. A held audience. He went about his business.

Then a sudden roar of rage: the beefy tattooed barman. He burst through the drinkers, but too late his swinging foot; a mighty kick that raised the man, who was a scrawny fellow, withered haunches, a good foot in the air. A cat-like squeal. He landed on all fours. The pub stood back in silence. The burly barman, it might be he was once a footballer; he booted the man up and down and up and down and out into the street.

'It must be why they've sawdust,' Winnie observed.

'He'll have a sore arse in the morning,' Rab said.

A barmaid emerged with a brush and shovel.

Rab began to laugh. It was quite the funniest thing – all of it, the squeals from the man, the sounds of a cat – that he had ever seen. But the rest of the pub, the drinkers; they downed their wine, the incident seemed forgotten.

'Ye don't think it happens often?' Winnie asked.

But Rab could not speak for laughing. A convulsive fit so that his thin frame shook. How the guy had squealed. Kicked out like a cat. But such contempt. A true 'fuck you' and if only he had fought. It would, to Rab, be an heroic deed if the man had fought. But how it was – he booted out, thumping kicks, as a squealing cat – it was turned into a farce. 'I've never seen nothing like it,' he said.

'And I don't want tae see nothing like it again,' Winnie said. 'The dirty thing.'

The barmaid poured some disinfectant. It smelled strongly of pine. At the far end of the bar a fight broke out, and again the tattooed barman. He appeared to have a talent for leaping the counter. This time with a club, what looked like an Irish shillelagh. But the fight broke of its own accord. There was nobody booted, or clubbed, out. The barman, a big fat arse, with what must be a practised vault of the bar, was again serving wine.

'But it's only winos he's dealing with,' Rab said. 'If a real man walked in he'd soon dance another tune.'

Winnie agreed. What else? But she was not so sure that Rab was right. The barman looked tough enough to her. She had heard his boot and roaring oaths.

'It's nothing tae dae wie us,' she said.

'But if a real man *did* walk in.'

'He would need tae be a *fit* real man,' Winnie said.

At that very instant, as Winnie spoke, the barman leapt the bar again.

'He's a big bully,' a woman told Rab. 'Just look at him.'

Rab did. Look. The energetic barman. This time, and for no apparent reason, the grip of a woman by the hair of her head. A peculiar hold. As hefting her out on his back. The woman up in the air, screaming by her pigtails.

'Why did he dae that?' Rab was honestly astounded; the caveman heave, and what, in this place, had gone before.

'She must hiv tried tae steal another body's wine,' the woman, a greasy looking hag, told him.

'He stands nae nonsense then,' Rab said.

'Ye don't think we should go?' Winnie asked.

'We'll have another wine.'

'Ye really think we should?'

'I'll go get them,' Rab offered.

But Winnie was already on her feet.

'She's yer mammy?' the hag asked Rab.

'Ye'd better not let her hear that.'

'Then it's as well that she's not here.'

The woman – Rab, with the wine, and so took-on with the barman, had not noticed her before – sat across from him, over a small, square tin-topped table. 'I should watch my mouth,' she said.

'It would be wise,' Rab said, a look at her head; the length of her hair. 'She's my lover.'

'And a fine figure of a woman tae.'

Rab lit a roll-up. The barman was back (a leap) at his station behind the bar, as if nothing had happened.

'Even if she had stole some wine,' Rab said.

'Ye don't know the half of it,' the woman said. 'Just look what he done tae Paddy.'

'He biffed me on the nose,' Paddy said.

'I kin see that,' Rab said. Paddy's nose, the bridge was smashed giving an upward tilt and a hog-like look.

'His fist did that?'

'One punch,' said Paddy, rather proudly.

Rab swallowed Winnie's wine. He would not want a nose like that. And Paddy looked a husky, strong guy. He had big rough hairy hands. 'Then he must be even stronger than he looks,' Rab said. 'He gave ye a snout like that.'

'And Paddy with only the one leg tae,' the woman said.

'It takes away the balance,' Paddy said. 'It's hard tae fight if ye have only one leg.'

'The fucking craw,' Rab said.

'Who?' Winnie asked.

'That barman.'

'I wish ye would forget him, Rab.'

'We were talking about Paddy,' the woman said.

'Look at his nose,' Rab said. 'Ye could go out for yer Halloween wie a snout like yon.'

'I think we should go, Rab.'

'We're going tae run away,' Rab told the woman. 'Winnie and me.'

'Yous are?'

'Tae London.'

'That's dead romantic,' the woman said. 'I always wished I'd been in love and run away when I was young.'

Winnie smiled: but sadly. 'Rab has not been well,' she said.

'Otherwise we might have been in London,' Rab said.

'Ye look a bit skinny,' the woman said. 'But then ye know what they say, the lean hungry ones.'

'He's skinny okay,' Paddy said. 'Do ye eat at all?' he asked Rab.

'I bet,' the woman said, 'he eats like a wolf.'

Rab, this talk about him, his complaint, wondered, the pair, were they trying to be funny? But, dear Christ, they could hardly talk: Paddy with his bashed-in nose, the look of a hog and a missing leg; and the woman – his wife? – she was lucky for even a guy like him.

Winnie – she was half seas over; so that her teeth were loose and her speech was slurred – said, 'Rab's right sensitive about his health, so he is. He used tae be a real fine build of a man.'

'But I got sick,' Rab said.

'My name is Pol,' the woman said.

'He nearly died,' Winnie said.

'I kin believe that,' Paddy said. 'He gave me a fright the look of him.'

Rab bristled, the hog-like bum. 'Have ye ever looked in a mirror?' he asked.

'Now. Now,' Pol said. 'We're all friends here. We don't want tae fight now, dae we?'

'That depends on him,' Rab declared, emboldened by the wine, and Paddy had only one leg.

'I told yous,' Winnie said, 'Rab's right sensitive.'

'And he's a right tae be,' Pol agreed. 'It's Paddy was in the wrong.'

'He was going tae go for the barman,' Winnie said, 'he thought that he insulted him.'

'I was in the wrong,' Paddy said.

'He might be a sick man, but he's proud. He didn't even want tae come out; he tried tae hide away he is so proud.'

'He was going tae got for Big Lurch?'

'If he's the barmen,' Winnie said, 'too true he was.'

Rab looked at Paddy's nose. He was? It demanded a taste of the wine.

'He looks like ye could blow him away tae,' Pol said. Then no wish to offend. 'But looks kin be deceiving.'

'Better him than me,' Paddy said.

'I told ye, the lean hungry ones,' Pol said. 'A skinny man will always beat a fattie.'

'Big Lurch is a beefy bastard,' Rab said, and quite loudly; this was him they were speaking about?

'Shoo,' Pol said. 'We all know he is but it's better we keep it quiet.'

At the bar a group of dossers began singing *Roaming in the Gloaming.*

'*Wie a lassie by yer side,*' Paddy chorused. 'But I'll never go roaming in the gloaming again,' he said.

'What happened tae yer leg?' Winnie asked.

'A lion bit it off,' Pol said. She nodded her head for emphasis. 'We're really gipsies, Paddy and me. It was the circus life for us. We went everywhere wie the circus. Everywhere.' Her head nodded again. It might be the help the wine. 'All over the world.'

'Only Europe,' Paddy said. 'But we were going tae South America; tae Brazil, when I got my leg bit off. Raja, that was the name of the beast. I'll never forget that one. Don't never think animals don't know.' Paddy drank some wine. 'Raja had it in for me and just waited its time. The bastard knew when I took a drink. It knew the nights when I was more drunk than others and the first time that I turned my back.' Paddy made a gnashing gesture; he had a few brown nail-like teeth. 'I wouldn't have turned my back only I was drunk.'

'How had it in for ye?' Rab asked.

'It thought that I'd sold its mate. Sheeba. The two of them was mates since cubs. She was one fine lion and I don't blame Raja, only it wasn't me. I even begged the circus owner not tae sell her. But he laughed at me. He didn't know lions and it wasn't him had tae go inside the cage. I didn't like it but I needed the money – the bastard threatened tae evict us from our caravan if I wouldn't train the lions – and I was scared of Raja and it knew I was scared and I got drunk and drunker and' – Paddy held his crutch aloft – 'ye see what happened.'

'I warned him,' Pol said. 'I warned him time and again – he got sometimes so drunk they had tae carry him inside the cage – but what kin ye dae wie a man that won't listen?'

'Is this all true,' Rab asked, engrossed by the story, yous two in a circus?'

'But I wished it wasn't,' Paddy said.

'I bet ye dae.'

'I still get nightmares.'

'He wakes up screaming,' Pol said, 'sometimes in the middle of the night.'

'Ye want tae be a man about it,' Rab rebuked Paddy. 'So ye lost yer leg, so what? It's no big deal – screaming like a sissy.'

Rab drank some wine. It was good stuff. He felt never so manly, tough; and he did not notice the look in Paddy's eyes nor the feel of Winnie tug his sleeve.

*

Anton, he lay over the rim of the pan; panting, thoroughly wretched, ruined. Spoiled. It would take a long, long time to heal, if ever. This violation. Mortification. And he could never tell no one what had happened. Not, scared beyond belief, the whole thing beyond belief, a cock rammed down his throat.

He felt bruised and battered, the edges of his mouth; his throat hurt, worse than worthless. That he might die, he did not much care, not, as he lay, and without protest, after what had already happened.

The foreman still with a mighty, a gigantic, hard-on; his victory complete, or almost. The naked, yielding boy. How he had *made* him. Parker felt to beat his chest. A warrior. There was blood enough, a tremendous battle. It drenched the prize, his skin; smooth belly and thighs, for all the more exciting.

Parker wished more time, more, with the boy; this almost crucifixion, to feast his eyes. But too long already; the fearful chance that he be discovered.

Anton levered, with his hands, the sides the pan; the attempt to rise.

Parker pushed him down. Easily. Contemptuously. The heel of his hand on Anton's forehead. 'Ye don't think it's finished yet,' he said. 'I'm going tae fuck ye proper.'

Anton's eyes widened.

'Up the arse,' Parker said. 'Ye've never been fucked before, I don't think.'

Anton pressed his thighs together.

'Ye don't think that'll help,' Parker said. 'Ye'll just get hurt some more.'

'If ye let me go now,' Anton said, 'I won't tell anybody.'

'But ye'll still not tell anybody after I've fucked ye.'

Anton, in this cubicle, stuck time, it seemed as a hundred years, the boy; he was surprised *how* innocent, trusting – for he saw it all so clearly now, Parker's mask – he once had been.

'I've fancied ye rotten,' Parker said, 'all the time, since ever I first saw ye.'

'*Please* let me go.'

'After.'

'I'll shout.'

'I don't think so.' Parker daubed his eye (the blood appeared no worse, but a steady, it must be an annoying, trickle) with the tail of his shirt. 'And I don't want ye tae struggle. Yer arse'll rip – have ye ever heard of a torn arse? – if ye even try and struggle.'

Anton lay sprawled out, his thighs still closed.

Parker said, almost as a dentist might to a tearful fearful patient. 'We don't want that, now, dae we?'

He stood over Anton, big; his bloated belly, as heavy as a sumo wrestler.

'I want ye to turn over.'

The cock; always that – he would never forget it. Its tilt and thrust, throb, full of veins, the purpled plum-like head.

'Come on. Come on,' Parker said, pulling at him. 'Who knows ye might even get tae like it.'

Anton, he was half-way up and, by Parker's hands, half turned over, *his* meat; he felt more a lump of mutton, sobbing like a baby.

He *felt* a baby; helpless, wet and dirty in the cradle.

Parker punched his head to shut him up. An almost reflex action. He was now so used to hitting the boy.

With the blow on his head, Anton saw stars; flashing, exploding in his eyes: blue and red and colours he had not known existed.

He began again to give some fight, so acquiescent, afraid till then; a new hot rage and hatred.

His ears burned hot; the exploding stars, he could almost smell the singe, hear the crackle; seeing colours never seen, for, in his agony, caught in shock, screaming his tortured soul, he swung out on a new dimension.

He tried to rise, his full height; to face Parker, for now he had no intention of turning over, but the foreman, a first alarm, felt a coldness, and punched him down.

It was the first, all the time, in the cubicle, the lavatory, that Parker took a backward step.

He forced though – even if going back; the sheer weight of his blows – Anton down on his hands and knees. But still coming in, and so gone that he did not feel the punches. This man had dragged, shifted him a million years, more wolf than human. Wrecked and wretched. Hurt so much that he could be hurt no more.

To Parker, it was, from a lovely yielding boy, to a demon sprung against him.

He backed to the door, a jelly of fright. This sudden swing, forceful as a storm; the boy, gnashing teeth, snapping as an animal.

Parker, his punches did not work, and he punched Anton's back; resounding blows, and the back of his neck with all his might, the attempt to push him down.

But the boy was too quick, too sweat-wet slippery he could not gain a purchase: use his weight. What had gone wrong? A blink from a monster victory now threatening disaster. And he would have run, he could; even, shamelessly, in his shirt-tail as he was. But he had blocked the door. What he had thought protection. The boy – such stupendous change – gnashing, hands as claws and teeth as fangs for already he was bitten and bleeding.

Anton, his rolling bobbing head, in and out; and his mouth was ghastly, streaming blood and he bit at random, where he could; a cannibal feast, and there seemed no end to Parker, elephant big, but soft and white and easy to bleed, full of smells; he could, heightened senses, whiff the slightest reek, the ebb and flow, as might a jackal, the strength drawn out of Parker.

'I don't need tae take his lip, a skinny fucker like him.'

'He meant nae harm,' Winnie said.

'Calling me a sissy.'

'But ye dae scream, Paddy,' Pol said.

Rab said, 'I don't think ye were a lion tamer either.'

'I'll fucking tame you,' Paddy said, and he knocked over the table in his attempt to rise.

The ruckus brought the barman, a swing-like vault, on his fingertips, over the top of the bar.

Rab said, '*He* might have worked in a circus.'

'He's wie ye,' the barman looked at Winnie.

'But it wasn't him,' Winnie said, she looked to the upturned table. 'We were only in for a quiet drink, is a'.'

Paddy said, 'He's been insulting me a' night.'

'So he has,' Pol said. 'I don't know who he think he is.'

'My name is Rab.'

'He's drunk,' Winnie said, looking at the barman. 'Ye see, he's been sick in bed and he shouldn't really be drinking.'

And indeed Rab shouldn't for, in mortal danger, that all could see but him, he began to laugh. 'A fucking lion tamer,' he said, looking at Paddy, 'ye couldn't tame a pussy cat.'

Paddy rose, his crutch aloft. 'I'm mighty handy wie this auld pal when I've a need tae be,' he said.

'Sit down, Mick,' the barman said. He looked at Rab. 'How did ye mean, I might have worked in a circus?'

'Because,' Winnie said, very smartly, 'of the way ye leap the counter.'

Rab was about to say, the barman, in the fucking monkey house, but Winnie cut him off: 'We'll be pleased tae pay the damage,' she said.

'Yous will?'

'And buy us all a drink. Yerself included of course.'

'That's the ticket,' Pol said.

'Good on yer,' Paddy said, and stamped his crutch. 'It was all just a wee misunderstanding.'

The barman, a long hard look at Rab; it was? Still the dame was smart, she had saved his hide; bought him out, the crack about the circus; a stay – if he was lucky, the look of him – in intensive care in the hospital. 'Four pounds,' he said, 'the damage. And I drink whisky.'

Winnie held him a five pound note.

'But it wasn't me,' Rab said, he saw the money; four pounds for what? The tin-topped table good as new and nothing, not even a tumbler, broken. 'I don't see how that we should pay.'

'Be quiet,' Winnie said and dug her elbow in his ribs.

'Ye'd be well advised tae listen,' the barman said to Rab. He looked at Winnie. 'I'll send the barmaid over. Four wines. And you have better watch yer friend. Any more shenanigans.'

'There'll be no more shenanigans.'

'All just a wee misunderstanding,' Paddy said.

'Ye handled him well,' Pol said; the barman, with a swing, was back behind his bar again. 'And it was worth the money, I'll tell ye that.'

'I know,' Winnie said.

Rab said, 'I still don't get it, four pounds for what?'

'Ye see my nose,' Paddy said.

'But we're running away tae London, we need all our money.'

'It was worth a broken head?' Pol asked.

'It's best,' Winnie said, 'I think, that we leave this place.'

'But first we'll drink our wine,' Rab said. 'We paid enough for it.'

'Then after the wine,' Winnie said, 'and only the one, I don't want tae be having tae carry ye out.'

'That shouldn't be tae hard,' Paddy said.

But the remark was lost on Rab. He was still bemused about the money. But if Winnie didn't mind then why should he? It could be, there might be a lot more where that came from. The thought cheered Rab. He was drunk for sure and unafraid, of the barman, Paddy's crutch, but still a miser's eye for money.

The barmaid – a fresh young girl for such a den, perhaps (a true contender) the crudest pub in Glasgow – came over with their wines.

Pol said, 'She's Big Lurch's fancy bit.'

'She is?' Winnie sipped her wine. It was the bold tipple. No wonder that Rab was drunk. For Winnie herself, it required the tightest hold, the fumes of the stuff, to keep her wits about her. One close call the barman. You could, for nothing, real or imagined, the slightest slight, get crippled in a place like this. It was madness they had stayed, drank still, and deeply, of the heady wine. 'He buys her lots of pretties,' Pol said. 'Bangles and beads and rings and things.'

'He would need tae, wouldn't he?' Winnie determined to elbow the company. They had caused nothing but trouble, a five pound note.

'This is awful good of ye, treating us a wine.'

'Yous kin treat us back,' Rab said.

'We're going,' Winnie said.

Rab said, his head on Winnie's shoulder, 'We're running away tae London, so we are.'

'Yous must have been saving up.'

'Aye,' Paddy said, looking at Winnie, 'ye must have a right fat purse tae be going away tae London.'

Winnie, she did not like the sound of this; the pair, who, with the help of the wine and the need for more, felt fit to hint, to (she saw Pol's eyes, black and hard) almost threaten.

'We have a wee bit put aside. In the bank.'

'But I think there's still another wee bit in yer purse.' Pol smiled. 'Don't worry, we're poor folks but we're honest.'

Paddy drained his glass, and, not a word, Rab almost asleep, his wine untouched, he drained that too.

Winnie said, 'That's one ye owe me.'

'Now don't be mean,' Pol said, 'and where would the likes of us be getting any money?'

'Not out of me,' Winnie said, her dander up, 'if that's what yous are thinking.'

Out on the floor, on the sawdust, some revellers, in jaunty rags, were forming a circle. A dance. Rab opened his eyes: 'What's this?' he asked.

Winnie said, 'We're leaving.'

'How?'

'We never done nothing,' Paddy said.

'I thought that we all were friends,' Pol said.

'We was only trying,' Paddy said. 'Ye can't blame us for trying.'

'Trying what?' Rab asked.

'It doesn't master,' Winnie said.

'Tee cadge a couple of drinks,' Paddy said, 'that's what we was trying.'

'Nae harm in that,' Rab said. He looked down at his empty glass. 'I could go another myself,' he said.

'But ye promised it was the last,' Winnie said, the drunken Rab; and she could have pulled her hair and needed a pee but was frightened to leave Rab alone. God knew what would happen. Paddy's crutch or Big Lurch and his shillelagh. It was nothing, this reunion, for what she had imagined.

'Who'll come in tae ma wee hoose, tae ma wee hoose tae ma wee hoose; for who'll come in tae ma wee hoose and make it a wee bit bigger?'

The circle; arms linked, a rag-tag lot, shuffled round, some kicks and whoops, and, Winnie, enough of it, this wild place, a pair of mooching vagabonds, hustled Rab up on his feet, surprised anew by his lightness; as a bird, for she was not strong, but his fragility (he could barely stand) gave the illusion of an amazon. But, for Winnie, it was only that, illusion, for, when she tried to move, she was a stuck; skunk-drunk with the wine, it struck her as a hammer, and caught in the circle, the linking arms, soon both she and Rab were dancing. Whirling. A merry jig. Round and round. Kicking and whooping. The night gone mad to soon be madder. The unhinged wine. Bamboozling. Treating Pol and Paddy. And she must have had five pees or six. Rab slept and danced. Paddy rolled his smokes for him. He spoke of ribs and cabbage. Big Lurch smiled on indulgently. He liked this; what his pub was all about, for people to let their hair down. Enough of his wine and the Pope would dance, swing his kilt – or whatever he wore – and clap his hands.

Winnie and Rab, whatever else; the sloshing wine, they kicked and whooped the party, it was not a night to be forgotten.

Tom Leonard

Honest

A canny even remembir thi furst thing a remembir. Whit a mean iz, a remembir aboot four hunner thingz, awit wance. Trouble iz tay, a remembir thim aw thi time.

A thinka must be gon aff ma nut. Av ey thoat that though – leasta always seemti be thinkin, either am jist aboot ti go aff ma nut, or else am already affit. But yi ey think, ach well, wance yir aff yir nut, yill no no yiraffit. But am no so sure. A wish a wuz.

Even jist sitn doonin writn. A ey useti think, whenever a felt like writn sumhm, that that wiz awright, aw yi hud to say wuz, ach well, a think ahl sit doonin write sumhm, nyi jiss sat doonin wrote it. But no noo, naw. A canny even day that for five minutes, but ahl sitnlookit thi thing, nthink, here, sumdayz wrote that afore. Then ahl go, hawlin aw thi books ootma cupboard, trynti find out hooit wuz. Nwhither a find out or no, it takes me that long luknfurit, a canny be bothird writn any mair, wance av stoapt. An anyway, a tend ti think, if it's wan a they thingz that *might* uv been writn before, there's no much point in writin it again, even if naibdy actually huz, is there?

It's annoyin – a feel av got this big story buldn up inside me, n ivri day ahl sit down, good, here it comes, only it dizny come at all. Nthi thing iz, it's Noah's if a even no what thi story's goany be about, coz a doant. So a thinkty ma cell, jist invent sumdy, write a story about a fisherman or sumhm. But thi longer a think, thi mair a realise a canny be *bothird* writn aboota fisherman. Whut wid a wahnti write about a fisherman fur? N am no gonny go downti thi library, nsay, huvyi enny booksn fishermen, jiss so's a can go nread up about thim, then go n write another wan. Hoo *wahntsti* read a story about fishermen anyway, apart fray people that wid read it, so's they could go n write another wan, or fishermen that read? A suppose right enough, thi trick might be, that yi cin write a story about a fisherman, so long as thi main thing iz, that thi bloke izny a fisherman, but a man that fishes. Or maybe that izny right at all, a widny no. But a do no, that as soon as a lookt up thi map ti see what might be a good name furra fishn village, nthen maybe went a walk ti think up a good name for a fisherman's boat, nthen a sat nworked out what age thi fisherman should be, nhow tall he wuz, nwhat colour his oilskins were, nthen gotim wokn iniz oilskins, doon frae thi village tay iz boat, ad tend ti think, whut duzzy wahnti day that fur? Kinni no day sumhm else wayiz time? Aniffa didny think that ti masell, if a jiss letm go, ach well, it's iz job, away out ti sea, ana big storm in chapter two, ahd tend ti think, either, here, sumdyz wrote that before, or, can a no day sumhm else wi ma time? An in fact, if a came across sumdy sitn readn it eftir a did write it, if a hud, ad tend ti thinkty ma cell, huv *they* got nuthn behtr ti day wi their time?

A don't no that am sayn whut a mean. But a suppose underneath everythin, thi only person a want ti write about, iz *me*. It's about time a wrote sumhm aboot masell! But whut? Ah thought even, ach well, jist write doon a lohta yir memories, then maybe they'll take some kinda shape, anyi kin use that ti write a story wi, or a play, or a poem, or a film-script, or God only knows whut, on thi fly. So that's whuta did. Didny mahtr thi order, jist day eftir day, writn doon ma memories. N ad be busy writn it, thinkin, whut an incredible life av hud, even upti noo. Then ad be thinkin, they'll no believe aw this hapnd ti me. Then a looktitit, najistaboot threw up. It wiz nuthin ti day wi me at all. Nthi other people ad be writin about, thi people ad met an that, it wuz nuthin ti day wi them either. It might eveniv been awright, if you coulda said it was about me nthem meetin, but you couldny even say that. It wiz jist a lohta flamin words.

But that's sumhm else. Yi write doon a wurd, nyi sayti yirsell, that's no thi way a say it. Nif yi tryti write it doon thi way yi say it, yi end up wi thi page covered in letters stuck thigithir, nwee dots above hof thi letters, in fact, yi end up wi wanna they thingz yid needti huv took a course in phonetics ti be able ti read. But that's no thi way a *think*, as if ad took a course in phonetics. A doant mean that emdy that's done phonetics canny think right – it's no a questiona right or wrong. But ifyi write down 'doon' wan minute, nwrite doon 'down' thi nixt, people say yir beein inconsistent. But ifyi sayti sumdy, 'Whaira yi afti?' nthey say, 'Whut?' nyou say, 'Where are you off to?' they don't say, 'That's no whutyi said thi furst time.' They'll probably say sumhm like, 'Doon thi road!' anif you say, 'What?' they usually say, 'Down the road!' the second time – though no always. Course, they never *really* say, 'Doon thi road!' or 'Down the road!' at all. Least, they never say it the way it's spelt. Coz it *izny* spelt, when they say it, is it?

A fine point, perhaps. Or maybe it izny, a widny no. Or maybe a think it is, but a also a think that if a say, 'Maybe it izny' then you'll turn it over

in your head without thinkin, 'Who does he think he is – a linguistic
philosopher?' Or maybe a widny bothir ma rump whether it's a fine point
or it izny: maybe a jist said it fur effect in thi furst place. Coz that's
sumhm that's dawned on me, though it's maybe wanna they thingz that
yir no supposed ti say. An thirz a helluv a lohta *them*, when yi think
about it, int thir? But anyway, what's dawned on me, or maybe it's jist
emergin fray ma subconscious, is, that maybe a write jist tay attract
attention ti ma cell. An that's a pretty horrible thought ti emerge fray
emdy's subconscious, coz thi nixt thing that emerges is, 'Whut um a – a
social inadequate?' N as if that izny bad enough, thi nixt thing that yi
find yirself thinkin, is, 'Am a compensatin for ma social inadequacy, "by
proxy", as it were?' An thi nixt thing, thi fourth thing, that yi find yirself
thinkin, is, 'If av committed maself, unwittingly, ti compensation "by
proxy", does that mean that a sense a inadequacy, unwittingly, huz
become a necessity?' An thi fifth, an thi sixth, an thi seventh thingz that
yi find yirself thinkin, are, 'Whut if ma compensation "by proxy" is found
socially inadequate?' and 'Ivdi's against me – a always knew it,' and
'Perhaps posterity will have better sense.'

   'Thi apprentice has lifted ma balls an cock,' said the plumber. Sorry,
that comes later. Am no sayin that these seven thoughts necessarily
come in the order in which av presented thim. Ti some people, ahl
menshin nay names, these thoughts *never* emerge fray thir subconscious,
particularly thi fifth, which is, yi can imagine, thi most terrible thought,
of thi lot. Often it turns out that thoughts six and seven are thi most
popular, though thoughts one ti five are largely ignored. But thi more yi
ignore thoughts one ti five, thi more thoughts six and seven will out. Coz
although thought five, 'Whut if ma compensation "by proxy" is found
socially inadequate?' never emerges fray yir subconscious, there comes a
day when, in a casual discussion about Literature in general, sumdy says,
'Your stuff's a lohta rubbish.' It might not even be so blunt – in fact, what
usually happens is, that in the foyer of a theatre or sumhm, an in thi
middle of a casual conversation about Literature in general, then sumdy
introduces you ti sumdy else, an thi other person says, 'Who?' An
although 'Who?' might no *sound* like a literal translation of, 'Your stuff's
a lohta rubbish,' nonetheless, in the thoughts of a social inadequate, it's
as near as dammit. So havin secretly thunk thought six, 'Ivdi's against me
– a always knew it,' yi hurry hame ti write sumhm, ti get yir ain back.
These ur thi symptoms. Coz yir that fed up wi ivdi yi know, so yi think,
that writin sumhm seems about thi only thing worth dayin. Then at least
when yir finished yi feel a hell of a lot better, coz whoever it was that was

gettin onyir wick before, yi can go upty an say, 'A don't gee a damn *whut* you think about me, coz av jist wrote a poem, an that's sumhm you huvny done. An even if yi huv, albetyi it wuz rotten.' Course you don't actually say all that – you don't *huvti* say it, even if yi could be bothered. An if it's sumdy that *did* say ti you, 'Your stuff's a lohta rubbish,' thirz no much point in goin upti thim anyway, is there? But yi can ey jist look thim in thi eye, in yir mind's eye, an think, 'Perhaps posterity will have better sense.'

'Ahma writur, your only a wurkur,' a said, to thi plumbir.

'Fux sake Joe stick wan on that kunt,' said the apprentice.

'Ball an cocks,' said the plumber, 'Ball an cocks. A firgot ma grammur.'

'Gerrihtuppyi,' a said, to thi apprentice.

'Lissn pal yoor tea'll be up na minit,' said the plumber.

'Couldny fuckin write a bookie's line ya basturdn illiturate,' a said, ti the plumber.

'Right. Ootside,' said the plumber. 'Mawn. Ootside.'

Sorry. That comes later.

Sian Hayton

from *Cells of Knowledge*

The woman takes up the thread of her story again.

My education began one day when I was in my eighth summer. I was in the weaving hall of my father's house. Like all my sisters I was taught to weave and spin almost as soon as I could stand and apart from the stuff we made for clothing some of us learned to make pictures by weaving them into cloth. We had taught ourselves to do this by studying garments my father brought from far countries. We had also learned to embroider from some Saxon women and to add all manner of detail to a picture to make it look like life. These pictures take us years to complete, and we never like to be watched while we are making them, for we each have our own tricks for giving life to a piece of work. At that time I was making a picture of hunters returning with kill on a winter's evening. I had sewn on little red beads to look like blood dripping from the deer's nostrils and the jaws of the dogs. The trees were to be black against the snow and the sky green, as it can be in winter. I showed the sun dipping into the sea, and I wanted to make the sight when light makes water seem like polished gold. I had thought to make it with gold wire but there was none in the basket. At once I was filled with a longing for the wire and I could not work on for thinking about it. I went to see my father for he was always the one who fetched it for us, but he was away from home and his servants did not know when he would return.

Concupiscence?

That night I could hardly sleep for thinking about the wire and when I went back to the weaving hall I stared at my work with a sickly gaze. Now the weaving hall was a long, narrow hall with the looms all down one side of it lying out from the wall so that each of us sat on our bench with our back to the one behind. On either side of the hall there were pairs of arched windows to let in a great deal of light, and these had all been glazed with round panes of green glass, so that even on the hottest day the room was cool and pleasant. Although it was our custom to pay no attention to each other in the weaving room, I noticed that the rack of oil lamps had been lit over a loom at the far end and could hear the sound of someone beating down a weft. From the position of the loom I knew that it must be my older sister, Olwen, working there, but as I had been taught, I did not turn the mirror over my loom to see if I was right.

That is a fine room to be set aside for weaving alone. It must be a very rich man that can let his women have such a well furnished place for their crafts. Are we to believe all this?

I began work at last, and went on well enough until a draught of air from the windows made my lamps flicker. Angry, I went to shut the casement. As I reached the window I saw a shadow approaching, and I leaned out. There I saw the gold and jewelled form of the Queen who lived in the fortress with us. The enamelled eyes of her mask seemed to stare right at me before she turned away and crossed the yard back to the hall. Her stiff golden skirts touched the ground, so that she did not seem to walk at all, but slid across the stones like a swan on the water. The crystals on her gold filigree crown shivered in the sunlight and the golden wrought flowers in her outstretched hand trembled as she passed over the ground. Behind me I heard a gasp, and I turned to see that Olwen had fallen against her loom. Being yet a child I was not troubled by the presence of the Queen, but the older ones among us could not withstand her closeness and suffered much distress. I went to see if Olwen needed my help. She had fainted and fallen against the loom and the warp was cutting into the skin of her face. It seemed to me that if I left her there her face would be scarred and the warp would become stretched, wasting months of work. Yet I knew I

O, Selyf, it was a bad day when you were disciplined against 'curiositas'. Who is the 'Queen'?

should not be looking at her, even now. I stamped my foot in perplexity as I wondered what to do for the best, and at last I decided to help her. I lifted her up and laid her along the bench.

I went back to my loom, but there was no help for me. I could only think about the gold thread I lacked; about my sister's rage when she revived and realised what had happened; about the Queen and the other wicked servants who lived in the castle with my father; and worst of all, I thought about the boy my father had brought to be my husband, who whenever he met me would grin and pull faces like a clown. At last I thought that the smith who made the wire could not live far away, for my father would visit him in an afternoon. It came to me that I could go for myself and fetch what I needed, and that it would be a very fine thing to get right away from the stronghold. With no more reflection I snuffed my lamps, found a slave who could show me the way, and collected some food for the journey. Essyllt, my oldest sister at the time, thought to stop me, but with the slave to guard me, young as I was, I could come to no harm, and her complaint was only a buzzing in my ear.

I ran across the plain of the stronghold and soon I was striding through the forest. Even though my father's servant accompanied me I was filled with joy to be away from his halls and from the stifling air which always surrounds them. It seemed that as long as I was at home a fog crept into my head and made it impossible to see clearly in any light. I used to feel it was some enchantment of my father's, but now I am sure it is a sickness in our souls.

The forest was brilliant in the colours of early summer, and the green of the trees was almost a pain to the eyes. The song of the birds was as loud as the sound of a mighty wind in the tree tops, and their wings thrummed as they flew about their nests. Once a flock gathered and mobbed my servant and I thought for a moment I might run and

Who are these servants and who is the Queen who poisons the older one and not the girl?

Why should birds mob a slave woman?

hide, but I did not yet know the road so I drove the birds off. We made good time and soon the track dropped down sharply towards a river. Then I knew I was near my destination, and the servant bobbed and bowed and left me alone. Soon I saw wheel-ruts in the road and followed this track downstream. I found a mound of baked earth which had been cut open to reveal burnt wood tightly packed inside. The wood was hard and black and like silk between my fingers. As I studied this strange sight I felt that someone had come close and I looked up to see a small man, no taller than myself, staring at me.

Charcoal.

He was dressed like a Saxon, with a plain belted tunic over a linen shift and drawers, and his legs were bound with soft red thongs of leather. He had fine brown shoes on his feet, and a long damascened knife at his belt. His face was wide and patched red. His cheeks and swelling forehead were pitted with specks of brown and blue where sparks had struck them. His pale blue eyes were scored all around with wrinkles from squinting into the forge, and under them the little bud of a mouth and the little wart of a nose looked as if they had been stolen from the face of an infant. The hair of his head was white and fine like flax. In a voice like a reed flute he asked me who I was, and I told him.

She was not yet ten years old and she must have been well secluded not to know that most farmers dress like this on market days.

He said, 'I hope you may be able to prove this is so, for I know how close your father keeps his daughters and – pardon me for doubting your word – you must see it is hard to believe.'

I saw the truth of his words, so I told him some things about our house that only those close to us can know. At last he seemed satisfied, for he said, 'Then you are the one your father told me to expect. You are thrice welcome, for he said that you are cleverer than all your sisters and the most eager to know the world outside your father's stronghold.'

It is clear there are some mysteries about her father's house we really should know about. I wish she had given more information.

Then he took me to his house, and showed me how he lived. The house was built in the bend of the river and made out of the earth so that grass and herbs grew right over the top of it. From any distance you would not have known it was there. The dwelling was dug deeply into the clay and rock of the river bank and in all the years I stayed there I never discovered how many rooms there were in all. The opposite bank of the river was a high cliff of many-layered red rock and trees were set along the top of it like a line of marching men. Up to that time the little man – Grig – had shared the house with his brothers, but they had gone away to serve the king of the Franks many years before and had not returned. He was all alone, and at the end of the day, when he had showed me all his workshops and answered my many questions, he asked me if I would like to stay on with him as his fosterling and student. I agreed to do so at once, for I had been happier that day than in all the days I could remember. When the servant came to fetch me we said that I would be staying and the message was taken to my father.

For the next ten years I worked harder than Grig and all his brothers together, and I learned how to set jewels, draw wire, to glaze and enamel; I learned how to work gold, silver, iron and copper, lead and tin; I also learned to ride a horse, plough a yard, make fish traps, milk a cow, and many other things about the land. And I learned to use weapons from a woman in the forest. With Grig I also saw my first sight of other men's dwellings. We would take things we had grown and things we had made to the towns to sell them at market there. At that time the pirates were not haunting the seas, and the Saxons had ceased to harry the land, so travelling was easy. Grig said that I was beautiful in the eyes of men, and he would load me with the jewellery we made so that people would see it to advantage. It was very pleasant to me to sit beside his booth and show the gold rings on my arms and fingers, and necklaces set with smooth green malachite and hot jasper. Grig, selling knives beside me would

---

This sounds as if it is on the river at Mailros, but that's a long three days away.

There was a king called Grig in Lothene beside the kingdom of one of the UiNial. It was said that his name was really Ciric and that he was called after the sainted father Cyricus. It appears that in his ninth year there was an eclipse of the sun on the first Ides of June which is the saint's own day. The people in consequence held that he was also a saint which is foolishness.

Where would they go for such markets? There are not many held now in this kingdom though I believe there were a lot in the days gone by.

laugh at the way people stared at such a finely dressed child. The jewels I wore to the common market place were not the best, for those were kept for the great lords whom Grig would visit alone. But I knew even then that fine jewels and clothing are of no value if the soul is sick. Grig knew this also for he said to me,

'Gold and silver are our servants, not our masters. Never let either of them tell you how to live.'

So you see he was not a foolish or wicked man. Further, we often saw monks and priests at the markets. We had little to do with them, for they rarely had any use for our wares, but Grig always pointed them out to me as good men, loyal to their oaths, benefactors of the sick and the poor. He said that if ever I were in trouble these would be the men to aid me, and he was right. Surely an adversary of God would not speak so?

While this is a crude and ill-informed version of the truth it could not be said to be malicious. From a pagan standpoint it is reasonable and just.

Now I will tell you about the only time I ever heard him speak of his mysteries. Sometimes in the making of jewellery we would use tiny globes of metal, and the making of them was something which has always puzzled me. Gold or silver would be heated till they ran like water, and at the same fire we would heat a perfectly round bowl of clay. Grig would make these bowls himself and would spend many hours grinding the surface till it was perfectly smooth. Into this bowl we would drop a little of the liquid metal and then the strange thing would happen. The metal would rush around the sides of the vessel like animals fleeing from a terrible, invisible hunter. Some pieces would even fly out of the bowl. I wondered if the metal was trying to escape from the heat of the bowl, but since it was itself hot I could not see how it would be aware of the heat.

This is very interesting. I must talk to Mochua at Cathures about it. He is the best smith in this part of the world.

I asked Grig what was happening and he said, 'If you had ever suffered from a fever you would not need to ask that question. You would know that in a fever skin is very tender so that anything placed on it causes anguish. Even when the skin is burning, a hot cup laid against it is agony. I conclude that it is the same for the metal. In its fevered state of heat the hot clay is unbearable to it and it tries to escape. When the metal is cool it falls on to the hot clay and slides slowly across it, and I know then it is feeling pleasure from the heat for it soon becomes soft and pliable like a contented infant.'

The only other time he spoke of such things, we were at the place where he found his raw iron and I had been with him for about seven summers.

One day when the stubble was yellow and the bracken lay like fire under the trees he came to me and said, 'It is time for you to see the place where iron begins. The womb of the earth where all the great metals come from has been a mystery of my family for many generations, and I am sorry to let an outsider into our secrets. But I see now that my brothers will not soon return, and I must take you with me in their place.

'If I went alone I would not be able to take all the mules I will need, and I will need your assistance at the minehead, also. You are coming into your full strength now, and you will be of much help to me.'

The strength of a girl of fourteen?

With so many mules the journey to the mine took many days. The first three days were easy, for we followed the river as it wandered downwards, but the morning came when we started to climb up a slope so steep that the branches on the upward side of the tree brushed against it. At the top we were so high that not even bracken grew there, only the thin white grass of the uplands. We followed a track that ran along the tops of the hills, and then sank again into gloomy forest which hung thick and silent round the road. I wondered that we had left the firm dry uplands for a dank forest, but I found that the road continued solid on a stony bank that lifted it well above the tangled forest floor. After a day's march we left the forest and returned to the trackless hilltops.

'Where the great stone road runs now the land has changed,' Grig told me, 'and if we were to follow it we would run into treacherous bogs. The earth moves slowly to work her will but in time she takes all things back to herself. The men who built the road were small and dark of skin and hair, and they came from far over the sea, thinking to leave their works where others would see and admire, but look what it all comes to.'

I looked where he pointed and saw that the road did indeed sink into the ground as if the earth had wrapped arms round it and dragged it down. Where it had been there was now only marsh grass and reeds. At the end of the fifth day we came to the mine and slept under the stars as we had intended. In the morning I woke to find my clothes sprinkled with snow.

'We will have to sleep in the bloomery,' said Grig, 'and that will be too hot.' He led me to a stone-built shed which held a furnace so big I could stand up in it. Grig left me to take the charcoal from the mules and hastened off to his mine. I started to fire the furnace with charcoal and the crumbling pink and yellow and black stone which stood in heaps at the minehead. About the middle of the afternoon Grig suddenly appeared from the mouth of the tunnel. My heart froze with fear: he was covered head to foot with blood.

'In the name of mercy, Grig, what has happened to you? Have you been crushed by falling rocks, or were there wolves in the cave?'

'I am not harmed,' he replied, laughing, 'this is only my mother's blood. The earth within the cave bleeds water and iron which form a fine red blood, and if her loving sons are not here to drive it out there is soon a great pool of it in the mine. I must stanch her wounds before I begin work, and the first day I am here I must be like a new-born babe, sodden and red. This will soon pass and my mother will let me into her bowels again.'

I am sure he means the Roman legions. The little man clearly did not know that they brought the word of God with them. That is an edifice more lasting than stone. The only road of the Roman type that I know of now is the one that runs north from the valley of the Nyd to the head of Clud water. It is said that this road was built by the Romans but I saw nothing like it when I was in Rome.

This is disgusting, but what can you expect?

Then from behind him, in the earth, I heard a rushing sound which made the hair on my neck stand up. Grig seemed truly to be more youthful, for he rushed joyfully from bloomery to mine and back many times. He showed me my duties, and there was much to do. As well as firing and minding the bloom I had to pack peat into thick trenches to make a poor charcoal. I had constantly to watch the passages around the fires on both of these to make sure the wind would blow through them, and at sunset I would fall to the ground in the stifling bloomery and sleep till sunrise. Grig hardly spoke to me, and I saw him only occasionally as he struggled out of the mine with his baskets of pink rock. But on the nights when we ran off the pure iron in a hot white stream with bright sparks flying round, it was so beautiful that all the labour was worthwhile.

I have learned that a 'bloomery' is where the rock containing iron is heated so that it runs like water and can be poured into ingots. These are called 'blooms' but they are far from beautiful.

After many days of this we had used all the charcoal we had brought with us, and what I had made, and at the minehead there was only fresh ore and the fresh peat I had cut.

Grig looked at this and shook his head. 'If my brothers had been here there would have been much more curing for next season,' and he pointed to the iron blooms stacked beside the furnace and said, 'and there would have been more than three times that number, nor would we have had to work like dogs to do it. In days past when we were all together it would have been a feast or a holiday. This week should have been the crown of our year. But this is not your fault – you have worked well. Come with me now, you have earned the right to see into our secret world.'

There is no invocation of spirits and no sacrificing to demons such as I have heard is common to miners in Franconia. If there is sorcery it may well be lawful.

Then he took a black oil-lamp and led me into the mine through the narrow slit of an entrance. The passage inside was so low that I almost had to bend double, and it was then that I realised that I had grown a lot of late, for I was much larger than the little man who danced along the passage ahead of me, splashing through water and kicking at rubble. The passage grew even lower and with each step my heart sank deeper and deeper in me for I was sure that the walls were closing in to crush me. Grig ran ahead, blithely, and once he disappeared round a bend to leave me alone in the breathing darkness. I tried to hear his step but all that came to me was the steady beating I had heard before, as if the living rock around me was flesh. Grig returned and led me by the hand to where I could stand upright. He held the lamp up high.

I saw a strange sight. The cavern around me was coloured like the rock ore, but the colour was stronger and more vivid with the water running over it. The red rocks looked like raw flesh bleeding, and lines of black ran across and through it like veins on a hand. At the back of the cavern where the light grew dim there were many thousands of glinting lights. Grig held his hand out to me and I saw he held a glittering stone that shone with many facets like a crystal.

'This is one of my mother's eyes, with a myriad of faces. Take it, and know she knows you, the first woman to see her secret self!'

Are these precious stones?

I took it, but with a heavy heart for I was dismayed to think of myself in the middle of a living being. This was no place of mine who had been raised in fire and light and air. I began to shiver in the damp winds of this womb world. But Grig was full of glee.

'Now you see her face to face,' he said, 'as only my brothers and myself have seen her before. She stands around you, a stiff, formless, meaningless pile. Everything we might ever need is here, but in what confusion! Everything is heaped together and mixed like wine in water, seeming inseparable. But she is not like water. She is hard and rigid and sullen. See how red and angry she is! Each kind of stone hates the other and vilely refuses to serve while it is hard packed against its brother. Helpless

What horror! I see the face of the Creator everywhere in His

creation, and He smiles at me. This dwarf loves his 'mother' yet he sees her as wicked and malicious.

How else could he see her? I did not see Vesuvio myself but I was told of its terrible rage, and of Ætna also. How much happier are we who have our loving Father watching over us. All this smacks of the heresy of Manichee, but since the woman is not party to it she cannot be stained, unless it is by association.

and meaningless. It is my great task to find out the nature of each one of them, so that all may find form and meaning. And then my mother loves me. Alone she can do nothing – she cannot bring them to birth unassisted. Sometimes in southern lands she tries to bring herself to fulfilment and then great fires pour out of her belly, and the rocks she would smelt gush down her flanks. But she cannot do it alone. All she can make is destruction and pain, and she must damp her rages down again before she tears herself apart.

'Even the Alfather who made her shuns and hates her. He leaves her alone here in darkness and misery and it is only by the hands of her loyal sons that anything good is made. We alone have the courage to face her malice. We return to her times without number and drag her separate parts aloft and work on them. We hammer and mould and draw. Her father and husband turns his face from her and we must do it all.'

Suddenly he fell silent, and the echoes from his voice swept downwards and away like the tide. I was chilled with terror, but he was exultant, his eyes great with tears, and his fists clenched. I had never seen him aroused like this before, even at the culmination of the most difficult tasks. I realised that I had seen a mystery whose whole meaning I could only guess at. I never heard him speak at such again.

'The devil reigns in all heresies but he has raised his throne in that of the Manichees.'

A few weeks after we returned I was idle for once and wandered into part of the house which was dug deep into the earth. Many of the rooms were empty and many held small beds and tables so that I thought they must have been Grig's brothers' rooms. I wandered on and at last opened a door on a sight that turned my belly to ice with fear. There, sitting on a high-backed chair, with her brow resting on her hand I saw the golden queen. I fled before she might lift her head and see me, and as I ran down the corridor the skin of my back crawled with the certainty that she was following.

I ran to the workshop where Grig was bent over his work and cried. 'When did she arrive? I did not see her coming.'

'She has always been here,' said Grig without raising his head.

'I am speaking of the Queen, the poisonous queen who lives at my father's house.'

'That is not she,' answered Grig smiling, 'but her sister who is like her in every way. I must tell you neither of them is living.'

'I tell you she is alive. She wanders about in my father's hall and when she passes we sisters fall sick.'

'I know what she does for I made her and the other who sits within. Come with me and see for yourself.'

He took a light and led me back down the passages to the room where she sat, and as I watched he took her head from her body. He unfastened the clothes at her back, and showed me the myriad tiny wheels and springs and wires that were fixed inside her head and body and made her move around.

She is an automaton. I heard that such creations were given to great Carolus by men from the east, or sorcerers. I was never in his capital to see.

'That is very great knowledge,' I said, 'could you teach me to make one like that?'

'Surely I could,' he replied, 'it will take many years, but you are an apt apprentice – I could ask for none better – I am sure you will learn.'

She is not over modest to mention his praise of her.

But it was not to be. That night the sickness of women came on me for the first time, and my father's servant was sent to fetch me home. I have always regretted that there was not time to learn to make such a creature.

James Kelman

from *The Busconductor Hines*

There's that instant a fraction before the alarm belts out and you've grabbed the thing and managing to shove down the stopper just at the warning click, knowing you're as fit as a fiddle and right up the lot of them; pushing out of bed and dressing in the black yet so swiftly, everything successful – the jersey in particular, seeming to pull itself on, settling round the trunk without even needing a tug. Pointless to eat; far better out on the road and walking. And the quick laying on the lips of lips for christ sake what does that mean –

kissing one's wife softly on the lips: that's what it fucking means. Then swallowing a half pint of milk prior to the silent farewell; an unknown moment of magical togetherness. Poor auld Sandra. Never to have felt these lips at that actual moment. Serves her right for being sound asleep. Women shouldnt go to sleep, it's a spoiler and we dont want that kind; what we do want is the fragrant aroma and soft flesh to be encircling one that one is pulled back beneath the sheets against one's will. Come on you I want to go to my work, stop it, stop it! let me get out into the harsh wintry wee hours of this my next moment of doom, that black black black of the

Jesus christ alfuckingmighty.

But it was almost halfway to the garage before the staffbus appeared he had been walking so quickly.

The driver was an imbecile. To talk to such a being is often out of the hands of Hines. And yet it was miraculous to have been there as it slowed to just that point beyond where he was standing that he had to be quickening to be jumping else no chance of getting aboard the thing. The public service omnibus is an amazing article. To be the driver of such a vehicle must certainly be a novel kettle of cabbage. Hines would have liked a buzz at it. Had his overall conduct been less abysmal he would easily have fulfilled the function quite as adequately as anyone.

He sat down.

Other members of the green were there. He greeted them cordially albeit with a concealed smile of superciliousness at the thought of himself there sitting there at this exact moment in the eternal scheme of things.

Consolation was his, however, deriving as it did, via his experience, of times verified via countless other mornings whence the ragings of a darkly brain had indeed given way to a calm but firm detachment. Had a mirror been handy he could have watched his face. It would have been interesting to witness the outward appearance.

The staffbus stopped in the garage yard and the greens strolled along into the office with Hines bringing up the rear in company with a driver by the name of Davis who has the fine habit of not talking for shifts at a stretch. It is astonishing how quickly the place could fill with smoke; Hines had been about to prise the lid off the tin but he returned it inside the pocket. An interesting observation: places used to smoke fill up with it more rapidly than other places. Take the topdeck of a bastarn bus where the eyes actually smart – although of course you've got the diesel fumes as well as the smoke, plus the extraordinary smells of the cunts farting, sorry jimmy, been on the guinness last night. Smoking is a malpractice. Consider the youthful Paul, how his lungs must resemble the inside of a fucking chimney, and him hardly 4½ years of age. Terrible. And the same goes for one's spouse. Although, having known of the habit prior to accepting the band of rolled gold, the question of an individual's freedom to form genuine decisions of an autonomous nature must enter the reckoning. The Deskclerk.

Davis had just signed for his duty and was walking to look at the duty-sheet on the wall. The Office was almost empty. Hines had taken the pen to sign for his own duty but he kept from pulling the book towards him; at last he looked at the Deskclerk: What's up?

The Deskclerk was smiling in a friendly manner.

Hines grinned.

Naw. I'm just wondering what you're here for.

Eh?

I mean there's no point signing the book, it's your day-off.

Hines sniffed; raising his right hand he scratched his hairline which seemed to be containing an enormous quantity of flaking skin nowadays. The Deskclerk continued to smile. He stopped the scratching, passed the hand over his forehead gently, as though not wanting to disturb the skin there lest it also flaked.

Honest Rab I mean that's what diaries were invented for; so folk can mark in their timetables!

Hh.

Anyway as it turns out, you've knocked it off, I'm short a couple of conductors this morning; you can switch days-off if you like.

Aw christ Harry ta.

16 duty; okay?

Great, aye, ta, thanks a lot.

The Deskclerk had pushed the book towards him and while Hines was signing he said, How's the stomach by the way?

Better.

The Deskclerk nodded, then he sniffed. Aye, I never heard till later on. You'd been stuck in the toilet for an hour because of it?

Well no quite ... Hines grinned.

Look eh ... I thought you were chancing it yesterday. That's how I eh ... He sniffed. I mean I didnt know it was genuine, when you came in to sign-off, otherwise I wouldnt've eh ...

No bother Harry.

The Deskclerk nodded. Right, day-off the morrow then – or Saturday? To be honest Rab it'd suit me better if you made it Saturday, you know what like Fridays are in this place!

Hangover day!

They both grinned.

Eh ... Hines was rolling a cigarette.

Aye?

Naw, just wondering, I mean yesterday and that eh I dont suppose I mean, changing it; what I mean, to a day-off.

What?

Naw I mean yesterday and that, you know how I had to go sick; I was just wondering, if it could be changed to a day-off I mean, so I could work Saturday as well ...

O Christ naw, naw Rab, that's no on, sorry I mean, it's just no on; it's through the books and that and you cant go back over it now.

Aw.

Aye, Christ, sorry.

Naw naw, okay Harry honest, no bother I mean I was just eh ... He sniffed, signed at the space appropriate to 16 duty; he lighted the cigarette and coughed sharply, and added, Thanks again Harry.

Aye eh ... The Deskclerk was gazing at a sheet of paper lying in front of him on the counter; he raised his head briefly to nod.

It has never been acutely necessary to think. Hines can board the bus and all will transpire. Nor does he have to explain to a driver how the bus is to be manoeuvred. Nor need he dash out into the street to pressgang pedestrians. Of its own accord comes everything. Not only are the passengers to be congratulated, so too must the creators and current administrators of the Public Transport System. It is all superb. Hines simply has to stand with his back to the safety rail beneath the front window and await the jerk of gear or brake to effect his descent to the rear and, with machine at the ready and right hand palm outwards to take in the dough, the left hand is extracting a ticket and dishing it up to the smiling person. Then though it be busy a lull always arrives, during which he can return to the front for a fly puff at a relaxing roll-up and, if of a mind, he can engage such as a Reilly in conversation. But a driver can be new. The Newdriver is a problem. One should tread warily in gabbing to such a being lest a lapse in concentration causes the bus to crash. Hines seems to get more Newdrivers than is his fair share. It is as though the Higher-ups view him as the 'deep-end' and thus they toss him the Newdrivers whenever available. They say to themselves: This busconductor Hines is a difficult kettle of fish; should the Newdriver survive a shift alongside him then this Newdriver is indeed the man for us. Hines will show them that which is the ropes. He will advise them what is the what. Let us continue to ensure that he remains the bus-conductor as opposed to a busdriver that we may continue to toss him the Newdrivers whenever he and his own driver are not on together. And gentlemen, let us also take pains to ensure that he and his own driver are not always on together.

Fucking shite.

But it's funny how he always seems to get lumbered with the cunts when Reilly's on the panel or whatever. They're all fucking idiots as well, this is the thing. 90% of their naivety is not connected with being Newdrivers; it is connected with being alive as persons. Hines cannot fucking understand how they have survived to the present. He signs for a shift and senses the proximity of a starched collar and tightly knotted black tie and there, in a quiet part of the Office, lurks the graduate, rocking back and forth on his heels while pretending fascination with the duty-sheets. What is the fucking point of such a carry-on. Useless talking. Hines leaves them to get on with it – which is no doubt why they get tossed aboard his bus. Some of them are cheery and some of them are not cheery, they chat and dont chat, but as the day progresses the latter always takes precedence. Because Hines doesnt fucking chat back! You think he wants to fucking die! Jesus christ!

Never disturb Newdrivers.

Even experienced drivers should not be disturbed. Back during the 1st

term of transport Hines was feart to glance suddenly at the driver in case
he caused a draught which might interfere with the steering mechanism.
Absolute nonsense. But the quick glance into the cabin could have the
driver reacting hastily that the possibility of disaster was reality. Hines
tries never to speak without firstly having made his presence known.
People can be deep in reverie. Some drivers have no idea where they are
at certain points on the road. They say, Christ I dont even remember
driving the last couple of miles! And these miles can embrace peak-hour
city centre streets. It makes you quite jumpy to consider. Imagine a bus
crowded with punters, standing room only both upstairs and down, all
giving each other the time of day under the mistaken apprehension their
lives are in a safe pair of hands. Now, these fucking hands might only be
2 days out the Training School for Busdrivers and some of them never
sat behind a wheel in their lives before arriving there for fuck sake. Hines
is sick of it. Apparently it isnt the fault of the Newdrivers themselves. But
the poor auld conductors are having to carry the burden. No wonder
certain shoulders will wilt. One pair should not have to support that kind
of thing.

Weans are the main hazard. Newdrivers feel able to be at home with
them. It is an error. They drive folk crazy. Newdrivers are simply
misjudging the situation. Experienced conductors have no truck with
weans. Weans are to be avoided at all costs. The most hair-raising
journeys involve them. On they pile maybe 6 to 8 at a time so that they
wind up getting jammed in the doorway and you have to be ready to
poke here and pull there. And they are out to con you into losing your
temper. One must tread warily. Three years ago a conductor by the name
of McManus had a stand-up fight with a team of them because they were
drinking wine on the rear seat of the topdeck. The full facts have never
come to light – although Hines has a hunch it concerned moral outrage.
McManus was an alcoholic. He always carried a half-bottle which he
wrapped in layers of toilet paper and stowed in his machine-case.
According to garage rumour he lost his temper because they refused him
a gargle but McManus was a whisky drinker and it was a bottle of wine
the weans had. Far more likely he wanted to warn them off the wayward
track. Anyway, whatever it was he was out of order and the weans were
right to object. So poor auld fucking McManus suffered a beating, then
lost his job into the bargain. The Department of Transport is opposed to
the boxing games where members of the green are involved. There is no
excuse. No circumstances are singular enough to warrant such action.
But obviously the beating was sufficient; he shouldnt have lost his job

into the bargain. And he wouldnt had the Union sorted it out properly. But the Union is not for discussing. Hines cannot discuss the Union. Yes he can. No he cant. Best leaving such a carry on to the likes of Reilly who is able to attend meetings and even get involved in the proceedings. Life is too elongated.

There is a road; and on this road there is much traffic.

He was journeying home by omnibus having spent the past hour watching snooker-pool. Greenly members play for cash. Hines doesnt; he has no money to play at snooker with. He can hardly play the fucking game anyway. During his earlier terms he failed to master it and has continued to fail ever since. Usually he gets the chance to play only when Reilly has nothing better to do. Reilly is good and prefers to play others who are good. He can win money. How does he manage it. He plays and then people give him money. Off he goes to buy cigarettes or rolls and fried egg – or maybe home to weigh in with Isobel who then sticks it all into the building society.

The sun has set; the streetlights have been on for a while; the slush, almost disappeared from the roads.

Hines sits on a damp bus, on the lower deck, having lacked the whatever necessary to climb to the top deck. He is being glanced at complicitly by an imbecile of a conductor who must have started in the job yesterday morning – he is upset at having a busy bus. Everybody gets a busy bus. There is nothing unique in the situation except that it may be so for him. Hines feeling obliged to raise the eyebrows occasionally, to convey interest, not wanting the cunt to suffer any sort of mental breakdown lest he is forced into donning the machine as substitute, until procuring an Inspector, and the ambulance. What a performance. At one stage the conductor slumped onto the seat beside him and began loud-mouthed complaints about the passengers he was getting. This loud voice going on and on and on, seeming to list the names and dates of birth of individual persons, in this voice which was grating on everyone – the heads of passengers twisting slightly to signal their awareness of what was being said.

Hines has enough on his plate. But there is no way through to some folk. A lot of drivers carry on in the same way, gab gab gab about the trials and tribulations of driving buses. Who's fucking interested. Hines is always getting cunts like that giving him their worries. Who wants to hear about irate punters at Hillington Estate. You finish your work and you expect a bit of peace, not some fucking imbecile battering your ears. This is what happens when you sit in the *Vale*; they all start yabbering about the morning's nasty events.

The wind was strong; he had to stride in a semi-sideways movement, frequently halting to catch his hat before it blew off his head; at one point he took it off but had to put it back on again because his ears got sore. Then the heat inside the nursery lobby, like a hospital. Even the smells of the place. Wiping his boots on the several mats he wandered down the corridor, seeing the work the weans had done pinned up on the walls. The hum of voices from the main play-area. He was still too early.

The Supervisor appeared; her tits very uncomfortable looking the way they seemed squashed together in the thing she was wearing. He nodded, stepping to one side as she passed, but she was frowning and barely noticed him. It summed up the place. Being a wean in the dump must have been no joke. Poor auld Paul right enough.

Near to the play-area door he paused at a print of the Chieftain of all the Britons. It was splendid. On the wall opposite were companion prints also splendid, of long canines with short legs, ideal goals for the kids. The Supervisor again. She hesitated. Hines raised his eyebrows, indicating the prints. Then she said: Paul isnt in today . . .

Although it wasnt a genuine statement it was nearer to that than a question. And she continued to look at him. Hines nodded, Aw aye, hh. He grinned, What a stupid . . .

As she pushed her way into the play-area he could hear her call to a child, or adult perhaps, before the door shut.

Along the corridor, ben the lobby, and out.

There were problems in what had been said but there might not be. There were other items – people for instance, as well as different things, needing to be considered. Plus the experiencing: the actuality. Even the pavement, dry bits and damp bits, hardly a sign of the snow now at all; and the condensation, on windows, of tenements and buses and other vehicles – those clear patches behind which the gazers, gazing. These fucking scary closes! Some of them are really evil. Strange dripping noises. Is it a burst pipe or what. A broken gutter. Just a tap with a faulty washer. And the concrete all cracked and treacherous for folk's feet. The auld yins there, having to tread with great caution, the lights in the close dim or not working except in periodic blinks; and that dogshit in dark corners

– the floor just swept too and suddenly littered with a mysterious black matter which is picked up for inspection, O my it's awful soft this whatever it is: Shite! help ma boab right enough. No wonder the auld yins crack up. Half a lifetime spent scrubbing and whiteclaying the concrete only to have to finally admit the uncontrollable stuff going on behind their stooped backs. It is a pity.

Two teenage girls at the corner, probably on the game the way they were standing, conducting a form of non-conversation, their gaze everywhere – even to Hines. Too early; they have no doubt forgotten today is only Wednesday, that tomorrow is the day when members of the putrid can be worth a glance. In fact they probably werent prostitutes at all, just girls having a chat before going up the stair for tea. But the district is definitely going downhill fairly quickly and not even a dyed-in-the-wool native of the dump could say any different. Hines is no dyed-in-the-wool native; he's a fucking incomer.

He clearly distinguishes the candlelight at certain windows, and the women resting their elbows on the sills, watching you walk by. One's offspring should not be reared in such a den. And yet according to local gossip it was once a sought-after area, green grass in a few backcourts; and all the local wee shops, a hive of bustling, good-natured activity. Evelyn Donaldson's mother had been born and bred here. And if it was good enough for her etc. it was certainly not good enough for sane citizens.

He paused at the traffic lights, staying very still, as though trying to remain untouched by the sharp gusts and eddies from the passing vehicles. One minute you can be heading along the street nice as nice and then the next you're fucked as usual, care must be taken. You get the poor auld fucking animals; they go hopping about with broken shoulders and backs with the punters yelling at the conductor to put them out their misery. What are they supposed to do at all. Smash their heads in with the fucking machine!

Darting out suddenly he made it to the other side, just as the green became amber. It is a habit he has picked up from them, the cats and the dogs. Dogs are better at it. They cross the busiest thoroughfares in a fine trusting manner, trotting quite the thing as though the space they occupy is bound to stay constant. Not so the cats. They know fine well there is no such thing as constant space and off they scud in the surefire knowledge the course they have chosen is 90% guaranteed to fail. What is astonishing is how neither species, once safely across, will pause to glance back over its shoulder. This fatalistic approach to life: no, it is not so good. At least once per month Hines sees something killed, animal or person. Being the best friends of people the deaths of dogs are reported to the polis so the van can arrive to cart them off. But cats are regarded like rats. On the first journey one gets run over and killed and coming back from the terminus its body is obvious. On the next journey out the shape can still be verified but returning in less easily so, and onwards, till with a bit of luck the rain is falling.

He ignored the newspaper vendor outside the pub. Another thief. He short-changes blind pensioners.

He rushed past the butcher and fruiterer.

All a load of shite. Ha ha ha.

Naw but, seriously, the depressed rectangles can be vicariously aloof. Pneumatic drills go blasting somewhere. Here you have this yin and there the other. What about the head though. The head is fine, fine. The head is a finely honed item; merely restricted at present. A gap-site is a delicate absence; a hunner years ago it was a brand spanking new section whose brightly white sandstone was quarried in Aberdeen perhaps, carted down by rail, the labourers and masons singing lustily, giving vent to their earnest endeavour via the traditional scotch worksong, while delivering then assembling the goods prior to collecting their wages and religious tracts from the builder's daughter at the end of the contract, a rosebudly wench of prim but lovely exterior, getting some practice in with the lowly before shooting out to the African jungle to sort out the converts, beautiful stuff, with the laced bodice and so on.

It would be hard to say what he was playing at. The volume control on the music-centre might have required decreasing, as also the gas-fire. He was still wearing the uniform, standing at the windows in the front room, the curtains parted as though night had yet to fall. His lips moved. He could have been mouthing the words of the song but if the song stopped he would be talking to himself if still doing it – maybe still singing right enough. The cashbag lay over his left shoulder. Although right-handed he always carries it thus. A point for possible discussion: do left-handed conductors carry their cashbags on the right. Or is it only those who smoke. Very few people dont smoke in the garage. Hines could have named almost all of them – at least those who worked on the same side of the shift as he did. Such people may have stronger personalities than the rest but they might just be stubborn. It is also noticeable how less eager the nonsmokers are to spend their dough willy-nilly. Or is this a case of yoicks tally ho on the part of Hines. In other words is he a bad loser. Because he still smokes and is aware he should not be. But if a poll was conducted in the bothy perhaps the percentage of nonsmokers who carried homemade sandwiches would be higher than that of the smokers. While the percentage of nonsmokers purchasing prepared food in the canteen would certainly be minimal. On the whole then, it would appear that nonsmoking members of the green are less inclined to spend money willy-nilly.

He continued to stand there once the LP stopped playing. Then he frowned and went ben the kitchen, and walked to the window. Some demolition equipment was lying about. It is surprising this should have been the case. Probably there was nothing of value else it would get stolen. The demolition men could even steal it themselves and say it had been stolen by nightprowlers. They could steal it each time it was replaced, until steps were taken. The firm would end up having to employ a nightwatchman and maybe even a daywatchman cause what would stop them stealing it during daylight, so the daywatchman would then follow them about during working hours ensuring the staff stayed on the premises.

He switched on the television, the gas-fire; returned to the front room and put on another LP record, switched off the gas-fire there. Before going back to the kitchen he listened to the opening of the first song. He drew his armchair nearer the fireplace, then hunched over it, sitting on his ankles the way Griff had done. What would three daughters be like. A quintet. A unit of 5 – plus the mother when she got out of hospital. If she ever got out. People rarely get out of hospital. They get kept in. They have their own wee incinerator down in the basement.

Amazing.

Hines can see their double chins, the way their jowls droop, the eyes saturated, while the bodies, groping towards each other in an effort to feel. Is that veins there. Actual blood pumping behind the greyly shadows. Living organisms of a reflective nature. Aw look, heh jimmy, a stain on the mohair suit, the cunt's pished himself and might rub against us; quickly quickly to the basement with the bastard or we'll never be the same again.

Hines can get closer in to them by flitting into Paul's usual kneeling position. Fine to drag a needle across the flesh, that thin bubbling line of blood, stripping them of their garments and sticking them into formation, tallers to the right and shorters to the left, single rank: size! Just so we can study them properly – see: here you have this yin and there the other. Essences: this yin's the essence of this and that yin's the essence of that. Out of it all you've got the individuals who perform the feats. Poke and you'll see them quiver. They hate getting poked right enough. And they dont like quivering in public either. And see how affected they get when you break their glasses, that sudden inrush of air; their eyes widening in terror, the streets coming jumping up at them – the accelerator james: let's get to fuck rapidly.

Or simply rearing questions, the answers of sociological interest to such as the adolescent Paul. And did you act in honest naivety. Or with thought malevolent beforehand. Or just as a genuine agent for whom the no-nonsense lack of shilly-shally is to bring forth universal benefit, as between two industrial captains – a singular contract for mutual expansion (if the sun doesnt rise tomorrow a balanced scale might simply slide, eh!). And how was it up there. Slippery. No time to relax. Aesthetically irksome, but compromise to some degree is always imperative if one is to gain a foothold, that footholds are seen as essential, that they are to be being continuing.

The uniform off he got into bed. He had turned off the television and the music-centre. He could have put on his jeans and a different jersey but he didnt. He was sitting beneath the quilt, on Sandra's side, with his back to the interior wall. From the recess the kitchen can be a peculiar experience since while being inside the subject is also outside. Should he have witnessed another Hines enter and go about his various bits of business it would have been very scary indeed, and yet also relaxing perhaps. Especially if the event took place during a long hot summer spell and he made straight to the sink to sluice cold water on his face and neck, washing off the sweat.

Steam issued from the kettle. The water was for his feet. He was going to wash his feet. He never bathes in the babybath. It is too small for him. One time he nearly got stuck in the thing. But it was a good buy, no question of that. And another time for fuck sake when Sandra was in it he saw a mouse. He was sitting on his armchair half-reading a book, half-watching her soaping herself and the mouse there, it must have come in beneath the door and it started along towards the tallboy but then stopped and stayed where it was, before returning to the door, and out. It was a bad yin, really, really bad. He didnt tell her; he has never told her: it is something beyond the pale.

He poured the boiling water into the basin, adding cold from the tap. It was as much to heat the feet as clean them, their being really fucking freezing for the past 12 hours or so. Is it 12 hours since he left the house.

It must be. Time shifts. That's the fucking trouble with nowadays; back when Hines was a boy

The water wasnt cold enough for the feet to enter immediately; he would be balancing them on the rim of the basin for the next 10 minutes at least, allowing the steam to get at them while enjoying the anticipation of actually sticking them under. He sat down on the armchair and started to greet. It was a strange thing. His face didnt alter and nor did his eyes redden, and he stopped it right away, balancing the soles of his feet on the rim of the basin, the water far too hot. He always allows the water to cool in the basin rather than adding too much cold to begin with. He likes to just sit there, the soles of his feet on the rim, sometimes with an additional kettle of hot water positioned at the fireplace which he can pour from, to protract the affair. He twisted the chair slightly, his shins having turned red from the heat of the gas-fire. O christ, he said and opened a book.

Hines is of the opinion that men have every right to greet though so far he has been unable to accomplish the practice in public. His most memorable bouts to date occurred after the death of his last surviving grandparent, and after his young brother had left for Australia. During the actual occasions he was the life and soul of the company; it was only a few days later the greeting took place.

He had brought three books from the front room, they covered a period of some 2500 years and spanned three continents. To plop them into the basin would be adjudged unusual. In itself his method of book-reading if not unusual would be adjudged irregular. He used to have a method he regarded as pertinent, as proper for the thing. He would place the book at the bottom of the basin and read the title page while rippling the surface of the water, gently, with a pinkie. If he had worn spectacles he could have placed those beneath the book.

Hines is an honourable fellow; if his wife has decreed the necessity of not being with him then she is entitled to have arrived at such a decision, even though it is to be taken literally i.e. that such a decision is irrevocably bound in with action. But they have survived bad patches in the past. And although he would probably argue that this is the worst yet, it is by no means certain this is true for Sandra. Nor is there anything to suggest that the current situation is a form of climax for it may yet prove nothing more than a further bad patch in a developing relationship. But it must be admitted that certain elements, unique elements, have already appeared. Prior to the other evening she had never stayed away without prior notice or something like it. That was the first time she had ever done that. Why did she do it. She knew he would worry, it was really strange, not like her. Tonight was like her. It was not like her. More, it was not, it was like as if, it was considerate though.

The note was propped against the wall above the mantelpiece, next to the gas-bill. His feet had entered the basin and he jerked them out, they had become red to the ankles.

There was no need to hold the note because he had read it at a distance. She had written 11 a.m. at the top as if this was the kind of information he would need to know at all costs. Maybe he did. What did it tell him. It told him she probably couldnt have managed it out to Knightswood and then got back into town in time for work. Was that anything. She could just have gone in late.

The soles of his feet were touching the water but he allowed them to remain there, the hard skin and so on. He lifted the tin and prised off the lid. Not much tobacco left but he had retained the price of more from the cashbag. Plus she had left £3 beside the note. The £3 for him.

This sort of escapade is beyond belief. Was it to be taken seriously.

Of course, shouted a voice. Whose fucking voice was it. Funny how voices come along and shout, just as if they were something or other, knowledgeable fucking parties perhaps, that knew what was going on. Because Hines doesnt. He doesnt fucking know. It is a joke. It is beyond talking about. Yet one obvious factor exists to substantiate the thesis that this is Sandra who's fucked off. This factor.

Wednesday is the fucking factor. Other women would have waited till wages-day. Not her. There is only one day out of every seven she can leave and this day is never to be Thursday. She can only leave that he is to be being fucking okay. He is such an imbecile he cannot be trusted to survive unless he has a full week's wages in the pocket. Such cash is not necessary for her and Paul. It is him who needs it.

He had the towel in his hands, raising the soles from the water. He dropped the towel to the floor. His feet were yet to steep. But he had been aware of this. It was not a moment of absentmindedness. Quite often he dries his feet without having washed them. Sandra nags at him and no wonder. Imagine being too lazy to wash your feet when you've gone and prepared everything, when you've sat for quarter of an hour with the cunts suspended above the bastarn basin, only to towel at the bottom portions, and see how the poor auld fucking skin goes skiting off into the basin because you havent washed them right. Terrible.

There ticks the clock; if it hadnt been wound then the ticking etc., it wouldnt be happening. And anyway, he had forgotten to bring the soap so this is a genuine reason not to wash them. Often it is the fresh socks he forgets to bring and sometimes the towel and sometimes more than the one item maybe even the fucking lot so that Sandra, having to get whatever it is, for him. O christ. And he doesnt like having to ask her if he has forgotten, he gets so sick of it, this forgetting, and the dependency. What happened last night. He came home. Things were not as they were. He comes home and things arent as they were. The things that should be fine. He of course did not go out to the Drum because he had been earlier on, christ, having advised her he was going in the evening which was why he couldnt take the wee man to the swimming like he'd been promising, always fucking promising, he had promised, to take him, but then couldnt, he was not able to do it, because he had to go out to the Drum and see wee Frank. Wee Frank was the thing of course. He had had to see him and he didnt turn up which was – fine really, because the next time it would be in the evening, definitely, and it could be sorted out with him. Not wee Frank, just Frank.

What is up in his head. As heads go. He told her a lie, another fucking lie, a non-telling of the truth; and not even to explain, even attempting it, to give something almost, close to it, something as close to what was really the case, something that was the truth.

Yet once upon a time

It should be remembered, however, that Robert Hines has accomplished nought. Even the present circumstances could have been rendered more amenable. A lick of fresh paint for instance, to hide the terrible wallpaper; a bit of polyfilla round the skirting board. He could have been getting rid of the mice. He could have called out the rodent exterminators. They would have sprayed their stuff. While awaiting their arrival he could have filled in the cracks. The last time they came it was a lassie along with a middle-aged man. The lassie was in charge. She spoke with authority and must have had qualifications in rodent control. She stealthily peered at the plethora of books while in the front room. Perhaps she would return alone: cups of coffee and a doughnut, a quiet conversation, with a brief account of the current problem, how items are not always going properly, becoming a wee bit overpowering at times. You can just go along okay, keeping upsides the world, not doing anything except taking part in a low-key kind of manner; you go to your work and so forth, until getting punched in the fucking mouth. An old story right enough. It happens to everybody now and again, you've got the incinerator at the foot of the stairs, a thing to be encountered every so often. The lassie is probably the same herself. Here she is having to chap at the doors of strangers, to wipe out their rodents and the rest of it.

Odd she should have taken Paul so readily.

That is definitely a something. One would have expected such a matter to be worthy of a little discussion.

Why is last night not this evening. She doesnt go last night and isnt here this evening when the actual item, the spur, is of last night. She goes this morning, first thing almost – 11 a.m. She goes to Knightswood, the home of her parents. Imagine going to the home of your parents! She must've been upset, otherwise, christ, the home of one's parents.

She goes to the home of her parents and takes her wee boy, leaving her man to accomplish that which he finds to be necessary in view of the current situation, whose circumstances though astounding are nevertheless not too astounding should one pause to consider the various eventualities. Now, these eventualities, are to be considered. One can consider them. One can sit; one's lower portions dangling over the hot water, one's tin etc., by one's side, and the trio of books, the towel and fresh socks. There are many items. A certain pleasure is to be gained from the world, its items, you have this yin here and a few more over there. Although predisposed toward the speculative musings, one is bound to say, having regard to that which is having gone before. One considers the Busconductor, Hines: now, here we have a fellow, from a spruce district.

How does she leave. How does she even fucking think a thing like that. How can she even think it for christ sake even think the fucking thing. Imagine it. For fuck sake.

It's beyond belief. It's actually beyond belief. Sandra makes it worse. This isnt her. She must've been really fucking, upset. When it all comes down to it, the way she is, so set in her ways, determined, thinking things out. Not like him. Hines is a fucking idiot: but she isnt, she's fucking – the way she thinks things out. This is what's so fucking ridiculous. Then just to grab Paul. Even doing that. The fucking selfishness, that's not her. Christ.

Hines had grinned. He stopped it, it wasnt right. He had dried the heel of his left foot. He gazed to there for a few moments. Then up to the clock, and then was drying both feet, and across to the tallboy, looking in at the drawers where she kept her stuff but they were always so jampacked it was difficult to know if she had taken extra, except if she had it couldnt have been much.

He was dressed and stuffing the tin and matches into his jerkin pockets. Before leaving he got the £3 from the mantelpiece and dumped the note into the rubbish bin then retrieved it, laid it face down on the mantelpiece.

And the front door key.

* * *

There was no point in phoning. You go there and phone and nothing is to be said. Best just having a couple of pints and then going fucking home. You stand there having trouble finishing the first, giving nods now and again to this old cunt standing next to you who keeps on making comments on the weather etc. Finishing it off and ordering another, the natural thing. A load of shite. You grab a hold of his lapels: Here auld yin my wife's fucked off and left me I mean what's the fucking game at all, your fucking daft patter, eh, leave us alone ya cunt for fuck sake. This isnt Hines who's talking. It's a voice. This is a voice doing talking which he listens to. He doesnt think like it at all. What does he think like. Fuck off. He thinks like anybody else, anybody else in the circumstances, the circumstances which are oddly normal. Here you have a busconductor by the name of Hines Robert whose number is 4729 and whose marital status. What's the point of fucking about. You leave half of the second pint and get off your mark.

Glasgow's a big city, all the life etc. The scraggy mongrels, they go moseying along near the inside of the pavement then to the outside and maybe off across the street to sniff other pastures. Hereabouts the district is a melter of sniffs. A myriad of things at your nostrils. The decayed this and the decayed that. A patch of tenements set for the chop. Imagine being drunk one night, as if that which is not to be doubted is on high authority, such that its existence can only be assumed such that the body is duty bound to endorse that assumption, fine, and sneaking into a derelict block for an illegal pish and tripping over a lump of concrete, cracking one's head on the floor, not badly, just enough to lope out of consciousness for an hour or so, to awaken in the wee hours, lying in the black, the smells surrounding you, then engulfing you the more aware you become; but not wanting to move in case your noise arouses other noise from a different room or maybe even the same one, that dark bit in the corner – it is your awareness sets it all going because these fucking noises man they were ever present, you just hadnt fucking realized them and now they come crashing in on you, indescribable noises; and how to escape how to escape, without your movement activating other movement. Better off razing the lot to the ground. And renting a team of steamroadrollers to flatten the dump properly, compressing the earth and what is upon and within, crushing every last pore to squeeze out the remaining gaseous elements until at last that one rectangular mass is appearing, all set for sowing. The past century is due burial; it is always been being forgotten.

There is a crack in the pavement a few yards from the close entrance; it has a brave exterior; it is a cheery wee soul; other cracks can be shifty but not this one. Hines will refer to it as Dan in future. Hello there Dan. How's it going? Cold yin the night eh! This fucking weather wee man. Never mind but, the ice and that, helps you expand. Pity cracks dont wear balaclavas right enough eh! One good thing about these old tenements, however, is the way they refuse to allow snow to hang about. A tough set of bastards so they are. No messing. None of your fucking good king wenceslas rubbish with them. The more mockit the better, where the air stinks and the absent horizons, the backcourts of a sturdy obscenity, these disused fucking washhouses whose brickwalls are liable to collapse on the offspring's skull at any moment. Fuck off.

Hines dislikes being a laughing-stock. The people he works beside are laughing-stocks. He is a laughing-stock. They are all laughing-stocks. Occasionally this being a laughing-stock is something not to be borne. He can lie awake at night, the head having started to bang. It is strange how they are content to remain objects of derision. Hines can see the faces. He can hear them discuss their children. What else does he do. He does a lot of things. It all gets a bit much. Very little time is left. There isnt the time to accomplish much. Should much be accomplished the time has shrunk. Should little be accomplished the world expands. To accomplish the little demands particular heads. Hines has not got a particular head. In his head the things go scratching against the outer shell. He can lie awake at night and breathe deeply, regularly, for the scratching to cease.

Sandra was in the kitchen. It makes no difference. With the gun in his possession movement will accelerate. The main problem is money. Hines was relying on his knowledge of Frank Sinclair to overcome this. A gun would probably cost 2 or 3 weeks wages but maybe as much as 4. Hines had no way of obtaining such an amount. The sum of £80 lay in the bank but could not be withdrawn by him. Yet no genuine reason exists for this situation. It is as much his money as Sandra's and Paul's. He just felt he should not be withdrawing it for selfish purposes. With £80 in hand he could probably get the gun quite easily, the additional cash to be advanced later on. Frank would arrange that.

Although in an obvious sense the £80 would have to be used for the gun. It belonged to the unit. As a symbol of that unity the money should be used to real purpose. Once Paul was old enough he would understand that. He could understand right now. If rupture within the home was the only alternative the boy would know fine well what had to be done; it would scarcely be a case of understanding or anything like it, just the natural order of things, that which the adult is obliged to do.

Of course Sandra was looking great, the jeans and the jumper, so reminiscent of how she used to look when pushing the pram; she used to push it down by the river to meet him coming home off early shift. If the day was fine they did this rather than him just taking a bus home. He used to run up the road, all the way from the garage, then down through the park. It was still a surprise seeing her shape, her lack of belly, fitting into the old outfits again. She looked really well, and sometimes he felt a bit of a cunt to be meeting her in uniform, an embarrassment, the daft cashbag and hat while she was looking the way she did, and the wee yin babbling away; walking home, along past the old flint mill, the trees and the bushes, the grass: right smack in the heart of the city she had found this place, an amazing spot where you could walk in a valley by the side of a river; an enclosed place, road bridges high overhead, no traffic sounds whatsoever.

Hines grabbed her. He increased his hold of her, he laughed abruptly, relaxing the hold and increasing the hold; again laughing and she began laughing, that chuckling sound; it begins from way deep in her throat and makes a noise like gloogle gloolg. He kissed her on the lips, his tongue along her lower teeth; he felt her relax, returning the kiss with genuine aggression, the kiss mattering in itself. She liked kissing him. This was the great thing; and probably an explanation of why their lips always fitted together so well – a kiss can be really erotic, one kiss and one kiss only, if that kiss is right, is enough to get things moving immediately. Her skin through the jumper; the actual texture of the jumper, lamb's wool maybe or something akin; the size a bit big for her, the upper trunk slenderish; her tits through it as though she had left off her bra altogether but probably because she buys good bras that their material resembles flesh almost or maybe just so thin the skin through it cannot be concealed. She could get him from nothing; just sitting in the same space and it altering, naturally enough an inter-something-or-other connected with radiation or something giving off from each other that one hand is moving to the other's hand, this drawing together as reaction, then the fitting together so exactly right. All parts of her. Those dances they used to have in just that kind of awareness, playing, dancing towards and dancing away, circling, an occasional touch, the tremble; then another record and sometimes when it was a slow one and they danced holding he got hard and they had to move from the floor, her shielding him.

Paul...

Asleep; he was dead-beat.

They kissed again. Over her shoulder he saw the gas burning in its steady flame; the arrangement on the mantelpiece seemed different, the note either not there or lying so flat it couldnt be seen; and the blind drawn at the window. She had maybe given the whole place a going over. She moved and he was aware of her jumper again, of how slender her body was, or just the jumper being that bit too big for her. But he felt he could put his arms right round her and still be touching the sides of his own body, as though she was eating less than she should be – skinny, not slender. He moved to look at her and they both smiled. He shook his head. Aw Sandra.

I'm sorry Rab.

Jesus christ. He clutched onto her now, his chin on her shoulder, his eyelids shut; she shifted to kiss him, she was beautiful; his hands beneath her jumper and lightly on her skin, his fingertips to that spot at the base of her spine, and moving upwards on her spine, to beneath the strap of her bra, then out and he brought his hands out from her jumper. Fancy going to bed?

She smiled.

What is it?

O ... She shook her head as she stepped to the armchair and began to undress.

How come you're so beautiful?

She stuck her tongue out at him, chuckling as she released the catch on her bra. Her tits jutted out as she turned to lay the bra on top of the chair.

He undressed and switched off the main light; she switched on the bedlamp. Lying down on his side he cupped his chin in his left hand, gazed at her until she moved nearer to him and he shifted so that she could lie above his left arm, it lying exactly beneath the pillow, within the space between her head and right shoulder, comfortably. She looked at him before they kissed. That can be a strange look. A look to see something or other – as though she isnt a hundred percent certain who he is. And when he broke the kiss she looked at him in the same way, before it continued, now pulling him more closely in to her. Sometimes he was unsure about holding her too tightly in case her breasts got too squashed by him, by his chest – one time years ago she gave him a kind of punch there, on the chest, and winced and rubbed her knuckles, not having been aware of how hard male chests can be. He manoeuvred her onto her back and they looked at each other. He kissed her throat and down to kiss her nipples, reaching to take down her pants; her head rose a little, her right arm lying over his back, to nibble at the lobe of his ear; she laughed and lay back on the pillow. Her legs parted as he positioned himself to enter. The opening felt so narrow.

God Rab you feel huge.

Hh.

It's because it's a while.

I'm no hurting you?

No.

You sure ... christ ... He breathed out and relaxed a moment then pushed up slowly. He opened his eyelids but hers were closed; he kissed the tip of her nose and settled onto her, but taking his weight on both elbows. He grinned. Dont move or I'll come.

O.

Ssh.

She made as though to speak.

Ssh ... He was having to smother a laugh. He placed his head on the pillow above her left shoulder. Think of churches. That old lady in the blue skirt walking up the path – Auvers, somewhere in France; where the sun shines. Going down some Rue, in the early evening, just the pair of them, heading for a meal, then onto some cafe for a chat and maybe a dance or something, Gaite Parisienne, the lassies kicking out, wee Toulouse with the sketch pad, the Seine in the moonlight, picked out on the ripples. Careful.

What d'you mean?

Nothing – a twitch, you twitched.

Sorry.

He was suppressing laughter.

Sorry! She began to chuckle.

They kissed now and he was moving and not able to stop, christ and he was having to thrust and come almost without an orgasm but having to cry out all the same.

He lay on her, still taking the weight on both elbows. It's okay, she said but he continued to take it. After a while he grunted and she said, Dont come out yet.

Okay.

God Rab it feels like the Niagra Falls.

He grinned and kissed her.

I forgot to bring in the tissues.

Use the sheet.

. . .

Naw, it'll be okay. Either that or you'll have to walk on your hands to the fucking cludgie.

O God.

They both began laughing until she cried: It's coming out, you're coming out. And he felt himself slipping out then was unsure whether he was maybe still in. He moved onto his side and got out of bed at once and dashed to the tallboy, into the top drawer for the box of tissues. She took a couple. She wasnt rushing. It doesnt matter now, she said. I suppose it's time the sheets were changed anyway.

Aaahh.

She glanced at him.

It's great to be alive.

She smiled.

He stretched, his fingertips to the ceiling, on tiptoes, muscles as tensed as they could be. He relaxed enough to breathe out deeply, prolonging it then breathing out again, the final old air, before gasping in the fresh. Aah. Christ. Fancy a coffee?

She nodded. See that bag over there . . .

He went to the kitchen-cabinet, the pull-down section lying out and the paper bag, containing two chocolate covered doughnuts. Absolutely fucking disgusting. I dont know how you buy this stuff Sandra I really dont.

Cheaper than tobacco.

Aye but christ sake I mean! When the water had boiled he made the coffee and placed the doughnuts and cups on the television set, beside the bed. Back between the sheets he stared at his doughnut and frowned. I have reason to believe that in certain sections of America one daubs one's erogenous zones with honey and one's partner licks it off.

Sounds interesting.

Aye, strange fucking place America: it's a doughnut-loving nation apparently.

It was me told you that.

Very sorry.

They dont have ordinary cakes, just assorted varieties of doughnuts.

Monopoly land, what d'you expect.

No but it's funny ... She studied the doughnut before taking the first bite. She was aware of him watching but continued as though indifferent, and she was managing to eat without getting any of the chocolate onto her face, except where a spot stuck to her upper lip, then out poked her tongue to ensnare it. It's actually quite tasty, she said. When he grinned she made a face at him.

How much were they?

I'm not telling you.

Dear but?

Yes.

A moment's silence; then he laughed and she grinned. Aye, he went on, life can be a startling item at times – I was just saying that very thing to a crabbit auld cunt who stepped onto my platform the other morning. Excuse me mrs I said I'm well aware your complaints are justified but in regard to the startling nature of the world, the ascendancy of certain stars and so on ... He grinned and ate his last mouthful of doughnut. He got out of bed, collected the tin from his jerkin pocket and paused to slap at the soles of his feet before returning. It's great to see you.

Hines had said it while prising the lid off the tin. And he added, I didnt expect it I mean eh.

She handed him her cup and while he leaned to put it on top of the television she put her arm round his back; he closed the tin and placed it next to the cups. How come you're so beautiful?

You're a terrible flatterer Hines.

Hh; cant even get telling the truth nowadays.

She slapped his chest.

Ah! She's beating me next!

They rolled together until she was on top of him and she raised herself, her tits drooping so well and perfect and he craned his neck to meet them, taking each nipple in turn between his lips; she moved onto her side eventually, then onto her back, Hines managing to shift position while keeping mouth to nipple. He came away and they kissed, her hand now between his legs and their tongues touching within the other's mouth; he was attempting the insertion and she moved for him. They were still kissing but his head now rested next to hers on the pillow, and his left foot steadying against the bottom wall of the recess. He began the thrust, she going with it. A rhythm was settled into. Later he was set to climax and halted; she had also halted. He listened to her breathing. A few moments just, then it would be right to resume.

Part Two

Liz Lochhead

Phyllis Marlowe:
Only Diamonds Are Forever

The letters lying there on the mat didn't exactly look as though if I didn't open them the world would stop.

I picked them up. I turned them over, squinting through the bloodshot marblings of my hangover and the tangled remains of last night's Twiggy eyelashes. It was back in sixty-six. Those days the world was a more innocent place.

I fanned out the fistful of manilla in my mitt. As I had thought. Zilch. A final demand from the Gas Board and a threat from Glasgow Public Libraries if I didn't return *The Maltese Falcon* and pay my seventeen-and-six fine they'd permanently withdraw my ticket and cut my left hand off. And what was this? I swallowed. I swallowed again. An appointment card, report today, today at two-thirty, the Brook Clinic, a discreet logo and address, a classy address in the city's ritzy West End.

I showered, shaved – shaved my legs – like I said this was back in sixty-six, the world was a more innocent place, those days no one accused you of anti-feminism if you were caught with a tube of Immac. I sniffed. I showered again.

I emerged from the bathroom a half an hour later in a cloud of Amplex Aerosol avalanched in Boots' 365 Talcum. The place looked like the ski-slopes at Chamonix.

I shimmied shivering to the bedsit, slotted another shilling in the gas fire and reached for the knob on the third drawer of the tallboy. I knew exactly what I was looking for, they had to be here somewhere, the one and only pair of knickers left uncontaminated in that disastrous load at the launderette, the stuff that had got washed along with that bargain-price bright-pink non-fast Indian-cotton mini-skirt from C&A. Some bargain, huh? These days I peeked out at the world through unevenly rose-tinted underwear.

I found them at last. Virgin white as the day they crossed the counter at Galls. I slid them on. Two-thirty, huh? I showered again.

Two-twenty-five found me on the steps of a slightly crumbling mansion in what the Estate Agents would call a highly desirable residential area. A simple brass plaque spelt out Brook Advisory Clinic. The whole place screamed Anonymity.

I pressed the bell. The door creaked open a couple of inches.

'Yes?' said a voice more frosted than its glass panels. I showed her my card.

'Two-thirty,' I barked.

She barked back, the door slid open wide enough for me to enter and I found myself in a roomful of dames all with rigor mortis of the third-finger-of-the-left-hand. Engagement rings. Woolworth's engagement rings, each a lump of glass as big as the Ritz. There was more imitation ice than in *The Ancient Mariner*, more gilt than in a psychiatrist's office, more rolled gold than in Acapulco.

Tonight these dames were going to have greener fingers than Percy Thrower.

Each broad had a Tame Boyfriend with her, like a poodle on a lead. All you could see of any of them was a pair of very pink ears sticking out behind old copies of the *Woman's Own*. Nobody in the place looked exactly relaxed.

I sat down. Dame opposite was wearing laddered black Beatle nylons – Jesus, nobody had worn Beatle nylons since sixty-four Chrissakes. She was reading *The Uses of Literacy*. Maybe she did have an honours degree in sociology, but she certainly was sixpence short in the shilling when it came to dress-sense. Still, somebody loved her. Otherwise she wouldn't be here. I slid my eyes over the gent she had accessorising her. Below magazine-level at any rate he was not painful to look at.

Over in the corner behind a gigantic desk sat this old bird who looked as though she had been there since Marie Stopes was pre-pubescent.

'Next!' she plainsonged and fixed me with an old-fashioned look from behind her lorgnette.

I sidled over. 'Name,' she stated.

'Marlowe,' I quipped. 'Marlowe with an 'e'. Phyllis Marlowe. 'Ph' for Phellatio, 'Y' for Yesplease, 'L' for Love, 'L' for Leather, 'I' for Intercourse, 'S' for—'

She looked at me as though I had said a dirty word.

'In here,' she said, 'remove tights and pants, lie up on that table. Doctor will be here to examine you directly.' She pronounced it Doktor with a 'k'. I gulped. I must pull myself together. I loosened my waistband and pulled myself together.

I found myself in a rough cubicle with a torn curtain hanging to approximately knee-height. Through this, various bits of anonymous female gooseflesh and, in the ringing tones of a Roedean Gym-mistress, Doktor's voice interrogating the bimbo-next-door about the ins-and-outs of her sexlife. The whole place was about as private as Grand Central Station on Glasgow Fair Saturday.

Five minutes later found me flinching and clenching, biting into the black vinyl of the couch as cold steel penetrated. I spat out a curse.

Ten minutes after that – I sat in triumph, six precious months' supply of the pill in my grasp.

Doktor wagged a metronome finger at me.

'You must take for twenty-one days religiously, stop for seven, always begin on the same day of the week, got it? Now, what do you do?'

'I'm a student at Jordanhill college doing Fribble,' I riposted.

She gave me a look, I returned it, she slammed it back, I caught it neatly, spun round and delivered a deft backward glance over my left shoulder.

Back in the waiting room it had gotten twice as crowded. Obviously there was a future in this business, they'd hit a nerve somewhere.

Then I saw him. Shoulder-length blond hair, embroidered cheese-cloth shirt, single strand of beads – I mean, beads but *tasteful* – a sensual hint of hash and patchouli, and midnight blue denims stretched taut then flaring over the longest, leanest bass-guitarist's thighs in Glasgow. Like, this guy's loons had *style*. I'd loved him for as long as I could remember. I'd have known him anywhere.

'Haw, thingmy,' he jack-knifed to his feet. 'Whit urr you daeing here?'

'I might ask you the same question.'

His Adam's apple slid up and down his throat like the lift in the Red Road Flats oughta, but don't.

'Hey, listen doll, great to see you, oh aye. Hiv tae git you roon tae wir new flat in Wilton Street, listen to a few albums, smoke a few joints. Fat Freddy's got some Moroccan in, really good stuff … toodle-oo!' he gabbled.

I looked over his shoulder. Coming towards him, big smile freezing fast, was this Julie Christie lookalike in Fringed Suede.

I smiled a lopsided smile. 'So long Blue-Eyes, see you around.'

Outside it was still raining. On my way through Kelvingrove Park I flipped my once-precious packet into a wastebasket and walked on.

Last I saw, a couple of hand-in-hand schoolkids had fished them out and were avidly reading the instruction leaflet. Probably disappointed to find it wasn't twenty-one tabs of acid. Sex is wasted on the young.

Back in my bedsit, I spooned bitter instant into my Union Jack-I'm-Backing-Britain mug – this was sixty-six, the world was a more innocent place – and sighed. I guessed I'd just have to swallow it strong and hot and black and bitter, I'd run clean out of Marvel. I ripped the cellophane off another packet of chocolate digestives.

Alison Fell

There's Tradition For You

Wanda eases herself invisibly under the skin, tense/release, tense/release, mainly the long muscles of your back and the fatty gluteus maximus and you think back to last Wednesday teabreak when you keeked at the paper and your old pal Lovat keeked right back at you, fatter now and most of his hair away but him and no mistake. Turns out some lassie's collapsed of an overdose two doors down from his flat, dancer it said, stripper it meant, Social Services at fault the headline said for the lassie's not eighteen and still in Care. 'I was shocked to discover the background to the case and will of course be pressing for an inquiry,' never set eyes on her in his life you thought to yoursel', aye that'll be right, well pull the other one mister Right Honourable randy Lovat. Gerald's got you posed with legs spread, one flat on the drapes, the other crooked up and the brocade's bumphling up under you – this idea of theirs that women lie around nude on old curtains gets on your wick but there's tradition for you. One arm's thrown back over your head – faces of course, don't interest them – at least back in the old days in the sculpture studio with its plaster casts of rude bits and Greek horses you'd hear all the wee ohs and ahs about the line of Wanda's thigh or Wanda's thorax, fucking fabulous, and if they didn't say it you'd see it in their eyes, Wanda, she's a humdinger. Planes and tones, Gerald keeps whispering, pencil angled in the air and chopping you up, planes and tones, and you smell the sweat of one armpit and wonder how a man like Lovat gets to be Undersecretary-for-whatever-it-is and what it was about him that got you anyway. That lick of colourless hair flopping down on you while he worked and worked for his thin wee fizzle, the light blue eyes rolling up, the chest hot and blotched with flat freckles. And him that first time squealing for your nails, Wanda, your fingernails, and you felt funny about it but you stuck them in all the same, try anything once; if it had stopped there, okay, but what didn't he need on top of that? Malt whisky, a finger up the gluteus maximus, Wordsworth and a clean hanky on the bedside table, and then in the bottom of the wardrobe the hat-box with the switch in it, ropes, the polaroid camera, you never knew whether he was going to read you poetry or tie you up or get you to leather his bum pink, maybe it was the surprises you went for, and that sexy voice he had, furry and English with rs in all the wrong places Americar amnesiar My Wife Cynthiar you never could resist foreign accents, look at Magnus and his Norwegian one, sly hand under the broom bushes making you wet that day up at Erskinehall where the boarding school was with the midges coming up and sniffing the pair of you but they liked foreign blood better so it was his bum they peppered, oh Magnus with his red cheeks and yellow hair you wanted to sail away to Norway and have his baby even tried to learn Norwegian from a library book Isla said you could always said you were clever and maybe you would have if Ray Beatty hadn't come along and that's another bloody story. Six weeks, they said, you've to keep the baby six weeks for the papers to come through so it wasn't worth giving him a real name when they'd only snatch it away and christen him Graeme or Neil or whatever, but there's bad luck long gone and Lovat taught you a thing or two, give him that, remember his red tongue that first time coming out like a snapdragon and slavering spittle round your nipples, no one else ever did that in broad daylight and made them stand up so straight you felt your whole womb tug when his finger slipped in and he's whispering all the time dirtiest stuff you ever heard then the rope goes round your wrists in a sheepshank good boy scout that he was hauling them above your head your ankles too, tied apart to the bedend so wide you're scared nearly seeing stars saying Christ Lovat, but he gets the camera out and snaps away smiling and purring while you feel yourself running wet and when he shows you the pictures one finger still fiddling you, there you were black and hairy under the swell of belly, pinkness keeking out and giving you a fright at first, like something slipped inside out, like a glove taken off and angry like piles or something, fancy that, you'd seen enough cows in calf, even had a full-term bairn tearing its way out but it wasn't you then looking at that inside red slithery flesh it was medics in white masks don't know what you thought you had down there; seeing again suddenly the wet flat hair on Fred's head, like Maisie the cat you buried in the garden by the gladioli, a slate for a gravestone and a sad ceremony until the rain came and flushed the earth away and there was Maisie's thin skull with the black hair wet and transparent and pink flesh showing through and it's not right no it isn't, that poor lassie in a coma and you up here spread out like a car crash or a murder chalk marks and all; what a greeter you were in those days though, crying for Lassie and calves stillborn and everybody's dead second cousin, Heartbreak Hotel howling for Magnus long gone, Stand By Me and Ben E. King soaking your hankies for Ray Beatty, until Lovat showed you that folded hole and somehow got you like red muck sucking at him with such a wet noise that you thought of the folds the tractor blades turned in the long furrows, colour of the earth dark purplish under the green grass clods toppling over, rainbow sheen of worms slipping back in for safety, and moles, too, sleeked and damp, and dead field mice sliced up in the baler, and your legs went up round Lovat's neck wanting him to plant you, you couldn't help it for with your eyes shut he wasn't lean white and clever any longer but a thick brown man hairy as a beast with a red cock spirting his stuff into you and you were ashamed but what the hell they took Fred away didn't they and a lassie's got a right to enjoy her sex hasn't she. And damn it all clean sheets steak au poivre made a nice change, remember speeding over the Forth Bridge with the top down, Radio Luxemburg on, he was no chicken then, must be fifty-five if he's a day but God was he wild, shouting drunk over the scregh of the wind about My Wife Cynthiar and the thirty-six teddy bears he never knew about till he married her thirty-six bloody teddies Wanda teddies on the bed teddies hanging off the mirror I shouldn't be telling you this Wanda, met her on Gleneagles golf course she'd an MA and bloody good legs and it was high time I settled down, never laid a finger on her until the nuptials as it were, some women don't like it you see, not like you Wanda not like you my lovely, swerving all over the shop while he gets his finger worked up under your suspenders, I can set you up Wanda a view on Kelvingrove a shower your own front doorkey why live in a pigsty say yes Wanda say yes my lovely, well what a lot of blethers I ask you. It'll be fair shares for his cronies and all you mark my words, said Isabella in the canteen that day but anyway he dropped the notion soon enough, not a peep out of the bugger that time you reckoned you were pregnant, I'm up to my ears in the by-election my dear so much for Wanda my lovely and I need you and the true blue confessions bit about My Wife Cynthiar. Aye you've had your problems Wanda hasn't everybody, look at the Glasgow models gone to pot already, Dorothy who used to be a lovely girl down to skin and bone in the brothel at Dundas Street and Isabella dead of drink at thirty, well, I've some information that might interest you Mister Maxwell, men like that'll always get away with it and there's a thought to get anybody off their arse and away down to Mayfair in the magnolia-smelling dark where streetlights kid on they're gaslamps and there are no dustbins alkies sweetiepapers or the like and then we'll see about amnesiar, could you picture his face if you stripped on his doorstep, very *déjeuner sur l'herbe*, absolutely fucking Manet wouldn't you say, you could get to be a right bitch Wanda if you wanted but never mind you needed the practice aye hell hath no fury but there's tradition for you

Margaret Elphinstone

from *A Sparrow's Flight*

'So you'll be on your way to the fair?'

Naomi looked at the woman in surprise. 'What fair?'

She received a look that could have been suspicious. The woman set down the tray on which she brought them food, and said questioningly, 'Surely you must know of it? Whatever road you came by, folk will have been on their way. And you carrying a fiddle with you. Don't tell me you didn't know.'

'No,' answered Naomi steadily. 'I didn't. We came by a little used way from the other side of the country, and just walked down the valley this morning. It's early in the year for a fair, surely?'

'For the cloth,' replied the woman slowly. 'They sell the weaving after the winter. It's not such a great event to an outsider, but whichever of these valleys you came down by, you must have heard of it, on any road. I never met a musician who would avoid a fair.' Her eyes rested on Naomi's pack as if she suspected something far more sinister within than a fiddle.

'I'll not avoid it now I know, certainly. Where is it?'

'At the end of this road, surely, where the two valleys meet. You're heading straight for it. You must have come that way to be in this valley at all. There's no other road.'

Naomi didn't answer that. 'You don't go yourself then?'

'My sister has gone from this household. But you won't find any folk in this village today. There'll be plenty of entertainment there tonight. Here's your friend.'

Thomas appeared at the door, his shoulders damp from the drizzle outside. 'Thanks,' he said, his eyes on the tray of food. 'That's very welcome.'

As soon as the woman had left them, Naomi turned to him. 'There's a fair at the end of the valley,' she said. 'Did you know of it?'

He looked puzzled, then remembered. 'For the weaving?' he said. 'Yes, it would be about now. Too far from my country, so I've never been, but I've heard of it. It's happening now?'

'Yes. She couldn't understand how I didn't know, so I stopped asking questions. Thomas, how far is it?'

He shrugged. 'Eight miles. Maybe more.'

Naomi sighed. 'I'm stiff all over. But so be it.'

'You want to get there? Today? We've come further than that already, and it's getting late.'

'Don't say it.'

'What?'

'I could have got up earlier. But I could do with something, Thomas. And you – your trade isn't so different from mine. Don't you want to go too?'

He shrugged, and stirred his soup. 'Yes. No. I could easily be distracted. I suppose I'd avoid it if I were alone.'

'And I would not. It's in such places I should be, not alone on a mountain top with only the birds to hear me.'

'I'm not a bird.'

'You think you're all the audience I need? You'd have to be more than one man for that.'

'I heard you playing this morning, and I never asked you to hurry, because I wanted to hear. I'm probably as good an audience as you'll get, although there's only one of me.'

Naomi leaned back, cradling her soup bowl. 'That could be true,' she admitted. 'I didn't even know you were listening. Why does it matter to you?'

Thomas shrugged again. 'Unworthy reasons, I suppose. It's my journey. I've a reason for wanting you and something to give you. Meanwhile, I suppose I don't want to share. Though it's not easy to admit to it.'

'You're more honest than you lead me to believe,' said Naomi, smiling at him. 'I like that in you. But the fact is, I'm not yours, not even for one journey. I've other business, which won't harm your plans. So I'll go to the fair, but I'll keep my contract with you, as I promised.'

'I've no right to ask more. In which case, we should push on. 'Have you eaten?'

'Nearly.'

'I'll give her something for it. No,' said Thomas, as Naomi was about to speak. 'I will. It's my journey, and all the currency you have is music, which I don't want to take the time for. Do you mind?'

'No. That's fair. I'll come in a minute.'

The woman who had given them the meal was right. As they went further it became obvious that they were on their way to an event. There were others on the road: people leading ponies, people driving carts, people with packs on their backs, and people with nothing to carry, dressed in their holiday clothes in spite of the persistent drizzle that hid the hills on both sides of the valley. The valley itself was opening out, and the river flowing alongside the road was growing gradually wider, meandering through lush meadows. There were many more settlements here, both hamlets and solitary farms, and only thin stretches of woodland between each cultivated clearing. The road was wide and deeply rutted, so that passers-by had trodden down the verges in an attempt to keep out of the dirt. Thomas and Naomi picked their way after them, occasionally overtaking slow processions of laden beasts and people.

At last the road diverged from the river, cutting across the foothills to the west. Naomi was really tired now. Her boots felt damp and tight, but she ignored her aching legs and led the way. Thomas trudged behind her, apparently inexhaustible.

There was another river below, with a humped bridge over it, and a small market town beyond. The field above the river was a mass of colour, a jumble of tents and animals and people. The noise that rose from it was like a hive of bees about to swarm in summer. Through the hum of people there were faint strains of music. Naomi held on to the straps of her pack to steady it, and began to run. Thomas stood and watched her go, looking a little bewildered. Then he walked slowly down to the bridge, and was caught up in a crowd of people going the same way. He hesitated at the bridge, as if debating whether to go on, but there were more people pushing from behind. He allowed himself to be swept along with the crowd, and the fair engulfed him.

He heard Naomi again before he saw her. It was already growing dark, and the place was lit with fires and torches. With the darkness the atmosphere changed, for no serious business could be done without daylight by which to see that everything was done fairly. The merchants' stalls were empty, and the seed sellers and drovers were gone. Instead, other tents and stalls had come to life, advertising gambling or fortune telling or various marvels within. There was music everywhere, mostly indifferent, all adding up to a dramatic confusion of sound, with a steady beat underneath coming from the centre of a crowd that had gathered round a huge fire on the far side of the field. The people who thronged the muddy alleyways between the tents were on holiday now. As Thomas wandered through the fair, children shoved past him and ran away, laughing, and couples drifted away towards the darker perimeter. Thomas ignored them all, only once stepping into the shadows to avoid a group of drunken men. He had left his pack in a safe place, and only carried a red cloth bag with a gold pentacle embroidered on it.

As he drew nearer to the fire, the crowd got thicker. Thomas slipped through it like a shadow, and few were even aware of his passing. He could hear the music now, not just the drum, but pipes and stringed instruments as well. And a fiddle. Thomas emerged at the front of the crowd, ducking under a fat man's elbow, and blinked in the sudden light.

He looked round, then without hesitation detached himself from the audience and went to sit right at the feet of the band, crosslegged on the ground with his bag beside him. From this vantage point he could watch the musicians without seeming to do so, although it was hardly the best place to hear the music. Thomas had other objects in view.

He didn't think Naomi had seen him. He wondered if she had known any of these people before. She seemed quite at home now. Earlier in the day he had realised that she was more tired than she was going to admit, and had slackened his pace accordingly. She hadn't appeared to notice. But there was not a trace of weariness about her now. Whereas he had spent the last two hours eating a large meal and drinking more beer than he usually did, he was fairly certain she had been playing from the moment she got here. This wasn't the sort of music she played when she was alone. This was fast and exciting, sets of reels and jigs slipping into one another, music for crowds and for dancing. People were dancing; a space had been cleared on the other side of the fire. The ground was slippery with mud, not all the dancers sober, but the pace was wild, and growing wilder. Someone nudged him, and he jumped. It was the flute player, handing him down a leather flask that was being passed around the band. So he was accepted. Thomas took it with a word of thanks, and raised it to his lips. It wasn't wine, it was potato brandy that caught his throat like liquid fire. Thomas choked, passed the flask back again, and took a bottle of water from his bag. There was a break in the music, and shouts for more. The dancers dispersed, and the crowd surged forward. Bottles were handed across to the band and passed around. He saw Naomi shake her head, and sit down to retune her fiddle.

There were more players now, another fiddle player among them. The flute player stepped down and disappeared into the crowd. The musicians consulted together, then took their places again. The crowd moved back a little, leaving a clear space between Thomas and the fire. He waited to hear the beat, then as they launched into another set he stood up, and opened his bag.

There was a murmur from the crowd when they saw him, and the circle formed round him, another part of the act. The drummer whistled at him from the stage, and the music swept on. Naomi glanced at him, and saw, not Thomas, but the juggler, dressed in yellow and gold, firelight catching at the braid on his jacket, coloured balls tossing in time to the music, yellow and red and orange. Naomi watched him as she began to play, as if he were giving her the beat, not the other way round. She hardly saw his hands move, but the balls were everywhere, all round him, like sparks of firelight round his head. The tune changed: the juggling moved to a different pattern, too fast to follow, with Thomas spinning round in the middle, turning apparently all ways at once, the crowd seeming to hold its breath. The set ended with a flourish, and he seemed to catch all the balls at once, so they vanished. There was a burst of clapping, and yells from the crowd. Thomas took off his hat and bowed to them.

The other fiddler called a tune across to Naomi. She nodded, and stepped forward. She found herself opposite a thin dark woman with heavy features which were faintly familiar to her. Something nagged at the edge of her memory, but she couldn't place it, and the woman was counting the time. Naomi concentrated on the music, and forgot.

When she glanced at Thomas again there was only fire: points of flame swirling with the music. She kept her attention, recovering herself, and glanced again. It was fire. Not coloured balls this time, but flaming torches, moving as fast as her music, making patterns in the air with the fiery tails they left behind them, circles and spirals, flames orbiting round him, the shadow of Thomas in the middle, a face caught in sudden flamelight, concentrated, then lost again in a whirl of light. The tune was growing faster, the whole band behind her, the drumbeat still with her, and the other fiddler who was good, but not as good as she, the music growing wilder and the flames leaping higher in front of her, following her lead, circling faster as she played them faster, and a blur of faces beyond, a crowd transfixed like the painted backcloth to a play.

The music stopped. There was sudden darkness. Then there was only Thomas, bowing again, taking another torch from his bag, a long thin taper, which he held over his head, exhibiting to the people. Naomi lowered her fiddle, and stared. Only the drummer went on playing, when he saw what was happening, a frantic beating, culminating in a roll of thunder. Thomas lit his taper at the fire, and held it aloft. His face shone with sweat. Naomi held her breath. Thomas threw his head back, opened his mouth wide, and the flames descended and vanished down his throat. There was a crash on the drums behind her. Then Thomas was swirling the taper round his head again, undoused, acknowledging the cheering of the crowd. Naomi let out her breath and raised her fiddle. This time she chose her tune, without asking anybody, and played alone. She could sense the uncertainty in their response, but she didn't care. This wasn't dance music; this was a lament, remote and poignant, solitary high notes full of longing unfulfilled. Then there was a response, the same tune played back to her by a single mandolin, notes echoing hers like clear drops of water. Naomi looked, and it was the dark woman again, her fiddle exchanged for a mandolin. Again, there was that tug of recognition, but it was lost in the music. The rest were silent, except for the faint crackling of the fire. Naomi played on, and the other woman played with her, following her lead and never taking her eyes off her. When they stopped there was a moment's quiet, then applause like a hailstorm. Naomi put down her fiddle, and brushed her sleeve across her eyes. Silly to play that tune here. She was too caught up in it all. Must be hungry, she told herself. You've eaten nothing since midday. You can't cry here, that's for sure.

They were passing round the drink again, but she refused. She was about to turn away when someone spoke just next to her. 'Naomi?'

It was the woman who played the mandolin. So there was something. 'Do I know you?' asked Naomi uncertainly.

'I don't suppose you remember. But I'd like to talk to you, when you've finished playing.'

Naomi looked round. There was temporary confusion on the stage. The musicians and the crowd were mingling, and nothing else would happen for a while. 'I have finished for the moment. I need to eat. Do you want to come with me?'

'Is that all right? They do a good meal in that tent over there.'

They had hardly stepped out of the firelight when they were over-taken. 'Naomi?' said Thomas. 'Are you going?'

To his astonishment she turned round and hugged him. 'Thomas,' she said. 'You're an artist. Not a fool – a magician. Would you like some supper?'

'You too,' said Thomas, smiling in the darkness. 'Not a fiddler, a magician.'

'Or a fool. I said, have you eaten?'

'Twice. But I'll come with you, if it's not private.'

'No. At least,' Naomi turned to her new companion. 'It's not private, is it?'

'Not to me.'

'Then come. I don't think I've got any secrets.'

There were only a few people in the tent, which was dimly lit by two or three lanterns set out on the tables. There was still hot stew being served from a big pot on a brazier by the door. Naomi took a large helping, along with a hunk of bread.

'Can I have a drink of water?'

'We have beer.'

'No, water please.'

'We'll have beer,' said Thomas cheerfully. 'Won't you ... I don't know your name.'

'Helen. Thank you. I will.'

'I still don't have any money,' remarked Naomi.

'They're passing round the hats now. You mustn't go without claiming your share.'

'I'm not bothered. I get my expenses paid, this trip,' said Naomi, and the other woman looked at her questioningly, but said nothing. They sat down in a corner, and Thomas fetched one of the lanterns over to their table.

'So tell me,' began Naomi, with her mouth full. 'How do I know you?'

Helen hesitated, as if wondering where to begin. Then she said, 'I'm sure you don't remember. It was all of ten years ago, in your own country. There was a festival at harvest, and we were playing. But there were a lot of musicians, and you were much better than me. I wouldn't bother to remind you, only I have a message.'

'But of course you should remind me! You're from my own country? You don't sound like it.'

'No, I was travelling, as you are now. Who I am isn't important. I'm a travelling player too, but not as good as you.'

She paused. 'But that's not the point. There was a party at that festival. There were a group of us, talking. You spoke about the man who first taught you, in your own village. You gave his name, and the name of the village on the west coast. You weren't speaking to me directly, I knew that, but all the same, I remembered.'

Thomas sipped beer, apparently abstracted, but he was listening intently. He sensed Naomi stiffen, suddenly on her guard. 'And so?' He was beginning to know that casual tone.

'I remembered. The years went by, and eventually I found myself travelling in that country. I began to ask about this fiddle player that I had heard of, who knew many tunes that were virtually lost to the outside world. I was moving slowly northwards into a wild and rocky country, where the living was very poor, and the villages few and far between. But I carried on, and in the end I met someone who'd heard about him.'

She waited, but Naomi said nothing.

'Well, to cut a long story short, in the end I came to the village, and I found him. He made me welcome. I stayed a while, and learned a great deal of music from him.'

'He would do,' said Naomi softly. 'He would make anyone welcome.'

'I appreciated it. I knew my limitations, and so did he, but he was patient. Naturally, he also asked me how I came to hear of him.'

'Yes,' said Naomi shortly. 'And you said?'

'I told him. And he said, would I ever see you again? I said I doubted it. I didn't think that you knew I existed, and the world is wide, and all roads long. It would be a rare chance that brought us together. He said, but if it happened that such a chance should come, he wanted me to give you a message.'

Naomi had stopped eating, and was sitting very still, her head propped on her arm so her face was shielded from the light. Helen waited for her to respond, then carried on with her story. 'He said, tell her this if you ever find her again: "You did the right thing Naomi, and no one is hurt by what you chose."'

'Oh,' said Naomi, so softly that only Thomas heard her.

'I stayed over a month in that village,' offered Helen presently.

Naomi raised her head. 'Tell me about the village,' she said imperiously.

Helen searched for words. 'It wasn't my sort of country. I suppose it hasn't changed much. It lies at the head of an inlet, and at the entrance there are great grey cliffs, and all the time you can hear the Western Sea beating against the rocks, and the cry of the seabirds that nest outside the bay. The sea is everywhere. When you lick your own skin you taste the salt on it. All the trees are withered by it, and the smell of it gets into everything. The sea provides a living for the people, for there is little richness in the land. I can understand why anyone should leave such a place, for life must be hard, especially in winter.'

'I don't think so.' Naomi's voice was cold, and Helen looked up quickly, as if she had expected a different answer. 'And Gavin – the musician – tell me more about him.'

Helen spread her hands helplessly. 'I don't know what to tell that you don't know. You believe me, I hope. He's a big man, taller than you. His hair is grey and curly, and he has a beard. He belongs to his sister's household, which is at the top of the village, next to the field gate. And he goes fishing. What do you expect me to say?'

'I believe you,' said Naomi. 'You must excuse me if I'm not gracious. How old are you?'

'Me?' asked Helen, nonplussed. 'Thirty. Why?'

'It's what happens,' said Naomi. 'The people who bring us into this world are not the same as those who see us out of it. My roots are in a time and place which no one in my present can perceive, and my end is hidden in the future. I stand half way, if you like, and when you speak to me about my past, you speak to me of ghosts. My beginning matters – it's who I am, but it's only in my head now, like a dream. You're like a messenger out of a dream, and I don't know how to receive you.'

'I don't think I understand,' said Helen.

'I understand,' said Thomas simultaneously, and Naoml glanced at him. He looked down. He had never seen her look so vulnerable, and he thought she would rather he didn't see it now.

'You don't have to,' said Naomi. She sounded cold and arrogant, and the other woman stiffened with annoyance. 'Tell me more about the village.'

'I don't know what to tell.' Helen sounded almost sulky.

'Did you meet anyone else?'

Thomas watched them both, and was aware that he was afraid for Naomi. Helen was perhaps offended, not surprisingly. Thomas suspected that she had been hoping by her news to claim an equality that she was far from feeling. Naomi wouldn't have noticed that, because such feelings were quite foreign to her. But if Helen were hurt, she might use what she knew to hurt back. Naomi might be strong, but she had no defences, not in this situation. Thomas listened; and waited.

'I met a lot of people. One in particular I wanted to tell you about, if you're willing to hear.'

Helen turned her mug round and round on the table, and stared down into the dregs. 'I was down at the jetty one day. I forgot to tell you it was late summer. There were people working on a boat on the beach below me. I was sitting on the wall, enjoying the sun. It was usually pretty cold, with the wind off the sea, so the sun was something special.

'Someone came up behind me and said my name. I was quite startled. It was a boy.'

Naomi leaned her head on her hand again, so her face was hidden. 'Go on,' she said.

'A boy about ten years old. He asked me if I wanted to come out fishing. I was doubtful. I asked if he had a boat, and if he were allowed out on his own, because I didn't know anything about the sea.

'He said, "I know this sea. I've had a boat since I was five. My uncle made it for me, after they caught me trying to sail out of the bay in a fish box. I can take you. You'll be safe with me."'

'"You like boats, then?" I asked him. He said "yes," and showed me his. It was just a tiny rowing boat, but there was room for two of us. He was very efficient. He rowed me right out to the mouth of the bay. I was scared. I said, "Surely we shouldn't go out into the open sea?" "Tide's right," he said, "and the saithe are out there. You're safe with me." He took me out a little way beyond the entrance, right under the cliffs where the sea had hollowed out great arches and caves. It was a calm day, and the tide was high over the rocks. The cliffs were sheer, overhanging us so the sound of the waves echoed back from the rock above us. I couldn't help asking again if we were safe. He just grinned at me, and said, "You should see it in winter." I asked him about that. He started telling me about the ocean, and about the sailing directions to unknown countries away to the west. He knew all about those. He said there were sailing directions remembered in the village, accounts of islands and strange countries that were forgotten by all the rest of the world. He wouldn't tell me them though. He said that was secret. And he wouldn't show me the signs on the hills that marked out the fishing grounds, though he told me they were there. Then he showed me how to fish with a handline. "It's easy," he said. "You just jig it up and down. Like this. And when you feel a tug, a kind of movement, pull in hard. You try." So I tried, and when I caught a fish he watched me bring it in, very critically. Then he said, "Can you take it off the hook, or are you squeamish?" I got the message, and I took it off, though I didn't fancy it much. He watched me do it, then he suddenly said to me, "Tell me about the woman who told you where to come".'

Helen stopped for breath, and glanced at Naomi, but Naomi didn't look up. 'Go on,' said Thomas sharply.

'I tried to describe you,' said Helen to Naomi. 'I told him what you looked like, and about the festival where I met you. I told you you were one of the best musicians in the west. He just nodded, and went on fishing. Then he asked me what you'd said about the village. "Nothing," I said. "She was speaking about the fiddler here. That was all." "I see," he said, and soon after that he suggested that we go back again. I agreed to it. I was getting pretty cold. That was all.'

This time Naomi did speak. 'There was no message?' she said hoarsely, without looking up.

'No message. I don't think it would have occurred to him. He was very young.'

'What was he like?' asked Naomi, as though the words were dragged out of her.

'To look at, do you mean?' Receiving no answer, Helen went on, 'Quite striking, I suppose. Red hair, very thick. And greenish eyes. Hazel, perhaps.' She glanced at Naomi, but Naomi's eyes were hidden. 'Not very big, but sturdy, and very handy with his boat.'

'What else?'

Helen was at a loss. 'I don't know what else. I'm not used to children. What is there to say, really, about a boy? I liked him.'

'Did he tell you anything about himself?'

'He told me his name.'

'Colin,' said Naomi harshly. 'Was that his name?'

'That was his name.'

Naomi stood up abruptly. 'Thank you. Thank you for the message. Perhaps I'll see you again. Perhaps not. Farewell.' She looked down at Thomas without seeming to see him, turned and picked up her fiddle, and left the tent.

Helen looked after her uncertainly. Then she turned to Thomas, as if afraid of his reaction. 'Perhaps I shouldn't have told her just like that,' she said, 'but she seemed so sure of herself, it made me angry. And all this happened six years ago. I forgot to tell her that.'

'I think she can work that out for herself.'

'Yes. She'd hardly forget how old he was.'

'No.'

'It can't be easy for her really,' went on Helen, fidgeting nervously with her mug. 'But I suppose you know all about it.'

'I know nothing.'

'But you're her friend!'

'I don't know,' said Thomas.

'I'm sorry. I've got myself into deep water. I don't know what this is all about. I could have been more sympathetic. Not being in exile myself, I could go home whenever I liked. It must make a difference.'

'It does.'

'So you do know?'

'I know nothing about Naomi. But I can't think of anything a woman could do to deserve being exiled from her own child.'

'You knew he was her child then? So she does talk about it?'

'I told you, I know nothing except what I heard you say.'

'Anyway,' continued Helen. 'She wasn't exiled. It was her own choice.'

'You said she was in exile.'

'By choice. She went away before I could tell her, but I went to her own household. I met her sisters, and her brother. They talked to me. They assumed I was her friend, I suppose,' said Helen, with a touch of bitterness. 'It would have seemed rude to disillusion them. So they talked to me.'

'I see.'

'Yes,' said Helen, apparently oblivious to his tone. 'It's not as if they didn't care about her. The way they saw it, she was young at the time, and confused. She knew all the time it was the music that mattered most, but because she loved the fiddle player, she chose to have a child. Having made the other choice already, you understand. And then she realised that if you take one thing, you lose another. She would never have become what she is if she'd stayed there, but her child belonged to her mother's household, and to be a mother to him herself, that was where she would have to stay. In my village, I think they'd have made her abide by the consequences. If she was old enough to have him, she was old enough to stand by him, you'd think. But she didn't, and they supported her. Only they made her agree that if she went away, she must stay away, so the choice didn't become confused again. Everyone could see, they said, that it was impossible to keep your heart in two places at once. Everyone except Naomi. Because she loved him – they kept telling me that. That was why she stayed till he was weaned, though it made it more difficult. Then she left. Her agreement with them was not to go back. And she hasn't.'

Thomas was silent.

Helen began to wonder if she had said too much. 'But you can understand it,' she said in a more conciliatory tone. 'There was the music. She knew what it could offer her. She knew what she might become. You can understand why she chose to leave her child. He's sixteen now, I suppose. Much too late to decide anything different.'

'No!' said Thomas suddenly, so passionately that she recoiled. 'No, I can't understand! I can't understand that at all!'

'I don't follow,' said Helen quickly. 'I thought you supported her. I thought you believed she'd done right.'

Thomas thumped his hand down on the table so that all the crockery clattered. 'I tell you, I know nothing! I know nothing at all. Why throw her private life at me like this? Why should I agree with you? I don't! I don't want to hear about it at all!'

'What do you mean?' Helen was angry now too. 'You both treat me like dirt, and all I've done is answer your questions. I'd have thought I'd get some thanks! What's it to you, anyway? You don't have to make any choice. You're nobody's mother! What right have you to judge?'

Thomas leaned on the table, all the fight gone out of him. 'Please,' he said. 'Leave me alone. And her. What's a mother? Do you suppose no man ever loved a child?'

She stared at him, bewildered, but he didn't look at her or speak to her again. She watched him pick up his bag with the pentacle, and sling it over his shoulder. He kept his face turned away from her, not in anger, she suddenly realised, but because he was crying. She watched him in horror, not knowing how to react, as he walked away, ducking under the tent flap, out into the night.

Liz Heron

Undue Haste

When he rolls up the blind there are blisters of rain on the windowpane. While he's waiting for the water to boil he turns on the radio and the forecast says downpours, with the likelihood of flooding. Summer's ending is abrupt, over-subservient to the calendar. He thinks of the Labor Day weekenders heading up to the Falls and how they'll be disappointed. After he finds his lighter, sunk in his dressing-gown pocket, it won't work, so he dips a dead match in the cooker's gas flame.

The downstairs apartment's dog is sitting on the back steps. They leave it outside most days; sometimes it's still there when he gets in from work. It looks up at Tom and gives a perfunctory bark, then drops its head in a pose of dejection. The rain hugs its fur, which looks shorter, darker. He feels sorry for the dog. But he has never made friends with it; he doesn't want them asking him to feed it, or it getting attached to him.

In the grey light the kitchen depresses him. The patchy dark green walls, the split wood of the draining board – where he'd left some tuna in an opened can last night – the 60-watt gloom, all depress him, like a scene from a life he has left behind. He should have gone by now, by today of all days. He remembers there are loose ends to be tied up first.

The cigarette steadies him, and the tea. He has lain awake for hours, hoping to get some more sleep before the alarm. When he woke he switched on the light to see the time and his first thought was that Jean would just have taken off. He wonders where the plane is now. Over Greenland, or nearly. She'll be looking forward to sunshine, picnics by the lake, all the things he wrote telling her about in the spring. For a few moments he buries his face in his hands, letting tiredness numb him.

People get the wrong impression about the weather here. They think of log cabins in midsummer heat with midges clouding the night air by the lakeside; fish leaping in the dark. They picture snug sleigh rides at Christmas, like in old black and white films. He hadn't bargained for the long Montreal winter, trudging in the snow from one employment agency to another. He was ill-clad and the wind bit at his ears and face. It stung his eyelids and pushed his breath back into him through raw nostrils and cracked lips. People called this twelve below and weren't shocked by it. They warded off the atrocities committed by the climate with central heating, fur coats and fleecy boots, hats with earflaps. He had money for none of it; his savings were being drained by the bare necessities.

He had been counting on Andy Curran to make things easier. Andy had been there a year and had written full of promises. Tom found him about to get married – to a French-Canadian girl. He'd thought he'd be staying with Andy, but after the wedding they moved out to the suburbs, and Josiane put her foot down about starting married life with a house guest. Sometimes she spoke to Andy in French when he was there, though he knew her English was fine. Once the baby came, he even felt awkward about going round at all. Andy fixed him up with a temporary job at the start. Two weeks, then nothing for a while. He told him to do more computer training if he wanted decent money. There were plenty of loading jobs going at the factory where his brother-in-law was a foreman, but Tom's game leg ruled that out as a stop-gap.

Montreal was a mistake. At Easter, hearing from a cousin who had come over on a college placement, he went down to Toronto to see how the land lay. He got a job right away. The Good Life came closer; here, he could almost see himself as Canadian. His letters to Jean were extravagant with optimism. He wrote often. He had been lonely for so long.

He needs to feel fresh, clean, more alive than his sleeplessness will allow. The needles of water on his back massage the tension out of his skin, but the flow gets too hot, it stabs at him too sharply, the shower-head needs replacing. He alters its angle, lets the water skim round him, and it builds a comforting cloud of steam.

When he shaves he nicks his chin in two places. He pats at the blood with the edge of the damp bath towel. Change happens to everyone, he reflects, his hand trembling a little, his memory adjusting to the present. Andy had changed, not just with marriage, but before that. The Andy he'd met when he arrived in Montreal was already different, as if looking over his shoulder all the time to see how things were working out. He even seemed smaller, his gangly frame striving to take up less space than it used to. And this was a big country.

There had been four of them: Tom and Andy, Jim Colvin and Phil Reid. The other three had looked out for him ever since school. He was always one of the boys without really being like them. He might lack their bravado, their physical quickness, their malice-tainted confidence with girls; it didn't matter, he was the outlet for their kindness. It came to seem in excess of what his limp, his orphaned childhood demanded. At twenty, he'd wondered when it was he'd signed the contract that led to the expectations he fulfilled. Nice Tom, rewarding the kindness he's given, careful to hurt nobody's feelings. Nice-looking too, fair-haired, open-faced, but able only to watch the way Andy could challenge a girl's eyes, could turn morose and the girls would find his sullenness exciting, fancy they could cure him of it. They confessed these things to Tom, sometimes on what he'd considered dates. He betrayed the girls' secrets, of course, judging their trust a form of contempt. What he knew was relayed without emphasis, as befitted a diplomat. Jean didn't know any of that crowd when he met her.

He has no umbrella so he turns up his collar and makes a dash for it, ducking in and out of doorways. Sal's Café is just on the other side of the block, but by the time he reaches it there's a fringe of wet hair plastered to his forehead. 'You could use a coffee, I bet,' drawls Sally, giving him a sideways wink. He suspects sometimes Sally drawls for his benefit, in a kind of mocking response to his own accent. There was something funny about hers, anyhow. Could it be she's trying to mimic him, doing it badly. He hasn't thought of this before, but is at once reassured by her smile. Sally likes him.

He has a bigger breakfast than usual since he's late today. Ham and eggs, pancakes and syrup, orange juice. He smokes and feels much better now. The day no longer intimidates him.

Jean was his first love. He'd glimpsed something of himself in her, although she wasn't quite an orphan; her father had walked out. When he remarried, her mother didn't want to be an onlooker, so she'd moved with her daughter to where they weren't known. They lived above a dry-cleaner's next to the shoe shop where Esther was the manageress; refugees from Renfrew in a place where 'incomers' stayed that way after twenty-odd years.

Mother and daughter had the same wiry alertness about them, an air of muscular determination. Jean swam well. There were dark hairs on her forearms and a shadow over her upper lip that excited him. Esther had kept her looks. She plucked her eyebrows and wore shoes in the house, medium-heeled, well polished. His aunt had always insisted on slippers; for the sake of the carpets.

Jean's interest was tepid for a while, but all the time he pursued her, Esther made him welcome. He would drop round there, and if Jean wasn't in, he would pour out his heart to her mother. She was on his side. No question.

Jean was different after he'd been away, so his year in London paid off in the end, though he came back jobless. There had been somebody else, but she'd got over it. It had helped her make her mind up about him. 'I took you for granted before.' When she said this he saw she relied on him. It was a new feeling.

It's funny to think he would be married to her now if she'd said yes there and then. No rushing into things for Jean. Canada had appealed to her, though.

On the bus to the air terminal he wonders if he still loves Jean. He knows he stopped missing her soon after he met Duna. That was in May, while he was waiting for Jean's answer, and still lonely. It has stopped raining, but the bus splashes passers-by from the gutter troughs. He watches people shrink back from the kerb; a woman makes a little skip to dodge the dirty water, and she slips.

Duna is a kind of person he has never known before; Duna's life is ready-made for him.

She is five years older, a difference the same as her son's age. Little Gary, whose dad died three years ago, of a heart attack at the wheel of the blue and yellow delivery van he drove. He was only thirty-three.

Duna is half-Armenian. Tom isn't sure where Armenia is, whether it's still a real place on the map, but he likes this about Duna. It seems to account for her vibrancy, the blue-black colour of her hair, a great dark nest he can lose himself in and pretend he's a little bird. When she shakes him free of it the hair sprays out across the pillow, covering it like smoke.

On the airport bus there are a few backpackers, English, Canadian, two with Glasgow accents. The other people look dressed up by comparison. Whoever they are, they've turned into airline passengers, glad maybe of the special anonymity that lets only appearances describe them. He hasn't forgotten what a big adventure it was leaving Prestwick in that Jumbo. He'd had no fear of flying.

What will Jean be wearing?

This reminds him about the dress. When she wrote saying yes, he could have answered right away saying he'd had second thoughts. But he hadn't known then how involved he'd get with Duna. How could he? When he did decide to make a clean breast of it he got the letter telling him about the dress. Ivory silk. Esther had helped her make it. Esther would be coming out too, eventually, when they were settled.

There's an Indian family on the bus, the three women in brilliant glitter-edged saris, shaming the other passengers' anaemic summer wear. Duna has an oriental hanging on the wall of her apartment. She loves colour. There are drawings, pine shelves with books and plants, ceramic pots, woven samplers. Some of these she has made herself, others were gifts from people at the daycentre where she's an occupational therapist. Things she helped them to make. Duna's artistic. She can turn an ordinary room into another world. When he saw her apartment it was as if he had always been looking for a place like that to belong in, without ever having imagined it. He plays with the boy while Duna cooks, he washes the dishes afterwards. There's oriental music or jazz on the stereo.

It's too small for him to move in there, just one divided room, and the boy growing. They're looking together for a bigger apartment. He hasn't told Duna about Jean, only that an old girlfriend of his would be in town for a week or two. He sees the folly of this lie.

For a moment he holds his breath and almost prays, bowed to the fervent wish that Jean won't really mind when he tells her, that she'll see the sights and go back home without a fuss. And save her wedding dress for another time. It's a stupid wish. It occurs to him to claim a letter got lost in the post, telling her, that is.

He'll tell her at the airport. He'll take her out to dinner. He's found her a place to stay well away from Duna's. She'll be tired, jet-lagged. She could have a holiday, maybe fly out to that aunt and uncle in Vancouver. He would pay something towards the fare. He lights another cigarette, his hand shaking.

He is one of the first off the bus. He follows the yellow signs pointing up the escalator. The bar is crowded; he elbows his way in and orders a whisky. He has never been a drinker but he orders another one straight away. The alcohol sears his gut but it fails to unknot the panic setting in there now that he is nearly face to face with her. The rain batters against the plate-glass windows. He's drowning in the sound of it, besieged by other noises: the electronic tinkling that precedes announcements he can't make sense of, the thousand conversations dissolving in a hellish buzz. He watches other people waiting to meet flights and yields to an envy that is total, self-annihilating.

He sees her, still some way off behind the barrier, a laden trolley in front of her. She is looking for him, her face flushed with the eagerness of arrival. She is in blue. She seems young, from long ago and another time in his life.

When she reaches him she is radiant and he returns her long, tight hug, almost in tears. He is unaccustomed to whatever this feeling is. He tries to retreat from it. His first reaction is to forget he is meant to tell her now. When he remembers he knows he has to wait until the shock of emotion subsides.

On the bus she spills out stories of departure, of leaving this and that behind, of parties and gifts, and final goodbyes, and hailstones are smashing on the roof. Under the wheels there's a heavy rush of water that gets heavier and half-way to town they slow down on a stretch that's waterlogged completely. He can see nothing through the windows. The world outside is a distant aquarium.

The bus starts again. He lowers his head and puts his face in his hands. Jean touches his shoulder.

'Tom, are you all right?' And her voice is light and sweet, its breath of anxiety for him alone.

Alan Spence

Brilliant

Shuggie's gaffer Tosh had been in a hurry to get home, so the whole painting squad had knocked off a few minutes early and by the time the factory hooter went, Shuggie was already in the toilet having a smoke, looking up, aimless, at the walls and doors of the cubicle where he sat. Somebody had spoken to Tosh about re-painting them, trying to brighten it up. It must have been years since it had been done, whitewash engrained with grime, patterns eroded by the damp, and over it all the slogans, messages, drawings. Years of them, names and dates, football scores, headless, limbless, naked women, giant cocks, gang-symbols, initials, invitations, challenges, claims; all jostled together, crowded each other out, layer over faded layer.

He liked to come across ones he'd written himself.

EVEN THEM WHO RULE SUPREME

SHITE IT FROM THE CRAZY GOVAN TEAM

He was pleased with that. It was good. The Govan Team was his gang. Across the top of the door he'd written SHUGGIE OK.

The whine of the hooter died away and he heard scuffling footsteps, then Eddie's voice. 'Izzat you at it again? Makes ye deef so it dis.'

'Away ye go ya fuckin arse-bandit!' shouted Shuggie.

'Right!' said Eddie. 'Here it comes. Wanker's doom!' He jumped up and threw an oily rag over the top of the door, down into the cubicle, just missing Shuggie's face and landing in his lap. Shuggie lobbed the rag back over the top, but as it hit the floor Eddie was already on his way out. Shuggie heard him laugh, the door banging shut behind him.

There was no paper in the toilet, so Shuggie took the folded newspaper from his jacket pocket and tore off a piece from the front page. The banner headline said BELFAST BOMB TERROR. Three dead. On the back of it was a picture of a girl in a bikini. Curvaceous 23-year-old Lynn Waters. Hobbies ski-ing, dancing, reading. Would like to go to America.

He wiped himself and flushed Lynn Waters away with the three Irish dead. He had a look to see what was on television. Nothing much. Then he remembered the advert. He found the page and read it over again.

JOIN THE PROFESSIONALS. A soldier with a machine-gun. Smaller pictures of the same soldier, playing football, jumping down from a tank, wandering through an Arab bazaar.

He tore round the advert, folded it carefully and put it away in his pocket. Then he stuffed the rest of the newspaper down behind the cistern. At the side of the wash-hand basin was a tin of stain-remover, thick and black. He scooped some out and did his best to clean the paint from his hands, before heading home.

Thursday was his mother's night out so he had to get his own tea. She'd be off with her friend to the pictures or along to the bingo at Cessnock. Shuggie's father had died four years ago, knocked down by a lorry. Shuggie had been twelve then. It seemed a short time, but already his father's memory was fading. Sometimes he couldn't remember his face.

(At other times he could see him clearly. His father sparring with him and his big brother Davie. His father giving them money. His father, drunk, singing 'Moonlight Bay'.)

Davie had served his time as a welder and gone to Australia, so now only Shuggie and his mother were left in the house.

On his way home he stopped in at the chip shop. It had only just opened, so he had to wait a bit for the chips to be ready. The woman before him in the queue was about thirty. Her hair was dyed blonde, lacquered and piled high on her head. He could smell her scent, even in the thick atmosphere of vinegar and smoking fat. Behind him, two small boys about ten, a girl a year or so older. The boys were grappling, the girl ignoring them. An older man came in, nodded to the woman.

'How's Maisie!' he said.

'How's John!' she replied.

She stretched and yawned, shook her head and smiled at the man. Above the deep-fryer was a long mirror, tarnished and blotched here and there. At either end were old faded adverts for Tizer (The Appetizer) and sparkling Vimto. Shuggie stared at the woman's reflection, but she was looking away, somewhere else. He shifted his gaze along to the top of Louie's shiny bald head, reflected. Louie was banging and shaking a basket of chips, lifting them clear of the bubbling fat. He shouted across at the boys to stop their fighting or he'd put them out. They stopped for the moment, sniggered, began prodding and digging each other quietly. The blonde woman bought some chips.

'See ye Louie,' she said. 'Cheerio John.'

'Cheerio.'

Shuggie bought a fish supper and a penny pickled onion. He hurried home the last few blocks, the greasy brown packet a patch of warmth, clutched against his side.

As soon as he got home he lit the gas fire in the kitchen and switched on the radio, letting music blare through the house, fill the empty space. Then when he'd gobbled his tea he kicked off his boots and slumped down into one of the armchairs. He sat there for a bit, stretched out, limp, staring into the fire. Then he remembered the advert in the pocket of his overalls. He looked at it again. If he joined the army he would maybe see a bit of the world. He had never been any further than a bus-run to Morecambe at September weekend. In the army he could learn a trade. That might keep his mother happy. Sometimes she moaned at him. If his brother could get a decent job, why couldn't he, instead of just labouring like his father.

Shuggie's father had been a labourer in the yards most of his life. For years he had worked in Harland's. Shuggie passed the site every day on his way home from work. The yard had closed down now and the buildings were gone. Just a wire fence and a flat expanse of concrete, here and there weeds growing, bits of rusted metal.

After a while he got up and put on a kettle of water, to wash himself at the sink. He looked out across the back court. Demolition had already begun on the tenements facing. There were no lights, the shape was ragged where walls had been knocked away, where bits had crumbled and caved in.

Soon the demolition would reach round here and Shuggie and his mother would be rehoused. He didn't like the idea of being put out to one of the schemes. Castlemilk. Nitshill. There was nothing to do. They were too far away from anywhere.

He looked down below to where a scabby-looking mongrel was snuffling and rummaging in the midden, poking among the tin cans and ashes. He remembered something he'd read in the paper about one of the schemes, Easterhouse or Drumchapel, where packs of wild dogs were supposed to be roaming the streets, fighting and chasing each other and even attacking people. The paper had blamed people who bought the dogs as pups. Then later, when they couldn't look after them, they turned them out. And now they were banding together, in packs.

The kettle was boiling. Before he washed, he dug out a blunt stub of pencil from his pocket and filled in his name and address on the army application form.

When Shuggie had washed and changed into his suit, he headed down to the corner where Eddie was already waiting, pacing back and forward, hunched, hands in his jacket pockets, looking about him, spitting through his teeth. Shuggie feigned a swipe at him and Eddie ducked, swung with his boot, just missing Shuggie. Then they both made as if to butt each other, and laughed.

'Good joab fur you ah'm in a good mood pal,' said Shuggie.

'Ach don't annoy me son!' said Eddie.

'Wherr ur we gawn the night?' said Shuggie.

'Don't know,' said Eddie. 'Mibbe wait'n see if any a the boays come roon. Ah fancy a wee bit bevvy 'n then up tae the dancin.'

'Nothin oan the pictures?'

'Naa, fuck aw,' said Eddie. 'Wan a they musicals or some pish lik that.'

'Whit aboot that horror picture?' said Shuggie.

'That's no oan till Sunday.'

The corner was where they always met, outside an old dairy that had closed down a few years before. Here too they had carved their names, sprayed their slogans, on the barred doors and boarded windows.

'See that wan wee Rab done,' said Shuggie, nodding towards the wall. 'Fuckin great but, intit.' Rab had sprayed an enormous symbol, made up of the letters RGT – Real Govan Team, the letters overlaid, the R and T contained within the great curve of the G. It was five feet across, bright red glowing paint, big sweeping strokes, and here and there, long trickled lines where the paint had dripped and run.

'Looks lik blood!' said Eddie.

'Ah wis thinkin it wis lik the Rangers badge,' said Shuggie. 'Ye know that RFC.'

'Rangers Football Club,' said Eddie.

'Rangers Fuck Celtic,' said Shuggie.

'If ye staun right back,' said Eddie, 'it looks lik Chinese writin.'

'Mao Tse-tung!' said Shuggie.

'Hoo Flung Dung!' said Eddie.

'Hey look at whit's comin!' said Shuggie. On the other side of the road Betty and Helen were passing by, arms linked, heels clicking in step. They had identical hairstyles, earrings, coats. Betty was slightly taller, thin, her features were sharp. Helen was smaller, more rounded, dark.

'How's it gawn!' shouted Eddie.

'No bad,' shouted Betty. She whispered something to Helen and they laughed.

'Gawn tae the dancin the night?' shouted Eddie.

'Ye askin?'

'Meet ye inside?'

'Gan ya big chancer!'

They walked on.

'See ye efter?' shouted Eddie.

'No if ah see you furst!' shouted Betty. Helen laughed again and looked back at them over her shoulder.

'Whit wid ye dae tae that yin?' asked Eddie.

'Ur wee pal's awright tae,' said Shuggie.

'Get right in therr Shug!' said Eddie.

If they stood at the corner long enough, just about everybody they knew would pass by, sooner or later. The girls had just gone out of sight when Aleck came round the corner. Aleck had been a friend of Shuggie's when they were at primary school but he'd gone on to a high school in town and Shuggie had gone to the local junior secondary and left at fifteen.

Aleck was wearing his school uniform. Over his shoulder he had a haversack full of books and under his arm he carried a flute in a long black case. He nodded towards Shuggie as he passed. 'How's Shug!' he said. Shuggie nodded. 'This you jist gettin hame fae school?' he asked.

'Ah steyed late fur band practice,' said Aleck. 'Then ah hid somethin tae dae in toon.'

He couldn't bring himself to use the word Orchestra to Shuggie. Band came more easily to the tongue.

'Izzat yer flute?' said Shuggie.

'Aye,' said Aleck.

'Kin ye give us The Sash yet?' said Shuggie.

'Oh aye,' said Aleck. 'Follow Follow as well.' He laughed, self-conscious.

'Ah seen ye up the dancin the other week,' said Shuggie. 'D'ye go up therr a loat?'

'Ach naw,' said Aleck. 'That wis ma furst time.'

'Wis that boays fae yur school that wur wae ye?'

'Aye,' said Aleck.

'Ye gawn up the night?' said Shuggie.

'Naw,' said Aleck.

'Huv tae stey in an dae yer homework?' said Shuggie. Eddie sniggered. For answer Aleck laughed again, the same embarrassed laugh, as he moved on.

'See ye,' he said.

'Aye,' said Shuggie.

'Whit ye talkin tae that poofin wee cunt fur?' said Eddie.

'Wee brainboax,' said Shuggie. 'Ach, e's awright.'

'Fucksake but!' said Eddie. 'E'll still be at school when e's whit … eighteen. Ah mean imagine that! Some wee shite ae a teacher giein ye the belt fur talkin! "Come out here Clarence and I'll warm your fingers. You naughty boy!"'

Shuggie laughed. 'Ach well,' he said. 'E'll come oot wi a good joab an that. Nae fuckin overtime fur him.'

He remembered the advert in the paper.

'Ah wis thinkin aboot joinin the army,' he said.

'Wur ye!' said Eddie.

'Aye,' he said.

'Might be awright,' said Eddie.

'Get me away fae here fur a while anywey,' said Shuggie. 'An ye kin learn a trade anaw. See a bit ae the world.'

'Mibbe ye'd get sent ower tae Ireland,' said Eddie, laughing. 'Get intae some a they cathlick bastards!'

'Ah mind a thinkin that when ah wis wee,' said Shuggie. 'Imagine the proddies and the cathlicks really fightin. Jist lik the aulden days. King Billy an aw that. Ah mind wan time ah wis it the ne'erday match wi wee Aleck an we seen these papes kickin fuck oot a Rangers supporter an ah says tae Aleck wintit be great if thur wis a real war wi thum ower in Ireland an the Orange Ludge went ower tae fight an we hid another battle at the Boyne.'

'Whit did he say?' said Eddie.

'He didnae fancy it,' said Shuggie.

'Ach!' said Eddie.

'Always wis a crapper when it came roon tae fightin,' said Shuggie.

Eddie began singing, prancing back and forward, stabbing his arms into the air as if he was brandishing a scarf.

> 'If the pope says no
> We will have another go
> On the banks of the Boyne
> In the morning.'

'Here's Pudge and Bugsy,' said Shuggie.

'Pudge is a cathlick,' said Eddie. 'Ye wanty get in some bayonet practice oan um!'

Bugsy and Pudge were the names they'd always been called. Most of their friends had forgotten their real names, or never knew them. Pudge was stocky and squat. As a child he'd been fat. Pudgy. Bugsy had always had nits when he was small. Bugs. (From time to time the school clinic would shave his head, leaving just a tuft of hair at the front, his head stubbly, dabbed with gentian violet, bright purple antiseptic.) He'd always been in fights, and usually he'd won. (Once, when he was about nine, he'd shoved another boy off the top of a midden and the boy had broken his leg. The headmaster had given him eight of the belt and called in the police, and Bugs had been sent to a probation officer.) At first Bugsy had hated the name. But later he'd thought it sounded like the name of an American gangster. Bugsy. Bugs. So he'd kept the name, made it his own. Nicknames were good to paint on the walls. Mental Bugsy. Bugsy Rules.

Eddie grabbed Pudge. 'Right Bugsy,' he said. 'You get is other erm. Shuggie's gonnae start killin cathlicks, startin wi this papish cunt.'

They pinioned him to the wall, laughing.

'Aw c'mon,' said Pudge. 'Leave us alane!'

'Fenian dog!' said Shuggie, and half-serious he began poking Pudge, slapping him and pummelling his belly, as he struggled and yelled and tried to break clear. Then Shuggie brought out his steel comb with the long pointed handle and pretended to stab him and finish him off.

They let Pudge go and he shrugged them off. 'Shower a mental bastards,' he said, annoyed at them all.

'Ach c'mon Pudge,' said Eddie, punching his shoulder, consoling. Pudge elbowed him aside and stuck out a boot at Shuggie, and he felt better for that, even although they were still laughing.

After a while, Pudge's young brother Frankie came sauntering past, a ball under one arm, comics under the other.

'C'mon son,' said Pudge. 'Gie's a kick ae yer baw.'

'You get!' said Frankie, still mad at him because they'd fought at tea-time.

'Aw!' said Pudge. 'The wee boay's in the huff!' He let Frankie go past, then pounced on him from behind, grabbing him round the neck. Bugsy punched the ball out from under his arm and ran clear with it. Frankie squirmed free, dropping his comics on to the pavement, and tried to tackle Bugsy who tapped the ball across to Pudge. Together they managed to keep the ball moving, always just out of Frankie's reach. Shuggie

had picked up the comics and was flicking through them. *Creepy Worlds.*
FBI. Superman. Sergeant Rock. He leafed over the pages of *Creepy*
Worlds, but it was one he'd read before. He stopped at the page of adverts.
Guitar Tuition. Hypnotism Made Easy. He'd often thought of learning the
guitar, but the few times he'd tried he'd given up, annoyed and frustrated,
unable to get it right. He wondered if hypnotism really was easy. He
could think of uses for that. He showed it to Eddie.

'Fancy bein a hypnotist?' he said.

Eddie laughed and waved his hands in front of his face. In a faraway
quavering voice he wailed, 'You will come wi me intae the back close an
drop your knickers.' Then in his own voice he said, 'Aye, that wid be
fuckin gemmie.' He looked at the page again and pointed at a half-page
spread on body-building. 'Imagine bein built lik that!' he said.

'Fuckin Tarzan,' said Shuggie.

The other adverts were ones they'd seen since they were small, each
advert in a box with a drawing and the price in American money. Itching
Powder. Black-face soap. Stink bombs. And something called a Seebacko-
scope, for looking behind you.

Bugsy and Pudge had tired of taunting Frankie so they'd given him
back his ball. He came over and snatched his comics from Shuggie, and
as he ran off he shouted back at Pudge, 'Ah'm tellin ma mammy 'n you.
An you'll fuckin get it!'

Pudge just laughed and turned to the others. 'Wherr is it the night
then?' he said.

'Dancin,' said Eddie.

'Gawn fur a kerry-oot furst?' said Bugsy, lighting up a cigarette-end
he'd found in his pocket.

'Aw aye,' said Shuggie.

'Gie's a fag Bugs,' said Eddie.

'This is aw ah've goat,' said Bugsy.

'Gie's a drag, well,' said Eddie.

'Aw c'mon fur fucksake!' said Bugsy. 'It's jist a wee dout. Lookit the
size ae it!'

'That's awright,' said Eddie. 'Ah'll remember that.' Then he saw Dan on
the other side of the road and waved across to him. Dan was a bit older
than them, nineteen or twenty. He too had been one of their gang, their
team, but now he was married and he'd quietened down.

'Been daein overtime?' said Eddie.

'At's right,' said Dan.

'Seen wee Rab?' said Eddie.

'Saw um doon the pub aboot hauf an hoor ago,' said Dan. 'Mibbe still therr.'

'Right,' said Eddie. 'See ye.'

'See yis,' said Dan.

'Bet e's daein overtime oan that wee wife a his!' said Pudge.

'Must be tremendous,' said Shuggie. 'Comin hame tae that every night. Nice wee single-end. Jist the two ae ye. Dead cosy.'

'Fuckin nice,' said Bugsy.

They were silent for a moment, imagining it. Shuggie felt a sudden emptiness, a lack. Then Eddie leered and said, 'Plenty a nooky!' He turned to Shuggie and said, 'Never you mind, Shug. Wance you're in the army you'll be gettin bags ae it!'

'You joinin the army?' said Pudge.

'Mibbe,' said Shuggie.

Bugsy coughed, almost choking as he sucked the last gasping drag from his cigarette-butt.

'Serves ye right ya mingey bastard!' said Eddie. 'Hope it chokes ye!'

'Ah jist minded a Dan the other week,' said Pudge, 'readin oot that book.'

'Aw aye,' said Eddie. 'That wis great. You wurnae therr Shuggie. Dan brought oot this book, the *Kama Sutra*, aw aboot different weys a gettin yer nooky. Some laugh!'

'Ah've heard aboot that,' said Shuggie. 'Ther's another wan tae. *The Perfumed Garden* ur somethin.'

'Thur supposed tae uv made a picture ae the *Kama Sutra* wan,' said Pudge.

'Need tae see that when it comes,' said Bugsy.

'Anywey,' said Eddie, 'ur we gawn doon the road the noo?'

'Aye, comin?' said Shuggie.

'Naw,' said Eddie, 'ah'm jist breathin heavy!'

On the way they passed the pub, so Eddie and Shuggie looked in to see if Rab was still there. He roared at them across the bar and made his way towards them.

'Wur jist gawn up the dancin,' said Eddie. 'Bugsy and Pudge ur ootside.'

'Great!' said Rab. 'Ah'll be wae yi in a minnit.'

He finished his pint and followed them out.

Further on they bought a carry-out from a licensed grocer's – a few cans of beer, some wine, a bottle of cider. They went into a back close to drink it, swigging back the beer, passing round the cider and the wine.

'Ah seen ye yesterday Shug,' said Rab. 'Oan the back ae a lorry ye wur.'

'Aw aye,' said Shuggie. 'Wan ae the drivers gave us aw a run doon the road.'

'It's great that,' said Eddie, 'when ye get a hurl oan a lorry. We sometimes go doon in wan tae dae a joab in toon. Fuckin tremendous!' (To be up there, gliding through traffic, looking around you, laughing, cursing, shouting at girls, straddling the edge of the lorry, balanced, holding yourself on with one hand; to feel like part of an invading army; like the feeling when you were on the supporters' bus and everyone stopped to look as you passed, scarves and banners streaming from the windows as the whole bus shook to your singing and stamping, together.)

'Dead gallus, intit,' said Rab.

'Pure fuckin brilliant,' said Shuggie.

And that was it. That was the way of it. Gallus. Pure Brilliant. That was the way for it to feel. In spite of everything, to be rollocking, alive. To be shouting, We are the PEOPLE, We are the REAL Team. To show them all. To let them know.

They threw their empty bottles and cans into the back court and went on their way.

They jumped off the bus at the traffic-lights because that was nearer to the dance-hall than the next bus-stop.

Before going in they had to file into a small ante-room where they were searched for weapons by one of the bouncers. Shuggie and Bugsy had to hand over their steel combs, Eddie his belt with the heavy metal buckle. 'Aw wait a minnit,' said Eddie, handing it over. 'Ma troosers'll faw doon!'

'Wull jist huv tae pit ye oot then,' said the bouncer.

'Never mind that,' said Rab. 'Good joab they never seen aw the chibs in yer poacket. Ye think theyda seen a cuppla knifes an a bayonet and a hatchet an a tommygun!'

'Fly man,' said the bouncer, not so much as a flicker on the hard, set face.

Rab went on, 'But ah don't know how ye could've missed that fuckin hydrogen bomb up yer jook!'

'On yer way!' said the bouncer.

Once they were in the hall, Shuggie felt good. The drink had hit him now, and the music was loud and familiar. Something rose in him, a joyful recognition; it rose and moved to the steady thumping rhythm. The song they were playing was an old one, but one that everybody still loved. Shuggie was singing along.

> This old heart a mine
> Been broke a thousand times ...

The dance-floor itself was circular, and round the perimeter were tables and seats. Above was a balcony, overlooking the floor. Eddie had to shout to make himself heard above the noise. He was saying he wanted to go up on to the balcony. Shuggie nodded and they all shoved their way up the stairs.

They leaned over the balcony, looking down at the packed floor below. The small stage where the group played was brightly lit in contrast to the rest of the hall. Revolving coloured lights threw shifting patterns of red and green on to a circle at the centre of the floor and on to the dancers who passed across. Just at the edge of this area Shuggie saw a group of girls dancing together, and as they danced, they moved round towards the centre of the floor and the circle of their dancing intersected the circle of coloured light. Then Shuggie spotted among them the two girls, Betty and Helen. He nudged Eddie and pointed them out. Rab had already decided he felt like dancing so they all moved back downstairs together. They made their way round to a table where they'd seen a few other boys from their team.

'Wull no ask thum jist yet,' said Eddie, looking over to where the girls were still dancing. 'Wull wait a wee while.'

Something about the songs always got to Shuggie. He had a head full of them. He only had to hear the opening bar and he'd be filling in the backing, playing every instrument, adding every voice. Sweet soul music. It lit something in him. It was something he wanted to spill out. He wanted to flail his arms and sing and laugh, sharing it. But he just stood, watching, bobbing his head, tapping his foot, looking now at the girls, dancing, now at the group, pounding out the music.

> Now it's the same ... old song
> But with a different meaning
> Since you been gone ...

Maybe he could learn the drums, he thought, instead of the guitar.

As he looked back to the floor he saw that two boys had broken the circle and were dancing with Betty and Helen.

'Fuck it,' he said, to Eddie.

'Disnae matter,' said Eddie. 'Wull get thum efter.'

But the girls stayed up with the two boys for the next dance, and the next, then they went and sat with them at one of the side tables.

'They look lik fuckin schoolboays,' said Shuggie. He was feeling restless and annoyed. Eddie seemed happy enough just to sit there, and that just irritated Shuggie all the more. Rab was dancing with a big redhaired girl called Rita. Bugsy and Pudge were leaning against a pillar. Shuggie noticed a small blonde girl standing by herself. He pushed over towards her and asked her to dance.

'Ah'm arready wae some'dy,' she said.

He turned away. He saw two girls dancing together. He stepped in between them.

'D'ye wanty dance wae me?' he asked one of them, his back to the other.

'Naw,' she said, shaking her head.

'We don't wanty get split up,' said her friend.

He went back to the table, scowling at Eddie.

'Never mind Shug,' said Eddie. 'Thur no worth it. Fuck them all!'

Across the hall Shuggie saw Betty and Helen going into the ladies' toilet. The two boys were hovering around, waiting for them.

'Ah'm gawn tae the lavvy,' he said, heading for the other side of the hall.

'Me tae,' said Eddie, following.

Shuggie saw the two boys as he came up to them. He singled out the one that had been dancing with Helen, and deliberately brushed against him as he passed.

'Watch who yer shovin son!' said Shuggie, pushing the boy again.

'Wait a minnit!' said the boy.

'Think yer a fuckin hard man?' said Shuggie, and he butted the boy in the face and brought his knee up into his groin. The boy's friend stepped forward but Eddie stuck in his boot, stopping him.

'We're the Govan Team pal, so don't fuckin mess!' said Eddie.

A few girls had screamed and there was a commotion round about as people backed away. Three bouncers were heading across, to see what the trouble was.

'C'mon,' said Eddie. 'Nae point in takin oan them as well. The boays ur aw away acroass the other side.'

Shuggie turned to the boy he'd hit and said, 'You're claimed ootside!' as Eddie dragged him on to the dancefloor where they split up and made their separate ways back to the others.

Betty and Helen came out of the toilet and looked around them, bewildered.

They had left a bit early and they stood across the road from the dance-hall, waiting; Shuggie and Eddie, Rab, Bugsy and Pudge, and two others, Jackie and Stu. Opposite, the big red neon sign that said DANCING flashed on and off, on and off, lighting up the pavement.

Through the doorway the crowds were beginning to spill out. Shuggie's eyes were fixed, watching for the two boys. 'Shouldnae be long noo,' he said.

'This should be good,' said Eddie. 'Didye see that wee guy's face when ah says we wur the Govan Team! Jist aboot shat is sel! That wis the best laugh. Fuckin tremendous!'

Shuggie laughed and reached into his pocket, feeling the steel comb with the long pointed handle.

'Mental!' he said.

'Brilliant!' said Rab.

Andrew Greig

from *Electric Brae*

Disappearing Gully

I push the rest of my beans away, feeling none too good, and glance at
my watch. She'll land in an hour and a half.

'Let's hit the road, kid.'

She sooks the last of her Coke.

'Soon come,' she says.

It's right dark outside. A whiff of snow off the high moors sets me
aching for a moment to be back in the winter hills again. Then in behind
that, like a punch in the guts after the smile to the face, comes the way it
felt then.

The salted road was a black tawse banged down on Rannoch Moor.
Whack! That'll learn you for dreaming, boy. I lit a cigarette and shook my
head. A violent culture, sure.

Early January '85 and at last the snow. Cold and hard outside the pits,
and a rough fortnight on the platform, my soberest Hogmanay on record.
Cokes and cigars and watching the folk at the Tron Kirk on telly. Still, it
had kept me from doing damage once Kim had tossed a coin and gone to
spend her New Year with Graeme in Wales.

A hoodie craw tilted across the road, veered into the wilderness in the
heart of Scotland. I thought of Lesley in Vermont, skiing with two fingers
of her right hand stuck out in a powerless V sign, instructing the young
and wealthy...

The white palm dipped under the blow and I wound down into
Glencoe, towards ancient grudges and betrayals, hands tight and careful
on the wheel.

I pushed into the Clachaig with my climbing gear and there were MacBeth,
Gypsy, old bauldy-heid Andy Clackmannan, the poet with her rinky-tink

mandola. A wave from Cathy and Shonagh, and Nick Fairer up from London with his side-kick Slide. My old, abusive, trusted winter climbing mates. Shake hands all round, our first meeting since the end of last winter.

'So how's it going, youth?' from Andy.

'Like *A Bat Out Of Hell*,' I said, 'way over the top.'

Ach, patter, patter. Still, he chuckled and made room for me.

'Well,' Gypsy drawled, 'didn't expect to see you *this* weekend.' He winked, nodded towards the bar.

He was standing there, back turned, neat in denim. My favourite Glaswegian, my old pal.

I should have walked out and driven to my brand new friend in Perth. But they were watching and they all knew, of course, no secrets in the climbing world. I stood like a stookie, trying not to show.

'McGlashan!' Gypsy shouted. 'Reckon you owe this man a pint.'

Graeme's lips moved like he was trying to whisper to me across the distance.

They were all watching. Show a moment's weakness and they're on you like wolves and as merciless. Except when it got really bad, then you could trust them with your life if not your lover, way beyond other folk.

'The usual,' I said and sat down among my friends, kept my hands out of sight a while.

He passed over the pint, sat down opposite. I raised my glass, nodded acknowledgement. Why the hell wasn't he still in Wales with her?

Then she walked in the door, brushing snow from her fleece jacket. Her eyes went to me, back to him, flicked over the expectant faces round the long table. MacBeth drew on his fag and looked down at the floor, squeamish at heart.

'Happy New Year, glad you made it,' Kim said and put her arm briefly round my shoulder, kissed my ear, then sat at the far end of the table, away from us both. She had her moments.

'So, you fixed with anyone for tomorrow, a ghràidh?' Shonagh asked. 'The Ben's in good nick.'

'I'm not fixed, m'eudail,' I managed.

I'd come up on impulse, to climb with whoever was around, or solo if necessary. My house was a wilderness till she next returned.

'Graeme's on his tod,' Cathy said. 'Why don't you two team up?'

I glanced at Graeme. He didn't want to, nor did I.

'Sure, why not?' I said.

'Suits me,' he said quietly. 'Where?'

Gypsy leaned back in his chair. Ice axes drawn at dawn.

He laughed and Graeme looked down at his hands. Small and strong, a bit hacked about, the hands that pleased and shared my lover. I watched myself smash the glass and put it to his face. A violent culture, sure, and I was part of it.

'Disappearing Gully,' I said and sat back while the poet fine-tuned her mandola and sang 'I Loved a Lass'. Just once her eyelid flickered my way. I took out my guitar and in Lesley's memory bopped through 'Walking After Midnight', and for the first time accepted it was down to me.

Kim's hand on my sleeve at the bar.

'For God's sake be careful!' she hissed. 'The two people I love most in the world.'

'Me too,' I said, 'but my heart's not big enough. I think I resign.'

She stared at me. Hail and farewell.

'Dinna fash yersel,' I said. 'I'll take care of him.'

We trudged apart up through the dark towards the foot of the Ben. Flurries of fresh snow swirled through my head-torch beam, mesmeric and bonnie but not a good sign. Six in the morning and a wild world. Way back Graeme's light bobbed and weaved, coming on slowly. He was a rock jock, not a mountaineer. Let him suffer.

I slugged up through deepening snow, wide-awake and calculating the next moves.

Dawn at the C.I.C. hut below the great crags, mist, a smirr of snow driven in the gale. A grey, bleak, unpromising day but climbing's no dafter than roping your happiness to someone else. Not her fault, she hadn't asked me too. It just grew that way.

I hunched in the lee and weighed the odds. This was no place for playing the hard men. They just get killed, and that's dumb not tough. If I pictured Disappearing Gully rightly, it would chuck down spindrift but nothing bigger. Getting off the top could be the hardest, a pure compass job in a full gale. Mountaineering, not climbing. For someone who hadn't been out much in bad conditions, someone like Graeme, it would be fairly desperate.

Ho hum.

On the other hand, we could just say sod this for a game of crazies and go back down to spend the day in the chalet with friends swopping yarns. Aye, and him and her, all day. If she touched him when I was there, I'd be shredded. Why even pretend to be tough?

Then again, I'd long wanted to do Disappearing Gully, and who better to do it with? Why, we might climb into it and just vanish altogether.

He staggered up, dropped his sack and a few curses. He looked pretty shagged, maybe she'd kept him up late.

'Does this make ony sense, pal?'

We talked it over but we were always going to do it. We strapped on crampons, took out an axe each and groped up into the Coire na Ciste. It was not an uplifting day but still better than being in Fort William in the rain. I led on past the Douglas Boulder, waiting for short breaks in the mist. Found the big gully then paced carefully.

Yup, this must be it. Disappearing Gully, a modern hard Grade V. A messy icefall soared into a dim chute then nothing. Spindrift slid down and blew in our faces with depressing regularity. Cathy and Shonagh had described it as 'interesting', meaning at the top end of my abilities. If it wasn't in good nick, we wouldn't get far.

We prepared in silence. I sorted out my rack of ironmongery along the waist loops of my harness. I took my time about it, getting into precision mode. Took out slings and karabiners, a screw-gate, the descendeur, still clumsy in my mitts but slowly remembering how this went. Finally I roped up.

'She's a bit twitchy about this,' he said.

He stood with his end of the rope in his mitt.

'Really,' I said.

'She says you've resigned.'

'Yup.'

The longest look at the foot of Disappearing while snow settled on our helmets like daft crowns.

'Yup, I've decided to untie. You two are on your own.'

'Jim, we never meant it tae be like this.'

I could kill him for that 'we'. I clipped a couple of ice-screws and drive-ins to my rack.

'But I'm crazy about her.' His voice was hoarse. 'Canni let her go.'

'Fuck solidarity, eh?' I said. 'No wonder you're losing the Miners' Strike.'

'Whit you haiverin aboot?'

'Need a couple of spare friends,' I said. 'Size 3 and 4.'

He handed over the spring-loaded cams and I clipped them in.

He hesitated then tied himself in, put me on belay. We were connected till the end of the day. I put my mitts through the wrist loops of both axes, looked up and took a few long breaths. Christ, it's a steep one. We loved each other once and we blew it.

'Climbing,' I said, and began.

Gradually I remembered how to do this. My axes investigated, stabbed, found good ice. Tested it, moved on up, breathing a bit fast. Nothing wrong with adrenalin when appropriate, like for fleeing, or fighting.

I hacked out some loose rubbish and it slithered down onto Graeme's bowed helmeted head. Left foot, right front points in, right axe lodged high, test, lean out, left axe in, pull up. Method and faith and some improvisation – climbing's like life, Cathy used to say, only easier. Her life was as much of a shambles as mine, but she sure was a better climber.

Forty feet up I found the crack I was looking for. After a bit of jiggling the nut held good. I clipped the rope through and relaxed a little. Down below, Graeme's red helmet glimmered through the mist and spindrift. He would stay there, patiently, until I signalled him.

I eased away from my temporary security.

It was slow going, the route not being in very good nick, just loose choss. I scraped, huffed and puffed, struck a few sparks as I groped from one iffy position to the next.

Time passed – the hardest, the best. Serious play. My world narrowed to textures of snow, opacities of ice, spikes of black rock inches from my face, the axes dirling in my mitts, the red and green ropes swooping down between my feet.

'Of course it's escapism,' Shonagh would say cheerfully. 'But at least the mountain isn't impressed by our bullshit.'

A tough Skye lassie, an ambitious hard climber with a streak of the necessary craziness, yet I'd seen her leave the Clachaig bunkhouse in tears over a man.

I pushed up on a nice mantelshelf move, whacked in the axes, leaned back and looked up. I'd seen few uglier scenes. But I could exit out of this, I could live without Kim. It had been less than six years together. A rough calculation suggested we must have made love some five hundred times. Very nice but no big deal.

I got a gobfull of spindrift and heard Shonagh laugh. *Bullshit, Jimmy!*

Yeah yeah. Couple of times I'd seconded her the winter before, an education that. She'd climbed a blinder but confessed her blues all the way back. We'd sat in the car outside the Clachaig till she'd stopped greitin and was ready to put her best face on and walk through the door...

My calves were starting to shake from too much teetering on front-points, and upper arms were burning and weak above my head. I'd surely run out most of the rope. Five hundred times seemed unlikely. I could remember perhaps a dozen occasions, but those would never leave me be.

Break-time.

A flared crack took a poor friend. Found some okay ice and got a drive-in half way in, tied it off. That seemed about it for belays so I clipped myself in and kicked out a ledge of sorts. Down looked fairly grim but it usually does.

He wouldn't hear me through the wind, so I sent down the sequence of tugs we'd established over the years. Took in the ropes and put him on belay, stuck a frozen Mars Bar in my gob, and waited.

He came up damn slowly. This was more awkward than anything he'd done in winter before, a big adjustment from hard rock. Sweat began congealing inside my thermals. A long pause. Finally he signalled for tight rope, slightly panicky, I thought.

I grinned and nearly dragged him up the awkward step. Suffer a bit, you bastard.

That wasn't very nice. Then again, I wasn't very nice. Certainly not the easy-going, reliable – heh, be honest, passive – Good Guy I'd tried to be for her for years. I was a howling spindrift of hateful thoughts and low-grade feelings. Not a good guy at all.

His fall was sudden. It jerked me forward and the friend flew out. The drive-in wobbled, held. The ledge started to crumple. Christ's sake, man!

The strain stopped. He'd re-attached himself to the face. I quickly jammed the friend back in, stomped out a marginally better ledge and, sweating now, faced out into the grey and took the rope in as he moved.

He appeared at last out of the gloom, grunting, swearing to himself.
'Steep?'
He rubbed a frozen mitt across his face, brushed ice off his eyebrows.
'Nae real. Bleedin nightmare.'
I nodded, shifted over and let him clip in to the belay.
'Thanks, pal. You caught me quick, but.'
'Ye near cowped me.'
He grimaced. We were now well into the throat of the gully. It soared

up into the grey, looked overhung but probably wasn't. Little spindrift avalanches gathered on our shoulders.

'What now?'

Good mountaineering is knowing when to say No. The triangle had had its moments. It could have worked.

'Push on,' I said. 'If it gets much worse, we abseil off. We can still crack this.'

He hesitated. With balaclava and helmet, each of us showed only a few square inches round mouth and eyes, and I watched his carefully.

'Ach hell,' he muttered, 'why not?'

'Consider the alternative,' I replied. It was one of our old routines.

'Sweet Fanny Adams!' he supplied the line and it suddenly seemed unfortunate. Kim, her body, her sex, passed between us and the moment was gone.

'Aye, well,' he said. 'Right then.'

He didn't like it but he was thrawn right through.

He started on up, awkward and unsure. He wasted a lot of time looking for belays – the long run-outs of winter climbing made him uneasy. Tension twanged down the ropes to me.

One little twitch, I thought, and he'd be off. And so would I, most like. So what? In time you can live without anyone, of course you can, but there's no joy in it.

Time passed. Occasional scraping sounds came down with showers of ice. I thought I heard a muffled shout, tightened instinctively, saw something grey fall past me, maybe just a clod of snow.

Waiting's the hardest. Admit you wake wishing you hadn't, drag yourself out onto the scaffolding deck, work on automatic day or night, and all the while your anger grinds like glass in the gullet, cuts deeper every time you swallow it. And you cannot shout or skelp her, not even be angry, because you hope to keep her. And these images of her delight in him . . .

I hunched my shoulders and waited. A culture of stoic suffering is limiting but has its uses.

Hours later, tugs came down the rope. I disengaged myself from the stance and stiffly put my axes to the test.

The climbing wasn't too bad but he took the slack in poorly. I kept having to stop and wait for the rope to come tight again. What was he playing at? The crux was awkward, with poor ice. A corner pushed me out into space, I felt like a bone stuck in the throat of the gully as it tried to swallow me down. Christ's sake, take in the slack!

Finally I pulled up into the ice cave, none too chuffed. Then I saw his right hand was bare, a white stiff claw.

'Dropped me glove,' he said hoarsely.

'Jesus.' So that's what had whirled down past me. No wonder he'd had trouble taking in the ropes. He could lose his fingers.

'Give me that,' I said.

He held out his hand. It felt like wood. I unzipped my jacket and carefully slid his white fingers under my oxter.

After a few minutes I gave him his hand back and he stuck it inside his pile jacket and stood there grunting, almost sobbing. Hot aches can make hard men cry. No shame in that.

Finally he looked across at me. His lashes were clogged with tears and snow, the dark eyes stared out from a long way back. He was being stripped to the bone and it hurt.

We were halfway up a serious route, the light was already dimming. He'd lost a glove and could lose a few fingertips and then he wouldn't climb too well again, nor paint, nor touch Kim the same.

I turned my back to him.

'Bottom of my sack,' I said. 'There should be a spare.'

He rummaged awkwardly, found it. Between us we jammed the Dachstein mitt over his half-thawed hand.

'One of hers,' I said. 'Good thing you've small paws.'

He almost smiled, I kinda shrugged.

'Keep working the hand,' I said. 'The belays here aren't good enough for abseiling down. We'll have to top out tonight.'

Coming out of that cave was hard, the ice steeper than I'd ever known but quality stuff. I climbed as fast as possible before the short day ended.

Then at the crux the ice went wrong. I tapped gently and it sheared off in plates. The snow on either side was just choss, and I sent it tumbling down the chute.

I made a couple more edgy moves and then ground to a stop.

I was thirty feet above my last runner which was iffy anyway, no secure points of contact and nowhere left to go. I couldn't reverse the last two moves nor go on. All I could do was bide in this impossible position till both of us froze to death, or let myself fall and pray the runner held.

I let my face fall against the ice.

Okay. I looked up and at full stretch scraped loose snow off a nick in the rock, just got the tip of my pick on it. All I need is just one good placement, one secure point of contact. Please.

It took five minutes to prove there was no such thing.

I settled for wedging my other pick into a crack off to the left, and twisted hard. It might hold. I'd have to torque hard on it while pulling absolutely straight on the right or it would skite off that nick and I'd be away, probably kill us both, for all the belays below were lousy.

Some of my friends could do it, but me, I was out of my league.

I closed my eyes.

'You're the two men I love most in the world,' she said.

I enquired within whether I was a man or a spineless invertebrate and received the usual answer.

Nevertheless I was going for it and pulling with all the power and control left in me. I rose up over the bulge, careful, careful, put my right boot out, lodged one front point. The axe wobbled, I was twisting desperately, pulling up. Left foot round and up, up, scraping on the lip, another inch, yeah! onto the ledge and stood right up on it and sank one axe high into pure ice, then the second, and stood there a moment, heaving. And as I powered on up towards the exit that had to exist, I was weeping.

I hauled him up that last pitch, mostly on tight rope. Didn't think he'd be too concerned about dignity at this stage. As he struggled with the crux I wasn't entirely in my right mind and idly considered untieing from him.

No point. I'd seen this movie somewhere before – two men, struggling on a mountain for a woman. But that was all old choss from the black and white days. Climbing wasn't like that. Kim wasn't like that. Men like that were dated as Mastodons in ice even if they didn't know it yet. No point at all.

He floundered through the cornice break and stood in front of me on the summit plateau, swaying slightly, caked in snow. At other times we might have hugged, the way we used to do after something specially gnarly and good.

'The Old Man of Hoy will be a piece of duff after this,' he mumbled. His jaw was frozen.

'Let's see the hand,' I said.

He pulled off Kim's mitt, I turned on my head-torch to see better. His hand was blotchy and red, but only the fingertips were white. He'd lose some skin, maybe the odd dead nerve, but he'd be okay. Better than Lesley, for sure.

'You played a blinder, pal,' he said and held out his hand. 'I'll leave her be.'

'Go to hell,' I said. 'She's no yours to give.'

He turned away and slowly walked out right to the edge of the cornice. He was a crazy man. It could break off any minute. Then I remembered we were of course still tied together and with me securely belayed he was risking nothing, just making gestures.

Then he stopped, turned to face me in the dimness, and slowly began to untie.

So I had to get off the belay, and stomped towards him through the wind and horizontal snow. I stopped a few feet short of the edge.

'Christ, you live dangerously, pal.'

He said nothing, just waited.

'You mad bastard,' I said. 'It's too late for that.'

'What am I tae dae?' He sounded bewildered.

'Win the next sodding Election, for all I care.'

'But can ye understaun it?'

'I understand it,' I said. Forgive is something else. 'Now can we get out of here?'

I turned and started plodding away. A pause, and then he followed me.

Working fast, we stuffed the gear away and tied in close to each other. It was now proper dark and we were alone in a winter storm on top of the Ben. I tried to hold the compass steady in my head-torch beam while the wind thrashed us. One hundred paces at 240 degrees then switch to 290 degrees and plough on towards the Red Burn descent. Miss the turn and you're over the edge; drift too far left and you're into Five Finger Gully, which is avalanche-prone and desperately dangerous.

'Now we do everything right,' I said.

Then we set off on the bearing. He broke trail in front, I followed with the compass, using him as a sight-line to hold our course when the wind blew us sideways. We were aiming for a hundred yard gap over a distance of three-quarters of a mile in a world without definition or horizon, and we had to walk that line without error.

It was hard, but nothing compared to what we do to each other.

Four hours later we dropped like sacks of tatties into my car and sat unable to speak or move. A full winter storm on Ben Nevis can be survived but scarcely comprehended. Me, I was wabbit, scunnered, dumfounert, forjeskit, then just weary beyond words.

He slumped back in the passenger seat with his eyes closed, arms hanging down at his sides. Melting ice dripped from his mitts. Even crossing the golf course we'd ricocheted around like pin-balls, slammed up against the fence and clung to it for the rest of the way.

I straightened up and fumbled the key into the ignition.

'Didni know it could be so hellish.' He tugged her mitt off with his teeth and cautiously waggled his fingers. A touch of frost-nip on two tips. 'Reckon I owe you wan.'

I giggled, began coughing, nearly threw up. He sat there nodding away like he had Parkinson's. Neither of us was entirely in his right mind.

'By God you do! But I'll settle for a pint and a shepherd's pie at the Clachaig.'

I manoeuvred cautiously out of the Siberian car park. After all, we're alive and these things happen. That's why they happen. Now let the bullshitting commence.

We walked more or less upright into the Clachaig around closing time. The place was packed and storm-bound, serious jollification squeezed within four walls. Drink, music, laughter, abuse and flirtation, all the human things. Outside for miles on end was the wilderness we'd struggled through. For a moment it blew in the door with us.

'Here come the long and the short of it!' the poet shouted. I wished she'd save her wise-cracks for her poetry.

'Shut that bleedin door!' Gypsy yelled.

Relief on the faces of our friends round the long table. I'd have been worried too. She looked like she was going to be sick. We were just too far apart for her to touch us both at the same time. She hugged him first and then me. It just fell that way.

'Don't you ever do that again,' she hissed. 'I'll no be a climber's widow.'

Graeme and I looked at each other.

'But you're no married,' I said.

'That's what you think,' she said and stomped off to the bar.

We dumped our sacks and sat down at the table to general abuse. Seeing the weather coming, they'd all had the good sense to do short routes or pack it in early.

'Dè a thachair?' Shonagh asked, but I buried my face in a pint to give myself time to decode that one.

'Diabhlaidh,' I managed at last. Hellish was about it.

'Thought you two had had it,' Andy Clackmannan murmured. 'I was hoping for your record collection.'

'But did you do the route?' Shonagh insisted.

I looked over at Graeme.

'Aa the way,' he replied. 'But I'd rather hae been in Fort William.'

We related our wee epic in the climbing manner – playing down the difficulties, exaggerating our fear and incompetence. She sat massaging his hand while I concentrated on the other end of the table. The poet pushed her granny glasses up onto her fringe, glanced at me.

'Maybe an old codger like you will ken the Incredible String Band's 'October Song',' she said and began. Only Clackmannan and I were old enough to know those words, and remember a time of soaring hopes however misplaced, of a joy now buried under winter. We sang as best we could, through choked throats, fortunate or otherwise.

Then Shonagh sang unaccompanied the old Gaelic heartbreaker 'Cumha na Cloinne', the Lament for the Children, and that about wrapped it up for me. After the shepherd's pie I went behind the bar and made a phone call, had a more or less satisfactory response. I came back and announced I was offski, was informed I was a crazy man. Eleven o'clock on a Saturday night, up since five in the morning and a howling blizzard outside – what's the hurry?

I kept my eyes averted from my own little corner of hell where Kim sat stroking his hand.

'Got a hot date in Perth,' I said, 'and the snowplough's just gone through.'

Shonagh shook her head and whispered in my ear.

'Come see me soon, a ghràidh. We'll do some easy routes together. Feuch gu fon thu mi. Promise you will.'

'Carson nach fon thusa mise?' I hacked my way through that lovely language.

'Keep the day job, doll. But thanks for trying.'

'Yeah, think I'd better listen to that cassette again.'

'Stick at it. Give Perth a good time, but remember where your friends are. Beannachd leat.'

'Aidh, beannachd leat.'

A good mate. As well I wasn't her kind of trouble, nor she mine. So I said my goodbyes, thanked MacBeth for the chalet doss. I was running on empty and desperate to get out of there.

Kim followed me out the door. We stood in the porch watching the snow blitz past. The melt dripped from her chopped dark hair.

'Like the ear-rings,' I said.

'He gave me them. Months back. I hope you're not affronted.'

'Haven't seen them before.'

The snow whirled past like some unwritten contract ripped into millions of pieces.

'I always took them off when I came to see you. Put on your ones instead. I forgot to change yours once and he went moody on me all weekend.'

I laughed quietly, then she did too.

'Do you have to, Jimmy?'

'We're not big enough. At least, I'm not.'

'Maybe it's just a fling,' she said into my shoulder. 'I'm oscillating like crazy.'

'I'd better away. My friend's expecting me.'

I brushed her lips. A dream, however braw and persuasive, is still only a fine example of a dream.

'Can I still come and see you?'

I stopped half-way to the car. She looked so small and weary my heart went to her. I wished she wouldn't do that.

'If you want to.'

I slung my gear in the back and set off before the road ahead vanished completely.

I played cassettes loud for energy and company. So wabbit I was, hallucinating with it, only the hands on the wheel felt mine.

When the snow plough turned off at the end of Rannoch Moor, I'd had it but pressed on anyway. Visibility was down to a few yards and sure enough I finally missed the road and buried the car in a ditch.

I mentally apologised to Perth and reached in the back for my sleeping bag.

Double yellow lights crept up from behind. I wound down the window and looked back. A Land Rover with snow chains. It stopped, the window came down and the inside light went on and a bull-like head peered out. Our old pal Mick DeTerre. I wasn't even surprised.

'Hi, man.'

*

'Kim fucked off then?'

We were winding slowly but steadily along Loch Earn. I grunted. He laughed quietly, put his paw on my arm.

'So it goes, man.'

So it seems.

'One crazy woman,' he said, 'but alright.'

I thought that was rich coming from him and said so. He laughed again.

'The Struggle continues.'

He asked after Joan. I said far as I knew she was living quietly in Shetland, running a salmon farm, sailing, being celibate. She was involved with Amnesty and the Church in Salvador, wrote a lot of letters and co-ordinated campaigns. I'd scarcely heard from her. He nodded several times.

'Yeah yeah,' he said quietly.

'Still got the guns?'

'Under my feet, as always.'

He tapped the floorboards with his Doc Martens, clicked his teeth.

He woke me. Lights in the distance. Perth. I checked my watch. Two in the morning.

'Is it a woman?'

I nodded, no energy to speak. My thermals were stinking. He stopped the Land Rover in a lay-by, switched on the light.

'Can't disappoint the lady.'

He laid out two generous lines of cocaine on a map case, looked at me and grinned.

'The guerilla's friend,' he said. 'And the lover's. We all have our roles to play.'

Liz opened the door. I was swaying but my head was now clear as ice, the untrustworthy kind. My new friend was in a towelling dressing gown, holding a book and looking warm, sleepy and rumpled. She smelled of bed and coffee and I longed to sink into her.

'A boring weekend so far,' she said. 'Went to a party and nearly got laid but thought of this new AIDS thingy and went to bed with Raymond Chandler instead. Yourself?'

'Eventful,' I said.

She hesitated.

'You'd better come in then.' She sniffed. 'Boy, do you need a bath.'

I opened my eyes. I was wearing Liz's dressing gown, in the hall, sitting propped against a radiator. She was slumped and snoring gently across my knees, auburn hair over her face. She looked vulnerable as we all do sleeping, though she said she could look after herself. I'd been known to say daft things like that too.

I smoothed her hair back, lifted the brandy glass I appeared to have in my hand, and toasted the wall in front of me. We'd been good to each other, it wasn't passion but there are other ways. There'd be Sunday breakfast on Sunday afternoon, then a walk, the papers, then more bed.

I stared at the white wall. Disappearing Gully. Soon I'd wake her and we'd get back to bed. Just sharing what there was to be shared, both of us hoping for more but guessing it wouldn't be with each other.

I sat on a while longer, curiously and briefly at peace, considering the movie so far, considering the lives we'd lost.

Here she comes, not so very late, through 'Arrivals'. The child breaks from me, runs under the barrier and into her arms. Assorted wifies smile and nod, a grave young man leaning on the rail looks like he's going to burst into tears. I go to meet her as all my prepared spontaneous quips go out of my head. It's been a fair while, an eternity by child's time.

We hug, her ear warm on mine, her breath on my neck. We hold each other long and close enough to be sure that the other's real, lightly enough to reiterate our limits. Irina clings to us both, babbling away her green coat and my Grand Slam T-shirt, and I imagine we make a pretty family picture.

'Welcome back,' I say.

'Good to be back,' she says. She's tired but her eyes hold mine and mean it.

Rina sits on the luggage trolley as we wheel it to the door. Lesley looks to me over her head.

'Thanks for holding the fort, Jimmy.'

'Ach, the Apache's settling down now. But I'm glad of the reinforcement.' She nods.

'The Apache's had a hard time,' she says carefully. 'I'm here to do the right thing.'

Frank Kuppner

from *A Very Quiet Street*

Let us follow him, then, as he climbs the reasonably presumed steps to the police station. I suppose he does not halt during his climb, and consider the possibility of going back home quietly and letting the matter rest there, or find its own level without him. After all, the newspapers have talked of a brooch stolen from the house of a murdered old lady, and a foreigner whom he perhaps finds unsavoury or dubious has been offering to sell his interest in such a brooch in a club which they are both members of. (The usual suggestion is that this object was haphazardly picked up by the murderer just before leaving, from a collection of similar pieces, to suggest theft as a motive – a silly and desperate move which turned out to be hysterically successful. (What thief would break a jeweller's display window, and remove a single plain ring from the periphery of a vast, expensive haul? It is perfectly possible, of course, but, unless the thief is mad, it can hardly be called simple theft. But the thief might have been mad. (But when the police arrested someone who was obviously not mad, and insisted that he was a thief, I suppose there are indeed many stupid thieves, or thieves who behave irrationally.)) Yet we should also, I think, keep in mind the possibility that the brooch never even existed. (We have only the word of a single, drastically unreliable witness – Lambie – that it was missing from its accustomed position in the first place. Or, if we have insufficient reason to think that Lambie invented the brooch, since it would be unjust to assume that she lied from sheer force of habit, we may think that, in the turmoil, she did indeed discover the brooch to be absent from its accustomed position. And then, perhaps a day or so later, she remembered what had become of it – or she may even have found it, say, unexpectedly attached to one of the dead woman's dresses (and, if so, she has a choice, does she not? Admit her mistake, and incur the wrath of so many people, or keep or dispose of the brooch. Very likely none of this happened, but, if it did, I think we may assume she had not a split-second of doubt about what she would do. (Good God, who would notice yet another ill-described brooch. Perhaps one of her relatives is still wearing it. Or threw it away decades ago as an object of no value, of whose history she was entirely ignorant.) *(In fact, a jeweller testified at the trial to the existence of the brooch in question. Its whereabouts, however, were to the best of my knowledge never resolved.)*

He has therefore, as a good citizen, no choice, whatever his personal wishes, but to continue manfully up the stairs and into whichever police-station it was, to give them his utterly worthless bit of information. (For how would he subsequently feel if it were to be discovered that the brooch was, in fact, the right one. (Or if time passed, and there was no progress made in the search: particularly if he found out, as surely he would – yes, as almost certainly he would – that Slater had left, bag and baggage, for America, within two days of the killing?)) After all, what harm can come of it? More to the point, if it were discovered that Slater's brooch could not possibly be *the* brooch (which was discovered at once to be the case), to what sane man would it even for a moment occur that the police might somehow surmise that, through presumably the direct intervention of Providence, the man involved in this trivial coincidence would turn out to be the killer anyway, despite the fact that there was not a single other material clue connecting him with the crime? Truly, one feels that, if the wife of the Lord Provost of Glasgow had been observed wearing a similar new brooch, the detective branch would, with equal aplomb, have decided that they need look no further. I should say so. Strange that, if he had paused at the top of the stairs, thought better of it, and returned to his modest abode, unwilling to get himself involved in such a business (as presumably did many other members of the Sloper Club, India Street, who also knew that Slater had been offering to sell a pledge for a brooch, but who, for one reason or another, did not share this priceless information with the police) Slater would probably have died in America, on a day when millions of others also died, utterly unheard of. But he opens the door, and goes in, and Slater dies, memorably, in Ayr. (Nothing more, I think, is heard of this MacLean.)

* * *

Slater's alibi is at once prosaic and fascinating, and would surely be some indication of innocence, were it not that the possibility of being guilty never even arises. (That is one of the fascinations of the case. A man came very near to hanging, and served, what, 18 years in prison, for a crime which it is not possible for a second to believe he was responsible for, even though the actual culprit remains unknown. How could the police possibly believe it was him? There was, I think it may be said, once the false trail of the brooch was cleared out of the way, absolutely nothing to connect Slater with the case, except for the fact that he lived in the neighbourhood. 10,000 other men could have been found guilty with as much logic. And, indeed, even the fact of his living nearby (the sole indicator of his guilt, except perhaps for his height, which was dead average (his weight, age and appearance all contradicted the original descriptions gathered from the witnesses)) loses some of its gloss if we recall the electrifying testimony of the attendant at Kelvinbridge Subway Station, about twenty minutes away from the scene of the crime, that a man hurried through the turnstile without buying a ticket, roughly half an hour after the crime was committed. The spotlight picks out the killer (or perhaps one of the two accomplices) for a moment.

(Perhaps. I am fairly sure that nowadays retribution from the authorities would be immediately forthcoming, if one tried to leap the electronic barrier. Kelvinbridge is at present the nearest station to where I live. (Interestingly, and it occurs to me only as I am writing this, the closest station to the scene of the crime is the next one down the line, at St. George's Cross, reachable very quickly from Miss Gilchrist's, in under two minutes at a sprint. (I should know: it was the station nearest to the house where my family lived for the first 16 or so years of my life. I remember the street well, in its previous incarnation. (It was being devastated for developmental, traffic-centred reasons around the time that we left.) The station was tucked in a corner, formed where the facade that lined the road suddenly dived back to create a pavement twice as wide. It was a curiously dark, mysterious little spot as I recall it, and I doubt if, structurally, it had changed much in the 50-odd years intervening, for all the X-million to-ings and fro-ings up and down the very steep, irresolute stairway – several of which manoeuvres, for all we know, may have been made by the murderer himself. (Was there anybody standing on the platform at the time of the murder? Almost certainly. And yet we will never know his, her, or their names – who are, after all, part of the story. Perhaps, had the murderer chosen a straighter course, they would have solved the problem at once. And so we probably *still* wouldn't have heard of them, since the case would sink back among all those appallingly straightforward murders, which it seems almost a crime itself to be interested in.)

No doubt the murderer did not choose that station, as it was altogether too near. Or, no doubt, by the time he could think straight he was nearer to Kelvinbridge anyway – although, if he had been thinking *really* straight, he would have paid for his ticket and become utterly immemorable, unless 7.30 in the evening was not as busy a time then as it is now.) But I would be interested to know what would have happened if a ticket-collector had asked to see his ticket. After all, this man had (probably *(actually it is far from clear that the man at Kelvinbridge had anything whatever to do with the case)*) lately committed a murder, probably without premeditation. It is likely that his response to a challenge would have been interesting.) But the man disappears unsuspected, and no-one notices the station at which he departs the train. Doubtless, wherever it was, it was conveniently placed for access to the house of at least some of the now deceased spinster's estranged relatives. (Which reminds me that I must try to find out who benefited from her will.) The judge however seemed to take the view that this personage tied in well with Slater, who took advantage of his great good fortune in living close by, by running to a comparatively distant railway station, presumably to brood over his doings on a journey the long way round the circle back to St. George's Cross.

(Slater was seen standing outside his home within an hour of the murder by a witness passing by. This witness was not called at the trial. Perhaps Slater merely took the short journey back one station, to St. George's Cross? The judge seemed almost to take the view that Slater was such a blackguard that he did not deserve to live, whether he was guilty or not; but he might as well be found guilty for neatness's sake.))) Slater's alibi was, that he was having dinner at home at the time of the murder. It is unfortunate for him that he had invited no guests, for a single pillar of the establishment, there for whatever (I grant you, implausible) reason, would surely have killed the case stone dead. But his (more or less) wife was there, and her maid; and although the judge chose to believe the latter's admission that her mistress sometimes received gentleman visitors in the evening ('gentlemen' here presumably meaning nothing more than 'male'), and based on it some disgraceful remarks in his summing-up, which eventually had the proceedings overturned on a technicality as a mis-trial 19 years later, he chose not to believe her testimony as to this modest, normal, familial meal. But, of course, it is as certain as anything in this case that it really did take place. One more meal, as innocent as most (what happened to the wife after the trial? – disappeared, I suppose); a few bites taken as a nearby door is opened; the plate nearly cleared as a nearby chair is lifted. (And intervening doors opening and shutting all the time. (Including some doors of the house where I was brought up. Who lived there then? Who was in the room where I was actually born? Is all this gone?) And chairs without number were being subtly rearranged – some brought closer to the fire, some moved slightly for ease in many places in a little procession of meals – and one now lying on a floor, soaked in blood, while its neighbours still stand by, in their previous attitudes of innocence.) They finish the meal, talking normally. His life will soon be shattered. They rise from the table and go into another room.

(In my rereading the next day, I learn that the fleeing passenger in fact flung down the required penny fare onto the ticket-counter, and thus did not defraud the Underground cashier of its legitimate revenue. But he did not stop for long enough to pick up his ticket (as, I suspect, legally required to do for the transaction to be a valid one), and thus he was still as open as ever to challenge by an inspector making an impromptu swoop (one chance in two? in five? in ten?) on the train in which he was travelling.)

*   *   *

How much, or how little, can I recall of the circumstances under which I first heard of Slater? I am fairly certain it will have been in the kitchen of the top-floor flat in West Princes Street where I lived from birth to mid-teens. (Not having been there for the last 20 years, I can nonetheless remember its lay-out fairly exactly, including the large recess in the wall to the right of the small entrance corridor from the door, doubtless originally for a bed, but now neatly accommodating the huge family table. (On the right of the kitchen-door was the door to a large cupboard. On the left that of a smaller room within which occurred the earliest events of my life which I know myself to remember.

(I remember standing in a cot beside the cot of my elder sister – both were rickety wooden affairs, supported by what seemed to me then to be high legs – and I was jumping up and down. (It was not clear to me in my recollection why I was jumping up and down (I think I assumed it to be sheer youthful high spirits and thought no more about it), but a few months ago I happened to mention this to my mother, and she, after an expression of surprise that I still remember that (somehow I had assumed that everyone must know I remembered it) told me that it was a favourite pastime of me and my sister to jump up and down in our cots, as we thereby managed, thanks, I assume, to the natural tilt of the floor, to travel some way across the room, towards the window.))))

I do not remember the circumstances of the discussion (after all, one talks confidently for decades, convinced that someone somewhere must be writing down what is being said, of such immense interest and importance is it), but at one point my mother broadened out the subject a little to mention that a famous murder had once been committed two doors away down the street. This seemed to us children (although who 'us children' exactly were, I forget) to be a bit too good to be true (possibly only myself and my elder sister again (it can hardly have included, in any receptive sense, my younger sister (and I have a brother too) who was born sufficient years after me, for me to have a fairly distinct, albeit mystified, recollection of that event also (of not being allowed into the kitchen, of strange comings and goings (no-one had told me anything, and I had no more notion of what was happening than if, well, than if a murder was being committed)). I mention this largely because it is my sister's 29th birthday in two days' time, and I have just put a card to her in the post-box on my way to the library this afternoon, half an hour or so ago, after phoning up my mother in her house on the west coast to find out my sister's new address in Edinburgh, which, we can add with confidence, is on the East Coast), but my mother insisted that such was indeed the case: that a famous murder had once been committed, just down the road, and (I think she added) that a man who had not been responsible for it had nonetheless been imprisoned for a long time. She then remembered that, when her husband ('your father') had just acquired the renting of the flat, she had written as much, very naturally, in her latest letter to our uncle who was living in England, and in his reply he had hoped that it wasn't the Slater flat. But no, she repeated: the Slater flat was two doors down the road. (One self-sufficient main door flat intervenes.) After which, I cannot remember hearing him mentioned for years. (Actually, the next clear recollection that I have is of mentioning this modest coincidence to someone who worked in the BBC building by the Botanic Gardens. He proceeded to tell me that his own father had been at the trial (!). (Apparently, as far I recall, he had returned home, distraught, after the verdict.))

* * *

It is, I trust, not too callous to point out that Miss Gilchrist, who was either 82 or 83 when she died, was, despite being the victim of an appalling and fatal attack, possibly the longest-living of all those who had anything to do with the case. (Slater himself, for instance, was 76 when he died, exactly twice the age he would have achieved if the law had taken its initially appointed course. (Indeed, for all we know it may even have been her sheer persistence in living which, by annoying someone, led to her demise.)) But if, say, three months earlier, she had fallen victim to a normal minor ailment of the aged, she would be no more to us now than any other of the little old ladies who must have died in West Princes Street, of whom nothing else whatever is known. And Slater too would have led a different life, and no doubt we would not know about him either: not that he visited Glasgow in 1901 (as did millions of others – it was the year of the Great Universal Exhibition in the city); or in 1905 (for obscure motives, like so much else in his life); or in 1909 (for a brief stay of two months before travelling on to, or so he supposed, San Francisco). But now we learn that, when the body was first discovered by Lambie, and, shortly thereafter, Adams, she was not yet dead. She made a final movement of her left hand. (Having reached her early eighties; fond of jewelry; unmarried; puzzlingly wealthy; a magazine abandoned for a moment still lying face-down upon the table.) If, even an hour earlier, she had simply fallen to the floor dead, without cause from elsewhere. If she had died, even in an appalling agony, we would have learned absolutely nothing about her. She could have writhed through a thousand devastating movements of pain, as no doubt others did, and we would still have heard nothing, seen nothing, and imagine nothing. We do not know, for instance, how the people died who were in the rooms of my house then.

(To revert to MacLean for a moment. *(In fact, he testified at the trial.)* I might mention, as I have since discovered, that, of the £200 so generously offered for the apprehension of Slater, this M'Lean received £40. It is difficult to work out quite how the portioning-out was arrived at, but I feel M'Lean would have had legitimate grounds for feeling aggrieved. It is true that he did not know the brooch-dispenser's surname, having only nodding acquaintance with a foreigner called 'Oscar', yet, without him, where could the police possibly have begun the search that would lead them triumphantly to Slater? (Can we assume he was horror-struck when Slater was finally released? (I must try to find out if he was still alive then.)))

* * *

Of Miss Gilchrist it may with some certainty be said that no part of her life is as well-documented as her dreadful death. Indeed, our knowledge of her previous 82 years in their entirety seems to come to far less, in precision and exhaustiveness, than our knowledge even of her fatal injuries. Simple arithmetic suggests her year of birth was 1826. Do we know where, or do we simply assume she was born in Glasgow? (Perhaps a dozen significant buildings already existing in that era still survive in the city.) It is odd to think that, while Beethoven dies in a thunderstorm in Vienna, some presumed parents are presumably cooing with half-disbelieving wonder at her first approaches to speech. Presumably the same rain cannot be falling. Or that, in the next year, as Schubert tries to find a way to lie at rest comfortably, not yet even dreaming that his illness is fatal, she has presumably mastered the art of walking. At this time, one trusts, her strange devotion to jewelry has not yet begun to manifest itself. (Of late, by the way, I have been desultorily reading Sir Walter Scott's journal. (Indeed, now that I think of it, the edition which I bought a few months ago (there seems to be no modern edition) was dated 1898 or some such year (certainly, late nineteenth-century) – published, that is, when both Slater and Gilchrist were alive (and Mary Barrowman was a very young girl of three or thereabouts, beginning to walk, talk, invent stories, etc.); the former not yet having visited Glasgow, the latter already an old woman of 70-odd, who had lived in West Princes Street for 20 or so years by now, and whose death in her sleep, need I repeat, would not have been the cause for much concern or comment anywhere.) I have not yet finished the book, but it is a little eery to consider that, doubtless on one of those myriad days when the good-hearted author spent eight or so hours in the library writing well below standard more or less non-stop (his day enlivened only by a long walk, or a couple of hours of jovial tree-felling) Miss Gilchrist put in her first appearance in the world. (I at length went over to the book-case, and found the requisite volume. There were no 'Gilchrist's in the Index, as there easily might have been, so normal is the name. It transpires that the date of the publication was, in fact, 1891, which affects all that I have already said so little that I need not bother changing it, since they were both alive during all those days anyway.) But by 1870, or 1871, when Slater was born (or rather, when an Oscar Joseph Leschziner was born in Oppeln, Germany, with whom it could reasonably be supposed that a Miss Marion Gilchrist of Glasgow would never have the least communication, be it the merest passing glance (and it seems likely that, in fact, they did not, although perhaps Leschziner once saw a little old lady on the other side of St. George's Road (or, perhaps more accurately, possibly she passed through his field of vision once))), we may, I think, assume that some sort of interest in expensive costume jewelry on her part had already made itself known. After all, she may have been 44 years old. (It was, more or less, the time of the Paris Commune. Perhaps, occasionally, she had begun to read an article about it in a magazine, but had had her attention distracted to something else – a knock at the door perhaps – had folded back the magazine, placed it face-down upon a table, and moved away. She may also have placed her spectacles down at its side, if she already wore spectacles, which is possible.)

* * *

Pursuing a little further the question of Miss Gilchrist and the architecture of Glasgow, we may remark that Blythswood Square, which is the only typically Edinburgh square to be found in the Western Metropolis (by the Edinburgh architect, John Brash) was begun in 1823, when Marion Gilchrist was not yet conceived, and was completed in 1829, when she was probably walking (and perhaps occasionally still falling) (although on none of these occasions did anyone then climb up onto her rib-cage and belabour her 50 or 60 times about the skull with a very lightweight hammer (which, indeed, despite the utterly ridiculous amount of time expended on this possibility at the trial, never happened at all)). Blythswood Square is still locally notorious as being the site containing the house in which the family of the architect Joseph Smith (1806–63) lived – a minor figure, but one responsible, for instance, for the workmanlike facade of the Treron building in nearby Sauchiehall Street (still there, passed by thousands every day (as surely Miss Gilchrist must time without number have passed it. (As surely must, in the 1860's, perhaps on the same side of the road as her, a locally domiciled doctor named Pritchard have done, who was hanged in 1865 for poisoning his utterly innocent wife and mother-in-law)). Indeed, I have walked past it time without number myself. *(And, in the last few months, I have often walked past its burned-out shell, gutted by a fire towards the end of 1986. Apparently the intention is to save it.)*

The family house is not, however, revered as a temple of the vital art of architectural design. It is to one of the architect's daughters, a dark decisive girl called Madeleine, that the locale owes its fame. She became involved in an illicit affair with a foreign gentleman (but this time French rather than German (remarkable how the European orientation of Scottish life surfaces everywhere (actually, he was from the Channel Islands, but a Frenchman all the same))), who became troublesome and a burden to her. She gave him cocoa to drink at some of their nocturnal trysts, and he died of arsenical poisoning. (She had of late been buying precisely this poison herself as a beauty treatment. (The trial of Madeleine Smith – she was, of course, acquitted – was the first of the four great Glasgow murder trials which occurred over half a century. All these murders took place within 10 minutes walk of Charing Cross. Slater's was the last. (Even though Miss Gilchrist was ten years older than Madeleine Smith. One wonders what her comments on such a scandalous subject were at the time of the trial. If she made none, she was possibly the only Glaswegian who didn't do so.) It is, I think, fair to say that in only one of them (Pritchard) was the murderer convicted. In one, the murderess (Smith) was found Not Proven. In the other two, guilty verdicts were indeed found against the accused, but, rather unfortunately, in neither case was the person thus sentenced to death the murderer. (Well, no legal system is perfect. And neither of them was actually hanged. (In one of these cases, the probable murderer was known by name, but, as he had acquired legal immunity through his role as the chief prosecution witness in the trial which found his accessory guilty (!), he could not himself be prosecuted, and thus escaped scot-free. His accessory after the fact, totally innocent of the murder, served ten years, so at least justice was partly seen to be done. The Slater case would seem to give additional weight to the principle evolved here that it doesn't much matter exactly who goes to prison for a major crime, so long as somebody does. Slater's case would seem to suggest that this person need not even have anything to do with the matter – although, of course, it is an advantage that he should live nearby.))))

I should add that quite a few people still believe in Smith's innocence. (I myself have been delightfully belaboured by one such.) This seems to me to be curious. (All the more so in that apparently, the 15-man jury which acquitted her found 10 for Not Proven, and 5 for Guilty. (In other words, no-one on the jury thought she should be found Not Guilty. We should note here that the voting in the Slater case was: 9 for Guilty; 5 for Not Proven; 1 for Not Guilty. (Decision was by simple majority – which is, I suppose, logical enough, if somewhat stark. (8 Guilty, 7 Not Proven – condemned. 7 Guilty, 8 Not Proven – acquitted. (Quite what, say, 5 Guilty, 5 Not Proven, 5 Not Guilty would be entered in the accounts as, is a question (like 7–1–7) which I have thought it better not to pursue, if only from the fear of losing a delightful fantasy.)

I have gazed at the photograph taken at the (Slater) trial: looking at the jury as if I might be able to see which of them was the wonderful man who found for Not Guilty (the jury were out for 70 minutes in all – 4.55 pm to 6.05 pm, 6 May 1909), but of course that is not possible. Allow me, nonetheless, to blow a kiss in roughly the direction of the heavens, as an inadequate expression of gratitude. (Note, please, that if merely two more had found for Not Proven, Slater would have been acquitted – 7 Guilty, 7 Not Proven, 1 Not Guilty. (Of course, ideally, for the last twist of the knife, 8 rather than 9 should originally have found for Guilty. (My earlier fantasies, I now realise are rather slight things. If a majority finds for Guilty, then such is the verdict. In the absence of such a Guilty majority, the accused is acquitted anyway, under whatever designation.)) (It seems to me, by the way, that three or four of the jury (I do not possess a copy of the illustrated transcript, and can only consult the one in the Mitchell Reference Library) bear a definite facial resemblance to Slater. It looks like almost pure chance that Slater is being tried for the murder, rather than one of them, for they all (I assume) had as little to do with it. (Well, I assume the murderer is not sitting on the jury, although he may be in or near the court. I mean, they are all Edinburgh men, or so I believe.)))))

Another point about Smith comes to mind. Although she nourished her superfluous lover with cocoa of her own inimitable preparation in Blythswood Square, their relationship commenced a year or so earlier, when the Smith family still lived in its previous house, which, if memory serves me correctly, was in the reasonably nearby India Street. (This street still exists, a short thoroughfare in a curiously overlookable location, but both of its sides are now devoted to monolithic modern buildings, and not a fragment of the old architecture that I remember remains. (Yet, even as late as 1968 things were entirely different. In the summer of that year, before going on to university, I worked for several weeks of casual labour in a hotel in that street. It was an old building (albeit with a hole in the ground for its immediate neighbour), and across the road stood old tenements. (I remember once being sent across the road with a tray of tea and biscuits, to take to the youngish hotel manager, who had a flat there. As I was climbing the fine stairway in the common close-mouth, one of the girls who normally worked at the reception desk or in the offices passed me quietly in the opposite direction. (I also remember quite clearly standing in one of the dark basement rooms of the hotel, and looking out at the railings above and beyond, and the sheer frontage of the sunlit buildings on the other side of the narrow street, and the continuous succession of passing people, and being struck by a sense of what?, of how much it took to fill a large city, in this street that I had known nothing of a week or so earlier.)) This presumably was, at least in part, the original Victorian architecture.)) Now, curiously, the club which Slater belonged to, and inside which he offered for sale his pawn-ticket for a valuable brooch, which so lingered in the memory of one Allan M'Lean, bicycle dealer, was also situated in this India Street.

Brian McCabe

Not About the Kids

He could just remember the apples and oranges careering around the kitchen. And the grapes – that's right, he'd just bought those grapes in the afternoon. He'd picked up a bunch of them in the fruit shop and felt their luxurious weight in his hand, half wondering if they could really afford them, what with being unemployed, and half thinking that the kids hardly ever got grapes. The way they'd scattered all over the floor – ricocheting around the kitchen like the beads of a broken necklace! In his anger he'd scooped the fruitbowl off the table and, in one sweeping movement, flung it at the wall. It exploded. Thank Christ the kids hadn't been there. He had to make sense of what had happened, or else here he was, driving through the night with no real clue about why he was here, in the middle of nowhere in Fife.

A light rain was beginning to fall and he switched on the wipers. He stared at the road in front of him. He was driving. He had to keep his mind on the road. It felt like he'd been driving for a long time, for years and years of his life. Now the road seemed to be coming at him out of the night, negotiating him rather than the other way round, as if it was testing him. If he could just concentrate on driving this car along this road, maybe all the other stuff would sort itself out. He'd had a row with his wife and now he was driving. That was all there was to it.

He braked to take a corner and heard the grinding screech of metal on metal. The break-pads needed to be changed months ago. Now the discs would be scuppered. The shocks needed to be replaced as well, and one of the rear coil-springs was broken. Age, the guy at the garage had told him, looking at him, not the car. But he hadn't had the money to go ahead and get the work done there and then. At any moment the broken spring could leap out, and the car collapse on to the rear axle.

It had been something so trivial, of course, some trivial little thing they'd disagreed about, not about the kids but about the housework – the household chores! Ruth had started getting at him about putting the rubbish out – was that how it had *started*? He'd been sitting there at the table, after the communal family meal. Bobby had been obstreperous as usual, throwing his food on the floor, insisting on drinking out of a glass like everyone else, then spilling his juice all over the table. Emma had been finicky and difficult and the food – an experimental fish curry – hadn't gone down well. She'd interrupted them with needless questions every time they'd tried to speak to each other. There had been a bottle of wine – his idea, along with the grapes. Ruth had declined the wine wearily, saying it was a waste of money. Maybe it had started with the wine, with the waste of money.

And, when the table had been cleared, with Bobby on his knee, popping a grape or two into the boy's mouth, he'd been aware of Ruth making more of a thing of doing the dishes than usual. The plates were crashing and colliding in the sink and she was smashing handfuls of cutlery down on the metal draining board. He'd asked her what the fuck was wrong with her. Nothing was wrong with her, she'd said, but in a tone of voice that seethed with resentment. Then she'd started sweeping the kitchen floor and shouting at Emma to get out from under her feet.

When he thought about it now, it came clearer that what he'd been trying to do was to woo her, but he'd tried to include the kids, when what was needed was not about the kids. What was needed was something else. And it was as if she held him responsible for trying but failing, as if the attempt had reminded her of how things would be but were not. The way she'd swept that floor, like some vengeful Cinderella.

Leave it, he'd said, just fucking leave it and I'll do it later on. Then she'd started dealing with the rubbish, tugging that black bag out of the bucket, tying it up so tightly. What was she trying to tell him? That he was neglecting this twice-weekly fucking ritual, normally earmarked as a chore of his in the demarcation of labour between them? She'd deliberately done one of his chores, encroached on his territory, so that she could get at him about it – could this be true?

He'd picked up Bobby and grabbed Emma by the arm and made for the door. Ruth had shouted something at him about the way he was handling the kids. Christ Almighty. He'd shouted back at her: No, this is not about the kids, this has nothing to do with the kids! So he'd removed them from the battlefield, running their bath and putting them in it before returning to wage war with Ruth about the rubbish. He'd tried to take over but she'd resisted and the two of them had ended up having a tug of war with the rubbish bag. It had split and all the food scraps and nappies and tin cans and eggshells had spilled over the floor, the floor she'd just swept. They'd stopped everything then to argue savagely. Then he'd smashed the fruitbowl and stamped out of the house, slamming the door. It was awful, it was desperate. But what was it all about?

He was finding it hard to concentrate on driving. He kept thinking of all the things he should've said but hadn't found the words for, the reasonable, rational things ... He came to a bend so sharp that he had to slow down to a crawl to take it. He didn't know this road and it kept surprising him, dipping and rising and twisting into the night unpredictably. He couldn't go back tonight, that was for certain. Maybe this time he wouldn't go back at all, maybe this was it, the final break, and they'd both remember this night like no other night in their lives.

Up ahead, just beyond the range of his dipped headlights, there was some kind of truck. One of its brake lights wasn't working. A truck or a lorry? It was hard to make out on that dark road. Even when he flicked his headlights on full for a moment, it was difficult to determine the exact nature of the vehicle. A loose tarpaulin was roped around the cargo, whatever it was. At every sudden summit, the truck made a lot of noise, as if its various parts had come apart for a second, only to crash back together as the truck roared on into the night. The way it seemed to veer from side to side unpredictably at every bend bothered him. He put his foot on the accelerator. He felt his heartbeat speeding up too. He knew that if Ruth had been in the car with him he wouldn't take the risk – but she wasn't.

Before he could level with the truck he saw, above the dark embankment at the side of the road, the light from an approaching car's headlights, so he braked and pulled back in. The bastard hadn't slowed down to let him pass – hadn't he stepped on it to make sure he couldn't? The approaching car dipped its headlights as it came round the corner. Even so, it dazzled him and he slowed down till it had passed. There was a moment when he could make out nothing but the red brake-light of the truck, dancing around in the night ahead, a taunting spark, then it disappeared. When his eyes had readjusted he saw that he was too far into the middle of the road as he took the bend, so he swung back out. This road was wild. It wasn't so much the blind summits or the hairpin bends, but the stretches in between, where the road wavered and couldn't make up its mind which way to go.

It was a dangerous road. Maybe it didn't go anywhere. He lit a cigarette and tugged open the overflowing ashtray on the dashboard. He'd been smoking too much and there was a sour taste in his mouth that reminded him of nights years ago, when he and Ruth had started up together, when they'd stayed up most of the night and gone to bed at dawn, making love as the birds were singing outside ...

He came over a rise and saw the truck there ahead, its one brake light

jiggling up and down, its tail-board rattling. It had slowed down. There
was a clear stretch ahead. He accelerated and signalled to overtake, but it
was taking longer than it should. The truck threw a spray of dirty
rainwater over his windscreen and snarled at him as he drew level with
it. He could feel the car jogging around on the uneven road. It was a relief
to get in front. Even so, the truck-driver had his headlights at full beam
and he could see nothing but the glare of them in his mirror. The truck
was gaining on him, so he put the foot down again and tried to leave it
behind.

A sharp bend in the road came at him and he had to brake hard to get
round it. The brakes screeched. The car skidded and swung too far into
the side of the road and scraped noisily against the barrier beneath the
sign with the chevrons. At the same moment he was dazzled by the
headlights of an oncoming car and he raised his right hand to shield his
eyes, trying to right the wheel with his left hand. The other car roared
past blaring its horn.

He went on driving, but his heart was hammering and he could feel
his hands and his arms shaking. He had to stop somewhere as soon as
possible.

As if the road had taken this decision, it wound downwards and
showed him a speed-limit sign and the nameplate of a village he'd never
heard of. He slowed down until he saw a pub just off the main street,
then pulled over and waited till the truck roared past. It was just a truck,
moving something from somewhere to somewhere else in the night. He
put his hand to his head, pressing his thumb and his forefinger into his
eyelids, and he sat like this for a moment before switching off the engine
and the lights.

There were only a few people in the pub and he felt conspicuous as
he walked to the bar. He was a stranger, and they didn't often get
strangers here. They stared at him with hostile curiosity. Some of them
seemed to dismiss him quickly, as if they knew he was from the city and
had just had a row with his wife.

The barman took too long to serve him. He was serving somebody
else but taking his time about it, having a conversation with some of the
men sitting round the bar. Apparently they were talking about birds,
birds they found living in the eaves of their houses. One man was
maintaining that when swifts made their nests they used their spit to
hold them together, and that swift's spit was the main ingredient in
bird's-nest soup.

He ordered a double and asked if there was a telephone. The barman pointed to the door that led to the toilets. He took his drink to a table by the window and drank half of it and smoked a cigarette. He thought about what he should say to her.

Ruth, it was the way you swept the floor.

Ruth, I demand custody of the kids.

Ruth, I think you should have custody of the kids. They can come to me half the week and stay with you the other half.

Ruth, we need to talk. Not about the kids. About us. What's happening to *us*, Ruth?

He looked at the only woman in the bar, as if this might help him to think of what he should say to his wife. She was sitting on a high stool up at the bar, next to a man – her husband? She wore a tailored leather jacket, the collar of which she held between her finger and thumb to illustrate her point. The man shook his head, raised his eyebrows wearily and slouched on his stool, over which he'd slung his nylon jerkin. They seemed a sad couple, trapped in their coupledom. But maybe they weren't a couple at all. And if they were a couple – what did that mean, exactly, when you got down to it?

The others sitting at the bar all seemed to know each other, though some wore muddied work boots and dungarees, others sports jackets or suits. Over in the far corner, two younger men in jeans and tee-shirts were playing pool and listening to the juke-box.

He took his drink and his cigarettes out to the telephone with him.

It rang and rang. Had she unplugged the phone? Eventually she answered:

– It's me.

– Oh.

– Sorry about the fruitbowl.

– So am I – not just about the fruitbowl.

– I know it isn't just about the fruitbowl. I'll get you another one exactly the same.

– Like hell you will. It was an antique.

– I know, I know, it's irreplaceable. I'm sorry. The thing is, I was angry.

– You were angry. Right. That explains everything, doesn't it? You were angry so you threw the fruitbowl at the wall. If the kids had been there –

– They weren't. I made sure of that.

– They could have been. Anyway *I* was there.

He apologised again then waited until she spoke.

– Where are you?

— Fife.

— What the hell are you doing in Fife?

— I don't know, I drove here.

— You must be out of your mind.

— I am. I am totally out of my mind.

— You're drunk.

— No, not yet.

— You're driving.

— That's right. I'm driving.

— You must be crazy.

— At this moment, you're right, I am completely crazy.

She didn't reply to that. He waited a minute, then he said:

— What's it about?

— What?

— All this. What's it all about?

— What do you think it's all about?

— That's what I'm asking you.

She sighed with fatigue and said wearily that she didn't know. He was glad she didn't. That gave him the initiative:

— It's something to do with me losing my job, isn't it?

— No. Of course not.

— I'm around the house too much. We're with each other all the time. I mean, sometimes a person has to go away just so that they can come back.

— Don't come back. Not tonight.

— Don't worry, I won't.

— I don't want to talk anymore. I'm tired, I want to go to bed.

— I'll tell you a bed-time story, then. Once upon a time, there was a boy and a girl, and they fell madly in love with each other. But they were young, just kids –

— I've heard this story before.

— Not this one, Ruth, this one is not about us, this one is about these kids, these kids who fell madly in love. In those days, Ruth, it was as simple as that. We're talking about a time when people went out with each other for a month, if it was serious. But these kids are so in love they manage to go on for a year, more than a year … That gives you some idea how serious about each other they are. But, as I was saying, they're young, too young to really know how to go on being in love, if you know what I mean, and after a while something has to happen.

The pips sounded, and he hurriedly pulled a handful of coins from his pocket, dumped them on the shelf and searched among them for a ten pence. He found one and put it in just as they were about to be cut off.

– Ruth? Are you still there?

– What's the point of all this?

– So, and this is the sad bit of the story, there comes a point when the boy begins to feel restless, he feels the need for change ... He's changing anyway, he's growing up, and the whole world is changing round about him. And so one night, out of the blue, the boy tells the girl he wants to finish with her. So they split up. Some time passes. The boy is totally miserable without the girl, but he is alone. He's himself and only himself. Then he goes back to her, and she takes him back with open arms. And they go on together again, pretty much as before except that everything has changed. In fact, nothing is ever quite the same after that brief separation. And soon the girl begins to feel restless, she feels the need for change ...

– You got what you deserved. What d'you want, sympathy?

– All I'm saying is sometimes people need the threat of separation, I mean so they can go on. The threat has to be real. But as soon as it is real it will never go away, it will always be there. D'you know what I'm saying, Ruth?

– You're saying it's time to split up.

– I never said that.

Maybe we should.

– Just remember it was you who suggested it first.

– What does it matter who suggests it first?

– It matters. Everything matters.

– Don't sound so gloomy about it.

– How should I sound – cheerful?

– I'm not saying that.

– What are you saying?

– I'm not saying anything.

– Well, why not? Are we communicating with each other here or what?

– I'm tired of communicating. We can communicate tomorrow.

– What about tomorrow?

But he could feel her attention slipping away from him. He tried to hold it.

– Are the kids okay?

– They're asleep, if that's what you mean.

– That isn't what I mean.

– What do you mean then?

— I mean are they okay? Come on, you know what I mean.

— They're okay, yes.

— Christ Ruth, I was trying tonight. I tried with the meal, I tried with the kids, I tried with us ...

— I know you tried. D'you think I haven't been trying? I'm always trying. Maybe that's the problem. Maybe it's just too much effort.

— You sound exhausted, Ruth.

— I am. My period's come.

— D'you think that had something to do with it?

— How do I know? Maybe, maybe not.

The pips went. He tried to tell her that he'd call her again in the morning, but he was cut off.

He took his drink back to the bar, finished it and ordered another. No one seemed to pay him any attention now, and they had become a meaningless blur to him. He didn't want to look at them, so he sat down in a chair that faced the window. He stared at his distorted image reflected in the marbled glass, and when he moved his head a little, his features disintegrated horribly.

Her period? Maybe, maybe not. But what, really, had happened? Maybe nothing had really happened. Maybe the threat was all that was needed. But then, maybe what he'd said to her was true: once the threat was there, it would never really go away.

If she could be here with him now ... but all that lay ahead was the night, a night spent alone, in a bed-and-breakfast in Fife. The utter pointlessness of it made him bang his glass down on the table as he finished his drink. Someone laughed at the bar, and he thought he heard a low-toned comment from one of the tables. He closed his eyes and listened. The clack of the pool balls, the music from the juke-box, the voices — all the noises in the bar seemed to swell inside him and engulf him, until he felt adrift in the world. He had to get out.

It had stopped raining, and the night was cool and clear. He walked to the car but didn't get in. He leaned against it and looked along the dark street of the village, at the haphazard silhouette of the rooftops. He imagined the swifts in the eaves, their nests being held together by spit, their eggs ... It reminded him vaguely of his childhood, although he had never lived in such a place.

Ronald Frame

La Plume de Ma Tante

My aunt was very famous in those days – the early 1960s – but famous in France where she lived, and because she was the black sheep of the family I was never encouraged to talk about her when I was young. The novels she wrote (in French) belonged to that period of 'new wave' films and elliptical jagged prose. They weren't translated, which was a relief to my mother and her other two sisters, as fewer people would realize that the earlier books referred to growing up in a genteel Scottish suburb, and not in favourable terms.

If my mother hadn't been a widow, and if money for holidays hadn't been tight after my school fees were taken care of, and if she hadn't happened to have had her head turned by the divorced father of a boy in my class, and if he hadn't been glad to get me out of the way for two or three days, then it's highly unlikely that when my aunt's invitation arrived – asking coyly if it would be in order for me to come and visit Paris over a weekend (at my aunt's expense) – I should have been given permission to go. My mother hummed and hawed at first, but maybe she thought that it would be a way of making up a little of all that lost ground with the renegade, and eventually she wired her terse agreement.

I was thirteen, and it was the first time I had been away from home without my mother. I went south by train; by two trains, one from Glasgow to London and then the night sleeper from Victoria, in a posh double-berth compartment I had to myself. In Paris I was met at the station by a driver and taken – in the back of a pneumatically sprung, glassy Citroën *Déesse* – over a stately bridge to the Left Bank, to a flat in a street of mellow-stoned mansion houses in the Seventh arrondissement. A woman came down to the courtyard to greet me. I presumed she was my aunt, whom I had never seen. Hearty laughter was her response to my mistake. She told me, in very practised English, that she was my aunt's – she hesitated momentarily – my aunt's 'companion'. She was dressed in neat corduroy pants and a cut-away tweed jacket, with a rich, chiffon scarf tumbling from the open neck of her silk shirt. A gamine haircut emphasized that the woman's looks were striking rather than pretty. Statuesquely built, she offered me a very firm handshake.

She showed me to my room next, and I gawped at the elegance of the flat. In the echoing *salon* we were served tea and English sandwiches and cake. I couldn't decide which of all the gilded chairs to sit on, but she indicated the one she meant for me, beside a table piled high with books. It was explained to me that my aunt had been 'delayed', that we would have tea by ourselves. So we sat, and I sipped and chewed politely, and we chatted. I felt I must be talking too much, but I was exhilarated just to have completed the journey successfully, in one piece.

Unfortunately my aunt was further delayed in the evening. After retiring to an adjacent room lined with bookshelves, her companion returned and announced that she would be taking me out to dinner. We dressed, and then we walked downstairs and out on to the street, and by a number of dog's-leg side streets we arrived at a restaurant in a garden of lilac trees. A table was waiting for us inside, at the back of the second room where it was quieter. My aunt's companion placed her large heavy handbag, with its catch undone, on top of the table and chided the waiter – playfully – loosening it from his grip when he attempted to lift it on to a chair. (I remember this in detail, because I am certain the incident is significant.)

For the first time in my life I tasted wine. I had two half-glasses in quite rapid succession. Under their influence I opened up, and how, although the following day I couldn't recall much of what I must have said. All about our lives at home in our well-to-do suburb, the one where my aunt had also grown up, which I suppose I described – without intending to – as a repository of hypocrisies and repressions. As I spoke of it then, it already seemed far far away, across water and great tracts of land, existing in the shadows of lowering purple mountains. Meanwhile ... The restaurant was supremely smart and tasteful; it appeared ineffably refined to me, like the clientele. I delighted in the discrepancy between my surroundings and what I was talking about. About school. My timetable subjects, the masters. My friends. Their parents and sisters. The two rival tennis clubs. My aunt's companion listened to all I said, paying close attention, steering me quite effortlessly from topic to topic. Occasionally she would depart to the *Mesdames*, carrying her big weighty handbag with her, and would hurry back, placing the bag – with its catch undone again – on top of the table.

I don't remember at what time we got back to the flat. Nor have I any recollection of how I changed out of my clothes into my pyjamas. Supine on the firm mattress in my room I dozed fitfully to begin with, then I dropped into the deepest sleep, and woke at nearly mid-day on the

Saturday. I jumped out of bed in a panic about how late it was, with a raging thirst for water, cold water. I threw on fresh clothes from my suitcase, gulped some bubbly mineral water straight from the bottle, and ran out into the corridor. When I presented myself in the hushed lofty *salon*, however, there was still no sight or sound of my aunt. I could hear her companion in the adjoining room, the study or library, talking on the telephone. When she walked back through, she didn't immediately see me. As soon as she did, a curious look creased her face – of puzzlement, perplexity, as if she was trying to place me. Me, in this chic apartment. Then of course she remembered, why it was I was here. Her face split into a smile, and almost simultaneously she whisked away from view a framed photograph of my aunt and herself standing close together, arm linked through arm. 'Now,' she said, slipping into a brisk cheerleaderish tone of voice, 'now I am going to show you the sights of our wonderful city!'

I never did get to meet my aunt. Her companion informed me that she had – she briefly hesitated – she had taken a cold. A bad head cold. While staying with friends. At Biarritz, by the sea, in the south-west of the country. I expressed my disappointment, although really I was enjoying myself just as I was, being looked after so well.

That day passed, and then the next came, Sunday, when we walked in a park in the morning and had lunch near L'Étoile in an American-style bar of bright chrome and white leather where the two women lunched every Sunday. My substitute hostess photographed me there with a flash bulb. Following that, some old photographs of my aunt's were retrieved from the handbag and spread out on the tablecloth and I was asked who certain people in them were, and probed about the locations. I obliged, answering every question, because it was quite easy for me and because I was only repaying their hospitality and because anyway I felt that I was looking down on Scotland from a very great height, like a bird in soaring flight. After lunch and our long discussion we returned to the flat in its quiet street of embassies, and I packed, and we both set off in the floating Citroën for the Gare du Nord and the first leg of my return journey.

In the sleeping compartment I was handed a present. I unwrapped it. A beautiful pale green lacquered fountain pen lay in a box lined with white satin. 'Your aunt never types,' her companion told me. 'She writes everything in longhand. She says a good pen makes her thoughts come more easily. They flow – ' and she demonstrated – 'in a long line, like this. Head. Shoulder. Arm. Wrist. Hand. Paper.'

I thanked her, as I knew to do, but she shook her head and assured me it was nothing. Just for a second or two, as she turned away, I thought her smile was being negated by the way it stayed so fixed in place, hooked up over her top incisors.

Two years later my aunt's new novel was published.

Six hundred and more miles away, *we* weren't to see it – no subsequent translation appeared and my mother had given up looking for the books – but it was advertised as being her most autobiographical to date. In the Parisian press, reviewers praised her memory for details. Apparently she had reproduced in French the drawly suburban accent of my sort very well, with its lockjaw inflections, its nuances and its slang. She had concentrated on the tiniest things in myopic and incantatory fashion, which precisely suited the French taste. Scotland acquired a more distinctive, more particular identity for her in the retelling than it must have had when she was a girl growing up there with my mother and her other sisters, when living was all that was required in our privileged suburb, not introspection nor even gratitude for the mercies of birth and upbringing.

When I was getting off the train at Victoria, I found a day-old Paris newspaper and tucked it into the pocket of my duffle coat. In the Glasgow train I opened it up.

On the society page was a group photograph taken at the Longchamp racecourse on Saturday, the day we'd toured the sights of Paris. My eyes were drawn to one woman's svelte trouser suit – and then to her face, which was uncannily like my mother's. A leash was wrapped round a strong wrist, and at the end of the leash a black Scottie sat on the paddock grass.

In the small print of the caption I wasn't as surprised as I thought I ought to be to discover my aunt's name.

Where were the wild Atlantic breakers hurling themseles at Biarritz's rocky foreshore? Longchamp is in the Bois de Boulogne, in Paris. In the photograph my aunt, modish and posturing, didn't look remotely like a woman going down with a common or garden head cold.

*

Concealed in the handbag – with, of course, its catch undone – there must have been a tape-recorder. And the same machine was doubtless hidden behind the books artfully arranged on the table in the salon where we drank our tea. My aunt's companion would have had a secretary's recall of minutiae, and – probably – a lover's dedication to the task my aunt had assigned her.

And the magnificent fountain pen?

It lies now on my own desk, in front of me. I use it every day in my author's work. Maybe from what my surrogate hostess told her on the telephone, my aunt intuited that I might have a little of her own aptitude for putting seemingly inconsequential things – which most people are content to take for granted, to overlook and forget – into a context.

One day, she hoped, I would understand what she'd been about. I might even find it was in me to grant her some measure of forgiveness.

My mother had me write a 'thank you' letter to my aunt with my new pen, although she conceded me a couple of days' grace, which she wouldn't normally have done: that must have been on account of her sister's behaviour, the ungracious and unapologised-for absence.

While I was working on my letter the telephone rang, and I listened to my mother talking in a high, dry, nervous voice to the divorcé who had been courting her for the past few months. I heard her reply 'no' to some question. The word was repeated, twice, more definitely. Then she suddenly replaced the receiver on its cradle.

By means of that one short call and the summary exchange, the past – her past, *our* mutual past – was rendered safe again. I'd noticed when I got back that my father's framed photograph had been brought out from behind the potted African violet on top of the sideboard and returned to its familiar position of prominence. Although their marriage hadn't been perfect, from now on my mother was going to adhere to the myth of it.

My aunt in Paris was busy demolishing myths, and yet to the two blood sisters the past – accepted by one, rejected by the other – was becoming the magnetic lodestone of both their lives.

Dilys Rose

All the Little Loved Ones

I love my kids. My husband too, though sometimes he asks me whether I do, asks the question, Do you still love me? He asks it while I am in the middle of rinsing spinach or loading washing into the machine, or chasing a trail of toys across the kitchen floor. When he asks the question at a time like that it's like he's speaking an ancient, forgotten language. I can remember a few isolated words but can't connect them, can't get the gist, don't know how to answer. Of course I could say, Yes I love you, still love you, of course I still love you. If I didn't still love you I wouldn't be here, would I, wouldn't have hung around just to go through the motions of companionship and sex. Being alone never bothered me. It was something I chose. Before I chose you. But of course, that is not accurate. Once you become a parent there is no longer a simple equation.

We have three children. All our own. Blood of our blood, flesh of our flesh etc., delivered into our hands in the usual way, a slithering mess of blood and slime and wonder, another tiny miracle.

In reply to his question my husband really doesn't want to hear any of my irritating justifications for sticking around, my caustic logic. He doesn't really want to hear anything at all. The response he wants is a visual and tactile one. He wants me to drop the spinach, the laundry, the toys, sweep my hair out of my eyes, turn round, away from what I'm doing and look at him, look lovingly into his dark, demanding eyes, walk across the kitchen floor – which needs to be swept again – stand over him as he sits at the table fingering a daffodil, still bright in its fluted centre but crisp and brown at the edges, as if it's been singed. My husband wants me to cuddle up close.

Sometimes I can do it, the right thing, what's needed. Other times, when I hear those words it's like I've been turned to marble or ice, to something cold and hard and unyielding. I can't even turn my head away from the sink, far less walk those few steps across the floor. I can't even think about it. And when he asks, What are you thinking? Again I'm stuck. Does it count as thinking to be considering whether there is time to bring down the laundry from the pulley to make room for the next load before I shake off the rinsing water, pat the leaves dry, chop off the stalks and spin the green stuff around the magimix? That's usually what my mind is doing, that is its activity and if it can be called thinking, then that's what I'm doing. Thinking about something not worth relating.

What are you thinking?

Nothing. I'm not thinking about anything.

Which isn't the same thing. Thinking about nothing means mental activity, a focusing of the mind on the fact or idea of nothing and that's not what I am doing. I've no interest in that kind of activity, no time for it, no time to ponder the true meaning of life, the essential nature of the universe and so on. Such speculation is beyond me. Usually when I'm asked what I'm thinking my mind is simply vacant and so my reply is made with a clear, vacant conscience.

I'm approaching a precipice. Each day I'm drawn nearer to the edge. I look only at the view. I avoid looking at the drop but I know what's there. At least, I can imagine it. I don't want to be asked either question, the conversation must be kept moving, hopping across the surface of our lives like a smooth flat stone.

… Thought is not the point. I am feeling it, the flush, the rush of blood, the sensation of, yes, swooning. It comes in waves. Does it show? I'm sure it must show on my face the way pain might, the way pain would show on my husband's face …

Do you still love me? What are you thinking?

Tonight I couldn't even manage my usual, Nothing. It wouldn't come out right, I try it out in my head, practise it, imagine the word as it would come out. It would sound unnatural, false, a strangled, evasive mumble or else a spat denial. Either way it wouldn't pass. It would lead to probing. A strained, suspicious little duet would begin in the midst of preparing the dinner and I know where this edgy, halting tune leads, I know the notes by heart.

(Practice makes perfect. Up and down the same old scales until you can do them without tripping up, without twisting fingers or breaking resolutions, without swearing, yelling, failing or resentment at the necessity of repetition. Without scales the fingers are insufficiently developed to be capable of … until you can do it in your sleep, until you *do* do it in your sleep, up and down as fast as dexterity permits. Without practice, life skills also atrophy.)

For years we've shared everything we had to share, which wasn't much at first and now is way too much. In the way of possessions at least.

We started simply: one room, a bed we nailed together from pine planks and lasted a decade; a few lingering relics from previous couplings (and still I long to ditch that nasty little bronze figurine made by the woman before me. A troll face, with gouged-out eyes. Scary at night, glowering from a corner of the bedroom.) Money was scarce but new love has no need of money. Somewhere to go, to be together is all and we were lucky. We had that. Hell is love with no place to go.

While around us couples were splitting at the seams, we remained intact. In the midst of break-ups and breakouts, we tootled on, sympathetic listeners, providers of impromptu pasta, a pull-out bed for the night, the occasional alibi. We listened to the personal disasters of our friends but wondered, in private, in bed, alone together at the end of another too-late night, what all the fuss was about. Beyond our ken, all that heartbreak, all that angst. What did it have to do with us, our lives, our kids? We had no room for it. Nor, for that matter, a great deal of space for passion.

An example to us all, we've been told, You two are an example to us all. Of course it was meant to be taken with a pinch of salt, a knowing smile but said frequently enough for the phrase to stick, as if our friends in their cracked, snapped, torn-to-shreds state, our friends who had just said goodbye to someone they loved, or someone they didn't love after all or any more, as if all of them were suddenly united in a wilderness of unrequited love. While we, in our dusty, cluttered home, had achieved something other than an accumulation of consecutive time together.

This is true, of course, and we can be relied upon to provide some display of the example that we are. My husband is likely to take advantage of the opportunity and engage in a bit of public necking. Me, I sling mud, with affection. Either way, between us we manage to steer the chat away from our domestic compatibility, top up our friends' drinks, turn up the volume on the stereo, stir up a bit of jollity until it's time to say Goodnight. See you soon. Look after yourself, until it's time to be left alone together again with our example. Our differences remain.

Do you still love me? What are you thinking?

Saturday night. The children are asleep. Three little dark heads are thrown back on pillows printed with characters from Lewis Carroll, Disney and Masters of the Universe. Three little mouths blow snores into the intimate, bedroom air. Upstairs, the neighbours hammer tacks into a carpet, their dogs romp and bark, their antique plumbing gurgles down the wall but the children sleep on, their sweet breath rising and falling in unison.

We are able to eat in peace, take time to taste the food which my husband has gone to impressive lengths to prepare. The dinner turns out to be an unqualified success: the curry is smooth, spicy, aromatic, the rice dry, each grain distinct, each firm little ellipse brushing against the tongue. The dinner is a joy and a relief. My husband is touchy about his cooking and requires almost as much in the way of reassurance and compliments in this as he does about whether I still love him or not. A bad meal dampens the spirits, is distressing both to the cook and the cooked-for. A bad meal can be passed over, unmentioned but not ignored. The stomach too has longings for more than simply to be filled. A bad meal can be worse than no meal at all.

But it was an extremely good meal and I was wholehearted and voluble in my appreciation. Everything was going well. We drank more wine, turned off the overhead light, lit a candle, fetched the cassette recorder from the kids' room and put on some old favourites; smoochy, lyrical, emotive stuff, tunes we knew so well we didn't have to listen, just let them fill the gaps in our conversation. So far so good.

Saturdays have to be good. It's pretty much all we have. Of us, the two of us just. One night a week, tiptoeing through the hall so as not to disturb the kids, lingering in the kitchen because it's further away from their bedroom than the living room, we can speak more freely, don't need to keep the talk turned down to a whisper. We drink wine and catch up. It is necessary to catch up, to keep track of each other.

Across the country, while all the little loved ones are asleep, wives and husbands, single parents and surrogates are sitting down together or alone, working out what has to be done. There are always things to be done, to make tomorrow pass smoothly, to make tomorrow work. I look through the glasses and bottles and the shivering candle flame at my husband. The sleeves of his favourite shirt – washed-out blue with pearly buttons, last year's Christmas present from me – are rolled up. His elbows rest on the table which he recently sanded and polished by hand. It took forever. We camped out in the living room while coat after coat of asphyxiating varnish was applied. It looks good now, better than before. But was the effort worth the effect?

My husband's fine pale fingers are pushed deep into his hair. I look past him out of the kitchen window, up the dark sloping street at parked cars and sodium lights, lit windows and smoking chimneys, the blinking red eye of a plane crossing a small trough of blue-black sky. My house is where my life happens. In it there is love, work, a roof, a floor, solidity, houseplants, toys, pots and pans, achievements and failures, inspirations and mistakes, recipes and instruction booklets, guarantees and spare parts, plans, dreams, memories. And there is no need, nothing here pushing me. It is nobody's fault.

I go to playparks a lot, for air, for less mess in the house and of course because the kids like to get out. Pushing a swing, watching a little one arcing away and rushing back to your hands, it's natural to talk to another parent. It passes the time. You don't get so bored pushing, the little one is kept lulled and amenable. There's no way of reckoning up fault or blame or responsibility, nothing is stable enough, specific enough to be held to account and that's not the point. The swing swung back, I tossed my hair out of my eyes and glanced up at a complete stranger, a father. The father smiled back.

We know each other's names, the names of children and spouses. That's about all. We ask few questions. No need for questions. We meet and push our children on swings and sometimes we stand just close enough for our shoulders to touch, just close enough to feel that fluttering hollowness, like hunger. We visit the park – even in the rain, to watch the wind shaking the trees and tossing cherry blossoms on to the grass, the joggers and dog walkers lapping the flat green park – to be near each other.

Millions have stood on this very same ledge, in the privacy of their own homes, the unweeded gardens of their minds. Millions have stood on the edge and tested their balance, their common sense, strength of will, they have reckoned up the cost, in mess and misery, have wondered whether below the netless drop a large tree with spread branches awaits to cushion their fall. So simple, so easy. All I have to do is rock on my heels, rock just a shade too far and we will all fall down. Two husbands, two wives and all the little loved ones.

Martin Millar

from *Dreams of Sex and Stage Diving*

The gig was nearing its climax. Elfish and Amnesia still swooped around like crazed eagles. In the morning Elfish would be a mass of bruises and abrasions but at this moment she was immune to all discomfort.

For the hundredth time Elfish was fighting her way back to the stage. She paused near two boys who still had cans of beer in their hands.

'Give me a drink,' said Elfish.

'No,' they replied.

Elfish would often ask strangers for drinks at gigs and was used to refusals so she would have thought nothing of this had not Amnesia at that moment appeared beside her.

'Give me a drink,' she said to the two boys.

Immediately they both handed over their cans to her and she drank from them. She offered one to Elfish. Elfish took it but her eyes were narrowed and she assumed that the boys had given Amnesia their drinks merely because she had long blonde hair.

Elfish was used to this and shrugged it off. She continued on her way, digging her elbows into those around her to make her way once more up on to the stage. The bouncers had by this time more or less given up and Elfish had an easy ascent. Once onstage, she kicked the lead singer's microphone stand over for fun then jumped mightily into the air. Elfish leapt in no particular direction but her keenness for this last jump carried her far and she crashed down close to the vacant space at the side of the stage. Only one person stood there and Elfish was fortunate to land on him rather than the concrete.

They both stood up and the person moved away, possibly feeling that this place was no longer safe. As Elfish looked up she saw that Amnesia was now onstage, preparing to jump. Amnesia saw her, waved, sprinted a few yards to the side of the stage and leapt directly at Elfish, intending to land on her, just as Elfish had previously landed on Amnesia in the same spot.

But Amnesia did not land on Elfish. As she sailed through the air Elfish stepped quickly to one side and the gap thus created was just large enough for Amnesia to crash head first on to the concrete where she lay without moving.

She was helped away backstage and later in hospital it was found that her collar-bone was broken and she was concussed. She was obliged to remain in hospital for several days.

Afterwards Elfish and Amnesia never spoke. There seemed little to say. Amnesia knew that Elfish had deliberately moved out of the way, and Elfish knew that she knew. Once recovered, Amnesia retired from the area, going to live in the suburbs for a while until her shoulder healed. While in the suburbs she thought often about Elfish, and always with great animosity. Elfish's behaviour had been treachery of the worst kind, a wretched betrayal of a friend and fellow stage diver.

'Why did you do it?' asked Aran later, but Elfish was unable to supply a satisfactory answer so did not try. It might have been pique at Amnesia jumping further than her, or it might have been annoyance that she kept landing on Mo and that Mo seemed to respond to her favourably. Or it might have been jealousy that the boys had refused drink to Elfish but supplied it to Amnesia.

It might have been none of these things. Elfish could not really say. When Amnesia was hurling towards her, she just felt like moving out of the way, and she could never honestly say that she felt very sorry about it.

* * *

Though Shonen's bulimia had improved after Elfish's encouraging news about the fund-raiser, it was a long way from being cured. Today she had been shopping in the supermarket and this had been a stressful experience from start to finish. Touring around the shelves pushing a trolley she experienced both the irresistible urge to stock up with some junk food and the certain knowledge that once she had eaten it she would feel bad and throw it all up again.

Driven by whatever childhood misery fuelled her disorder, she swept supplies into the trolley. As she did so, she practised excuses and reasonable stories in case anyone asked her why she was buying so much food; Shonen's guilt about eating extended to a paranoia that other people knew all about it and were watching with disapproval.

'I have a large family to feed,' she would say, if challenged by the checkout woman. 'I rarely get the chance to shop, I am buying provisions for a month. The woman next door to me fell down and broke her leg and I'm shopping for her as a favour. I am having a dinner party for twelve people and they are all big eaters.'

Unchallenged by the checkout woman, or the manager, or the store detectives, she bundled her food into a collection of flimsy carrier bags and struggled home. She was so encumbered with food that on the outskirts of her estate it took her much time and effort to find her purse to give a little money to a hopeless-looking woman with no place to go who sat begging beside the children's playground. Shonen always gave money to beggars.

Once home she wolfed down a meal, vomited, ate, vomited, ate, vomited, then collapsed. She was on the verge of plunging into total despair when she remembered that things were not entirely without hope. Elfish was coming to the rescue. Elfish was going to put her theatre group back on the rails. These days the thought of Elfish had become very inspiring, looming large over Shonen's hopelessness like a benevolent goddess.

Shonen cleaned up the toilet, resisted the urge to eat again, and forced her bulimia from her mind. With an effort of will she made herself think positively about a new production. This was such a pleasant thing to contemplate that not long afterwards she was on the phone to the rest of her group, practically bullying them out of their own defeatism with enthusiastic plans for the future.

Despite being neurotic, depressed and defeated by life, Shonen was not one of Brixton's lonely characters. She had many friends and was frequently in contact with the various members of her theatre group.

These fellow performers were surprised by the sudden change in her. She had organised their appeals for funding and sponsorship and now called them up to organise planning meetings for a new season. She invited them round for drinks and launched into enthusiastic discussions about writing and rehearsing a new play and taking it to next year's Edinburgh Festival. And, she said, if the Edinburgh Festival did not work out then they could do it free in a pub somewhere. Anything to perform.

When the members of the acting group asked her what had brought about this abrupt change in her demeanour, this sudden enthusiasm for life quite uncharacteristic of her recent behaviour, Shonen unhesitatingly gave all of the credit to Elfish. Elfish had taken the trouble to find someone who could actually help them and she appreciated this immensely. Not only that, Elfish's strident endeavours to bring her own ambitions to fruition had acted as a powerful inspiration to Shonen.

'If she can overcome her difficulties, then so can we,' she told her theatre group.

'Elfish is so determined. She is inspiring. If she says she can find us someone to look after our funding then she'll do it because Elfish does not give up.'

Mo was at this moment thinking much the same thing, although not with kindness. He had learned from Irene Tarisa that Shonen was helping Elfish with her speech, and that May and Casaubon were playing in her band. Aisha was even painting a backdrop for her, which seemed like a sure sign that Elfish was confident of success.

Mo was perturbed, so perturbed that he spoiled his band's rehearsal that day by continually picking faults in each musician's contribution till the rehearsal ground to a halt in animosity and bad-tempered recriminations.

* * *

Artemisia was Queen of Halicarnassus in Asia Minor. She sailed with Xerxes, King of Persia, against the Greeks in 480 B.C. She was unique, being the only woman to fight in the war, a war which involved millions of men. She did not have to do this. Her husband had died, passing the sovereignty to her, but she had a grown-up son who could have led her forces. Artemisia was moved by the spirit of adventure.

Herodotus gives a very favourable account of Artemisia, possibly because he too came from Halicarnassus. Artemisia led a small squadron of ships, captaining the flagship herself, and gained a reputation for her prowess in war. The Greeks particularly hated the fact that a woman was fighting against them and offered a large reward for her capture but she was never taken.

Artemisia also gained a reputation as a shrewd adviser to the King. She was the only one of Xerxes's counsellors who advised him against fighting the battle of Salamis, saying that the huge Persian army should continue the war on land rather than sea. Xerxes did not take her advice and went on to suffer a catastrophic defeat at Salamis. His fleet was routed and his entire plan to conquer Greece suffered a severe setback. This increased Artemisia's reputation because her advice was proved to have been correct and Xerxes realised he should have paid heed to it.

Another event occurred during the battle which further increased her reputation. The vast Persian fleet, being outfought and outmanoeuvred by the superior Greek navy, was in full retreat. Artemisia's ship was fleeing along with the rest and she found herself hemmed in between a Greek pursuer and a ship of her own fleet which was blocking her retreat.

Without hesitation Artemisia rammed this ship even though it was on her side. It sank with all hands. Her Greek pursuer, seeing this, presumed that Artemisia's ship must in fact be on his side and ceased the pursuit, allowing Artemisia to escape.

Xerxes was watching the battle from a hill near the shore.

'Do you see how well Artemisia is fighting?' said one of his advisers. 'She has just sunk an enemy ship.'

Xerxes, distressed about the destruction of his fleet, at least had one thing to be glad about, and made a comment which was to become well known. 'What has happened to my army? The men have turned into women and the women have turned into men.'

He later entrusted Queen Artemisia with the safe conduct of his children back to their home, which was a task of great importance and some danger.

Artemisia's immediate descendants built the Mausoleum, a famous building in Antiquity, parts of which can still be seen in the British Museum. 'It's my favourite story from Herodotus,' said Aran. 'Would you like to hear my favourite story from Thucydides?'

'No,' replied Elfish. 'You know I can only listen to one story at a time.'

'Very well,' said Aran. 'I'm going to put Artemisia into my video game. Would you like to play my video game?'

'Absolutely not. I detest your video game. Help me with the speech.'

*   *   *

Elfish's two remaining friends and pool partners, Tula and Lizzy, were also friends of May's. Not as close friends as they were of Elfish, but they had visited May during a trip to Ireland last year and she had received them very hospitably.

They were therefore pleased to learn from May that Elfish was finally providing her with a secure home in England.

'Secure for a while anyway,' said Lizzy, as they sat waiting their turn on the pool table. 'Although I see the government is bringing in a law making it illegal to squat.'

This was to happen soon. In Brixton, a council flat would be just about affordable to rent but these were no longer given to single people, only to families, if they were fortunate. A private flat was so far out of the reach of most people it was not worth thinking about. Even an unpleasant bedsit was beyond the range of many people unless they could manage to have the rent paid by the social security, but this was hard to organise, and anyway landlords always wanted a deposit and a month's rent in advance so this was more or less out of the question as well.

This left squatting, and as the council had many unused flats it seemed like a sensible solution. The government, however, had now resolved to make squatting, the one remaining safety-valve, illegal, and turn even more people out on to the streets.

A strong article by Chevon in her prospective newspaper had pointed out that this was very bad timing. The streets of London were already fully occupied. Homeless people were everywhere, as were beggars.

Distressingly, in recent years, these people had become far more lost and hopeless-looking than before, due to the government's triumphant new policy of emptying and closing mental institutions, moving the occupants from these institutions out into the community. Whether or not the actual intention of this 'Care in the Community' policy was that the mentally ill should now be slumped in hopeless and degraded poverty in shop doorways everywhere was not clear, but this was certainly the effect. Many of the beggars who now held out their hands in Brixton were people who were clearly unwell and obviously unable to look after themselves. Some of them were not even able to hold out their hands. They just sat in silence on the pavements, and might sit there till they died. A few would shout and run about wildly. Who was now meant to be looking after these people, nobody knew.

Those who, despite being poor, displayed strong mental health by finding an empty place and squatting it were now to be turned out to join in the throng.

Already there were fewer squats in Brixton; soon there would be none, and a small epoch would have ended. As the people involved were not very important the question of where they were actually meant to live was not one that anyone had bothered answering.

May, however, would be secure in Elfish's house, at least for a while.

'Where is Chevon moving to?' asked Lizzy.

'She isn't moving,' Elfish told her frankly, but in this she made a bad misjudgement. She presumed that Tula and Lizzy would see immediately that it was a worthwhile deception in order to get May playing guitar on Saturday. They did not. They were outraged that Elfish was building up May's hopes falsely.

'May is in a really bad way,' protested Lizzy. 'When she finds out you've lied to her and there is no place for her to live she'll collapse completely.'

Elfish, too obsessed to see the danger, merely shrugged. Tula and

Lizzy were upset. They gathered up their leather jackets and left after lecturing Elfish briefly on what they saw as appalling behaviour.

Thus Elfish's last remaining friends walked out of her life, leaving her with only a depressed brother and a band of people she had lied to for her own purposes.

'Well, fuck them,' muttered Elfish, and proceeded to wipe out her next opponent on the pool table, putting five balls down from her first break and finishing the game off on her next visit to the table.

In the pub people looked surreptitiously at her as she played.

'That is Elfish,' whispered one person to another. 'The woman who is so obsessed with naming her band Queen Mab that she is going to recite forty-three lines of Shakespeare on stage before Mo's gig on Saturday.'

Everyone who knew Elfish informed everyone who did not that it seemed very unlikely that she could manage it, and interest in the whole proceedings continued to grow at an alarming rate. Complete strangers would stop Elfish to ask her about it. Unable to think quite what to say, Elfish would merely grunt at them. If they persisted with their questioning she would tell them brusquely to mind their own business. This was enough to silence most people but Elfish's aggressive manner made no impression on Mo and his friends. They laughed at her quite openly. Elfish no longer felt entirely comfortable in this pub although she had been coming here for some years. There were too many people whom she suspected of mocking her and looking forward to her downfall.

She would not stop coming though, even though it might mean standing by herself now that Tula and Lizzy would no longer come drinking with her. To abandon her usual haunts would mean accepting a defeat, which she would not do.

It was not pleasant drinking on her own, however. Even Aran would be some company but he would not come with her to this bar. As well as being too depressed to leave the house, he was worried that he might run into his old girlfriend, an event which he said would be too much for him to cope with.

* * *

John Mackie sat alone in his shop. There were no customers. He was watching a small television which rested on a chair behind the counter. Business was still bad but he was rather more cheerful than he had been.

This was due to Elfish. In the past few days she and May had been calling in constantly for leads, plectrums, a tuner, two fuzzboxes, a microphone, a sustain pedal and various other bits and pieces they needed for their band. Everything they bought was the cheapest there was and even then part of the cost had to be put on to Elfish's bill but John Mackie found that he did not mind. He had become infected with Elfish's enthusiasm. It felt good that a woman who reminded him of his sister was coming into his shop, talking about her plans and generally being positive. Her visits gave him something to look forward to. Extending her credit was undoubtedly poor business practice but as things were so bad it made little difference and it brought him pleasure.

When she called in they would talk about what she required for the gig at the weekend and though he was not fully conversant with Elfish's overwhelming need to call her band Queen Mab, John Mackie was aware of the gig's importance to Elfish. He was willing to do what he could to help. The enthusiasm that this generated inside him was the first that he could remember for many years. Arriving at his shop that morning he had felt positively cheerful as he gave a little money to the homeless beggar who huddled in his doorway. The pavement outside John Mackie's shop was a popular place for homeless beggars. John Mackie took his Christian charity seriously, and was sorry for them, and gave them money.

The television news switched to a report from Sudan.

'Here the famine is becoming more serious every day,' said a reporter, as the screen showed bodies thin beyond belief stumbling hopelessly in search of nourishment.

These pictures troubled him, and he resolved to donate money tomorrow to the famine relief fund at his church.

Aisha was watching the same programme while she painted the backdrop. 'How terrible,' she said, but what she really thought was, they could all die if only my boyfriend Mory would come back, and she carried on painting to block it out of her memory.

Aran too was watching the news.

'How terrible,' he muttered, but what he really thought was much the same as Aisha. He switched off the TV and studied his cigarette cards to take his mind off his ex-girlfriend.

He frowned. Despite buying and smoking an immense amount of cigarettes he had not yet collected all twenty cards. He was stuck on eighteen. He had more than one of each of these. Of some of them he had as many as four. Yet his collection contained not a single example of either number three or number twenty.

'There is definitely something funny going on here,' he mumbled. 'I don't believe the company is distributing the cards fairly.'

Various schemes whereby the cigarette company could cheat its customers and deny them their five pounds' reward floated through his head. There might not be any cards numbered three and twenty. This was a diabolical thought and brought Aran close to despair.

Musing further on this, though, he rejected it eventually as too risky for the company. If they did not print up any of one card then someone might notice. A disgruntled employee might talk to the newspapers. Word would leak out and the Serious Fraud Office would investigate. Altogether too dangerous for the board of directors.

They might, of course, only print up a tiny number of certain cards. It could be that there was only one number three in the whole country and it had been sent to Glasgow. That seemed quite likely, and Aran again felt desolate. Even more fiendishly, the company might be printing up an equal number of each card but ensuring the cigarette packets containing certain cards were sent only to carefully controlled locations. Every single card number twenty might at this minute be in a warehouse on the Orkney Islands, awaiting distribution to only one local tobacconist. Orkney Islanders, smoking away keenly to claim their reward, might find that every card in their collection was number twenty. And what legal redress would a person in London have against the company? None whatsoever. They did not say anywhere in their advertising that the cards were sent evenly around the country. Aran could now see clearly that the whole thing was a plot, fixed from start to finish.

'It's no use,' he sighed. 'These companies are too powerful. There is no way of winning against them.'

Elfish appeared, looking extremely dirty and demanding a poem. To her surprise, Aran had one ready.

'From Milton's "L'Allegro",' he told her. 'Have I ever told you the story of Milton's life? He was—'

'Shut up and give me the poem,' ordered Elfish, and held out her hand.

> Till the livelong daylight fail,
> Then to the spicy nut-brown ale,
> With stories told of many a feat;
> How fairy Mab the junkets eat;

'What's a junket?' asked Elfish. 'Never mind, don't tell me. This is fine. It will do to counter the painting of Ben Jonson's Mab. I'll go and put it through Mo's door right away.'

* * *

The storm abated but there was no respite for the exhausted occupants of the raft. The edge of the world was now in clear sight and the noise of the ocean falling away into the void rolled over them like thunder. With their situation growing ever more hopeless they began to bicker.

'Haven't you fixed the rudder yet?' complained Cleopatra.

'I'm doing my best,' retorted Botticelli sharply.

'Well, it doesn't seem to be having much effect.'

'I'm a painter, not an engineer.'

'I'm sure Leonardo could have done a better job,' said Cleopatra.

'So who are you to criticise?' demanded Botticelli. 'All you do is strut around giving orders. I haven't seen you actually working yet. And this from a woman who lost a whole empire just because she picked the wrong Roman.'

'Mark Antony was not the wrong Roman,' retorted Cleopatra. 'We were just unfortunate to lose the battle of Actium.'

Bomber Harris, interested in this, started a conversation about wartime tactics through the ages but he was interrupted by Red Sonja.

'Shut up and keep working. It won't be long till the gryphons come back.'

'Don't you tell me to shut up, you ignorant barbarian. I didn't notice you having any notable success when you tried to mend the sail.'

'Stop bickering,' said Ben Jonson, who was trying to nail the mast together. 'We'll only get out of this situation if we all work together.'

He looked pointedly at Mick Ronson, who still sat idly in the middle of the raft.

'I refuse to work any more,' said the musician. 'There's no point. We can't win. I'm going over the edge of the world strumming my guitar.'

He launched into the solo from 'Moonage Daydream', a song he had recorded while playing with David Bowie in 1972. This solo was full of long, high, lingering notes, building up on each other to beautiful effect.

'Ship ahoy!' screamed Cleopatra, and everybody looked in alarm, assuming it was some new enemy come to torment them.

'I recognise that ship,' cried Pericles, great statesman of Athens. 'It's Queen Artemisia.'

He drew his sword, preparing to repel boarders, but it soon became clear that Artemisia was not going to attack. Her ship sailed on by, back towards the far distant shore.

Aran was programing the task for the next level. The raft had to somehow attach itself to Queen Artemisia's trireme. If they could do this they would be towed all the way back to safety. When the occupants of the raft realised this they made frantic efforts to make ropes from whatever material they had available, fixing Red Sonja's sword to the end as a grappling hook. They paddled frantically after the ship while Sonja prepared to cast the line.

Naturally it was hopeless. There was no way for the raft actually to come close enough to make the connection.

'You Failed,' said the caption on the screen, after Sonja's repeated attempts to reach Artemisia's ship with her grappling hook all fell short. 'You are now plunged into the next level, right at the Edge of the World.'

* * *

Mo's long hair lay over his face and the carpet and Shonen sat over Mo, fucking him by the light of the television. She did this quite slowly. Her movements were noticeably more relaxed than normal.

Mo, who had been drinking, lay passively for a long time as Shonen rocked back and forth on top of him.

After a while he seemed to gather up his energy and reached up to take hold of her small breasts before dragging his body into a sitting position so that Shonen was kneeling on his lap and they kissed.

Mo had had no hesitation in asking Shonen to sleep with him towards the end of his first visit. Shonen had agreed because although she rarely had sex and thought about it seldom, there was something about Mo which she found attractive. Possibly it was the fact that he did not really care if she was alive or dead. More than one person had found that attractive about Mo, including Elfish. Another attraction was that he would leave immediately afterwards without bothering her for details of her personal life.

Shonen slid her hand between their bodies to grip Mo's penis lightly between two fingers as it entered her. Mo wrapped his arms round Shonen and slid his finger up her anus. Locked together, they rocked gently backwards and forwards in the dim light of the television.

When Mo was close to orgasm he brusquely shoved Shonen off his lap and on to her back and fucked her as hard as he could till he came, then lay momentarily on top of her, dripping with sweat.

He left soon afterwards. Shonen had not come, which was frustrating. There again, sex had taken up more than an hour during which time she had had no desire to eat or vomit.

Later, however, she felt anxious lest Elfish should find out she had been having sex with Mo. Shonen knew that Elfish would not like this and she did not want to offend her.

Elfish was in her thoughts because Mo had questioned her about Elfish's progress with the speech. He had intimated that Shonen was unwise to help her. Shonen had explained to Mo that Elfish was doing her a favour in return although when she explained what it was Mo snorted and said that Elfish was certainly lying because no theatrical fund-raiser lived anywhere near her and anyway Elfish was a born liar.

Shonen did not believe Mo. She trusted in Elfish's efforts to aid her. Her physical theatre group was too important for her not to believe in Elfish. Even as Mo's semen was still trickling out of her body she was back at her sponsorship documents, and giving some thought to their next production.

For his part Mo had gained the impression that Elfish was close to success. He resolved to do something about it.

Candia McWilliam

Seven Magpies

The train was passing between still, high fields of standing corn. The light over the fields had a talcy glow that lightened and ceased to shimmer a yard or so into the sky. From time to time a small area of field flicked under a switch of wind, the specific unanimated flick of a creature's pelt. Rangy wild oats over the wide crop and flimsy poppies at its edges were the only intimations of natural disorder. Nothing much was moving but the train through this thinly chivalric part of England.

'Girls are like people, I realised it late on,' said the younger man to the older, who resembled him too much not to be linked to him by blood.

'It will have been my fault you did not see that before. Though I can't see the good it will do you to know it now.'

'Why do you say *now*?'

'You've already done your harm and it is late to begin any undoing.'

'You know more than most that there is no undoing. At least I need do no more harm now.' The young man spoke as though harm were something simple, like hammering.

The older man stood to open a window, with such urgency that he seemed in want of new air. The air that entered the train brought nothing new with it but dust more rural than the dust within.

'You dramatise yourself, Findlay, a pointless thing to do in your profession and very tiring in hot weather.' Sitting down, the older man pinched his trousers and flung his right leg over his left as though this gave depth to his paternal but unfatherly dictum.

'Gum?' rejoined his son, loosening a white tooth of chewing gum from its packet with his thumb and offering it gingerly to his father. It might have been the elegant old man in his old cream linen who had been uncouth. But the reprimand was lost on Robert Meldrum who sat now looking at his son over his own, just touching, fingertips.

Knowing that his father was waiting for him to offend, Findlay shot five bits of gum into his own mouth and began to champ until his throat was flooded with minty saliva and his jaw was aching. Would it be the professional or the private life that was coming into the old man's sights, he wondered, with the same dishonourable curiosity that led him to encourage people to repeat themselves indefinitely and to tell him stories he already knew.

'I followed a trade all my life and I fear you are too good for that.' The word 'good' carried none of its customary decent replete weight. Nor did it imply its opposite, merely something lightweight, skittering, inconsiderable.

'Father, your life is not over,' said Findlay, hoping to divert attention from his own life, still, he felt, hardly begun. He almost forgot himself and began to flatter the hard old man, as he might have someone he loved less and trusted more, enticing him into discussion of the past with some welcome slipway down into memory, 'And what a life it has been, eh...'

'No, you can't catch me like that. Are you hungry at the stomach or is it the chewing you favour? If so, how odd. How unnatural indeed. You are like that.' Findlay knew his father meant 'you' the young. He himself was seventy-two; Findlay forty years younger. 'You are all appetite and no hunger. All temper and no rage.'

Only a man as stagy-looking as his father, black-browed, blue-eyed, white-haired, elongated but without idle languor, could speak in this public manner in a private place without self-consciousness. The natural dignity of his appearance had throughout his life lent authority to the actions and sayings of Robert Meldrum. Replacing the words in the mouth of a notional short man with clumps of hair, a man whom Findlay had begun to keep about him as a companion in subversion as a boy, was the way to subtract the awe inspired by his father's stern Scots glamour. Although he would have denied the word, the older man exploited the quality, as a preacher might have, in mixed vanity and good faith.

Findlay was slighter than his father, but like him tall and blue-eyed, the eyes seemingly set in the sockets by sooty fingers. His hair was black as his father's had been, but with needles of white at the back and sides. He was less dapper than his father, and as evidently clean to the pitch that actually repels dirt, rather than the holiday smartness that draws it and is ruined. Neither man wore a colour much beyond the neutral, although there was in Findlay's inner jacket pocket, when it flapped open, a row of pencils, crocus yellow, each with a small pink eraser bound to its top with a band of gold metal. Once or twice his right hand went up to these pencils and rolled them like a toy or an instrument. Their small geared hexagons made a noise only Findlay heard.

None the less he failed to notice when his father, in a train, in summer, in England, leant his fine head against the rough blue nap of his seat, drowsed, slept, and, sometime before arrival at their undesired destination, died.

'It's unfortunate you married a man so far superior to yourself,' said her husband.

There was a choice of replies to be made, but since it was breakfast time and their two children were watching Morag to see how she took Daddy's joke, she said, 'That is so, I'm afraid.'

Edward's comment had been made in front of the children before, but never before, as now, stripped of the pretence of levity. It was clear that today would continue the bleak barracking of the night before, until he was out of the house. On his return it would, as clearly, resume. She began to attend to his wants with an assiduity that was part of the ugly bargain she had some months ago made with fate: she would tend to him scrupulously if one day she might be delivered from him. She squeezed oranges down on to the juice extractor as though they were the breasts of the martyred St Agatha.

The table had no place, indeed no room, for her, and it was her pleasure to wait on her family. The thought of eating with them confused her; who would fetch things if she sat down? If she did sit down, she would surely have to rise, so it was easier not to. She thought these small acts of abnegation would attune her children at an early age to the deceits of family life and, even more importantly, the real place of women: these inoculations she, being ironic, took as salutary, and they, being innocent, took for example.

When told she was inferior, it came naturally to scrutinise the superior object. Morag was inferior to a large man nearing forty who sat like a stranger among his possessions and children and whose umbrella, had this been a normal day, he would later forget, causing him to return and feel obliged to kiss her.

In the garden below their first-floor kitchen window a cat moved with rumpy stealth towards a fit-looking magpie that had settled under the denuded roses, among petals lying profuse over the sodden grass. The cat kept its belly from touching the ground, as it would not have on a dry day. Its dark tail and ears cast their shadow in the fresh wet sunlight, its creamy body appearing too blurred and soft to be stockinged and tipped in so sharp a mode. All through the grass were spiders' webs still, though where the cat had been there was a bright trail through the webs' slick silver.

When the Siamese laid low the maggot-pie the squawks and cawings came from both. The cat batted the smart but loutish bird, deriding it to death, then crunching at it with a besotted look as if to say, 'Doesn't it suit me?' The big bird, now without its life, looked frivolous as a hat, but for the dainty giblets and bladders the cat was discarding from its feast. All the while wet petals fell with no sound and up in the kitchen the children, silenced by this pleasant domestic diversion as they had not been by their parent's contained wretchedness, watched, staying their eating only to exchange old saws:

> 'One for sorrow, two for joy,
> Three for a girl, four for a boy,
> Five for silver, six for gold,
> Seven for a secret that's never been told.'

Morag caught the boiling milk as it reached its height and poured it for her husband on to the freshly brewed decaffeinated coffee. On noticing that there was a drop of coffee on the saucer, she fetched a clean cloth and wiped it, making sure that she took the cloth from the pile that was composed of cloths that touched clean surfaces only; not floors, the sink, the table or anything that had not already been washed at least once – a system instituted by Edward.

So as to prepare Edward's breakfast without distressing him, for he had washed his hair this morning as usual, she lit a candle, and set it in the sink to consume the frying smells from the children's breakfast. No one could say she had not colluded in her own demotion from love object to servant. The extravagant acts of obedience and enslavement had, she thought, been a conduit of intimacy between them. Now these actions had set into resented habits and their certainly fetishistic significance had fallen away. Sometimes, when Edward was far from home and she was able to think about him with the balance bestowed by distance, she suspected that she had invented some of his more demanding stipulations in order at first to have more ways of pleasing him, and at length to have more things to blame him for.

She extracted the unsalted butter that only he was permitted, and cut off a small nut or knob, as the books told one a small piece of butter was dubbed. It was not to her especially lubricious stuff.

The butter went into its own brick-shaped, lidded pot, to avoid taking on the smells of other substances. The openness of butter to corruption is extreme, Edward had taught her; only let it see garlic, or melon.

In the early days of their marriage the serene freedom from confusion that her husband had represented, with his distaste for muddle or inappropriateness and his almost mystical sense of what was proper, had been a relief to her: like entering clean sheets for good. A man who knew where things should be put was a man to honour in untidy times.

Now, though, Morag had come to think of mess as having an energy if not sublime at any rate fully human. She had begun to cultivate people who lived in a manner abhorrent to Edward, so that she might sit at their sticky kitchen tables to hear them unpick their troubles as they cleaned their children's faces with their own spit and a paper handkerchief and shook out cat litter, birdseed, flour and currants with impartial, unwashed hands. She fancied she saw a nobility and vigour she did not find in her own house in whose kitchen she never entertained.

'What are these?' Edward asked one evening after his bicycle ride home, his first bath and their wary kiss, during which he smelt her carefully and could guess almost her entire day from what he smelled.

Morag had once made an ebullient – the word occurred to her as she pitied herself for living with a man who did not love fun – an ebullient flower arrangement that included beautiful, fat, complicated globe artichokes. She had thrust their thick architectural stems deep into a vase and starred them about with blue cornflowers and asters the colour of plain chocolate.

Edward flinched when he saw it, at the whimsy as much as at the waste.

She set today's egg before him, and ten toast soldiers. He had never stipulated that he liked ten, but in complaining to a friend one day of her husband's ways, she had invented this one, and found herself complying.

'A man so attentive to detail must be attentive in other ways,' her friend had said, not wrongly, but displeasing Morag who was attached to her hobby of resentment. Her friend was anyway not to be trusted in the matter of men, changing her walk and lifting her tail and walking round the room only to stop, and softly pick things up to hold them against her cheek in the manner of a girl in an advertisement.

'You two go and clean your teeth,' Morag said to her children. She had retained enough tact not yet to enjoy displaying the faults in her marriage to its children, a stage that comes as a rule when the children can least begin to bear it.

Hearing her voice change, she said to Edward, while she took the crusts off his second piece of toast, placed it on a clean plate, and took away the used things before setting down a fresh knife, 'Would you like a second egg?'

He had never said 'Yes' in answer to this question and did not do so now. He did not take more than three eggs in the week, making sure to include in this tally units of egg that might have been incorporated into other things he ingested, for example cakes. Morag's question about the second egg therefore had to his ears something of the murderous in it.

'If you want to kill me,' he said, 'continue to behave precisely as you have done for the past three months. You will find no one as good as me . . .'

She left before she heard this sentence end with the words, 'for you.'

She left the house with her raincoat, her handbag and a pair of painful silver shoes she had worn to annoy Edward that morning, but which by the end of a day that included the plane south, a journey on the tube that had been almost alarmingly smooth, as though she would never have human feelings again, a hot train journey through a part of England that made her homesick already for Scotland, and a promising period of eavesdropping that ended with one of its participants' disappointingly quiet death, annoyed her much more and burned her too, by virtue of their metallic finish.

Hard along the house's dusty yellow length the scaffolding was set, carrying all the blows taken to fix it tight together up to Jean's open window in the form of longitudinal shudderings and breathy irregular chimes. She was resting in a position that she had taught herself during the years of living in other people's houses. Braced everywhere but the neck, her body was arranged in the least comfortable chair in the room. This choice might not have been understood by people unashamed of their own ease. Her wrists and hands curled, ready at any moment to push her up, over the chair's splint-like arms. The plumbing of the house clanked and hissed without cease. In the sash window-frame of Jean's thin high room lay flakes of paint like peeled bark. A tentative persistent lichen grew in on the sill. The scaffolding seemed bold, an expression of someone's intention to hold things up against time.

Fresh yet heavy with the summer that sleeps low around an English river, the air brought into Jean's light sleep noises that came always at this time of day. She did not know she heard them but her closed eyes told her pictures as each noise came. The pictures were clear as illustrations in a first alphabet. She saw a cow, yeast-coloured, on a green field. Pigeons arrived in pairs behind her eyes as their cooing took her back to other houses of which she had become a part, and then fallen away at the given time when another job at the heart of a family withered.

Behind her warm lids, a train came, complete with funnel, condenser, signalman, smuts. She awoke with a start and a taste in her mouth like sucked coin. Morag was coming to stay here. She was arriving this afternoon, in the train.

Jean woke, remembering that Morag had left behind Edward and, more deplorably, Ishbel and Geordie. She wiped the sleep from her face with a rough flannel as you clean the bloom from a plum, and prepared herself to see her daughter and look her straight in the eye. Morag would no doubt make free of a taxi from the station. Edward would already be beginning to pay for whatever his sin had been. Jean was made unsteady by the reasons Morag gave for leaving, as if there could be reasons for an unreasonable thing. The confusion of love with marriage was no help. Jean held love, in Morag's sense, to be what you felt before you knew a person well enough to know when they were lying. What came after that knowledge might have less fire but it was warmer also, she on principle imagined.

She filled her kettle from the wash basin and made a half cup of instant custard, watching the glowing pink flour melt to a suffused yellow, breathing in the smell of vanilla, sugar and starch. Quickly the custard set, with the spoon upright, as though in a cup of plaster of Paris. She powdered her face in a sketchy way, looking at the mirror's flecks and motes and not at her own, which did not interest her. Before leaving the room, she spooned and smoothed a layer of cooling thick custard into the half coconut that hung at her window for the birds. She could not bear to give the birds nothing, and had not the facilities or way of life that produced bacon rinds. It was a vegetarian household, had been so for eighty years.

'Mother, come down, I'm arrived. Or we are.'

The voice came from under the window. Jean looked down through the scaffolding.

'Do you want me to climb down to you?' asked Jean, in an admonitory whisper that subtracted the intended irony. In the heat the creeping plants that embraced the house were reaching tendrils towards the scaffolding, pitting their minute continual subversion against the clumsy man-made optimism of its structure. Should it remain too long, the plants would wind it about and bring it down.

'Shall I actually come in this way?' said a male Scots voice, perhaps drunk. Jean looked along the house. Just to the side of her own bathroom window, over the workroom of Ludovina her employer, was a man over thirty standing rather crouched in the hot box of air between the first-floor scaffolding bars. His colour was bad. It was hard to believe that here was a romantic motive for Morag's morning dash from Edinburgh, but it was Jean's duty to ask.

'Had you intended sharing a room? Ludo would not mind but I am not for haste in these things,' she said to the starling-coloured head of her daughter below. Morag was standing thigh-deep among blue agapanthus and the long belts of their leaves.

'Mother, I left my husband under twelve hours ago, and not because I don't love him. I may.' Morag began to look for a cigarette. She had taken up smoking in the last two hours. It had seemed impolite not to smoke in all the dejected rooms she and Findlay Meldrum had been put into after the finding of his father's body. There had been so little all these strangers could offer, it would have been unkind not to take their cigarettes.

'Have one of mine. You light the end that you don't put in your mouth,' said the man in the scaffolding, dropping a cigarette that fell some feet wide of Morag, and seeing the ineptitude of his throw, he burst into tears for the first time that afternoon, and fell limp out of the rungs down on to the deep lawn of moss where he lay on his back weeping at the English sky in gasps for his father as Jean and Morag looked down at him from their two heights, and, from her workroom in this house where she had been born, Ludovina heard what she had not for more than twenty years, the intractable grief of a man.

The obvious thing, to gather him up in comfort, was evidently up to Morag; but she only knew more about him, she did not *know* him any more than did her mother or Ludovina. Shy of any first touch, she wanted him and his misery, and the way it might bind them for even these hours, to be gone.

She had chosen this as her own day for drama, and events had eclipsed her. Things do not know when to happen, she thought, they are ruthless like children. Cheated of a weeping declamatory scene with her mother, she did not at that point choose to consider why she had not minded becoming involved with Findlay Meldrum's long distressing afternoon with the railway authorities, the police, the hospital.

Curiosity had made her listen to Findlay's conversation with his father. But the sight of him had passed into her with a speed and heat she had forgotten through the years of discipline and some kind of peace with Edward. This made harder the thought of gathering him to her as he beat his head back on the ground – to put it out of its misery, it seemed – and poured tears for his loss of a man she did not know. If she had thought of holding him it was not to give ease, or not at once.

In the end it was Ludovina who dealt with Findlay. Her presumption of competence always endowed her with it. She was good at the extreme states of others since they offended her sense of the stable, measured, discreet and sober way a rational life should be led. She was a satisfied atheist, a type that will take swift decisions without later compunction; her greatest impatience was against timewasters and ditherers. The rock of her unbelief had never once let her down.

Letting herself out by the apple-house door, she moved over the lawn in her sandals and djellabah, her stout decisive form at once becoming the focus of the group; the other two women were distraught at the sight of a man unmanned. Ludovina took over. She was at her best in a crisis, her certainty and bossiness becoming buoyant and purposeful, not chilling.

She thought aloud in the drawling unembarrassed tones that had served her perfectly well through eighty years of privileged activism and rash adventurous travels: 'Jean, you make a bed and a drink for him, if you would. Somewhere he can shout and howl without disturbing us. What's your name? Ah interesting, you are a Scot too then, at any rate at the start of your history. I live here because this is the house of the parents of my mother, and the house where I was born, but I owe myself to Scotland.' Here she spoke of what she found best in herself, her toughness, her independence, her sentimental effective brusqueness.

Ludovina remembered the urgency and stopped, delighted to be at the heart of things that were happening, not to have to kill time with talk. 'Morag, this is sudden, but I am pleased to see you. Since he is not your lover, don't be so foolish and hold his head to stop him doing that.' Ludovina knew well that a mistress would hold a lover who wept. She had herself conducted passionate rational adulteries throughout her long successful marriage.

Findlay had rolled on to his stomach and was beating his head down on the edge of the grass where it met the path of gravel and cinders. His shiny hair was dimmed by black dust. He began to like the distracting pain of smashing down his head among the sharp small stones. Morag squatted, sank and caught him under the arms so that his head was held in her lap where he lay tense and resisting until the reminder of life that

came with being held for no reason but humanity entered him, and
restored to him the superficial social emotions of a man watched by a
short, composed octogenarian woman as he breathes in a stranger
through her skirt wet with his own tears. Ludovina nodded as Findlay
calmed down. She took her time. Her hard but inky hands were on her
thick waist.

She had the thread of a new story almost in her grip. She could not
wait to return to her pen, with which she had a further three hours to
spend that day, before she went out to dig the evening's potatoes.

'I'm sorry,' Findlay said, apologising also to his father who, he thought,
would have deplored every one of the actions taken by his son since his
death. 'I had not known it would be like this. You are kind.' It was not
easy to say these things lying down and into the lap of a woman he did
not know, who smelt of lemon soap, ironing, cheese and pickle, blood
and, on the fingers of her right hand that was now stroking, not holding
rigid, his left shoulder, the beautiful autumnal domestic dirty smell of
extinguished candle.

Janice Galloway

from *The Trick Is To Keep Breathing*

I watch the ceiling till it's light enough to make lists. Sunday Mornings I make a lot of lists.

I stay in bed because it's warmer and pile the cover with books, magazines and bits of writing paper, drinking tea till I'm sloshing like a water bomb. Then it's time to get up for the Sunday papers – I can spend a while cutting out things to put in the post. I listen to The Archers, Pick of the Week, Desert Island Discs. I make more tea and eject the week's newspapers, the debris of last night's clippings then carry the junk to the kitchen.

On Sundays, I bake.

The kitchen scales are good ones, a present from Ellen. Fractions of ounces and grammes if I need them: I like to be meticulous when I bake. I make good gingerbread, wonderful sponge. My shortbread melts in the mouth because I take care. I think of mouths when I'm baking, digging my fingers into the flour and fat, blending eggs and sugar and milk. Greasing tins makes my hands reek and clogs my nails with melting margarine.

The glass jars are polished every day, so the kitchen glitters. Muscatel, Lexia, pitted dates, candied peel, cherries and chocolate chips; quicksands of brown sugars. The powders make clouds: wholemeal, wheatmeal, strong plain white and brown, granary, rye and buckwheat for blinis. I'm very adventurous. I fold and whisk and knead for hours among the jars, dropping blended mixes from spoons into the shining tins. I read the ingredients and the method out loud for the beautiful sound of the words. In two hours there will be a Dundee cake, Ginger squares, Oatmeal scones and Fresh Orange Tarts. After that I might make preserves. A good wife going to waste.

I lived with a man for the better part of seven years. We met at school: fifth form romance. Our first date was in a café when we should have been in French. We ate salad rolls and doughnuts that tasted like sacred wafer because we were out of school and we both liked the same things: doughnuts and salad rolls. Once we went late into school eating opposite ends of an eclair, giggling, faces too close, smeared with chocolate icing and cream. Half way across the playground, a stray teacher caught sight of us. He shouted SEPARATE YOURSELVES and sliced the air between us with the flat of his hand. We separated. He said we were a terrible example.

I wiped the cream off my nose as defiantly as I could and said I couldn't see why. He stopped short.

Pardon? he said.

Look, I said. You're holding a cigarette. That's a worse example to impressionable young minds than anything we're doing.

I knew it wouldn't make things any better but I couldn't stop. Paul kept his mouth shut and looked apologetic. We got hell. Paul never ate eclairs in the playground with me again. He always did have a better instinct for keeping out of trouble.

We had bad times and we had good times on and off over the seven years. I learned to cook good meals and run a house. The fridge was always well stocked and the cupboards interesting. I cleaned the floors and the rings round the bath that showed where we had been but I knew there was something missing. I felt we were growing apart. We were. It was called growing up but I didn't know that at the time. I tried to talk to him because the magazines I was reading said communication was important. He was reading different magazines: his magazines told him different things altogether. I thought the answer was soul-searching and he thought it was split-crotch knickers. Stalemate. We were unhappy. He punished me for his unhappiness by refusing to touch me. Night after night. I punished him for my unhappiness by not speaking but I hadn't the same willpower. His willpower lasted out for months. A year. More. Practice was making him perfect and me desperate for kisses. I had an affair. I couldn't see it wasn't the sex I missed so much as someone to care whether I missed it or not. The affair didn't help. Paul found out because he read my letters when I wasn't in and knew everything I was doing. I didn't know he was doing that and thought he had xray vision. I thought I was going crazy. I started writing my diary in code. I started thinking in code because I thought he could tap my brain. I became afraid to leave the flat in case he could tell things by feeling the walls when I was out or maybe through supervision. I thought he was Superman. I couldn't live with Superman without thinking

a) Superman's weaknesses are my fault (like Kryptonite)
and
b) I was vastly inferior in every respect.

He talked to me even less and I talked to myself more and more. He still
ate my meals and let me make the beds, do his washing and attend to
the Superflat but it wasn't the same. Now there was no talk at all, only
the sound of two people suffocating into different pillows. We were killing
each other. There was nobody to ask for help because I was too proud
and too ashamed I wasn't fit to live with. My mother was dying and it
wasn't right to speak to her about this kind of thing. That was a romantic
idea. Even if she had been well, I wouldn't have said anyway. Besides, I
needed his car to supervise my mother's dying. They always build
hospitals a million miles away from people.

The day of the funeral, he shook my hand in line with everybody else
waiting outside the crematorium. I looked at his face and couldn't think
who he was for a minute. It didn't feel better when I remembered. It felt
worse. But still I stayed in his flat, where there was nothing of mine,
nothing of me. I got more and more guilty about sapping his Superpowers
and thought I couldn't cope. I knew I had to leave and I had to get help. I
found a shoulder to cry on. The shoulder thought I might be more
comfortable crying in bed. Paul found out about this too. He wanted to
hurt me so he told me he was screwing everything in skirts within a
fifteen-mile radius. I told him it was a source of comfort to know I hadn't
inflicted permanent damage on his erectile tissue. That was when he
played his ace.

I don't need you for anything, he said, loud and flat. I don't need you
for a thing.
I racked my brain to find something to prove it wasn't true. I came up
with the only answer left.

Look, I'm going to make us something to eat. At least I can do that
much. You need me all right. You need me because you can't cook. You
can't fucking cook. I yelled too.

He went out slamming the door but I made something anyway. Pasta with
seafood sauce, garlic bread, olive and pepper salad: his favourites. I didn't
have favourites: I liked what he liked. I thought he had great taste. He'd
come back sooner or later.
He came back an hour later with a carrier bag. A Chinese take-away. For
one. He ate it without looking at me but I heard the message loud and clear.

SHOVE YOUR FOOD

It took me a month to find somewhere else to live. He was right. He
didn't need me for a thing.

I don't think I ever came to terms with the shock. Even while I decorated
my new home, I took time out to make him a cake now and again, some
homemade preserves. These days he stays away. He has someone else
who cooks his meals. The cupboard under the sink bulges with chutney.

The cakes come, transformed from the oven. The scent of them cooling
on the wire rack makes me feel weak. When they stop steaming I can
wrap them in silver foil because they are gifts, and put them away in the
cupboard. They make me feel secure in there: ready for other people to
eat and me to ignore. A strength. That gives me a lift.

I make a note about the appointment with Dr Stead tomorrow because
I'm confident after the baking. I can handle thinking about him right
now, so I make my list of things to say tomorrow so I don't forget
anything while I'm there.

DO I HAVE TO TAKE THE RED THINGS?

(I read in a magazine anti-depressants make you fat. I've been terrified of
them ever since.)

> PLEASE STOP SENDING HV
> ARE THE SLEEPING PILLS SUPPOSED TO WORK?
> STILL NO BLEEDING.

It looks assertive because of the capitals. I'll need it tomorrow. I need all
the help I can get with Dr Stead.

ooo

I put the heating on and my skin starts rippling. The house is clean from
Friday but I polish a little extra to be sure. Then I go to the shop at the
end of the road and buy cheese, bread, milk: things to make the fridge

look populated. By five the water is ready. I go upstairs. It's time for the bathing ritual. Preparation for the nightvisitor.

Dear Kathy,
I know you're going to think this is a silly worry but it's not to me. I have a very understanding boyfriend and we both want to make love, but every time the occasion arises, I'm not able to 'let go'. I can't tell him what it is because I'm too ashamed. But I'm scared he'll be repulsed when he sees me or that I'll do something stupid. Even when we're kissing I worry about being a mess afterwards, not what he thought I was under the make-up. Please help me. This is ruining my chance of happiness.

All sorts of people came at first. I wasn't even in the right place but they found me. People can be very kind. It screws me up. Marianne did the talking and they paid calls. Some of the people I thought would come didn't but others came to take their place. There were compensations.

Sam came.
He had a new bike and a new face: scrappy bits of beard and broken veins on his cheeks. He took me out to see the new bike: silver and red, shiny chrome, smell of hot grease. I wore Michael's leather jacket and we went out, way out along the coast to some pub or other. Mhairi and Sean were there, Frank and Joyce. Me with my hair plastered down and my eyes streaming from the wind. Sam bought me gin. Sean bought me gin. Frank, Joyce and Mhairi bought me gin. We sat round a space-invader table and looked at the shapes moving, luminous green and yellow through the glass top. Sam took me back on the motorway to open her up and wind rushing towards us took my breath away: I yelled all the way to the estate.

It was a surprising time. I spent nights rambling in strange cars, eating meals with people I hardly knew. But I was relieved when it tailed off. It made me worry too much and I was never as grateful as I wanted to be. It made me tense and anxious wondering why they came, why they did it. I got guilty about wondering. I kept thinking there is no such thing as a free lunch and wondering when the price came. It didn't but I was easier when it stopped anyway.

There is No Such Thing as a Free Lunch.
There is no such thing as Lunch.
Joke.

Now I have particular visits. I don't like to take anything for granted. This Sunday night he's coming round. Maybe I will be embraced, entered, made to exist. The physical self is precarious.

The Bathing Ritual.
The bathwater must be hot: warm isn't good enough. I wait till the water is scalding and run the bath as evening falls, getting rid of the day's clothes: standing in the steam, acclimatising.

I pour oil into the scalding water. My skin gets creaky and dry as I get thinner, like tracing paper: the oil will make me smooth. I step into the water, careful because of the heat. The mirror cuts off my head as I sit and steady my lungs, feeling the flesh under the surface turn raw. When sweat breaks on my upper lip, I can't see the mirror for steam. The scent of the oil is lost among the clouds.
On the white bath rim, the wash glove
                    the soap.
   The glove is made of matting, knotted in rows. I dip it once into the water and pass it over the soap: only once so the hair doesn't coat, flatten out against the cloth.

When I finish, the skin sizzles: my whole surface sings. I stand up in the bath draining away the ordinariness that floats with the scum on the water, rinse myself with fresh water from the taps. The cold water runs on while I sit and soap each leg in turn, then lift the razor, checking the edge is keen. It gives a better finish slicing upward, against the hair: it severs more closely. I have to be careful it doesn't catch or draw blood. That would be unsightly. The water runs down each foreleg while I shave, carrying the shed animal hair away down the black hole under the taps. Fleeced, I turn off the taps and step out to rub my skin hard with the flat loops of the towel till it hurts. This makes me warmer. Then I stoop to wash my hair over the basin, pouring lukewarm cupfuls till the water is clear again. Twice. I wrap the damp hair in a towel and wipe a place in the misted mirror.

Boxes and bottles on the bedroom floor: creams, fluids, cotton and paper. Moisturiser. To keep in the juice. Glutinous stuff for my elbows, knees and knuckles in case they're rough. I pluck my eyebrows, the single hair on my upper lip. Nail-scissors to make my pubic hair neat. Perfume for my ears, my neck, my wrists and navel; the flat space between my breasts, tips of my spine, between the toes. I file my nails, hands and feet with emery and pumice, pushing back the cuticles, defining whiteness with chalk. I paint my toenails. The radio mutters a play under the fallen bedspread. I paint them again. Then each fingernail the same way. I leave my armpits free from chemical interference: deodorant matts, it tastes bad. This is my token to naturalness in case this is what he prefers. I stand and pad on some talc from a canister instead, dripping white dust onto my knees and belly, puffs of smoke across my chest. I put on my prettiest underwear: net lace and satin, ribbon straps. Black. I wear a lot of black.

I pick up the hairdryer.

Not long now. I sit on the bedspread and spread out the things for my face. This has to be subtle; just enough makeup to make my eyes seem more, the lips rounder, bleach out the circles and lines growing like a web under the lashes. I have to tint my face because I am pale in cold weather, powder blue. This is unappetising and nothing to kiss. I tint myself Peaches and Dream, stain my eyelids lilac, brush the lashes black. I smear my lips with clear wax from a stick (red is too vivid and leaves marks, so may make him cautious). I am to be entirely inviting in case. In case. I check the watch again. I never know what to wear. I'm still combing and fixing earrings by the time I hear the grind of wheels outside, the low purr of the engine.

Sunday Night 9.05
It's important not to think about Monday.

Bright light flashes past the window and the engine cuts. I think about his hands on the wheel, red hair at the rim of his cuff. He is always late, but he comes. The engine stops as I test a smile in the mirror; it is difficult to pull the thing together, to see all of the offering and not a jumble of separate parts. I don't think I want to anyway. Footfalls thud on the boards downstairs. I smile at the woman in the mirror. Her eyes are huge. But what looks back is never what I want. Someone melting. And too much like me.

She switches out the light and opens the door.

In the white corridor
over and over, the same thing
something thudding
thudding solid behind the door

> *say there's nothing*
> *say there's nothing say there's*
> *jesus*
> *jesus*
> *jesus*

a tall dark boy comes towards me
heavy accent and these still brown eyes
and there's a terrible sound of

my mouth is open

> *jesus*
> *say there's nothing*
> *say there's nothing*
> *say there's*

>> *terrible sound of*
>> *thudding in my chest and someone*

>> *screaming*
>> *screaming*
>> *scream*

ooo

Mondays

The smoke out of my hair, the creases of leftover makeup under my eyes, aftershave and stale perfume. Pile-up on the M6, beached whales in Alaska, earthquake in Chile. Screams and falling in the dark.

sometime

Blaze through work by all means but be circumspect. You'd be surprised how much cumuppance tends to follow even little mistakes. Scottish Education: apportion blame that ye have not blame apportioned unto you. It wisny me, it was you/him/her a wee man and he ran away. No relief when the bell rings. My lift with the women tells me *Dennis wouldn't eat the liver after all what did I tell you not even with the onions and Evelyn Little's wedding eh must be at least thirty six by this* etc etc. They never open the windows and me in a poloneck to hide the weals, the way adolescents do. The car goes too near to the verge when she says he *never speaks he's out on that garage or the golf course the whole time and never speaks at all.*

Leaves scratch at the window.
You raise your hand to touch them before you remember.

ooo

Seven minutes early.
The appointments line snakes right out the door and into the drizzle. I go to Dr Stead too often and feel bad about it. I always think I'm wasting his time and I hate that so sometimes the visits are acrimonious. So I always go early and make notes. It's supposed to make me businesslike and brisk. It's supposed to save his time and my anxiety about it, but it never works out like that. It works out like this:

DOCTOR How are things/what's new/how's the week been treating you?

I try to remember the things in the notepad. They get jumbled and I think I'm going to cry. This is terrible so I say anything.

PATIENT I'm not sleeping. I'm still not sleeping.

DOCTOR Try taking the yellow things an hour earlier in the evening. And the red things later. There's nothing left to do to the green things on this theme. Keep them as they were. [Already writing prescription] Do you need more?

PATIENT Thank-you. I feel terrible.

DOCTOR Well, let's leave it for a while, see how you are next week. One thing at a time, eh?

I come out like a steamrollered cartoon: two-dimensions to start with then flattened some more till I'm tissue. I walk to the bus stop with my head down. Even on warm days I take a scarf to hide my face.

Dr Stead's in the upstairs surgery today.
He's never anywhere else but the receptionist always says it as though it's a temporary arrangement for the doctor to be in the upstairs surgery. It proves her indispensability as the only one who knows for sure where he is. You know she's hoping one day you get too cocky and go upstairs without her say-so and find someone else there instead. So I always take the advice as if it's news: I'm not going to be the one who gets caught out.
Take your cards with you please.

I take them and say nothing. Once, I called her Mrs McKay by mistake. It says Mrs McKay on her lapel badge so I thought it would be all right. She looked right through me as if I wasn't there and shouted NEXT so maybe it wasn't her name at all, or if it was, she just didn't like people using it. She likes to keep the patients on their toes. Or maybe it's her revenge for all the coughing and wheezing and scratching she has to put up with. Anyway, I don't speak now, just names and dates. I take my cards and go upstairs to wait.

Preparation for the Doctor
A short exercise lasting anything up to forty minutes

[The surgery is blue. The patient stands while the doctor scratches his neck, sits, rifles through pieces of paper. Some of the pieces of paper fall and he picks them up, sighs, grins tightly to himself, scratches the back of his neck with his ring finger then looks up.]

DOCTOR   Sit. [Pause] So how are things what's new who are you anyway?

PATIENT   I'm tired and I still need somebody to talk to. I need to get less angry about everything. I'm going nuts.

DOCTOR   Don't tell me how to do my job. Relax. You can talk to me. I made a double appointment so we can have twenty minutes. Go ahead. I'm listening.

PATIENT   What can I say that makes sense in twenty minutes?

DOCTOR   Try. You're not trying. You're looking for something that doesn't exist, that's why you're not happy. Look at me. I'm under no illusions. That's why I'm in control.

PATIENT   How can I be more like you?

DOCTOR   That's not what I meant. That's not what I meant at all. Envy is a destructive emotion. Besides I had to fight hard to get to feel like this. I'm buggered if I'm giving away the fruits of my hard work for nothing. You must tell me how you are.

PATIENT   I don't seem to know how I am except bad. There's nothing there but anger and something scary all the time. I don't want to get bitter because it will ruin my looks.

DOCTOR   Maybe a hobby would help. Facetiousness is not an attractive trait in a young woman.

PATIENT   I know I know. I can't help myself.

DOCTOR   OK. We'll try these green ones for a change. And step up the anti-depressants. Don't drink or drive. Make an appointment for a few days' time and try to be more helpful in future.

While I try to imagine him shouting the last bit, he comes out the surgery and takes in a little boy with a huge sty on one eye. Maybe he guesses I sit out here rehearsing.

IMPATIENT   OK, let's talk straight. You ask me to talk then you look at your watch. What am I supposed to take from that? This whole thing is ridiculous. Can't you send me to someone who's paid to have me waste their time? You don't know what to do with me but you keep telling me to come back. And stop sending that woman to see me. All it does is make me guilty and secretive.

DOCTOR   Look, this is reactive depression. I don't see that sending you to a specialist will help things. Talk to your family if you can't talk to me.

IMPATIENT   I have no family.

DOCTOR   Don't be melodramatic.

There's a click and a scuffle. Dr Stead is standing in the doorframe of the surgery waiting with his appointment sheet. He looks smaller than he was in my head. Crow's feet are beginning to dent his temples and his nails are bitten into the quick. We try to be at ease and go through the routine about the pills, the anxiety, the sleeplessness, etc. There is no consensus, no conclusion. No answer. When he reaches for the prescription pad, something like warm fingertips slither under my chin. They gather, cool and drip making dark spots on my trousers. This is unavoidable but still humiliating. I leak steadily over his nice chair.

There's another prescription here for when you leave. He sighs and holds out a kleenex. I'm his last patient and it's probably been a long day.
Are you listening to me?
I nod and he goes on. I don't want to look up. He must see a lot of this sort of thing. Like me, he is familiar with it. He gives up with the kleenex and we each pretend to the other it isn't happening. Professionals.
Good. No word from the referral yet? I shake my head.
Let's see. Nearly a fortnight. I still don't agree with you about the usefulness of Health Visitors but it's obvious things aren't getting much better. We'll hang on for Foresthouse.

I think about things not getting any better, knowing fine that THINGS = ME. He sighs. I know he's hating this. He knows I know.
You must understand they're always busy, though. They'll take a few days to write. Hospitals always do these days.
It's already been a fortnight.
He stands up. I gather up the prescription and follow him to the door. He always opens it for me: one of the old school. Just before he opens it, he reminds me not to expect miracles.
No, I say.
No.

An old man is sitting in the corridor. He pulls his coat tighter and looks across to me, irritated at being seen waiting.
I've been waiting half an hour. He coughs.
Bloody doctors. Think you've nothing better to be doing. He is not talking to me. He is talking just in case anyone is watching, waiting to

call him to account. Or just for something to say. When the doctor comes the old man will say nothing. The doctor is an educated man. He is doing his best. The old man is merely old.

Bastards, he says.

He has to blame someone. He blames the empty corridor. When the doctor comes he will be like the rest of us and smile. When the doctor says he's sorry to have kept him waiting, he'll say Not at all, doctor, not at all. I keep my head down, expecting something sudden to fall from the sky at any minute. I jerk, ducking the impact that never comes.

ooo

A fortnight before she left, Marianne took me out in the car. We had a huge bottle of cheap wine. I held it cooling out of the window while she drove. Irresponsible. It was very late: hardly any cars. We went for miles into the country past Kilmarnock till she cut the engine and we sat in the dark drinking the wine and looking up at half the moon. She was worried about going and wanted to make me think about lasting through. We drank lots of wine and decided it was all about lasting through, just getting on with the day to day till it got less terrible. I wanted to know what would happen if she hated the States.

I'll come back, she said.

Her shoulders tightened. She was being flippant because she was worried too. She was worried about lasting out at least a year in a strange place with people who would make a big thing out of not understanding her accent. Even if it was the worst job in the world she wouldn't be able to quit: she had signed contracts that said so.

We had some more wine.

At least I'll be paid good money for hating it.

This time it came out bitter. We ran out of things to say so we went home, weaving down the centreline on the road back, over the motorway and down onto the sand of Irvine shore. She stopped the car to look at the sea: there is no sea in Kentucky. Then she turned and looked at me.

Just last out. Last out for me. It has to get better eventually.

I know, I said. I know that.

The sound of the waves carried all the way across the dunes.

But what will I do while I'm lasting, Marianne? What will I do?

I don't want to

                 listen to the radio
                 watch tv
                 have a bath
                 listen to records
                 read
                 write letters or visit
                 go for a walk
                 sew
                 go out for a meal
                                 for reasons I already explained.

That leaves the phone.

Marianne is one of life's natural phoners. My own feelings are mixed. My mother didn't have one at home: too expensive. I spent my whole teenage life without a phone. But I thought they must be wonderful. I thought everybody had one but us and owning one was a sure sign of success. Smooth plastic casing, seductive coil of wire and complacent purr when you lifted the receiver: the whole thing was desirable. I didn't really think about what it was for: that wasn't the point.

The point was
The point was
The point

I didn't know the point. Only the desire mattered.

There was a phone in Paul's flat, ready fitted. One of these little Wimpey numbers with just one big room to live in but there was a phone. Already, attachment to a man meant better things. I was upwardly mobile: phone number all my own. More or less. I couldn't call my mother since she still didn't have one but I could call the speaking clock and the operator. I could call work to say when I was ill: this didn't happen often. Not then. I would get excited if it rang and run dripping from the bath to find out who was on the other side. Most times it was Paul saying he was working late. Then I paid for my mother to have a phone: she was ill and I thought it was a good idea. She called me more often than I called her. She called me since it seemed ungrateful not to after I had paid all the money. She always held it too far away from her mouth and shouted. Sometimes it rang in the middle of the night and scared her. She was never sure who it was. Overnight, she left it off the hook. In case. Soon, I had to phone the hospital to talk to her. More than once she didn't know who I was. This must have been frightening but I kept doing it. I called her once from the top of a mountain, shouting I'M CALLING YOU FROM THE TOP OF A MOUNTAIN as if it was significant. She hung up. She didn't remember when I told her about it a week later. Someone rang me at work the day she died. I went to the house and checked the phone, the one I paid for, on the hall table. It was off the hook.

I got a phone for the cottage the day I moved in. After all, I thought, everyone needs a phone. You can't live nowadays without a phone. Michael would call late in the night after his wife had gone to bed and whisper down the line to my bedroom. Then there was the call that began with only two words.
  She knows.
When he put the receiver down I threw up. I just missed the phone.

I phoned Norma straight off the Spanish flight at Heathrow. A noisy callbox, waiting for the Glasgow connection. I wanted her to know what I did. First hand. Rumour and speculation can do awful things.

Marianne phoned people all the time after that to let them know. Norma was doing a lot of the same thing. You could hear the embarrassment in their voices at being told again. She had plenty of time. It took three weeks to get him back in a lead-sealed box. All that time, she was phoning.

The phone is an instrument of intrusion into order. It is a threat to control. Just when you think you are alone and safe, the call could come that changes your life. Or someone else's. It makes the same flat, mechanical noise for everyone and gives no clues what's waiting there on the other end of the line.

You can never be too careful.

Iain Banks

from *The Bridge*

'You know I had that damn record for three years before I realised Fay Fife's name was a pun; you know; "Where are you from?" "Ah'm fay Fife,"' he told Stewart, shaking his head.

'Aye,' Stewart said, 'Ah ken.'

'God I'm so stupid sometimes,' he breathed, gazing sadly at his can of Export.

'Aye,' Stewart nodded. 'Ah ken,' he said, and rose to turn the album over.

He looked out through the window to the view of the town and the distant bare trees of the Glen. His watch said 2:16. It was getting dark already. He supposed they were near the solstice now. He drank some more.

He'd had five or six cans, and it looked like he'd have to stay over with Stewart, or get a train back to Edinburgh. A train, he thought. He hadn't been on one for years. It would be good to take a train from Dunfermline and go over the old bridge; he could throw out a coin and wish that Gustave would kill himself, or that Andrea would find herself pregnant and want to bring her child up in Scotland, or –

Cut it out, you idiot, he told himself. Stewart sat down again. They had talked about politics. They'd agreed if they were sincere about what they said they believed in they'd be out in Nicaragua, fighting for the Sandinistas. They'd talked about old times, old music, old friends – but never about her. They'd talked about Star Wars – SDI – which Britain had just signed up for. It wasn't that distant a subject for them; they both knew people at the university who were working on optical computer circuits; the Pentagon was interested.

They'd talked about the new Koestler chair of parapsychology at the university, and about a programme they'd both seen on television a few weeks earlier, on lucid dreaming; and also about the hypotheses of causative formation (he said sure it was interesting, but he could remember when Von Daniken's theories had been 'interesting').

They'd talked about a story mentioned on television and in the press that week, about an *émigré* Russian engineer living in France who'd crashed his car in England; a lot of money had been found in the car and he was under suspicion of having committed a crime in France. He had apparently gone into a coma, but the doctors seemed to think he was faking. Devious bastards us engineers, he told Stewart.

They had talked, in fact, about almost everything except what he really wanted to talk about. Stewart had tried to bring the subject up, but each time he had found himself sliding away from it; the programme on lucid dreaming had come up because it was the last thing he had had an argument with Andrea about; the causative formation hypothesis because it was probably the next thing they'd argue about. Stewart hadn't pressed him on the subject of Andrea and Gustave. Maybe he just needed to talk, about anything.

'How're the kids anyway?' he asked.

Stewart had something to eat and asked him if he wanted anything, but he didn't feel hungry. They had another joint, he had another can; they talked. The afternoon darkened. Stewart felt tired after a while and said he'd have a snooze. He'd set the alarm and be up to make the tea later. They could head out for a pint after they'd eaten something.

He listened to some old Jefferson Airplane on the headphones, but the record was scratched. He looked through his friend's collection of books, drinking from the can and finishing off the last joint. Finally he went and stood by the window, looking out across the slates to the park, the glen, the ruined palace and the abbey.

The light was slowly going from the half-clouded sky. Streetlights were on, and the roads were filled with parked or slowly moving cars; doubtless full of Christmas shoppers. Light-sapped skies hung over the glen. He wondered what this place looked like when the palace was still a place for kings.

And the Kingdom of Fife. A small place now, but big enough then. Rome had been small too, to start with, and it hadn't stopped her; what would the world have been like if some part of Scotland – before such a state existed – had blossomed the way Rome did ... No, there wasn't the background, the legacy of history here at that time. Athens, Rome, Alexandria; they had libraries when all we had were hill forts; not savages, but not civilised either. By the time we were ready to play our part it was already too late; we were always too soon or too late, and the best things we've done have been for other people.

Well, sentimental Scottishism, he guessed. What about class consciousness rather than nationalism? Well, indeed.

How could she do it? Never mind that this was her home, that this was where her mother lived, her earliest friends, where she had so many of her earliest memories formed, and her character; how could she leave what she had now? Forget about him; he would willingly leave himself out of the equation ... but she had so much, to do and to be ... How could she do it?

Self-sacrifice, the woman behind the man, looking after him, putting herself second; it went against all she believed in.

He still hadn't been able to talk to her properly about it. His heart beat faster; he put the can down, thinking. He didn't really know what it was he wanted to say, only that he wanted to talk to her, to hold her, to just be with her and tell her everything he felt for her. He ought to tell her all he'd ever felt, about Gustave, about her, about himself. He should be totally honest with her, so that at least she would know exactly what he felt, be under no illusions about him. It was important, damn it.

He finished the can, put the roach into it, then folded the red tin neatly. A little beer dribbled onto his hand from the folded corner of aluminium. He wiped his hands. I ought to tell her. I ought to talk to her now. What was she doing this evening? They were at home, weren't they? Yes, they both are; something I was invited to, but I wanted to see Stewart. I'll call her. He went to the phone.

Engaged. Probably another hour-long call to Gustave; even when she was here she still seemed to spend half her time with him. He put the phone down and paced the room, his heart thumping, his hands sweating. He needed a pee; he went to the bathroom, washed his hands afterwards, gargled with some mouthwash. He felt all right. He didn't even feel stoned or drunk. He tried the phone again; same signal. He stood at the window. The Jag was visible, if he stood close to the glass and looked right down. A white, curved ghost on the dark street. He looked at his watch again. He felt fine; perfectly straight. Just ready for a drive.

Why not? he thought. Take the albino Jaguar off into the gloaming; head for the motorway and blast over the road bridge with the sounds cranked up high as they'll go; an arrogant grin and a blast of aural pain for whatever poor bastard takes your toll ... shee-it; very *Fear and Loathing*, very Hunter S. Thompsonish. Belay that, laddy; damn book always did make you drive just that little bit faster afterwards. Your own fault for listening to *White Rabbit* a few minutes ago; that's what's done it. No, forget about driving; you've had too many.

Aw hell; everybody does it at this time of year. Damn it, I drive better drunk than most people do sober. Just take it easy; you can make it. Isn't as though you don't know the road, after all. Drive real careful in the town, just in case some kid runs out in front of you and your reactions are affected, then nice and easy on the motorway; legal limit or even less, none of this blowing away the local boy-racer in his Capri or giving nasty surprises to glassy-eyed BMW drivers; just don't get intimidated, just maintain concentration, don't think about Red Sharks or White Whales, testing the suspension over concrete walls or controlled drifts round an entire clover leaf. Just take it easy, listen to the sounds. Auntie Joanie maybe. Something soothing; not soporific, but steady, not *too* exciting, not the sort of thing the right foot just hears and floors on; nothing like that ...

He tried the phone one last time. He went through to see Stewart; he was sleeping quietly, and rolled over when he looked in, away from the hall light's glow. He wrote him a note and left it by the alarm clock. He took up his old biking jacket and the monogrammed scarf and let himself out of the flat.

Getting out of town took a while. There had been a shower; the streets were wet. He was playing *Steeltown* by Big Country as he edged the Jaguar through the traffic; it seemed appropriate, in Carnegie's birthplace. He still felt fine. He knew he ought not to be driving, and he dreaded to think what he'd register on a breathalyser, but one – undrunk – part of him was watching and evaluating his driving; and he'd do, he'd get by, providing his concentration didn't slip and he wasn't unlucky. He wouldn't do it again, he told himself as he at last found a clear stretch of road, heading for the motorway. Just this time, because it is important after all.

And I'll be very careful.

It was dual carriageway here; he let the car leap forward, grinning as his back pressed into the seat. 'Oh I just love to hear that engine snarl,' he murmured to himself. He ejected the Big Country tape from the Nakamichi, frowning at himself for exceeding the speed limit. He let the car's nose drop again, slowed.

Something not too raucous and adrenalin-encouraging for the approach and traverse of the great grey bridge. *Bridge Over Troubled Water?* he thought to himself, grinning. Haven't had that in the car for yonks, Jimmy. He had Lone Justice, and Los Lobos' *How Will the Wolf*

Survive? on the other side of the tape; he picked it up, glanced at it as he approached the motorway itself. No, he wanted the Texican boys right now, and he didn't want to wait for it to spool back. Just have to be the Pogues then. *Rum Sodomy & the Lash*; fuck nice steady driving tunes. Nothing wrong with a bit of raucousness. Keeps you awake better. Just don't try to keep pace with the music all the time. There we go...

He joined the M90, heading south. The sky was dark blue above the patchy clouds. A very mild evening; hardly even cool. The road was still wet. He sang along to the Pogues and tried not to go too fast. He felt thirsty; there was usually a can of Coke or Irn Bru in the door pocket, but he'd forgotten to replace the last one. He was forgetting too much these days. He put his main lights on after a few people flashed him.

The motorway crested a hill between Inverkeithing and Rosyth, and he could see the road bridge's aircraft lights; sudden white flashes on the spires of the two great towers. Shame, really; he'd preferred the old red lights. He pulled over into the nearside lane to let a Sierra past, and watched the tail-lights disappear, thinking, You wouldn't get away with that normally, chum. He settled back in the seat, his fingers on the small steering wheel beating in time to the music. The road headed for a stepped cutting through the rocks which formed the small peninsula; the sign for North Queensferry flashed by. He might have gone down there, to stand under the rail bridge again, but there was no point in making this journey any longer than it had to be; that would be tempting fate, or irony at least.

What am I doing this for? he thought. Will this really make any difference? I *hate* people who drunk-drive; why the hell am I doing it? He thought about heading back, taking the road down to North Queensferry after all. There was a station there; he could park, take the train (in either direction) ... but he'd passed the last turn-off before the bridge. The hell with it. Maybe he'd stop on the far side, at Dalmeny; park there rather than risk this expensive paint job in the pre-Christmas Edinburgh rush. Come back for the damn thing in the morning and remember to set all the alarms.

The road cleared the cutting through the hills. He could see South Queensferry, the marina at Port Edgar, the VAT 69 sign of the distillery there, the lights of Hewlett Packard's factory; and the rail bridge, dark in the evening's last sky-reflected light. Behind it, more lights; the Hound Point oil terminal they'd had a sub-contract on, and, further away, the lights of Leith. The old rail bridge's hollow metal bones looked the colour of dried blood.

You fucking beauty, he thought. What a gorgeous great device you are. So delicate from this distance, so massive and strong close-up. Elegance and grace; perfect form. A quality bridge; granite piers, the best ship-plate steel, and a never-ending paint job ...

He glanced back at the roadway of the bridge as it rose slowly to its gentle, suspended summit. The surface was a little damp, but nothing to worry about. No problems. He wasn't going all that fast anyway, staying in the nearside lane, looking over at the rail bridge downstream. A light winked at the far end of the island under the rail bridge's middle-section.

One day, though, even you'll be gone. Nothing lasts. Maybe that's what I want to tell her. Maybe I want to say, No, of course I don't mind; you must go. I can't grudge the man that; you'd have done the same for me and I would for you. Just a pity, that's all. Go; we'll all survive. Maybe some good –

He was aware of the truck in front pulling out suddenly. He looked round to see a car in front of him. It was stopped, abandoned in the nearside lane. He sucked his breath in, stamped on the brakes, tried to swerve; but it was too late.

There was an instant when his foot was jammed down as hard as it would go on the brake, and when he'd pulled the wheel over as far as it would go in one twist, and he knew there was nothing else he could do. He would never know how long that instant was, only that he saw the car in front was an MG, and that there was nobody in it – a ripple of relief on a tsunami of fear – and that he was going to hit it, hard. He caught a glimpse of the number plate; VS something. Wasn't that a west coast number? The octagonal MG sign on the boot of the broken-down car floated closer to the Jaguar's mascotless snout as it dipped, dug in and started to skid all at once. He tried to go limp, to relax and just go with it, but with his foot jamming the brake to the floor that wasn't possible. He thought, You foo—

The customised white Jaguar, registration number 233 FS, smashed into the rear of the MG. The man driving the Jaguar was thrown forward and up as it somersaulted. The seat belt held but the small steering wheel came pistoning up to meet his chest like a circular sledgehammer.

Joseph Mills

Watch Out, the World's Behind You

'Remember the sabbath day, to keep it holy. Six days shalt thou labour, and do all thy work: But the seventh day is the sabbath of the Lord thy God: in it thou shalt not do any work, thou, nor thy son, nor thy daughter, thy manservant, nor thy maidservant, nor thy cattle, nor the stranger that is within thy gates; for in six days the Lord made heaven and earth, the sea, and all that in them is, and rested the seventh day; wherefore the Lord blessed the sabbath day and hallowed it.'

'And on the *third* day,' William said, '. . . we got The Dog.'

'The *Dug*,' Robert corrected.

William opened the Harrods Super Deluxe Photo Album at a double page spread headed THE DUG in individual silver letters. Beneath which: photos of Robert and The Dug, William and The Dug, Robert and William and The Dug.

'Oh and there's us seeing ye aff at Central Station.' Robert's ma pointed the picture out to her husband. Mr and Mrs Murray were sitting either side of William, on the big settee; in front of them a coffee table supporting a huge pile of photo albums. The table was a pretentious affair which William had dared Robert to buy. Instead of legs to support it, there was a big bronze Hercules shouldering the smoked glass. He seemed at that moment to be sweating. Certainly the bronze was glossier than usual. Robert sat opposite with an upside down view of the proceedings.

'That's a gid yin,' Mr Murray said, looking at the Central Station photo. 'Who took that wan?'

'That's one of mine,' said William. 'I take all the arrivals and departures; Robert takes all the important ones.' He slid the picture out of the tinted protective cellophane. 'Gorgeous, isn't it? You should see it on the projector.' He handed it over to Robert. 'We really *must* get the slides out later.'

Robert examined it. Yes, it really was a great picture: Robert's ma and da with The Dug on Renfield Street, at the corner of the station. William had stood well back up the street so he could get into the picture the big neon IRN BRU sign which William, a twenty-one-year-old Southerner, had decided was the nexus of all Glasgow, Scotland, just as the COKE sign on Times Square was the centre of New York, New York.

As always when he saw those neon night photos of Glasgow – even more so when it was the aerial postcards kaleidoscoping the city – Robert found it hard to believe that he was looking at the same place he'd grown up in, a place that corresponded much more, he was sure, to the old black and white tenement pictures they didn't seem to take as much any more. But William's picture really did, Robert remembered, look great on the slides, where you could lighten and darken the scene so it was even better than the real thing, like a memory.

'Remember,' William said, taking the photo back, 'that was the night we were going to London.'

'Of course I remember. It was only two months ago. Show them the new fire in the bedroom.'

William snapped the album shut.

'Do you want to see it now?'

Robert's parents dutifully stood up. They always deferred to William's English middle-class politeness; through enchantment, claimed William, through cultural intimidation, said Robert.

'We turned the fire on earlier so it could build up to its best effect,' said William as he led them away, turning back to Robert. 'It's probably warmer in there.'

Robert turned the photo album around and flicked through the pages.

God, all this nostalgia.

But he had been trying to remember something himself.

The kitchen door was open. He couldn't help noticing the overflowing laundry basket waiting to be emptied; the hoover plugged in and ready to rock; half-written letters and unpaid bills on the desk.

Fucking Sunday. The rubbish tip at the end of the week, where all the undesirable chores of life pile up, demanding immediate attention. How could anyone like a Sunday?

Sundays

Robert had always hated the last day of the week. He had got off to a bad start with Sunday right from the beginning. It first became distinct to him as The Day Before School, throughout which the week in prospect lingered at the back of the mind like a death sentence – whether he had homework to do or not. Having to do Sunday chores was bad enough – although compared to the nine to five of weekdays it should have seemed like heaven. Worse was the depressing realisation that the weekend had gone, all too quickly, and there was the huge five-day sentence in store before another. Curiously though, once he actually started serving the sentence it was never as bad as the anxiety that preceded it. But, of course, he forgot this every Sunday, as completely as a reincarnated soul is said to forget all its past lives.

Mass was always the low point of the day. Robert went dutifully, although he didn't know why he had to. Neither did his parents, but when he asked they told him: 'Because you're a Catholic.' His Protestant friends didn't have to go. They probably loved Sundays. They never had to make the big decision: Morning Mass or Evening. Neither alternative was attractive. If you left it till night time you had it hanging over you all day; if you got up early, the day was that much longer, *and* you had to mingle with all the Happy Sundays, the ones who went to mass because they enjoyed it, not, like the majority, because they were terrified of Hell.

Mr Murray always got up for the 10 a.m. show, which made Robert feel guilty, since Sunday was his da's only day of rest, the weekdays being spent taking the place of a piece of machinery in a factory, and Saturday afternoon working part-time in the betting shop. The countdown also began for Robert's da on a Sunday, the countdown to Friday night, when he would be in the pub, young.

Everybody's young on a Friday. Friday is blind youth – all that time in front of you! Saturday, with Sunday on the horizon is middle-age; Sunday, old age and death. Monday to Friday night is the dutiful pre-independence period, when we grudgingly do what others tell us, because we think it will be good for us in the long run.

Robert looked through the double glazing on to a late afternoon Glasgow Sunday. Depressing stillness. Nearly all the shops shut. An early winter sun dying painfully.

He left the lights down low and switched off the photo album lamp. It should have been one of those sultry Barry White/Luther Vandross soulful moments, like the ones they try to evoke in the ads for 20 LOVE SENSATIONS. Instead, being Sunday, the atmosphere cried out for a bland waiting-room soundtrack: sterile saxophones, tuneless muzak getting nowhere by intention. Cheap nostalgia.

Robert had another look at the Central Station picture of ma, da and

The Dug. William's furry glove was clearly visible by the edge of the photo. He could never quite take a flawless picture.

Something about the glove.

What *was* he trying to remember?

He dug out some of his old Woolworth's photo albums: Robert Abroad.

By leaving Glasgow Robert had managed to obliterate Sundays altogether, but the process had begun before that. Choosing jobs that involved shift work meant he worked through the weekends, getting paid double into the bargain. And there was the reward of sweet midweek holidays: getting up at eight in the morning just to go out and buy a big 'Sunday' breakfast and watch all the zombies at the bus stops. Somehow all the normal Sunday things became luxurious during the week: the long lazy meal, three hours over papers and magazines, black and white 40s films. So it wasn't, he discovered, that he hated not working. It was that all-encompassing Sunday rut that was so hard to endure, when everyone, no matter what the circumstance, is expected to come to an abrupt halt for twenty-four hours and take part in the great collective rest.

Take the worst aspects of Christmas and New Year – the obligation to walk slower, smile for nothing, reflect – multiply by fifty-two. Answer: Sunday. *The Day The Earth Stands Still.*

And not that he hated the prospect of a working week. At least not since he found a job that suited – the photojournalism that ultimately destroyed the Sabbath by taking Robert here there and everywhere until there were no more days of the week at all, just assignments and in between assignments.

Here there and everywhere eventually became New York, whose inhabitants, at least those worker ants that Robert mingled with, could ignore pneumonia if it got in the way of progress; so Sunday was a piece of cake – or rather, Sunday was Central Park jogging, performing, hosting, spectating, culturing, *doing.*

He made a lot of money there.

'There's a rerr heat aff that fire, Robert,' his ma said, coming out of the bedroom. But she still made for the big Real Coal affair in the living room, rubbing hands. They had obviously set the bedroom fire too low.

'We've made this smaller bedroom into a gym,' William was saying, leading Mr Murray there. The tour had only just begun. Robert's ma quickly left the fire to follow them.

The money embarrassed Robert, after all the early poverty – which he could now review with the same sense of detachment usually summoned up for his snapshots of Third World Misery.

Tenements

Snap One: the outside toilet, unlockable door hanging open, overflowing with used toilet paper and urine, beetles crawling up the walls. Snap Two: Brother, two sisters and parents sharing a cramped room (males) and kitchen (females). Snap Three: The same rooms two months later with the furniture rearranged to make it look new. Snap Four: The raganbone man handing over a few shillings for beans and cheese biscuits on the day before payday. Snap Five: His da, furtive, embarrassed, handing over the pay packet at work to Robert on Friday afternoon because they couldn't afford to wait till he got home.

Even though he had easily managed to buy his parents' council house for them, clear off all their debts and free them from money worries until the end of their days, Robert still felt guilty. He had more money than them and he always would have. If he gave them every penny he had they wouldn't know what to do with it. He could never make them as consumerist as he had become; as his generation and class was becoming he discovered on his return to Glasgow in the 80s. They were too old to get on that roundabout.

'What time is that now?' Robert could hear his da asking. All the clocks and watches in his parents' house were running either too fast or too slow, to varying degrees, so that you had to check all of them at one go to calculate the exact time. But only Mr and Mrs Murray knew the rates of imprecision, so the secret of time was theirs in their own home. Outside of it their watches were useless.

'It's only just after six,' William said.

He'll be worrying about missing the news, Robert guessed. Mr Murray was an absolute news junkie. He watched all the main programmes on all channels – one o'clock, five-forty, six, seven, nine, ten, *Newsnight*, and all the in-between bulletins, from TV AM to *Through The Night* on STV. Like so many working-class pensioners, untrained for a life of leisure, he had a thoroughly informed opinion on all those issues of the day he could do zero about. Except vote every five years, in a country that had been voting in huge Labour majorities throughout the decade and had been 'democratically' governed by the Tories for its troubles. So zero right enough.

Robert's da almost escaped back into the living room.

'Oh, but one last thing,' William stopped him. 'You must see in here.' He took them into the little studio they had set up: a dark room for Robert, and a wall of tape machines, synthesisers and video equipment for William. The plan had been that together they would create avant-garde audio-visual poems. But William hadn't counted on Robert's art burn-out from his years in Greenwich Village. As far as he was concerned, Lennon was right when he said, 'Avant-garde is French for shit.' So William had to settle for a video collage of Robert's best pictures, synchronised to William's beat. And thus was the creative fusion of their relationship achieved, not to William's complete satisfaction, but well within the time limit set for it.

Robert pitied his poor parents having to sit through that. And his sisters and bemused brothers-in-law seven days earlier. Embarrassed friends the week before that. This Remembrance Sunday was definitely becoming a fixed routine.

When had it begun? It must have been on the Anniversary. Four weeks ago. Six months they celebrated. To the day. According to plan. They were where they said they would be six months before. So it wasn't only a period of time together they were celebrating, but a success. A job well done.

It was definitely something about the early days Robert was trying to remember. Maybe as far back as Day One, the day they officially charted the beginning of their life together from; or further back still, the few weeks before that (which William chose to ignore), that limbo spent cajoling Robert into marriage, into bed for god's sake. The weeks that those who weren't there never believed existed.

No one who saw the sandy-haired twenty-one-year-old William with the stencilled-in stomach muscles would ever have imagined that he would have to *pursue* a reluctant Robert, twice his age, greying, balding and thickening all over. None of what friends Robert had left at the time believed it, any more than they believed his claim to have been celibate for the ten years before he met William. Celibate not just in any old decade, but in the fun-loving, hedonistic 80s, when the British were just beginning to learn about conspicuous consumption – or at least were beginning to learn to yearn for it. But it was true. And he wouldn't have believed it of himself in the 70s. When he went quite mad.

Robert's 70s

For a working-class Scot to make big money was reason enough for
merrymaking – they celebrate enthusiastically enough on factory wages
– to travel, even more uninhibiting. But to let loose a near virginal faggot
on The States Of Desire in the decade of The Golden Age – *well.* Robert
enjoyed The Dancers and The Dance to the full. To the extent of addiction
really. But being addicted to sex, love, drugs, money in those places at
that time was like being 'addicted' to tea or beer in Glasgow. You would
never have dreamed of looking at it as such, since the medicine was so
readily available, and nobody was asking you to watch the dosage.

Ironically, the one narcotic he did attempt to be Scots-thrifty with –
love – was the one that proved the hardest to kick. Sex, drugs, booze,
money were all consumed in copious amounts with never a thought to
the morning after. But he did try to economise on the currency of
Romance: the looks, gestures, declarations, tears and admissions, attempting to save something for some far off Right Time.

'Postponing happiness Robert, *really,*' William had said when he told
him all this. 'How *very* middle class.'

And of course the plan was doomed to failure. Love was the one thing
that couldn't be rationed or controlled, and the overdoses, withdrawal
pains and eventual immunity had ultimately led to his austere decade.
But it was the thing he gave least thought to that started him off on the
road to abstinence.

Sex had at first been easy, uncomplicated, fulfilling. And safe – until
the little bug arrived, whenever. Somehow he had been one of the lucky
ones, but if he hadn't tired eventually of the consequences of overindul-
gence the bug would certainly have found him too. For Robert got
everything going. Friends watching him prepare for a night on the town
would joke: They're out there waiting for you Robert, all those little
germs and bugs with the big red 'R' on their backs. He began to get fed
up with the increasing number of weekends which had to be endured in
agony before he could get hold of his doctor; days spent passing razor-
blades through the bladder, and clawing at red skin (why did he always
ignore crabs until it was too late); bedtimes spent drifting in and out of
nightmares at the thought of those creatures living off him, even after
he'd given in and shaved every hair off his caveman body. And come
Monday, the flesh-rending cures were just as bad – 'A mild stinging of a
transient nature' indeed. His doctor had begun to tire of Robert's

indulgence shortly before Robert did, signalling his lack of sympathy by yanking foreskin back, and demonstrating just how heavy-handed you could be with a cotton swab.

'I knew the Scots had to be famous for something,' he would complain sarcastically.

Robert was giving the Homeland a bad name. He decided to slow down. And when the physical illnesses were compounded by more severe emotional ones, he decided to stop altogether.

'He's dreaming of Alberrr again,' William said. The tour was over and his parents had been brought up to date on WillyRobertland. They brought tea in with them.

'It's no ferr leavin' William to do all this himself,' Mrs Murray said.

'Five minutes,' said Robert, 'and you'll have my undivided attention.' He locked himself in the bathroom.

His head was buzzing with unanswerable questions.

What am I trying to remember?

Why all this reminiscing?

What else is there to do on a Sunday?

Do angels spend eternity gazing down from heaven at their imperfect earthly shadows?

Longingly?

How Robert's 70s ended

1979: he was falling out of love with love. He had endured one too many hello/goodbyes; and all that other nonsense: please stay/better off without me, I/you need more space/time/relativity. He had experienced, directly and indirectly, too many emotional couplings, too many insights into the whys and wherefores of Romantic Love. Like a scientist nearing the end of an experiment, the data was becoming all too familiar, trial results repeating themselves over and over again. Far from rationing love, by the end he was consuming and processing it at an alarming rate. An attraction that could have sustained itself for several years at school in mystery and luxurious frustration was now digested and excreted in a week or a night, so efficient had his emotional metabolism become. No sooner did he begin some attachment than he rushed to see the end of it, rose in one hand, telescope in the other.

This state of affairs had come about through necessity. He had decided he needed to stop loving because he was too sensitive to romantic failure. The non-starters or enforced partings were bad enough. Even worse were those grey areas when agonizing choices had to be made: whether to maintain a difficult but intense relationship or not.

Torture.

It was then he wondered why everyone made all the fuss about sex and none about love. Why did authorities meticulously define sex crimes but ignore love in their law books. The consequences of sex – VD, pregnancy, AIDS – are so foreseeable and preventable that it's impossible for a consenting, careful partner to be unexpectedly affected by them. But how many emotional virgins are trapped by experienced cynics into passionate affairs, only to be dumped by the expert when he tires of what was, for him, a diversion, for the virgin, everything.

'Alberr' – Albert – had duped and dumped Robert. Had he been warned, he would have thought twice. Had someone said: You will fall in love with Albert, but he will never be able to fall in love with you, then he would have taken precautions. But he was not a consenting adult, and he bitterly told those who would listen that they should take the pretty police out of the toilets and put them in cafés and wine bars where love crimes were being committed every day.

Albert, contrary to William's belief, was not the major entanglement, simply the first of many disasters – those attractive intellectuals and artists who fascinated him with a language which seemed way above his head (until the same quoted authors turned up again and again, the same quotations); the models and B-movie actors who turned out to have brains in inverse proportion to beauty.

He learned. It became easier. And he began breaking hearts himself, knowingly and without consent. And he got sick of himself, after all those moralising Catholic teens. Anyone, it was now obvious, could be a puritan in a block of ice. And then he began forgiving himself, and all the others, and ended up feeling calm, all-knowing. And middle-aged. 'Another Brick in the Wall' was the appropriately bland tune that was number one the day he dramatically decided to have a rest from it all: New Year's Eve 1979. At a mad orgy of Village People lookalikes in New York. Which left him with yet more germs and bugs with the red 'R' on their backs; but this time the creatures were much more tenacious. Which, in retrospect, was a blessing in disguise: he would surely have fallen back into old habits but for the enforced three-month layoff. After which he realised that he did not miss the sex as much as he would have thought, told himself to grow up and get on with Other Things.

Robert's 80s

Success in his career intensified his resolve. The assignments were already mounting up since he switched from journalism to showbiz. All the contacts he'd made led to contracts for pre-production work on major movies. Making a small fortune became the biggest kick of all. And then he found himself in with one of the echoes of the Warhol crowd, where celibacy was chic in the early 80s, and you had all the drugs to help.

And just as the notion of dipping his toes back in the water emerged there were the first rumblings of the AIDS volcano and he decided to wait just that little bit longer till they got it sorted out. Then it got worse and he was convinced he had it. He had a test. It was negative, which was a surprise, a relief, a message. The doctors had their four-year plan for a vaccine or cure; he had a similar length plan for lifelong financial security. His plan worked, theirs didn't. They were still saying 'four years' almost a decade later. And throughout that decade the chance of moving from positive to full-blown moved from one in ten to nine in ten, and he decided he didn't trust his willpower, having never practised 'safe sex' in his life. Anyway, the rest would do him good.

No. It wasn't anything to do with that period either he was trying to remember. It was definitely to do with William and him and Day One.

Robert joined William in the living room. He was not, as Robert had feared, showing off their joint address book: look how many people we know! They had decided very early on that Good Friends were a must-have component of the population of their world.

Parents were in the kitchen. TV was on.

William handed Robert a cup of cold tea. 'What's with all the off-stage philosophising?'

'I don't know. I feel as though I've got a tape loop of The Robert Murray Story reeling through my head today. It's all your fault,' – he indicated the photo albums piled high – 'And all this grand tour nonsense.'

'Well we worked hard for it. Why not show it off?'

Robert sipped the cold tea and made a face. He sat down, back, and closed his eyes. William sat beside him, took his hand and rubbed it vigorously.

'Now, now. We don't want to lose you again. I know the Scots are supposed to be dour and impenetrable but this is ridiculous.'

Robert opened his eyes and sat up. 'Sorry. Sundays just make me feel so lazy.' He opened one of the earliest photo albums. 'I bet you didn't realise what you were taking on back then. I bet you thought: nothing else doing tonight, so I'll take on this old thing, even though he's twice my age, balding—'

'Attractively.'

'Greying—'

'With distinction.'

'And putting on weight all over.'

'Very attractively.'

'You make middle age sound ... attractive.'

'You make it sound like Lourdes.' William measured the considerable expanse of Robert's shoulders. 'I thought you were James Bond.'

'Only because you were in a Scottish gay bar.'

'No. It was the hairiness that did it. First I noticed the arms, then the bits peeking out over the top of the T-shirt. I thought: I bet he's got that fab Sean Connery chest. I could see you had the build. It doesn't matter how heavy you get with bones like yours.' He offered Robert a plate of cakes.

'I'm not into that type at all,' Robert said, taking the plate.

'*Now* you're not. What about before.'

'I suppose it's more attractive when you're younger. Come to think of it,' he smiled and licked all the cream out of a huge cake, 'I used to *love* Jean-Paul Belmondo when I was your age – those big French Kissing lips.' Robert had a repertoire of teases he could practise on William: the mention of anyone called Albert, of course; Albert cakes, Albert Square (through which any reference to *EastEnders* became suspect); *Alberto Balsam*, Prince Albert and any connectives; anything French.

'So you found Jean-Paul in New York and I found Sean Connery in Glasgow.'

' – as James Bond,' said Robert, opening a photo album. 'Life imitates Art.'

'Imitates life,' said William, pointing out a picture he had taken of Robert dressed up as Sean As Bond.

Robert studied the picture, feeling better about himself. Quite sexy: shirt and trousers tight in all the right places, good strong shoulders and neck, big dark-eyed glare. He could have come all over a picture like that twenty years ago, when he really was into the Jean-Pauls, Redfords, Newmans, and, well, almost anything older than he was. When the last thing he wanted was a fragile, middle-class English boy. The accent alone would have put him off at that time, when it was still associated with authority figures or Scots trying to act posh. But he lost those prejudices abroad, when he discovered you could be rich, educated *and* unpretentious. And the Socialist English were becoming defensive about the Scots' perceptions of everybody south of Manchester being Thatcherite yuppies. You could be sure their distaste for such people was one of the first things they let you know about themselves. It was certainly one of the first things Robert found out about William that first night.

How Robert's 80s ended

It was going to be just another night in the Waterloo. Robert had continued to frequent gay bars throughout his celibacy, with friends, a sister or two, his mother. The brother had long before joined the Yups down under with his Economics degree. (When asked if she had any children other than Robert his ma would invariably reply: 'Two girls and an insurance salesman.') It was all just a good drink and a scream in the 80s for Robert. If ever he felt the old urges return he could easily remind himself of the many benefits of celibacy, the principal of which was how much easier it was to relax in gay bars with no concerns about success or failure, no anxieties about looks or performance.

Ironically, predictably, this relaxed aura was transmissible and made Robert seem much more approachable than most of the other customers, whose assumed air of nonchalance was exposed as fake by their ever-attentive eyes and ears, their acknowledgement of every entrance and exit. So the greatest drawback of celibacy turned out to be the necessity of dodging the evening's drinking partner at closing time. He often felt like a pop star trying to escape after the concert at which he's just spent two hours giving the illusion of eternal availability. An illusion he would repeat with a different audience every night. If Robert didn't make good his escape, there was indignation bordering on violence. Especially with older, plainer types who were more pushy since they lacked the self-assurance of the attractive youths who thought all they had to do was wait patiently and they would be asked. So even if Robert hadn't already decided to join the party again he would have chosen to speak to William, the only youngster there that night.

'Do you remember the first night we met?' Robert asked William as his parents returned to the room.

'Oh God, do I!' William rolled his eyes theatrically, turning to Mrs Murray. Mr Murray had sat in front of the television.

'He starts rambling on about the Berlin Wall coming down, and how much everything was changing and he was stagnating, and if he didn't touch another human being soon he'd explode.'

'I was really drunk.'

'And after all that it was four weeks before I even saw him in his underwear.' William looked a bit embarrassed by what he had said, remembering the company. But Robert's da seemed engrossed in the religious TV programme, and his ma knew more than William did about that period, by virtue of the drink and gossip sessions Robert and she had indulged in since he came back from abroad.

'I was beginning to think you were going back with Gordon,' she said.

'No. There was no chance of that.' Robert turned to William. 'Gordon was just another person, he wasn't as special as I made out at the time … *he said defensively,*' he said defensively.

Gordon

'I met Gordon in Boston in '78. You've seen his picture.' He nodded towards the cupboard where the old Woolies albums were kept. 'I bumped into him – literally – a couple of months before we met. He was the first old affair I'd seen in years – one advantage of making all your mistakes in one continent then leaving it for another.'

It had been running into Gordon and his new lover that convinced Robert that his period of celibacy must end. He had turned the corner into Sauchiehall Street one night and come face to face with that stunning face, the wild blue eyes, gelled back black hair; Gordon's face, framed by night colours, seemed to have picked up only a few laughter lines on the journey from twenty-three to thirty-five. The night colours tinted the white T-shirt Gordon had on. And they were both wearing shorts at eleven p.m. And it was summer and hot and the whole scene brought back desire from the dead just like that.

They were on a European holiday, just off to Bennets. Their obvious happiness with each other intimidated him, filled him with jealousy. He declined the invitation to go to the dancing, but couldn't help kissing Gordon lightly on the cheek as they parted.

The collision seemed to have jogged Robert's senses back into action, because he found he was hypersensitive to Gordon's musky smell in the warm evening air, his firm tingly skin, aftershave taste.

Twenty minutes later he found himself moving along the Glasgow streets at jogging speed. He stopped, noticed he was almost at Partick, miles from where he was headed. This unthinking, heart racing, blind running had only ever happened twice before: the first time when he got the contract for his first job abroad, the second when he just missed being run over by a truck.

First night

'You looked so confident that first night,' William said. 'As though you owned the place.'

'He's spent enough money in it!' Robert's da said. 'He'd be as well fucking owning it!'

Robert ignored him. 'I was terrified. That's why I drank so much. As soon as I decided I was back on the market again all the old places became frightening. Even the good old Waterloo. It was like walking into your classroom on exam day – you know how you start noticing things you never did before–'

' – lopsided pictures,' said William helpfully. He was always amused when Robert began getting dramatic.

'And don't forget I was forty-three, not thirty-three. I was afraid I'd wasted the best years of my life.'

'That was a great film,' Robert's da said. They were singing hymns on the TV.

'Liza Minnelli!' said William. 'That's how we got talking.'

'She wasn't in it,' said Mr Murray.

'Judy Garland, yer thinking of,' said Mrs Murray.

'No her either,' Mr Murray said. 'It wizny that kinda film.'

'No. Robert had just put a Liza Minnelli record on the juke box. "Losing

My Mind." And I said, Oh that was great on *Top of the Pops.* And he said—'

'The best thing since "Starman".'

'Another great film,' said Mr Murray. 'Jeff Bridges—'

' – Who's a doll,' said William. 'Anyway, that's how we got talking, about this record. I said I had been really disappointed when it went down the chart from six to seven since I had been listening to the top forty specially because I thought it was going up to number one.'

'And I had been listening to the same show, with the same thought, and we both realised we'd been experiencing the exact same emotion the year before at exactly the same time. Me in Glasgow, he in London.'

'What did we do after the Waterloo?' said William.

'Burger Bar,' said Robert's da. 'Heard it.'

'Just you keep watching the priest on the telly telling ye what to do,' said Robert. There was the usual pious figure of the cloth, dispensing moronically simplistic parables in a condescending voice.

'God, who the hell do they think they're talking to?' Robert said.

'*Me,*' said William.

'You're not telling me you get anything from that.'

'Who would you rather be listening to – the Marxist Minister for the God-awful truth, no matter how depressing?' Robert's da was nodding in agreement. 'I mean they're not doing any harm. At worse they're just telling nice fairy stories to cheer people up.'

'Proves my point,' said Robert. 'You tell children fairy stories; why do they have to make it so obvious they're talking down to you? You don't talk to an adult like that – or an equal.' Robert was sounding more bothered than he actually was. He had only brought the subject up because it was the one thing that William and his da could gang up on him about, giving at least the illusion of some sort of bond.

'We're not back to the old tyrannical middle classes abusing their power over the lower orders are we – like in the Burger Bar.'

The Burger Bar Story

'He looks at the menu,' Robert said. Mr Murray turned off the TV.

'He looks at the menu, and there's about a dozen dishes with little pictures next to them. And one without a picture. So he has to ask about the *one dish* that isn't pictured. I mean it was something like deep fried pineapple burger and he had no intention of ordering it. He just had to show that he was the paying customer and was going to make sure he got everything he was due. That's so middle class. Why do you always have to remind yourself of whatever power you have?'

'Firstly,' said William, 'It's not middle class, it's me – my sister's just like you – she would eat a pickled rat if it was put down in front of her rather than "make a fuss". Secondly – what about the working class? What about the chip shop?'

'That was just one particular guy – to use your own argument.'

The Chip Shop Story

'We'd been standing in this chip shop ten minutes before the assistant showed his face. I could see him in the back telling his pals, "Am no servin' him." Then when somebody else came in he served him before us!'

'It was that stupid fairyish pink scarf roon yer neck.'

'That widnae go doon too well in Argyle Street, William,' said Mrs Murray.

'That's right: it was gay prejudice, nothing to do with class.'

'Rubbish. As soon as I open my mouth in this place I get the big chip on the shoulder treatment.'

'Or chip shop in this case,' said Robert. 'It's your Englishness that annoys us anyway, not your class. You're paranoid.'

'So are you.'

'I'm surprised you ever agreed to meet each other again after all that,' said Robert's da, irritated. He hated listening to stupid arguments, unless he'd started them himself.

'I didn't think we'd ever meet again,' said William. 'If we couldn't even manage to buy something to eat together without an argument . . .'

'But strangely enough we met again the very next night. In the very same place.'

'Well I had just moved to Glasgow, obviously I was going out every night to get familiarised. What was your excuse?'

'The heating broke down.'

'Like tonight?' said Mrs Murray, rubbing her hands.

'Oh I'm sorry,' said William, jumping over to the central heating gauge. 'I keep forgetting the coal fire isn't enough for a room this size.' He glanced over at Robert. 'And the weather here is so changeable.'

'A wee dram's the quickest way I know of heating the blood,' Mrs Murray said. 'Right Robert?'

'A wee hauf,' Robert agreed, was the very thing.

They opened a bottle of whisky. And spent twenty minutes arguing about what music to put on. Mrs Murray (The Carpenters) won, but she couldn't get over the novelty of the CD remote control and kept changing tracks.

'God this is what Robert and me did the second time I met him – argued all night about what records to put on the juke box. Then I asked him to go home with me and he refused. I thought I wasn't his type.'

'You were, sort of, by then.'

'You thought he looked like that boy, the blond one in *Brideshead Revisited.*'

One of the problems with Robert's alcoholic confidences with his mother was that she often regurgitated his confessions with scant regard for accuracy. Especially on her third whisky.

'No. I never liked him – the look of him, anyway. Too smug and spoiled.'

'That poor boy,' said Mrs Murray, shaking her head. 'Oh the drink's a terrible thing.' She downed her third whisky and headed for the bottle.

'That was the only thing that was interesting about him,' said Robert, 'the drink, the melancholy, rebellion.' He turned to William, smiling. 'Until I saw that programme I didn't realise that middle-class people drank.'

'Oh, come on.'

'Well, I didn't know they *enjoyed* it.' He was laughing but William was getting annoyed. He knew Robert didn't give a toss about creed, class or country but he couldn't stop arguing back if there was someone else there.

'He wasn't middle, he was upper class. And anyway he can hardly be said to have enjoyed it–'

'Don't take that aff!' Mrs Murray shouted. Mr Murray had gained control of the CD player and was trying to eject Carpenters and inject *Cabaret.* Mrs Murray went over to stop him.

'So,' William said. 'You were hoping I'd be a tearaway lapsed Catholic alcoholic–'

' – with a *huge* dowry.'

'But it surely wasn't the fact I wasn't that put you off sex.'

As he said this, William had a terrible sense of *déjà vu.* He knew that Robert's reply would be and what he would say after that. This had all been sorted out the day they agreed to go with each other, but more and more they were going over old ground, as when they had re-examined the perfectly functional old fire in the bedroom with ever greater scrutiny, willing some hitherto unnoticeable imperfection on it.

'I was terrified of AIDS – especially with a Londoner, and a youngster. I mean, *I* could never have been careful at your age.'

'But we "youngsters" are more scared of people your age. And what's London compared to Edinburgh?'

'That's mostly straights. Anyway, Edinburgh's not Glasgow. You're as bad as the Yanks. They think Scotland is part of England.'

'It's a miracle right enough we did eventually get together.'

Day One

William was convinced that the only thing holding Robert back from taking the plunge into the whirlpool of sex and love was the simple fact that he had left it so long. But it took him four weeks to persuade Robert. Four weeks of endless drunken conversations in the pub or at Robert's home. Conversations with no conclusions. Robert would always put the case for the defence first (which was basically his life story up to that point). But before William could state his own case, before Robert even finished his own story, the alcohol gradually made useful conversation impossible: in the pub the music demanded ever more attention, at home, drinking spirits, they simply fell asleep. Court was adjourned.

Of course, William eventually worked out another line of attack. He realised that Robert was intentionally dodging the issue. On those nights at Robert's house when they drank themselves into a stupor he would awake, thirsty, at dawn, to find himself shoeless and blanketed, lying on the couch; Robert's bedroom door was firmly closed. He never tested it, but he would not have been surprised to find it had been locked as well. Robert never lost control no matter how much he drank. He knew exactly what he was doing.

After four weeks of this, William stopped Robert's monologue one night and condensed the rest of it into a few sentences, ending with 'and now it's 1990 and you have a very simple choice to make.' They were at home. It was only nine o'clock. Robert had no choice but to listen.

'Don't tell me you can't have sex with me because of AIDS. You know I've been on the scene less than a year, that I've never done anything stupid. What do you want – a certificate to prove it? Even if we both had tests we could go right out the next day and get fucked stupid. You know we can do it safely. Or we can do anything; and trust each other. I'm willing to believe your story. You have to trust me.' William refilled Robert's whisky glass. 'Coping so far?'

'Go on.'

'But I think that sex is the least of it. I think you've just got so used to being in control, of living this bland, safe lifestyle that you're afraid to rock the boat again. You're afraid you won't be able to cope with the emotional traumas that were difficult even fifteen years ago, when you were more confident that something else would make itself available. Am I on the right lines?'

'More or less. But you don't realise how *tired* you can get. It's different when you're younger, jumping into affairs with your eyes shut. But I know what's going to happen. It takes a lot of energy.'

'You see that's your problem. You think you know everything.' William was annoyed. 'How can you possibly know me? How can you be so sure things will continue to happen the way they always have?'

'OK. You've stated the problem. What's the solution?'

'As I said before. You have a simple choice to make. You can *never* have a sexual emotional relationship with someone else again. Or you can. That's what it boils down to in the end. Your circumstances aren't going to change in any way to make it easier – quite the reverse, as you know yourself. Either you take a chance or you don't. If you don't take a chance now you're saying you're never going to take a chance ever. For the rest of your life.'

The fact that Robert's fear had nothing to do with AIDS was proved that night when they finally did have sex, and 'safety' was the last thing on either of their minds. They both awoke the next morning, lips bruised and numb, dicks blistered and swollen ('Wish they would stay that way').

'I think that was a perfect lesson in how *NOT* to do it safely,' Robert said. William smiled: he knew now that Robert trusted him. They stayed in bed till it got dark. Which, in fact, was only two hours after they awoke. But a romantic two hours.

And productive. They made up there and then their plan for the next six months. They would get married. They *were* married. They would make this marriage work by leaving nothing to chance. Pooling their respective experiences they decided on all the factors that were essential for the perfect relationship and worked out a battle plan. Communication was, as all good agony aunts tell us, essential. Day One was, conveniently enough, since they were in bed and had exhausted the only other two things you could do there, Talk Day. Each had to tell the other of all previous affairs: good, bad, mediocre and why, why, why.

'What do you want more than anything in a lover?' William asked first.

'I better not say. It's too sugary.'

'Tell All. Remember?'

'I hope you're not diabetic.'

'Come on. I'm getting interested.'

'Shh,' Robert said, and drew back a curtain above the bed headboard which revealed windows throbbing beneath a rain waterfall. 'Someone to listen to the rain with.'

'You're right. It is too sugary.'

'I want a divorce.'

Day Two

On the Second Day, William bought Robert a little toy James Bond ring. Robert got him a Wizard of Oz watch. 'It was the nearest – portable – thing to Liza Minnelli I could get. You either wear this on your wrist for the rest of your life or the video of *Cabaret* round your neck.' William read out the inscription on the back: For giving me the heart, the brain, *de noive.*

Day Three

On the Third Day they were moving William's stuff into Robert's house when a pack of mangy mongrels crossed their path, examining William's possessions with dirty paws and scarred noses.

'Dugs!' screamed William in his best Billy Connolly accent. 'And look – there *is* always a three-legged one.' Sigh. 'A genuine three-legged Glasgow dug.'

On the Third Day Robert brought home Rusty, The Dug. And William saw that it was good. And the creators of this little world were beginning to feel pretty damn pleased with themselves.

And then it was fixing up the house, installing the gym, helping each other get fit, the abortive attempt at co-creativity (whose relative failure was really a success, of course, since it showed them the parameters of their life together), the dual record, book, video collection, the search for friends who could fill the spaces their divergent interests created – musicians for William, journalists for Robert. And so on. For six months. And on the Seventh they rested.

The Seventh

On the Seventh they looked at photo albums. And drank whisky. Which was running out, according to Mr Murray. Robert served up the last drops to his parents before they left. The TV was on again. Iraq's invasion of Kuwait. 'The beginning of the Holy War,' Mr Murray was explaining, that he had been predicting all along would be The Next Thing.

'Thank God you're not taking pictures in places like that any more,' Mrs Murray said. Robert wondered if he was thankful. If he'd rather be taking pictures than looking at them.

After the parents had gone, Robert shoved on an old Velvet Underground LP. On the record player.

'What's wrong with the CD?' William asked.

'I want to hear the LP, with all the clicks and pops. Twenty-three years I've had this, and I can remember where every scratch came from. You'll never be able to do that with a CD. They're *too* perfect.'

William brought in coffee from the kitchen. 'You won't be saying that about me in twenty-three years. I bet people would buy CD versions of other people if they could, to keep them perfect.' He began to sing:

'*Another fine edition of you oh yeah, and boys will be boys will be—*'

'Roxy Music. *For Your Pleasure*. 1973.' Young people were always impressed when you could identify pop stuff, Robert found.

'I must have heard it in the nursery,' William said.

It did not escape Robert's attention that William had just made his first ageist joke at his expense. He hoped they weren't going to get into one of those stupid Sunday night arguments again. The last few weeks it had been the same: too much drink, days of tension and irritability building up, demanding an outlet. Who started it this time? Me, Robert decided. Stupid dragging out The Velvets like that. He kept forgetting these days how much the age thing affected William in a way it no longer did him, despite the occasional (occasionally truthful) protestation to the contrary. He'd gone out with all age groups and had come to realise how little it really mattered if the older guy had more experience/knowledge/lovers than you; or the young guy less lines/body fat/grey hairs.

That remark about a 'new model'. Maybe William really did think he was getting bored with him. The daft thing was, this was supposed to be the best time, the secure time.

Robert had announced, excited, on Day One that they should send out invitations there and then for their first anniversary party to prove how confident they were that they would last together. Then he got carried away and the party was to be only six months away and by then William would have a job, the house would be sorted, everything would be just right. And it was. But before everything was just right, Robert would have been more sensitive to William's anxieties. He wouldn't have started blabbing on about Twenty-Three Years Ago without reassuring him that Now was better than ever.

There was a long, loud crackle from the speakers.

'*Watch out the world's behind you,*' sang William, along with the record: 'Sunday Morning'. Surely a contradiction in terms, he thought. He too was examining the discontent in the air.

Complacent; resting; retired. He never thought he would ever associate those words with Robert. But he couldn't help thinking that something *was* behind them. And it was Robert's obsessive fault: ten years' indulgence, ten years of deprivation. Six months 'getting things right'. For what? So they could spend the rest of the time getting it wrong? But it was his fault too. He had worked at least as hard as Robert and rested as hard now too.

Strange, William thought: Robert had always refused to take those big, sickening wedding photos with all the diverse generations, grudges and jealousies, frozen together in false unanimity. And now here they all were trapped in the same glossy charade: the lovers, their parents, relatives, animals, friends, possessions, labelled and stuck in a scrapbook, preserved in transparent foil.

Work.

Rest.

There would have to be a bit of creative fusion again. This time he would insist.

In the bathroom getting ready for bed it occurred to Robert at last what it was he'd been trying to remember all day. He had awoken that morning anxious and paranoid, thinking that things were slipping away from William and him. Then, like the marriage guidance counsellors tell you to do, he began to try to remember the thing that had been good about their relationship in the early, successful days, the thing that had convinced Robert to go with William, despite so many misgivings. He got into bed still trying to remember this thing, feeling almost as anxious as he had that first night together.

Then William did the thing he had done that first night that convinced him.

He held his hand.

It wasn't one of those perfunctory, Oh-it'll-be-all right-you'll-see squeezes you give to a dying relative; William had turned round in bed, in that moment just before sleep, with no conscious effort, and entwined all five fingers round Robert's. It was a prehistoric, animal gesture, which requested and granted reassurance in one movement. It startled Robert now the way it had done that first night. It said: *Come on.* I belong here and you know it. It was a gesture that existed before language, one that revealed its inadequacies. A picture worth a thousand words. Or a month of Sundays.

Robert looked down at the hand. William was still wearing the Wizard of Oz watch.

It was Monday.

Part Three

Irvine Welsh

from *Trainspotting*

The First Shag in Ages

They had spent most of the day getting stoned out of their boxes. Now they are getting pished in a tacky chrome-and-neon meat market. The bar is fussy in its range of overpriced drinks, but it misses by miles the cocktail-bar sophistication it is aiming at.

People come to this place for one reason, and one reason only. However, the night is still relatively young, and the camouflage of drinking, talking and listening to music does not, at this point, seem too obvious.

The dope and drink has fuelled Spud and Renton's post-junk libidos to a rampant extent. To them, every woman in the place seems to look outstandingly sexy. Even some of the men do. They find it impossible to focus on one person who might be a potential target, as their gaze is constantly arrested by someone else. Just being here reminds the both of them how long it has been since they've had a shag.

– If ye cannae git a Joe McBride in this place, ye might as well call it a day, Sick Boy reflects, his head bobbing gently to the sounds. Sick Boy can afford detached speculation, speaking, as he generally does in such circumstances, from a position of strength. Dark circles under his eyes attest to the fact that he has just spent most of the day shagging these two American women, who are staying at the Minto Hotel. There is no chance of either Spud, Renton or Begbie making up a foursome. They are both going back with Sick Boy, and Sick Boy alone. He is merely gracing them with his presence.

– They've got excellent coke man. Ah've never had anything like it, he smiles.

– Morningside speed man, Spud remarks.

– Cocaine ... fuckin garbage. Yuppie shite. Although he has been clean for a few weeks, Renton has the smack-head's contempt for all other drugs.

– My ladies are returning. Ah'll have to leave you gentlemen to your sordid little activities. Sick Boy shakes his head disdainfully, then scans the bar with a haughty, superior expression on his face. – The working classes at play, he derisively snorts. Spud and Renton wince.

Sexual jealousy is an in-built component in a friendship with Sick Boy.

They try to imagine all the cocaine-crazed sex games he'll be playing with the 'manto at the Minto', as he refers to the women. That is all they can do, imagine. Sick Boy never goes into any details about his sexual adventures. His discretion, however, is only observed in order to torment his less sexually prolific friends rather than as a mark of respect for the women he gets involved with. Spud and Renton realise that three-in-a-bed scenes with rich tourists and cocaine are the preserve of sexual aristocrats like Sick Boy. This shabby bar is their level.

Renton cringes as he observes Sick Boy from a distance, thinking about the bullshit that is inevitably coming out of his mouth.

At least with Sick Boy, it is to be expected. Renton and Spud are horrified to note that Begbie has bagged off. He is chatting to a woman who has quite a nice face, Spud thinks; but a fat arse, Renton bitchily observes. Some women, Renton considers with a malicious envy, are attracted to the psychopathic type. They generally pay a high price for this flaw, leading horrible lives. As an example, he smugly cites June, Begbie's girlfriend, who is currently in hospital having their child. Proud that he didn't have to go far to make his point, he takes a swig of his Becks, thinking: I rest my case.

However, Renton is going through one of his frequent self-analytical phases and this smug complacency soon evaporates. Actually, this woman's arse isn't that fat, he reasons. He notes that he is operating his self-deception mechanism again. Part of him believes that he is by far the most attractive person in the bar. The reason for this being that he can always find something hideous in the most gorgeous individual. By focusing on that isolated ugly part, he can then mentally nullify their beauty. On the other hand, his own ugly bits don't bother him, because he is used to them, and in any case, can't see them.

Anyway, he is now jealous of Frank Begbie. Surely, he considers, I can't fall any further from grace. Begbie and his new found love are talking to Sick Boy and the American women. These women look pretty smart, or at least their tan-and expensive-clothes packaging does. It nauseates Renton to see Begbie and Sick Boy playing the great mates, as all they generally do is to get on each other's tits. He notes the depressing haste with which the successful, in the sexual sphere as in all others, segment themselves from the failures.

– That's you n me left, Spud, he observes.

– Likesay, eh, yeah ... it looks that way, catboy.

Renton likes it when Spud calls other people 'catboy' but he hates being referred to in that way himself. Cats make him sick.

– Ye ken, Spud, sometimes ah wish ah wis back oan the skag, Renton says, mainly, he thought, to shock Spud, to get a reaction from his hash-stoned, wasted face. As soon as it comes out, though, he realises that he actually means it.

– Hey, likesay, fuckin heavy man ... ken? Spud forces some air out from between tightened lips.

It dawns on Renton that the speed they'd done in the toilet, which he'd denounced as shite, is now taking effect. The problem with being off smack, Renton decides, is that they are stupid, irresponsible fuckers, taking anything that they can get their hands on. At least with smack, there is no room for all the other crap.

He has an urge to talk. The speed is a good lap ahead of the dope and alcohol in his system.

– Thing is though, Spud, whin yir intae skag, that's it. That's aw yuv goat tae worry aboot. Ken Billy, ma brar, likes? He's jist signed up tae go back intae the fuckin army. He's gaun tae fuckin Belfast, the stupid cunt. Ah always knew that the fucker wis tapped. Fuckin imperialist lackey. Ken whit the daft cunt turned roond n sais tae us? He goes: Ah cannae fuckin stick civvy street. Bein in the army, it's like bein a junky. The only difference is thit ye dinnae git shot at sae often bein a junky. Besides, it's usually you that does the shootin.

– That, eh, likesay, seems a bit eh, fucked up like man. Ken?

– Naw but, listen the now. You jist think aboot it. In the army they dae everything fir they daft cunts. Feed thum, gie the cunts cheap bevvy in scabby camp clubs tae keep thum fae gaun intae toon n lowerin the fuckin tone, upsettin the locals n that. Whin they git intae civvy street, thuv goat tae dae it aw fir thumsells.

– Yeah, but likesay, it's different though, cause ... Spud tries to cut in, but Renton is in full flight. A bottle in the face is the only thing that could shut him up at this point; even then only for a few seconds.

– Uh, uh ... wait a minute, mate. Hear us oot. Listen tae whit ah've goat tae say here ... what the fuck wis ah sayin ... aye! Right. Whin yir oan junk, aw ye worry aboot is scorin. Oaf the gear, ye worry aboot loads ay things. Nae money, cannae git pished. Goat money, drinkin too much. Cannae git a burd, nae chance ay a ride. Git a burd, too much hassle, cannae breathe withoot her gittin oan yir case. Either that, or ye blow it, and feel aw guilty. Ye worry aboot bills, food, bailiffs, these Jambo Nazi scum beatin us, aw the things that ye couldnae gie a fuck aboot whin yuv goat a real junk habit. Yuv just goat one thing tae worry aboot. The simplicity ay it aw. Ken whit ah mean? Renton stops to give his jaws another grind.

— Yeah, but it's a fuckin miserable life, likesay, man. It's nae life at aw, ken? Likesay whin yir sick man … that is the fuckin lowest ay the low … the grindin bones … the poison man, the pure poison … Dinnae tell us ye want aw that again, cause that's likesay, fuckin bullshit. The response packs a bit of venom, especially by Spud's gentle, laid-back standards. Renton notes he's obviously touched a nerve.

— Aye. Ah'm talkin a loaday shite. It's the Lou Reed.

Spud gives Renton the kind of smile that would make old wifies in the street want to adopt him like a stray cat.

They clock Sick Boy preparing to leave with Annabel and Louise, the two Americans. He'd spent his obligatory half hour boosting Beggar's ego. That is, Renton decides, the sole function of any mate of Begbie's. He reflects on the insanity of being a friend of a person he obviously dislikes. It was custom and practice. Begbie, like junk, was a habit. He was also a dangerous one. Statistically speaking, he reflects, you're more likely to be killed by a member of your own family or a close friend, than by anyone else. Some tubes surround themselves with psycho mates imagining that this makes them strong, less likely to get hurt by our cruel world, when obviously the reverse is true.

On his way out the door with the American women, Sick Boy turns back, raising one eyebrow at Renton, Roger Moore style, as he vacates the bar. A speed-induced flash of paranoia hit Renton. He wonders if perhaps Sick Boy's success with women is based on his ability to raise the one eyebrow. Renton knows how difficult it is. He'd spent many an evening practising the skill in front of the mirror, but both brows kept elevating simultaneously.

The amount of drink consumed and the passage of time conspired to concentrate the mind. With an hour to go before closing time, somebody you wouldn't think about getting off with becomes acceptable. With half an hour left, they are positively desirable.

Renton's wandering eyes now keep stopping at this slim girl with straight, longish brown hair, slightly turned up at the edges. She has a good tan and delicate features tastefully picked out by makeup. She wears a brown top with white trousers. Renton feels the blood leave his stomach when the woman puts her hands in her pockets, displaying visible panty lines. That is the moment for him.

The woman and her friend are being chatted up by a guy with a round, puffy face, and an open-neck shirt which strains at his bloated guts. Renton, who has a cheerfully undisguised prejudice against over-weight people, takes the opportunity to indulge it.

— Spud: deek the fat radge. Gluttonous bastard. Ah dinnae go fir aw that shite aboot it bein a glandular or metabolic thing. Ye dinnae see any fat bastards on tv footage fi Ethiopia. Dae they no huv glands ower thair? Stroll on. Spud just responds to his outburst with a stoned smile.

Renton thinks the girl has taste, because she cold-shoulders the fat guy. He likes the way she does it. Assertively and with dignity, not making a real arse out of him, but letting him know in no uncertain terms that she isn't interested. The guy smiles, extends his palms and cocks his head to the side, accompanied by a volley of derisive laughter from his mates. This incident makes Renton even more determined to talk to the woman.

Renton gestures to Spud to move over with him. Hating to make the first move, he is delighted when Spud starts talking to her mate, because Spud never normally takes the initiative in that way. The speed's obviously helping, however, even though he is somewhat distraught to hear that Spud is rabbiting on about Frank Zappa.

Renton tries an approach he considers is relaxed but interested, sincere but light.

— Sorry tae butt intae yir conversation. Ah jist wanted tae tell ye that ah admired yir excellent taste in kicking that fat bastard intae touch just now. Ah thought that ye might be an interesting person tae talk tae. If you tell us tae go the way of the fat bastard, ah won't be upset though. Ah'm Mark, by the by.

The woman smiles at him in a slightly confused and condescending way, but Renton feels that it at least beats 'fuck off' by a good few furlongs. As they talk, Renton begins to get self-conscious about his looks. The speed kick is running down a little. He worries that his hair looks daft, dyed black, as his orange freckles, the curse of the red-headed bastard, are prominent. He used to think that he looked like the Ziggy Stardust era Bowie. A few years ago, though, a woman told him that he was a dead ringer for Alec McLeish, the Aberdeen and Scotland footballer. Since then the tag had stuck. When Alec McLeish hangs up his boots, Renton has resolved to travel up to Aberdeen for his testimonial as a token of gratitude. He remembers an occasion where Sick Boy shook his head sadly, and asked how some cunt who looked like Alec McLeish could ever hope to be attractive to women.

So Renton has dyed his hair black and spiked it in an attempt to shed the McLeish image. Now he worries that any woman he gets off with will laugh her head off when he removes his clothes and she is confronted with ginger pubes. He has also dyed his eyebrows, and thought about dyeing his pubic hair. Stupidly, he had asked his mother for her advice.

— Dinnae be sae fuckin silly, Mark, she told him, nippy with the hormonal imbalance caused by the change in life.

The woman is called Dianne. Renton thinks that he thinks she is beautiful. Qualification is necessary, as his past experiences have taught him never to quite trust his judgement when there are chemicals racing around in his body and brain. The conversation turns to music. Dianne informs Renton that she likes the Simple Minds and they have their first mild argument. Renton does not like the Simple Minds.

— The Simple Minds huv been pure shit since they jumped on the committed, passion-rock bandwagon of U2. Ah've never trusted them since they left their pomp-rock roots and started aw this patently insincere political-wi-a-very-small-p stuff. Ah loved the early stuff, but ever since *New Gold Dream* thuv been garbage. Aw this Mandela stuff is embarrassing puke, he rants.

Dianne tells him that she believes that they are genuine in their support of Mandela and the movement towards a multiracial South Africa.

Renton shakes his head briskly, wanting to be cool, but hopelessly wound up by the amphetamine and her contention. — Ah've goat auld NME's gaun back tae 1979, well ah did huv but ah flung thum oot a few years back, and ah can recall interviews when Kerr slags off the political commitment by other bands, n sais that the Minds are just intae the music, man.

— People can change, Dianne counters.

Renton is a little bit taken aback by the purity and simplicity of this statement. It makes him admire her even more. He just shrugs his shoulders and concedes the point, although his mind is racing with the notion that Kerr has always been one step behind his guru, Peter Gabriel, and that since Live Aid, it's become fashionable for rock stars to want to be seen as nice guys. However, he keeps this to himself and resolves to try to be less dogmatic about his views on music in the future. In the larger scheme of things, he's thinking, it doesn't matter a fuck.

After a while, Dianne and her pal go to the bogs to discuss and assess Renton and Spud. Dianne can't make her mind up about Renton. She thinks he's a bit of an arsehole, but the place is full of them and he seems a bit different. Not different enough to go overboard about though. But it was getting late ...

Spud turns and says something to Renton, who can't hear him above a song by The Farm, which, Renton considers, like all their songs, is only listenable if you're E'd out of your box, and if you're E'd out of your box it would be a waste listening to The Farm, you'd be better off at some rave freaking out to heavy techno-sounds. Even if he could have heard Spud, his brain is now too fucked to respond, taking a well-earned rest from holding itself together to talk to Dianne.

Renton then starts talking personal shite to a guy from Liverpool who's up on holiday, just because the guy's accent and bearing remind him of his mate Davo. After a while, he realises that the guy is nothing like Davo and that he was wrong to disclose to him such intimacies. He tries to get back to the bar, then loses Spud, and realises that he's well and truly out of it. Dianne becomes just a memory, a vague feeling of intent behind his drug stupor.

He goes outside to get some air and sees Dianne about to enter a taxi on her own. He wonders with a jealous anguish if this means that Spud's bagged off with her mate? The possibility of being the only one not to bag off horrifies him, and sheer desperation propels him unselfconsciously towards her.

— Dianne. Mind if ah share yir Joe Baxi?

Dianne looks doubtful. — Ah go to Forrester Park.

— Barry. Ah'm headed in that direction masel, Renton lied, then told himself: Well, ah am now.

They talked in the taxi. Dianne had had an argument wi Lisa, her pal, and decided to go home. Lisa was, as far as she knew, still bopping on the dancefloor with Spud and some other cretin, playing them off against each other. Renton's dough was on the other cretin.

Dianne's face took on a cartoon sour look as she told Renton what a horrible person Lisa was, cataloguing her misdemeanours, which to him seemed petty enough, with a venom he found slightly disturbing. He was appropriately crawling, agreeing that Lisa was all the selfish pricks under the sun. He changed the subject, as it was bringing her down, and that was no good to him. He told her jocular stories about Spud and Begbie, sanitising them tastefully. Renton never mentioned Sick Boy, because women liked Sick Boy and he had an urge to keep the women he met as far away from Sick Boy as possible, even conversationally.

When she was lighter-hearted he asked her if she minded if he kissed her. She shrugged, leaving him to determine whether this indicated indifference or an inability to make up her mind. Still, he reasoned, indifference is preferable to outright rejection.

They necked for a bit. He found the smell of her perfume arousing. She thought that he was too skinny and bony, but he kissed well.

When they came up for air, Renton confessed that he didn't live near Forrester Park, he only said that so that he could spend more time with her. In spite of herself, Dianne felt flattered.

— Do you want to come up for a cup of coffee? she asked.

— That would be great. Renton tried to sound casually pleased rather than rapturous.

— Only a coffee mind, Dianne added, in such a way that Renton struggled to determine what sense she was defining terms in. She spoke slyly enough to put sex on the agenda for negotiation, but at the same time assertively enough to mean exactly what she said. He just nodded like a confused village idiot.

— We'll have to be really quiet. There's people asleep, Dianne said. This seemed less promising, Renton thought, envisaging a baby in the flat, with a sitter. He realised that he'd never done it with anybody that had had a baby before. The thought made him feel a bit strange.

While he could sense people in the flat, he couldn't pick up that distinctive smell of pish, puke and powder that babies have.

He went to speak. — Dia . . .

— Ssh! They're asleep, Dianne cut him off. — Don't wake them, or there'll be trouble.

— Whae's asleep? he whispered nervously.

— Ssh!

This was disconcerting for Renton. His mind raced through past horrors experienced first hand and from the accounts of others. He mentally flipped through a grim database which contained everything from vegan flatmates to psychotic pimps.

Dianne took him through to a bedroom and sat him down on a single bed. Then she vanished, returning a few minutes later with two mugs of coffee. He noted that his was sugared, which he usually hated. but he wasn't tasting much.

— Are we going to bed? she whispered with a strangely casual intensity, raising her eyebrows.

– Eh … that would be nice … he said, almost spluttering out some coffee. His pulse raced and he felt nervous, awkward and virginal, worrying about the potential effects of the drug and alcohol cocktail on his erection.

– We'll really have to be quiet, she said. He nodded.

He quickly pulled off his jumper and t-shirt, then his trainers, socks and jeans. Self-conscious of his ginger pubes, he got into the bed before sliding his underpants off.

Renton was relieved to get hard as he watched Dianne undress. Unlike him, she took her time, and seemed completely unselfconscious. He thought that her body looked great. He couldn't help a football mantra of 'here we go' playing repeatedly in his head.

– Ah want to go on top of you, Dianne said, throwing back the covers, exposing Renton's ginger pubes. Fortunately, she didn't seem to notice. Renton was pleased with his cock. It seemed so much bigger than usual. This was probably because, he realised, he'd become accustomed to not seeing it erect. Dianne was less impressed. She'd seen worse, that was about it.

They began touching each other. Dianne was enjoying the foreplay. Renton's enthusiasm for this was a pleasant change from most of the guys she'd been with, but she felt his fingers go to her vagina and she stiffened and pushed his hand away.

I'm well lubricated enough, she told him. This made Renton feel a bit numb, it seemed so cold and mechanistic. He even thought at one stage that his erection had started to subside, but no, she was lowering herself onto it, and it was, miracle of miracles, holding firm.

He groaned softly as she enclosed him. They started moving slowly together, penetrating deeper. He felt her tongue in his mouth and his hands were lightly feeling her arse. It seemed, it had been, so long; he thought that he was going to come straight away. Dianne sensed his extreme excitement. Not another useless prick, please no, she thought to herself.

Renton stopped feeling her and tried to imagine that he was shagging Margaret Thatcher, Paul Daniels, Wallace Mercer, Jimmy Savile and other turn-offs, in order to bring himself off the boil.

Dianne took the opportunity, and rode herself into a climax, Renton lying there like a dildo on a large skateboard. It was only the image of Dianne biting into her forefinger, in an attempt to stifle the strange squeaks she made as she came, her other hand on his chest, that caused Renton to get there himself. Even the thought of rimming Wallace

Mercer's arse couldn't have stopped him by that time. When he started to come, he thought that he'd never stop. His cock spurted like a water pistol in the hands of a persistently mischievous child. Abstinence had made the spermcount go through the roof.

It had been close enough to a simultaneous climax for him to have described it in such a way, had he been one to kiss-and-tell. He realised the reason he'd never do this was because you always get more stud credibility from the enigmatic shrug and smile, than from divulging graphic details for the entertainment of radges. That was something he'd learned from Sick Boy. Even his anti-sexism was therefore overlayed with sexist self-interest. Men are pathetic cunts, he thought to himself.

As Dianne dismounted him, Renton was drifting off into a blissful sleep, resolving to wake in the night and have more sex. He would be more relaxed, but also more active, and would show her what he could do, now that he had broken this bad run. He compared himself to a striker who had just come through a lean spell in front of goal, and now couldn't wait for the next match.

He was therefore cut to the bone when Dianne said: — You have to go.

Before he could argue, she was out of the bed. She pulled on her pants to catch his thick spunk as it started to leave her and trickle down the insides of her thighs. For the first time he began to think about unprotected penetrative sex and the HIV risk. He'd taken the test, after he'd last shared, so he was clear. He worried about her, however; thinking that anyone who would sleep with him would sleep with anybody. Her intention to banish him had already shattered his fragile sexual ego, turning him from cool stud back into trembling inadequate in a depressingly short time. He thought that it would just be his luck to get HIV from one shag after sharing needles, although never the large communal syringes favoured in the galleries, over a period of years.

— But kin ah no stey here? He heard his voice sound puny and biscuit-ersed, in tones that Sick Boy would mock mercilessly, had he been present. Dianne looked straight at him and shook her head. — No. You can stay on the couch. If you're quiet. If you see anybody, this never happened. Put something on.

Once again, self-conscious of his incongruously ginger pubic hair, he was happy to oblige.

Dianne led Renton through to the couch in the front room. She left him shivering in his underpants before she returned with a sleeping-bag and his clothes.

— Sorry about this, she whispered, kissing him. They necked for a bit and he started to get hard again. When he tried to put his hand inside her dressing gown she stopped him.

– Ah have to go, she said firmly.

Dianne departed, leaving Renton feeling empty and confused. He got onto the couch, pulled the sleeping-bag around him and zipped up. He lay awake in the dark, trying to define the contents of the room.

Renton imagined Dianne's flatmates to be dour bastards who disapproved of her bringing someone back. Perhaps, he decided, she didn't want them to think that she would pick up a strange guy, bring him back and just fuck him like that. He bolstered his ego by telling himself that it was his sparkling wit and his unique, if flawed, beauty, which had swept her resistance away. He almost believed himself.

Eventually he fell into a fitful sleep, characterised by some strange dreams. While he was prone to such weird dreams, these disturbed him as they were particularly vivid and surprisingly easy to recall. He was chained to a wall in a white room lit by blue neon, watching Yoko Ono and Gordon Hunter, the Hibs defender, munching on the flesh and bones of human bodies which lay dismembered on a series of large formica-topped tables. They were both hurling horrendous insults at him, their mouths dripping with blood as they tore at strips of flesh and chewed heartily between curses. Renton knew that he was next on the tables. He tried to do a bit of crawling to 'Geebsie' Hunter, telling him that he was a big fan of his, but the Easter Road defender lived up to his uncompromising tag and just laughed in his face. It was a great relief when the dream changed and Renton found himself naked, covered in runny shite and eating a plate of egg, tomato and fried bread with a fully clothed Sick Boy by the Water of Leith. Then he dreamt that he was being seduced by a beautiful woman who was wearing only a two-piece swimsuit made out of Alcan foil. The woman was in fact a man, and they were fucking each other slowly through different holes in their bodies which oozed a substance resembling shaving foam.

He woke to the sound of cutlery clinking and the smell of bacon frying. He caught a glance of the back of a woman, not Dianne, disappearing into a small kitchen which was just off the living room. Then he felt a spasm of fear as he heard a man's voice. The last thing Renton wanted to hear, hungover, in a strange place, wearing only his keks, was a male voice. He played at being asleep.

Surreptitiously, under his eyelids, he noted a guy about his height, maybe smaller, edging into the kitchen. Although they spoke in low voices, he could still hear them.

— So Dianne's brought another friend back, the man said. Renton didn't like the slightly mocking intonation on the term 'friend'.

— Mmm. But shush. Don't you start being unpleasant, and jumping to the wrong conclusions again.

He heard them coming back into the front room, then leaving it. Quickly, he pulled on his t-shirt and jumper. Then he unzipped the bag and threw his legs off the couch and jumped into his jeans, almost in one movement. Folding the sleeping-bag neatly, he stuck the settee's displaced cushions back where they belonged. His socks and trainers were smelly as he put them on. He hoped, but in a futility that was obvious to him, that nobody else had noticed.

Renton was too nervy to feel badly wasted. He was aware of the hangover though; it lurked in the shadows of his psyche like an infinitely patient mugger, just biding its time before coming out to stomp him.

— Hello. The woman who wasn't Dianne came back in.

She was pretty with nice big eyes and a fine, pointed jawline. He thought he recognised her face from somewhere.

— Hiya. Ah'm Mark, by the way, he said. She declined to introduce herself. Instead, she sought more information about him.

— So you're a friend of Dianne's? Her tone was slightly aggressive. Renton decided to play safe and tell a lie which wouldn't sound too blatant, and therefore could be delivered with some conviction. The problem was that he had developed the junky's skill of lying with conviction and could now lie more convincingly than he told the truth. He faltered, thinking that you can always take the junk out of the punter before you can the junky.

— Well, she's more a friend of a friend. You know Lisa?

She nodded. Renton continued, warming to his lies, finding the comforting rhythm of deceit.

— Well, this is actually a wee bit embarrassing. It wis ma birthday yesterday, and ah must confess ah got pretty drunk. Ah managed tae lose ma flat keys and ma flatmate's in Greece oan holiday. That wis me snookered. I could have just went home and forced the door, but the state ah wis in, ah just couldnae think straight. Ah would probably have got arrested for breaking intae ma own flat! Fortunately, ah met Dianne, who was kind enough to let me sleep on the couch. You're her flatmate, right?

— Oh … well, in a way, she laughed strangely, as he struggled to find out the score. Something was not right.

The man came and joined them. He nodded curtly at Renton, who smiled weakly back.

— This is Mark, the woman told him.

— Awright, the guy said, noncommittally.

Renton thought that they looked about his age, perhaps a bit older, but he was hopeless with ages. Dianne was obviously a bit younger than the lot of them. Perhaps, he allowed himself to speculate, they had some perverse parental feelings for her. He had noted that with older people. They often try to control younger, more popular and vivacious people; usually due to the fact that they are jealous of the qualities the younger people have and they lack. These inadequacies are disguised with a benign, protective attitude. He could sense this in them, and felt a growing hostility towards them.

Then Renton was hit by a wave of shock which threatened to knock him incoherent. A girl came into the room. As he watched her, a coldness came over him. She was the double of Dianne, but this girl looked barely secondary school age.

It took him a few seconds to realise that it was Dianne. Renton instantly knew why women, when referring to the removal of their makeup, often say that they are 'taking their faces off'. Dianne seemed about ten years old. She saw the shock on his face.

He looked at the other couple. Their attitude to Dianne was parental, precisely because they *were* her parents. Even through his anxiety, Renton still felt such a fool for not seeing it sooner. Dianne was so much like her mother.

They sat down to breakfast with a bemused Renton being gently cross-examined by Dianne's parents.

— So what is it you do, Mark? the mother asked him.

What he did, at least work-wise, was nothing. He was in a syndicate which operated a giro fraud system, and he claimed benefit at five different addresses, one each in Edinburgh, Livingston and Glasgow, and two in London, at Shepherd's Bush and Hackney. Defrauding the Government in such a way always made Renton feel virtuous, and it was difficult to remain discreet about his achievements. He knew he had to though, as sanctimonious, self-righteous, nosey bastards were everywhere, just waiting to tip off the authorities. Renton felt that he deserved this money, as the management skills employed to maintain such a state of affairs were fairly extensive, especially for someone struggling to control a heroin habit. He had to sign on in different parts of the country, liaise with others in the syndicate at the giro-drop addresses, hitch down at short notice to interviews in London on a phone tip-off from Tony, Caroline or Nicksy. His Shepherd's Bush giro was in doubt now, because he had declined the exciting career opportunity to work in the Burger King in Notting Hill Gate.

— Ah'm a curator at the museums section of the District Council's Recreation Department. Ah work wi the social history collection, based mainly at the People's Story in the High Street, Renton lied, delving into his portfolio of bogus employment identities.

They looked impressed, if slightly baffled, which was just the reaction he'd hoped for. Encouraged, he attempted to score further Brownie points by projecting himself as the modest type who didn't take himself seriously, and self-deprecatingly added: — Ah rake around in people's rubbish for things that've been discarded, and present them as authentic historical artefacts ay working people's everyday lives. Then ah make sure that they dinnae fall apart when they're oan exhibition.

— Ye need brains fir that, the father said, addressing Renton, but looking at Dianne. Renton couldn't make eye-contact with the daughter. He was aware that such avoidance was more likely to arouse suspicion than anything else, but he just couldn't look at her.

— Ah wouldnae say that, Renton shrugged.

— No, but qualifications though.

— Aye, well, ah've goat a degree in history fae Aberdeen University. This in fact, was almost true. He'd got into Aberdeen University, and found the course easy, but was forced to leave mid-way through the first year after blowing his grant money on drugs and prostitutes. It seemed to him that he thus became the first ever student in the history of Aberdeen University to fuck a non-student. He reflected that you were better making history than studying it.

— Education's important. That's what we're always telling this one here, said the father, again taking the opportunity to make a point to Dianne. Renton didn't like his attitude, and liked himself even less for this tacit collusion with it. He felt like a pervert uncle of Dianne's.

It was just as he was consciously thinking: Please let her be sitting her Highers, that Dianne's mother smashed that prospect of damage limitation.

— Dianne's sitting her O Grade History next year, she smiled, — and French, English, Art, Maths and Arithmetic, she continued proudly.

Renton cringed inside for the umpteenth time.

— Mark's not interested in that, Dianne said, trying to sound superior and mature, patronising to her parents, the way kids deprived of power who become the 'subject' of a conversation do. The way, Renton shakily reflected, that *he* did often enough, when his auld man and auld doll got started. The problem was Dianne just sounded so surly, so like a child, she achieved the opposite effect of the one she was aiming for.

Renton's mind was working overtime. *Stoat the baw, they call it. Ye kin git put away fir it. Too right ye kin, wi the key flung away. Branded a sex criminal; git ma face split open in Saughton oan a daily basis. Sex Criminal. Child Rapist. Nonce. Short-eyes.* He could hear the psycho lags now, cunts, he reflected, like Begbie: – Ah heard thit the wee lassie wis jist six. – They telt me it wis rape. – Could've been your bairn or mine. Fuck me, he thought, shuddering.

The bacon he was eating disgusted him. He'd been a vegetarian for years. This was nothing to do with politics or morality; he just hated the taste of meat. He said nothing though, so keen was he to keep in the good books of Dianne's parents. He drew the line at touching the sausage, however, as he reckoned that these things were loaded with poison. Thinking of all the junk he had done, he sardonically reflected to himself: You have to watch what you put into your body. He wondered whether Dianne would like it, and started sniggering uncontrollably, through nerves, at his own hideous *double entendre*.

Feebly, he attempted to cover up by shaking his head and telling a tale, or rather, re-telling it. – God, what an idiot ah am. Ah wis in some state last night. I'm not really used to alcohol. Still, I suppose you're only twenty-two once in a lifetime.

Dianne's parents looked as unconvinced as Renton by the last remark. He was twenty-five going on forty. Nonetheless, they listened politely. – Ah lost ma jacket and keys, like ah wis saying. Thank god for Dianne, and you folks. It's really hospitable of you to let me stay the night and to make such a nice breakfast for me this morning. Ah feel really bad about not finishing this sausage. It's just that ah'm so full. Ah'm no used tae big breakfasts.

– Too thin, that's your trouble, the mother said.

– That's what comes ay living in flats. East is east, west is west, but home is best, the father said. There was a nervous silence at this moronic comment. Embarrassed, he added: – That's what they say anyway. He then took the opportunity to change the subject. – How are ye going tae get into the flat?

Such people really scared the fuck out off Renton. They looked to him as if they hadn't done anything illegal in their lives. No wonder Dianne was like the way she was, picking up strange guys in bars. This couple looked so obscenely wholesome to him. The father had slightly thinning hair, there were faint crow's feet at the mother's eyes, but he realised that any onlooker would put them in the same age bracket as him, only describing them as healthier.

— Ah'll jist huv tae force the door. It's only oan a Yale. Silly really. Ah've been meaning tae get a mortice for ages. Good thing ah didnae now. There's an entry-phone in the stair, but the people next door will let me in.

— Ah could help you out there. I'm a joiner. Where do you live? the father asked. Renton was a little fazed, but happy that they had bought his bullshit.

— It's no problem. Ah was a chippy masel before ah went tae the Uni. Thanks for the offer though. This again, was true. It felt strange telling the truth, he'd got so comfortable with deception. It made him feel real, and consequently vulnerable.

— Ah wis an apprentice at Gillsland's in Gorgie, he added, prompted by the father's raised eyebrows.

— Ah ken Ralphy Gillsland. Miserable sod, the father snorted, his voice more natural now. They had established a point of contact.

— One ay the reasons ah'm no longer in the trade.

Renton went cold as he felt Dianne's leg rubbing against his under the table. He swallowed hard on his tea.

— Well, ah must be making a move. Thanks again.

— Hold on, ah'll just get ready and chum you intae town. Dianne was up and out of the room before he could protest.

Renton made half-hearted attempts to help tidy up, before the father ushered him onto the couch and the mother busied herself in the kitchen. His heart sank, expecting the ah'm-wide-fir-your-game-cunt line when they were alone. Not a bit of it though. They talked aboot Ralphy Gillsland and his brother Colin, who, Renton found himself pleased tae hear, had committed suicide, and other guys they both knew from jobs.

They talked football, and the father turned out to be a Hearts fan. Renton followed Hibs, who hadn't enjoyed their best season against their local rivals; they hadn't enjoyed their best season against anybody, and the father wasted no time in reminding him of it.

— The Hibbies didnae do too well against us, did they?

Renton smiled, glad for the first time, for reasons other than sexual ones, to have shagged this man's daughter. It was amazing, he decided, how things like sex and Hibs, which were nothing to him when he was on smack, suddenly became all-important. He speculated that his drug problems might be related to Hibs poor performances over the eighties.

Dianne was ready. With less makeup on than last night, she looked about sixteen, two years older than she was. As they hit the streets, Renton felt relieved to be leaving the house, but a little embarrassed in case anyone he knew saw them. He had a few acquaintances in the area, mainly users and dealers. They would, he thought, think that he'd gone in for pimping if they came across him now.

They took the train from South Gyle into Haymarket. Dianne held Renton's hand on the journey, and talked incessantly. She was relieved to be liberated from the inhibiting influence of her parents. She wanted to check Renton out in more detail. He could be a source of blow.

Renton thought about last night and wondered chillingly what Dianne had done, and with whom, to gain such sexual experience, such confidence. He felt fifty-five instead of twenty-five, and he was sure that people were looking at them.

Renton looked scruffy, sweaty and bleary in last night's clothes. Dianne was wearing black leggings, the type so thin that they almost looked like tights, with a white mini-skirt over them. Either of the garments, Renton considered, would have sufficed on its own. One guy was looking at her in Haymarket Station as she waited for Renton to buy a *Scotsman* and a *Daily Record*. He noticed this and, strangely enraged, he found himself aggressively staring the guy down. Perhaps, he thought, it was self-loathing projected.

They went into a record shop on Dalry Road, and thumbed through some album sleeves. Renton was now pretty jumpy, as his hangover was growing at a rapid rate. Dianne kept handing him record sleeves for examination, announcing that this one was 'brilliant' and that one 'superb'. He thought that most of them were crap, but was too nervy to argue.

— Awright Rents! How's ma man? A hand hit his shoulder. He felt his skeleton and central nervous system briefly rip out of his skin, like wire through plasticine, then jump back in. He turned to see Deek Swan, Johnny Swan's brother.

— No bad Deek. How ye livin? he responded with an affected casualness which belied his racing heartbeat.

— No sae bad boss, no sae bad. Deek noted that Renton had company, and gave him a knowing leer. — Ah've goat tae nash likes. See ye aroond. Tell Sick Boy tae gie us a bell if ye see um. The bastard owes us twenty fuckin bar.

— You n me both mate.

– His patter's pure abysmal. Anywey, see ye Mark, he said turning to
Dianne. – See ye doll. Yir man here's too rude tae introduce us. Must be
love. Watch this punter. They smiled uneasily at this first external
definition of them, as Deek departed.

Renton realised that he had to be alone. His hangover was growing
brutal, and he just couldn't handle this.

– Eh, look Dianne ... ah've goat tae nash. Meetin some mates doon in
Leith. The fitba n that.

Dianne raised her eyes in knowing, weary acknowledgement,
accompanying this gesture with what Renton thought were some strange
clucking noises. She was annoyed that he was going before she could ask
him about hash.

– What's your address? She produced a pen and a piece of paper from
her bag. – No the Forrester Park one, she added, smiling. Renton wrote
doun his real address in Montgomery Street, simply because he was too
out of it to think up a false one.

As she departed, he felt a powerful twinge of self-loathing. He was
unsure as to whether it came from having had sex with her, or the
knowledge that he couldn't possibly again.

However, that evening he heard the bell go. He was skint so he was
staying in this Saturday night, watching *Braddock: Missing in Action 3* on
video. He opened the door and Dianne stood before him. Made-up, she
was restored in his eyes to the same state of desirability as the previous
evening.

– Moan in, he said, wondering how easily he'd be able to adjust to a
prison regime.

Dianne thought she could smell hash. She really hoped so.

Robert Alan Jamieson

The Last Black Hoose

There was no feeling like it. Nothing to compare with this feeling of homecoming, of the moment when the steamer would come round the headland at the Knab and reach the shelter of the harbour, of the moment when his feet would be upon the pier. This was his place, this island. *Bon hoga.* The ferry ploughed northwards, courting the shadows of the wintery peat hills around Cunningsburgh and Quarff. He turned away from the rail and went below to fetch his bags from the cabin.

When he reached the purser's office laden down with his cases, a number of fellow passengers had already assembled with their luggage around them, like walls to keep the strangeness of travelling out. The boy sat down on a long red vinyl seat and waited for the engines to slow. That was the sign that the berth was in sight. One or two people he knew were standing nearby but he couldn't be bothered with talking, so he took a book from his bag and pretended to read. Out the porthole through the salt spray he saw the lighthouse at Bressay slip silently past.

The door in the ship's side was open and he pushed forward in the disorderly queue. The tide was high and the boat well above the pier. Through the gap, over the shoulder of the deckhand making ready to take the gangway from below, he saw his father, wandering slightly bent-backed along the pier, looking up at the faces on board.

The boy took hold of his luggage and got in the line of people going ashore. In front of him, a huge fat man with two great cases and another two bags slung over his shoulders kept getting stuck between the narrow sides of the gangway. The steps rattled and swayed as he went down. The damp harbour air was like a wash under a cold tap.

His father stepped forward to meet him, a welcome on his face. It was four months since he'd last been home. Fæder's large calloused hand slapped him on the shoulder.

— Boy, fu is du?

— Aaricht. An you?

The polite form of the pronoun, reserved for social superiors and the plural. His father gestured sameness and moved off towards the van.

— An hoo's da University gyaain, dan?

University. The word was alien here, as this world was alien there. The two tongues in the boy's head struggled for space, seeking after individuation. He didn't answer, but shrugged. Together they walked from the pier to the car park. Opening the back door of the van to put his cases inside, the smell of unwashed wool rose powerfully to meet him. It was the smell of his father's work, shocking and familiar to him at the same time. Rolls of hessian sacks used for packing the wool lay in the middle of the metal floor. He shoved them out of the way, put his bags inside and tried to close the door, but the lock sprang open. His father signalled him out of the way, and shut it with a flourish, as a forklift whined by on its way to unload the steamer.

Inside the van, his father spoke.

– Aald Robbie o' Snusquoy de'ed last nicht. I met da doctor on da wye here.

– Robbie? The boy thought of the house at Snusquoy, the last black hoose in the toonship. The caddy lamb under the stove, the wet peats in the porch, the hens traiking in and out through the open doors. The two sisters, one of them that couldn't talk and the other that wouldn't, at least not unless it was absolutely unavoidable. They said that she just pointed to the things she wanted in the shop.

– We'll hæ t'gying t'da funeral, his father asserted, drumming his fingers on the steering wheel, while he waited for the exit from the car park to clear.

– Ja.

The boy would go. Robbie had been a kind man, despite the family's straitened circumstances, contributing to all the collections, always giving the bairns a shilling or two if he was down from Snusquoy at the Post Office. He had the respect of the folk, even them that most abhorred the filth they lived in at Snusquoy. The boy could hear him yet, hooting down on the awe-filled peerie faces staring up at the tall ragged figure with the silver in his hand: *Buy yoursels a bit o chocolate. It's good stuff you ken, keeps oot da caald.* Never with a patronising tone like some, or with a warning to be good, but always with the same short inhalation of breath as might precede the sharing of a secret, followed by the almost surreptitious passing of the coin.

Fæder cleared his throat and lit a cigarette.

– Dær'll be gød turnoot, mark du me. He wis weel lækit wis aald Robbie.

The boy felt no shock at this death. He had experienced many, as the community grew older and the houses fell vacant. Crofts were signed

over and amalgamated into larger units by the few that had the energy
or the vision for a better way of living. But the number of folk was
dropping away, and the boy knew that communities could die. That had
been the fate of his mother's birthplace, when the car and van replaced
the boat as mode of transport. And just the previous year, she had gone
with the others, leaving the north end of the house a mausoleum, full of
all her things that no one in the family had the heart to throw away.

The van traced a two-tyre pattern on the dewy road to the west. It was
early and only the odd car passed on its way to the toon and the work.
The boy knew the bends in the road with his eyes shut. As a child, he
had often kept them closed as a test of memory. The sequence of these
rolling motions was a sign of return.

It would be difficult telling his father that he wasn't going back to
Edinburgh. It would come as a kind of rejection of his mother's will. She
had so much prized that education, which she as a girl from a poor
crofting family during the war could not aspire to. But the boy knew that
he would have to do it. He glanced at his father's face to see if there
might be present some clue as to the right approach.

The face was as it had been, for almost as long as he could remember.
Heavy pendulous skin hanging from cheekbones lineless, broken only
by a soft fleshy mouth and bulbous nose. The eyes bright to the point of
becoming opaque. Only the white hair marked it as older, though that
was thick as it had ever been and still swept back in a curve established
years ago by a hair cream long discarded. The soft mouth opened.

—I wis trying t'tink whit'n an age o man Robbie wis, he frowned. Then
grinning, — Fir aa da dirt dey lived in, yon Snusquoy folk ir no døn bad. I
mean dær's aald Frankie, he wis seeventy-tree, and Robbie widna been
muckle less. An bæth Annie an Jessie ir been draain da pension fir
twartree year noo. Hit mak's de tink, sn it? Dær's some dat'll live in spite
o demsels an idders – he hesitated – weel I canna help tinkin o dy pør
midder, boy, never drank a drap, never even smokkit a fag and she never
even saa fifty. Quhile aald Robbie's sookin awa on a bottle o horse
lineament.

— Horse lineament? He drank dat?
— Ach weel so some fok say. Did du never hear o dat?

Astonished, the boy turned away to gaze out the side window as the
van climbed up the side of the hill of Weisdale, through pale sunlight
now filtering through the foggy morning. The shapes of the many tiny
islands lying in the mouth of the voe formed a grey blue abstract puzzle
which his memory sought to complete.

The last miles home passed silently. Just inside the hill dykes of the toonship, they passed the house at Snusquoy. The doctor's car was outside. The boy looked in the but end window and saw the solitary bare lightbulb, the only speck of contact with the world of electrical marvels. A black and white sheepdog came tearing out from the porch and chased snarling after the van until it was outpaced.

— Damn føl dug, said Fæder.

The boy looked back to the dog, where it had stopped in the middle of the road, still directing an occasional bark after them.

— Dey hæ næ use fir it noo. Hit'll be better aff if dey hæ it pittin doon.

The van pulled up at the side of their house. It looked shabbier than it had, even four months before. The honeysuckle which had wrapped itself around the porch was gone, lying hunched into a great ball of stem and leaf at the side of the house.

— Whit happened t'dis?

— Ach, it cam doon wi da last gæl. I never hed ony time t'see t'it.

They went into the but-end and took their jackets off. Fæder emptied the tea-pot and put a kettle on the rayburn to boil. The boy went to the door, saying he would take his bags to his room up the stair.

Once outside with the door closed, he didn't mount the stair, but hesitated. He opened the north end door. Everything was as it had been, save for an increase in the dust. The photograph of Grobsness still hung above the fireplace, next to the old American clock. On the mantel stood the photo of her as a young woman, a picture that had always intrigued him because in it she still had her own teeth. Furniture, clothes, ornaments, all lay as it had four months before. He stood a moment taking in the sight, then closed the door behind him and went up the stairs with his bag.

Fæder had made the tea when he got back down to the but end. He was listening to the eight o'clock news. They ate from a packet of biscuits while the radio voice told them what the world was like today. Fæder was silent. Maybe he knew the boy had been in for a look.

— I'll hæ t'gying. I've somebody comin wi oo, he said, standing up.

— I'll gie you a haand, the boy offered.

His father fetched him out a pair of overalls from the cupboard and they went out the back door, up the brae to the old byre, now bereft of kye. It was here that Fæder worked, sorting out the wool clips from the crofts and packing them up for shipping to the mainland mills.

The morning had come good. The sun shone clear and bright now. The sea was still and the rush of waves from the nearby beach was soothing. Fæder stopped and looked out over the meadow land. The boy did the same. He knew every undulation of the treeless landscape intimately, could have drawn it from memory as quick as a glimpse.

In the distance a tractor was at work, with two figures perched on the planter, setting tatties. The stillness of the morning allowed the distant sound to echo across the thin coastal strip of arable land.

– Du can hear da bell ringin on da planter, boy, Fæder said as he lit a cigarette, and stood a moment staring into space.

– Aathing's aaricht is it, wi da University. Du's been very quiet aboot it, he asked.

Surprised, the boy couldn't answer immediately. Fæder sensed the problem, it was clear. The boy sighed.

– It's juist dat, weel I'm no saa sure its richt fir me.

– Richt fir de? Surely du means is du richt fir it? Fir du's da wan dat'll hæ t'change, no hit.

– I dønna ken if I can.

Fæder laughed. – Aabody can change, my boy. An maist o wis hæ tæ. Du's næ different in dat.

He stared at him as if he was giving a backward pupil a necessary lesson. The boy blushed.

– Bit dønna let it happen tae de if du's no ready. Da mær times du bends, da mær brittle du gits. Du's young yit. Tak du dy time.

A small blue van approached, and came to a stop outside the byre. The back doors were tied with a bit of rope and between them the sacks of wool bulged out. A woman got out the driver's door.

– Mimie, is dis de? I wis expectin Lowrie.

– He's no been weel, man, she answered.

– Sam aald trouble?

– Ja ja, juist yon weary back o his.

She walked round to the back doors and began unfastening the rope.

– I see dir settin tatties roond here already, she observed.

Fæder grinned. – Ja. Trang wirkin fok roond here, no læk yon Glimmerwick crood.

Mimie laughed. She turned to the boy. – Sam aald Bobby. Alwis pullin da leg.

They carried the bags one by one into the shed and started weighing, hooking them up onto a balance hanging from a rafter. The smell of the animals was strong. Fæder claimed he knew the breeds by that alone.

He sniffed and spoke.

– Blackface an Cheviot again dis year, Mimie?

She made a face and snorted. – Ja, ja, but du kens, boy, du gits sicna size o lambs.

– Coorse bruck o oo, though.

They agreed an overall weight, to be graded later, and Fæder settled back on the bags of wool to get the news.

– Did du hear, lass, aald Robbie o'Snusquoy's de'ed.

– Aald Robbie?

– Ja. Last nicht it wis.

– Weel, dang me, I never tocht he wis still livin. He most a been a terrible age?

– Seeventy plus, I reckon.

– Is dat richt? An him still livin in yon aald black hoose.

Fæder nodded. – Black aaricht. Da last teckit røf roond here.

– Hed he ony fæmily?

– Twa sisters still itida hoose.

– Nane o dem merried?

– Na, nane o dem ever merried. Guid kens whit'll come o dem noo. En o dem's a dummy, an da idder en, tho she can spæk, says precious little. Hardly gying oot o da hoose, da pair o dem. I canna see dat dey'll lat dem gying on livin yondroo noo dat Robbie's gien.

Fæder went with Mimie to the van. The boy stayed in the byre. When Fæder came back they started sorting the clip, the boy opening the bags and emptying the contents onto the floor, while his father threw the fleeces onto different piles. They worked silently until the last bag was spilled out. Fæder stooped to pick up a fleece which was rolled up tight like the others, but which was clearly different from its colour and its web.

– Well, weel weel, he muttered. – Wid du look at dat.

He unrolled it and held it up to the beam of light coming through the small sash window. Here and there, peat dust trapped in the fibres gave it a faint reddish tinge. When it was opened out fully the boy saw in it a pattern so naturally perfect that he pictured a piece of lace work. Certain areas of the fleece were clumped into little peaks, while in others the strands of wool were drawn out so thinly as to be virtually transparent. The pattern of these occurrences was beautiful.

– See? Even in da worst clip du sometimes fins wan. Pure Shetland dat. No a drap o cross near it. And turning he laid it carefully in a place by itself, under the window. The boy stared at it for a while. – Beautiful, he said, not thinking.

The work over, Fæder leaned back against the door of the byre.

– Did du ken, dey say dat Shetlan oo is owre fine t'be spun commercially. Dey say dey hæ t'mix some coorser oo in wi it, so da yarn will hadd tagidder. Bit I'm no sæ sure. I mean, whit did da aald fok use if it wisna pure Shetlan, eh?

The boy nodded. – Most hæ been.

– Noo I ken a muckle modern frame is no da sam as a peerie spinnie, bit still if du took da time t'do it richt, eh? I reckon it cood be don.

Fæder stood back from the door. – Gying du if du wants tæ. Hæ a bit o a waandir. I'll be gittin som dennir aboot wan.

The boy walked down over the links to the beach. He was thinking about what his father had said about the wool and about old Robbie, the old man's charitable ways and the darkness of his life in poverty and dirt. Was it possible for the two to be separated out? Was it possible for that pure yarn to be spun on modern equipment, or would the thread just snap and recoil?

The links had been eaten away by the sea over recent years, till the narrow neck of land that separated the freshwater loch from the ocean was no more than a stone's throw in width. He walked around the shoreline till he came to the derelict Haa, where the lairds of old had lived. In the distance he could see the house at Snusquoy. Yes, this was his place. That would always be so. But if he stayed would the spectres of isolation and death hang over it, so that he could not avoid the chilling sense of loneliness he knew so well; but if he left, could he remain himself outwith this place, pure spun, without the necessary coarse addition?

There was a way to find out.

The funeral drew an army of men to the kirk. Cars covered the ground outside the dyke and far back down the road beyond. Figures in dark cloth stepped into the kirk, removing hats and picking up hymnaries. Neither of the sisters were there. They had been moved out of the black hoose, to an old folk's home in the toon.

The minister made much of Robbie's generosity and humility. He read the story of the widow's mite and said that the dead man had given of his labour and himself freely, that he had embodied a spiritual contentment rare in the modern age, regardless of worldly goods. There was no need to make a point of the cleanliness of his soul, in contrast to his environment.

After the service, the fleet of cars drove in convoy through the village

at a respectful speed to the place of burial. The Post Office was shut for
the duration of the ceremony. The children were kept indoors and all
work in the rigs was suspended.

The kirkyard was a half-mile off, yet when the hearse reached its
destination, the last of the line of cars had not left the kirk. Fæder and
the boy came somewhere in the middle. They stood a little way off from
the graveside. During the ritual throwing of earth, the boy caught sight
of his father's eyes as they strayed to the stone that bore his mother's
name. Their vision momentarily met. When the burial was done, they
moved towards the gate with a new sense of union. Fæder turned to him
and spoke.

— She'd hæ been prood, du kens, o de at da University. She used t'say
du'd go far.

The boy nodded, a ball of guilty feeling blocking his throat.

— It sood o been her, no me. It wis her dræm, no mine.

— Mebbe, boy, mebbe. So du's no gyaain back?

— No.

— Whit'll du dø?

— I tocht mebbe we cood see if dis spinnin frame wid wirk.

Fæder raised his eyes and sighed, with a smile on his face.

— Mebbe.

As they passed a group of men at the gate, the boy overheard them
discussing the great revelation of the day when the district nurse had
gone to pack the sisters' gear for them to take away with them. She had
found in a kist under the bed, in the traditional place, a small fortune in
uncashed pensions and neatly folded notes.

Fæder nodded his head firmly. — Dær's wan thing we hæ t'dø, boy. We
most gying ina yon nort room an sort it oot. Will du help me?

The boy nodded.

— Ja.

Ian Rankin

A Deep Hole

I used to be a road digger, which is to say I dug up roads for a living.
These days I'm a Repair Effecter for the council's Highways Department.
I still dig up roads – sorry, *highways* – only now it sounds better, doesn't
it? They tell me there's some guy in an office somewhere whose job is
thinking up posh names for people like me, for the rubbish collectors and
street sweepers and toilet attendants. (Usually they manage to stick in
the word 'environmental' somewhere.) This way, we're made to feel
important. Must be some job that, thinking up posh names. I wonder
what job title *he's* given himself. Environmental Title Co-ordination
Executive, eh?

They call me Sam the Spade. There's supposed to be a joke there,
but I don't get it. I got the name because after Robbie's got to work
with the pneumatic drill, I get in about things with the spade and clear
out everything he's broken up. Robbie's called 'The Driller Killer'. That
was the name of an old horror video. I never saw it myself – I tried
working with the pneumatic drill a few times. There's more pay if you
operate the drill. You become *skilled* rather than unskilled labour. But
after fifteen seconds I could feel the fillings popping out of my teeth.
Even now my spine aches in bed at night. Too much sex, the boys say.
Ha ha.

Now Daintry, his title would be something like Last Hope Cash
Dispensation Executive. Or, in the old parlance, a plain money lender.
Nobody remembers Daintry's first name. He shrugged it off some time
back when he was a teenager, and he hasn't been a teenager for a few
years and some. He's the guy you go to on a Friday or Saturday for a few
quid to see you through the weekend. And come the following week's
dole cheque (or, if you're one of the fortunate few, pay packet) Daintry'll
be waiting while you cash it, his hand out for the money he loaned plus
a whack of interest.

While you're only too happy to see Daintry before the weekend, you're
not so happy about him still being around *after* the weekend. You don't
want to pay him back, certainly not the interest. But you do, inevitably.
You do pay him back. Because he's a persistent sort of fellow with a good

line in colourful threats and a ready abundance of Physical Persuasion Techniques.

I think the chief reason people didn't like Daintry was that he never made anything of himself. I mean, he still lived on the same estate as his clients, albeit in one of the two-storey houses rather than the blocks of flats. His front garden was a jungle, his window panes filthy, and the inside of his house a thing of horror. He dressed in cheap clothes, which hung off him. He wouldn't shave for days, his hair always needed washing... You're getting the picture, eh? Me, when I'm not working I'm a neat and tidy sort of guy. My mum's friends, the women she gossips with, they're always shaking their heads and asking how come I never found myself a girl. They speak about me in the past tense like that, like I'm not going to find one now. On the contrary. I'm thirty-eight, and all my friends have split up with their wives by now. So there are more and more single women my age appearing around the estate. It's only a question of time. Soon it'll be Brenda's turn. She'll leave Harry, or he'll kick her out. No kids, so that's not a problem. I hear gossip that their arguments are getting louder and louder and more frequent. There are threats too, late at night after a good drink down at the club. I'm leaving you, no you're not, yes I am, well get the hell out then, I'll be back for my stuff, on you go, I wouldn't give you the satisfaction, well stay if you like.

Just like a ballet, eh? Well, I think so anyway. I've been waiting for Brenda for a long time. I can wait a little longer. I'm certainly a more attractive prospect than Daintry. Who'd move in with him? Nobody, I can tell you. He's a loner. No friends, just people he might drink with. He'll sometimes buy a few drinks for a few of the harder cases, then get them to put the frighteners on some late-payer who's either getting cocky or else talking about going to the police. Not that the police would do anything. What? Around here? If they're not in Daintry's pocket, they either don't care about the place anyway or else are scared to come near. Daintry did a guy in once inside the club. A Sunday afternoon too, stabbed him in the toilets. Police came, talked to everyone in the club – nobody'd seen anything. Daintry may be a bastard, but he's *our* bastard. Besides, there's always a reason. If you haven't crossed him, you're none of his business ... and *he'd* better not be any of *yours*.

I knew him of course. Oh yeah, we went to school together, same class all the way from five to sixteen years old. He was never quite as good as me at the subjects, but he was quiet and pretty well behaved. Until about fifteen. A switch flipped in his brain at fifteen. Actually, I'm lying: he was always better than me at arithmetic. So I suppose he was cut out for a career as a money lender. Or, as he once described himself, 'a bank manager with menaces'.

God knows how many people he's murdered. Can't be that many, or we'd all have noticed. That's why I thought all the information I used to give him was just part of his act. He knew word would get around about what he was asking me for, and those whispers and rumours would strengthen his reputation. That's what I always thought. I never took it seriously. As a result, I tapped him for a loan once or twice and *he never charged me a penny*. He also bought me a few drinks, and once provided a van when I wanted to sell the piano. See, he wasn't all bad. He had his good side. If it hadn't been for him, we'd never have shifted that piano, and it'd still be sitting there in the living room reminding my mother of the tunes dad used to play on it, tunes she'd hum late into the night and then again at the crack of dawn.

It seemed strange at first that he'd want to see me. He would come over to me in pubs and sling his arm around my neck, asking if I was all right, patting me and ordering the same again. We'd hardly spoken more than a sentence at a time to one another since leaving school, but now he was smiles and reminiscences and all interested in my job of work.

'I just dig holes.'

He nodded. 'And that's important work, believe me. Without the likes of you, my car's suspension would be shot to hell.'

Of course, his car's suspension *was* shot to hell. It was a 1973 Ford Capri with tinted windows, an air duct and a spoiler. It was a loser's car, with dark green nylon fur on the dashboard and the door panels. The wheel arches were history, long since eaten by rust. Yet every year without fail it passed its MOT. The coincidence was, the garage mechanic was a regular client of Daintry's.

'I could get a new car,' Daintry said, 'but it gets me from A back to A again, so what's the point?'

There was something in this. He seldom left the estate. He lived there, shopped there, he'd been born there and he'd die there. He never took a holiday, not even a weekend away, and he never ever ventured south of the river. He spent all his free time watching videos. The guy who runs the video shop reckoned Daintry had seen every film in the shop a dozen times over.

'He knows their numbers off by heart.'

He did know lots about movies: running time, director, writer, supporting actor. He was always a hot contender when the club ran its trivia quiz. He sat in that smelly house of his with the curtains shut and a blue light flickering. He was a film junkie. And somehow, he managed to spend all his money on them. He must have done, or what else did he do with it? His Rolex was a fake, lighter than air when you picked it up, and probably his gold jewellery was fake too. Maybe somewhere there's a secret bank account with thousands salted away, but I don't think so. Don't ask me why, I just don't think so.

Roadworks. That's the information I passed on to Daintry. That's what he wanted to talk to me about. Roadworks. *Major* roadworks.

'You know the sort of thing,' he'd say, 'anywhere where you're digging a *big* hole. Maybe building a flyover or improving drainage. Major roadworks.'

Sure enough, I had access to this sort of information. I just had to listen to the various crews talking about what they were working on and where they were doing the work. Over tea and biscuits in the canteen, I could earn myself a few drinks and a pint glass of goodwill.

'How deep does that need to be?' Daintry would ask.

'I don't know, eight maybe ten feet.'

'By what?'

'Maybe three long, the same wide.'

And he'd nod. This was early in the game, and I was slow catching on. You're probably much faster, right? So you know why he was asking. But I was puzzled the first couple of times. I mean, I thought maybe he was interested in the ... what's it, the infrastructure. He wanted to see improvements. Then it dawned on me: no, what he wanted to see were big holes. Holes that would be filled in with concrete and covered over with huge immovable objects, like bridge supports for example. Holes where bodies could be hidden. I didn't say anything, but I knew that's what we were talking about. We were talking about Human Resource Disposal.

And Daintry knew that I knew. He'd wink from behind his cigarette smoke, using those creased stinging eyes of his. Managing to look a little like his idol Robert de Niro. In *Goodfellas*. That's what Daintry would say. He'd always be making physical comparisons like that. Me, I thought he was much more of a Joe Pesci. But I didn't tell him that. I didn't even tell him that Pesci isn't pronounced pesky.

He knew I'd blab about our little dialogues, and I did, casually like. And word spread. And suddenly Daintry was a man to be feared. But he wasn't really. He was just stupid, with a low flashpoint. And if you wanted to know what sort of mood he was going to be in, you only had to visit the video shop.

'He's taken out *Goodfellas* and *Godfather 3*.' So you knew there was trouble coming. Now you really didn't want to cross him. But if he'd taken out soft core or a Steve Martin or even some early Brando, everything was going to be all right. He must have been on a gangster high the night he went round to speak with Mr and Mrs McAndrew. In his time, Mr McAndrew had been a bit of a lad himself, but he was in his late-seventies with a wife ten years younger. They lived in one of the estate's nicer houses. They'd bought it from the council and had installed a fancy front door, double-glazed windows, you name it, and all the glass was that leaded criss-cross stuff. It wasn't cheap. These days, Mr McAndrew spent all his time in the garden. At the front of the house he had some beautiful flower beds, with the back garden given over to vegetables. In the summer, you saw him playing football with his grandchildren.

'Just like,' as somebody pointed out, 'Marlon Brando in *The Godfather*.' This was apt in its way since, like I say, despite the gardening Mr McAndrew's hands were probably cleaner these days than they had been in the past.

How he got to owe Daintry money I do not know. But Daintry, believe me, would have been only too happy to lend. There was McAndrew's reputation for a start. Plus the McAndrews seemed prosperous enough, he was sure to see his money and interest returned. But not so. Whether out of sheer cussedness or because he really couldn't pay, McAndrew had been holding out on Daintry. I saw it as a struggle between the old gangster and the new. Maybe Daintry did too. Whatever, one night he walked into the McAndrews' house and beat up Mrs McAndrew in front of her husband. He had two heavies with him, one to hold Mr McAndrew, one to hold Mrs McAndrew. Either one of them could have dropped dead of a heart attack right then and there.

There were murmurs in the street the next day, and for days afterwards. Daintry, it was felt, had overstepped the mark. He was out of order. To him it was merely business, and he'd gotten the money from McAndrew so the case was closed. But he now found himself shorter of friends than ever before. Which is probably why he turned to me when he wanted the favour done. Simply, he couldn't get anyone else to do it.

'You want me to what?'

He'd told me to meet him in the children's play-park. We walked around the path. There was no one else in the park. It was a battlefield, all broken glass and rocks. Dog shit was smeared up and down the chute, the swings had been wrapped around themselves until they couldn't be reached. The roundabout had disappeared one night, leaving only a metal stump in place. You'd be safer sending your kids to play on the North Circular.

'It's quite simple,' Daintry said. 'I want you to get rid of a package for me. There's good money in it.'

'How much money?'

'A hundred.'

I paused at that. A hundred pounds, just to dispose of a package ...

'But you'll need a deep hole,' said Daintry.

Yeah, of course. It was *that* kind of package. I wondered who it was. There was a story going around that Daintry had set up a nice little disposal operation which dealt with Human Resource Waste from miles around. Villains as far away as Watford and Luton were bringing 'packages' for him to dispose of. But it was just a story, just one of many.

'A hundred,' I said, nodding.

'All right, one twenty-five. But it's got to be tonight.'

I knew just the hole.

They were building a new footbridge over the North Circular, over to the west near Wembley. I knew the gang wouldn't be working night-shift: the job wasn't that urgent and who could afford the shift bonus these days? There'd be a few deep holes there all right. And while the gang might notice a big black bin-bag at the bottom of one of them, they wouldn't do anything about it. People were always dumping rubbish down the holes. It all got covered over with concrete, gone and quite forgotten. I hadn't seen a dead body before, and I didn't intend seeing one now. So I insisted it was all wrapped up before I'd stick it in the car-boot.

Daintry and I stood in the lock-up he rented and looked down at the black bin-liner.

'It's not so big, is it?' I said.

'I broke the rigor mortis,' he explained. 'That way you can get it into the car.'

I nodded and went outside to throw up. I felt better after that. Curried chicken never did agree with me.

'I'm not sure I can do it,' I said, wiping my mouth.

Daintry was ready for me. 'Ah, that's a pity.' He stuck his hands in his pockets, studying the tips of his shoes. 'How's your old mum by the way? Keeping well is she?'

'She's fine, yeah...' I stared at him. 'What do you mean?'

'Nothing, nothing. Let's hope her good health continues.' He looked up at me, a glint in his eye. 'Still fancy Brenda?'

'Who says I do?'

He laughed. 'Common knowledge. Must be the way your trousers bulge whenever you see her shadow.'

'That's rubbish.'

'She seems well enough, too. The marriage is a bit shaky, but what can you expect? That Harry of hers is a monster.' Daintry paused, fingering his thin gold neck-chain. 'I wouldn't be surprised if he took a tap to the skull one of these dark nights.'

'Oh?'

He shrugged. 'Just a guess. Pity you can't...' He touched the bin-bag with his shoe. 'You know.' And he smiled.

We loaded the bag together. It wasn't heavy, and was easy enough to manoeuvre. I could feel a foot and a leg, or maybe a hand and arm. I tried not to think about it. Imagine him threatening my old mum! He was lucky I'm not quick to ignite, not like him, or it'd've been broken nose city and hospital cuisine. But what he said about Brenda's husband put thought of my mum right out of my head.

We closed the boot and I went to lock it.

'He's not going to make a run for it,' Daintry said.

'I suppose not,' I admitted. But I locked the boot anyway.

Then the car wouldn't start, and when it did start it kept cutting out, like the engine was flooding or something. Maybe a block in the fuel line. I'd let it get very low before the last fill of petrol. There might be a lot of rubbish swilling around in the tank. After a couple of miles it cut out on me at some traffic lights in Dalston. I rolled down my window and waved for the cars behind me to pass. I was content to sit for a few moments and let everything settle, my stomach included. One car stopped along-side me. And Jesus, wouldn't you know it: it was a cop car.

'Everything all right?' the cop in the passenger seat called.

'Yeah, just stalled.'

'You can't sit there forever.'

'No.'

'If it doesn't start next go, push your car to the side of the road.'

'Yeah, sure.' He made no move to leave. Now the driver was looking at me too, and traffic was building up behind us. Nobody sounded their horn. Everyone could see that a cop car was talking with the driver of another vehicle. Sweat tickled my ears. I turned the ignition, resisting the temptation to pump the accelerator. The engine rumbled, then came to life. I grinned at the cops and started forwards, going through an amber light.

They could probably arrest me for that. It was five minutes before I stopped staring in the rearview mirror. But I couldn't see them. They'd turned off somewhere. I let all my fear and tension out in a rasping scream, then remembered the window was still rolled down. I wound it back up again. I decided not to go straight to the bridge-site, but to drive around a bit, let all the traffic clear along with my head.

I pulled into a bus-stop just before the North Circular and changed into my work clothes. That way I wouldn't look suspicious. Good thinking, eh? It was my own idea, one Daintry had appreciated. I had a question for him now, and the question was: why wasn't he doing this himself? But he wasn't around to answer it. And I knew the answer anyway: he'd rather pay someone else to do dangerous jobs. Oh yes, it was dangerous; I knew that now. Worth a lot more than a hundred and twenty-five nicker, sixty of which were already in my pocket in the shape of dirty old pound notes. Repayments, doubtless, from Daintry's punters. Grubby money, but still money. I hoped it hadn't come from the McAndrews.

I sat at the bus-stop for a while. A car pulled in behind me. Not a police car this time, just an ordinary car. I heard the driver's door slam shut. Footsteps, a tap at my window. I looked out. The man was bald and middle-aged, dressed in suit and tie. A lower executive look, a sales rep maybe, that sort of person. He was smiling in a friendly enough sort of fashion. And if he wanted to steal my car and jemmy open the boot, well that was fine too.

I wound down my window. 'Yeah?'

'I think I missed my turning,' he said. 'Can you tell me where we are, roughly?'

'Roughly,' I said, 'roughly we're about a mile north of Wembley.'

'And that's west London?' His accent wasn't quite English, not southern English. Welsh or a Geordie or a Scouser maybe.

'About as west as you can get,' I told him. Yeah, the wild west.

'I can't be too far away then. I want St. John's Wood. That's west too, isn't it?'

'Yeah, not far at all.' These poor sods, you came across them a lot in my line of work. New to the city and pleading directions, getting hot and a bit crazy as the signposts and one-ways led them further into the maze. I felt sorry for them a lot of the time. It wasn't their fault. So I took my time as I directed him towards Harlesden, miles away from where he wanted to be.

'It's a short cut,' I told him. He seemed pleased to have some local knowledge. He went back to his car and sounded his horn in thank you as he drove off. I know, that was a bit naughty of me, wasn't it? Well, there you go. That was my spot of devilry for the night. I started my own car and headed back onto the road.

There was a sign off saying 'Works Access Only', so I signalled and drove between two rows of striped traffic cones. Then I stopped the car. There were no other cars around, just the dark shapes of earth-moving equipment and cement mixers. Fine and dandy. Cars and lorries roared past, but they didn't give me a second's notice. They weren't about to slow down enough to take in any of the scene. The existing overpass and built-up verges hid me pretty well from civilization. Before unloading the package, I went for a recce, taking my torch with me.

And of course there were no decent holes to be found. They'd been filled in already. The concrete was hard, long metal rods poking out of it like the prongs on a fork. There were a few shallow cuts in the earth, but nothing like deep enough for the purpose. Hell's teeth and gums. I went back to the car, thinking suddenly how useful a car-phone would be. I wanted to speak to Daintry. I wanted to ask him what to do. A police car went past. I saw its brake lights glow. They'd noticed my car, but they didn't stop. No, but they might come back round again. I started the car and headed out onto the carriageway.

Only a few minutes later, there was a police car behind me. He sat on my tail for a while, then signalled to overtake, drawing level with me and staying there. The passenger checked me out. They were almost certainly the ones who'd seen me parked back at the bridge-site. The passenger saw that I was wearing overalls and a standard issue work-jacket. I sort of waved at him. He spoke to the driver, and the patrol car accelerated away.

Lucky for me he hadn't seen the tears in my eyes. I was terrified and bursting for a piss. I knew that I had to get off this road. My brain was numb. I couldn't think of another place to dump the body. I didn't want to think about it at all. I just wanted rid of it. I think I saw the travelling salesman hurtle past, fleeing Harlesden. He was heading out of town.

I came off the North Circular and just drove around, crawling eastwards until I knew the streets so well it was like remote control. I knew exactly where I'd effected repairs, and where repairs were still waiting to be carried out. There was one pot-hole on a sharp bend that could buckle a wheel. That was down as a priority, and would probably be started on tomorrow. I calmed myself a little with memories of holes dug and holes filled in, the rich aroma of hot tarmac, the jokes yelled out by the Driller Killer. I'd never worked out why he'd try telling jokes to someone wearing industrial ear protectors beside a pneumatic drill.

Seeking safety, I came back into the estate. I felt better immediately, my head clearing. I knew what I had to do. I had to face up to Daintry. I'd give him back the money of course, less a quid or two for petrol, and I'd explain that nowhere was safe. Mission impossible. I didn't know what he'd do. It depended on whether tonight was a *Goodfellas* night or not. He might slap me about a bit. He might stop buying me drinks.

He might do something to my mum.

Or to Brenda.

I'd have to talk to him. Maybe we could do a deal. Maybe I'd have to kill him. Yeah, then I'd just have the *two* bodies to worry about. In order to stop worrying about the first, I stopped by the lock-up. This was one of a cul-de-sac of identical garages next to some wasteland which had been planted with trees and was now termed a Conservation Area. The man in the High Street had certainly conserved his energy thinking up that one.

There were no kids about, so I used a rock to break the lock, then hauled the door open with my crowbar. I stopped for a moment and wondered what I was going to do now. I'd meant to leave the body in the garage, but I'd had to break the locks to get in, so now if I left the body there anybody at all could wander along and find it. But then I thought, this is *Daintry's* garage. Everybody knows it, and nobody in their right mind would dare trespass. So I hauled the package inside, closed the door again, and left a rock in front of it. I was confident I'd done my best.

So now it was time to go talk with Daintry. The easy part of the evening was past. But first I went home. I don't know why, I just wanted to see my mum. We used to be on the eleventh floor, but they'd moved us eventually to the third because the lifts kept breaking and mum couldn't climb eleven flights. I took the stairs tonight, relieved not to find any of the local kids shooting up or shagging between floors. Mum was sitting with Mrs Gregg from along the hall. They were talking about Mrs McAndrew.

'Story she gave her doctor was she fell down the stairs.'

'Well I think it's a shame.'

Mum looked up and saw me. 'I thought you'd be down the club.'

'Not tonight, mum.'

'Well that makes a change.'

'Hallo, Mrs Gregg.'

'Hallo, love. There's a band on tonight, you know.'

'Where?'

She rolled her eyes. 'At the club. Plenty of lovely girls too, I'll bet.'

They wanted rid of me. I nodded. 'Just going to my room. Won't be long.'

I lay on my bed, the same bed I'd slept in since I was ... well, since before I could remember. The room had been painted and papered in the last year. I stared at the wallpaper, lying on one side and then on the other. This room, it occurred to me, was probably the size of a prison cell. It might even be a bit smaller. What was it, eight feet square? But I'd always felt comfortable enough here. I heard my mum laughing at something Mrs Gregg said, and pop music from the flat downstairs. These weren't very solid flats, thin walls and floors. They'd knock our block down one of these days. I liked it well enough though. I didn't want to lose it. I didn't want to lose my mum.

I decided that I was probably going to have to kill Daintry.

I packed some clothes into a black holdall, just holding back the tears. What would I say to my mum? I've got to go away for a while? I'll phone you when I can? I recalled all the stories I'd heard about Daintry. How some guy from Trading Standards had been tailing him and was sitting in his car at the side of the road by the shops when a sawn-off shotgun appeared in the window and a voice told him to get the hell out of there pronto. Guns and knives, knuckle-dusters and a machete. Just stories ... just stories.

I knew he wouldn't be expecting *me* to try anything. He'd open his door, he'd let me in, he'd turn his back to lead me through to the living room. That's when I'd do it. When his back was turned. It was the only safe and certain time I could think of. Anything else and I reckoned I'd lose my bottle. I left the holdall on my bed and went through to the kitchen. I took time at the open drawer, choosing my knife. Nothing too grand. just a simple four-inch blade at the end of a wooden handle. I stuck it in my pocket.

'Just nipping out for some fresh air, mum.'

'Bye then.'

'See you.'

And that was that. I walked back down the echoing stairwell with my mind set on murder. It wasn't like the films. It was just ... well, *ordinary*. Like I was going to fetch fish and chips or something. I kept my hand on the knife handle. I wanted to feel comfortable with it. But my legs were a bit shaky. I had to keep locking them at the knees, holding onto a wall or a lamppost and taking deep breaths. It was a five-minute walk to Daintry's, but I managed to stretch it to ten. I passed a couple of people I vaguely knew, but didn't stop to talk. I didn't trust my teeth not to chatter, my jaw not to lock.

And to tell you the truth, I was relieved to see that there was someone standing on the doorstep, another visitor. I felt my whole body relax. The man crouched to peer through the letter box, then knocked again. As I walked down the path towards him, I saw that he was tall and well-built with a black leather jacket and short black hair.

'Isn't he in?'

The man turned his head slowly towards me. I didn't like the look of his face. It was grey and hard like the side of a house.

'Doesn't look like it,' he said. 'Any idea where he'd be?'

He was standing up straight now, his head hanging down over mine. Police, I thought for a second. But he wasn't police. I swallowed. I started to shake my head, but then I had an idea. I released my grip on the knife.

'If he's not in he's probably down the club,' I said. 'Do you know where it is?'

'No.'

'Go back down to the bottom of the road, take a left, and when you come to the shops it's up a side road between the laundrette and the chip shop.'

He studied me. 'Thanks.'

'No problem,' I said. 'You know what he looks like?'

He nodded in perfect slow motion. He never took his eyes off me.

'Right then,' I said. 'Oh, and you might have to park outside the shops. The car-park's usually full when there's a band on.'

'There's a band?'

'In the club.' I smiled. 'It gets noisy, you can hardly hear a word that's said to you, even in the toilets.'

'Is that so?'

'Yes,' I said, 'that is so.'

Then I walked back down the path and gave him a slight wave as I headed for home. I made sure I walked home too. I didn't want him thinking I was on my way to the club ahead of him.

'Short walk,' mum said. She was pouring tea for Mrs Gregg.

'Bit cold.'

'Cold?' squeaked Mrs Gregg. 'A lad your age shouldn't feel the cold.'

'Have you seen my knife?' mum asked. She was looking down at the cake she'd made. It was on one of the better plates and hadn't been cut yet. I brought the knife out of my pocket.

'Here you are, mum.'

'What's it doing in your pocket?'

'The lock on the car-boot's not working. I'd to cut some string to tie it shut.'

'Do you want some tea?'

I shook my head. 'I'll leave you to it,' I said. 'I'm off to bed.'

It was the talk of the estate the next morning, how Daintry had been knifed to death in a toilet cubicle, just as the band were finishing their encore. They were some Sixties four-piece, still performing long past their sell-by. That's what people said who were there. And they'd compensated for a lack of ability by cranking the sound system all the way up. You not only couldn't hear yourself think, you couldn't *think*.

I suppose they have to make a living as best they can. We all do.

It was the assistant manager who found Daintry. He was doing his nightly check of the club to see how many drunks had managed to fall asleep in how many hidden places. Nobody used the end cubicle of the gents' much; it didn't have any toilet seat. But there sat Daintry, not caring any more about the lack of amenities. Police were called, staff and clientele interviewed, but no one had anything much to say.

Well, not to the police at any rate. But there was plenty of gossip on the streets and in the shops and in the lifts between neighbours. And slowly a story emerged. Mr McAndrew, remember, had been a lad at one time. He was rumoured still to have a few contacts, a few friends who owed him. Or maybe he just stumped up cash. Whatever, everyone knew Mr McAndrew had put out the contract on Daintry. And, as also agreed, good riddance to him. On a Friday night too. So anyone who'd tapped him for a loan could see the sun rise on Monday morning with a big wide smile.

Meantime, the body was found in Daintry's lock-up. Well, the police knew who was responsible for that, didn't they? Though they did wonder about the broken locks. Kids most likely, intent on burglary but doing a runner when they saw the corpse. Seemed feasible to me too.

Mr Andrew, eh? I watched him more closely after that. He still looked to me like a nice old man. But then it was only a story after all, only one of many. Me, I had other things to think about. I knew I could do it now. I could take Brenda away from Harry. Don't ask me why I feel so sure, I just do.

Andrew Crumey

from *Pfitz*

Schenck was a cartographer, and had worked on Rreinnstadt for ten years, ever since its inception by the Prince. Originally, Schenck was drafted into the Accounts Department, calculating the wages of some of Rreinnstadt's notional inhabitants. But it was observed that his penmanship was good, and so he was soon moved to the Cartography Office.

The ability to write well and copy accurately was one of the chief skills needed for his new job. Since the object of study was a city which did not exist other than on paper, the cartographer need no longer worry over such things as surveying or taking measurements. No need now for him to stand in wind and rain, his plumb line blown off course as he tries to set up his theodolite. Now it was only other maps which he would survey; his first aim being to maintain total consistency with everything which had been done before – not only the existing maps showing the simple positions of buildings and streets, but also those others which indicated height above sea-level, and others yet which showed the successive buildings, in order, which had occupied a given spot (for already by now the city of Rreinnstadt had become a thing with its own history; it had become an entity capable of transformation and development). On the shelves of the Cartography Office, there were maps of such a scale that only a single room of a single residence was shown, or a small portion of a room (every item meticulously charted and illustrated – the contours of a silver plate, or a cup upon a table; the bearings and co-ordinates of a Turkish rug spread across a floor). There were maps of finest rice-paper which could be overlaid, one upon the other, so as to show in ever-deepening layers the cross sections of the city at successive heights, and maps which indicated not only positions in space, but in time also – plans showing the location of individual citizens on particular days, at particular times (individuals whose lives were at that moment being chronicled by the Biographical Division).

It was amongst such documents that Schenck had lived and worked for the last ten years. The table from which he ate his lunch each day was an atlas placed upon his lap, and at night his dreams were laced with sweet filaments of latitude and longitude. The world itself had become for Schenck a great chart; its rich vocabulary of contours and features, a text which was completely self-contained, completely consistent, and yet endlessly perplexing. And the future which he foresaw for himself was a gradual traversing across the uncertain surface of the map, drawn at the moment of his birth, which defined his own destiny in every detail.

One day, Schenck was sent upstairs to deliver some plans to the Biographical Division. This was situated in a great high-ceilinged room, lined with galleries of shelves, amongst which the Biographers circulated endlessly, as they brought into existence the citizens of Rreinnstadt. Here was the place where new life was created; memories, dreams and speculations. It was work of inestimable importance (as the Biographers kept reminding everyone else), and when Schenck found the person he was looking for he was curtly thanked and then dismissed as if he were no more than a servant.

Schenck made his way back along the gallery, looking down at the rows of Biographers sitting at their desks. The only sounds were those of nibs squeaking, of pens being dipped into inkwells, or of pages being turned. They even had to wear special overshoes, so as not to disturb the others whenever they needed to go and search for documents.

And then he saw her, sitting amongst the others, and it was a kind of revelation.

She was wearing green. Her hair was red, her skin pale and marked in places with a fine network of lilac veins – marked in those places where the skin is thinnest, as for example where it stretches across the protuberance of a clavicle. This was the part which the Cartographer now watched, as she sat bent over her writing. He watched from a distance that taut area of pale skin, and the threads of veins like some hypothetical system of roads, or rivers. And he watched the thickening of the skin, its deepening, as his gaze fell southwards, beneath those chilly regions, towards the warm promise of her bosom.

If she were to lean further forwards, or else perhaps to adjust the position in which she was sitting, then he would see more. New contours would be revealed, new regions of that inviting surface. Much later, in his memory, he would compare what he saw then with his subsequent, more detailed survey.

Schenck knew that he ought to leave, now that he had completed his errand. But no one was paying any attention to him (they were always like that in Biography). And he was fascinated by what he saw; the arresting contrast of thick red hair against her white neck, and the green dress. Her pale skin called to mind a map he had once seen, of the Earth's polar regions. If she leaned further over her work, he might see more of her bosom. This hope, mingled with fear, kept him fixed in awe. He remained where he stood, motionless, his mouth dry, his stomach tightening with an excitement bordering on dread.

So that now, on the map of Schenck's life, a new feature had appeared; a snow-capped vision of mountainous beauty. And the seismic impression of this moment would send tremors to the very edges of his existence; across the distant years, he would come to recall those ridges of half-remembered dreams, gulleys of distorted memory, appearing and then vanishing again without warning. Everywhere he might choose to look on his life's map, whichever way he should turn now, he would see her indentation upon the landscape, like the hollow which remains upon a pillow after the head has risen.

Then at last she leaned forwards; aware already, he now felt sure, of his observation. She leaned forwards, consenting to his momentary mapping of her body – or rather condescending. And as she moved, everything changed – a shifting topography of skin, flesh, mass displaced. Her breasts swelling, shrinking, falling slightly, as if in offering (only a moment!). Pendulous memory. He would think of it later, as he worked on his maps. And the question formed in his mind: how would he be able to prolong this pleasure, repeat it? How would he be able to come closer to this unknown woman who intrigued him so much?

Now she raised her head, and for a moment he was able to see her face in all its beauty, as she looked up towards the gallery. He felt her gaze discovering him, and her expression conveyed a look of quiet triumph. The Cartographer lowered his eyes, and made to leave. But by walking towards the spiral staircase at the furthest end of the gallery, he would be able, after descending its steps, to choose a route which would take him close to her desk. He prepared himself, as he began to make his way down the steps, for the imminent encounter; the brief proximity (perhaps even the possibility that he would brush against her, that some unspoken gesture would manifest itself and communicate a message of complicity, of gratitude, and the promise of further similar meetings); the narrow gap of closeness through which he had to pass – the pregnant opportunity of this moment, as he approached the object of his fascination, her head bowed once more; drew close with his eyes fixed on the door ahead, while his gaze concentrated on the mysterious figure at the periphery of his vision. And then at last he was walking past her, breathing the air in which she lived. Daring briefly to look down at her hair, and her neck, and the work before her, there were many things for him to try and assimilate in the slim wedge of time available; many pieces of information he should have liked to acquire amongst the shards of delight which were now prickling him. But from the paper on which she was writing, he could gather only a single name, spelt out in her neat blue script. *Count Zelneck*. He walked on until he reached the door, and the name remained fixed in his mind as he went back downstairs to the Cartography Office; a word whose silent repetition on his lips felt almost like a kiss. It was the key which had allowed him to gain entry into a small corner of her existence; a piece of common ground now, whose investigation might bring him closer to that great act of exploration he longed so much to carry out.

Who might he be, this Count Zelneck? If Schenck could discover anything about him, then he would immediately be drawn closer to that fragrant circle which he longed to inhabit. The name seemed vaguely familiar, but this may have been illusory – like the sensation he had felt on seeing the Biographer; the profound impression that here was some-one he had met before, in some other life, and whom he had known intimately, though all trace of memory had been erased. And the Count, also, seemed already like an old friend – a treasured mutual acquaintance. Schenck had to learn more about him. He decided to consult his maps.

He soon ascertained that the Count had no residence in Rreinnstadt, and so concluded that he must be one of those visitors who are regarded as significant enough (because of their status, or their links with Rreinn-stadt citizens) to warrant biographical treatment in their own right. Schenck then went to the section of the Topographical Directory showing the locations of Non-Residents and itinerants.

This was no easy feat. The Section (in four volumes) contained a huge number of maps, on which were indicated (amongst other data) the positions of individuals within Rreinnstadt at various times, over a period covering several years. To find one person amongst this transient crowd would be impossible, without some further clue to his possible whereabouts.

But luck was on the Cartographer's side. Later that day, he was in the Map Room when he met Gruber, who was looking for a road plan giving indications of traffic at the time of the Festival of the Swan (the great annual celebration which attracted large numbers of visitors to Rreinn-stadt from the surrounding country). Gruber said that someone in Biography had requested it, and Schenck saw an opportunity to pay another visit to the solemn place upstairs with its intriguing treasures.

'Thanks for offering,' said Gruber, 'but I'd rather take it myself. It's a pretty piece of work who wants it.'

Schenck was filled with excitement and agitation where he heard this; the very suggestion of the woman he longed to see again made her seem as vivid as if she had walked into the room. But also he was seized by jealousy at the thought that Gruber might be about to beat him to his goal. He had to satisfy himself that Gruber was actually referring to another biographer. 'What's she like?' he asked.

'Redhead. Just my type.'

He would have to act quickly. There was no chance of delaying Gruber, but he could at least try to obtain as much information as possible without letting Gruber suspect his intentions.

'Let me help you. Exactly what date does she need?'

Gruber told him the day and year, and even explained that the Biographer was planning Count Zelneck's journey from his country seat, wishing to avoid those roads which would be most congested with travelling peasants and vagabonds.

'Here it is,' said Gruber, who had found the map he was looking for. Then he began to flatten his hair with his hand, and straighten his cravat as he walked out with the book under his arm. 'See you later!'

Schenck felt sick at the prospect of being usurped by this oaf. But at least he knew now the exact time of Zelneck's visit. He returned to the Directory, and studied every chart of Rreinnstadt for the appropriate day. Finally, after more than an hour of frantic searching, he found the Count.

There he lay, on a map of the Tischner Quarter of Rreinnstadt on the first morning of the Festival of the Swan. It was a map set in the early morning, the sun hardly risen, and everyone still asleep, save a few insomniacs who were marked, their names minutely inscribed, in the streets and parks where they walked. Spurned lovers, perhaps, or dazed revellers, or possibly even criminals (who had already, at that time, begun to appear in Rreinnstadt). And in a tavern on Schlessingerstrasse (how many such taverns Schenck had previously searched!), in an upstairs room, the pale blue rectangle showing the bed in which the Count lay. Her Count. Looking at that neatly drawn symbol, it was as if Schenck were gazing straight into the Biographer's own heart. And he thought once more of that fascinating rectangle of neck and bosom, that perplexing map of a territory whose features had been represented to him in a code which he was still attempting to decipher, as he reworked its memory again and again.

Schenck almost wanted to pick up the book and hug it. Here was the

Count – here was the beginning of his entry into the Biographer's life, her world. At this moment, she too was thinking about the Count – weaving the fabric of his existence, bringing together the events which would shape him; deeds of heroism or nobility which might mould him, memories he would carry with him as he made his journey towards that bed where he would sleep, in a Rreinnstadt tavern, on the morning of the Festival of the Swan.

Everything about this tavern was now fascinating. He consulted other maps, found the floor plan of the building; studied its every detail, explored the rooms in which the Biographer too might find herself, once she had brought her Count to his destination. And he studied over and over that chart which showed him sleeping in his bed, and all the other Non-Residents and itinerants; the beggars in the parks (marked in grey), and all the additional topographical detail, minutely encoded. A pile of leaves, soon to be blown away. A beer barrel – fallen from its wagon – cracked and spilled across a street. The beer (symbolically) lying uncleaned in that early morning, and giving off its beery fumes to the sleeping citizens (this malodorous cloud being of ill-defined extent, its representation being decoded in the marginal Key). Even the roaming dogs were frozen in their tracks, marked by tiny crosses.

And the tavern, its guests located and named. The Count was not alone in his room. On the floor beside him Schenck saw an irregular figure of roughly human proportions, erased and redrawn, along with a pencilled inscription which Schenck could not easily decipher. Pfitz, it looked like. This must be the Count's servant. And the Cartographer felt even greater joy, that his researches should have taken him slightly further into the life of the Count.

But what about Gruber? Schenck had not seen him again; he could only speculate on the kind of success which he might already have achieved with the Biographer. For the rest of the day, he pursued his work with a troubled heart – contours were badly drawn, bearings misnumbered. He could think only about the Count, and Pfitz, and the lovely Biographer.

As evening approached, Schenck packed his things and began to make his way back to his lodgings. He followed the streets blindly as he took his usual route, hardly noticing the waggoners, the flower sellers, or the couples walking arm in arm. But as he came past the iron gates of the park, he was brought rudely from his dreams. At the far end of the street, he saw Gruber and the Biographer. She must have agreed to let him walk her home. Schenck began to follow, trying to ensure that if either of them should turn he would not be seen. In any case, it was already growing dark, and the two figures up ahead seemed too engrossed in their conversation for there to be any chance of them looking back. Schenck cursed his bad luck. If only he were in Roads and Thoroughfares, instead of those cursed Aquifers, then it would have been he, not Gruber, who would have been charged with finding the Biographer's map. And then it would be he who was walking beside her now, feeling her delicate arm in his.

As he followed, his attention remained fixed on the two figures ahead; their closeness, the symmetrical motion of their limbs, their swaying bodies as they walked slowly together, like reeds in a common current. He fancied that he saw the death of all his dreams. Yet still he followed them, along successive streets. What did he hope to discover? Would he eventually find himself standing in misery beneath a window in which he would see their two figures embrace?

They were in a dark alley now, lined with tall overhanging houses. It was not one of the better areas of the city, and Schenck might have felt nervous to walk here, were his attention not so preoccupied with the couple who went before him. There was no one else about, nor was there any traffic, and so Schenck gave a start when he heard and then saw a carriage speed past him. It was going far too quickly for such a narrow street – and as it approached Gruber and the Biographer, Schenck saw its wheel mount the pavement. They would be hit! Everything happened too quickly for Schenck to have to decide whether to call out in warning. Already the high wheel of the carriage had pushed Gruber off his feet and against a wall; he was lying on the ground, cursing loudly at the escaping vehicle, while the Biographer was helping him to get up again. Mingled with shock, the Cartographer felt a malicious pleasure at the sight of Gruber, a ridiculous figure brushing the dirt from himself and limping with aching limbs. Gruber did not appear to be seriously hurt, but he and the Biographer were in danger now of looking round and seeing Schenck – perhaps even suspecting his involvement (such was Schenck's delight, that he felt somehow responsible). Schenck quickly went back to the corner of the street, where he turned out of sight. As he walked briskly back to his lodgings, he congratulated himself that the random motion of a badly driven carriage had made Gruber look comical and absurd, spoiled his plans, and given new life to Schenck's hopes.

Jackie Kay

from *Trumpet*

He never hit me. Never raised a hand or a fist. A belt, a buckle or a boot. Once. Hardly ever raised his voice. Didn't need to. Never hugged me either. Never sat me on his knee and bounced me up and down. He'd hold my hand in the street. Liked that. Holding my hand in the street for people to see. Father and son out and about in the street. Sometimes it looked like me and him could be good friends. Sometimes we were strangers. Total strangers who happened to look alike. People that didn't know I was adopted said things like, You're your father's spitting image, you are. Made my father roar, my mother smile. What I wanted when I was a kid was to look like my father. You could write a list of things after his name. Goodlooking. Talented. Plenty charisma. Couldn't write fuck all after mine. Colman Moody the guy who tried to be an au pair in France and got knocked back. The guy who did two years of a four-year course. The bloke who hung out in India for a year taking people on trips in his rubber dinghy. The guy who flopped his A levels first time round. Colman Moody, son of Joss Moody, the famous trumpet player. You know the one. The one who pretended to be a man and fetched up a woman at his death. Pulled the wool over his own son's eyes. That boy must have been thick. Two planks. Colman Moody the guy who didn't do nothing.

Not a lot you can say about me. I can tell you things. I'll tell you things, no problem, anything that interests you, right. But my life isn't all that eventful. Scandals don't make events happen do they? I mean it's only become eventful now; after his death. After he died, my life, the one I thought I knew I'd lived, changed. Now I don't know what I lived. It suddenly isn't the same life. It's a whole different ball game. Know what I mean. I haven't got the same life.

It's pretty ironic really. When I'd tell people I was adopted they'd say things like, you could have been brought up in another part of the world, with rich parents, poor parents, Mormons, Trotskyites. Lucky you ended up where you did. I'd like to find some of those fuckers now. Ask them what they think of this. Charlie McIntosh. Horace Saunders. Margaret Miller.

The children of lovers are orphans anyway. I forget who it was that said that. Some bright spark.

It about sums me up. My parents – I've got to still call them that. The habits of a lifetime. Something you don't usually have to think about isn't it? What to call your parents. It's mum or dad isn't it? And the trendy kids can use first names. But I was a traditional boy. I'd have never dreamed of calling my mother Millie. My household was unconventional – I don't mean the fact that my father was not who he said he was. I mean the jazz. A lot of my childhood was spent on the road. Touring. Place to fucking place. I'd have been happier at home watching Star Trek with a bowl of cornflakes. Too much, it was. All that razzamatazz. Other kids envied me and I envied other kids. That's it. Grass always greener. Kids of bohemian parents long for a square meal on the table every night at 5:30. My mate Sammy knew that Tuesday was fish pie day and Wednesday was steak and kidney. I'd have loved that. When I stayed in my mate Sammy's house, I loved everything being regulated. But Sammy hated it. I kept saying we could swop. I mean I'd already swopped from the mother who had me; so why not again. But Sammy lost his bottle and couldn't ask. I suppose I was boring as fuck. I'd have liked to have been made to have a bath every night in the same house in the same town. My mother was strict about my homework. Had to take it around with me wherever we went. I remember practising reading in dingy old jazz clubs before my father went on. I liked that. Sitting at a brown table with a coke and a book. A lot of the time my mother would not want to go with my father on the road on account of my schooling. But he was unusual for a jazz man. He wanted his family with him. As much as possible. If we didn't go with him, he'd come back with a hangover and a hang-dog look on his chops. He got nervous or superstitious if we didn't go. And pissed.

I used to think he had affairs at times like those. All men are disloyal. I used to think I was quite cool being able to think of that. Once, I even asked my mother how she'd feel. Just to stir things up a bit. Send the dust flying. She said he never would be unfaithful and gave me an odd smile that makes perfect fucking sense now. See that's what I mean. I'm going to have to go back over my whole life with a fine tooth comb and look for signs like that. I've got to do it. Jesus. It's embarrassing, that's the worst of it. Pricks saying, Really Cole, didn't you know? Bastards asking me questions. I'm so embarrassed I could emigrate. Just get the fuck out any fucking where. That's what I wanted to do when the shit first hit the fan. Just get the fuck out of this country.

I couldn't miss his funeral. No matter what he'd done to me. Just couldn't miss it. I considered it. Kept me awake the whole night before the morning of his funeral. But I'm too superstitious.

I never liked jazz. Much. I OD'd on it. When I was a kid. Everybody who came to our house, all they ever talked about was jazz. It was a big pain in the ass. If I was a fanatic I'd have been over the moon. But I wasn't. Some of my father's friends were all right in themselves. They liked me enough. Probably thought I was a bit moody when I was covered in acne and having a change of voice. But I didn't care. I was in my own world. All I ever wanted was for my father to be proud of me. As a man. A black man. I fucking worshipped him.

I goes in my father's bedroom. I am six years old. I opens their wardrobe. My daddy keeps his trumpet in here. I opens the big silver box, and there it is, all shiny inside. I touched it. I did touch it. Then I strokes it like I've seen my father do and it purrs. I runs my fingers over they keys then along the fur, the purple fur in the box. My fingers are burning hot. I tells it a story about a magic trumpet like itself. Then my mum finded me. I can't make anything up. She says, Colman what are you doing. Get out of your father's trumpet. So I close the silver lid and push it back into the wardrobe. Daddy must have forgotten to take his trumpet, I says. I hope it doesn't make him bad luck, I says. As if I was worried about it.

How did they pull it off? How did they pull it off? I mean you have to get a marriage certificate and stuff like that. How did they do it? I'm not sleeping nights trying to work this one out. Part of me thinks, Chuck it in Cole. Give it up. But the other part of me is pure obsessed with it. Every time I try and put it out of my mind, some other fucking question pops up like a fucking Jack in the box.

How did they get me? I mean no adoption agency would have done that then, would they. I mean they don't even do it now all that easily. I was reading some rumpus about some couple of blokes that wanted to adopt this little boy. I mean fair enough; good luck to them, it's not my problem. This is though. This is my fucking problem, that's for sure. And there's nobody else. No brothers or sisters. Just got me. They got me from the Scottish Adoption Agency in Edinburgh. 1962. I was born in 1961 but they had to wait a few months. They told me that the agency was well pleased with them given my colour. They said the agency called them 'a find' as I remember. A find. I am the same kind of colour as my father. We even look alike. Pure fluke. Or maybe I copied his smile so much I look like his carbon copy. Anyhow this was long before all this transracial adoption business. So it was an accident. A fatal accident if I think about it now. I'd rather have had some bod that was an army officer, some wanky accountant, some bland businessman, man, any fucking ordinary man would have done. I think the agency thought they'd have had trouble placing me if Joss and Millicent Moody hadn't come along.

We moved from Morton to London when I was seven. I got rid of my Morton accent. My father clung on to his. Determined that everyone would know he was Scottish. When I came home with my Cockney accent, my father got all cut up. He'd shout, 'Speak properly!' Seriously. He was quite nationalistic, I think you'd say. It was a fucking nightmare moving down here with that accent. I got ribbed. Non stop. Got it both ways. London was dead racist. Felt like shit. I don't remember much about Morton. I remember the inside of my Gran's house. All her ornaments. The smell of her mints on her breath. Her big high bed. That's about it. And a bike I got once for my birthday. Must have been six. It was bright red. Brand new. I thought I'd never learn to cycle, then one day I suddenly did. That's it. My father kept telling me I was Scottish. Born there. But I didn't feel Scottish. Didn't feel English either. Didn't feel anything. Now I feel even less like anything.

I'll go down their house and look for the important papers bag. My mother kept anything important in an old leather bag that looked like a doctor's bag. All the shit is in there. Do people get a marriage certificate? I fucking don't know. There must be birth certificates though. I've got no idea what it says on my father's death certificate. I suppose it must say Joss Moody. I'll need to find that out too.

I've never been a nosey bastard in my life. That's the fucking truth. I'm not interested in other people's business. Candid Camera. Know what I mean? I wasn't the sort of kid who hung about and earry-wigged at the door or at the top of the stairs. Wasn't my scene. If something forced me to listen, I'd listen. But this. This is different. I've got a fucking right to be a nosey bastard now. It's my life. I can go and snoop and prowl and sneak about the place. I can take things out and not put them back. I will. I'll do any of it. I don't care who it upsets. I'm upset. I'm the one who is upset.

My father was nice to everybody. Even though he was famous. He was pleasant to people. Smiled and talked to fans. Wrote bits of letters to people. See all those people, they'll be as flabbergasted as me. The fucking Joss Moody Fan Club will have to close down, man.

We were poor till I was ten. I didn't get hardly anything new. Well except that new bike. Everything else had been worn by somebody. Know what I'm saying? I wore other people's kids' clothes that my mum got at Oxfam. I used to imagine the boys that had worn the dufflecoat before I did. What their life was like. I used to imagine them as I was doing up the toggles. My dad hung out in those really grotty jazz bars. More dens than bars. I liked them. I used to find them exciting when I was very little. He always practised in the top room of some pub because the Morton Jazz band, or the Delta Swingers, or the whatevers I forget all the different names he had for himself, couldn't afford a decent place to practise. He was always coming back then, looking deflated because some pub had turfed him out and said they needed the room for some function. That way of living seemed to go on for ages. We went to Torr every summer because it was cheaper. My dad was always counting his takings. He'd get me to sit on the floor, spread out a newspaper, and build pounds, towers of sixpences, threepenny bits, crowns. I liked doing that; it made me feel rich. I didn't like when my father took all the money and put it in a plastic bag to be taken to the bank. I never understood why the bank deserved our money. I'd get a shilling for a pokey hat from the van.

When we moved down to London I still called an ice-cream a pokey hat when I was with my parents and called it an ice-cream with my mates. There were lots of words like that that I used because it cheered them up. I was practically schizophrenic. But now I come to think about it, I wasn't nearly as schizophrenic as him. Saying mocket to one and dirty to another is a whole different thing from being a man to the whole world and a woman to yourself. My father did all the so-called manly things. He was pretty handy about the house, putting up shelves and shit. He was good with electrical things. I mean he was practical for a jazz musician.

If he was angry with you, you knew about it. It was worse than a slap or a slinging match. He'd just go all cold and quiet on you and it'd give you the creeps. He'd say things like, 'Colman, I'm disappointed in you'. Once he was really angry with my mother and my mother was all upset. She put a tea towel over her face and cried underneath it. I tried that. Put a tea towel over my face and cried when he was angry with me. I made big sighs behind it like I'd seen my mother do. Big sighs, made the cotton breathe with me. But my father never seemed to feel guilty like we wanted him to. If he was angry, he was justified. The tea towel never stopped him. Throwing the towel in. When he was seriously angry his face darkened like the sky when it's about to pour down. Heaveeee.

Some people have got good memories. I haven't. There's hardly any particular times I could talk about. Everything gets all jumbled up. I haven't got a fucking clue what happened when I was nine. Don't remember my ninth birthday. Not really. One time I do remember was when I was on this bus with my mother and this black man got on. This was in Morton. So I'd be six or something like that. And somebody said something horrible to him, called him a fucking ape or some shit like that. And my mother, in a fucking flash, was on her feet giving the guy dokey. Saying she was ashamed to come from the same country as him and that he was pig ignorant. Pig ignorant. I remember that expression because it made me laugh out loud. Then I remember him staring at me, the nasty man, and saying to my mum, 'No wonder', or something. And the black man who had been called an ape, I couldn't take my eyes off him, was just sitting with his eyes low, looking at the bus floor. Embarrassed as fuck I expect. Then my mum grabbed my hand and we got off that bus and walked home. We'd got off too many stops early and I had to half-run to keep up with her fury. I don't think she told my dad about that one. Just as well it hadn't been him. I remember wishing my mum had just kept her mouth shut and not said anything. I stared at her and I was scared and people were staring at me. It made me look at my own colour of skin when I got home. Maybe that was the first time I really noticed it. And I was sort of surprised by it. That's about the longest memory I've got and unfortunately it doesn't really involve my father, does it?

It was just like having an ordinary mother and father except I was adopted and my dad was into jazz, except for that it was just ordinary. I could never have guessed. I never saw nothing. If I had, I'd have thought I'd been seeing things. It really fucking gets to me that they didn't just tell me. Sometime. I'm thirty-three. I'm not some adolescent or some 'wee boy'. There was plenty of times they could have said something. I never had a bath with him or saw him or her naked. But then plenty kids never saw their parents naked. That isn't all that unusual. I mean some parents were just uptight. Kept their fucking privates to themselves. Sammy got to see his Dad's willy. Sammy's family were dead casual about all that. Once I saw Sammy's mum's bra hanging on the back of a chair in their living room. I stared at it for fucking ages. Sammy said his Dad's willy was so big it worried him. He didn't want one that big, he didn't think it looked nice. He made it sound really horrible. Said it was the size of a big carrot and had lots of dark hairs at the top. Wild. I was appalled and fascinated. I tried for a couple of weeks after Sammy saw his Dad's dick to get to see my dad's, but it never happened. And I was probably a bit relieved. I never pulled it off.

Just as well. Imagine I'd been confronted with a big frigging mound of venus.

I never had many friends home except Sammy, my parents liked him. Sammy was the only one to get to come to Torr with us. I wonder where he is now and if he has seen the News. I used to be convinced that my father liked Sammy better than me. It made me jealous. Sammy and my dad talked more, laughed more. Once my father even gave Sammy a shot of his trumpet which drove me mad. He told Sammy he'd got the hang of it really quickly.

Things are falling into place. He never taught me to swim. No wonder. Where would he have got changed? Said he couldn't swim. He never went to the Doctors, said he was terrified of them. Even the urinals. He never fucking used the urinals. Said they were common and you could catch things and there were unsavoury men who could be dangerous. When I stop to think about it; which is what I have done; stopped to think; stopped my whole life just to think about this, talk about this; stopped seeing my mates; stopped my job; stopped sleeping at night; when I stop to think about it, it is spilling out all over the place. Everywhere I look it rears its head. Waves a menacing hand, says Hello There, I'm over here. I've made a complete arse of myself. I am what my father called an eejit. Eejit. I wonder what the first eejit on the planet did to get called an eejit. I wonder if he just went about the place with his eyes shut.

Before I became Colman Moody, I was William Dunsmore. If I'd stayed William Dunsmore all my life I'd have been a completely different man. Definitely. I mean a William Dunsmore's smile would be different from a Colman Moody's smile. Certainly. All my facial expressions would have been different. If some fucker's saying, Hey Willy to you, you're bound to look a bit grim. I bet even my walk would have been heavier if I'd been William Dunsmore. Heavy footed. Maybe a bit lopsided. That was one of my favourite things when I was a kid and my mother first told me that name, imagining what I'd have been like if I'd kept that name. I was pleased to be called Colman, not William. Really fucking chuffed. Now I'm not pleased, not pleased at all. There's not that many Moodys around. You just need to mention Moody and people think of the trumpet man that turned out to be a woman.

In fact if my father had wanted immortality, he couldn't have connived a more cunning plan. This one puts the tin lid on it. If the jazz world was so 'anything goes' as my father claimed, then why didn't he come clean and spit it out man? The 1960s were supposed to be cool. Flower people. Big joints. Afghans. Long hair. Peace. Why not a woman playing a fucking trumpet, man, what was wrong with that?

When I became a man, you'd think my father would have told me then, wouldn't you? Most fathers have a special chat, don't they? Mine, instead of philosophising about the birds and the bees and all that crap, could have sprung that on me. Why didn't he? Just tell me the truth when I was old enough to completely screw up my adolescence.

I never fancied boys; no. I've always been one hundred per cent heterosexual, except for those times when I was about sixteen and my mates and me would have a joint and a communal wank listening to Todd or Genesis or Pink Fucking Floyd. Or watching the Old Grey Whistle Test on the box. I don't like that hippy music anymore, man. It was just a phase.

Why do people want to make other people proud? What's that about? It's neurotic isn't it? Kids get fed that crap before they walk. Even walking for your parents is something to be proud of, your first wobbly steps. It's a load of balls, that's what it is. I spent too much time saying, Look at me Daddy, so much that I never fucking looked at him.

We didn't talk a lot about me being adopted. I wasn't that interested in my real parents. I mean my thinking was if they weren't interested in me, then I wasn't intersted in them. Simple as that. My mother would tell me that this other woman would have loved me and found it hard to give me up, I just said yeah, yeah and privately thought, Bollocks. I mean if you love a kid you keep them, if you don't you give them up. Simple. Money don't matter, what people think don't matter. If you want a kid and you get a bun in your oven, you'll fucking cherish the whining squirming brat, or not. If I'd got the chance I'd have probably liked to see a photograph of my mother and one of my father. I don't even know which one was black or where the black one came from. Haven't got a clue. People are always coming up to me and asking if I'm from Haiti, Morocco, Trinidad, Tobago, Ghana, Nigeria, Sierra Leone, Jamaica. Some asshole the other week was convinced I came from Haiti. You look identical to the people there, he said. Stopped me dead in the street and says, Hey are you from Haiti? I dunno, I says. Then I thought the next fucker that asks me where I come from, I'm going to say yes I come from Haiti, Morocco, Trinidad or any place they ask. What does it matter anyway? My father always told me he and I were related the way it mattered. He felt that way too about the guys in his bands, that they were all part of some big family. Some of them were white, some black. He said they didn't belong anywhere but to each other. He said you make up your own bloodline Colman. Make it up and trace it back. Design your own family tree, what's the matter with you? Haven't you got an imagination? Tell me really, that's what I kept saying, tell me where your father was really from. Look Colman, he said. Look Colman, I could tell you a story about my father. I could say he came off a boat one day in the nineteen twenties, say a winter day. He came off a boat on a cold winter day, a boat that stopped at the port of Glasgow. The port of Glasgow when Glasgow was a place where all the ships wanted to go. He came off that ship and although it was cold and grey, he liked it. He liked Glasgow, so he settled. Or I could say my father was a black American who left America because of segregation and managed to find his way to Scotland where he met my mother. Or I could say my father was a soldier or a sailor who was sent here by his army or his navy. Or I could say my father was from an island in the Caribbean whose name I don't know because my mother couldn't remember it. Or never bothered to ask. And any of these stories might be true Colman. It drove me mad. Which one, I said. Which one is true? Doesn't matter a damn he said. You pick. You pick the one you like best and that one is true. It doesn't change me who my father was or where he came from and it certainly doesn't change you, he said.

He was wrong about that. He was wrong. The stupid bastard was wrong. I'm sure he used to be right. I'm sure when I was a little kid he was right about everything. He was so right his face shone. His hair looked clever. He was so right then and I went about the place trying to remember all the things he told me and the way he told them. I'd copy some of his big words. Kidology, that was one. Or colossal, that was another. Or impertinent, facetious, irreversible.

My father didn't like discussing his family. He had no old photographs of himself when he was a kid, not one. I suppose if I look in their house I could find some photographs of Josephine Moore hiding somewhere. Unless he cut himself up or burnt himself to hide the evidence. I hope he didn't. I hope I can find some. If I saw a photograph of her, I could convince myself that I'm not living some weird Freudian dream, some fucked-up dream where I don't know my father, my mother or myself. I don't know any of us anymore. He has made us all unreal. It doesn't matter where your father came from Colman he said. Like fuck it doesn't. For all I know there could be some custom in one of those Caribbean islands, some annual carnival where everyone changes sex, dresses up as their opposite. Some big island carnival where all the transvestite island-ers play steel bands and float on floats, heavily masked and made up so that no one can recognise anyone. I can't believe the stuff I'm thinking now. It's crap. Pure crap. I know it's crap, but that doesn't stop me from thinking it, from it floating into my head – all the scum and shit, drifting and sliding through my filthy mind.

He was wrong. He was wrong about everything.

I'm not bothered about knowing about those blood parents of mine. My mother told me a few bits about what they did. All they do is cause pain – parents, blood parents or Mickey Mouse parents, all they do is mess with your head. Not to be trusted, man. Shit I wouldn't have kids. No way.

All I did was get born. I came into this world weighing a modest 6lbs and 2ozs according to my mother. I've always remembered those num-bers; I was a lightweight. But my mother told me there was a big fucking hurricane around the time I was born. Blew the trees in our street down and several slates off the roof. Made quite a commotion. The winds were stark mad when I arrived at the Elsie Ingles hospital in Edinburgh. I'm still a skinny fucker. No meat on me. Tall as fuck and skinny. When I went to India I looked like the walking dead man. Got the runs and lost a stone and a half. My father said to me when I got back, you need to put on some weight, Cole. He called me Cole when he was being nice. My mother always called me Colman. I didn't ask to be born. I didn't ask to be adopted. Why should I be grateful to anybody? I was born under a sleeping star. An inebriated star. Somebody wasn't paying no attention. First this, then that. That's the story of my life. Nobody was watching out for me. They were too busy watching out for each other.

That's about all I can figure out. Some people get all the luck. There were guys like that at my school. They'd get chosen for the sports teams, they'd get the best-looking girls, they never wore glasses, especially not those extra thick ones, or trouser patches, or naff shoes. They just looked cool. I wore glasses. Don't anymore as you can see. I'm vain as fuck now. Whoever invented contact lenses ought to be knighted. I got a double barrel name: Darky-Specky. I always thought it funny when teachers tried to explain racism to kids by saying, You wouldn't like to be called Freckles or Specky now would you? But all that seems nothing to this. Nothing.

My father had tits. My father didn't have a dick. My father had tits. My father had a pussy. My father didn't have any balls. How many people had fathers like mine? Which chat line could I ring up for this one? Imagine it flashing up on the screen after a programme about father/ mothers, trani parents or whatever the fuck you'd call them: if any of this relates to you and you need someone to talk to, please ring blah blah blah. The line will be open for the next 24 hours. Some things those fuckers haven't dreamt of, I'm telling you. I could ring round the whole country and never find anybody that's gone through what I'm going through. I bet you.

I'm going to track him down. I'm going to track my father's life down, back to when he was a girl in Morton, under the unassuming name Josephine Moore. Josey. Jose. Joss.

But where did he get the Moody? Or was that just moody blues. I'll write his fucking biography. I'll tell his whole story. I'll be his Judas. That's what Oscar Wilde said isn't it? My dad often quoted it and laughed. 'Every man needs his disciples but it's Judas that writes the biography.' I used to be my father's disciple. Not any fucking more mate. I've gone over to the other side.

I went into that funeral parlour and the man, the funeral man, takes me aside. He's got a look on his face I know I won't forget. Half-awkward, half pure glee. Like things are suddenly looking up for him. He calls me Mr Moody. I think maybe he doesn't get all that many famous dead bodies and he's dead chuffed. Mr Moody he says, I'm not quite sure how to put this but it had better be me who tells you rather than the media, I am assuming of course that you don't know already. He waits. I see him reading my face. Know what already I say, thinking the guy's a pillock. When I undressed your father to perform my routine duties, I dis- covered... I'm waiting for him. I think he's going to say he discovered my father had died of some other illness or that he discovered some weird mark on his body or that he discovered my father had committed suicide. I'm waiting. He's drawing it out. What the fuck has he discovered, that my father is still alive?

When I undressed your father, Mr Moody, I discovered that she is a woman. I had to have him repeat that sentence. The sentence sounded wrong to me. She. She is a woman. I thought the guy must be getting paid to perform some sick joke on me. Perhaps they have organizations where instead of sending a live kissogram to a birthday party, you send a weird deathogram to a funeral parlour. The man must not be the real man. I tell him I want to see the real undertaker, the mortician, whatever the fuck you call it, your boss. I said, is this your idea of a joke you sick bastard? Who has put you up to this? I'm shaking him. Pulling his stupid thin lapels back and forth. This is all quite understandable he says. Don't fuck with me, I says. He takes me through to where the body is. Through to the cold parlour and shows me my father. I see him naked and it is only now that I realise that this is the first time in my life that I have seen my father naked. The funeral man shows me some surgical bandages that he says were wrapped tightly around my father's chest to cover his 'top'. I take a quick look. But that look is still in my head now. It has stayed in my head – the image of my father in a woman's body. Like some pervert. Some psycho. I imagine him now smearing lipstick on a mirror before he died.

I walked out of that place as fast as I could. I said thank you for letting me know to the funeral man. The sky was bright blue that day and it was sunny. Hot. I was sweating. Everyone was complaining about the weather. I remember wondering if I'd ever be able to talk about anything so ordinary again. What a fucking luxury it seemed to stand around and say, Isn't it hot? A woman in a white top said to an old woman who was dressed for winter, 'Isn't this insufferable. Freak hot weather. Freak's the word.' I ran along repeating that to myself, 'Freak's the word.' I stopped and hung down to my toes and took a deep breath. My heart racing. Then I started up again. I was soaked. My hair was stuck to my head. My trousers were wet. The streets were on fire. Maybe I could just melt, I remember thinking, just melt away.

That's my Daddy. The one with the orange tie. See. See, standing next to the man with the big drum. He is My Daddy. See his trumpet? That's his. His third trumpet. Slim Fingers, his friend, give it to him. That is his favourite. He looks smart, doesn't he? He is good to the trumpet. His eyes close like he sleeping. My daddy finish and people clap. Clap, clap, clap. I stands on my chair and claps too. I have on a sailor suit. I just gets it. My mummy says, Sit Down Colman. But my Daddy comes and picks me up, swings me in the air, high, high, through all the big smiles. Then sits me on his big shoulders. Says, All right, wee man. Everybody crowds round us. Smacks my dad in the back. I'm going to fall off. I could. They could make me fall off doing that. All right, wee man.

Yesterday I got rat arsed. This morning I woke up with a disgusting taste in my mouth. Like that Billy Connolly joke: your mouth's like a badger's bum. Too many fags and pints, but it was the whisky that finished me off. I could never take whisky. I went into a pub I've never been into where I knew nobody and just sat myself down in a stool at the bar like I've seen depressed guys do in movies. I don't know how I got home. Woke with a fucking crashing headache, thumping, and tightening the screws, going into my temples deep. Took a couple of panadol. My stomach felt like a wobbly egg. Nothing in the cupboard. I went round the corner and bought some bread, but forgot to buy butter. Dry toast. Dry toast and tea. I'm feeling so sorry for myself, I hate myself. It's not a nice feeling, feeling sorry for yourself. It's stupid. My morning story. Hardly fucking breakfast at the Savoy, but there you go. I've always been a 'moany wee shite' – his words. Now he's given me something to moan about.

I can't remember much of what I was saying yesterday. Sammy. I remember talking some crap about Sammy. You can run, but you can't hide. I'd discount a lot of that as junk. I think it's better to start all over again. From the top. When I went to the shop this morning I saw the back of some woman that looked like my mother and she made me feel like shit. She had a scarf over her head and was hurrying because the rain just started coming down. I don't know where she was going, you never know where people are going, do you? All these people rushing about, they're all going somewhere. London's full of fuckers rushing to some place. Even early in the morning, you can't avoid them. I can't get my head around it. Suddenly the rain was coming down vicious and I lost her, the woman that looked like my mother. They kissed each other often enough. I'd catch them in the kitchen, or on the stairs, kissing. Sammy's sister is a lesbian. Sammy told me that one day out of the fucking blue. We were seventeen. He just said, My sister's a bender Cole. And I said, That right, and he said, Yeah man, and we left it at that. We didn't think much of it.

All we were was anti Culture. We hated stuff being shoved in our faces. Who to read, listen to, look at. Who's in. Who's out. Glossy mags. Being written about, interviews, bollocks. We just took the piss. We liked shit nobody else liked. We liked rap before it took off then didn't like it when it did.

My mother got into a double bed every night for the past thirty odd years and slept with my father, a woman. I am not small-minded. Seriously, I am not. Not anti-gay or anything. But I'd have probably been cool if I'd known what was going on.

What is it?

What is it that is eating me? I'm not a bitter man. Don't get me wrong. Please. It's probably the fact that my father didn't have a prick. Maybe it's just as simple as that. No man wants a fucking lesbian for his father. Maybe for his mother. But for his father! My father wasn't a man like myself, showing me the ropes and helping me through puberty when everything was mad and changed at the same time. When your voice suddenly goes like something falling through a floor. When your face gets itchy and rough. When you wake in the morning, rub your cheeks and get a shock at the stubble. A fright. And then you remember you are becoming a man. These changes are normal. I thought my father had had those too. The shock of pubic hairs arriving unannounced, one at a time, then suddenly they've all sprouted like alfalfa. The boy you were gets lost. Now the man I was is lost too. My father once said to me, I know what it's like son, when I was going through some fucking teenage torment. I remember it myself. But he didn't did he? That was an out and out lie.

What did he remember?

My mother always told me it was all right for me to be naughty sometimes, but lying, lying was the scourge of the earth, the worst thing for a child to do. Own up Colman. I think that was her expression. I am cut up. Since my father died I've been walking around, half-alive myself, sleepwalking, with this pain chiselled into my chest. Jagged. Serrated. Nothing makes it disappear. Not Milk of fucking Magnesia. Nor Rennies. There's an animal inside me, slobbering.

A mate of mine's mother was carted off to the loony bin when he was eleven. He wasn't told nothing. Your mum's gone off for a little holiday. He knew it was no fucking holiday from the wild look in her eyes.

Will I ever forgive them? No.

He is sitting on the edge of my bed, my Daddy. He pulls my yellow blanket back. I am too hot. I am too hot and it is too early for bed. He gives me a spoon of medicine. I open my mouth wide and wait for the spoon to be put in my mouth and wait for my Daddy to say Brave boy. Because it is nasty horrible stuff. My Daddy smells of his trumpet club. He takes my hand and sings, Dreams to sell/ Fine dreams to sell/ Angus is here/ with dreams to sell. Then my Daddy is sleeping. He does a loud snore. Then he catches his breath and suddenly wakes. He pats my head. Strokes my head. Hair just like mine, he says. Then he pulls my cover right up to my chin, says, Coorie in Son, Coorie in. I am still not sleeping. I hear voices under the floor. My Daddy is singing another song to my Mummy. I hear next door's dog bark like he is angry. I hear children playing out in the street. I hear Sammy shouting. Then they drop their voices. Then I hear the house breathe.

My father had a lifelong terror, phobia whatever, about hospitals. Makes a lot of sense in hindsight. He was so scared of doctors, he passed that onto me. That's what parents exist for: to pass their phobias on generation to generation. Fuck, if I so much as saw a white-coat man, I'd wet myself and have a big Marks and Spencers. That was our family word for tantrum – I had my first big tantrum in Marks and Spencers apparently in the food bit. I went bananas because my mother wouldn't buy me some fancy chocolate bar. My mother said that her ears went bright red with shame. I was doing some high pitch scream and jumping up and down on her feet at the same time. So every time after that when I was about to lose it my mother would say, Don't you do a Marks and Spencers on me. My father thought of doctors as a whole breed apart; he had a million different words for them. And jokes. What's the difference between God and a doctor? God knows he isn't a doctor. Shit like that. As many words for doctors as notes on his trumpet. If he wanted to insult somebody he'd say they wrote like a doctor, talked like a doctor, smiled like one. Needless to say, when he got ill, he just point-blank refused to see one. This is 1994. I'm still not sure what he had wrong with him. Something to do with his liver. He said, the last time I saw him, My number's up Cole. Like life was a fucking game of poker. I was destroyed. I tried to persuade him to see a doctor, but he was having none of it. I read somewhere that dying women are braver than dying men. He was definitely brave. But not brave enough to tell me the truth. And my mother didn't want me to stay the night, that night. She wanted to be on her own with my father.

So I went out with my mate Brady who has left nine messages on my machine, man. The first one just said, Fucking Hell Cole. Ring me.

The day I went to the funeral parlour I still had the remains of a hangover. I puked in the toilet of the creepy place before I left. I puked everything up until I'd nothing left but bile. Bright yellow bad tasting bile. I'd never seen a dead person before. Never seen someone there and not there like that. Still and stiff. Unreal. The smell of disinfectant not the smell of people. The cold air spinning round the room. The sick noise of that big fan, its arm whirling around like some mad dancer.

My father looked fake. Everything about him. His breasts looked like they were made of silicone. His eyes were closed, but I got the feeling that if someone opened them, the bright orange eyes of some huge doll would scream out at me. His hands looked like plastic gloves as if they had never ever held a trumpet, as if the trumpet was just a dream the dead body had. I wanted to touch him to check he was real and not some waxwork, but I couldn't. I was too freaked out. I was scared shitless. I've never been so frightened. Someone had put powder on my father's cheeks. I don't know if it was the funeral man or someone else. The funeral man told me my mother was expected in later in the day and she was going to bring his suit, his best suit. That's what she wants her to wear, he said as if it was all beyond him. I'd forgotten my mother. I'd forgotten all about her. That meant she knew. Well of course she knew. I went to the toilet and then I ran and I kept on running through streets I didn't know in that unforgiving heat.

I phoned my mother and said things to her I can't now remember. She begged me to come round and see her. I told her she'd be lucky if I went to the funeral. I could feel how hollow her silence was, like I'd just scooped out her voice. But I couldn't stop. Ranting man. Fucking ranting. She said some balls like Colman try and understand. And she said sorry over again till that made me sick too. Colman I'm sorry. Sorry Colman. Colman. Colman. Colman. I started feeling dizzy at the sound of my own name.

I did go to the funeral, as you know. So did the jazzmen, all the old troopers from way back. Blokes I dimly remembered. Men from all the millions of bands my father formed before he stuck with Joss Moody. Can't remember their names now. Delta Swingers. Red Hot Dixies. All American-sounding names. I think he was even in one once called the Sweet Potatoes, but I might have made that up myself. I remember The Jazz Witnessers because it took me till I was ten to pronounce it. Anyhow. I never saw so many men cry in my life as at my father's funeral. Fucking Jesus. They all had huge big proper cloth handkerchiefs. I didn't cry. I just sat listening to them playing my mother's song.

I snatched a look at her. I wasn't sitting next to her, but I could see her from four rows behind. I knew she wanted me next to her, but I just couldn't. I was too mad. I sneaked a look at her when Tobias was playing her song and she was crying, not like how you'd expect, passive crying like the tears were something that was happening to her. Not big heaving sobs. Just futile little tears man going down her face slow. Seeing her like that, I half-thought of going and standing next to her. That would have been enough for her. Just for me to have stood next to her. But then I remembered my father in that parlour, naked, and I thought, Nah, why should I?

When people left, my mother left too. She didn't stand shaking hands as they went out like she did for my grandfather's funeral. Then I saw her leave in her big black Limo, alone. She turned round and looked at me and tried to smile. I looked away. That's the closest I came to crying, man. Not managing to look at my mother. I was surprised at how many people turned up actually. Everyone in double fucking shock. Coat collars turned up and this is the summer. Looking like winter. Everybody looking like winter.

The other thing that surprised me was that my father had changed again. Seriously. I don't know how that fucking happened. His coffin was open for people to pay their last respects. There he was dressed in one of his designer suits. He was well into the clothes. Flashy tie. Back to normal. In his clothes, he looked real again.

My father was born a girl on the 6th of November 1935. He was christened Josephine Moore. He was known as Joss Moody when, on the 29th of June 1994, he died.

Gordon Legge

Life on a Scottish Council Estate Vol. 1

Chap. 1

... and I'm playing some records and dancing about and generally enjoying myself when there's a knock at the door. It's Wee Harry and his problems. He tells me Wendy's chucked him so I let him in and make him a coffee and prepare to hear his life story for the millionth time. Just as we reach the part where his mam used to serenade him with 'Nobody loves you/ you're nobody's child', Edwyn and English Edgar arrive. Edwyn skins up and English Edgar says my flat's fair stinking of oranges and Marlboro. Just like California, I tell him. We take our cue and slap on some Beach Boys records. Wee Harry feels we're ignoring him (which we are) so him and his problems take their leave. The Tank is next to appear. He's got a few cans and joins us singing along to 'California Girls'. Edwyn and English Edgar depart when the dope and the bevvy run out... The Tank dives into my records... He comes out with The Stones, Cheap Trick, Alice Cooper and Guns N' Roses (the closest I've got to AC/DC). We get out the golf clubs and mime guitar solos and use them as microphones. The Tank says 'Is that the door?' It is. It's Stuart this time. Stuart is looking for Edwyn and English Edgar cause he heard they had a bit of dope. We tell him that they were here but that they left when the dope and the bevvy ran out ... Stuart is distraught... He skins up the roaches while wondering aloud who would be prepared to sell him hash on tick. This is difficult since Stuart owes money to everybody. Stuart is a divorced psychiatric nurse in real life. The Tank pisses off cause he can't stand Stuart ... Stuart gives it the really paranoid bit about how nobody likes him. This is true. Nobody does like him. There is a knock at the door. I look out. There's no one there. I look down. Ah, it's the kids (Aaron, Jason, Abigail and Veronique) and a dog called Bongo. They come in and head straight for my Scalextric. Stuart makes up his mind to go and says he's off to Steve and Sara's. They've always got hash and he only owes them a fiver. I make myself a coffee and play Scalextric with the kids and a dog called Bongo. I soon discover that Stuart has taken my full box of matches and left his empty one. Shit! I look out the window to see if the ice-cream van is there. It is. This is my daily exercise. I go bombing down the stairs and out the front door. AAAAAAAAAAAAA AAAAHHHHHHHHHHHHHHHHHHHHHHHHHHHHHHH!! I scream for my dear life and leap ten feet in the air as the biggest fucking Alsatian you have ever seen leaps out from our bundle of bin-bags... I compose myself and see that the Alsatian belongs to two guys with baseball bats and balaclavas who are presently engaged in smashing to bits a car belonging to one of my neighbours. They ask me if I've got a problem. I say 'Nnnn-nnnn-nn-no' and shrug my shoulders and try to look really uninterested. When I reach the ice-cream van, however, I say to Total Trevor – the English ice-cream man – 'Did you see that?' He shakes his head, does his Manuel and goes 'I know nuuuuu-ting.' Typical. So I get my matches and a snowball, a Mars bar, a packet of McCoys, a coconut Boost, a packet of white Buttons and a ten pence mixture. I also get ten pence mixtures for each of the kids and a dog called Bongo. (See if I'd have given as much money to charity as I have to the ice-cream van, I'd have shaken hands with Princess Anne by now.) Back at my flat I make myself another coffee and demolish my munchies... I am bloated. The door goes. It's Wendy. She tells me Wee Harry's chucked her. The kids say 'Ahhhh' as Wendy cries and I try to comfort her. The kids and a dog called Bongo can't stand the slushy bits so they decide to leave. They remind me I've got an all-night babysitting session on Friday and depart to plot my downfall. I return to Wendy. I put on this specially compiled Prince tape I made up for comforting distressed women... It works and before the end of 'Condition of the Heart' she's going, 'Gordon! Gordon! I want to have your babies' and we're partying like crazy through in my spare bedroom... In the afterglow there's a knock at the door. *Oh, no, it's my psychotic big brother!* My psychotic big brother drinks Newcastle Brown to make him violent and whisky to make him maudlin. Wendy departs screaming as my psychotic big brother batters fuck out of me and says sorry at the same time... After he's finished, I wash myself and nurse my injuries whereupon Hamish arrives and offers to sell me records I've already got. He says, 'They're really cheap, but.' He then tries to sell me a camera. Grant puts in an appearance. Grant comes round on the off-chance of bumping into Wee Harry. He wishes to befriend Wee Harry and gain a subsequent introduction to Wee Harry's wee sister, for whom he carries a horn of almost Alpine proportions... Grant circles my living-room... He offers me a fag. He makes polite conversation for three seconds... Then he says, 'Seen Wee Harry recently?' I say he's been and gone. Grant gets up and leaves. (He's pretty serious about this wee lassie.)

Hamish chases after him shouting, 'Do you want to buy a camera? Do you want to buy a camera?' I make myself a coffee but before I reach the comfort of my settee the door goes again. It's my pal Mikey. He's just up from London and heads straight for my records. He selects Steely Dan's *Countdown to Ecstasy* (he's dead nostalgic when he gets back to my bit) and we mime all the solos and remember all the words. Then we have a singles battle. We each seek out a record and defy the other to find a better one. This ends up with us arguing and damned near falling out. My pal Mikey says, 'I recognise that knock – IT'S THE BIG MAN!' And it is. The Big Man is an airline pilot in real life. (You think I'm joking!) He earns £30,000 a year, wears ludicrous Noel Edmonds jackets and is just back from Mexico. He's got a massive carry-out, a carrier-bagful of munchies and a bit of dope the size of Gibraltar. 'You know how those old Mexican geezers always look completely out of it?' he says with a megagrin on his face. Me and my pal Mikey say 'Ye-essss.' 'Well,' says The Big Man, 'this is the stuff that does it.' Me, my pal Mikey and The Big Man get stuck into the bevvy and the munchies and investigate the dope... We are soon looking like old Mexican geezers. My pal Mikey says he can't feel his legs or his eyelids. He crashes out in my spare bedroom. Me, I don't feel too good. For the first time in my life, I fail to finish off munchies. I tell The Big Man just to crash out in my living-room. He looks pleased with himself, now that he's turned us into zombies, and says he's just going to roll himself a single-skinner to ease him off to sleep. History has told me that he only managed to smoke half of it before achieving the desired state. Leaving the other half to start a fire which would in turn burn my fucking flat down.

Chap. 2

So the blessed council rehoused me, and now I'm sandwiched between a couple who watch videos of *The Hit Man and Her* and a right weird-looking guy who spends all his time at the bookie's and owns only one record – Dire Straits 'The Walk of Life'. Thankfully, we managed to save my records and The Big Man kitted me out with a new suite and a top-notch TV, hi-fi and video. It was the least he could do. My family and friends have been very good to me. They're great, as Big Tony the Tiger says. Edwyn and English Edgar arrive. Bad news. They have chapped the doors of the thirty-three places in our wee town that you can buy dope and have come up with nothing. Big fat zero. Stuart comes round. He empties my buckets, hoovers my carpets and ransacks my furniture but there are no roaches to be found. I am keeping my new flat very tidy. The Tank brings round one of his videos to entertain us. It features a black woman constantly screaming, 'Shit on my chest! Shit on my chest!' The plot develops to incorporate a series of guys – who look like my dad's neighbours, incidentally – and they, you guessed it, shit on her chest. Wee Harry appears. (At the door, like, not in the film.) He says we are depraved. The Tank says it's all right but it's not as good as *Anal Inferno*. The Tank is a window cleaner in real life. Wee Harry says he knows where we can get a bit of dope but first we have to listen to something that is very important to him. This we agree to do. Wee Harry goes over to the hi-fi, removes a tape from his pocket and puts it in the machine. It is Mahler's Ninth Symphony. It is sad and depressing with the good bits few and far between. It is the story of Wee Harry's life ... Wee Harry and English Edgar depart to get the dope. *Chap! Chap!* The new kids (Winston, Lee, Emma and Nicola) and a dog called Bongo (that's right, the same darn dog!) are at the door. Bad news, they say. My psychotic big brother has found out my new address. *Oh, no.* They tell me he got it off Hamish when Hamish was trying to sell him a camera. I thank the kids for letting me know and they remind me I'm babysitting on Friday night. I tell them it would be best to check again tomorrow. My visitors express their sympathies when I tell them the news. Wee Harry and English Edgar return with Grant, a half a ton of Bombay mix and a bit of dope. But there is to be no party. I tell my visitors I have to face this alone and ask them to leave. This they do ... I am alone. I am absolutely pissing myself and absolutely shitting myself. I hear 'The Walk of Life' coming up from below and find myself singing along. I'm just a bit disillusioned. The door goes. It's Carmel. She is looking for my pal Mikey. I tell her my pal Mikey is back in London and isn't due a visit for another couple of months. She is disappointed and horny. She puts on my specially compiled Prince tape and starts coming on really strong. I tell her about my psychotic big brother finding out my new address. (I also suspect that fear has made me impotent, but I do not tell her this.) Needless to say, she departs pronto. I make myself a coffee and think about things ... I'm thinking ... I would really like a fish supper. A fish supper with two pickled onions. A fish supper with two pickled onions and a Mars bar. There are five fish supper establishments within five minutes' walk of my house but I stay glued to my settee. I hear the ice-cream van but still I do not move ... *I recognize that knock – it's The Big Man!!* He heard about my psychotic big brother finding out my new address and he's come straight back from the Middle East. He hands me a sports bag and says it's the best he could do. I open the bag. It's a fucking machine-gun! The Big Man explains the mechanisms, praises the specifications and lists the various conflicts in which it has been put to use. 'Just kill the fucker,' he says. The Big Man's heart is in the right place. Respectfully, I ask him to leave. He does so. I get back to my settee and look at the machine-gun. Self-defence? An accident? I could hit him with it. Oh, I could hit him with a lot of things. Somebody chaps my verandah door. I think really fast. fkjfidkfjdkrick58djrifjjdj jfjgjjkkrj. The Big Man must have locked the close door. Now I live three flights up. Only one person would have the audacity to climb that. *My psychotic big brother*. The door gets chapped again. If I blasted off a few rounds that would be the end of it. But my mum wouldn't speak to me if I killed my psychotic big brother. And God knows what she'd do to me for ruining the curtains. 'What do you want?' I enquire. 'It's me, Hamish,' says Hamish. Whhhh-ooooh. I let him in. I tell him about all the trouble he's caused. He laughs and says it was all part of his masterplan. I point the machine-gun between his legs and say, 'What masterplan was that, like?' Hamish goes on to explain what happened. My psychotic big brother saw Hamish trying to sell the camera and approached Hamish with the intention of buying said camera. Once they were alone my psychotic big brother then inflicted various forms of torture upon poor Hamish in order to find out my new address. (I expect these acts of torture were never required to go beyond threats, but, anyway.) So Hamish gave him my address and my psychotic big brother appropriated the camera to boot. At this point, Hamish looks like he was the bloke who just invented the wheel. He goes on to say what he did next was to phone the police and tell them he'd seen a guy with a stolen camera. But the camera wasn't stolen I point out. Eh, says Hamish, it was … cause he stole it from his work. It was in the papers. So, continues Hamish, the police caught up with my psychotic big brother as he was preparing to come round and see me, i.e. getting tanked up on Newcastle Brown and whisky. There ensued a struggle and my psychotic big brother, five policemen, two Alsatians and three civilians have ended up in hospital. My psychotic big brother will be facing several charges and will almost certainly spend a while in prison, Hamish, who knows about such things, assures me. I have been reprieved. I go out onto the verandah and holler 'YEE-HAA. BEEZER CITY, MAN.' Hamish asks me what I intend doing with the machine-gun. He says he could sell it to somebody over the old town and offers to go halfers. I shake my head. Hamish is married with two children in real life. My visitors return. There is much celebration. The Big Man has bought me a fish supper with *three* pickled onions and a Mars bar. We party well into the night. Grant pesters Wee Harry about his sister. The Big Man and The Tank have a kid-on fight. Hamish and Stuart have a real fight when they accuse each other of hogging. Edwyn and English Edgar party through in my spare bedroom. I play my records at ridiculous volumes and we finish off by having a game of indoor football... Within the week I am evicted for making too much noise.

Chap. 3

So I've got a new flat and the good news is there are two spare bedrooms (one for the Scalextric, one for the shagging) – but the bad news is it's the lowest of the low on the difficult to let list in the heart of Dodgy Cunt City wherein my neighbours look like the cast of *The Name of the Rose* with tattoos, and the kids come to my door, shout, 'KILL THE WILLY!' then punch me in the balls and run away. This close is wild, man; even a dog called Bongo doesn't come round here ... Anyway, there's a knock at the door. It's the post with a package from my pal Mikey in London. My pal Mikey's wrote me a letter and sent me a tape of the Stone Roses and Happy Mondays. He says I'm going to love this tape. He says I've got to give it twenty listens cause it's one of those – growers. He tells me we've got to get hold of ecstasy. He says it's the greatest drug of all time. Eh? Now my pal Mikey's pretty much like myself, a records/football/ shagging man, and for him to be raving about a drug is pretty much akin to my grannie raving about drugs!... Edwyn, English Edgar and The Tank come round. I tell them the news and play them the tape ... We're into it. The Tank says, 'That boy's some guitarist.' (The Tank says things like that.) Edwyn and English Edgar take it upon themselves to contact The Big Man and get him to organize the ecstasy. They set out on their mission. Wee Harry comes round. He's jacked in his job, he's left Wendy and he's just botched up an attempt at slashing his wrists. No problem, we tell him. Party, the night, my bit, be here. Ecstasy, we tell him. My pal Mikey's raving about it. Wee Harry says it's his last hope. He leaves to tell Wendy. Hamish arrives. He doesn't have any money but he wants an ecstasy. We tell him he's got till The Big Man arrives. Can Hamish do it? Time will tell. Stuart is next. 'Party?' he asks. *Party*, we tell him. He's got a new jumper and a wee bit of dope. The Tank tells him to save the dope till later. Stuart is distraught again. The more people present the less he'll

get. We wait . . . .
. . . . we're waiting . . . .
. . . . waiting for The Big Man. Stuart's staring
at his wee bit of dope, The Tank's fast-forwarding a Michelle Pfeiffer
video to get to the shagging bits and I'm making coffee. The door goes.
It's Carmel. She says she wants an ecstasy. She's heard it makes you
horny. This is incredible! If Carmel gets any hornier the paint'll come off
the walls. Carmel is a primary school teacher in real life. Wee Harry and
Wendy arrive. They're together but they're not talking to each other. I
politely ask them not to smash my windows or my hi-fi and not to throw
my records at each other. The door goes yet again! It's Grant and Wee
Harry's wee sister. This is their first night out together. The air of tension
and expectancy is incredible. We're waiting . . . .
. . . . we're standing about like workies . . . .
. . . . waiting for The Big Man. 'I RECOGNISE THAT
KNOCK' we all scream at once – but it's only Edwyn and English Edgar
pretending to be The Big Man. Edwyn's been on his uncle's phone and
fax machine all day and everything's set. The Big Man is due. Piggy banks
have been raided, accounts have been overdrawn and families have been
borrowed from. There's an apologetic knock at the door. 'Oh no, he
couldn't get any,' we all groan at once. But it isn't The Big Man ... *it's my
psychotic big brother*! He says, 'Hello, Gordon.' I say, 'Hu-hu-hu-hu!' He
asks if he can come in. I let him in cause he's wearing flares, a hooded
top and hundred-and-twenty quid Reeboks. Something is very strange.
He tells me he's stopped drinking, gives me a hug and tells me that he
loves me. This is all very emotional and all very weird. He's never
embraced me – he's only ever hit me. He says 'Hello' to everybody and
asks what's happening. I tell him we're waiting for The Big Man bringing
up the ecstasy. 'Brilliant,' he says. He says he did tons of the stuff when
he was in prison. My *ex*-psychotic big brother goes on to say that there's
at least three hundred places in Glasgow manufacturing ecstasy. (Really,
and I thought all they did was walk greyhounds.) He says a lot of it's bad,
though, and a lot of it's dodgy. (That's more like Glasgow.) We tell him The
Big Man'll get us good stuff. 'Good,' he says and tells us he's got a couple
of acid-house tapes in his bum-bag. (*He's wearing a bum-bag!*) They'll do
for later on, he tells us. We wait . . . .
. . . . there is no more exciting place in
the world to be the night than my bit . . . .
. . . . the guy who's going to be
shagging Madonna is bored out of his skull by comparison . . . .

.... we're waiting for The Big Man. Outside I hear a car tooting its horn. I RECOGNISE THAT TUNE. IT'S THE BIG MAN! I rush to the door and let him in. He's got a taxi here straight from the airport. *Prestwick airport!* He's got the ecstasy, enough for everybody. 'You call them E's,' my ex-psychotic big brother tells me. The Big Man says they're good ones. My ex-psychotic big brother says they look good. They look like aspirins to the rest of us. The Big Man says he got them off one of his fellow pilots. He says all the pilots are 'on one'. You call it being 'on one' my ex-psychotic big brother tells us. Wendy asks if it's like acid/mushies/speed. The Big Man says, 'No/No/No.' We all breathe a sigh of relief because we don't want to end up like Stuart. 'There's no paranoia,' says my ex-psychotic big brother, who, like most nutters, used to be pretty moralistic about drugs. He says it isn't crude and the comedown's beautiful. The Big Man says he could do with a smoke of dope. We tell him all we've got is Stuart's wee bit. 'Pity,' says The Big Man – then he looks round him, like we're on a mission or something, and says, 'Okay. Let's drop the E's.' We wait ....
.... we're waiting ....
...........................we're waiting to see what happens. There's a knock at the door. It's two sixteen-year-olds the size of giants in police uniforms. They ask to be let in. I let them in. They ask me to turn down my music. I turn down my music. They eye my visitors. My visitors smile back. They ask my name, my date of birth and how old I am. I'm really polite and cool and tell them. All of a sudden The Tank says, *'Fucking hell, man'* and planks himself down in the corner. He looks like Buddha doing an impression of Yogi Bear. Wee Harry starts dancing to the Happy Mondays. Really dancing, like an African. *Wee Harry never dances!* He listens to Gustav Mahler and *Leonard Cohen Sings Peter Hammil* and reads Sylvia Plath for breakfast. Edwyn and English Edgar ask if they can go through to my spare bedroom. 'Just for a minute,' they say. *They never ask!* They usually just disappear. Wendy and Grant and Wee Harry's wee sister start dancing with Wee Harry. *Really dancing!* Carmel's running her fingers through her hair and moaning gently. *The paint is seriously coming off the fucking walls, man.* She's so into herself, it's unreal. The Big Man says, 'Yeah, I'm well into this' and sits himself down beside The Tank and gives him a cuddle. The last time I seen that grin on his face was when he got the love-bites from Wee Jeannie Wright on the school trip to Switzerland. Stuart looks cool. As if he's savouring something. *Stuart looks cool!* Stuart never looks cool. *Never, never, never.* He's sitting two feet from two policemen, he's got dope secreted about his person and

he's looking cool. Like he's normal or something. My ex-psychotic big brother is going round asking everybody if they're all right. He asks the policemen if they're all right. The police don't look all right. They're filling their notebooks. I turn the tape over. This is my twentieth listening of The Stone Roses LP – *fucking godlike*. I'm grinding my teeth and I'm telling the police The Stone Roses are fucking godlike. The police note this down then leave. I see them to the door. Me, I like the police. They lock up nutters. More power to them. I watch their car leave the court then rush back to my living-room and turn up my music. Stuart skins up his dope. Edwyn and English Edgar reappear. They now wish to be known as The E Boys. Wee Harry and Wendy head off to the spare bedroom. They're best pals again. There's a knock at the door. It's Hamish. He asks, 'Was that the feds?' I tell him it was but everything's cool. I ask if he got the money all right. He says, 'You're not going to believe this but I've just won on the big bandit up the club. I'm fucking loaded. Fucking hell,' he says when he sees everybody. '*Give me some!*' Everybody is pleased to see Hamish. Everybody loves Hamish. *Eh?* The Big Man asks if Hamish has any dope. Hamish tosses a lump over to The Big Man then he does his Blue Peter and removes a two-foot-long joint from his coat pocket and says, 'And here's one I prepared earlier.' I ask Carmel how she's doing. She says she thought she'd feel really horny but the only person she's into is herself. Pity, I says to myself. She starts that moaning again. *She's glowing, man.* She's glowing. Every breath brings it back on. Wee Harry reappears. He's wearing only his Y's and announces emphatically, 'I understand the sixties! This stuff is important!' That's all he says, then heads back through to my spare bedroom. There is a wonderful atmosphere. Everything's worked out all right. Nobody's fighting or falling out or being sarky. *Why? … Ecstasy?* My ex-psychotic big brother points to The Tank, The Big Man, Hamish and Stuart (who are passing round the big joint) and says, 'That's called chilling out.' He points to Grant, Wee Harry's wee sister, Carmel and The E Boys (who are dancing) and says, 'That's called vibing out.' I cuddle my ex-psychotic big brother and he says, 'And this is what it's all about.'

(to be continued)

James Meek

Get Lost

A bright constellation, Orion the hunter, shone through the skylight as I raised a glass of reservoir water and drank the tablets down.

Throughout my body veins and arteries began to pulse with painful pressure and sparks flickered in my eyes.

Swimming through thick air I floated into a chair and switched on the TV.

I clutched the armrests and tried to focus on the wobbling screen.

Jackie Bird was there but she'd turned into the Central Belt. Her hair was the flares of Grangemouth, her teeth were luxury bungalow developments in Falkirk, her private parts were a Japanese seafood factory in East Kilbride and her legs were the Clyde all the way to Dunoon.

Somebody was beckoning. It was Eddie Mair, tapdancing along the M8. I was following him, mounted on the shoulders of a punchdrunk boxer. And finally, said Eddie, dancing in front of a juggernaut which hit an Escort which hit a Fiesta which rammed into a schoolbus which crashed into a petrol tanker which exploded destroying a Fiat 125 and a Chrysler Alpine, throwing bodies into the landscaping where the crows were waiting. The night was lit by blue flashing lights and we all climbed into ambulances, Eddie still dancing, till we were ambushed by Young Conservatives, who beat the drivers senseless with baseball bats and took the ambulances for United Biscuits plc, but we escaped up the verge and rolled down the other side into a new town with a licence, where every house had a bar and poets of choice were scribbling on the backs of whisky labels and children were taught to swim in pools of Tennents lager and men and women slept where they fell and the bins and the gutters overflowed with puke and empties. And then we found the really bad side of town, where the only man with a job was showing tourists the longest waterfall in Scotland, twenty-five years down the back of his lounge, when a plane carrying live lobsters from Stornoway to Paris crashed into the estate, and the streets rang with the screams of starving Scots fleeing from edible crustaceans. And we saw Rabbie Burns renamed Rabbie Sideburns in a stetson and a bootlace tie telling a girl that condoms were for mummies' boys, and we asked him the way out of town, and he said no no no no no no

No going westward, a group of leading businessmen has the Government franchise to siphon off your blood and market it worldwide under the Quality of Scotland label of excellence.

No going eastward, a member of the house of Windsor is setting fire to every building built since 1918 and torturing and hanging architects in one of his well-appointed residences.

No going southward, the road's blocked with a drift of skeletons, of women burned by Scottish kings and men murdered by Scottish aristocrats and people made slaves by a Scottish parliament and a boy poisoned by a badly defrosted Scotch egg.

How d'you no go north, said Rabbie.

Aye, north, said the boxer, let's away up north.

Look north! said Eddie, and his dancing feet went spare tapping, and the moon rolled up over the Grampians and knocked the clouds aside like skittles, and millions were crawling on all fours towards the mountains, hiding their faces.

My heart was pounding and sweat was running down my face and I slipped off the boxer's shoulders into a sealoch where environmental freedom fighters were clubbing fish farmers to death and liberating caged salmon, and the salmon were being eaten by seals and ospreys and the freedom fighters were being eaten by killer whales and I tried to swim to safety but one of the whales grabbed me by the leg and offered me a free portable TV if I'd attend a timeshare presentation, but I struck out for the shore and saw the catseyes of the A9, which weren't catseyes but Chernobyl lambs' testicles, and it wasn't the A9 but a disused airfield where the SAS was providing weapons training for a squad of youngsters applying to be god, the favourite could preach like Ian Paisley and tackle like Willie Miller and dress like a taxi driver from Bridge of Allan and make decisions like the Convention of Scottish Local Authorities and punish like a dogfight trainer and reward like a smiling old woman from Glamis, and the young gods were looking at me for target practice and I dodged into a corrie where three social workers were gathered round a giant bubbling potnoodle, and I tried to speak but my words were drowned out by a squadron of jet fighters practising their wartime role by flying between my legs, and the social workers turned to me and sang a ballad of community care, Neurofen and Lemsip, paracetamol and Aspirin, Novocaine, Askit, Haliborange, Rennies...

And the first one said Fuck away with you, leave this deadend place and go to bigger brighter countries at the junctions of cultures and peoples and changes

And the second one said Get a grip and stay at home and work and learn and act to make it good, the best place to visit is a handmade homemade future

And the third one said Go up into the mountains in winter on your own and find a rock as big as yourself and punch it with your fists until your hands bleed and put your hands in the snow until you can't feel them anymore and punch the rock again and put your hands in the snow again until the pain makes you cry and then come back into town and do anything you like.

Ali Smith

The Unthinkable Happens to People Every Day

I'm sorry son but there's no one of that name lives here.

The man hung up, stood in the phone box and breathed out slowly. Without warning London surrounded him, widening round him like rings in water with its scruffy paintpeeled shops, its streets leading into other insignificant streets, its anonymous houses for all the grey seeable distance. Someone rapped on the glass, a woman scowling from under her umbrella, and as he came out he saw people waiting in a line behind her. He crossed the road and stood outside a television shop with the sets in the windows showing one of the daytime programmes where two presenters and an expert discuss an issue and viewers phone in and talk about it. That was when he went inside the shop and within a few minutes had smashed several of the sets.

Now the man was driving too fast for his car, he could hear it rattling and straining under the tape of The Corries, the one tape that had been in the glove compartment when he looked. Above the noise there was a hum in his ears like when you wet your finger and run it round the rim of a glass. He thought that's what it had been like, like going into a room full of wine glasses. Nothing but wine glasses from one end of the floor to the other, imagine. As soon as you got into a room like that, he thought, the temptation to kick would be too strong. The same as when he was a boy and they visited the McGuinnesses, when he was handed that china saucer and the cup with the fragile handle, with the lip of it so thin against his own that it would be really easy to bite through. As soon as a thought like that came into your head you wanted to try it. That ache in his arm to twitch suddenly and send the tea into the air. That would have made his folks laugh. They might have been cross to start with, but after that it'd have been something to remember.

He had stepped inside the TV shop to get out of the way of passers-by. Sleek new televisions were ranged in front of him, small ones on the top shelf, larger ones in the middle, massive wide-screen sets on the floor on metal stands. All except two were showing the same picture and the sound was turned up on one; he heard the presenter hurrying a caller off the air so as to bring the next person on. The woman he was hurrying had apparently just told them about a wasting disease her daughter aged nineteen had been diagnosed as having and the bespectacled expert, presumably a doctor giving advice, was shaking his head dolefully at the camera. The presenter said, well thank you for that call Yvonne, we hope we've brought a little bit of comfort to you on that, and your daughter too, but now let's go over to Tom who's calling from Coventry, I believe he's just heard he's been found HIV positive, am I right, Tom? The maps on the screens flashed where Coventry was.

The man leaned forward and tipped the television in front of him off its shelf; it crashed onto the top of the television below it. Its screen fragmented and there was a small explosion as all the sets in the shop went blank. In the time it took the young woman serving another man in the video section to get to the door of the shop, he had launched a portable cassette radio through the screen of another set and sent a line of small televisions chained together hurtling one after the other simply by nudging the first.

I'm sorry, it couldn't be helped, was what the man said. The woman told her boss Mr Brewer this, and that before she had a chance to call for help or anything he was off and because she was so shocked she didn't see which way. What the woman didn't tell Mr Brewer was that actually the man had stood in the debris before he left and had slowly and carefully written down an address and a telephone number on one of the price display cards as he apologized. She had the piece of card folded in her back pocket and could feel it pressing against her as she spoke to Mr Brewer. Maybe the man hadn't given her his real address. That was something she didn't want to know. Maybe he had, though. That was what she didn't want Mr Brewer to know.

Side two of The Corries ended again and the machine switched automatically back over to side one. The last sign had flashed past before he'd had a chance to see where he was. In the middle years of his life, in the middle of a dark wood. He couldn't remember what that was from. In the middle lane of the motorway in the middle of the night. In a service station in the middle of nowhere in the middle of a cigarette. He held his coffee and stared out into the dark. He ought to phone his wife, they'd maybe be frantic. Or perhaps he could try the number again. There were three payphones by the exit. Think about just picking up the receiver, putting the coin in, pressing the number he knew the shape of like he knew the shape of his own hands, the telephone ringing there in the dark. But look at the time, he didn't want to wake anybody, that wouldn't do, and so he drained his coffee and headed back to the car.

At first light the road was so full of steep drops and sudden lifts that it was like being at sea; he had to travel most of it in second gear. It was light enough to read the word Scotland on the big rock as he passed. The Corries snapped near Pitlochry in the middle of the Skye Boat Song. Since Scotland is only a few hours long, it was about ten when he tried the number again, this time from a call box in sight of the house.

He lifted the receiver and pressed the numbers, he closed his eyes tightly and opened them again to try to get rid of the dizzy feeling. The garden, the walls, the door. The tree, much bigger. The lawn, the hedge. The next door. The whole block. The sky above it. The bus-shelter, the grass where the bus-shelter met the concrete, the little cracks in the edges of the kerb, different, the same. The same, but new houses had been built at the back where the field had been. The windows of the new houses, with their different kinds and colours of curtains. Even before the phone was answered, he knew.

No, I'm sorry. Look, is it not you that's phoned a few times already? I'm sorry, I can't help you there son. There's nobody of that name here.

I know, he said. I won't call again. I'm really sorry to have bothered you. I'm just being stupid.

After that it was random. Soon he was coasting the wet green carsick roads of the north; a little later he saw that the petrol he had bought in Edinburgh was almost gone. His car eventually ground to a halt on a gravelly backroad next to a small loch. The man wound down the window and as the sound of his car in his ears died away he heard water and birds. He opened the door and stood up. Further down the beach a child was crouched like a frog on the stones, her hair hanging; behind her was a big white-painted house converted into a roadside restaurant, closed for the season. A pockmarked sign on the roof of the house said HIELAN HAME, underneath in smaller letters BURGERS BAR-B-Q TRADITIONAL SCOTTISH FARE LICENSED. Behind this a mass of trees, behind them in the distance two mountains still with snow on the peaks, then the sky, empty.

The man walked across the stones and stood in the litter at the edge of the water. The car door hung open behind him, and the engine clicked as it cooled down. A bird sang in the grey air. Water seeped cold over the sides of his shoes.

*

It was the Easter holidays and the girl was out on the stones looking for insects or good skimmers. Sometimes if you turned a big stone over you could find slaters underneath, it depended how close to the water it was. The real name for slaters was woodlice. The girl had decided to collect insects for various experiments. She wanted to try racing them, she also wanted to try putting different kinds in a tupperware box together and to see which kinds survived when you left them in water. Last summer she had discovered tiny tunnels in the back garden and she had followed one to an ant colony in the manure heap. To see what would happen she had poured Domestos from the kitchen cupboard onto it. First a white scum had come and some ants had writhed in it, taking a long time to die. The others had gone mad, running in all directions, some carrying white egglooking things bigger than themselves. They had set up another colony on the other side of the heap and for days she had watched them cleaning out their old place, lines of ants carrying the dead bodies away and leaving them in neat piles under one of the rosebushes. She was very sorry she had done that thing. This year she was going to be more scientific but kind as well, except to wasps. If they were stupid enough to go in the jam-jars and drown it was their own fault.

Here was a good flat stone. As she stood up to see how many skims it would have she saw the man who had left his car in the middle of the road walking into the loch. He sat down in the water about ten feet out. Then his top half fell backwards and he disappeared.

She ran along the bay to look for him; she heard a splash somewhere behind her and turned round. The man was sitting up in the water again. He looked about the same age as her uncle, and she watched him take some things out of his pocket and fiddle about with them. As she got closer she saw he was trying to light a wet cigarette.

Mister, excuse me, she said, but your car's in the middle of the road, people can't get by.

The man shook his hand away from himself so he wouldn't drip water down onto a match.

Excuse me mister, but is it not a bit cold, the water? Anyway your matches are soaking – my mother's got a lighter. I know where it's kept.

The man looked embarrassed. He pulled himself to his feet unsteadily and wiped his hair back off his face, then stumbled back through the shallows. The girl watched the water running off him. She didn't know whether to call him mister or sir.

Are you drunk, sir?

No, I'm not drunk, the man said smiling. Water from his clothes darkened the stones. How old are you then? he asked.

The girl kept her distance. I'm nine, she said. My mother says I'm not to talk to strangers.

Your mother's quite right. I've got a daughter your age. Her name's Fiona, the man said, looking at his feet and shivering.

I told you it was cold, said the girl. She twisted round to skim her stone.

I could show you how to skim stones, said the man.

I know how to skim stones, the girl said, giving him her most scornful look. She expertly pitched the stone against the surface of the loch. The man scrabbled about at his feet to find himself a good stone and she stepped out of the range of the drips that flew off him when he threw.

Not as good as you, said the man. You're an expert right enough.

That's because I do it every day, said the girl so the man wouldn't feel too bad. I live here, so I can. Are you on holiday here? Where do you live? she asked.

The man went a funny colour. Then he said, well when I was your age I used to live not far from here.

You don't sound very Scottish, said the girl.

That's because I've lived in London for a long time, said the man.

The girl said she'd like to live in London, she'd been there once and seen all the places they show you on TV. When she grew up, she wanted to work for TV, maybe on programmes about animals. Then she asked the man did he know that Terry Wogan owned all those trees over there.

Does he? said the man.

Yes, and a Japanese man whose name she couldn't remember owned the land over there behind the loch.

Who owns the loch? the man asked.

Me, I do, said the girl. And my father owns the house and my mother runs the restaurant. Are you redundant? My uncle was made redundant.

The man told the girl that no, he wasn't redundant and that, believe it or not, he worked for television. Had she ever heard of the programme called The Unthinkable Happens To People Every Day? The girl said she thought her mother watched it. Then she said suspiciously, I don't recognize you from off the TV.

No, said the man, I'm not *on* the TV. I work in the background. I do things like phone up the people who write to us and ask them to come on the show to talk about the unthinkable thing that's happened to them.

Then I add up how much it'll cost for them to come, and decide how long they'll get to talk about it.

The girl had grown respectful and faintly excited about talking to someone who might work for TV. She couldn't tell whether the water running down the man's face was from his eyes or his hair. He looked very sad and she suddenly felt sorry for him even though he wasn't actually redundant. She decided to do something about it.

Would you like to come up on to the roof? she asked the man.

Would I what? he said.

Would you like to come up onto the roof and throw some stones? I know this really easy way to get up there, said the girl.

The man filled his wet jacket pockets with stones the girl selected. She showed him, springing up lightly, how to climb from the coalshed roof onto the extension. From there the man could heave himself after her up the drainpipe.

You have to be very quiet or my mother'll hear, said the girl. It's a wonderful view even on a day like today, isn't it?

Yes, the man whispered.

The girl pointed at the HIELAN HOME sign twenty feet away. She was obviously a good shot; the paint had been chipped in hundreds of small dents.

It's two points for big letters and five points for small ones. There's a special bonus if you can hit the c of Scottish, she said. But *your* arms are probably long enough so that you could even reach the loch from here if you wanted, she added hopefully.

Right, said the man. Taking a stone as big as his palm, he hurled it. They watched it soar in silence, then there was a distant splash as it hit the water.

'Yes! cried the girl. Yes! You did it! Nobody's ever done that before. Nobody ever reached the loch before. She jumped up and down. The man looked surprised and then very pleased.

Anne-Marie! called her mother at the thumping. Anne-Marie, I've *told* you about that roof. Now get down here. If you're at that sign again you'll feel the back of my hand.

The girl led the man down off the roof, watching that he put his feet in all the right places. Her mother, angry at first at a stranger being up on her roof, was soon amazed and delighted to meet someone who worked on The Unthinkable Happens To People Every Day. She made him tea and a salad, apologizing for the fact that the restaurant was closed and there wasn't anything grander, and she dried his suit off for him. He told her that he was sort of a local boy really, but that he'd lived in England for a while. She said she could spot it in his accent. Had he been up visiting his parents, then? No, they were both dead, both some years ago now. He'd been up for a drive and to look at the place again. She asked him how he'd got wet. He said he'd fallen into the loch. He filled his car from a tank of petrol in the garage and before he left he promised the girl that he'd get the autographs of some famous children's TV presenters for her when he got back to work.

Some weeks later a packet arrived addressed to the Hielan Hame. Inside was a thank-you letter for the girl's mother and several photographs of celebrities all signed To Ann Marie with best wishes. The girl took them to school and showed them to all her friends. She didn't even mind that they'd spelled her name wrong.

These are from the man who hit the loch, she told her friends. He works for the TV and he's been up on our roof.

Frank Shon

The Farmer's Wife

For a long time Thomas Robertson suffered from pains in the face. Sometimes they lasted ten minutes, sometimes half an hour, but when they happened his whole body was locked in an agonized paralysis. Then one day the condition suddenly and inexplicably worsened. The pains became more intense, like a steel bit drilling into the jawbone; and what was worse, they came more often. Between the attacks he became drowsy and feverish. So in the first week of June, which is a busy time for a fruit farmer, Thomas Robertson went into hospital.

Anna Robertson and their small son Tomas travelled up to Dundee every day to see him. At first they went in the evenings, too. Then Thomas Robertson said it did not make sense to come twice and thereafter they came only once, in the daytime. They sat with him for an hour or two in the warm hospital ward, the sun lying across the foot of his bed and his face in shadow, and then they went out into the fresh air and enjoyed themselves. Now, Anna Robertson did not use the time as you might expect. She went nowhere special, saw no one and did nothing illicit while her husband was out of the way. She simply enjoyed the sensation of being – at long last – alone. Of course the boy was with her, but that was just the same as being by herself. For she still thought of him as part of her, as though the cord connecting them for nine months had never been cut. She performed all the necessary little daily tasks with a new pleasure, and was happy that he should be there.

In the mornings they walked down the length of the raspberry field, past the pickers with their children, past the tractor with the scales on it, all the way down to the yard at the bottom where there was a little office. There were the shipments of fruit out to the factories to be kept track of, occasional phone-calls to make or answer, payment schedules to be kept up, and other matters connected with the crop. But usually they could finish at twelve. Willy the foreman looked after everything else and let her know well in advance when more money would be needed to pay the pickers. In the winter Willy was a drinker, but in the summer he could be relied on absolutely. And always little Tomas was with his mother. When they went into Arbroath to pick up some money he helped her carry the bags.

When they were finished in the office they walked back up the field to the house at the top and had lunch. It was a beautiful June and they nearly always ate outside. From the back of the house you could look out and see all the way down to the coast. There was nothing but fields all the way, greens and yellows, rising and falling. There was no wind and the sun blazed on the flagstones. They lay in it like a hot bath and fell under its spell. And there they would stay until a look at her watch told Anna it was time for them to go up to the hospital. Sometimes the boy pretended to be asleep. Then she would shake his little naked shoulder gently as he lay in the big canvas chair and they would go into the house. They dressed, she combed his hair for him, and they left.

Visiting time lasted two hours in the afternoon. Sometimes she took him a book, but more often a newspaper. Thomas Robertson wanted to keep in touch with the world. Above all, he didn't want to let go of it. So every day he asked his wife how business had been, if the fruit was of good quality, if Willy was doing his job properly without himself there to keep an eye on him; he asked details of the volume of fruit picked the day before and what parts of the field had yielded the most, what were not quite ripe yet. Usually all this took up at least the first half-hour. Thomas Robertson was visibly pleased when she did not have the answer to a question immediately to hand; it reassured him that the business could not really function properly without him. He also took a certain pleasure, now more than ever, from the fact that his wife was younger than himself. She was tanned from the sun, and her hair, which she wore long, had lighter streaks of brown in it. She looked strong and healthy. And sometimes when he pretended to listen to her he cast a furtive little glance around the ward to see if the other men were looking at his wife. Often they were.

Thomas Robertson, from his wife's point of view, looked different. He was a big man, still powerful for his age. Yet there was something in his features that suggested a new delicacy, even fragility, as if the sum of his existence had in some ineffable way diminished. Certainly there were noticeable physical changes. His face seemed a little thinner; some of the colour had gone out of his cheeks. But it was in his eyes that she saw the greatest and most subtle change. For despite his exhibition of acuity, in his eyes there had been a peculiar softening. They sparkled darkly with a lustre she had never seen in them before.

She took in his features with occasional glances while he looked elsewhere. And then it came to her clearly, even as he whispered that he missed her and gave her his suggestive smile, that this figure sitting up in bed issuing his orders and asking questions was nothing other than an old man. For a moment she resisted the idea, then it drew in the man that had been and swallowed him forever. And just as a physical change in someone's appearance takes an initial moment of adjustment before it is accepted, it took Anna only a short time to take in and accept this alteration. The new man was born, the old forgotten. And in bed with half his beard shorn off, proudly wearing the silk pyjamas he bought himself the Christmas before, the new man was suddenly rather absurd.

He leaned over from the bed and said: 'What is it, Tomas?' The boy had been staring at him. But now he said nothing, only looked back to his mother who was sitting on the side of the bed. 'It's the beard,' she said. 'He hasn't seen you without the beard before.' Thomas Robertson said nothing but smiled, and looked at them together, his wife and son. The boy had put his hand on her lap.

Afterwards they went back home. When the business for the day was finished Anna Robertson liked to sit outside in the warm evening with a magazine. There was a big rectangular pool, not deep, which Thomas Robertson had stocked with ornamental fish. About two weeks after he went into hospital it was the brief focus of attention. Anna had drifted into a half-sleep in the canvas chair. Tomas was playing in a little fenced area full of sand. Then all at once there was some splashing and Anna sat up, abruptly. Her dog, a Jack Russell bitch, was in the middle of the pool, jumping and snapping at the water with its sharp little muzzle. The level of the water was low because the pump had broken down and the cycle of drainage and replenishment had stopped. The water had simply drained down to the level of the outlet and stayed there. The dog went after the fish, which had nowhere to go, and because the level of the water was so low it was catching them.

Anna went over to the pool and shouted, but of course the dog ignored her. For the dog knew she did not care about the fish. And there was even something in her voice, a tiny element, that suggested she was only half serious. Then Anna lost interest and at the same moment saw that the boy had come over to the other side of the pool and now stood there, laughing. There was the splashing, gulping sound of the dog killing the fish and behind it the sound of his laughter. And then she found herself laughing along with him. When it was over the dog climbed out of the water and skulked over to a corner. The last of the fish floated on their sides in the dirty green water, their orange and black bodies glistening in the evening sunlight, except where they had been torn.

When she told him about the fish Thomas Robertson didn't shout, as she had expected him to. He didn't even seem angry. He simply nodded and lay back on the upright pillows. His face, from being thin, had become swollen. He said dreamily that the doctors did not understand what was happening to him, but that it was getting worse. The best theory was that the jaw had been fractured some years before and that this fracture had become the seat of the infection. But exactly what it had been infected with they were unable to say. The treatment, likewise, was uncertain. And then he said once, in a quiet, desperate voice, 'I'm scared...' and Anna touched the sleeve of his pyjamas. But she could bring herself to do nothing more. And she knew that beneath the pity that glowed momentarily, there was nothing in her heart for this sick creature. She felt awkward, almost embarrassed by him, as if he were a stranger. The quiet human drama of it shocked her, as though it were something extraordinarily vulgar, inappropriate. She looked at him now, stroking the top of his hand with the tip of her finger, and she saw the dull, animal fear in his eyes.

She sat in a chair beside the bed, just as the boy had done all along. Thomas Robertson's interest in the outside world had collapsed. No more exhibitions of acuity. The newspapers she had brought him every day lay unread in the locker by his bed. A shadow lay across his puffed-up face like a blanket. Once he opened his eyes wide and looked at her with a frightened, accusing look, then at the boy, his head starting up off the pillow. Then he sank back down and did not wake again that afternoon. Anna and Tomas hurried silently away half an hour before the end of visiting time, oppressed by the weight of the shadow that was on him, by the unbearable warmth of the place.

It was late in the afternoon but the water at the coast was still warm. She ran into it with the boy and swam for a few minutes. That was long enough, long enough to wash off the uncleanliness that clung to them both from the place. It hung on them like a tangible odour; the shadow of death had settled on her like a colourless film and must be scrubbed off with the salt water and the sharp little breeze that had sprung up at the edge of the water. Tomas wasn't a good swimmer yet and had no natural aptitude for it. He feared the water and when he could no longer feel the bottom with his feet he looked to her for help. She saw his frightened little face above the water and once, when he got into difficulties, stepped forward and took him in her arms and guided him back towards the shore. Yet not before waiting, just for a moment, but for a real interval to pass before she went to him. He saw her wait, saw her watch him struggling there, hung in the water like a helpless, unearthly thing, and for a minute he hated her. Then she took him in her arms and walked with him to the shallower water, stroking his head, talking to him, smiling. It had been washed off. They were clean now, awakened again into the daylight and the world of life. And little Tomas seemed to know what it meant, this moment of loneliness when she held back from him, that it was their bond. When they were home again and standing under the shower he shut his eyes. And as she washed his hair, he unconsciously leaned against her.

They operated on Thomas Robertson's jaw the next day. They scraped off a small amount of bone and took it away for examination, then stitched up the hole and sent him back to the ward. When Anna visited him she was genuinely shocked. He lay back, his arms very still at his sides over the top of the coverlet. His head lay resting on its good side so that the side of the jaw that had been operated on, thoroughly bandaged, was facing upward. His eyes were open, but they were smoky. When she asked him how he was feeling he could not bring himself to speak; he simply raised his open left hand a little in a gesture of resignation.

Now that it was gone, Anna realized that the beard had made him look younger. It had been light brown in colour and slightly pointed, and had given something vaguely elegant to his face. Now that it was gone and the lower half of his face was obscured beneath the bandage, she saw the incipient decay of his features and charted the path they would surely take before long. The outline of the eyesockets announced itself plainly as she sat there looking at him; the wrinkles, usually palliated by the healthy colour of the skin, stood out starkly from the pale background tissue; the eyebrows were grey, quite suddenly and completely grey, and the hair above would follow before long. The life seemed to be seeping out of him like a fluid even as she watched, and Anna found herself disgusted by the palpable corruption. For a minute she had been standing over him, looking down into his eyes. And as she leaned over she was aware of a finger on his left hand coiling through her palm. She wanted to withdraw from it but could not. Simply could not. She looked down at the quivering digit that now linked itself to her index finger, so insistently. Anna looked around the ward. Still the finger tugged at her, and there was something suddenly indecent in the gesture which revolted her. It gripped her tightly, a gesture, a symbol of their continuity – he and she. 'If it happens,' he whispered. 'If I go...' But she wrenched her hand free before he could finish.

It was raining outside. Anna and Tomas (for he always went with her) came away from the hospital feeling exhausted. They drove back to the house, about twenty minutes away, and immediately went for a walk. They walked down the long field, following the line of the pine wood. The rain hung quietly about the trees and sometimes woodpigeon flew out as they passed by. The ground was full of muddy brown pools. Anna had pulled down the hood on her jacket so that her head would be soaked, and Tomas did the same. He walked beside her, stabbing at the pools with a piece of stick he had picked up. The field was empty and the wide rows of raspberry canes ran down its length like ribs. The smell of the pine wood and the rain soaked through the air and she breathed it deeply, like a tonic.

When they had married, six years before, the difference in their ages had seemed unimportant. In itself it presented no great obstacle to fulfilment. Thomas Robertson was still healthy, he could still father children. And whatever had to be endured in the making, a child was worth it. Indeed Tomas was the reward for that nightly sacrifice she had made of herself on the altar-bed; for the solemn rigour with which she had enacted their conjugal absurdities. Tomas was what it had all been for, and without him it would have all been for nothing. The man had made the boy and now the man must wither.

The next day there was a marked improvement in Thomas Robertson's condition. When Anna and the boy came he was sitting up in bed looking at a newspaper. 'It was the drugs,' he explained. 'They had me pumped full of drugs.' He spoke indistinctly because of the bandages but his voice was firm again. She asked him if he was in much pain. 'Not much,' he said cheerily. 'They gave me something for it.' His features had regained their animation. The future was where it belonged again, no longer written on his face. Like a sacred text, it had been glimpsed once and put away.

'I can only vaguely remember your visit,' he went on. 'You held my hand, didn't you?'

'Yes. I wasn't sure whether to call the doctor, you looked so bad ...'

'I am glad you were there with me,' he said. He squeezed her hand. As usual Tomas was sitting on the chair by the bed. While his parents were talking he looked around the ward. An old man lay in the next bed and he winked manfully at the boy. Tomas looked around the beds, where clusters of visitors were gathered. The sounds of their voices mingled with the soft music coming from an old-fashioned radio speaker positioned above the doorway of the ward. Slowly he became aware of something, a voice talking to him, saying his name. He turned. 'What about it, Tomas?' His father's eyes were smiling. His mother, looking faintly embarrassed, leaned down and took the boy's hand. 'What about it, Tomas, are you missing me?' Tomas looked at his mother, as if he had not quite understood the question. The expression hurt her, and she felt a sudden surge of shame as though she had failed him. 'Of course he misses you,' she said, not looking at her husband. She had led the boy forward, encouraged him; she could not turn back on him now. The lie must come from her lips. 'He talks of nothing else but when his father will be well ...'

The father leaned over and ruffled the boy's combed hair with his big hand.

'What have you been doing with me out of the way, eh?'

'Nothing unusual,' said Anna. 'In the office with me. Then we go for walks, don't we?' She looked at Tomas but he didn't answer; he was looking down at the coverlet.

'I dreamt the dog had killed all my fish,' Thomas Robertson said. 'Saw it quite clearly in my head.'

'I told you that a couple of days ago, before your operation.'

'What, all of them?'

Anna nodded. 'We were in the kitchen when we heard the splashes. By the time we got outside it was too late.'

He was quiet now, and Anna could see the cloud settle over his features. 'Please,' she said. 'Never mind about the fish. Tell me what the doctors say.'

The cloud began to move away. 'They think they're close to cracking it.'

'You mean they haven't yet?'

'Not yet, no. I get injections twice a day, and pills.'

She coughed. 'Do they say how long – before they get it under control?'

'They don't know, but soon now. Definitely soon.'

Anna nodded thoughtfully. Thomas Robertson thought she looked unsettled. 'What is it?'

'Oh, nothing really,' she said. 'I'd just like some idea ...'

'Don't worry about me,' he said, interrupting her. 'I'm on the mend. Look at me.' She smiled complaisantly, and he thought: perhaps this has not been for nothing, perhaps this illness of mine had brought us a little closer together ...

Over the next few days Thomas Robertson's improvement continued, so that at the end of the end of his fourth week in hospital the doctors began to discuss his discharge. They did not know exactly what the illness was which had overtaken him, but they had faith in the treatment they were prescribing. Every day when Anna Robertson and Tomas went up to the hospital to visit him they were told that it would not be long before he would be home. And indeed every day he looked a little better. The colour returned to his face and although the bandage remained on his jaw the swelling had all but disappeared. Then at the end of the fifth week a date was set for his discharge, to be the following Friday.

The last few days drained quickly away and, taking on a fugitive quality like the last days before an execution, were spoiled. A shadow had been cast over the woman and her son. On their walks the silence that absorbed them was no longer contented, but filled with frustration. The three little worry-lines were never very far from Anna Robertson's forehead. Tomas became moody. Their equilibrium had been fractured, disturbed by the impending presence of a third. Two was a harmony, an evenness; three was discordant, an oddity. Not even a question of will, she thought, not even of demands. It would simply be the man's presence, the presence of a third element which would destroy their happiness and their perfection.

The boy didn't hold her hand any more, but lingered behind. Often she had to stop and wait for him, and when she looked at him she saw in his child's face all the sullen resistance of a human being to the inevitable undoing of life. She stepped forward and put a hand on his neck and leaning down, kissed the crown of his head. He, unmoved, stood rigid and unassailable, receiving her offering like a priest or a child-monarch, and despised her. And when he looked up into her face his eyes were cold and full of that accusing male pain she had come to know. And then she knew their lives would return to what they had been. The solitude that bound them together had already begun to dissolve. The dream was nearly over. She could feel the flow of it, carrying her irrevocably towards the future. There would be nothing apocalyptic, of course, only the slow dripping away of her life. If she had had inside her what she saw in those hard little blue eyes it might have been different. But she did not. And she had known all along that she did not. So now she must begin to forget the dream. For grown human beings can forget with remarkable facility. But not a child. A child does not forget, nor forgive.

On a clear day you could see the house from far away, even out to sea. Sometimes the fishermen noticed it on their way back to harbour, a long low structure like a Spanish hacienda, curiously misplaced and white against the dark country that surrounded it. For there was nothing near it, nothing for half a mile down the little tree-lined road. There were only the rows upon rows of raspberry canes, pared back now and tied to their wires and posts for the coming winter. At the bottom of the field was the yard, with its loading-shed where the fruit was sent out in barrels, and the house where Willy the foreman lived, and the little office. After it reached the yard the little road went off towards Arbroath.

There had already been a lot of rain and the earth was black and heavy with it. There had been strong winds too but these had not damaged the canes because of the narrow strip of pine wood that shielded the seaward side of the field for most of its length. Back up at the top of the field, in front of the white house, there was a potato field. It ran down from the house and stopped when it came to a couple of old wooden sheds. Every year the pickers used the sheds to shelter in. It was late September now and Thomas Robertson had begun turning the earth over with a tractor. He ploughed away from the house so that the pickers who followed behind would have the advantage of the slope. The farthest and lower end of the field was damper than the rest and he knew the potatoes there were often rotten. So he always had the pickers start on the high ground, and they went along on their hands and knees in the sodden grooves clawing potatoes into baskets. Many of the pickers, whole families sometimes, had been picking Thomas Robertson's fruit in the summer. Many of them had also come to his field for ten years or more and knew Thomas Robertson quite well by now. They knew he didn't like to work them too hard, as Geddes down the road did, and that he could be trusted to pay them on time, which Geddes could not. Thomas

Robertson didn't pay exceptionally well – not even as well as Geddes. But he didn't pay badly either, and because they could trust him and did not have to work too hard with him they remained his pickers and returned to him every year.

Thomas Robertson was glad to be working again, especially to be working like this on his land, as a man should. His jaw was healed and his beard had grown over the small interruption to the line of his face. He could almost forget the sudden phenomenon that had nearly carried him off. Of course it had been a close-run thing. Even the doctors said so, in unguarded moments. Understandably, they took the credit for a successful treatment. But when the question arose – as it did more than once – of what the vanquished illness had actually been called, they smiled at the innocence of the question, like possessors of some profound truth, muttered in their mystic language and moved on, still smiling.

This had annoyed him at the time. He never could bear to be patronized, and besides, he wanted something specific to tell his friends. Yet now, sitting on the tractor with the wind against him and the damp cloying odour of the turned earth in his nostrils, Thomas Robertson was glad that they did not have so much as a name for it. An aberration, a moment of chaos, a mere accidental gust had blown his life off balance. But he had recovered now. The time that had seemed so very extended while he was in hospital had miraculously snapped back into perspective, so that now he could look back on it as a short spell of treatment. Six weeks, that was all. It didn't sound much when you said it. It had been just a short interruption to his continuity, nothing more.

So it was that after only a couple of months he had begun to bury the whole matter. In another few months his memory of the event would start to fall apart, and in a few years he might come to deny that it ever occurred at all. Better by far, he said to himself, to get on with the business of making a living. It was inadvisable, he thought, to 'dwell' on matters, a habit he regarded with deep suspicion. Often he would say that introspection was the enemy of achievement. It was something he had read somewhere and he made the pronouncement with the certain air of authority that farmers and businessmen in general often adopt on the subject of 'getting things done'. Thomas Robertson was a doer, not a thinker, never an intellectual, and he didn't mind saying so. Not that he was verbose: most often when he made any comments on such matters he addressed them to himself.

And yet despite his manful wariness of such things he could not, as he ate his lunch, stop his mind from turning on the night before. Why had she wept like that, he wondered, afterwards? It always made him feel uneasy when it happened and some vague guilt bubbled to the surface of his mind for a while, a few hours perhaps. But guilt for what? That was always when he became confused and secretly rather irritated with her. After all it was supposed to be a pleasurable thing, certainly nothing for a grown woman to cry about. For a moment he considered the question from a technical point of view (it always helped him find his bearings in matters of this sort – that is to say, matters of some awkwardness). Had he done anything wrong, anything clumsy? He remembered as best as he could and could think of nothing … no, nothing wrong in that department. Then he thought of how her dog had died, killed on the road outside, and she had cried then, not just at the time but for days and weeks after. There was no doubt about it, she was a cryer. Some people are just like that, he mused. The sort who cry at weddings out of happiness. And the idea triggered something in his mind and he thought, that is it. It was after all the first time since … yes, he had moved back into the main bedroom now, and with a vengeance. She had cried from happiness. And he heard again the stifled little moans she had made the night before, and laughed to himself. Women, he thought. Women … and carried on eating his lunch.

Duncan McLean

Hours of Darkness

He came striding out of the north just as darkness was falling. Away to his right dark fields stretched out, black furrows creased across the red earth, boulders tumbled in by the dykesides, gangs of crows and gulls picking over the broken ground. A step to his left the cliffs plunged down to rocky coves scattered with cracked slabs split from the cliff-face, and already deep in shadow. From time to time there was the sound of a tractor inland, and always the blattering of the sea below, beating on the cliff-foot, raking through the pebblebanks.

He walked on. The grass on the heuch-head was short and had a spring to it, and his boots made no sound as they fell. It was good there was no vegetation to kick through or trip over, but still he had to watch out for sudden incuttings of the cliff and tummocks of bracken or gorseroot that could catch his feet.

A few yards ahead an empty fertiliser bag lay across his path, weighted down by a puddle of water and black ooze. He slowed down and stepped forward carefully, then raised the landward edge of the bag with the toe of his boot. The puddle ran away into the grass, leaving a circle of sooty particles on the weathered plastic, and immediately the bag began to stir in the faint uprise off the cliff. He lifted his boot another few inches and the bag leapt up into the air then slid off his foot towards the cliff-edge; for a second it rested there, then slipped out into nothingness, hung momentarily, then folded in on itself and fell quickly towards the sea. It was lost in the darkness long before it reached the bottom.

The ground was rising again in front of him, steadily but quite steeply, and his breathing was getting heavier; he hooked his thumbs into the shoulderstraps of his backpack and kept up the pace. The sun was well down behind the hills in the west. Skeins of high cloud were running in from the same direction, their bellies rodden, carrying over the hills and moving quickly down the length of the howe and towards the sea. If they kept coming and spread and thickened, and if low cover followed, some of the day's heat might be retained. Otherwise it was set for a chilly night out. But if the cloud did come, the last of the light would go quickly. He had to ignore the pain in his feet and keep moving while he could still see: he had to get off the cliff-top before it was total darkness.

After a time, the cliff swung up and out into a headland with some kind of cairn or triangulation point on top. He avoided the steep climb and walked on in the lee of the dykes and fences that marked the end of the farmlands, eyes on the ground in front of him. Sudden loud birdnoise made him raise his head and scan the nearest park. Two hoodies had turned on a gull and were jabbing for its eyes with their beaks, lifting their broad dark wings and louping around as they did so, blocking the gull from taking off. As he watched, the gull seemed to give up the struggle, stopped flapping and mewling, and cawked a stream of stuff out of its open maw. One of the hoodies immediately went for the spewings, caught them up in its black neb and swallowed with jerking movements of its swack feathered neck. The other crow seemed not to have seen what the gull had done, and continued attacking it, stabbing with its thick parted beak, beating its wings, screaming and cawing loudly.

He watched for a few seconds, then lifted his hands clear of the straps and brought them together in a sharp clap, at the same time pursing his lips and whistling a piercing high note. The gull whipped its head round, and as it looked at him the hoodie struck it hard on the side of the skull just behind the eye. The gull staggered sideways, then lifted a wing and seemed about to steady itself, when the crow struck again and the white bird was tipped over a dreel into the deep furrow that separated two ploughed rigs in the park. Immediately, both crows were onto it.

A few minutes later he was going downhill towards the lights of the village. There weren't many lights, only half a dozen streetlamps amongst the buildings down near the water and a few more zigzagging up the steep hill at the head of the bay. Under each of the hillside lights a small piece of narrow road was visible, tacking in angles up the slope, climbing steeply. He walked on, keeping his eyes on his feet most of the time, though the path was now fairly well trodden and wide, and the drop from the cliff-top to the dark water below was lessening all the time. He paused, looked ahead, then went on down the long steady descent at an even pace, till the path dropped away sharply in front of him in a slide of mud and rocks that tumbled down to a small pebble beach. At the far end of the beach was a jetty, with a broad open area of flat ground at the head of it, then the village. He paused again and looked across to the lights. The strange thing was how few house-lights there were: only three or four lighted windows could be made out amongst the black shapes of the houses; most of the village was in darkness.

As he stood at the pathfoot, the sound of a fast-moving car rose over the sifting of the waves, then died down, then got louder again. The car slowed, changed to a lower gear; now his eye was drawn to the road at the bayhead by headlights at the top of the hill. The lights suddenly dived, and the car changed gear again and started down the brae, still travelling fast. After a few seconds, there was a screeling of tyres, and the lights swung round at a sharp angle and were pointing towards the far side of the bay. A couple of seconds later and the car switchbacked again, the lights catching his eyes. He looked down, studied the slide in front of him, then scrambled quickly downwards across the scree and started walking along the beach.

The sound of the car's motor was hidden by his boots crinching through the mowrie, but half-way along the beach three blasts on a carhorn sounded out, and shortly afterwards the headlights emerged from the seaward side of the village, wove across the open ground, then disappeared. He carried on walking.

The far end of the beach was marked by a grassy rise. He walked up and over this, and found himself at the start of the village. One straight street led away in front of him, low houses with small windows lined along each side, shacked up against each other, their doors opening right onto the roadway. He headed down the middle of the street, his breathing evening out after the trachle across the beach. There were no cars about, not even parked, and at this end of the village there were no streetlamps at all; it was almost pitch-dark here, down in the hollow of the bay. Fifty yards ahead, though, the road seemed to open out, and there were lights on there.

It was the village square. Directly opposite the street he'd come along was a small hotel, windows beaming out yellow light; a few cars and a lorry were standing in the middle of the square, and there was a post-box set into a white-harled wall. An opening on the left headed towards the jetty and the sea, and one on the right was the road that led to the hillclimb at the bayhead. There were a couple more modern-looking houses up in that direction with lights on, or the telly flickering through uncurtained windows. But still there was no one to be seen.

He crossed the square and went into the porch of the hotel, scrubbed his boots on a mat there, and unslung his pack. There were burrs of gorse and grass-ears stuck to the shanks of his breeks, and patches of reddish mud dried on his knees; he bent down and brushed at the mud, knocked the worst of the burrs off, then straightened up, wiped his hands under the arms of his jersey, and opened the door marked BAR.

He stepped in. There was a slight pause in the conversation, but it didn't stop: one guy, at the end of the bar, was telling a funny story, and two others were laughing at it and adding comments of their own. The three of them had glanced over as the walker entered, but turned back to their drinks and their yarn almost immediately. In two steps he was leaning on the bar. There was no one behind it. A door at one end led to some kind of unlit backshop, but nobody came through it. He moved along the bar and parked himself on a high stool there, letting his pack drop to the floor by the bar footrail. He eased his shoulders slowly up, back, down, and forward to rest again; he circled his head round, loosening his neck; he stretched his arms up in the air, arching his back at the same time. Then he sat still: upright on the stool, hands flat on the edge of the bar, feet twitching occasionally in their heavy boots as they rested on the footrail.

The storyteller was talking louder, getting to the end of his tale. Another thing about New Zealand, he said, See what this guy tells me? He says the burns are stappit full of salmon – fairly hoaching with the buggers! – and you can hardly get moved through the country for the grouse and, eh, kiwis aneath your feet!

So you can just reach out and pick them like tatties, said one of the listeners.

The storyteller ignored him, except for forcing a wider grin and raising his voice. And see what this boy says? he went on. See all these beasties? Well you can just go out with your gun and shoot as much as you like. No gamie bastards or nothing! Anything you see, the old twelve-bore, bang bang, you don't need no bugger's permission. It's a hell of a place New Zealand, he said. Fairly puts Scotland in the shade. Christ aye, I said to him. Permission? You need permission to pish on a dyke in Scotland!

The storyteller laughed, and half a second later the others joined in. One of them repeated the punchline, shaking his head. After a few moments' laughter, the storyteller leant forward on his elbows, still chuckling to himself, and said loudly down the length of the bar, Are you needing a drink son?

Eh, aye, a pint, said the walker. I'm needing a pint.

Ha! The storyteller laughed again. He had a fat neck and face, and when he laughed his jowly cheeks vibrated. Hold on a minute, he said, then slid backwards off his stool, walked over to a door marked PRIVATE at the far end of the room, and went out. There was the sound of heavy footsteps treading up a flight of stairs.

One of the storyteller's friends cleared his throat. Aye man, he said, and nodded down the bar. He had a baseball cap on, and the peak of the cap cast a band of shadow across his eyes.

Eh, hello . . .

The other man nodded too, then looked away, shaking his head. Permission to pish, he said quietly. What a load of shite!

Christ I ken, said the one in the cap. No one tells me when to pish or not! He's in a world of his own, that bugger.

The other one pulled a fag out of a pack lying in front of him on the bar. He nipped one end of it between the nails of his thumb and forefinger, ripped the filter off and flicked it to the floor. He lit up, smoked hard for half a minute with his head thrown back, then lowered his gaze, looked down the length of the bar and said, You ever been to New Zealand son?

The walker looked up. Me? No, I've never been anywhere.

The smoker inhaled, narrowed his eyes, and exhaled. You must've been somewhere, he said. I mean you're not from round here, are you?

Not exactly, said the walker, But not far away. Not New Zealand anyway!

The smoker rested his fag on the edge of the whisky ashtray, stared at it for a second, then snatched it up and pointed down the length of the bar with it, pincing it like a dart. I'll tell you something for nothing, he said loudly. Fat Boy's never been there either!

He's a lying bastard, the one in the cap said.

Eh . . . but surely he never said he'd been himself? Was it not some guy he'd met who was saying all that stuff?

The smoker jabbed the air with his fag and snorted, Ach, that's a load of shite as well. Who would talk to him?

He's a lying bastard. He doesn't ken fucking anybody.

Fat arse and a big mouth, that's him. He kens fuck all about New Zealand, but anything to run this place down . . . Christ! The smoker leant to one side for a moment and spat on the floor. He straightened up. Not an ounce of patrioticness in his whole fat fucking body! he said.

A pause.

It's nothing to do with me, said the walker.

It might be, the one in the cap said quickly. Just don't believe everything he tells you, that's all.

There was the sound of footsteps descending the private stair.

That'll be Fat Boy now, said the smoker. Watch this: ten to one he spouts some shite about shagging the barmaid up in her room . . .

The door opened and the storyteller walked in. He clapped his hands together. Now then, he said. He stepped round the back of his two friends and, lifting the hatch, squeezed in behind the bar. The lady of the house is busy at the moment, he said, and, half-turning to his friends, added, Getting her knickers on!

The two of them laughed, not meeting his eye, then the smoker lifted his head, eyebrows raised, and said, See?

See what? said the storyteller, looking round at his friends, frowning, then quickly back.

The walker shrugged.

I was just telling the boy that Anne would likely be busy, said the smoker.

She's aye busy when you're needing a fucking drink, said the one in the cap.

Oh aye. The storyteller laughed, a frown still on his face. Is that right? he said suddenly, leaning over the bar.

Eh ... aye, that's what we were talking about, said the walker, looking into the frowning jowly face.

The storyteller drew himself up, laughing quietly. It's just I wouldn't like to think you were talking about me behind my back.

The one in the cap whispered something to the smoker.

The storyteller whipped his head round. What was that?

The two of them stared at him. Nobody moved. Eventually the one in the cap let out a long loud sigh and said, Nothing, nothing. Fuck all.

The storyteller stared at him.

The walker coughed, turned it into a clearing of the throat.

Christ, will you look at that. The smoker pointed down the bar. The laddie's parching for a drink.

That's just what I was fucking saying: empty glasses man! The one in the cap lifted his empty pint tumbler and shook it in the direction of the man behind the bar. Are you going to serve us or what, eh?

The storyteller clapped his hands together again, unwrinkled his forehead and said, Aye aye, I'll pull them the now till Anne gets down, no bother. But I'll get our visitor first, okay lads? Hospifuckingtality, ken? He turned away from his friends. Now, what'll it be pal?

Well, I was thinking actually ...

The fat man had scooped a glass up from under the bar-top and was tossing it up in the air, catching it again as it spun down past his chest. He grinned. What were you thinking?

I was thinking time was getting on, ken, and I was actually needing to get going fairly soon. The walker coughed again, scanned the back of the bar. So maybe I'll just have a bit of grub, and then head off. Whatever you've got...

The storyteller placed the glass down on the bar and looked along at his friends. The smoker blew out a cloud of smoke, and the other one pushed his cap to the back of his head, twitching his eyebrows and blinking.

So, eh, have you got any food? I mean do you ken if there is any? A pie maybe? Or a bridie?

Silence.

I was looking around for one of those heated cabinets with the grub in it, the walker went on, Or a toastie machine or something. I'm wasting away here!

The storyteller had sat down on a seat behind the bar. He was shaking his head, cheeks puffed out and wobbling. Then he said, No, you're out of luck. There's nothing. They don't do food at this time of year.

What, nothing at all? Are you sure?

The storyteller shook his head again, sighed, and looked down at his feet.

Here, said the smoker from the end of the bar, There is pickled eggs...

The storyteller looked up, eyes half-closed, and gazed into space for a moment. Aye, he said slowly, Pickled eggs... He got to his feet and went ben the backshop.

And nuts! called the one in the cap, There's crisps and nuts as well! He laughed, and the smoker joined in. Christ aye, he continued, There's no need to go hungry in this day and age.

The storyteller stuck his head through from the backshop, grinning. Success on a plate! he said, and held out a big glass jar with half a dozen eggs sloshing about in a few inches of cloudy vinegar. So, how many'll you have son?

I think, eh, two; I reckon I'd manage two. Well, how much are they?

They're twenty-five pence, said the smoker.

Aye, that's about it. So fifty in total, eh? The storyteller slid the jar across the bar-top. I'll tell you what: choose your own. How's that for service? Whichever ones you like.

Right. Ehm. Have you got a fork or a spoon or something?

Oh... The storyteller scratched his cheek. Hold on a minute. He disappeared into the backshop but came back through again straight away. There might be something through there, he said, But it's too dark to see: fucking light's gone.

There could be anything through there, said the one in the cap. I mean we've only your word that Anne's upstairs.

The storyteller frowned. What are you getting at?

Ah well, said the smoker, half-smiling and winking at the walker, Maybe you're keeping her tied to a bed of beer-kegs through the back and giving her a sly poke every time you nip through there.

Aye man, we all ken how she's daft for you: you've tellt us often enough!

The two friends laughed loudly. The storyteller took a step towards them, then stopped, rubbing the palms of his hands up and down the flanks of his thighs. His big cheeks were blotched with red. Ha! Pair of jokers! he said, forcing a laugh, then turned back to the walker, clapped his hands and cried, A fork!

Well I need something, said the walker, not looking down the bar. I mean... He lifted the jar up to eye level and looked at the eggs bobbling about in the vinegar.

Ah-ha! said the storyteller, Bright idea! He turned his back and started rummaging through some stuff on the shelf under the gantry: matches, fags, dart-flights and other pub gear. After a few moments he turned round. Ah-ha! he said again. He unscrewed the top from a small plastic tube he'd picked up, held it six inches above the bar-top, and shook. Several dozen cocktail sticks tumbled out and fell in a pile on the bar. That'll do you pal, eh? he said, beaming.

Aye. Great. The walker pulled one of the sticks out of the heap, examined it for a second, then took the lid off the jar, dived his hand in and speared one of the eggs. Vinegar ran down the back of his hand and up his sleeve as he lifted out the egg. He let it drip for a moment, then stuck the whole thing into his mouth, pursing his lips around the cocktail stick as he pulled it out. He chewed. Then he picked out another egg and ate it in the same way. This time it took longer to chew the mouthful. Eventually he wiped the back of his dry hand across his lips, reached into his pocket, and came out with a handful of coins. Fifty pence you said?

The storyteller was screwing the lid back on the egg jar. Ach forget it, he said. The bastards are out of date anyway.

Outside, it was even darker than before. As he stepped from the porch, a streetlamp on the far side of the square flickered and went off. He swung the rucksack up onto his back and walked out.

There was still no one about and no cars moving, so he walked slowly across the roadway into the middle of the square then stopped and looked up at the surrounding buildings. A lot of the walls seemed to have been harled recently, or at least freshly painted, and the roofs of the buildings had bright red pantiles in snug rows, none missing or cracked, no moss growth, no soot and water stains. But the buildings weren't modern, they were old, really old-looking, with small narrow windows and low doors, and all of the angles seeming not quite straight. And the corners of everything – windows, doorways, steps, gables – were rounded, like they'd been worn down by years and years of salt wind off the sea, or maybe rounded up by years and years of painting and patching. But all the buildings were empty: no lights on inside, no curtains in the windows, no names on the doors ...

In the middle of the seaward side of the square was a tall thin tower with a pointed roof and a clockface three-quarters of the way up; there was only one hand on the clock, and it was hanging straight down, as if it was about to fall off and spear down any minute. On each side of the tower was a small one-storey building with bars on the windows and fresh white harling on the walls. The two buildings leant into the base of the tower as if they were buttressing it up, or maybe as if they needed to lean on it for support. Also joined to the tower was a set of stairs that stuck straight out into the square and led up to a small round-topped door let into the wall at first-floor level. Above the door was a notice of some kind, a plaque maybe, stuck onto or carved into the wall: there was writing on it, and a group of symbols.

He crossed over towards the tower and started to climb the steps. They were very worn in the middle, trodden down to half their original height, and he stumbled over one of them in the dark. The sound of his boot scuffing on the worn stone then thudding on the step below echoed round the square for a second, then quickly faded away and was covered by the noise of the moving sea drifting up the narrow street from the shore. He gritted his teeth, and carefully carried on up.

The round-topped door looked old and thick; black iron diamonds studded into the dark wood. He stood on the top step and looked at the door for a second, then reached out and put his hand through a ring of iron that stuck out of the door at waist height. He moved his hand, first one way then the other, feeling for give, then grasped the ring with both hands and twisted it clockwise. From the other side of the door came a rattling, grating noise. He put his shoulder against the door and shoved. Nothing happened. He twisted at the handle again, first clockwise, then the other way, all the time shoving at the door with the whole of the side of his body. There was a slow rasping sound, two pieces of rusty metal dragging against each other, but the door didn't budge; and now the iron studs were pressing into the flesh on his shoulder and arm and hip, digging through his clothes and pressing sharp edges into his body. He stopped shoving, leant away from the door, breathing heavily, then took a step backwards onto the next stair down. Shit, he said. He was getting his breath back now. After a few seconds more, he lifted his head and gazed at the carving on the wall above the door.

The stone panel was worn and crumbling, but he could make out a coat of arms there: three swans sailing along in a triangular formation with a big five-legged star in the middle. On a separate upper panel of the carving was an inscription. This was worn too, like the stone was slowly flowing in and filling the incised letters, and he had to stare for a long time, moving his head to catch the light from the streetlamps around the square. Eventually, he worked out what it said:

> THIS FABRIC WAS BUILT
> BY EARL JAMES BRAIDON
> AND TOWN, FOR CRIBBING
> OF VICE AND SERVICE
> TO CROWN: 1593 A.D.

He stared at the carving for a while, then said aloud to himself, For cribbing of vice. Town and crown. He frowned. Cribbing...

A crash, a loud crash behind him, and angry shouting following: instantly he was crouching down and hugging in to the shadow of the wall up the stairside. More loud bursts of shouting across the square. He slowly shuffled round on his hunkers till he was facing out the way. In front of the hotel, some kind of scuffle was going on. The fat storyteller was standing in the road, swaying, looking back at the door into the hotel porch, which was being blocked by his friends. Bright lights had been switched on inside the porch, and the two of them were cut out in sharp black silhouette as they stood there, motionless, while the storyteller stottered in front of them, shouting in short angry blurts and shaking his fists at them in between. The storyteller shouted again, waving a hand towards the upper storey of the hotel, where one window was lit. One of the men on the steps, the one in the cap, said something in reply, jerking his thumb at his chest as he spoke, then the fat man made a run up the steps, dived between the two of them and lunged at the hotel door. In an instant the others had grabbed the sleeve of his jacket and his hair, and were pulling him away from the door back level with themselves. Then the one in the cap shoved him in the chest and the smoker struck the side of his face, and the fat man tumbled backwards down the short flight of steps and fell onto his back on the roadway. He lay still. For a few seconds his friends looked down at him, then one of them turned and went in the hotel door. The other followed. The fat man lay on the road.

The stone of the tower steps was cold, and now there was a dampness as well, seeping through to his skin. Slowly the walker got to his feet, looking all the time at the body lying on the road across the square. It wasn't moving at all. Oh shit, he said again. Poor bastard.

Then the fat man moved. He raised his left arm into the air directly above him, then his right, held them there for a second wiggling his fingers, then brought both hands down behind his head. He started to shout again, lying in the road, head pillowed from the cobbles by his hands. I'm . . . not . . . worried, he shouted. Ha! Ha! Ha! He fell silent.

Suddenly the fat man jumped to his feet and started walking quickly towards the tower steps, shouting as he came, FUCK YOU! I'LL FUCKING KILL YOU! His voice was almost screeching. It echoed round the square. The walker watched, backed against the studded door, as the fat man strode towards the tower. YOU'RE FUCKING DEAD! FUCK HER! YOU'RE ALL WASTED, YOU FUCKERS! Ten yards from the foot of the stairs he stumbled, came on more slowly for a few steps, then stopped altogether. For a moment he just stood there, then ground his head round over his shoulder to look back the way he'd come. He looked to the front again. He shook his head. He seemed to be chuckling to himself. You stupid bastard, he said in a quiet voice, then chuckled some more. It's a joke! It doesn't worry me, he said, then turned on the spot and walked quickly off across the square, passing the hotel without a glance, staring straight ahead, walking swiftly across the square and disappearing up the road that led to the hillclimb. In half a minute the echoes of his footsteps had faded away completely.

The light in the hotel porch went off. A few seconds later the light in the upstairs room went off too. There were no other lit windows in the square, and there was no one going about: from the top of the tower stairs the square looked big and empty, its corners lit by streetlamps but the buildings in between dark and the central area dark too. The walker went down the steps, turned left then left again into the narrow street that led to the sea.

He was walking quickly, keen to get away from the square, and he headed straight down the middle of the road, ignoring the narrow pavements in by the low windows and doors of the houses. But there was something about those windows... He steered in to the side of the road for a minute, walking in the gutter, staring at the housefronts as he passed. He looked to the front again, frowning, keeping moving. Then he stopped. He stepped sideways onto the pavement, then half-turned and stood gazing at the nearest window. After a moment he shook his head, bent forward from the waist and gazed at the window from a foot away. Suddenly he straightened up, laughed, and said, For God's sake! He reached out and knocked on the window-pane with his knuckles: there was a dull wooden thud. He laughed again, and slowly turned to look up and down the shadowy street. It was clear now, obvious once you knew. None of the windows really were windows: they were all boarded up. Instead of frames and glass in the window-holes, black-painted boards had been slotted in, then thin white lines marked on, one down the middle and two crossways, so now – on a gloomy dark night, from the corner of an eye, or with a straight look even till you knew – they really looked like real old windows. He laughed. It was typical, typical clever stupidity: service to crown!

He started walking again, back in the roadway, striding along. He was heading for the darkness ahead, beyond the endhouses, where the sea was moving against the shore.

At first it seemed there was nothing but darkness in front of him. He stopped. After a few moments he was starting to make things out: some of the light from the village streetlamps carried this far, and several tall thin objects in the foreground were faintly lit by it, less dark than the total darkness between them. There were no stars, no moon; the cloud had come over fast and was lying very low: his footsteps had been dull as he walked the length of the street towards the shore, deadened before they could echo back off the freshly harled walls and the boarded windows. Now he was walking on grass, short grass over flat even ground: a kind of links between the houses and the sea. The sound of the sea was deadened too: there was no crashing of breakers or rattling of battered pebble shoals, just the thud of lumps of water landing on wet sand and stone, weights of water heaving up then thumping down on the sodden shore.

He walked forward slowly through the damp, heavy air. After a couple of steps a pole loomed up directly in front of him, tufts of reedy grass around its base, its top stretching up into the darkness further than he could see. He stretched an arm out and moved towards it, a step, then another step. His thumb hit wet wood and he grasped it, the pole, half-circled it with his fingers. His grip slipping on the greasy wood, he swung his weight half round the pole and looked back the way he'd just come. The village seemed brightly lit now, though there were still only the few streetlamps in the square and a scattering of others through the village, mostly towards the hill end. But compared to what his eyes had got used to, the pitch-darkness where he was heading, the village looked very well lit.

He completed his circle about the pole then let his fingers slide from round it and walked on into the dark. It was really deep black now, he couldn't see a thing: he shouldn't't've let himself look back at the village lights. But he kept slowly on anyway, blinking his eyes to ease the dazzlement. The sea was dead ahead, still thudding on the wet beach, the sound dulled by the damp air and the clouds overhead, and he was heading straight for it. He couldn't go on much further, but he couldn't stop either: the links were too open, the poles gave no shelter. Here he was nowhere. He kept on moving.

Soon he could make out poles off to both sides and up ahead as well: he was right in the middle of them. One appeared right in front of him; he reached out an arm and pulled himself towards it, then leant there, both arms round the pole and back to touch the sides of his body, listening. His breathing was loud. He hadn't been moving fast, but something about walking through darkness, and the pain from his feet as well maybe, made his lungs feel heavy and his breathing hard. He waited till it quietened, then listened again.

Voices. He heard voices. Talking. Somewhere in the darkness there were voices talking, two or three voices. Off to the right maybe. Ahead and to the right. It was hard to tell with the thuds of the sea and the sounds dulled and flattened by the hanging damp. He let go of the pole and set off for the next one on the right. He paused when he reached it and listened some more. Now the voices were definitely closer, still to the right and still ahead, but closer too. He stared into the dark then started off towards the next pole ahead, crossed from there up a slight rise to one on the right, then one more to the right, then stopped.

From down in the ground twenty yards ahead bright flickering lights shone upwards, red lights and yellow: a fire, faint tails of flame rising up from the ground, flitters of pale light crossing the turf in front of him and fading away into black. The voices were coming from down in the ground too. There was talking and laughter, and some of the talking was female, at least one woman's voice, no, two female voices and one male as well, all youngish sounding. He could hear them clearly now. And now he could smell it too, a reek of damp smoke, burnt woodsmoke in the wet heavy air, salt and ash on his tongue as he drew breath.

There was a pause in the talk, then a muffled thump and an immediate burst of crackling and fizzing: something had been chucked on the fire. After a few moments the voices started again; they floated up and over the links with the smoke and the faint firelight, up out of the ground, up from under the level of the links. It was a harbour. Twenty yards in front of him the links ended in a drop edged with stone, and the edge reached away round to the right, holding the earth and grass from crumbling and washing into the anchorage; and out on the left the edge became a wall, a jetty wall stretching out over the black water, the waves dunting against its base. And down on the bed of the harbour the fire was burning, in the crook of the jetty arm.

He dropped to a crouch and moved forward slowly, keeping his face to the ground. Ten yards on he got down on all fours and raised his eyes to look around. Now he could see the stretch of links beyond the landward edge of the harbour; a car was parked there, scrapes in the paint and an unmatching door showing up in the light from the fire. But the folk who had parked it were still out of sight, hidden down inside the harbour, burning their fire and laughing. The grass was dewy on his hands, and wetness was soaking his breeks. He couldn't stay stuck here forever. He moved, crawling on slowly towards the edge, keeping low to the ground but knees bent, ready to turn and run into the dark if he had to. Three yards from the edge he could see it all. The harbour was filled in, or silted up, aye that was it: a high bar of sand closed off the mouth, and from there to the edge where he was crouching the sand sloped down steadily, strewn with odd bits of driftweed and rubbish, a single long pool of dark water at the foot of the seaward wall. In the centre of the sand sat two women and a man, all about his own age; they were gathered round a wide low bonfire, a couple of bags beside them, a scatter of odd pieces of wood drying by the edges of the fire. As he watched, one of the women passed a bottle of clear stuff to the other woman, who took it, smiling, then drank; then, lowering the bottle from her mouth, she wiped her lips and said something, rolling her eyes. The man sitting beside her gave her a shove, and the other woman laughed, shaking her head.

The walker was cold from the wet grass now, and the fire looked fine and warm. And if they had drink they'd maybe have food as well. He slowly stood up and took a couple of steps forward. Hello there! he called out.

The three faces turned towards him, red in the flamelight of the fire. The bottle had disappeared.

Who goes there, friend or foe? shouted the woman he'd seen drinking.

I was just passing and I saw your fire. He shrugged, opening his hands wide towards them.

The three of them looked at each other across the fire for a moment, then the other woman called, Come on down, there's a rare heat off this thing, plenty to go round!

He took another pace forward; his toes were at the edge of the drop. How do I get down? he said.

There's some steps just over there, said the second woman, and lifted her arm to point backwards into the darkness behind her.

Right... He walked in the direction she'd indicated. Halfway round the landward edge he found a ladder-top, clambered round, and started down it into the harbour. The ladder felt like it was falling to pieces as he climbed down, coming away from the wall with the weight of him; a couple of rungs from the bottom he stepped backwards and jumped down onto the sand. He turned and walked towards the fire, bowing his head to examine the palms of his hands in its light as he approached. Flakes of red metal were sticking to his skin, and brown powdery stuff lined along the creases across his palms and in his finger-joints. He stopped a few feet away from the fire, nodded at the three of them sitting there, and held out his hands to them. Look at this, he said. That ladder's rusted away to nothing: I'll never get up it again.

The woman on his right laughed. You shouldn't've come down that old thing. God! I said the steps; there's proper steps over there at the end, past the ladder: solid stone jobs!

Oh. I didn't see those. It was too dark. I just saw the one way down.

Never mind that now, she said. Come on and have a seat, that's the main thing.

He took his pack off and dropped it behind him, then nudged a couple of stones away with the toe of his boot and sat down on the sand, his feet close to the fire's edge. On his left was the man and one of the women, sitting close together; on his right was the other woman, the one who'd pointed out the steps. Her hair was hanging long over her face, and now she pushed it back behind her ears, half each side, and looked across at him.

Well, she said, It's not often we get anybody dropping in on us here, is it?

The other woman looked out into the darkness. Mind you, we could fairly do with some new company, she said. The man beside her sighed.

I wasn't expecting to find anyone here, said the walker. He started to rub his hands in front of the fire. Hih, I thought I was the only human life for miles around.

The other man smiled. Ach, you are, he said. Me and Claire are aliens and Melanie here is a hologram. He twirled his hand at the woman next to him. I mean to say, how else could you get such perfect beauty in female form?

Melanie groaned, but turned back towards the fire, half-smiling. Aye, not that you're drunk or anything Ray!

I am not drunk. Happy maybe. You can call me happy, that's fair criticism, but not drunk. No way.

Okay, not drunk then: bleezing.

Ray was about to say something back, but Claire broke in. Och, shut up you two, shut your cakeholes! She laughed. Here, mind when you used to say that, when you were a bairn? Cakehole! Shut your cakehole Mel!

My God, you're blootered as well! cried the other woman, but then she joined in laughing with Claire.

During the laughter, Ray leant back behind Melanie and pulled forward a shoulder-bag from a few feet beyond the firelight. He lifted it onto the sand in front of him and unzipped it, then looked up, grinning. He clapped his hands, then said in a fake slimy voice, Well ladies, shall we continue?

Aye, said Claire.

What were you doing? asked the walker.

Ray pulled out a half-empty bottle of vodka.

Nothing, said Melanie, Nothing at all. It's just the way he says it makes it sound interesting.

Ray had taken a drink from the bottle, and handed it to Claire, who was now upending it. Next, Ray took a bottle of diluting orange out of the bag, unscrewed the top, and took a gulp. The vodka was passed to the walker. Ta, he said. Voddy for the body. He took a short scoosh then passed the bottle on to Melanie.

She took the bottle, gazed at it for a moment, then said, Well, I hope he's not bloody HIV.

Claire lowered the orange bottle into her lap. You can't catch it off saliva, she said.

Still... Melanie looked at the walker out of the side of her eye, wiping the top of the bottle with her sleeve at the same time.

Silence.

Here, Claire, said Ray. See if you can't catch it off saliva? Does that mean you won't mind if I spit on you?

Everybody laughed again, and Melanie took a drink of vodka.

The walker cleared his throat. Listen, he said. It's good of you to be handing round the bevvy and that, but what I'm really needing is some grub. I'm not on the scrounge; I'm just asking if there's anywhere around here I can get a feed.

The three of them looked at each other. After a second Claire said, There's nowhere around here. That's the thing about this place: there's nowhere for a couple of miles, nothing.

Unless you tried the Arms, said Ray. See what Big Anne could rustle up for you.

Aye, you could try there, said Melanie, Up in the square...

The walker shook his head. I've been there already.

No go? said Claire.

A pickled egg and a packet of nuts... The others laughed. The walker pulled a blue bag of peanuts out of his pack sidepocket. Ah well, he said, and tore a corner of the bag off with his teeth. He held the nuts out towards Melanie and Ray, but Melanie shook her head and Ray was drinking from the vodka. He offered them to Claire, and she reached over and held her palm out in front of him. He put the bag in it.

No, no, she said. Just pour us out a few, I'm just needing a taste.

The walker hesitated, then tipped the bag up and emptied a heap of nuts into her hand.

Enough! She sat back and started to chuck them into her mouth one by one. She chewed slowly, gazing into the heart of the fire.

The walker put his head back and poured in a big mouthful of nuts. After a few seconds' chomping he accepted the vodka bottle from Melanie, gulped down the nut-mush, then took in a mouthful of drink, swilled it round his teeth and swallowed. He carefully wiped some particles of peanut from around the neck of the bottle then passed it on to Claire.

I must admit, he said, I kind of screwed up as far as the food was concerned, I should've planned it better. Hih. Well, I thought I had planned it, but it turns out my plans have gone off agley, as they say.

How, what happened like? said Ray.

Well, just that I thought I'd be able to get some grub here. I was remembering that Haven o' Braidon was a fair size of a place, the kind of place that would have a pub and a chippie and a Spar shoppie even.

Dear oh dear! Ray chuckled.

You picked the wrong place to look for bed and board, said Claire.

The Haven's nothing but a big black hole in a cliff, said Melanie. There's nothing here. It's a shitehole. I tell you, I'm just going to piss off from here completely, go to London or Glasgow or somewhere. This place is fucking rubbish!

Ray stood up, stepping apart from Melanie. He began to say something, then shut his mouth and looked away. There's a petrol station up over the brae at the junction with the big road, he said at last. They've got a microwave that heats up burgers and that. He lifted his left leg and waggled his foot; sand shook out from the turn-ups of his jeans.

Ach, they'll be closed years ago, said Claire. It must be nearly midnight.

Ray shrugged. Ah well, he said, and turned away into the darkness. I'm off to get some more wood for the fire. Anybody coming?

Nobody spoke.

Ah well, suit yourself. Don't finish the vodka before I get back. He walked away into the dark. After a moment there was the sound of him walking up some stone stairs, then his footsteps on grass, then silence.

Right, said Melanie, Let's finish the vodka before he gets back.

Claire looked across at her. Was that not a bit of a hint from Ray the Rave there?

Melanie snorted. He can hint all he likes, I'm biding here. She shook her head. I'll tell you pal: he's a long, streaky bastard. I hope he falls over a fucking cliff.

Och Mel! Claire turned to the walker. She loves him really, she said.

The walker raised his eyebrows. Is that what you call it?

Melanie picked up a bit of stick and started poking about the edge of the fire with it. Let's talk about something else, she said. On second thoughts, let's not talk about anything. Who's got the voddy?

They sat without speaking for a couple of minutes as the bottle was passed round and the last inch of vodka split between the three of them. Melanie took a swallow of the diluting orange and gave the bottle to the walker, who handed it straight on. Claire took a sup, then screwed the top back tight and wedged the bottle into the sand beside her. She pushed her hair back behind her ears again and turned to the walker.

Tell you this, she said, I reckon you'll need to get yourself a new map.

I mean, if the one you've got now has Haven o' Braidon down as anything more than a rickle of stones and half a dozen inbred alkies, well, it's useless. Worse than useless!

Hih. The walker chuckled, then looked up at her. Do you want to see my map?

Aye, come on, said Claire, leaning forward. Show us where you've come and stuff.

The walker nodded. He reached down to his feet, stretching his back slowly, and untied the laces on his boots. He yarked the laces on the left one out of their holes down to past his ankle, gave the tongue a pull, then shoogled at the boot, gradually working it down over his heel and off his foot.

Melanie looked up from the bit of the fire she was poking at. I thought you were going to show us your map, she said, Not the holes in your socks.

He didn't reply, but took off the right boot in the same slow way, grimacing.

What's the matter? said Claire. Blisters?

He shook his head, eyes closed, and started to peel off his right sock, rolling it down the ankle, lifting it over the heel, and leaving it bunched up around his toes.

Claire and Melanie looked down at his foot. He was holding it up off the sand, balancing on the bones of his backside. He peeled down the other sock. Both feet were in a similar condition: there were only a few bits of pale, clean skin visible; most of it was covered with reddish stuff, blood, rubbed into the pores and creases, matting the hairs. Some parts were in a hell of a state: all around the right heel were patches of red-raw flesh, and the soles of both feet were worn away too, big flaps of white whorled skin hanging off like strips of cloth. Claire drew a breath in through her clenched teeth, and held it.

Don't worry, said the walker. They're not sore at all. They're kind of numb. It's not a problem, not as bad as it looks, anyhow: half that bleed is probably dye out of my fucking cheapo boots! He held up a finger. Wait ... A wad of paper had fallen out of his left sock as he pulled it down; he picked it up off the sand. Another one the same was hanging down from the base of his right heel, stuck on with a mess of dried blood; he took hold of the paper by one corner and tugged at it gently a few times, then gave a sharp jerk and pulled it clean off. A shaky noise like a laugh came out of his mouth.

Christ, your feet are in a hell of a state ...

You don't say, Melanie! Claire was frowning. Maybe we should wash them or something. Here, we could seal up the wounds with alcohol like they do in the films: pour some of the vodka over them.

Could we what! said Melanie. Anyway, it's finished, unless the rich kid's splashed out and got another bottle planked somewhere.

Forget it, said the walker. They're fine. Look at this though. He moved round into a kneeling position, then started to unfold on the sand in front of him the wads of paper he'd taken from inside his socks. The one from the left sock unfolded easily, it started to come apart along the creases as he laid it out; the other one he had to pick at with his fingernails to get started: the leaves were matted together with dried blood and hard to separate. Eventually he spread that piece out on the sand too and lined it up with the other half. The two parts made up a map of Scotland. It was hard to make it out at first, as the paper was covered in a grid of thick white lines where the map had been folded and the print worn away; where the lines of the grid intersected, there were holes worn right through the paper. There were also stains of sweat and dye all over, and on the north half of the map, which had been under his right foot, there were large patches of blood, dried-in browden red and yellow, even dark brown where there were thick gatherings in the folds of the paper. One of these brown crusts lay right over the north-east coast from Aberdeen to Montrose, covering all the bays and cliffs and villages down the coastline, and spreading out into the blue of the sea.

Now you know how I went wrong, said the walker, kneeling and looking over the tattered map. I just had to go on what I could remember before it got knackered: this morning, up at Muchalls, before I put it in my boots.

The others looked from his feet to the map and back again. Claire pointed at the side of his heel. Look, she said, There's a whole bit of it printed onto your skin: there's Inverness and the Black Isle!

I ken I'm thick, said Melanie, But was it not a pretty daft place to keep your map in the first place?

Aye, no doubt. He shrugged. But I needed some padding, see? My feet were just getting blistered to fuck, these socks are that skinny.

They're worn away to nothing, said Claire. You should take better care of yourself ...

Melanie was away to add something but stopped, cupped a hand up round her ear, and peered out beyond the fire.

What is it? said Claire.

Shh... Melanie listened some more, then said, It's just, I thought I heard something, somebody creeping about out there...

The three of them sat in silence, turning their heads out to the darkness. Suddenly there was a loud rattle of kicked rocks. Quickly, the walker folded up the torn pieces of map and shoved them into his jacket pocket.

At that moment footsteps came down the stone steps and across the sandy bed of the harbour, and Ray walked into the firelight, carrying an old fishbox piled up with an assortment of driftwood. He dropped the box at the far side of the fire then started to unload it, throwing the branches and plank-ends and lumps of wood onto the sand. Melanie and Claire spread them out in a single layer all around the fire, and at once the walker could see trickles of steam rising up from the wet wood in the firelight. When Ray had emptied the box, he stood up again and crashed his foot down on the corners of it, wrenching off the side panels; then he lifted the bottom of the box and broke it over his knee, cracking it into three slats. He flung all the pieces down at the edge of the fire, then walked round and flopped down in the sand by Melanie.

The worker returns! he cried, slapping his hand on Melanie's thigh. Right, where's the... Fuck's sake! He stopped, staring at the walker. What are those things on the ends of your legs?

Eh, plates of meat?

Christ, that's terrible: cover them up quick, before I spew!

The walker laughed. I was just going to, he said. It's getting a bit warm down here: the heat from the fire'll be giving me chilblains. He started to pull on his socks, then leant further forward and slowly fitted his feet into the boots.

Ray was shaking his head. How the hell did they get into that state?

Och, just wear and tear. I've been walking.

Christ, I can see you've been walking, but where from? Timbuktu?

Close, said Melanie, Muchalls.

Claire looked away as the walker laced up his boots. You're mad, she said. You should leave them out for a bit, relax them...

Nah, they'll swell right up if I leave my boots off. Hih, cribbing, that's what they need, good tight cribbing. Ha! But talking of relaxing, my, eh, bladder could do with a bit of a relax: where do you go when you're needing a pish around here?

Just go up and over the harbour wall, said Claire, placing a big bit of driftwood on the fire.

There's seaweed for bog-roll, said Ray.

Right. Thanks. He got slowly to his feet, checked his inside pocket, and walked off towards the steps that Ray had used earlier. Behind him he could hear Melanie asking Ray if there was any more drink, and rummaging in the bag, and just as he was reaching the foot of the steps, Ray shouted, Hey, watch out for the famous leaping lobsters of Braidon Bay! I hope you've got some protection! Then there was laughter, and when it stopped Claire called, If you're not back in an hour we'll send out the coastguards!

He carried on up the steps, crossed the top of the harbour wall, and went down some more steps on the far side, down out of the last of the light from the fire.

He was squatting with his trousers round his ankles when he heard someone coming down the steps behind him. He didn't look up, but slowly withdrew the needle from his thigh, releasing the lump of flesh he'd pinched up with the other hand, then slapping his leg there a couple of times.

Is that you? It was Claire.

Eh, aye, I'm over here. He put the syringe away in its clear plastic case and laid it behind a rock off to one side, then rose, yanked up his breeks, and turned to look at Claire standing halfway down the steps.

Where are you? she said.

He stepped sideways out of the dense shadow of the harbour wall. Tara!

Christ, there you are, I didn't see you! She came down another step. Maybe just as well, eh?

Hih, aye, maybe just as well... He bent his head to do up the buckle on his belt.

She stepped down onto the pebbles and came towards him. I wasn't trying to catch you out or anything, she said. I just had the feeling that Mel and him wanted me to piss off for a bit. So I thought I'd come and see if you'd finished, eh...

... pissing off?

She laughed. Aye, I suppose so.

I'm finished all right, aye. I just have to... Hold on a minute; could you... He waved a hand towards the end of the beach and she nodded and turned to look off along there. He knelt into the shadow of the harbour wall and felt around at the back of the rock he'd been squatting beside.

Have you lost something?

No, no, he said. I'm just ... His fingers touched the smooth plastic. Got it!

What is it? said Claire, turning and looking at him as he stepped out of the shadow and examined the case in the moonlight for a second.

He glanced up, found her staring. Nothing, he said, at the same instant slipping it back inside his jacket pocket.

No, hold on, she said. What was that?

Honestly, nothing. It's just ... I should be more careful.

Shit, she said, and took a pace backwards, then another one, till she reached the foot of the steps.

Sorry, he said. It's nothing, nothing at all.

That's not what I'd call it, she said, and backed up the steps, her hands feeling for the wall as she went, her eyes fixed the whole time on the walker.

Listen, he said, It's nothing, really.

She stopped, stared at him for a few seconds, then said, Is that all you can say, bloody *nothing*?

He opened his mouth, then shut it again and shrugged. What's the point? He stared into the darkness beyond her for a second, then shifted his gaze back to her and said, I know that look on your face: you've made up your mind. What can I say that'll matter?

Anything! Say anything! I mean that was a needle there, wasn't it? What is it, the works you call it? And after Mel talking about AIDS and that. Jesus, say anything!

He paused, looked down at the ground and kicked a pebble with the toe of his boot. I'm diabetic, he said at last.

Claire looked at him, then sat down suddenly on the steps. She rubbed both hands into her forehead, then looked up. What did you say?

Ehm ... I'm diabetic. It was a needle, but for insulin, that's all. He patted his jacket over the pocket. I have to stick a dose of this into me a couple of times a day, or else I get a reaction, ken: I flake out.

Shit. She leant back against the stair, throwing her head back and resting on her elbows. Sorry, she said. She raised her head to look at him again. I'm really sorry.

You don't have to feel sorry for me, he said, sticking his hands into his jeans' pockets. It's nothing. I wish I'd never mentioned it.

No, no: I'm sorry for jumping to the wrong conclusion there. I was worried, that's all. I mean I don't know who you are or anything ...

He was silent.

I don't. I don't know anything about you, what you're doing here . . .

So you just thought the worst thing possible straight away. He shook his head, looked down again. Folk are always doing that.

She gazed at him for a moment, then jumped to her feet and started to come down towards him again, her eyes on the shadowy steps. At the bottom she put her hand on his shoulder and rested it there for a second before pressing down on it as she jumped off and onto the beach beside him. I should've known better as well, she said. There was a girl in my class at primary school was a diabetic – Tracey Coutts – and she was really bad for it: she kept running out at playtimes and buying all this chocolate and Love Hearts and stuff, and then she'd scoff the lot and go into this kind of fit . . . what do you call it?

A hypo. He coughed.

Aye, hypo, that's it. She'd eat all these sweeties and then start shaking all over and kind of faint, take one of these hypos.

He cleared his throat and seemed about to say something, but turned instead and walked away from the lee of the harbour wall, through the greasy black rocks there and onto the mowrie beach. Claire followed after him, and fell into step at his side. Aye, he said after they'd walked for a while, Your diet's very important. It's a balancing act: you have to keep the sugar at a certain level in your blood, or else – doosh! – blackout.

It must be a worry having that hanging over you, the thought you could just black out at any minute.

Ach, I don't think about it anymore. You just have to concentrate on the regular food and the regular jags, and put the hypos out of your mind. I don't worry about hypos at all anymore. They don't worry me. It's always there, but I don't worry about it. I just don't. Anyway: blah blah blah. It doesn't worry me.

They walked on in silence. After a few moments Claire started humming something under her breath. Then she came to a halt and crouched down. It's amazing how your eyes get used to the dark, she said. When you come away from the fire it seems like it's pitch-black out here, but after a wee while you start to make things out.

He looked down at her. What can you see?

I was just wandering along in a dwam there when I noticed this patch of stones, a really good lot of skimmers. Look!

He poked the toe of his boot into the patch of flat slatey stones. That's the good thing about walking, he said, You notice a lot of things you'd never see in a car or on a bike.

Aye, like you notice your feet are bleeding to death! She picked up a couple of the skimmers and weighed them in her hand. Come on, let's have a go. I bet I can beat you, I can do seven!

Never.

Aye, look. She balanced herself, half-kneeling, then drew her arm back slowly and flung it forward, sending a stone spinning out over the water. One, two, three, four ... ach!

What?

Four: not bad for starters.

That was never four.

Aye it was! Look, I'll beat that this time. She waited for a lull in the waves then skimmed another stone out across the water. One, two, three, four, five ... Five!

Come on, how can you say five? I only saw one; it's too dark to see after that.

Ah-ha!

Ah-ha what? Don't ah-ha me with your fives! It probably sunk straight after the first bounce.

No, I could hear it. There were definitely five splashes.

He laughed. You're a joke! Here, let me have a go. He felt around amongst the pebbles at his feet, then half-straightened up and spun one out over the waves. One, two, three, four, five, six ... I got six!

That's nothing! She shook her head, her hair swinging. I can do seven, any day.

Oh aye, seven? Just listen to this then. One, two, three, five, eight, seventeen, twenty-three ... Twenty-three! A new world record!

She hooted with laughter, he carried on shouting about his twenty-three skims, hobbling a dance at the edge of the water. Eventually he stopped still and laughed too, then paused to shout, It's probably in Norway by now: hello vikings! He laughed again.

Claire grabbed him by the arm and dragged him after her, up the narrow sloping pebbly beach to where it ended in a small bank of sand with a mat of grass rooted in along the top of it. Hup! she said, and pulled herself up on top of the bank. She turned to sit with her legs dangling over the edge, then held her hand out and hauled him up alongside her.

For several minutes the two of them sat quite close together, not speaking, just getting their breath back, occasionally letting go a laugh or two, and looking out over the dark sea. The cloud cover had started to break up some time before, and now there were long rips appearing right across the sky, and through the holes in the cloud a few stars were visible; every so often, as the tears shifted and widened momentarily, ragged sheeds of moon would appear, high overhead, and the tops of the waves diving in the sea would be picked out for a second, curves of white silver appearing then crumbling into black, rising again and falling again, silver into black.

There was a faint sound away over to the left, and both of them turned and gazed at the dark harbour walls with the glimmer of the fire glowing inside. They listened, but there was no more sound from there, only the waves raking through the stony shingle on the beach in front of them.

Then he said, I've got another packet of peanuts in my bag back at the fire.

Do you want to go and get them?

Well...

It's just the main reason I came after you was to leave the two of them by themselves for a while. Let them patch things up a bit.

What, are they fighting?

She turned to him, pushing her hair back and arching her eyebrows. Could you not tell?

Ach, I'm out of practice at that kind of game. But I suppose I did think Melanie was being hell of a sarky all the time.

Oh aye, taking the male side immediately!

What? No, I just...

Tch, I'm only kidding. Mel does come across as awful bitter sometimes. She's fed up with this place you see. But Ray's quite happy: he's got a job. She looked down. Old arguments...

I suppose I don't like the place I live either.

Where's that? South somewhere?

Eh. He frowned. I can't remember. I've been walking too long.

She laughed. Can you not remember your name either? You went out of your way not to tell it earlier on.

Did I? Hih! He swung his legs round onto the grass and jumped up. Talking of going out of our way, he said, Let's walk a bit more: my toes are throbbing away dangling in space there.

Claire got to her feet and started after him. We could easily go back for your nuts if there's any danger of you taking a hypo thing. Cause look: I'm really sorry about back there. Am I forgiven?

Nah, he said after a moment. I'm fine. Anyway, I've got these glucose tablets in my pocket; if I start to feel woozy at all, I'll just have a couple of those: pure energy! I feel fine now though, like I could walk forever: all the way! He started singing, Keep right on to the end of the road...

She laughed.

They walked along the grassy links till they got so narrow – a rising heuch on one side and a rocky part of the beach on the other – that they had to stop. They stood there for a few seconds, then Claire pointed to a patch of clear sand over beyond the rocks, just where the cliff swung out towards the sea, high and craggy, the southern edge of the bay. They clambered down and started picking their way through the sharp rocks and black pools towards the light circle of shingle.

He paused and looked up at the cliff looming in front of them. What's on the other side of that? he said.

She stopped just behind him. Doolie. Where we live.

Is that the same as Inverdoolie on the map?

Aye, but everybody just calls it Doolie; saves wasting time on the place.

They headed on towards the patch of sand again. So is this what you Doolie folk do? he said. Drive out to your local beauty black spot and sit up all night getting rat-arsed?

You can talk! Walking about net-greens in the dark? Jumping out on folk just minding their own business? Is that what you do?

He laughed. Well, it's hard to meet folk these days. Jumping out on them's my last resort: it's all I'm left with.

Here we are. She stepped high over the last of the rocks and onto the sloping circle of sand beyond. It wasn't as big as it had looked from up at the end of the links. She turned and gave him a hand as he stumbled over the rocks after her. There are friendly folk about, it just depends how you look for them. She smiled at him as he stepped onto the shingle beside her.

Ach, I reckon I've given up looking. Too many knockbacks. Just keep on walking, that's my philosophy.

Christ, talk about Mel being bitter!

I'm not bitter. Cause it doesn't worry me. I like being by myself. Just walking on, I like it. On and on.

She looked at him. Oh aye?

Aye.

I don't believe you.

It's true. I'm used to it. I like it.

She laughed and took a step towards him. Well, if you like walking so much, come on, let's go on further!

There isn't any further, is there? Unless we go round the head?

Ah-ha, just look over there though. She stood beside him and pointed to the foot of the cliff twenty yards ahead, close to where the waves were raking the shore. Do you see them? she whispered.

See what?

Look.

He looked. The cliff was dark and split up and down with cracks and shadows of rocklums, and ledges and shelves cut sideways shadows, deep against the dark rock too. But down at the base, where the cliff joined the shore, was a solid black band, a long low slot in the rock, totally dark in the faint star and moon light.

What is it? he said.

Come and see. She crossed the sand to the point nearest the cliff-foot, then paused. He stopped just behind her. Ahead were piles of black shattered crag-stone and pools of glinting water. Watch this, she said, then picked up a pebble and tossed it underarm into the black hole in the cliff. There was a sharp crack, then a rattling noise, then the echoes of the crack and rattle, a fainter series of echoing patters, then silence.

Christ, he said after a second, It's a cave.

Aye! Brilliant, eh? Well actually it's three caves, it kind of widens out and splits once you get in the entrance there. I used to come here with my folks when I was a kid. Picnics on the beach, ken? I haven't been up this end of the bay for years though.

It looks a bit spooky. Does the water not come up into it?

She looked out to sea. The tide won't be turning for a couple of hours yet. Come on, we should have a look inside. Well, we won't see much, but we can feel our way in: you'll get the atmosphere of the place anyway.

For a few seconds he didn't reply, then he said quietly, Claire, will you hold my hand?

What? In there? Scared of the dark are you? She laughed. Aye, sure, come on.

She stepped out of the circle of sand, setting one foot down on a flat boulder and looking ahead for the clearest route to the cavemouth. Suddenly he reached out and grabbed her elbow, pulled her back off the boulder and towards him. He said something under his breath: Now, now, now... She half-lost her balance and fell against him, pushing her free hand against his chest to keep herself upright. He was still holding her other arm tightly.

What are you doing? she said.

You know fine well what I'm doing, he said in a hoarse voice. He took hold of her free arm, and held her still while he lowered his head and half-turned it to press his mouth to hers.

She jerked her face away, his breath hot on it, and tried to shake her shoulders free of his grip. You've got the wrong idea, she said. Let go of me, now.

No, no, it's the right idea. He moved one of his arms round her back and bent to kiss her again. Please, Claire, please. I just want to ... a kiss in the dark. No one'll see. Please?

No! Let me go!

Claire! He was raising his voice now, and breathing loudly too. His boots were kicking up sand as he struggled to keep hold of her. Come on! Claire, into the cave, come on! Please ... He pulled her against his body. COME ON!

Suddenly he staggered off to one side, yowling with pain, still holding onto her arms. She flung a glance down and now brought the ridged heel of her monkey-boot down on his other foot. He yelled again, and she twisted and dug down onto his toes and the top of his foot, shaking him off her shoulders at the same time. He started to fall over backwards, and let go of her, throwing his arms out behind him to break his fall. He yelped loudly as he landed amongst the jaggy rocks, one arm twisted behind his back.

Quickly, Claire stepped backwards across the circle of sand. Fuck you, she said in a steady voice, and he heard the sound of her spitting, then her turning and moving off through the rocks, sliding on pockets of pebbles, splashing in hidden pools, heading straight for the narrow tang of the links.

He closed his eyes and lay back. He hadn't felt her spit hit him, but his back and left arm were already soaking, drookit in the cold water of the rockpool he'd fallen across.

He was sitting in the middle of the circle of sand, looking out over the sea. A small yellowish light had appeared from behind the headland and was moving slowly northwards across the dark water. He followed it with his eyes for a long while, shivering from time to time: the whole back of his jacket and large parts of his breeks were soaked through, and it was cold sitting about, away from the fire. He shivered again. Suddenly he frowned, put a hand up to his forehead, and felt it damp with sweat, chill sweat. He held the hand out in front of him and gazed at it for a second, rubbing his fingertips together, then shook his head a couple of times and looked at his hand again. He wiggled his fingers about in front of his eyes in the half-dark.

He got to his feet, staggering slightly as he rose, and thrust his hands into his jacket pockets. His left hand came out empty, the right one clutching a wad of tattered, bloody paper: his map. He looked around the sloping circle of sand; it was churned up with footprints all over, but there was no sign of his glucose tablets. He checked his inside pocket: nothing. He fell to his knees and scrabbled about in the sand where he'd been sitting the past while, howking up damp handfuls and flinging them away to each side. After a minute he stopped, leaning on all fours over the foot-deep hole he'd dug, breathing hard. The bottom of the hole started to fill with water, sucking sand in from round the edges, collapsing the walls he'd scooped out. He got slowly to his feet, wiped the sweat off his forehead, and started to search carefully amongst the rocks that surrounded the patch of shingle.

Almost immediately he found what he was looking for. In the middle of the shallow pool he'd half-fallen into earlier on, lay the yellow and red wrapped tube of glucose tablets. He shoved his sleeve up to the elbow, stuck his hand in the cold stingy water and pulled out the wrapper and its contents. It squelched in his fingers. Kneeling at the side of the pool, he peeled open the paper tube; a dribble of grey mush ran out over his hand and down onto the sand. He clapped the hand to his mouth and licked the stuff off his skin, working his mouth on the traces of grainy slush and trying to swallow. Straight away he was retching, down on his knees, his hands flung out to steady him against the nearest rocks. He retched, relaxed for a moment, then retched again. He lifted his right hand to wipe sweat from his brow and found he was still clutching the remains of the map.

He sat back on his heels and gazed at the folded wodges of paper in his fingers. His hand was shaking. He started to unfold one of the pieces, but the leaves were welded together with dried blood starting to soften and run after the dooking; he flung that half of the map away, and it skited onto the dark water of the pool in front of him, rested on the surface for a moment, then zigzagged to the bottom, disappearing in the drumlie depths.

He was concentrating on the other piece of map. He was trying to get his fingers in between the folds of the paper, but the paper wasn't keeping still, and there wasn't enough light to see properly. His fingers were trembling too, fumbling over the damp edges of the map, rough now with stuck grains of sand from the times he was dropping it.

He was feeling tired out with the effort. He paused to rest and looked up. The sea was moving in front of him, but it was all very dark now, and hard to make out where the sea ended and the shore began. He remembered he'd been watching the light of a ship a moment before, and he scanned the black face of the water for it, but it was nowhere in sight. It must have gone down over the horizon.

He had something in his hands. It was a wad of paper. He looked at it briefly, then laughed to himself and tore it in half and in half again. He tried to tear it a third time but his fingers couldn't hold all the pieces, he was too tired. Fragments of white paper tumbled down onto the sand. He watched them fall, then swung his arm out and flung the remaining pieces towards the sea. They flittered towards the rocks in front of him, some of them floating down onto the dark water of the pool; he watched them resting there, white sprinkled on the black, trembling, floating and soaking through, and sinking slowly into nothingness.

There was a roaring noise. It was the sea.

He was walking. So tired now, he had to have a lie down. He made his way across a field of jagged rocks, slipping often, dunting his boots and banging his shanks. His eyes were beginning to close over.

The night was very dark now. It wasn't the night, it was the cliff glooming above him.

There was a roaring noise. It was his head.

He walked on into the cave mouth.

He walked on.

Bridget Penney

Incidents on the Road

Police block

It was as if I'd been exposed to an electric shock. All the revulsion I'd felt for my job over the past months welled up at once and I started to walk towards the door, past the whining machines beneath the bright light and the figures bowed above them, transfixed by the continual rattle of coins.

— Where are you going, Judy?

— Piss off.

She flushed and stepped across me to bar my way. I stood there, mute, and glowered at her. She regained her calm, and spoke steadily;

— Not with those things.

My fingers seemed very large as I fumbled with the knots that held the overall in place. Her face was still. As knots unravelled, the rolls of money dug into my stomach. I pulled the garment over my head and used my arm as a spindle, closing the money within a tight roll of cloth in a gesture that became increasingly futile as I sensed the smile spreading across her face.

— Judy!

I tossed the roll at the ground where it struck her ankle, and brushed past out into the salt air, following the line of the wooden planks until I'd quit the pier and was heading along the esplanade, between the sea and the afternoon traffic. It was hot and I began to sweat. As I slowed, the wind off the sea caught me, and my clothes felt like ice.

A car pulled up. I glanced at it involuntarily and caught the eye of the woman leaning across as if to ask me directions.

Her eyes were watery and bloodshot. She had reddish hair and pale skin that looked firm and healthy. I found myself saying

— I'll show you,

and saw her hand move to unlock the door, smiling as I opened it and slipped inside.

— This is very kind of you, she said as the car pulled away from the kerb. I wriggled slightly in my seat. The overheated upholstery was sticking to the back of my legs.

— Can you put on the seat-belt, she said, taking one hand from the wheel to indicate it – in case we get stopped.

I bent forward, and stole a glance up at her. A private smile played around her lips, which were pale and dry, giving the impression they had not enough skin. Her chin was sharp, but blurred by a suggestion of fat.

— There are some cigarettes in there.

I took the hint, lit one, and passed it over. She held it gingerly, inhaled deeply, and coughed. Then she opened the window and threw it out. I found a packet of pastilles in the glove compartment and passed her one. She sucked noisily for a second, then spat it out.

— Thanks, she said. Her cough had gone.

She changed gear as we turned off the coast road and headed uphill. I leaned back in my seat: the cold wind ventilating the car made it quite pleasant. I smoothed my clothes and undid the top button of my blouse, scraped my hair up from my neck and let it fan out over the back of the seat. Then I teased off one shoe with the toe of the other, rotating my heel to study the clinging patch where a blister had burst against the dark nylon.

— Why don't you take your gloves off?

I laughed out loud and glanced down at my hands encased in black cotton. Looking up again, I caught her eye. She shook her head and smiled a bit, then turned away.

— It was part of my job, I said, fumbling with words for what already seemed remote. Staring down at my hands as if I couldn't quite believe in them, I laughed again, rather oddly.

— What was your job?

— Changing people's money in the arcade so they could lose it in the games machines.

— Sounds terrible.

I gestured self-consciously. Without removing her eyes from the road she gave me another quick smile, and pulled across into a different lane. Idly I raised my hands, then lowered them.

There was activity up ahead. The traffic had come to a halt, and there were lights across the road, blinking ineffectually against the glare of the sun setting over in the west. They cast weak shadows upwards, elongating the trees at the roadside so they threatened to close over. I rolled down the window and stuck out my head to look along the column of cars. There was a restless movement next to me as she drummed at the steering wheel with her fingers.

— There's a man coming. A policeman.

She raised her shoulders indifferently and sighed.

— There must have been an accident.

He went to her side of the car, asked for her licence. She handed it over with a flippant gesture. He straightened up, and studied it for some time before passing it back.

— What's wrong with it?

His face showed that he resented her tone. He glanced from her to the car and back.

— There's been a murder.

It barely showed but he succeeded in rattling her.

— Two young women had their throats cut in the North Wood.

— That's the other side of town, I interposed, leaning across her. – Why are you stopping people here?

— We've got men on all the roads.

As my gaze met his, he looked irritated, insecure. Then he turned and walked back along the column, his shadow brushing up against the cars.

— You all right? I asked the woman. She shrugged impatiently. I put my gloved hand on hers where it rested on the wheel, lightly touching all her fingers. After a second she removed it and didn't look at me.

The policeman returned with another, older man. I could see them arguing as they came along.

— Sorry to bother you, girls.

She passed a hand across her forehead.

— What's the matter, officer?

He gave her a warily sympathetic look, then glanced at his colleague, who stubbornly resisted the glance and addressed himself to us.

— Someone described a car like yours parked near the wood.

The woman raised her head and spoke scathingly.

— You mean someone said they saw a black car. There are thousands.

He looked as if he might have shrugged.

— The description was more specific than that.

There was a moment of silence.

— Are you going to arrest me? she asked softly.

Her eyes flickered from one to the other. I stirred in my seat, disconcerted by the directness of her challenge.

The older man cleared his throat, and addressed me.

— Perhaps you can tell us something about yourselves.

— We came down from London this morning.

I glanced at her as if for corroboration. — We were going to drive along the coast, then find somewhere to stay.

— What's your name?

— Judy Smith.

As I met his glance, he gave me a tired smile.

— All right, girls. We shouldn't keep you much longer.

I watched him walk to the head of the column. The younger man had gone to check on the cars behind us.

She sighed and scratched her head.

— I don't like the police.

It was practically dark in the car, and the shadowed outline of her face made me feel somehow peaceful. I let myself stretch out as far as the seat allowed. A gratifying, almost titillating exhaustion spread through my limbs.

— What's your name? I said on the verge of a yawn.

— Laura.

River

We drove for most of the night. Slight changes in the engine's pitch made me aware, in my semi-conscious state, where the road varied. Sometimes I raised myself to look as a white wall flashed by.

Just before dawn we pulled on to a rough track, then slithered across grass. Something brushed the roof of the car as we came to a halt.

I must have slept again for when I woke it was light. Laura was doing something at the front of the car. For a moment I lay still, eyes half-closed, to listen to the faint sounds she made. Then I stretched my neck tentatively, and my limbs, one by one until cramp receded and I opened the door and got out.

We were parked underneath a tree. On either side the boughs bent down gently to cloak us, creating a barrier of leaves through which the diffused light shone green. I walked to the edge of the circle and ran my arms up along the branches until a satisfying coolness drenched my clothes and the scent of the leaves made me giddy.

— Feel better?

I turned. She was standing behind me. There was a smear of oil on her left cheek and her eyes were barely open.

— You should have woken me if you wanted help.

She smiled and shook her head.

– You must have been tireder than I was.

Her tone was friendly, but there was a slight reserve which might have been due to exhaustion. I stepped back a little and looked around.

– Why here?

She shrugged.

– I don't like to park too near the road. You get people coming along.

– How did you find your way in the dark?

She gave me a guarded smile and said

– You don't have to bother about that, Judy.

She turned quickly, leaving me at a loss, and walked back to the car, her light shoes making little sound. The green shadows gave everything an eerie tint. Slowly I rolled up my wet sleeves. My forearms glowed as I parted the curtain of leaves and stepped outside.

We were on the bank of the river. The sun was still low in the sky but the last traces of mist were already dispelling. My feet sank into sodden grass. I tried to gauge the time from the sun's position and let my failure yield to a sense of pleasant aimlessness. Any noises I could hear were much too faint to provide a clue.

I studied my surroundings with passive deliberation, gaining such satisfaction from the way I moved that I felt the desire to do something extravagant fill me with a slow excitement that was hard to contain. The field behind me was empty, the road invisible.

On the opposite bank rushes grew close to the water. I stared at the coal-black mud, castellated by the river's progress. Its current was hard to discern: just a few faint ripples indicated a tug towards the far bank. My head turned to look along. The river became a flat stretch of grey, running straight where the bank had been improved. Then a smudge of trees, and it vanished, curving slowly beyond my sight.

I took off my clothes and slipped into the cold water. Its first shock forced the air from my lungs, then I kicked out strongly, loving the feeling of moving through water the sun had not yet begun to warm. It had a silky texture that would be unbearable later in the day. I hadn't felt so good in a long time. My legs and arms pumped through the water in perfect tune.

– Oh, Laura, this is marvellous! Come in.

She was standing on the bank with her arms crossed, watching me. Her presence made my satisfaction a little more deliberate. I kicked out my legs in a mighty splash, conscious of a desire to tease her, and saw her flinch as a few drops of water fell dangerously near in the sunlight.

— I'll teach you to swim, I persisted, generous in the sense of my advantage.

As she shook her head the sun caught her face and the furrow between her brows.

— I think you can drown enough for both of us.

I laughed. As I heaved round on my stomach to tread water, her expression took on a complexity that puzzled me.

— Let's get on our way. Can you drive?

I nodded. As I climbed up the bank she looked at me with a glance in which amusement mingled with something else.

— Where are we going?

She made a casual gesture. — I've got some stuff stored in a place a few miles from here.

— And then?

I was drying my feet with excessive care. As I straightened up it was as if her eyes had moved away from me rather sharply.

— Oh. Her manner was offhand. — Anywhere you like.

I donned my clothes soberly, feeling slightly ashamed of playing her up. As I walked with her back to the car her expression was warm but brittle. She was more nervous than I had suspected or perhaps tiredness exaggerated her reactions.

I really liked her. She was tricky, which I appreciated, and made me less worried about being moody myself. She had a car, and wherever I might end up it was better than stewing on the pier all summer.

House

It was a long time since I had handled a car, and I experienced a steady, if rather remote, excitement as the road smoothly disappeared before me. Laura dozed in the passenger seat, her chin pressed right down against her neck. Occasionally a stifled snore escaped her. When this happened I would glance across, and moving my eyes back, would catch an almost conspiratorial look in the mirror. Her hands lay limply in her lap. A slight swell of fat at the wrist was swiftly contained by buttoned cuffs which had that shiny look clothes get when they've been worn too long.

She opened her eyes with difficulty and sat up.

— What is it? she asked, seeing me grin.

— You, I said truthfully.

She wasn't quite sure she liked that.

— What about me?

I smiled and shook my head, devoting exaggerated care to the tension of the wheel between my hands.

We turned down a lane that rapidly petered out into a track. I had a dim glimpse of a pond, overhung by trees. When Laura put her hand on the wheel, I braked a little too quickly and turned to her. She smiled.

— Do you want to come?

— Your stuff's here?

She raised her eyebrows at my surprise and slipped out of the car. She walked ahead with a slightly floundering motion, dipping and jerking to avoid the deposits of mud that lingered though there'd been no rain for a week. Mosquitoes and flies swarmed around us; I kept my hand up in front of my face to swat them away.

We came level with a broken paling. She stopped.

— Here? I echoed.

She bent her shoulder to lift a gate which hadn't been disturbed for a while. I followed her through onto a path that led up to a house of incredible decrepitude.

— I used to live here, she said, as if needing to explain.

It was all right inside, which worried me, because I felt that when it started to crumble it would do so very quickly. I followed her through the rooms, fitting my footsteps to her own in the obscure hope of minimising disturbance.

— I was here as a child, she said. — My parents moved to London when I was eight.

— I would have been relieved.

A sideways smile suggested my desire to leave had reinforced her need to talk. She went on apologetically.

— I hated moving. As soon as we got to London my cat ran away.

For a moment she fidgeted uneasily.

— I'm sure she came back here. I wanted to come and look but they wouldn't let me.

Her voice went very small. I gingerly avoided leaning back against a door.

— It was only a cat, Laura, I said, trying to comfort without feeling any sympathy.

Silence ensued. A nervous desire to laugh was tempered by vague horror as I stood there looking at her in the almost ruined house.

At last she sighed very quietly and said

— My stuff's in here.

Two suitcases and a grip, which she wiped casually before handing me the larger case. Without further words we left the house. I wasn't tempted to look back and don't know whether she was.

Café

We were sitting together in a café drinking ice cream sodas. Being Saturday morning, it was full of prospective teenage couples who made me self-conscious. Laura, who was either oblivious or better at concealing her reactions than I, was gurgling with her straw at the last pink fragments. After a couple of sips at mine, I stirred it aimlessly, wishing I'd held out for a cup of coffee. I was impatient for Laura to finish but as she showed no signs of hurrying I picked up the paper a previous customer had left and glanced at it.

– Look, I said to Laura – about those girls who were killed.

I folded the paper appropriately and passed it across. A slight frown creased her brows as she read, then shoved it back to me.

– So they caught someone.

– Seems so.

She shrugged. – Can I have your soda?

I passed it across without a word, watched with amusement as she meticulously replaced my straw with her own.

– I keep expecting you to say you used to come here when you were fourteen.

– Oh but I did, she said, in such a way that I was unable to tell whether she was joking.

I plaited my fingers together on the table and leaned forward.

– Do you often revisit your past?

She sucked up the last of the soda appreciatively and raised her head.

– Judy, she said with great solemnity – it's in your honour.

We looked at each other, and simultaneously faltered. Her tone was so close to mockery that for a moment we both doubted whether it was. She cast down her eyes and fiddled with her glass, but her composure was gone. I craned round the room with such a start I found it hard to believe we hadn't both become instantly noticeable.

– I do like you, Judy.

She spoke from just above the rim of the glass. I hardly dared reply or look at her.

– In all sorts of ways.

This time she looked up and met my gaze with a disconcerting smile. I found something very sweet in her voice and was conscious of a desire to prolong all the implications of that moment.

If this showed on my face it made her laugh.

— Judy, she said — let's go.

She pushed some coins beneath her saucer and abstracted the two straws with a sleight of hand I was expected to see. Then another smile, kinder because less challenging, and possessed of a gravity I'd have found it hard to assume.

— Judy, she said again.

In some obscure way I'd already lost out. A flicker of concern across her face betrayed the panic I'd let show in mine.

— Laura, I . . .

It was all bewilderingly clear. There was a hint of tenderness in her smile. I passed out of the café with the strongest commitment to something I knew nothing about.

The Bridge

We went into a shop to buy provisions for our journey. Laura selected biscuits and several cartons of fruit juice. While I half-heartedly added a loaf, Laura took jam and a sheaf of chocolate bars. She paid with a large note and I found myself carrying the bags. Laura walked slightly ahead, whistling thoughtfully and twirling the bunch of keys round one finger.

— It's too hot to drive now, she called back at me. — What do you say we dump this stuff in the car and set off this evening?

She gave me a slightly teasing smile as if to indicate what a good idea this was. I smiled agreement — it was her car, after all.

We reached the entrance of the underground car park. There were narrow concrete steps at one side for pedestrians, but Laura ignored them in favour of the ramps the cars went down, seeming careless of any danger we might incur. She took the bag from me and swung it as she walked with a slight swagger down the middle of each slope through the chilly petrol-saturated gloom.

We put the stuff in the back, beside her luggage. As she was locking up, I was taken by a feeling of awkwardness, partly sad and partly reckless, as if I didn't really know what to do but was being overtaken by events against my will. Staring at her back outlined by the coat in the flickering light I had a confused impulse towards her, in which an almost

violent tenderness was dominated by something else that made no sense
to me. Turning, she smiled at me thoughtfully, and taking my arm, led
me up the steps into the sunlight.

— What would you like, Judy?

— Somewhere quiet.

She rubbed her free hand across her face as if tired or trying to think.
For some reason this aroused my suspicion, and I gave her a quick mulish
glare which she evaded, seeming about to say something sharp, then
changing her mind.

— I don't really know my way round here.

— Neither do I.

We looked at each other, then smiled.

— Let's wander.

She took my hand and squeezed it lightly. I looked down on her
fingers which were white and slightly plump. We both seemed to have
recovered our good humour. As we walked along, we responded to a
sense of complicity which took the form of throwing a mystery round
ourselves, emphasising our behaviour in peculiar ways and engineering
a private joke that permitted us to laugh at everything around us. We
covered the main streets in this way, but when we came into the quieter
suburbs we were more subdued, and strolled in silence along the
tree-lined streets, occasionally glancing at each other, but mostly self-
contained, soaking up the dull warmth of the afternoon.

— Look Laura, I said suddenly – there's a bridge.

It poked up a little oddly behind the houses. She gave me a look as if
she was trying not to laugh at me. I grew self-conscious, and stopped.

— Come on, she said – let's look at your old bridge.

It was at the end of the street. She took my arm again and led me on.
She seemed amused with the whole thing. I didn't like her being amused
with me, but it would be worse if I demurred.

We climbed a flight of iron steps, then lolled against the sides of the
walkway that spanned the tracks and platforms of a station. She peered
over the edge, and I looked at her. As a train pulled in underneath she
raised herself on her toes with a slight exclamation of surprise.

— It's hot, Judy.

I made my face as nonchalant as I could manage and she gave me a
look perhaps intended for mystification. I followed her across the bridge,
listening to the slightly mannered taps her shoes gave out against the
iron.

At the bottom of the steps a narrow lane ran straight along beside a high wall. From the bridge I'd glimpsed trees and thought it was a park, but when we found the gate and entered, it was a graveyard.

— Put on your gloves, Judy, Laura murmured. – And be a young widow. I'll support you.

We proceeded in that way. The place was overgrown, with the thick foliage of early summer already wilted by the scorching heat. But the paths had been freshly cleared, so the clipped-back bushes presented a vivid uniform wall of green, and the impression was rather that of a well-maintained maze than a cemetery. It was a place for assignations: every turn suggested a glimpse of someone slipping out of sight.

We passed slowly among obelisks and angels. The masquerade added a curious potency to our progress. Laura held me tightly, she stroked my hair and I buried my face in her shoulder. She was laughing very softly, right down in her chest, which I could hear because my head was pressed so close. Her heart beat slightly fast, and the sense of it pumping round all this warmth that surrounded me put a choke in my throat and an urgency in my grasp from which Laura wordlessly disengaged herself, pulling me to one side of the path where the leaves partially covered us.

She seemed to swallow before she spoke.

— Two kinds of people haunt cemeteries, she said. Her tone was light and dry but her eyes were anxious. – Ghouls and lovers. Which are you?

It was as if I was a stranger. Her eyes seemed to search my face over and over rapidly but reach no conclusion.

— A widow, I replied, falling in with her formal banter, and touched her hand.

— Why then you're both, she said in a tone at once grave and playful. She turned my hand palm upward and seemed to study it for a moment, then stared at me, slightly embarrassed. I kept my eyes steady and did not betray the strange focus of emotion within me. Then she looked aside, abruptly, and gave a sort of half-smile to distract us both.

— What a place for it, she said, almost under her breath.

She made as if to step onto the path but I caught her hand and held her, determined to take the initiative for once.

— Judy, she said, and there was both alarm and annoyance in her tone.

— I love you, I said stubbornly. I could repeat it without looking at her, and did, trying to get some sense into the words so she could see what I was at.

— Not here, Judy, she said.

Her face registered bafflement and panic.

— There are other places, but not here.

I let her bring me out onto the path. Then I looked up and said with great calmness
— I don't respect the dead.
She looked as if she didn't quite understand me.
— You don't respect them, she said as if making it clear for herself.
— Perhaps you should.

Hotel

We were in the foyer of a cheap hotel. Laura was talking to the clerk while I stood by the stairs, gazing up at the short twisted pillars of honey-coloured wood that formed the banisters gradually rising from sight. We had been driving all day, and I was stiff and sweaty from being in the car.
Laura came over.
— Third floor, at the front.
— Sea view, I suggested, beginning to climb the stairs.
— If you look far enough over the roofs.
She sounded tired. I felt a twinge of guilt, moulded into protective compassion. I took one of her bags. My own was very light for there was little in it.
At the top of the shaft a smeared pane admitted the late glow of the sun. Our door was painted white. Once inside, I wedged the window open at the top and pulled the curtains across.
Laura was taking off her shoes.
— Are you hungry? I said on a curious impulse.
— No. Are you?
She looked at me straight for the first time in a while. For a moment I hesitated then smiled and shook my head. I got rather a tight smile in exchange.
— I'm going to sleep, she said and curled up under the coverlet.
I slipped through to the bathroom, ran the tub full of water and soaked there for a long while, topping it up when it threatened to cool. No sound came from the adjoining room. To avoid disturbing her I switched off the bathroom light before opening the door. A faint draught moved the top of the curtain, outlined by a whitish glow that seemed unnervingly precise.
It was some time before I realised I wasn't watching it alone. Then I was careful not to betray my knowledge, relishing the bond that common object gave us. So I was still. And then she turned, and looked at me.

— Couldn't sleep?

— Bad dreams.

I went to sit with her. She sighed, moving up in the bed, then rose abruptly and went to stand by the window. I followed her with my eyes, then looked down, conscious of something I could not share.

— It's cold there, Laura. Come back into bed where it's warm.

She shook her head. I resolved to watch her, then realised with a start that I'd been asleep for a while.

It had been raining for hours. The window was open and she was leaning there, deep in thought, with her chin in her hands.

Alan Warner

The Man Who Walks

Away in one of the Far Places, The Man Who Walks comes over the hills from The Back Settlement. He moves down those slopes with a camping pack on his back and his unlit pipe upside down in his mouth, to stop it filling with the rain. On the end of each long arm dangles a carrier bag. Both bags are filled full of water, the plastic handles straining against his hands and he has to hold the bags out to get them clear of his moving legs.

The bag he holds with his left arm has a large dead salmon floating inside, curled around against the plastic so's you can see its sliver flank of scales. The other bag just has water in it that splashes out in response to his erratic walk.

It's still raining when The Man Who Walks arrives outside The Hotel. In The Hotel carpark, next to two parked buses, The Man Who Walks tips out the water from the bags. He wraps the salmon in one and lays it by his boot then using two fingers, The Man Who Walks reaches up to his left eye and removes it. It's a glass eye. After he's taken out the glass eye he pokes in to the dark recess of the socket and from beneath the little flap of skin he removes a small tinfoil package of cannabis resin. He unwraps it, uses his thumb nail to split away more than half then swallows a piece of the resin. He wraps the remaining portion and puts it back in the socket behind the eye, which he replaces. The Man Who Walks then picks up the salmon and crosses to the door of the lounge bar. Inside The Hotel is busy with tourists from the buses, who will be staying there that night.

When he gets to the bar The Man Who Walks says, 'A score of nips.'

'A score? You want twenty whiskies?' The barman slides out a tray then lifts up three tumblers.

The Man Who Walks shouts, 'In *one* glass man; in one glass.'

The barman looks at him, reaches for a large tankard and begins filling it with repeated shots.

The Man Who Walks slaps down the salmon on the bartop. 'Cash or fish?' he asks.

The barman says, 'Look, Sir, barter went out with the Middle Ages, it'll have to be the legal tender'.

The Man Who Walks takes a very large wad of wet one pound notes from his overcoat pocket and with one eyebrow raised, peels the paper notes; a few tear in half they are so sodden but The Man Who Walks sticks them down on the wooden bartop. The barman collects over twenty of the soaked notes and doesn't put them in the till but lays them to dry on the radiator beside some beer crates. The barman rings up the till and puts change down beside the dead fish. 'Can you take *that* off the bar please,' says the barman.

The Man Who Walks takes the fish off the bar and puts it inside the plastic bag. 'What a big beautiful fish,' a nearby tourist says. The Man Who Walks removes his glass eye again and grins at the tourist then says, 'Look into my mind.' The tourist moves sharply away.

The Man Who Walks takes a small case from inside his overcoat. He opens it and removes his drinking eye. This glass eye is similar to his other but the white of the eye is specially rivered with reddened blood vessels designed to match with his living eye after the consumption of twenty whiskies. He fits the red eye in.

An hour and three quarters later it's after closing time and the lounge bar is deserted apart from The Man Who Walks whose tankard still has a good dose of whisky in the bottom.

The barman repeats, 'Come on now Sir. I'll have to ask you for your glass.'

The Man Who Walks picks up the carrier bag: the upside down dead eye of the fish and its gaping mouth are inside, pressed against the greyish-looking plastic.

The Man Who Walks lifts the salmon out by its head, clamping the gills with his grip, he gently tips the whisky from the tankard into the open mouth of the dead fish then bangs the emptied tankard down on the bartop. '*Good night!*' says The Man Who Walks and he steps out of The Hotel into the rainy darkness and holds the big fish's mouth up to his own then tips the head back and gulps whisky out from the insides of that fish. When he's emptied the fish, The Man Who Walks turns his face up to the wind-driven splatters of water coming down from the slates on the overhang above. Then The Man Who Walks takes the salmon's tail in both hands, swings back and gives the big bastard a good fling across the road. The fish goes spinning through the night then lands with a bump on the roof of one of the buses – no doubt leading to a lot of shitey speculation among the tourists in the morning.

But meanwhile The Man Who Walks is off – striding into the wet

black of nightimeness with his thumbs under the straps of his camping
pack. Moving along the backroads, across The Concession Lands,
between the outlying homes he makes his way through the darknesses
until he climbs up on an old wire fence which squeaks along some of its
length. He jumps down into a flat field and strides into the blackness.
There is a large crack and a blue explosion as he walks into an electric
cattle fence cranked up to the max. The Man Who Walks yowls, falls
backwards on his arse. He can't see a thing in front of him, behind him,
to his left or to his right, so he does not know where the electric fences
are...

So he sits still in the raining field and chuckles in the dark then, later,
lets out a sound like a sob. The Man Who Walks leans forward and
swings the backpack off. He pulls out a set of poles which clink together
and sound like tent poles. *But they are not.* The Man Who Walks is
unfolding the plastic walls and roof of a child's Wendy House which he
uses for his camping expeditions. The Man Who Walks tries to get up on
his feet to pitch the Wendy House but he is mortal as a newt and slumps
back on his arse each time. Eventually he unlaces his boots and removes
them then lies back and just pulls the Wendy House plastic up to his
chin like a sheet. He starts snoring. In the darkness is the sound of big
raindrops pattering down on the plastic and in the morning The Man
Who Walks' boots are filled with water...

It's stopped raining and there is weak sunlight so The Man Who Walks
packs up and makes his way along the electric cattle fence. Hung along
the wire are the electrified, decomposed shells of hoody crows and moles
fixed there by the gamekeeper to display his boundless industry.

The Man Who Walks crosses a stile in the corner of the pasture beside
the extra booster batteries for the fence. In one of the lower policies
where the river flows in to the loch, The Man Who Walks sees a tractor
with the gamekeeper sat up in the cab. The shovel attachment at the end
of the tractor's telescopic antler has been lowered into the waters of the
delta and is baited full of cattlefeed pellets. A frenzy of fish are churning
up the muddy water inside the shovel. The Man Who Walks hears the
tractor engine start. The shovel attachment lifts up out of the water and
the tractor reverses backwards, splashes coming over the edges of the
shovel. Then the shovel falls forward and a cloud of water blows across
the tractor cab; its windscreen wiper goes on while a mass of flicking
silver fish bump onto the green grass and begin thrashing there, reflecting the dull sunlight. The first seagull comes gliding in from the delta,

leans backwards on its wings and lands among the fish. Soon a mass of gulls, pecking and hacking, are moving among the squirms of fish. The tractor cab door catches the sun as it opens and the gamekeeper, wearing a camouflaged hat and sunglasses slowly emerges and fires both barrels of a shotgun from his hip. About ten seagulls vanish in an explosion of feathers and mutilated fish.

In the afternoon sun, carrying a new bag of water, The Man Who Walks comes down off the hills and into The Back Settlement. He enters Old Greyhead's General Store to get provisions. The Man Who Walks places things on the counter beside the till, spilling water from his bag all over the floor as he moves. He buys four cans of South Atlantic Pilchards and one can of North Atlantic Pilchards. He buys Clann Tobacco, two copies of the *Daily Telegraph*, two copies of the *Observer*, two copies of the *Scotsman*, two copies of the *Herald* and two copies of the *Independent*.

'It's brightened up a lot now hasn't it?' says Old Greyhead.

'Shut your mouth and give us a carrier bag,' says The Man Who Walks who has forgotten to change his drinking eye so he has one red eye and one clear one.

Old Greyhead hands over a bag to The Man Who Walks. Although The Man Who Walks stinks, shouts, spills water, and once shat pilchard skitters on the floor of the shop then wiped his arsehole with a dead pigeon, Old Greyhead holds The Man Who Walks *in-the-highest-regard* because of the quality newspapers he reads.

'Good afternoon now Sir,' says Greyhead, following The Man Who Walks' heels with a swishing mop.

The Man Who Walks moves up the paths to his one-storey house on the hill. He empties the bag of water into an already full 45-gallon drum in the overgrown garden. The Man Who Walks opens the front door to his house. Afternoon sun still shines over his shoulder but it's dark in there: pitch dark. The Man Who Walks shuts the door behind him, gets down on all fours and dragging the carrier bag of provisions he crawls forwards through the network of filthy papier-mâché tunnels and igloos he has constructed inside the rooms and corridors of the house; the papier-mâché made from years and years of unread, quality newspapers.

1988

A. L. Kennedy

from *Looking for the Possible Dance*

Margaret is sleeping now.

It is three o'clock in the morning and the sparrows and dunnocks are trying out their songs. Windows along the street have full dawn against them and Margaret Hamilton lies behind the dark of her curtains, asleep.

A week ago, Margaret was still employed and today she is not. Because she was prepared for this, she had her railway ticket ready and this morning she will travel away from here. Probably, she will come back, but this is not certain. She is going away to think about things like that.

Asleep, she is surrounded by waiting. In her kitchen, her half-packed holdall is waiting to be filled, the kettle waits to be boiled and the curtains are waiting to be drawn. In a street a mile away, the sleepy taxi driver who will take Margaret to the station is waiting by a hamburger van with his radio turned off. And away in the city the railway station is expecting her.

At almost exactly seven, Margaret wakes up.

Without an alarm clock or other assistance, this is quite hard to arrange, unless you know the trick of it. Margaret's father taught her how. Just before you fall asleep, when the lights are out and everything else is done, you must hit your head off the pillow, once for each hour of the time when you wish to wake. Margaret hasn't done this since she was a girl. When she was ten, her father bought her an alarm clock to use instead.

But yesterday evening, alarm clock broken, her preparations for sleep sounded quite like this:

PFFUPH, PFFUPH, PFFUPH, PFFUPH, PFFUPH, PFFUPH, ... PFFUPH.

Or this:

Alright then, seven, it could even be half past, but you can't do halves. At least, I don't think so.

ONE.

And I want to sleep tonight.

TWO.

Please.

THREE.

Train tomorrow. London.

FOUR.

God, I'm too tired to sleep.

FIVE.

South. Do I really like the English.

SIX.

Who cares? Nobody cares. The English don't bloody care. Sleep, fuckit.

SEVEN.

The English don't *know*, so of course they don't care. I didn't tell them I was coming. I'll have to ask someone to watch the flat. I should have thought of that. No point in just watching, they'd have to come in. I couldn't ask Colin, not now. No nonono no no. Sleep. Everything's fine. Sleep.

Seven o'clock, I'll wake.

Clever Daddy. I wonder how he knew.

And Margaret does sleep and doesn't stir once until almost exactly seven the following morning.

Usually, for a journey, she will dress in something practical like a sweater and maybe jeans. Today, she will put on a suit, as if she were travelling to London for an interview. This is because, in the job she has lost, she was almost always dressed in jeans and sweaters and now she wants a change. Margaret is making a new start and intends to feel different and formal when she and England's capital meet. Also she knows it isn't good to let yourself go when you don't have a job; she's seen what can happen when people do that.

Margaret is wearing perfume; one made new by lack of use. It surrounds her every time she moves and has given her wrists a slightly bitter taste. As the day progresses it will change and fade.

Her taxi arrives a little early and she darts out to sit the back, feeling odd and not wanting to speak. She is still waking up and the city which passes by her is curiously unconvincing. Buildings like tall, heavy ships swing round about her, shining with glass and blasted sandstone; scaffolding and sails of plastic sheet.

A very few people are out walking, their faces lit by a sky which is the strident blue of plates. Inside the cab, music is playing and Margaret feels; as she sometimes does; that she has inadvertently started to be a film.

As soon as she reaches Central Station, this feeling intensifies. Margaret pays the driver quickly, lifts her bag and leaves the taxi with the kind of smooth and purposeful speed that cameras might expect. Her impetus carries her far into the body of the building before she can recover herself.

The station is nice, she likes it. The period wood-panelling and glass, ripped out several years ago, is slowly being replaced by imitation wood-panelling and glass. The pale, hard floor, beefsteak tomato seats and the more or less garish shop-fronts combine peculiarly as amplified music washes down and a high, black indicator board rolls and pulses hugely. This could be a place of worship.

Over by the photographic booth, two drunks are quietly cutting each other's hair in the mirror provided. People with an air of going to work are running and striding and straggling as Margaret simply walks, but the majority of figures here are still. They are standing like an operatic chorus awaiting revelations from above. Their positioning is beautifully regular, their postures both relaxed and alert, as they gaze at the platform numbers, destinations and arrival times, all crossing the board from nowhere into nowhere, constructed out of tiny yellow squares. The crowd seems very much at peace, very focused, just a little unnerving.

Margaret peers up just enough to see her platform number and is careful not to pause. The train is snug by the platform and while Margaret searches for the carriage labelled H, four policemen take away the barber drunks.

Although there is no one sitting near her, Margaret settles herself quickly and then pretends to fall asleep. No one will talk to her if she's sleeping. Only a ticket inspector will even try.

Margaret hears feet and a distant child and luggage, the traditional whistle blast, and then the tug of movement begins. In a way she does not understand, a murderous electric current pulls her and the carriage out of the station and away.

If she opened her eyes to look out and down the river, Margaret would see a layering of bridges, stretching east before and then beside and then behind her as her own bridge is crossed. Everything is blue, the sunlight and the water, the sky behind the dark blue bridges and their shiny blue buses and cars. The river always turns its mornings blue.

Margaret settles her head more firmly between the window and her hand and when the horrifying speed of her progress has ceased to alarm her she begins to fall asleep. Before she passes Motherwell, she is dreaming.

From one sleep to another, there she goes.

*

Late in his life, Margaret's father forgot how to sleep and of all the people who knew this, he was the least concerned.

'It isn't as if I'm still working. It isn't as if I can't nap. I can nap if I want to, any time. If I needed to sleep, I'd be tired, wouldn't I?'

Because no one was with him all of the time, no one knew if he napped. Nobody could be certain, when they saw him, still and with his eyes closed in the easy chair, if he was thinking, or napping, or simply humouring them.

When Margaret came to visit him, he seemed only slightly changed. It seemed there was only a very thin callous of time across the father she had as a child and the one she had now. If she nudged her daddy down beside her on the sofa and they talked, their heads resting back, inclining towards each other, they could have been speaking in any time. If she called through from the kitchen and heard his voice, only his young man's voice, he could have been speaking to her from one of their after-school discussions. They might have been planning an outing, or what she would like for Christmas, bearing in mind that she wouldn't get it because Christmas should be a surprise.

'Alright, then, what would you like?'

'Nothing.'

'You'd like to have nothing?'

'No.'

'You'd like to have something?'

'No. I *wouldn't* like one of those things that you blow down and press the keys.'

'You mean a saxophone.'

'No. These things are plastic. They sound like a paper and comb would, only better?'

'Mmm. I thought you might hate to have a telescope. Funny.'

'Oh, I'd really hate that. Yes.'

'Good, good. Well, you'll not get that, then. That's a relief. And now.'

He folded his hands round her waist, nearly tickling, but not quite. He bristled his stubble against her cheek, blew on her nose.

'Who do you love? Just out of interest. Anyone?'

'I love you. I love you.'

'Only me?'

'Only you.'

'You're a good girl.'

Their wee catechism.

He would always begin it softly, at the tail end of something else, as if he wasn't sure of what to say. Margaret would always answer twice, to make him sure.

'I love you.' Loud and firmly, a quiet shout, and then, 'I love you.' Softly, to give him all the feeling and stop him being frightened by the shout. This became the only way she could say these words to anyone, although she didn't notice this for some time.

When they had finished speaking, he would touch her head or stroke her face and never be as happy as she hoped.

Margaret was happy with the telescope. It combined things for her pleasantly. She loved the fresh autumn nights near her birthday, their hungry smell and that obscure excitement they made her feel. She loved to disappear into watching, to be nothing but eyes. She loved the peace of doing something by herself. It wasn't like school, or even being home with her father. Two of you couldn't watch; it was impossible for you to see the exact same things. She could look through the one eye of the telescope, the only person there, or needed there, and she could be peaceful and enjoy the night.

She sat in her room while the rows of rooftops and streetlights spread away into shadows and dots; a blush of orange rubbing up beyond the hills. At night, the hills seemed just humps of black nothing, but she knew what they really were. Her light was off and her window opened right up, the door was shut and muffled with her quilt, and she sat in the full feel of the outside and the dark, inside the house and there with her. She watched the colours of the stars and planets and the nothings in between and felt they were lifting her to them. This was the time when the path was opened, when she could choose to walk out from her window and up and into the moon. Asleep, she would dream of running on air. Thin, unscented air.

Her father thought it was too lonely to sit by yourself and look at bright things so far off. He had hoped to be with her, holding her shoulders and giving the little scatters of light their right names, but she didn't want to know what she should call them. She just wanted to watch the stars turning and think of the bigness of distance and of time and then look at the patterns of streets round her house and be sure they could never change.

Deep in the long winter term at school, Margaret would only feel real when the sun had gone down and she was alone by her window, looking up.

In retrospect, her schooling seems absurd.

Margaret's education was in no way remarkable, it merely took the Scottish Method to its logical conclusion, secure in the knowledge that no one would ever complain because, after all, it only affected children.

Margaret, like many others, will take the rest of her life to recover from a process we may summarise thus:

THE SCOTTISH METHOD
(FOR THE PERFECTION OF CHILDREN)

1. Guilt is good.
2. The history, language and culture of Scotland do not exist. If they did, they would be of no importance and might as well not.
3. Masturbation is an abuse of one's self: sexual intercourse, the abuse of one's self by others.
4. The chosen and male shall go forth unto professions while the chosen and female shall be homely, fecund, docile and slightly artistic.
5. Those not chosen shall be cast out into utter darkness, even unto the ranks of Her Majesty's Armed Forces and Industry.
6. Pain and fear will teach us to hurt and petrify ourselves, thus circumventing further public expense.
7. Joy is fleeting, sinful and the forerunner of despair.
8. Life is a series of interwoven ceremonies, etiquettes and forms which we will never understand. We may never trust ourselves to others.
9. God hates us. In word, in thought, in deed we are hateful before God and we may do no greater good than to hate ourselves.
10. Nothing in a country which is nothing, we are only defined by what we are not. Our elders and betters are also nothing: we must remember this makes them bitter and dangerous.

Funny old things, schools. Margaret can easily imagine her headmistress, even now – a piercing, yellow mouth, craned across the black wood of a desk.

'Don't you want to die for your country?'

Margaret couldn't understand the question.

She only remembers standing in a gravel playground each year, each second Friday in September. Rehearsed to the point of hyperventilation, the Pipe Band would advance in long-haired sporrans and white spats. They played 'The Flowers Of The Forest' and 'Scotland The Brave' and the Brownies fainted.

The Brownies always fainted. They would be marched out in close order through the dark of the morning, a full two hours before anyone else, and stood to attention, brown and taut in cotton dresses and knitted hats. The honour of their pack was in the balance.

As the bugler blew the reveille from behind the Domestic Science block, forward came the columns of girls and the columns of boys, all searching for their special marker Brownie. Each column would string itself out behind its Brownie, safe and still. Without the marker, they would have to wander, lost and incorrect, perhaps halting in entirely the wrong place, perhaps never halting at all.

Usually, the Brownies would last until the opening prayer. Then emotion, the swing of the kilts, or simple exposure would begin to take their toll. By the time Margaret first made her dot in the Armistice Day Photograph, a special team of Brownie bearers had long been a vital element in the display. As the morning progressed they would lift up their little fallen comrades and carry them away. They had bright faces and stepped in time.

For older members of the staff, the symbolism of these moments would sometimes prove too great. Lowered heads and coughing often hid a tear.

Margaret can't quite describe her school; if she tries, things seem to get away from her. She can't be sure if what she remembers is totally true or not. Her head fills with marching columns and the Twenty-third Psalm and she seems to have always been marching or singing, as if she were in preparation for some kind of war. Over the years, she has invented sequences for effect, but only because the reality makes no sense.

She can shut her eyes and watch a huge, square-headed man gradually take off his jacket to belt a boy. The boy has blond hair and is almost obscenely smaller than the man.

'Sometimes, when I belt a boy, I only take my arm back to here.

'Sometimes, when I belt a boy I lift my arm, right up, as far as it will go.

'Sometimes, when I belt a boy, I take my jacket off.

'For you, boy, I'm going to take my jacket off, then I'm going to roll up my sleeve and then I'm going to make you very, very sorry.'

The horror of it stayed with the class, all day. No one would go near the blond little boy, in case whatever badness he had around him would spread to them.

Such merry brutality soon became commonplace. Margaret smiles as she thinks of the maths teacher, the one with the greasy hair and the uncertain fly, who would beat a boy or two almost every day. The boys responded by spitting, smoking and starting casual fires in their desks. It seemed a natural part of things. For half their time, Margaret and the others would observe themselves like strangers, just to see how far they'd go. The rest of their day, they gave to the fight. It was a way of life they were so used to, they almost believed they'd invented it.

Margaret only realised that she didn't like her school on one of those marching, drizzling Armistice Days. A real Armistice Day with real Brownies. It was that terrible Day when Frazer MacTaggart, the chosen Pipe Major, flung his six-foot ornamented staff high through the layers of rain and then didn't catch it.

Every face in the columns of faces tilted up to watch the staff in flight and suddenly knew that Frazer MacTaggart would miss. The faces turned towards Frazer and made him know. He stuttered only a little in his marching, before the staff point caught him a wheeling blow on the shoulder and he fell.

The rest of the band marched around him, not knowing what else to do, and a group, perhaps of Brownies, ran out to help him away.

Margaret's was the only face that laughed. It wasn't spite, at least she didn't think so, she was simply very happy. Her school would have to be ashamed now. Not her; her school. An act of God had hurt its pride. Clever God.

It was hard for Margaret to tell her father what it was really like out there, away from his home. She didn't know if he could understand. When she

came home crying because the lady who taught them sewing had
spanked her, she already knew that he wouldn't be able to help. She told
him that she couldn't use a thimble because it made her stitches go all
wrong and Mrs Parker would shout at you for that, but if you sewed
without your thimble, she shouted, too.

Daddy held her on his knees with his nose in her hair and didn't say
anything. His breathing felt very hot and she imagined it would make
her head less sore, so it did.

'Come on, now. No more crying. You've made my shirt all wet.'

'Sorry.'

'It's alright. It's alright. Here you go.'

She took his huge, fresh handkerchief and wiped her face and he
looked at the window, beyond her head.

'We'll have to buy you a thimble and you can practise.'

'I can't do it.'

'If you practise. It's only that you've never used one. Your mother
would have had one, I think she did. You have to please these people
sometimes, even if they're silly. She's silly. You know that?'

'Mm.'

'Who's silly?'

'She is.'

'Who?'

'Mrs Parker.'

'Mrs Parker is silly. Go on. All together.'

'Mrs Parker is silly.'

To please him, she giggled. Thinking of the chalky fabric smell of Mrs
Parker and how she would always win, Margaret giggled. Daddy seemed
convinced.

Margaret's father walked her down to the chip shop after that. They
looked at all the other gardens and her daddy's was still the best.
Sometimes she wanted to cry again, but she knew that she couldn't
outside, because people would see and they would think it was her
father's fault. She wondered if he'd known she wouldn't cry outside and
that was why they'd come.

That night, she thought she heard him very late, walking about in the
living-room by himself.

Probably, Margaret could say the sound of her daddy, up and pacing
out the night, had run through her thinking for something like twenty-

three years. Through her presence and her absence in his house, it ticked out her worries which were his and his worries which were hers. The space where she expected his sound to be was still unoccupied in her head.

As she dreams in the train, there may be the hush of slipper footsteps, still walking through her mind. Something like her breath or her heartbeat, or the sound of a slow dance step.

One November, Margaret phoned her father. They were both near the end of those twenty-three years they had together. Twenty-three years. As long as a marriage, maybe two.

'How are you?'

'Fine.'

'Are you sleeping?'

'I'm fine, Margaret. Just fine.'

'That's good. You'll be sleeping at night then. That's good. I had thought that, if you weren't sleeping at night, it might be a wee bit boring. I thought you wouldn't like a video recorder. To pass the time. I thought that would be no use to you.'

'They're very expensive.'

'Good thing you don't need one.'

'Too expensive, love.'

'Well, like I say. Anyway, what are you doing with yourself? How's my Daddy these days?'

When the video came, he seemed happy; he bought tapes and hired films from the garage across the street. He read the leaflets on how it worked. If he wanted to record a programme, he had to kneel down and lean on his elbows, then squint at the little green numbers, press little keys. He found that all quite difficult to do. His knees were stiff. And it seemed his fingers were very large for the remote control. The keys were certainly small and close together, so close be would often press two of them at once. The thing was not intended for his size of hand. It was a shame, he would have used it, if he could.

* * *

Colin liked to talk most on the move. He liked to do things moving. This hadn't been the case before he went away. When they first met it took Margaret several months to get used to Colin's kind of stillness. He could sit sometimes, not blinking, not breathing, muffling his pulse, and she would be frightened that he was dead. Afterwards, she asked him what it felt like and he couldn't tell her, didn't know.

Perhaps the drugs altered his pace. Certainly, you could imagine him throwing something and seeing it curve and fall at half the speed, maybe slower, still under the influence of his hand. His conversations seemed to hover and lose themselves as the spaces between the words ran into silence. Questions could take days to answer, so she didn't ask them. All she could do in the end was interpret his range of quietnesses. To be honest, she couldn't say if they meant a thing.

At least she couldn't complain he annoyed her with snoring. She often woke in the night to find his chest neither rising nor falling, exhaling an absence of breath. But if she touched him, he might speak.

'Hands off McCoag. It's sleeping.'

Whether he woke at these times was uncertain. In the mornings, he never mentioned being disturbed.

Now, he had changed his speed. He was certainly still thin, but now it looked intentional. He trained. There were tracksuits and sweatshirts, plain black, or freckled grey, which might be worn at any time. There were shorts for his running, or working in the gym, and she got used to his smell being altered with the sharpness of frosty grass, of new sweat and swimming pools. Undressed, his muscle pressed beneath his skin, like an anatomist's drawing, or maybe a butcher's chart. He was hard to the touch; soft skin but hardness beneath it.

Outside and dressed he strode along beside her like a very tall dog, conversing on the run, talking down the pavements, discussing through shops. Even indoors, he could be restless, like a child.

'Sit down.'

'What, love?'

'Why don't you sit down.'

'Aye, I was just thinking.'

'Well, take the weight off your brain for a while, you're making me dizzy.'

He walked to the sofa, letting one arm slip behind her as he sat and resting his chin quite gently on her head.

Margaret likes that; that's why it happened.

'Are you comfy now?'

'Uh huh.'

'So what were you thinking about?'

'Och, I was just out this morning, having my wee run, and this auld fella's down by the bridge. He quite often is. I don't think he's a drunk, you know, he doesn't seem like that, he just looks as though he's off his head.

'Sometimes he's curled up sleeping and I wake him when I pass, but usually he's sorting through the papers and the leaves, making them neat. I thought he was saving them up until I watched him throwing a load in the river one time – I think that's what be always does. He stacks everything neatly, then throws it away.

'Anyway, he was there again this morning and his face was covered in blood – fucking big lump out his head, blood in his hair, still running over his eyes. I mean, he didn't seem upset. I stopped in case he was dying or something, but he was just rubbing his shirt sleeve over the blood, then sucking it clean. Over and over. He was speaking. He was saying, "It's me. I can't waste it. It's me. I can't waste it." Out of his mind. Completely.'

'Poor man.'

'I came back from London to get away from that – dafties and weans and beggars all over the street. Lepers and plague carts on the way. And guess what I find up here.'

'Is that really why you came back?'

'No. I wanted to come back. I'd wanted to for months. I knew you were here.'

'How?'

'Somebody told me. I mean, I asked folk and one of them told me. I wanted to be here, I didn't like the atmosphere down there and I did think I might see you. Well, more than that, I hoped, but at least to see you. I did that the first week I got here.'

'I know, you came to the Centre.'

'That was when you saw me. I was there another time. A couple of weeks before that, I followed you home. Lesley and her boyfriend locked up –'

'She doesn't have a boyfriend.'

'Aye she does, wee Sammy. Did you not know? Jesus Christ, you work with them, I thought at least you'd know that?'

'Seriously?'

'Aye, I'll tell you later. So Lesley and Sammy lock up and you're off down the street to choose between the corpy and the deregulated bus. You waited for quite a while.'

'You're guessing.'

'Nope. There was a wee boy at the bus-stop in a red jersey, he asked you for a cigarette and you told him you didn't smoke. You looked thinner than I thought you would and you were tired.'

'I don't know if I like you watching me.'

'I do it all the time.'

'But I know about it now.'

'I only ever do it to make sure you're safe. And because you look nice. Give us a kiss.'

Margaret gave him a kiss.

'And let's dance.'

'What?'

'Dance with me, Maggie. Go on.'

'I don't think I've got any music we could dance to.'

'No, no, no. What we do – I hold you, like this. Waltz position. Mm hm?'

'I'm still here.'

'That's good. I'd hate it to be someone else. Because now we lie down and we dance. No music.'

They steered each other towards the sofa.

'I don't think this is called dancing. I think dancing is something different.'

'We can try it your way next time.'

That was faster, too: like being approached by a bulldozer, a hard mind. Margaret thought she might prefer it slow.

The evening after she came home from the dentist, Margaret asked Colin again.

'Why did you come back?'

'Hm?'

They were almost sleeping, neat in her bed together, a good fit. His head had been lying across her arm just long enough to make it sore.

'Why did you come back?'

'I'm not back, yet, I'm still catching my breath.'

'Not just now; then.'

'Hm hm, mm hm, huh.'

He gave a little cough that moved them both and then turned to face her.

'Why I came back? From London?'

'Uh huh.'

'I wanted to see you again.'

'And.'

'Why should there be an "and"? Why should there have to be an "and"? Are you not worth coming back for, all by yourself? Or do I lie to you so often that you can't believe me when I say that I came back for you?'

'Alright.'

'No, it's not alright. I came back because of you. I've tried every way I can to prove it. I can't do anything else.

'It wasn't great in London and I'll admit, I didn't like it there but it wasn't all that bad either. I ended up lodging with my Uncle Archie and he sorted me out. He ran a fish shop. "You canny be a useless dope fiend and work in a fish shop." That's what he said. At least that's what he said to me. Personally I still reckon it's the only way to do it and stay sane. Archie was entirely off his head – all that radiation and raw sewage, to say nothing of the actual fish. But it could have been worse and there wasn't anywhere else that I could go. You think it's hard to find a place to live up here? A nice wee job in the city? Down there it was impossible. Everything was impossible. There was nowhere I could go. There was no one I could be with that didn't mean trouble.

'I had to stay with Archie and he did a lot for me. He spoke to my mother and I saw her before she died – we made friends again. Archie even offered to leave me his wee fish shop, to make me a partner. I said I was coming back here. He told me I was crazy. "I'll go anywhere you like for any reason but I'll not move a half an inch for a woman. Not me. I've the smell of them every day at my work and that's more than enough." That's what he said.'

'I'm glad you came.'

'Are you really.'

'Yes.'

'OK.'

Margaret didn't like it when they argued in bed. You were meant to be peaceful and nice to each other in bed.

It was also the place where they slept.

'Colin? McCoag?'

Margaret's voice seems louder in the dark.

'Mm hm.'

'Colin?'

'Awwff. I'm no gonny get any sleep tonight am I?'

'Don't be cross.'

'I'm not. I'm fucking tired, it's some ridiculous time of the night in fact it's in the morning, and I want to be asleep. I asked if I could sleep with you. I know that involves a wee bit of staying awake as well, but I would like to sleep. At least try to. Or how about molesting my body instead of my mind.'

'I just wanted to tell you something.'

'Is it something exciting?'

'Come here a minute.'

He reaches to touch her face.

'What's wrong, love?'

'Come here.'

Margaret fits her head against Colin's shoulder, feels his hand curl round to rest along her waist. She's always thought he does that very well.

'What is it?'

'I just wanted to say I'm glad you're here. I mean here in general. Not just in bed.'

'I'm not going to go away. Unless you want me to.'

'I don't want you to.'

'Good. I'm going to sleep, now. Night, night.'

Margaret lies in the thick of the dark and thinks of something she cannot tell Colin, something she cannot explain which sometimes wakes her in the night, like a cry springing up from out of clear water.

She was in her room. Twenty-one years old, newly graduated, and reading in bed with the little brown lamp on; the little brown lamp that Margaret chose to take away with her to England; the old lamp she has slept beside, on and off, for a decade or more. The lamp lit what she remembers and cannot say, because it is probably unsayable.

She was reading a book she had borrowed from her father, because most of her books were still in England and she couldn't go to sleep without reading, at least for a while.

When a knock came at the door, she had almost forgotten which house she was in, was almost unsure of the country around her. Her father's face seemed surprising as it edged round the door.

'I'm sorry, Margaret, I've surprised you.'

'No. No, it's fine.'

'Can I sit on the bed?'

'You always used to.'

'Well, you're bigger now. I have to ask.'

They were quiet for a while, until Margaret brushed the back of his hand.

'Mm hm, well, you see, I was thinking about what you said at dinner, there. About going back down south and I thought you might, maybe put it off. There are some nice wee jobs going up here, I've been looking for you. I mean, you'll be staying up here, in the end. You should probably have my room now – it's bigger and you'll make it the way you'd like. We'll sort it out. Don't worry.

'I need to go back down.'

'Of course, you'll have friends and – You'll soon make friends up here again. I see that Susan and Barbara quite often. Remember, from school? They ask about you.'

'Dad. Look, I might not come back. At least I will come back, but not to stay. I'll probably live down there.'

'No.'

'Some of us have got a flat together. It's very nice. You could visit me.'

'No.'

'Dad.'

'You never told me.'

'Well, I'm still not sure.'

'What's he called?'

'No, it's not like that.'

'I knew there was someone, but I thought you would have told me, I thought I must be wrong, because you would have said. You didn't say.'

'Dad. I would have told you if it was serious.'

'He's not touched you.'

'Dad.'

'Don't tell me he's touched you. I don't want to know if he's touched you.'

'It's alright, you'd like him.'

She felt his hand tightening round hers, the skin smoothed with age. Strong bone. His voice was very soft when he spoke again and he didn't look at her.

'Please don't go. Just don't leave me. Please. Please. Margaret, please. I can't – I was waiting for you to come back. Please.'

He fluttered his free hand towards the lamp and she turned it off. She let him cry in the dark. When she held him, she could feel him trying to pull in breath and his tears on her neck, just below her ear and running down. When he spoke, she felt that, too, as the sound moved in his throat and chest.

'Please. You were always such a good girl. If you leave me, I don't know what I'll do. I can't bear it. Your mother went away. She never came back. You'll never come back.'

His breath flailed out again.

'Of course I'll come back. Silly. I'll come back. Mum can't come back – she died. I love *you*. I still love you.'

'She didn't die, she fucking left me. Did you think I would tell you that? Your mother was a fucking slut? She ran away the first chance she got because I was no bloody good? She might as well have died. Leaving her baby. Leaving me. You're like her, you know that, you always were like her. I knew it.'

'I love you, Daddy, I love you.'

There seemed to be an absolute silence, Margaret couldn't say for how long. And then her father breathed, spoke.

'Don't cling to me. You don't need to cling to me. I know where I am now. I know just where I am.'

He pulled her away, but she lifted her hands to his head, gripped it, held it still, and kissed him. He stopped moving.

'I'm fine, Margaret. You go to sleep, now. I'm fine.'

He touched her shoulder and then stood up from the bed. All she saw was the block of light when he opened the door and the dark shape he made. She didn't sleep.

In the morning, he called her down for breakfast in the way that he always had and they ate in silence, while their plates and cutlery battered and scraped.

Then, 'Margaret, I'm sorry. I say things that I don't mean, I'm getting old. Forget what I said about your mother, she did the best she could and I never should have told you otherwise.'

'It's alright.'

'No. It's not. Finish your tea. We should go to the shops this morning, buy you some clothes. You'll want to look nice when you go back south.'

'Dad.'

'I know, I know.'

But Colin had gone to London and that was that. Margaret had to come home again and explain. Her daddy was sympathetic. She knew he was also pleased.

'I'm sorry. I am sorry. If he's for you, he'll come back. If he's not there'll be someone else. You're very pretty – you'll able to pick a nice one. Come on, don't be sad.'

'I can't help it. What do you want me to do?'

'Don't make yourself alone. No one has to be like that. It's not a good habit to have, love. Don't be alone.'

He hugged her, gave her that silence again. The one that happened sometimes when they touched.

Mark Fleming

St Andrew's Day

They crept on all fours, Devlin squinting through the nippy smoke from the roll-up poked between his lips, Kareen grim-faced and imagining they were soldiers in Bosnia. Until she burst out giggling again.

'Rap it!' Devlin hissed through teeth that might well have been gripping an invisible knife instead.

'It's just the way your arse is wriggling ... Makes me want to give each cheek a huge chowie! Just as well it's not been raining, too. Your new Versaces and that, like? Eh, Dev? Your knees'd be fucked! Heh! Imagine if there was puddles? The two of us trying to duck in here all hunched up like that ... What was his name? That American comedian? From the old days ... The glasses and moustache? The cigar and that. They were brothers or something, I think. Eh, Dev?'

'Sssh, Kareen, fuck's sake! I'm just asking you to zip it for five fucking minutes. Right, sweetheart?!'

Kareen watched him flick the expired smoke off into the darkness.

'They Regal King Sizes you're smoking the night smell funny.'

'Kareen...'

Devlin stopped; he lay stretched out by a van's bonnet. Kareen squirmed alongside. Seven cars were arranged ahead of them, waiting in the cold for owners supping beyond the arc of light from the pub windows.

Devlin stared past Kareen. He tried to picture this car park in daylight. His memory conjured a large concrete square; similar to those all over the city where there had once been green squares. The pub was a large pillbox with glass. Condensation had crept over the windows to keep the concrete square masked. The shifting figures inside seemed like apparitions.

Kareen saw what Devlin was watching. 'That's like my telly when it needs tuned.'

He turned to her. The light was catching her profile, her small hooked nose and her blonde bob that night-time had turned to silver. His eyes dwelled on her cleavage. He saw how it trembled with her weight on her elbows. He murmured: 'I think *you* need tuned in half the fucking time. You Muirhouse bam!'

Kareen's whisper carried across the car park. 'I'm not from Muirhouse, you. I was born in Lancs, as you well know. Bet I'm the first Lancastrian you've humped. Apart from Racquel off Corrie that is, in your dreams.'

'Never denied the bam bit.' He shook his head at her, then more vigorously, eyes screwed shut. 'Quite a fucking wicked hit, man. That skunk. Fuck your astroturf... It's much better being on grass, ken?'

Kareen nodded. 'Uh-huh. Magic. Here! You listened to that tape I gave you yet? The last mix that Hectic done on the radio?'

Devlin looked at her, faced the pub again. He had tensed. A silhouette was moving just inside the doorway, tugging at a cigarette.

'Mind that song Grim up North?' she persisted. 'Few year ago, it came out. The boy reels off the names of all these Northern towns, like. Manchester and Crewe and Rochdale and that. Oldham, too...'

'Naw, Kareen. Christ...'

'That's why I liked that one. Hectic's 'Grim up North Embra'. Sound mix it is, by the way, Dev. Wait till you hear it. Specially if you're ripped, like.'

'Aye. DJ Hectic. You know all about that cunt, eh, Kaz? Let the cat out the bag on that score, you did, sweetheart. When I got you pished in *Slammers* that morning.'

'Not exactly a state fucking secret, Devlin.'

'Moving to the Hectic beat...'

'Hah.'

'Bonking to the Hectic beat...'

'Fuck off.'

They remained rigid by the van wheels like accident victims. Until Kareen's jaws got going again; up, down, sideways, smacking her gum.

'Get fucking back inside, you ... Fucking bugging my happiness, this cunt.'

'Heh ... What's this cunt about, Devlin?'

'Ssh. Don't know. Just watch, sweetheart. Keep your eyes well peeled.'

The man was hunching his shoulders, tossing his cigarette to the deck, grinding it in. Another man emerged from the shadows. They started arguing. This was obviously a continuation of what had begun inside; it escalated.

Devlin and Kareen gaped at the action, mesmerized. Presently a third person stepped into view. This man was drunk and his slurs were aimed at the man who'd been smoking. He poked his finger towards the smoker's chest. The smoker brushed the finger aside but it came back, then back again, the smoker wafting it off like a midgey.

The less drunk of the two facing the smoker grew bored with this display. His bunched right hand crashed into the smoker's face.

'Aaah!' the smoker growled, his head whiplashing sideways.

'Oyah!' Kareen whispered from where they were lurking.

The smoker and the hitter performed a tentative and elaborate squaring-up, like a matador practising in a mirror. The drunk kept his thumb raised at the hitter while staggering on the spot as if he'd been struck himself.

But the smoker had only been taken by surprise. His reaction came all at once. His arms flayed at the two bodies ahead of him, the drunk crumpling when the first hook connected, the hitter cowering, attempting to block the rain of blows, screaming: 'No, son! No, son! Christ, no! Enough.' More shapes tumbled from within.

'Deek this lot, Kaz ... It's the fucking wild west. Like the films ... I swear John Wayne'll steam through the lot of these cunts any minute. Sounds like a fucking wedding reception.'

He couldn't believe their luck. A shrill woman's voice added to the masculine battle cries, yelps of pain and the dull smacks of skin against bony skin: 'I'll fucking chib you, John! Touch your father once more and I'll fucking chib you, d'you hear?'

Devlin gave Kareen's backside a quick pat. 'Let's do it.' They heaved themselves to their feet, keeping their backs arched. Devlin began to weave through the cars. Kareen held back, continuing to spectate, listening to Devlin's soft curses at wheel locks or blinking alarms. Eventually he called to her: 'Kaz ... Kareen. Quick!'

She whipped round to see him giving the okay sign. He'd stopped by the driver's door of the car furthest from the pub battle. He held his left hand out to her, beckoning.

'All clear, eh?' he whispered, looking over the light shining across the curve of the car's roof.

'Aye,' Kareen replied. She sprinted on tip-toe, ducking down at the car. She began jigging her body, bobbing on her trainers. She murmured lyrics that were floating through her mind, snippets of Hectic straddling his decks amongst light sabres and sweet clouds of dry ice: 'Gonna take you to the limit, take you to the top, baby baby baby, gonna never gonna stop. You know it's grim up Granton when the horneys they crawl, but I'm sorted, I'm mental, life's one fucking ball...'

'Kaz!'

She shut up but her jaws persisted with the gum. She gazed at Devlin hovering by the car door. 'Watch you don't disturb some Tory cunt shagging a tart, likes, Dev!' She fired a glance back towards the melee. A different tune implanted in her brain, a punk chorus that an older cousin used to bawl out. She gave a muted version under her breath. 'Yeh yeh, Industrial Estate. Yeh yeh, Industrial Estate. Yeh yeh...'

'Kaz. This is fucking serious shit, you wee radge. Don't fucking know about you but this is pure freaking me out, man! The fucking state I'm in, likes. Pure fucking wasted, likes. It's bad enough facing your old dear when I'm as fucking ripped as this. But twoccing some cunt's wheels, ken? Fucking serious shit. Plus those fucking clowns over there'll have the horneys down on this place fucking...'

'Settle, Dev ... You know the pigs never show till they've given whatever stushie there is a good twenty minutes to cool off. Ready?'

Devlin rubbed his palms up and down his jeans. 'Right. Tape?'

She dug into the pockets of her jacket. Producing the thick brown reel she pressed it into Devlin's gloved hand. She hunched over him, eyes darting between the pub's exit and the approach from the main road.

'That's it, sweetheart. Just keep on keeping shottie.'

Once Devlin had achieved his criss-cross pattern, Kareen backed off as he stepped back. He stood with his arms outstretched, glanced once towards the pub, flashed his steel toe-caps towards the orange from the lamp-post behind the car. The dull gleam spread smiles across their faces.

Devlin's expression twisted, the grin vanishing into a constipated grimace. Snatching his breath in he moved each black hand outwards, making a hypnotic motion with his outstretched fingers.

Kareen's heart flipped once when Devlin's leg lashed for the door, his body perfectly angled. His Tai-Kwan-Do kick struck the window dead centre. There was a muffled splintering.

Devlin repeated the trained movement. His mind had turned that square of shards and tape into the beergut of a fat Hearts supporter. He cracked right to the rib cage a third time, a fourth, until his left foot ceased balancing him and he tumbled back onto the car park.

'Dev!' Kareen's stare checked the drunken violence, then went back to his collapsed frame. She shoved her hands over her mouth and doubled up. 'The state of you, Dev. Fucking ... Van Damme on drugs. Jean-Claude Van Devlin. Ha hah!'

Devlin sprang up. He rubbed at his backside. Marching over to the car he fisted the window until it had fallen inside. He poked around for the handle, heaved the door open. He heaved the destroyed pane out and to one side, pausing before he jumped in. 'Fucking hate this bit, ken? That fucking Rotty ... Must've thought its dreams'd come true and a huge fucking human shish kebab had just poked into its owner's car, eh?!'

Kareen chuckled. They'd screwed in a car the night before and afterwards she'd tenderly caressed Devlin's scarred right forearm. The previous weekend's snarling guard-dog hadn't locked its jaws but had snapped twice at his 'KAZ' and 'YLT' Indian Inked flesh.

'I'll never forget that, Dev ... You nashing away from the car like you're in the Benny Hill Show with a sleeve missing off your brand new Stone Island top!'

He was crouching inside. Hand reaching again, he said: 'Torch.'

'I've forgot it, Dev. Sorry, man!'

He snapped his fingers once. She lifted out the small black cylinder and handed it over, peering back at the pub. Various bodies were being restrained. Three people kept the smoker arm-locked; he was firing verbal insults at the woman who had now folded into hysterical greeting.

'The evils of legal drugs, Devlin.' She could make out that someone had selected Boyzone on the jukebox.

'Not that fucking gash again', she murmured. She turned to the beam of light beneath the dashboard where Devlin would be clawing into the car like a surgeon. She found herself joining in with part of the song's chorus. A voice inside followed suit.

Before the Irish quintet had completed their work, Dev had completed his and a grand and a half's worth of motor transport changed ownership. As he wired the engine into life Kareen bent double into a stupid walk, round through the headlights, towards the pub, turning sharply for the passenger side.

'Fuck's sake ... Heh! Groucho Marx, Kareen! That's who you were trying to think of. That was fucking nipping me, that!' Adding a triumphant yelp like a movie Indian clutching a fresh scalp he stretched over. He wrenched Kareen's door open.

The two youths caught one last glimpse of the smoker wriggling free of his guards to lunge at the female. She produced something from inside her jacket. Devlin stomped on the accelerator before they could see what she'd drawn and whether she'd managed to use it.

Christine stubbed out her cigarette as the camera on *News at Ten* panned the debris inside a Bosnian house. She pressed the mute button. Getting up from the settee she stepped along the hall to glare at the debris of her daughter's bedroom again.

The quilt remained discarded. A trail of clothing led to the Caterpillar boots, their labelled tongues sticking out at her as a reminder of the amount that she'd had to fork out for them after weeks of huffs and tantrums that had verged on method acting.

She was angry at the state that the bedroom had been left in, at her daughter having been out all day and at knowing that she could expect a phone call at any time which would state: 'Staying at Debbie's, Ma. Her Ma says it's okay.' Click. She knew that it was absurd but she also felt angry that Kareen was out there somewhere without these boots.

Before switching the room back into blackness she shuddered. These crumpled bed covers and strewn clothing had made her picture that farmhouse after having been ransacked by Serb militia, not much older than Kareen, enflamed by cheap vodka.

Once she returned to the settee she fired the remote control at the screen. The activated volume introduced men seated around a conference table. Little flags and nameplates were poised next to jugs of water before them. Each one was poised for his turn to speak earnestly into microphones. Cameramen jostled in the background like crash spectators.

A man with wild grey hair took the floor, the caption giving him a Transylvanian Count's name. He represented the Bosnian Serbs. He started to wag his finger at the world.

Christine sighed and checked the time on the video's digital display.

Kareen staggered out of the doorway and sniggered when she tipped several chips down onto the pavement at her feet. Devlin made a lunge at the contents of her newspaper parcel. She laughed even more as she pulled them out of his reach with a customary: 'Fuck off you!'

Devlin halted by the front of the car, watching Kareen sway over to the passenger side. She heaved her door open and landed onto the seat, jolting the car.

'Watch my suspension, Kaz!' He scowled as he ducked in.

Kareen leaned over and tugged his hood back from his head. She ran her slender purple-tipped fingers down his stubble, stroking. Sucking in breath she shouted into his ear '*Your* suspension? That's one of your more beautiful beauties, Devlin, you cunt! Just like all they pairs of 501s you used to wear in your drainpipe days when I first met you were *your* jeans. No fucking receipts, though, but. Neither had those radges you used to buy them off. Car fucking boot sales outside Gladstone's after closing time, eh?'

Devlin gave her another look, poked a finger into his ear-hole, drawing it free to toy with the large gold hoop dangling from its lobe. 'Kaz. You're bammy as fuck, by the way. I'm just speaking at my normal forty-five, ken? But you! You're at fucking seventy eight' Where's my fucking smokes, by the way?' He patted his pockets, coughed and spat through the window frame.

Kareen was laughing in between mouthfuls. She watched Devlin checking the floor below the dashboard. While his head was bowed she dug into her jeans and tugged the fags from where she'd hidden them after pick-pocketing him in the chippie. She placed the packet on the dashboard behind the steering wheel. She nudged him.

He scowled over at her but noticed the blue and white flash in the corner of his eye. 'Right before my fucking yacks the whole time, eh? That'll be shining fucking bright!'

Kareen nodded, gulping her food down. 'Well crash the ash then!'

'One thing at a time, Kaz. Christ. Finish your scran, at least. Time to hit the yellow brick . . .'

Kareen chewed a handful of greasy chips as Devlin got the purring engine back into gear. She lunged towards his frowning eyebrows and smothered his lips with her own, her tongue darting across his teeth, probing the gaps. He used his own tongue to ward hers off, giving her a noisily smacking kiss. 'You taste of salt and sauce, daftie.'

'You taste . . . All nicotiney. Here, d'you want another one of my chips?'

'Nah, sweetheart. I'll just get this fucker shifted again. Fucking . . . It's fucking Bertie Auld enough the night without having any glass in my fucking window, ken?'

The car jumped forward. Swinging the wheel round towards the main road Devlin jerked his left arm, climbing up the gears.

Kareen eased back into her seat, stamping her left trainer out onto the dashboard as she finished the last mouthful of her food. Crushing the papers into a ball she peered out the window for a while, now chewing the gum that she'd kept wedged between teeth and cheek until the chips were finished. She unwound the lever. Once the window came down to halfway she bowled her wrapper out towards the verge flashing past. Grabbing at the handle again she twisted it back up, her greasy fingers doing the Acid House smile in the condensation.

'Sound motor this, Devlin. She can move, eh? A pure gem, she is. I don't know where you get so much bottle. Big fish like this, like, right down to the tiddlers. I mean. Mind that old guy at the bar? When was it, Dev? A week past Tuesday? Nah, Monday. Aye, Monday … Cause I'd wanted to see my home team on Sky. Oldham Athletic…'

'You casting up me tipping that yuppie cunt's drink over?'

Kareen nodded slowly. 'Oldham against the bastard Gooners. I was feeling shit at the time … Coming down from the weekend and that and watching the Latics getting fucked again by those Southern scum was making it really fucking shit … You just wanted to slag Ian Wright for being such a posing bastard. Just cause he can afford to walk into shops and actually take his gear over to the bird at the till and not have to do the fucking Linford Christies along Rose Street Precinct, eh Dev?'

'Now you're casting up the Saturday morning before the old Hibees done the business against the Tims? Going radge on the Parkhead terraces with my Kickers after doing nought to fucking twenty out the fucking Schuh changing room. Those bastard shoes got scuffed to fuck, too. Parkhead's a bigger fucking tip than that fucking Gorgie slum, eh sweetheart? These weedjie cunts. They're fucking scoobied about looking cool, likes, Kaz. You can see them through the fucking segregation fence. The closest they've got to Casuals're a couple of gadges who've stookied some cunts at a golf course and robbed their fucking Pringle jerseys. Thereafter it's a sea of green scarves, Irish flags and blond streaked hair.'

'Just imagine all their pairs of white towelling socks, Dev? Slip-on shoes. Poundies trainers.'

'Exactly. Parkhead and fucking Ibrox're the only two grounds you still get young cunts in Snorkel jackets. I swear it, Kareen.'

'What?'

'These fucking hideous anorak things with furry hoods. Soap dodgers! I blame their dress sense on all that fucking Buckfast and glue sniffing. I was reading this sound magazine article. About the Gorbals part of Glasgow. Before they knocked it all down and shipped them out to the towers in the sixties, Kaz. In the *olden* days the fucking weedjies used to pipe fucking gas from the mains into pints of milk and throw that down their necks…'

'Dev?!'

'And the Tims call their ground Paradise, too … Fucking *Paradise*. Imagine they Bounty adverts. A taste of Paradise. Instead of a beautiful desert island these supermodel cunts find theirselves in the middle of fucking Easterhouse … And what about that fucking Rod Stewart song that was on your radio last night? Fucking … Can't mind what it's called, but he goes on about Celtic, Rod Stewart.'

'Another fucking Londoner bastard, he is. What's he like with his tartan scarves?'

'You're Celtic and you're Man United, cunt was singing to one of his birds. Well, Kareen, my sweetheart. You're Hibs and you're Man City.'

'City fuck all, pal. I'm a Latic, like. I was telling you about the Oldham game. And you being a game cunt … Last Monday, like? The Latics might've been gubbed by Arsenal and heading back up the M1 with fuck all but thanks to my loving boyfriend I was on the last number six with a fucking score in my sky rocket that I'd never had when Wright was doing his fancy patter. You cunt! Just watching you going up the bar and tipping that half-pint down that snobby bastard's Pringle jacket, flapping over the cunt with a bar towel, then fucking off to the toilet with the bar towel wrapped around the boy's wallet and fucking off out the fire exit … I'm telling you, Old Fagan would've been proud of you!'

'Old who?'

'Oh, nowt. It's that musical I was telling you about. That we're supposed to be doing at school the now. I'm a pick-pocket. In Victorian times. The Artful Dodger, like.'

'Never did like musicals, Kaz. Quadrophenia was all right. That video we seen up at Gabby's on Tuesday.' He paused, checked his wing mirror. 'Christ this fucking van's almost right up our arse. Fucking cowboys. Shouldn't be allowed on the road half the cunts … Sorry, Kaz. You were on about the Artful Dodger? That's that well dodgey pub near Wester Hailes, is it not?' He was grinning at her.

'Ha ha, Devlin. I've drunk in the Dodger before. When I went out with Mark Hunter just after last Christmas. I liked it. Used to go there all the time. Even after I chucked him same night he got himself barred.'

'What? You bevvying all the time? Last Christmas? All of fourteen you must've been.'

'I've always been tall for my age, though. Long legs. Long blonde hair. A low-cut lycra top that shows me off to cunts. What's it you say? Two good handfuls, Devlin, you cunt?! That's what the barmen see first, like … Then they ask theirselves do I want to worry about the off chance the CID might show up or do I give blondey the benefit of the doubt and get in a good night's fucking leching? You only get asked for ID if you get tipsy on two halfs of cider and can't stop giggling and drop your glass or fucking boak without bothering your arse to get to the bogs. Like Carri-Anne's capers the other night.'

Devlin was hooked on his stoned impression of the scene ahead, the white lines drilling underneath, the bright shapes that the headlamp beams were carving out of the darkness.

Kareen was getting her own impressions; the orange streetlights blinking over Devlin's face. She thought that it was like a mask on a stage, a slow strobe light catching the features. She watched this for a while, riveted. The gaping window frame had been tossing his hair out of place so he'd pulled his hood over. Now she was thinking that he looked like some wartime fighter pilot.

'All you need's a white scarf and you could be that Biggles cunt, Dev.'

'Eh?'

'Nowt. Thinking aloud, just, likes.' She could still smell their last spliff, the glorious sweetly pungent skunk that they'd smoked after driving out to Port Seton to the Forth; watching the white of the waves endlessly curling over, their new car dwarfed by the power station. Her mouth was dry from that grass; her tongue had gone numb. She felt that she had to continue talking to keep it exercised. Then she thought that there was so much to say anyway.

'What the fuck you going to do with this motor?'

'Do with it, Kaz? I thought we could take her out to Cramond, ken? Out to the sea again . . .'

They cruised past Portobello police station. He glanced into his wing mirror, easing their speed down for one gear change.

'Cramond?'

'Aye, Kaz. The sky'll be pure clear as a bell out there the night. I'll point out Orion with his belt up in the sky, arms up in the air giving it laid as I crank the volume up to max. I'll skin up and we'll just stare at the lights on the Forth, ken? Reflected in the water. Like a painting. The lights from Kirkcaldy or whatever the fuck's on the other side. You can try another one of your radge handstands. See if the picture looks the same. Ha ha.'

'Like that radge painting we seen in that shop window? That was well upside down, that painting. And you'd have to have won the Lottery to have afforded the pictures in that shop. Pure sad what some minted cunts throw their poppy at . . .'

'Never mind paintings, Kaz. What about Gazza? A boy who's worth millions and his best mate's some bevvy merchant called Five Bellies!'

Kareen shut up. Her lips kept on with their relentless smacking at her gum. After they'd made the next amber lights she poked into her mouth and tugged a portion of the gum out to toy with in her fingers. She stopped this when she noticed that her fingertips were giving the once-mint gum a nicotine tinge.

'Gross,' she murmured.

'What's that, daftie?'

'I was just thinking, Dev. These cunts that try nicotine-flavoured chuddie or they daft fucking patches, man. I mean. What the fuck? The way I see it is ... One out of every four smokers die from smoking. Lose one of their fucking lungs at least, like. That's what they said on the telly the other night, like. According to some scientist. If you're still hooked when you're forty-odds then either your next pack's got your name on it or it hasn't. If you're one of the three who don't get cancer you could get ran over, or get bayoneted, or catch the virus, or live on to be like my Na-Na who thinks she's one of the fucking Royal family. Ha! That's gospel, by the way, Dev. Did I not tell you? I have to curtsy now when I go up to visit her in her home. If you're a member of the Royal family where's your fucking yuppie lover hiding I say to her? Where's the swarm of fucking News of the World photographers outside this fucking sheltered scheme, Na-Na?'

She halted, chewed some more, stared out the windscreen.

'Joppa!' Kareen announced a street-sign that had just whipped in and out of sight. 'What a daft fucking name, eh? Joppa ... Joppa. Sounds like a martial art, eh? Karate. Kendo. Judo. Joppa. Seen Van Damme's Joppa video? Taught me a few tricks, I'll tell you. These Hearts Boys from over Saughton Mains were outside the chippie pure getting wide so I said to the cunts okay then square-goes now you HIV cases and the cunts kicked off but I fucking banjoed the radges with this move I learnt off that tape last week and that, you know?'

'Steady, Kaz. You know you've not shut up for a second since we left Port fucking Seaton. Not even to draw breath. What, have you got gills or something? Don't tell me you turn into a mermaid at midnight? That's why you like chilling out near the sea, eh?'

'I talk when I'm happy, you know? Like a dog wags his tail, I fucking wag my tongue. And when I'm out my face it pure wags like fuck!' And here she picked up on the DJ mix currently blaring out of the speakers. She wriggled her body, elbowed Devlin. 'Here ...'

'What? And fucking sit still. You're putting us off, man. All these fucking double parked clowns, man.'

'Dev, baby. Once we hit Ferry Road, which'll be any second now the way you're burning rubber, like, I'm going to duck when we go past Drylaw Road, right? I'm supposed to be grounded. Since my Ma came back early from The Doo-Cot and found you raking about in the kitchen with just your scants on, man!'

Devlin lifted one hand from the wheel as he burst out laughing. He unzipped his jacket's top pocket. 'Here, Kaz. Might as well drop this the now. Only a quarter, babe, but what the fuck? Enough for that wee buzz.'

'Sound, Devlin.' She reached out for the tiny corner of paper, then watched him producing a cassette from a lower pocket. Swallowing quickly, she went on: 'What's this shite you're hitting us with?'

'Shite, fuck all, you. I snaffled this at that car boot sale over at Duddingston, ken? At that school.'

'Snaffled? From a car boot sale, Dev? What about that pride you love to go on about, like? Probably would've cost you ten pee or something.'

'Just stick the fucker in so's I can get give it a listen, Kareen. I never fucking coughed up for it cause I don't even know if I'll like it.'

'Who is it, like?' She squinted at the cover in the gloom.

'Happy Mondays. An early yin, likes. Squirrel and G-Man or some fucking shite. From about ten year ago, likes.'

'Ten year ago? I would've been at Primary, still. Didn't even know where Edinburgh was, probably . . .'

'Aw. Sweet. Imagine you being sweet, Kaz?'

'Fuck off. And don't you dare mention those fucking horrible photos my Ma's got pinned up.'

'Wouldn't fucking dream of it. I've bad enough bruises on my arm from being attacked by that fucking Rottweiler. Fucking . . . Just stick the Mondays in, eh? Let's see if Sean Ryder's singing was just as fucking chronic in they days.'

'In a fucking minute, man. I love this bit coming up. When fucking Prodigy comes in. Here it is . . . I'll take your brain to another dimension! I'll take your brain to another dimension!'

'Aye. If you don't stop distracting me I'll take us both into another dimension. That starts six feet fucking under!'

Christine hovered by the phone, bottle in hand. She slugged the last of the 20/20 and grimaced when the fortified strawberry-flavoured drink bit into the back of her throat. Her hand reached to the receiver, snatching it up.

As the other end purr-purred away she stared at the carpet, trying to keep its pattern in focus. She'd had her usual three bottles of the liquor, the 20/20, the fruit-flavoured brain-cell obliterator and was therefore drunk, or sixty-sixtied as she liked to describe it. The carpet went all blurred again.

Her thoughts were drifting everywhere so she was surprised to hear her voice on the other side of the room, sounding slurred and shaky, amidst a frantic squealing of feedback, like the music she'd heard on the radio when tracking through the dials to uncover Radio Forth that had sounded like The Who when they were finishing a song and smashing up their instruments at the same time, this noise having been described as Sonic Youth to which she'd murmured: 'Chronic Youth'.

Christine was steaming and trying to hold an earnest conversation with Andy on the Radio Forth Open Line. Once she'd followed his request to switch off her radio, she began to ramble.

'... And how am I on this first day of Christmas, you said, Andy? Well ... Well I'll tell you ... I'm a bit tiddly the night, but ... But my problem is my daughter's boyfriend. He's the problem. And it's driving me up the bloody walls and that. Pat. Pat Devlin, in case he might be listening to this. He's got my wee baby out there. Thing is, Andy. He came to pick her up two ... three weeks ago in a red car, a Volvo. The next again week it was a Blue ... Cavalier. What's it the papers call it? Joy riding? Can't be much joy having some hooligan steal your car for ... for kicks, likes, Andy, eh? I mean ... My girl's not even old enough to be doing what they do in the back of a car, let alone a stolen car. You know, Andy? And she's so wrapped up in him ... Her wee face ... She'll be scowling at the telly and not speaking to me one minute, then he'll phone up and it's like she's schizophrenic or something the way her face lights up soon as she hears from him ... Christ, Andy, I think she might've fallen in love. Can you believe it? In love at fifteen! And when she's explaining to me where she's been when she's not got in till God knows what time it sounds like she's been brainwashed ... As if this Devlin's a cult leader or something, likes. Occult leader, more likes. He's got this wee devil tattooed on the back of his hand, you know? And the way he says "Cheers Christine, doll" when he's leaving messages, if Kareen's not back from the school or at the shops for me or on the odd occasion she still sees one of her own pals, likes. The way he says that ... Sets my teeth on edge, Andy ... That's the way Kareen's dad used to say things. He'll be saying the same things to his Filipino girlfriend, likes. Met her in a restaurant, the bastard, but that's another story. Sorry for swearing on your radio show, Andy. You should hear the radio station they pair listen to, plays that dance music all night long, that rave stuff. Cause it's a pirate job and they don't have a licence the DJs can f and blind it ... Kareen ... What if she falls pregnant, Andy? I mean ... I don't know what I mean ...'

Without waiting to hear Andy's words of conciliation she hung up. The pattern below had become garish as a seventies disco floor. There was a single cigarette lying in the middle of the carpet. She couldn't remember the tantrum that had involved throwing it there. She plucked it up.

She went back to her chair, checking that there was still fags in the packet, ensuring that she would have one to wake up to with the alarm in the morning. This was as much a morning ritual as cleaning her teeth.

She switched off the TV. Confronted by the living room's silence she burst out crying. Tears began to stream and she made sounds as if she was being strangled by the silver necklace which she was tugging between her fingers. Her jewellery snapped. One hand mopping at her cheeks she threw it towards the TV screen. It lashed across the surface. Static crackled, then it was gone, falling somewhere in the carpet's thick pile.

She sobbed and looked towards the mantelpiece where Kareen posed in various fashion phases. Her swimming eyes rested on Kareen in 1st Year colours and herself, a Chester Zoo polar bear a white shape behind bars in the background. She stepped closer to the photograph. She felt caged herself. She stared at this blurred scene: Kareen and herself occupying the two-thirds of the frame up to the frayed edge where the third person had been torn away.

But there was a noise from Kareen's bedroom. She checked the time on the video: 00.40. Hurrying along the hall she felt for the light switch, anticipating Kareen's blonde mop suddenly twitching to life as the masked face mumbled: 'I've been in bed for hours, mum. You were dozing on the settee.'

The room remained as it had been during *News at Ten*. Except that a poster had fallen from the wall to drape over the pillow. Christine went over to it and turned it to face upwards.

She looked at the five young men posing there. It said: Inspiral Carpets. Cool as f**k. She aimed a fist at the skinhead nearest the legend. The force of her blow tore his cheek wide open. 'How cool as fuck's that, son?'

By the time she got back to the living room it was 00.44. All the lights in the room seemed so bright. She must have been staring at the screen for too long. And she was forever giving Kareen a row for that. The way she could sprawl forward on her bed clutching her portable's remote and channel-hop all evening, that button taking her from East Drylaw to the East End, to Manchester, to Australia.

She tidied, stuffing the *Daily Record* with the last article she'd read, entitled 'Drew Barrymore – Hollywood's Wild Child' into the bucket. She noticed the date again. Today had been St Andrew's Day. Now it was December.

She shuddered to think what Kareen thought that she might be getting for Christmas. Last year the request had been Armani jeans and Christine had sent her younger brother out for these and he'd returned with a pair that were blue denim but had stated Chipie on their label. Craig had told her: 'These were seventy, Christine. And that wasn't far off *two thirds* the price those ones my daft niece was after ...' Kareen had tugged them out of their wrapping with a smile right enough but Christine had overheard her daughter on the phone a few weeks later saying: 'I know, Tara. But Chipie's well out, man!'

Christine turned to the corner where they would be putting up the tree. She felt angry and sad and frightened and suddenly shivered with the coldness that she was feeling. So she kicked off her slippers and scurried back down the hall, barging into Kareen's room where she fell onto the bed and crawled under the downie. It smelled of sweat in here. The only thing missing were the post-coital tissues. 'Devlin, You *bastard*,' she spat out.

But all that she could think of was that she wanted to be nowhere other than underneath these covers, Kareen's covers, in Kareen's bed, keeping its warmth in. She would stay here as if cocooned, cosy beneath the poster that said in a voice that she could hear her daughter repeating: 'Cool as fuck.'

After Kareen had shoved Devlin's cassette deep into a pocket of her jeans she flipped the present tape over. The hissing from the four speakers indicated that the music to follow would be loud. Devlin turned the wheel and the car sped into the Crewe Toll roundabout. Then his foot stamped for the brake with such force that Kareen had the absurd notion that a rat had somehow got into the car and was at their feet.

As the impact came, this stuck in her mind, along with the recognition of the DJ doing this next mix: Hectic, her favourite DJ, doing her favourite dance track of all time, Spinning on XTC, the one she'd first heard at *9C*; her pal Tara had gone out with DJ Hectic, and once when she'd chummed Tara round to his bit at Magdelene to muck around with his new deck, they'd dropped enough mushies to get buzzed and Tara had spent two hours locked in the toilet while her and DJ Hectic, or Richard, who was famous for his spinning at 45, had spun at 69 on his settee as they'd listened to Tara's muffled singing through the door then they'd dressed and danced, really freaking out to Hectic's sounds and when Tara had re-appeared she'd dyed her blonde locks red and it was still dripping down her cheeks like some vengeful Carrie until she'd caught her reflection in the mirror and creased herself and they'd joined in, Tara's face going as red as her running dye, Richard compounding her state by nashing round from his turntables to undo her bra-top but Kareen had felt so cool and when she'd closed her eyes tightly there had been sparkling lights like along George Street at Christmas and now her thoughts were whizzing along as fast as the line of lights on the horizon was going vertical.

It was like *ER*. Flowing with this trolley, peering up at the ceiling and the faces bowing over. Something came back to her for a second: she wondered if the rat had bitten Devlin to fill him with the same poison. The thought slipped away.

Kareen had never felt so light-headed, so out of it. She tried to make a fist; she thought that this would stop her floating along this way, it would take her back to the trolley. The trolley was solid, supporting.

She wanted to tell these men in white overcoats to release Devlin. Right now. Because she would need to be jellied for coming down from all of this.

Andrew O'Hagan

Glass Cheques

Every other morning, just after milk but before the start of painting, Tubs McAllister would raise his thick hand and whisper 'I'm needing'. Those on either side of him made faces, behind him they pegged their noses, and the rest of the class twisted from side to side clutching their throats, poking their tongues out, pretending to puke. Tubs, as his hand lifted off the desk to begin its sorry ascent, would have a beamer, a brasser, a burn-on, a reddy – would, whatever you call it, have a face so red, and so crumpled with bubbling tears, that he looked fit to burst open any second.

Mrs Curry would swoop in and hurry him out of the class. Though nobody felt for Tubs, everybody felt for her – holding the warm hand of the boy who always spoke too late, the shitey fatso, the one with the vile lump at the back of his shorts, the spaz, the spanner, the skittery dipstick Tubs McDumper. The auxiliary kept spare white pants in a tub at the back of the cloakroom though, sometimes, McAllister would mess himself so bad there'd be nothing to do but send him home.

'It's lava,' Catriona Kelly said on the fourth day of the new term, 'lava going down his legs.'

Mostly he'd go off on his own, his classmates craning their necks to watch him out the window as he went. There he'd go, down the school path, up over the railway bridge leading into the scheme, waddling along, legs apart, like a little cowboy bereft of his horse. The kids would fall about, and Mrs Curry would stand at the front of the class, thin-lipped, saying nothing.

Mrs Curry came just after the summer. They gave her three classes in one, three year groups in one class; and though her term in charge of them was cut short, she managed to build up a reputation for craziness, for neatness, for oddness and coolness, that – to some minds – had no rival in any other class or school or in any other time. Things started perfectly. From the very first ring of the morning bell, Mrs Curry, walking nimbly over the playing fields towards the hut that was to be her classroom, saw that everything would be just fine, that it could well be OK.

'Our new teacher's like a cartoon,' said Michael Elderley, spying her from the playground as she marched across the grass.

Curry was albino; the children in her class called her Beano. Everything in the hut was darker than her, including the milk by the door and the chalk in a saucer sat on a runner under the blackboard.

With her light hair, she looked like a papier-mâché angel whose mouth and eyes had been freshly drawn in with damp crayons. And she had one of the finest, by which people meant the thickest, moustaches ever sported by a lady teacher in East Kilbride. The sun glinted off it, the smaller kids thought it lovely: some of the boys were intrigued, they fancied her; the girls, the leading girls, rubbed furry pencil cases across their small mouths, wondering what it would be to be so fancied.

They all sat in rows, heads lolling on shrugging shoulders, whilst the great new Miss sounded out new words from a gap somewhere under that smouldering, smoky bush of a sash. A shushing, teaching thing, Beano stormed into the minds of her youngsters, filling corners which used to be happily dark, naming and placing furniture previously covered in white drape. She flooded them – and then left them before the year was out, by simply vanishing.

Beano's classroom was done up like some sort of palace in a water-coloured dream, inside a hut at the edge of the playing fields. She encouraged them to cover their jotters, squared ones and lined, with wallpaper and drawings so long as they wrote in their name, their class (P3–6) and the words St John-of-the-Cross R.C. The blue, wooden walls of the hut would rumble and creak at times of the day when trains went by, or when lorries and buses ran past on the road outside. It happened too when workers at a quarry on the other side of the bypass let off explosives to break up the ground. The hut was a thing in itself, a place apart from the rest of the school and the houses which lined up around it: it was their world, the children felt it was theirs, and Beano's first, unworried days were spent helping them celebrate the shapes and colours of their new freedom.

'Mint. Walk now children, between the desks, and think of smelling mint.'

'Mint Cracknel mint? The chocolatey mint? That kind Miss?' shouted Marie Nugent, walking the length of the back wall with her hands clapped over her eyes.

'Yes Marie, indeed,' she said, 'whatever kind of mint you see in your head, if you can see it, then go ahead and smell it too.'

Marie, with the rest of the class, went chewing and sniffing to the

sound of Beano's semi-singing voice. Bumping this way and that, their
nostrils flaring out to meet Beano's lovely-sounding smell, they eventually opened their eyes in turn to see their teacher standing on an
upturned bucket out front, waving her arms around her head like
someone lost in the conducting of a great orchestra. The hut was
smothered in trees; they grew up and along the side of the railway
banking which bordered the east side of the school, their branches
dipping down to the flat roof. Beano called it 'the tabernacle of your
primary education, the seat of your learning'. Nobody knew what she was
on about, though they liked the way she said it. She'd turn up the palms
of her hands (one hand had a glove on it, the hand she used to write on
the board with), she'd blink, and after a while her head would tremble,
and then she'd say it, sometimes twice, before telling them to get on with
something quiet, something usually requiring paints. 'I'm stepping out
for a moment. Stay silent,' she'd say. 'Just for now.' Then she'd go into the
cupboard.

As the weeks went by Beano, having sparked everything off, saw less
and less of the kids in their moments of discovery. She'd get them going
then slip quietly into the cupboard. They got used to that. They'd fill
their time doing up the hut; drawing out a thought and colouring it in
with felt tips. With egg cartons and bin-liners they invented a funny
world; teaching themselves, for the most part, how to create and inhabit
a place of their own making – a rare place, built up from snatches of time
when Beano had stepped out.

'Mrs Curry said to use your fingers like your tongues, your tongue,'
said Catriona to Mark Orr, who was messing about with Play-Doh,
pushing it through the neck of a plastic bottle. 'We're too old now to roll
it – Mrs Curry – but she said, she said to touch it and taste its colour but
not to eat it Mark.'

Catriona Kelly loved bossing and telling the others what to do. She
walked around talking and talking and saying 'Mrs Curry' and putting
shells up to her ear when she couldn't think of another thing to say.

'Mrs Curry – you can hear the wind, whispering – Mrs Curry said – a
story,' said Catriona, eating a chew and lying on the teacher's desk with
the shell to her ear, balancing it there, without hands.

Everyone stuck painted card on the wall and wrote in their jotters. The
hut was a tardis spinning through time, a space garden, an Indian
reservation outside Glasgow, a street filled with customized trucks at the
North Pole, a Chinese temple encrusted with egg-carton-dimple-shaped
rubies. Only once, when a boy called Samson chipped a girl's ear with a

ruler, did Beano lose the rag. She belted him with a borrowed strap, making him place one hand neatly under the other, and the sound of six heavy, nippy slaps filled the hut. She put him outside for an hour.

Outside it was cold, and he strolled over to the other side of the playing field. A horse called Dobbin stood by a hole in the railway fence; he fed it cold fistfuls of grass torn out of the field. He could see his own face, his face like a potato, bending up and down in the horse's watery eye. He stretched his palm out, with the grass on top, feeling the nice way the horse nudged its teeth and lips into the stinging cup of his hand. The others watched him from the window. He'd been belted.

After that, when Beano went into the cupboard (a thing she did more and more often) she'd hand her glove to one of the older boys, a boy with plenty of brothers – the Grimes – some who were known to run in gangs and deal stuff around the scheme. He'd been staying on in the hut after dark sometimes, just hanging around to talk with Beano. They called him The Boy David. His name wasn't David – it was Fergus – but they called him The Boy David after seeing a programme on TV about a Peruvian boy who was born with a funny mark in the middle of his face. Fergus only had a tiny mark, a birth mark, but the name got to him all the same. So there he was, The Boy David, standing in front of the class several times a day, and now and then turning to face the board. He'd pull the glove tighter before turning with the chalk. Someone had rifted or farted or shouted and that meant he'd to write up their name and the nature of the crime.

The coming on of Fergus, the funny-looker who became the Grass, was the start of the trouble in Beano's hut. He loved the job, he chalked his head off: every mutter and parp noted in the knowledge that Beano would slap or belt the guilty ones when she came out. Some of those named, staring at The Boy David with pleading, hateful eyes, would break down in the minutes before her return. Even McAllister – snottery, shitey Tubs McAllister – paid close attention when the child Fergus stood before the class, legs apart, arms folded, like the King of Siam.

They couldn't believe it. Something had gone wrong, Beano'd gone mad, everything changed quicker than they could say. In the run up to Christmas, just as there was a whole new seasonal world to paint, a chill set in. Beano was pacing inside the cupboard more than ever and The Boy David was on the rampage. Many of the kids couldn't think to draw, some just sat staring. Beano had started paying her deputy, giving him empty lemonade bottles – and not just lemonade, but Red Cola and Tizer – in return for his good work with the chalk. He always had one or two in his schoolbag. Kids who used to be pals with him were sick, ashamed; standing in the main yard at playtime they'd spit on the ground as he tripped past, empties clanking on his back.

'Any glass cheques?' they'd shout. 'Any bottles?'

Most of them, without saying it, felt that glass cheques – the returnables most people felt too embarrassed to return – were exactly the right kind of payment for a dick like Fergus, The Boy David, the ugly Peruvian who grassed on his mates.

In class Mrs Curry looked at Fergus with her watery, blinking, rose-coloured eyes as if there was some big joke going on that only they could get. They'd stare each other out, half-smiling, thinking the rest of them couldn't see. Him with his face, her with hers, stripping the very colour off the walls. Catriona started putting her head on the desk all the time, Marie Nugent kept having sore stomachs and wanting to go to the medical room and Michael Elderley just sat bored, trying to get his fingers stuck in a hole he'd worn out in the inside of his desk.

'We should treat each Christmas as if it was our very last,' said Beano one morning. This began a few days which were like the class's first days with Beano. McAllister hadn't dumped in class for three mornings running, Beano brushed up her hair 'in lieu of snow' and, for a reason nobody knew, The Boy David didn't get his hand in the glove so much, so was sulking over by the window. Something had happened. He hated the sound of the class, the sound of them getting excited and he hated Beano's laughter. Beano, the turncoat, had gone this way and that. He had his head leaning on the backs of his hands, his elbows propped on the desk, and with his fingers he secretly turned up the top lids of his eyes, pulling the skin up over the lashes so the red bits showed.

'Fucking freaky Beano-eyes,' he whispered to himself.

A plastic Santa was placed at the front of the class, on a board normally used for rolling Plasticine on, and everyone was asked to put their tuck money through a slot in its beard. As they did so, the children were told to send a prayer to Mary and think of how the 'blessed, black babies' would spend the money. Beano got everyone going. Rifling through coat pockets at home, going round the doors asking for money in the evenings, the kids looked to put colour back into their hut by pleasing the blessed gnome sat at the front of the class. The coins came in, and Beano set the count for 22 December.

An aeroplane, on its way to America, crashed into a street of houses not far away on the night before the count. In the morning, the younger group were full of questions and wanted to draw the news, but Mrs Curry just sat on a chair at the back, asking them to listen while she sang a hymn in praise of 'the people who fell from the sky'. Catriona Kelly said she'd make up a song for the people who died when the plane fell on top of them.

'Now they're in the sky,' she said.

'Who is? Who's in the sky?' asked Beano, looking up.

'The ones who weren't in the sky but were in the house. The plane came on top of them. Now, they are in the sky,' said Catriona, before asking if anyone had seen the picture of the upside-down woman, with her seat belt still on, sat on top of a chimney stack.

'Shush now,' warned Beano. 'Shush, and say your rosary while I step out. Be as quiet as you can.' The blood vessels glowed in her eyes, pinker than ever and wetter, as she slipped behind the cupboard door.

No one watched over the class as they said their rosary. McAllister, on the third Hail Mary of the second decade, quietly peed himself and had to wait, all wet, for twenty minutes till Beano came back in, and then another ten while she went searching for the tub of pants.

When they filed into the hut after lunchtime, Michael Elderley, cracking his fingers and whistling, was the first to notice that the Santa was missing. The Plasticine board was there, but no Santa. Beano exploded. They'd never seen her, never like this. Wild and in tears, she blamed everyone in turn; she was so angry that, for a second, a bit of red seemed to colour up her face. She shook some by the shoulders, poked at others, throwing pictures into the air, sand on to the floor, demanding that someone among them find the missing Santa. She'd gone all wrong. She took down the metal crucifix from the wall and toured it round the desks, making each of them kiss it and swear they didn't know the whereabouts of the money box. When she got to Fergus's desk, she lifted her head and hesitated. She offered him the crucifix and they stared long into each other's eyes.

'No Miss,' he said.

At least half the class, especially McAllister and the wee Primary Threes, cried and shook. Some of the older ones, the bigger girls, bit on their bottom lips and twisted their hair, feeling excited. Beano started hammering on his desk with the crucifix, each blow peeling another strip off the surface, revealing a much softer and cleaner wood underneath. She raised the cross over her head each time. Eventually, her teeth bared and her face glistening, she brought it down on his desk and held it there with both hands. He sniffed and turned away.

'Mrs Curry, you have the Santa,' he whispered to the wall.

She dragged his schoolbag from under his chair and threw it across the room, towards the corner, where it smashed down, the bottles inside breaking one on top of the other. Beano ran after them, panting, as if to get at them before they hit the floor. Then she leant against the door, holding on to herself, her expression blurred and amazed.

The Boy David walked over to the cupboard, turned the door handle, and pushed the door forward as far as it would go. Those tall enough could see in. The top shelves had one or two piles of jotters and a few flat boxes of pencils. But the lower shelf had nothing on it but a few short bottles – bottles of Temazepam – around which lay dozens of squeezed-out capsules, some of them strewn over the floor looking like crushed, sun-dried beetles. There was a length of flimsy rubber pipe and some other things wrapped in a length of moist cotton wool. The liquid innards of the capsules, the little that remained, sat in a tiny metal dish shaped like a kidney.

The Boy David strolled in and lifted a black handbag off a hook, bringing it out and placing it on the teacher's table. Many of those in tears couldn't work it out: they were crying about the Santa, or was it the plane crash or the sight of the altered Mrs Curry, now staring at the floor, her face so white against the hut's linoleum; Mrs Curry, who'd so suddenly, so certainly stopped liking them? Fergus lifted the bag upside down and let the things inside fall on to the table. The Santa eased out slowly; a black stopper on its base popped and coins spilled over the desk and on to the floor. Fergus picked up the glove and the chalk and wrote the words 'Curry does jellies Beano is a junky I saw her'.

The hut was noiseless till McAllister, quietly at first but with a sound that steadily rose, began to chuckle deep into a clenched fist. When the class turned their heads from the board their teacher had gone.

Biographical Notes

IAIN BANKS was born in 1958. His first novel *The Wasp Factory* was published in 1984. Since then he has published several others including *The Bridge, The Crow Road, Espedair Street* and *Whit* (1995). He also publishes science fiction under the name Iain M. Banks. He lives in Fife.

ANDREW CRUMEY was born in Glasgow in 1961. He read theoretical physics and mathematics at St Andrews University and Imperial College, London. His first novel, *Music, in a Foreign Language* (1994), won the Saltire Best First Book Prize. His other novels are *Pfitz* (1995) and *D'Alembert's Principle* (1996). He lives in Newcastle-upon-Tyne.

BILL DOUGLAS was born in 1934 in Newcraighall, outside Edinburgh. In the fifties he did National Service with the RAF in Egypt. During 1959–60 he was a member of Joan Littlewood's Theatre Workshop at Stratford East. He is best known for the trilogy of films which he wrote and directed: *My Childhood* (1972), *My Ain Folk* (1973) and *My Way Home* (1978). His only other full-length feature film was *Comrades* (1987). He died of cancer in 1991.

DOUGLAS DUNN was born in Inchinnan, Renfrewshire, in 1942. He is Professor of Scottish Literature at the University of St Andrews and has published two collections of stories: *Secret Villages* and *Boyfriends and Girlfriends*, as well as nine collections of poetry. He edited the *Oxford Book of Scottish Short Stories* (1995).

MARGARET ELPHINSTONE was born in 1948 and has lived in Scotland since 1970. Her novels include *The Incomer* (1987), *A Sparrow's Flight* (1989), *An Apple from A Tree* (1991) and *Islanders* (1994). She has also written two gardening books and edited *A Treasury of Garden Verse* (1990).

ALISON FELL was born in Scotland and lives in London. Her novels include *The Grey Dancer, Every Move You Make* and *The Bad Box*. Her poetry collections include *Kisses for Mayakovsky* and *The Crystal Owl*. She is also the editor of several anthologies including *The Seven Deadly Sins* (1988).

MARK FLEMING lives in Edinburgh.

RONALD FRAME was born in Glasgow in 1953. His novel *Penelope's Hat* (1989) was shortlisted for the McVitie's Prize and the James Tait Black Memorial Prize. His other fiction includes *Bluette* (1990) and *Underwood and After* (1991).

JANICE GALLOWAY was born in Ayrshire in 1956. Her first book, *The Trick is to Keep Breathing* (1990), won the MIND/Allen Lane Book of the Year and was shortlisted for the Whitbread First Novel Award. *Foreign Parts* (1994) won the McVitie's Prize. Her collections of stories are *Blood* (1992) and *Where you find it* (1996).

ALASDAIR GRAY was born in Glasgow in 1934. He is a painter and writer. His works of fiction include *Lanark* (1981), *Unlikely Stories, Mostly* (1983), *1982 Janine* (1984), *The Fall of Kelvin Walker, Lean Tales* (with James Kelman and Agnes Owens), *McGrotty and Ludmilla, Something Leather, Poor Things, Ten Tales Tall and True, The History Maker* and *Mavis Belfrage* (1996). He has also published the polemic *Why Scots Should Rule Scotland*.

ANDREW GREIG was born in Bannockburn in 1951. His volumes of poetry include *Men on Ice, Surviving Passages* and *The Order of the Day*. His two novels are *Electric Brae* and *The Return of John MacNab*. In addition he has written non-fiction accounts of Himalayan expeditions.

SIAN HAYTON was born in Liverpool in 1944 and has lived in Scotland since she was a child. She went to the Royal Scottish Academy of Music and Drama. Her novels are *Cells of Knowledge* (1989), *Hidden Daughters, The Governors* (1992) and *The Last Flight*.

THOMAS HEALY was born in Glasgow in 1944 and lives there. He has published two novels, *It Might Have Been Jerusalem* (1991) and *Rolling* (1992). *A Hurting Business*, his memoir as a lifelong boxing fan, was published in 1996.

JOHN HERDMAN was born in Edinburgh in 1941. His *Pagan's Pilgrimage, Clapperton* and *A Truth Lover* were collected in *Three Novellas* (1986). *Voice Without Restraint* (1982) was a book about Bob Dylan's lyrics. His most recent books are *Imelda* (1993) and *Ghost Writing* (1996).

LIZ HERON grew up in Scotland and went to Glasgow University. She lived in Paris, Madrid and Venice before settling in London in 1976. *A Red River* (1996) is her first book of stories. Her non-fiction includes *Truth, Dare or Promise* (1985, as editor), *Changes of Heart* (1986), *Streets of Desire* (1993) and (as co-editor with Val Williams) *Illuminations: Women Writing on Photography from the 1850s to the present* (1996).

ROBERT ALAN JAMIESON was born in Lerwick, Shetland, in 1958 and brought up in the small crofting community of Sannis. His first novel was *Soor Hearts* (1984). He worked for a long spell at Sullom Voe oil terminal and went on to write *Thin Wealth* (1986), which is subtitled 'a novel of the oil decade'. His most recent novel is *A Day at the Office* (1991). In addition he has published a widely praised collection of poems, *Shoormal* (1986).

JACKIE KAY was born in Edinburgh in 1961 and brought up in Glasgow. Her work includes two plays, *Chiaroscuro* (1986) and *Twice Over* (1988), and the collections of poems *The Adoption Papers* (1991) and *Other Lovers* (1993). Her poems also appear in the anthology *A Dangerous Knowing* (1985) and *Penguin Modern Poets Eight* (1996). She lives in London.

JAMES KELMAN was born in Glasgow in 1946. He has published fourteen books of fiction including *A Disaffection* (1989), which won the James Tait Black Memorial Prize and was shortlisted for the Booker Prize. *How late It Was, How Late* won the Booker Prize in 1994. He has also published a book of plays and *Some Recent Attacks: Essays Cultural and Political.* He lives in Glasgow.

A. L. KENNEDY was born in Dundee in 1965 and has lived in Arbroath and Coventry (while studying at the University of Warwick) before moving to Glasgow. She has published three collections of stories – *Night Geometry and the Garscadden Trains* (1990), *Now that you're back* (1994) and *Original Bliss* (1997) – and two novels – *Looking for the Possible Dance* (1993) and *So I Am Glad* (1995). She also wrote the screenplay for *Stella Does Tricks* (1996).

FRANK KUPPNER was born in Glasgow in 1951. His prose includes *A Very Quiet Street* (1989), *A Concussed History of Scotland* (1990), *Something Very Like Murder* (1994), which won the McVitie's Prize, and *Life On A Dead Planet* (1996). His poetry collections are *A Bad Day For the Sung Dynasty, The Intelligent Observation of Naked Women, Ridiculous! Absurd! Disgusting!* and *Everything is Strange.* He lives in Glasgow.

GORDON LEGGE was born in Grangemouth in 1961. His first novel, *The Shoe* (1989), was shortlisted for the Saltire First Book of the Year Award. His first collection of stories, *In Between Talking About the Football* (1991), became a cult success and has finally been reprinted. His second novel is *I Love Me (Who Do You Love ?)* (1994). He has fiction in the anthology edited by Kevin Williamson, *Children of Albion Rovers* (1996). He lives in Edinburgh.

TOM LEONARD was born in Glasgow in 1944. His *Six Glasgow Poems* were published in 1969, followed by *A Priest Came on at Merkland Street* (1970), *Poems* (1973), *Bunnit Husslin* (1975) and *Three Glasgow Writers* (with Alex Hamilton and James Kelman) (1976). In 1984, Galloping Dog Press of Newcastle published his *Intimate Voices* (Selected Work 1965–83). He has edited the anthology *Radical Renfrew: Poetry from the French Revolution to the First World War* (1990) and written *Places of the Mind* (1993), a biography of James 'B.V.' Thompson. His *Reports From the Present* (Selected Work 1982–94) was published in 1995. He lives in Glasgow.

JOAN LINGARD was born in Edinburgh in 1932 and grew up in Belfast, living there between the age of two and eighteen. Her first book, *Liam's Daughter*, was published in 1963. She has published eleven adult novels as well as more than twenty books for children. Her recent adult fiction includes *After Colette*, *The Women's House* and *Sisters By Rite*. She lives in Edinburgh.

LIZ LOCHHEAD was born in Motherwell in 1947. She trained as a painter at Glasgow School of Art then worked as an art teacher for eight years. *Dreaming Frankenstein* (1984) collected her poems from 1967. *True Confessions and New Clichés* (1985) is a compilation of raps, prose and performance pieces. She has written many plays including *Blood and Ice*, *Mary Queen of Scots Got Her Head Chopped Off*, *Dracula* and *Tartuffe* (in Scots). She lives in Glasgow.

BRIAN MCCABE was born in Edinburgh in 1951. His works of fiction include *The Lipstick Circus*, *The Other McCoy* and *In a Dark Room with a Stranger*. He lives in Edinburgh with his wife and three children.

CARL MACDOUGALL was born in Glasgow in 1941. He edited the literary magazine *WORDS* and has had several collections of stories published including *Elvis is Dead* (1986). His novels are *Stone Over Water* (1989), *The Lights Below* and *The Casanova Papers* (1986).

WILLIAM MCILVANNEY was born in 1936 in Kilmarnock, Ayrshire. His fiction includes *Remedy is None* (1966), *A Gift from Nessus* (1968), *Docherty* (1975), *The Big Man* (1985) and *The Kiln* (1996). He has also written three novels featuring the Glasgow detective Jack Laidlaw. His stories are collected in *Walking Wounded* (1989), which won the *Glasgow Herald*'s People's Prize, and his essays in *Surviving the Shipwreck* (1991).

DUNCAN MCLEAN was born in Fraserburgh, Aberdeenshire, in 1964. In the 1980s he was a writer and performer in the Merry Mac Fun Co. His first book was a collection of stories, *Bucket of Tongues* (1992), which was followed by

Blackden, Bunker Man and the non-fiction *Lone Star Swing.* He now lives in Orkney.

CANDIA MCWILLIAM was born in Edinburgh in 1955. Her novels are *A Case of Knives* (1988), *A Little Stranger* (1989) and *Debatable Land* (1994).

ALLAN MASSIE was born in Singapore in 1938 and brought up in Aberdeenshire. His first novel, *Change and Decay in All Around I See*, was published in 1978. Since then he has published many novels including the prize-winning *The Death of Men* and a book of non-fiction, *The Caesars.*

JAMES MEEK was born in London in 1962. His family moved to Scotland when he was five and he later went on to Edinburgh University. His works of fiction are *Mcfarlane Boils The Sea* (1989), *Last Orders* (1992) and *Drivetime* (1995). Since 1985 he has been a newspaper reporter and is currently Moscow correspondent for the *Guardian* and *Scotsman.*

MARTIN MILLAR was born in Glasgow and lives in Brixton, London. His fiction includes *Lux the Poet, The Good Fairies of New York, Milk, Sulphate and Alby Starvation* (1987), *Ruby and the Stone Age Diet* and *Dreams of Sex and Stage Diving* (1994).

JOSEPH MILLS was born in 1958 and attended Glasgow University as a mature student. His novel *Towards the End* was published in 1990 and various short stories have appeared in magazines and anthologies. He lives in Glasgow.

ANDREW O'HAGAN was born in Glasgow in 1968 and grew up with the seagulls and submarines on the Ayrshire coast. For several years he was an assistant editor of *London Review of Books.* His book *The Missing*, part personal history, part investigation of cases of missing children, was published in 1995. He divides his time between London and Glasgow and writes regularly for the *Guardian* and *Esquire.*

AGNES OWENS was born in Milngavie in 1926. Her first book was the novel *Gentlemen of the West* (1984). *Lean Tales* (1985) collected some of her stories with those of Alasdair Gray and James Kelman. She has published two further novels, *Like Birds in the Wilderness* and *A Working Mother*, and the collection of stories *People Like That* (1996).

BRIDGET PENNEY was born in Edinburgh in 1964. She has been writing full-time since she was twenty and lives with her partner and two children in East London. *Honeymoon with Death and other stories* was published in 1991. She has just finished writing her second volume of stories.

IAN RANKIN was born in Fife in 1960. He is mainly a crime writer and his series of novels featuring Inspector John Rebus began with *Knots and Crosses* in 1987. He is married with two sons and lives in Edinburgh.

STANLEY ROBERTSON was born in Aberdeen in 1940 into a travelling family. He is the nephew of Jeannie Robertson, the great Aberdeenshire ballad singer. His books include *Exodus to Alford* (1988), *Nyakim's Windows* (1989) and *Fish-Hooses* (1990).

DILYS ROSE was born in 1954 in Glasgow. She has published collections of poetry, including *Beauty is a Dangerous Thing* and *Madame Doubtfire's Dilemma*. She has published two books of stories, *Our Lady of the Pickpockets* (1989) and *Red Tides* (1994). She lives in Edinburgh with her husband and three children and has just completed a novel.

FRANK SHON was born in Arbroath in 1963. For several years he worked as a labourer in factories, building sites and in horticultural nurseries. He went on to train as a teacher.

ALI SMITH was born in 1962 in Inverness. She has lived in Aberdeen and Edinburgh. Apart from writing fiction she has published poetry and had several plays produced in London and at the Edinburgh Fringe. She now lives in Cambridge. She published *Free Love and Other Stories* in 1995, and her novel *Like* in 1997.

IAIN CRICHTON SMITH was born in Glasgow in 1928 and raised on the Isle of Lewis. He has published many collections of poetry both in English and his native Gaelic. His *Collected Poems* were published in 1992 and a large selection of his stories came out in 1993 as *Listen to the Voice. Consider the Lilies* (1968), about a woman evicted from her croft during the Highland Clearances, is one of his best-known novels. His most recent novels are *In the Middle of the Wood* (1987) and *An Honourable Death* (1992).

ALAN SPENCE was born in Glasgow in 1948. His books of fiction are *Its Colours They Are Fine* (1977), *The Magic Flute* (1989) and *Stone Garden* (1995), which won the McVitie's Prize in 1996. In addition he has written two books of poetry and the plays *Sailmaker*, *Space Invaders* and *Changed Days*.

JEFF TORRINGTON was born in the Gorbals, Glasgow, in 1935. His novel *Swing Hammer Swing!* (1992) won the Whitbread Prize. *The Devil's Carousel* was published in 1996.

ALAN WARNER was born in Oban in 1964 and brought up in Connel Ferry, nearby. His first novel, *Morvern Callar*, was published in 1995 and his second,

These Demented Lands, in 1997. He also has fiction in the anthology *Children of Albion Rovers* (1996). He lives in Ireland.

IRVINE WELSH was born in Edinburgh in 1958. His works of fiction are *Trainspotting* (1993), *The Acid House* (1994), *Marabou Stork Nightmares* (1995) and *Ecstasy* (1996). A highly acclaimed film of *Transpotting* came out in 1996.

DUNCAN WILLIAMSON was born on the shores of Loch Fyne in 1928, of traveller people. He worked for fifty years in jobs such as peatcutting, fishing and crofting. His *Fireside Tales of the Traveller Children* (1983) has been reprinted many times. Among his other books are *Tales of The Seal People, Don't Look Back, Jack* and *A Thorn in the King's Foot.*

Acknowledgements

Every effort has been made by the publishers to contact the copyright holders of the material published in this book, but any omissions will be restituted at the earliest opportunity.

AGNES OWENS. 'When Shankland Comes' first published by Serpent's Tail in *The Seven Deadly Sins*. Reproduced with permission.

IAIN CRICHTON SMITH. Extract from *In the Middle of the Wood* first published by Victor Gollancz Limited. Reproduced with permission.

DUNCAN WILLIAMSON. 'Mary and the Seal' by Duncan Williamson from *Fireside Tales of the Traveller Children* first published by Canongate Books Ltd, Edinburgh. Reproduced with permission.

JOAN LINGARD. Extract from *After Colette* published by Sinclair-Stevenson, Reed Consumer Books Limited. Reproduced with permission.

BILL DOUGLAS. 'My Childhood' (adapted from Douglas' original film script) first published in *Bill Douglas: A Lanternist's Account*. The films comprising *The Bill Douglas Trilogy* were produced by BFI Production. Reproduced with permission of the Bill Douglas Estate.

ALASDAIR GRAY. 'Kenneth McAlpin' from *Lanark*, published by Picador. Copyright © Alasdair Gray 1969, 1981, 1985. Reproduced with kind permission of Canongate Books Ltd.

JEFF TORRINGTON. 'The Fade' from *The Devil's Carousel* first published by Secker & Warburg Ltd, 1996. Copyright © Jeff Torrington 1996. Reproduced with permission.

WILLIAM MCILVANNEY. 'At the Bar' from *Walking Wounded*, first published by Hodder Headline plc. Reproduced with permission of Hodder Headline plc and Curtis Brown USA.

ALLAN MASSIE. 'In the Bare Lands' reproduced with permission of Allan Massie and Curtis Brown.

STANLEY ROBERTSON. 'A Monk's Tail' from *Fish-Hooses*, first published by Balnain Books. Reproduced with permission of Stanley Robertson and Balnain Books.

JOHN HERDMAN. 'Original Sin' from *Original Sin and other stories*, first published by Polygon. Reproduced with permission.

CARL MACDOUGALL. Extract from *The Lights Below*, first published by Secker & Warburg Ltd. Copyright © Carl MacDougall 1993. Reproduced with permission of Secker & Warburg and the author c/o Rogers, Coleridge & White Ltd, 20 Powis Mews, London W11 1JN.

DOUGLAS DUNN. 'The Political Piano' from *Boyfriends and Girlfriends*, first published by Faber & Faber Ltd. Reproduced with permission of the author, Faber & Faber and Peters Fraser & Dunlop Group Ltd.

THOMAS HEALY. Extract from *It Might Have Been Jerusalem*, first published by Polygon. Reproduced with permission.

TOM LEONARD. 'Honest' from *Intimate Voices: Selected Writings 1965–1983*, first published by Galloping Dog Press, reprinted by Vintage. Reproduced with permission of the author.

JAMES KELMAN. Extract from *The Busconductor Hines*, first published by Polygon. Reproduced with permission.

LIZ LOCHHEAD. 'Phyllis Marlowe: Only Diamonds Are Forever' from *True Confessions and New Clichés*, first published by Polygon. Reproduced with permission.

ALISON FELL. 'There's Tradition for You' from *Sex and the City*, edited by Marsha Rowe, first published by Serpent's Tail. Reproduced with permission.

MARGARET ELPHINSTONE. Extract from *A Sparrow's Flight*, first published by Polygon. Reproduced with permission.

LIZ HERON. 'Undue Haste' from *Red River* is reprinted by kind permission of the publishers, Virago Press.

ALAN SPENCE. 'Brilliant' from *Its Colours They Are Fine*, first published by HarperCollins Publishers Ltd. Reproduced with permission.

ANDREW GREIG. 'Disappearing Gully' from *Electric Brae*, first published by Canongate Books Ltd, Edinburgh. Reproduced with permission.

FRANK KUPPNER. Extract from *A Very Quiet Street*, first published by Polygon. Reproduced with permission.

BRIAN MCCABE. 'Not About the Kids' from *In A Dark Room With A Stranger* (Hamish Hamilton, 1993) copyright © Brian McCabe, 1993. Reproduced by permission of Penguin Books Ltd and Curtis Brown.

RONALD FRAME. 'La Plume de Ma Tante' reproduced by kind permission of the author and Curtis Brown.

DILYS ROSE. 'All the Little Loved Ones' from *Red Tides*, first published by Secker & Warburg Ltd. Reproduced with permission.

MARTIN MILLAR. Extract from *Dreams of Sex and Stage Diving*, first published by Fourth Estate Ltd. Reproduced with permission of Fourth Estate Ltd, Mic Cheetham Literary Agency and the author.

CANDIA MCWILLIAM. 'Seven Magpies' first appeared in *New Writing 4*, edited by A. S. Byatt and Alan Hollinghurst, published by Vintage. Reprinted with kind permission of the author.

JANICE GALLOWAY. Extract from *The Trick is to Keep Breathing*, first published by Polygon. Reproduced with kind permissioin of Polygon, A. P. Watt Ltd and the author.

IAIN BANKS. Extract from *The Bridge*, first published by Macmillan (London) Ltd. Reproduced with permission.

JOSEPH MILLS. 'Watch Out, The World's Behind You' from *The Ten Commandments* edited by Tom Wakefield, first published by Serpent's Tail. Reproduced with permission.

IRVINE WELSH. 'The First Shag in Ages' from *Trainspotting*, first published by Secker & Warburg. Reproduced with permission.

ROBERT ALAN JAMIESON. 'The Last Black Hoose' from *A Writer's Ceilidh*, edited by Aonghas MacNeacail, first published by Balnain Books, Edinburgh. Reproduced with permission.

IAN RANKIN. 'A Deep Hole' from *London Noir* edited by Maxim Jakubowski, first published by Serpent's Tail. Reproduced with permission.

ANDREW CRUMEY. Extract from *Pfitz* first published by Dedalus Books Ltd. Reproduced with permission.

JACKIE KAY. Extract from *Trumpet* to be published by Picador. Produced with kind permission of the author.

GORDON LEGGE. 'Life on a Scottish Council Estate Vol. 1' from *In Between Talking About the Football and other stories*, first published by Polygon. Reproduced with permission.

JAMES MEEK. 'Get Lost' from *Last Orders and other stories*, first published by Polygon. Reproduced with permission.

ALI SMITH. 'The Unthinkable Happens to People Every Day' from *Free Love* is reprinted by kind permission of the publishers, Virago Press.

FRANK SHON. 'The Farmer's Wife' first appeared in *Scottish Short Stories* published by HarperCollins. Reprinted with kind permission of the author.

DUNCAN MCLEAN. 'Hours of Darkness' from *Bucket of Tongues*, first published by Secker & Warburg. Copyright © 1992 Duncan McLean. Reproduced with permission.

BRIDGET PENNEY. 'Incidents on the Road' from *Honeymoon with Death and other stories*, first published by Polygon. Reproduced with permission.

ALAN WARNER. 'The Man Who Walks' first appeared in *Rebel Inc* and is reproduced by kind permission of the author. Copyright © Alan Warner 1995.

A. L. KENNEDY. Extract from *Looking for the Possible Dance*, first published by Secker & Warburg Ltd. Reproduced with permission.

MARK FLEMING. 'St Andrew's Day' first appeared in *Scottish Short Stories* published by HarperCollins. Reproduced here with permission of the author.

ANDREW O'HAGAN. 'Glass Cheques' from *A Junky's Christmas* edited by Elisa Seagrave, published by Serpent's Tail. Reproduced with permission.

The editor would like to acknowledge the assistance of Christine Kidney, Duncan McLean, Murdo Macdonald, Simon Cartledge, Francesca Dunfoy and Rachel Heath. And to John Barker for mentioning and not mentioning it.